Nazi E

The Oak Sacrifice of the Judeo-Christian Worldview in the Holocaust

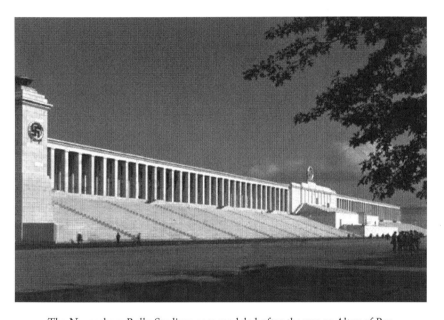

The Nuremberg Rally Stadium was modeled after the pagan Altar of Pergamum that German archaeologists excavated from Turkey. When they began the excavation in 1878, the altar was embedded in a grove of oaks. The Greek god Zeus was otherwise known as the god of the oaks. In Revelation 2:13, the phrase "Satan's throne" is most probably a reference to the Altar of Pergamum (Photo Credit: bpk, Berlin, Karl Kolb 1938, Art Resource, New York).

By R. Mark Musser

Also by R. Mark Musser
Wrath or Rest: Saints in the Hands of an Angry God

DEDICATION & THANKS

This book is dedicated to Charles Clough, the founder of Bible Framework, for his strong encouragement at the very beginning of this project.

A special thanks to Cliff Kincaid of Accuracy in Media. He was a tremendous encouragement for the first edition.

I would like to thank Dr. E. Calvin Beisner for his constant encouragement.

Thanks also to Tom McCabe who volunteered many long hours to help edit the book.

Finally, thanks also to my uncle, Charles Edenstrom, the first enthusiastic reader of my rough draft when it was still in its infancy.

This picture (Courtesy Buchenwald Museum) was taken in 1944 at Buchenwald concentration camp. Buchenwald means "Beech Forest." The SS enjoyed a nearby zoo just outside the camp. The tree in the middle of the picture is an oak tree. It was known as Goethe's Oak. The famous scholar Johann Wolfgang von Goethe (1749-1832) blazed the trail for the German Romantic movement. Today, Romanticism is known as environmentalism. Goethe spent much time around the environs of this particular oak tree, the destination of his favorite forest retreat. It was located near a wilderness area at the time. When the Nazis cleared the ground for the construction of the Buchenwald Concentration Camp, they saved the oak tree. The tree died during an Allied bombing raid. Today the stump still remains at Buchenwald.

"But for Your sake we are killed all day long;
We are considered as sheep to be slaughtered."

Psalm 44:22; quoted in Romans 8:36

READER COMMENTS

"*Nazi Oaks* is one of those important books that is unlikely to get the kind of mainstream media coverage it deserves."

– Alan Caruba, Warning Signs

"*Nazi Oaks* has given me a whole new perspective on religion and the environment."

– Steve Milloy, Junk Science

"Mr. Musser exposes the powerful religious and philosophical undercurrents that are sweeping the *green* tsunami over our political landscape. In a day of sound-bite rhetoric and fundraising memos obsessed with the latest scary story of alleged damage to Mother Nature, we often are too overwhelmed to see the flow from big ideas to big consequences. As one trained in modern environmental studies and experienced in actual environmental policy regulations, Musser ably deconstructs the Third Reich's green connection—a sobering exhibit of what happens when ancient Baalist nature-worship coalesces with modern totalitarian bureaucracy. This is a lesson that Biblically-green *creation care* must learn, or suffer the consequences of ignoring it."

– Charles Clough, B.S., Massachusetts Institute of Technology;
M.S. in atmospheric science, Texas Tech University;
Th.M., Dallas Theological Seminary;
Founder of Bible Framework.

"Mark Musser has produced a valuable work showing the clear connections between Romanticism, the National Socialist ideology and the rise of modern ecological religion. *Nazi Oaks* explains how romantic Mother Earth-loving vibes are no guarantee for pleasant outcomes, for mankind or the earth."

– Dr. James Wanliss, author of the Green Dragon.

"Mark Musser's research into the Nazi elements in the environmental movement is unique and absolutely needed to understand current events. He demonstrates that radical environmentalism is an effort to control peoples' lives and that the Nazis used it for that purpose. Ominously, he also proves that the Nazis used environmentalism to target groups of people they wanted to eliminate from the face of the earth. We cannot allow government to acquire this kind of power again."

– Cliff Kincaid, Accuracy in Media

"*Nazi Oaks* is a tour de force, patiently accurately unearthing the explicitly anti-Biblical worldview and philosophical roots of modern environmentalism in the renewal of pagan nature worship inherent in German Romanticism a la Goethe and Wagner, racism a la Haeckel, existentialism a la Heidegger, and nihilism a la Schopenhauer and Nietzsche. If, as the Bible says, good fruit cannot come from a bad tree, and bad company corrupts good morals, then it's time for Christian—indeed for all—environmentalists to take a sober look at the roots and branches of the tree on which they perch. Rev. Musser's book shows both historically and philosophically how and why ecologism bore fruit in Nazi totalitarianism, racism and the Holocaust, why those dangers remain inherent in modern environmentalism, and why ecologism's worldview remains incompatible with Judeo-Christian morals. It also shows how and why ecologism led then, as it does now, to the corruption of science and its enslavement to political ideology. Those who read *Nazi Oaks* will be surprised, and shocked, to see how even many of their heroes were nourished by the sap of that tree, and how heavily European and North American environmentalism today remain tied to and ideologically predetermined by the anti-Christian roots from which it sprang. Thoroughly documented and insightfully argued, this book shows all the earmarks of having been written by someone who has become a complete master of the ideas and the history he explains."

– Dr. E. Calvin Beisner, founder and national spokesman,
The Cornwall Alliance for the Stewardship of Creation

"It is a good guide and helpful book."

– Dr. Martin Erdmann, Verax Institute

"While Musser's well-researched book is jam-packed with information gleaned from dozens of sources, the text is smooth and readable. It explains the Nazis better than a shelf-full of 'official' histories ever could."

– Mike Gray, American Culture

"This ... text easily passes as a piece of professional academic scholarship. More importantly, Musser definitely contributes something valuable to the conversation about environmentalism with his pantheism-versus-Christianity thesis."

- William Kay, Environmentalism is Fascism blog

"A very informative and fascinating look at Nazi ideology. It's amazing that I have heard about the evil Nazis all my life but never heard about what they actually believed, except, of course, for their anti-Semitism and German racism, but I didn't really understand those things either until after reading *Nazi Oaks*! I especially like the way Nazi thought is traced back to things like Romanticism. That's very relevant to today's scene. We are in a very neo-Romantic time now with all this environmentalism and religious mysticism, which should concern us Christians especially, since it's seeping into the church, too."

– Prof. Bruce Davidson, Hokusei Gakuen University

"Mark has written an invaluable book for anyone who wants to understand how a rejection of the God of Christians and Jews led the Nazis to worship other, grimmer, false gods. It is not a book that radical environmentalists will want you to read, which is precisely why it is indispensable reading for sane and decent people today."

– Bruce Walker, author and columnist

"Great read and very insightful."

– David Pepe, The Ignorant Fishermen blog

Der Stürmer

Nürnberger Wochenblatt zum Kampfe um die Wahrheit

HERAUSGEBER : JULIUS STREICHER

| Nummer 48 | | Nürnberg, im Dezbr. 1927 | | 5. Jahr 1927 |

Der vergiftete König

Reichstagskandidat
Dr. Hermann Luppe

Wie wir von gut unterrichteter Seite hören, beabsichtigt Luppe, sich in den kommenden Reichstag wählen zu lassen. Im Wahlkreis Franken soll er als Spitzenkandidat aufgestellt werden. Er hat bereits von den Sozialdemokraten, von den Demokraten und von der bayerischen Volkspartei (!!) im Nürnberger Stadtrat sich die Einwilligung zu seiner Kandidatur eingeholt.

Diese Fraktionen sind also damit einverstanden, daß der „Bombenfabrikant" auch noch im Reichstag herumwuschelt. Sie finden nichts dabei, wenn demnächst der 1. Bürgermeister der Stadt — dem die Nürnberger Steuerzahler ein Jahresgehalt von 36000 Mark zahlen müssen — praktisch für die Stadt nichts mehr arbeiten wird.

Es sind dies die gleichen Fraktionen im Rathaus, die nichts dabei finden, in geheimer Sitzung dem Juden Dr. Süßheim ein Extrahonorar von 6000 Mark zu bewilligen.

Wie wir weiter hören, ist Dr. Hermann Luppe dazu ausersehen, demnächst den Herrn Reichswehrminister Dr. Geßler abzulösen. Daß er zum Reichswehrminister eine ganz besondere Eignung hat, ist bekannt. In Frankfurt war er Feuerwehrhauptmann und während des Krieges hat er sich im Frankfurter Rathaus das Eiserne Kreuz II. Klasse am Heimatbande erworben.

Ein Freimaurerverbrechen
Dr. Wichtls Enthüllungen sind bestätigt

Im Jahre 1919 schrieb der 65jährige Oberstleutnant Dr. Friedrich Wichtl ein Buch gegen die Freimaurerei. Es trägt den Titel: „Weltfreimaurerei, Weltrevolution, Weltrepublik". Die geheime, verbrecherische Tätigkeit der Freimaurer ist darin enthalten.

Als dieses Buch an die Öffentlichkeit kam, da ging ein entsetzlicher Lärm los. Die Judenpresse heulte vor Wut. Sie nannte Wichtls Buch eine „Schmutzschrift", eine „gedruckte Roheit", ein „widerliches Gebräude". Der Wiener Großjude ließ veröffentlichen, es sei „eine Unverschämtheit, daß dieser Mann von der öffentlichen Achtung noch nicht niedergezwungt sei". Es dauerte nicht lange, dann wurde Dr. Wichtl tatsächlich niedergezwungt. Nachdem die Kugeln eines gedungenen Mörders fehlgegangen waren, wurde Dr. Wichtl im Jahre 1922 vergiftet.

Das Werk des Toten aber wurde ist der Öffentlichkeit

*) Das Buch ist über 300 Seiten stark. Es ist in Halbleinen gebunden und kostet RM. 4.50. Zu beziehen durch die Großdeutsche Buchhandlung.

Wenn das Ungeziefer tot ist, grünt die deutsche Eiche wieder!

Die Juden sind unser Unglück!

In 1927, the National Socialist tabloid Der Sturmer portrays the gassing of what was considered to be Jewish vermin in the crevices of an oak tree that was damaging its roots, "When the vermin are dead, the German Oak will flourish again."

"The point of *Nazi Oaks*, documented with extraordinary information about the Nazi Party's connection to conservationism, nature worship, environmentalism, social Darwinism, and loathing for capitalism, is that all of these things are still very much alive and kicking among socialists around the world who reject the Genesis story of man being superior to nature. *Nazi Oaks* has given me a whole new perspective on the evil Third Reich with its undeniable connection to environmentalism today. Everyone needs to read *Nazi Oaks* – even those with no faith at all. *Going green* and all its ugly implications are absolutely incompatible with Christianity."

– Chriss Rainey, Catholic reader

"R. Mark Musser's book explores the historical roots of modern environmentalism, its connection to the Nazi regime, Hitler's obsession with wolves, Haeckel's *volkisch* environmentalism influence on modern Greens in Germany, the economic wastefulness and physical damage of renewable energy to the land, the bizarre and inexplicable environmentalist love for trees but not for people, the Romantic movement that stressed nature, the Biblical view of human autonomy over nature, and the Protestant Reformation and the Enlightenment's utilitarian view of nature. The oak is more than just a symbol of German nationalism. It is an expression of the 'brown road to Auschwitz that was lined with green trees'—trees nourished by the sweat and blood of innocents who were deprived of their freedom and of their right to live."

– Dr. Ileana Johnson Paugh, author,
columnist and radio commentator

This oft photographed oak stands just inside the gated entrance of Auschwitz Camp I in behind the infamous sign which reads, "Work makes you free." At Auschwtiz, Zyklon B, a pesticide used to kill rats and pests, was used to murder Jews.

"The Jew ... is a parasite in the body of other peoples. That he sometimes left his previous Lebensraum (living space) has nothing to do with his own purpose, but results from the fact that from time to time he was thrown out by the host nations he had misused. His spreading is a typical phenomenon for all parasites; he always seeks a new feeding ground for his race. . . . The Jew's life as a parasite in the body of other nations and states explains a characteristic which once caused Schopenhauer, as has already been mentioned, to call him the 'great master in lying.' Existence impels the Jew to lie, and to lie perpetually, just as it compels the inhabitants of the northern countries to wear warm clothing."

Adolf Hitler, Mein Kampf

"Our epoch will certainly see the end of the disease of Christianity. It will last another hundred years, two hundred years perhaps. My regret will have been that I couldn't, like whoever the prophet was, behold the promised land from afar. We are entering into a conception of the world that will be a sunny era, an era of tolerance. Man must be put in a position to develop freely the talents that God has given him. What is important above all is that we should prevent a greater lie from replacing the lie that is disappearing. The world of Judeo-Bolshevism must collapse."

Adolf Hitler, Feb. 27, 1942

"North Africa was once a heavily wooded territory, and Greece, Italy and Spain too, at the time of the Greco-Roman era also had many vast forests. In passing judgment on European history, too, let me advise caution. Like Greece and Italy, Egypt also during the period of her glory was a most habitable country with a most equable climate. So when a people began to cut down their trees without making any provision for reafforestation — and thus rob nature's wise irrigation system of its most essential prerequisite — you may be sure that it is a sign of the beginning of their cultural degeneration."

Adolf Hitler, July 7, 1942

TABLE OF CONTENTS

O Lord, our Lord, How majestic is Thy name in all the earth, Who hast displayed Thy splendor above the heavens! 2 From the mouth of infants and nursing babes Thou hast established strength, Because of Thine adversaries, To make the enemy and the revengeful cease. 3 When I consider Thy heavens, the work of Thy fingers, The moon and the stars, which Thou hast ordained; 4 What is man, that Thou dost take thought of him? And the son of man, that Thou dost care for him? 5 Yet Thou hast made him a little lower than God, And dost crown him with glory and majesty! 6 Thou dost make him to rule over the works of Thy hands; Thou hast put all things under his feet, 7 All sheep and oxen, And also the beasts of the field, 8 The birds of the heavens, and the fish of the sea, Whatever passes through the paths of the seas. 9 O LORD, our Lord, How majestic is Thy name in all the earth!

Psalm 8

FOREWORD

Mark Musser's *Nazi Ecology* provides a convincing answer to questions which are almost never asked: Why Germany? Why the Holocaust? His answer: the joining of the German version of Darwinism with Germany's transition to green environmentalism—the idea that humans are merely part of nature, no different from the rest—from the Judeo-Christian foundational concept that humans are creations of God in His image and charged by Him to populate the Earth and have dominion over nature.

Musser attributes this transition to the output of the *great* German thinkers whose writing led Germans to view the world as either pantheistic or godless, populated by nations of which the German nation is the greatest, that populations be improved by employing the 'scientific' principals of eugenics, that non-Germans should be cleared from the land adjacent to Germany to make room for Germans, that peoples inferior to Germans should be enslaved and that the Jews—those responsible for the commercial values which lead to the corruption of nature and the Judeo-Christian morality which obstructs the path of Germans from achieving their manifest destiny as rulers of the world—should be removed from the world.

Nazi Ecology demonstrates that it was no accident that the Nazi government's implementation of the ideas of the *great* German thinkers provided the ideas that promoted Germany's aggression, its policy of Lebensraum, its genocide of the Jews and its enactment of the world's *greenest* legislation.

Whereas Musser provides a detailed pedigree of the ideas that provided the Nazis with the rationale for their actions, for the post-Nazi period the roles of Germany's thinkers and government in promoting *green fascism* receive hardly a mention. I would recommend caution in accepting this as reflective of reality.

In my own research I have found that a little digging usually reveals the role of Germany-connected/directed individuals and organizations in promoting long-held elements of Germany's agenda in the United States and throughout the world. Thus, to suggest—as Musser seems to—that Al Gore Jr. promoted on his own, without Germany's encouragement, the idea that catastrophe-producing global warming would be caused by CO2 emissions, ignores the Gore family's (Sr. and Jr.) long-exercised practice of accepting gifts for services.

Similarly, it would probably be a mistake to believe that *environmentalists* on their own, without the active participation of Germany's government 'created parallel governances' by 'appropriating state resources and integrating them with movement-controlled state-like entities in the private sector.' I have found strong indications that 'the deliberately inscrutable jumble of quasi-government tribunals and councils conjoined to thousands of environmentalist non-governmental organizations,' which are attributed to *environmentalists*, are in fact largely the product of German planning and funding.

Dr. Robert Kaplan, Jerusalem, Ph.D. in European history
and author of the Soros Connection, July 2017.

THE GREEN NAZI MOTIVE OF THE HOLOCAUST

For the past 200 years in both North America and Europe, the Judeo-Christian worldview has been specifically targeted by modern environmental thinkers for being anti-natural. Much of this green opposition originally came forth from the dark and chilly northern forests of Germany and New England. The cool, remote and isolationist environmental mentality of the north has somehow captured the romantic imagination of modern environmentalism. Their romance with the natural world stands in direct opposition to the warmer and cultured Judeo-Christian civilization of southern Europe, born in the sunny Middle East. That this northern environmentalism would later become infatuated with the cult of global warming,[1] dressed up in modern green science, is thus perhaps not so curious. Such an ecological agenda that has been able to politicize the weather and the climate shows just how far this movement has come. Romantic love is often blind. This is nowhere made more evident than in the environmental infatuation, if not worship, of a natural world which the modern greens will never be able to save no matter how totalitarian the movement becomes.

In fact, much like the ancient Canaanite nature religion eventually suffocated Israel and Judah in the Old Testament, modern environmentalism is well on its way to completely smothering the contemporary western world as well.[2] Author Steve Milloy of *Junk Science* rightfully points out, "There is hardly any area of your life that the greens consider off limits to intrusion. There is almost no personal behavior of yours that they consider too trivial

---

[1]   The "Climategate" email scandal, uncovered by computer "hackers" who "hacked" into CRU computer files in the United Kingdom on Nov. 20, 2009, shows evidence of abuse of power, fraud and data manipulation on the part of the so-called climate experts committed to the Global Warming/Climate Change agenda. Another round of compromising emails was exposed in November of 2011.

[2]   See *Blue Planet in Green Shackles*, by Vaclav Klaus. Washington DC: Competitive Enterprise Institute, 2007.

or too sacrosanct to regulate."[3] The worship of nature and strict asceticism, with occasional bouts of human sacrifice, often went hand in hand in the ancient world. Similarly today, with all of the land use regulations already on the books, ecological asceticism is increasingly becoming the moral ethic for both Europe and America under environmentalism. People will be not only expected, but required to make substantial sacrifices for the sake of the environment.[4] Environmental asceticism is well on its way into becoming a total replacement of the Judeo-Christian ethic in the western world. Even the publication of Green Bibles, which highlights a smattering of environmentally friendly Scriptures in green,[5] is potentially just another nail driven into a sacrificial coffin built for Judeo-Christian values.

Many modern greens loathe the Judeo-Christian worldview and the western cultural superstructure built on its foundations. At root of this particular controversy is Genesis 1, where man is not only made in God's image, and hence crowned as the king of creation, but he is also commanded by God to "subdue" and "fill the earth" (Gen. 1:28; cf. 24-31). In the creation story, God granted Adam and Eve a substantial amount of autonomy and liberty over the natural world. This ecological foundation laid in Genesis 1 is thus extremely controversial from an environmental point of view. Many environmentalists believe the Biblical commands to subdue and fill the Earth are the primary reasons why the present-day planet lies in ecological ruin. The word *subdue* is a very strong term in Hebrew. This coupled with the command, "Be fruitful and multiply" (Gen. 1:28) essentially means to tame nature with the civilizing influences of work, marriage and procreation.

---

3   Milloy, Steve. Green Hell: How Environmentalists Plan to Control Your Life and What You Can Do to Stop Them. Washington DC: Regnery Publishing, 2009, p. 3.

4   Bramwell, Anna. *Ecology in the 20th Century: A History*, Yale University Press, 1989, "The cultural and political criticism known as political ecology involves substantial ethical and moral claims, and proposes drastic and apocalyptic remedies," p. 8.

5   Work, Telford, "Meager Harvest," in *Christianity Today*, is unimpressed with the new *Green Bible*, "The two testaments central concerns—covenanted Israel, anointed Jesus, and missional church—are pushed aside by the green passages that testify, or are made to testify, on environmentalism's behalf. Yet if the editors narrowed their criteria or applied them strictly, much less of *The Green Bible* would be in green, and that would give the false impression of biblical indifference. This double bind makes *The Green Bible* an awkward witness to the strong theological case that can actually be made for creation care. Despite the publisher's intent, spending time with *The Green Bible* makes me more aware than ever of the gulf separating ancient Israel from the Sierra Club and warier of forcing environmentalism, anti-environmentalism or any other contemporary agenda into passages of Scripture," p. 30, Feb. 2009.

Environmentalists think that latent within the Biblical commands to subdue and fill the Earth is the concept that people may exploit nature for selfish or even greedy purposes. In a famous environmental essay written in 1967, Lynn White Jr. lectured, "Christianity, in absolute contrast to ancient paganism and Asia's religions, not only established a dualism of man and nature but also insisted that it is God's will that man exploit nature for his proper ends."[6] Environmentalists insist that such an attitude has led to a dominating view of nature that has vandalized the planet of its ecological purity. Worse, there are now too many people living on too small a planet. This great problem has been further exacerbated by both the scientific and industrial revolutions that flowered under the culture of the Christian West.[7]

Contrary to popular opinion, modern science was born under a Judeo-Christian milieu precisely because it celebrated man's dominion over nature. The scientific technology employed in the industrial revolution brought about a mastery over nature on a scale never seen before in human history. However, the unprecedented growth in wealth and living standards in the West seemed to be everywhere matched by the spread of black smoke, dangerous contaminants, poisoned waters and dirty cities.[8] Thus, many in the green movement hold western Christianity in contempt, "As we now recognize, somewhat over a century ago science and technology—hitherto quite separate activities—joined to give mankind powers which, to judge by many of the ecological effects, are out of control. If so, Christianity bears a huge burden of guilt."[9]

The book of Genesis stands as the exact antithesis of what most environmentalists believe and promote these days. The Biblical account says that while the creation of the world was ultimately made for the glory of God, it was also made for man since he was made in God's image. This Biblical view of man and nature means that nature was specifically made for man to subdue and fill the Earth under the Divine blessing of marriage. Marriage has

---

6   White, Lynn Jr., "The Historical Roots of our Ecological Crisis," *Science*, Vol. 155, No. 3767, March 10, 1967, p. 1205.

7   Ibid., pp. 1,203-1,207.

8   The scientific revolution was rooted in the natural theology of the Christian Middle Ages. Natural theology is distinct from Biblical theology. Natural theology is based on nature. Biblical theology is based on the Scriptures. Even as early as the Middle Ages, natural theology itself tended to overlook the great historical crisis brought on by sin and the subsequent fall of man and nature. By the time of the Enlightenment, the creation story and the fall of mankind was increasingly treated as a myth.

9   White, p. 1,206.

an overall Divine purpose in the world—to subdue it and fill it with population. It thus becomes the basis for all subsequent human history in contrast to the natural world over which it has dominion. The dichotomy between nature and history was thus born in the opening chapters of Genesis, and matrimony is at the heart of the matter. The Bible thus favors men, women and their children over nature, a theme which continues throughout from cover to cover. Environmentalists characterize this humanistic emphasis found in the Bible as anthropocentrism, i.e., man-centered. "Especially in its western form, Christianity is the most anthropocentric religion the world has seen."[10]

More striking, Genesis 1 also implies that nature was considered unkept and in need of human interference, even in its original fresh purity. Adam was never called to be in communion with nature. Rather, he was to subdue, fill and rule it (Gen. 1:26-31). In fact, his job was to turn the wilderness into a garden using the garden of Eden as his model.[11] While it is true that the subsequent fall of Adam and Eve into sin greatly complicated man's dominion over nature, the Genesis mandate is still in effect today. God never rescinded it (Ps. 8). However, man's dominion over nature is now saddled with much blood, sweat and tears (Gen. 3:16-21). The natural world was cursed with death, thorns and thistles to discipline man's rebellion (Gen. 3:17-19).[12] It was no longer benevolent as it was originally. It also became subject to corruption and pollution. Hence, both man and nature co-exist in a fallen state. Because of Adam and Eve's rebellion, God, man and nature are all alienated from each other as corruption, disease, mutation, increasing chaos, competition and death rule as a way of life in the natural world. Adam and Eve were removed from the garden paradise of God—never to return.

As the creation story in Genesis has increasingly been treated as a myth, the notion that sin is the root cause for all the alienation that exists in nature (Hos. 4:1-6; Jer. 14:1-22) has increasingly fallen by the wayside. In its wake, environmentalists have found a different scapegoat to blame—the industrialized Western world itself, improperly built on the foundation of an alien, transcendental Judeo-Christian ethos that emphasizes man's

---

[10]   Ibid., p. 1,205.

[11]   See especially *Where the Garden Meets the Wilderness: Evangelical Entry into the Environmental Debate*, by Dr. E. Calvin Beisner. Grand Rapids, Michigan: William B. Eerdmans Publishing Co., 1997.

[12]   Genesis 3:18 perhaps records the first biological mutation in history.

dominion over nature. Environmentalists believe such an attitude is what is allegedly most responsible for the degradation and exploitation of the environment. "Both our present science and our present technology are so tinctured with orthodox Christian arrogance toward nature that no solution for our ecological crisis can be expected from them alone."[13]

The great controversy here is the Biblical view of man and nature strongly implies an autonomous, utilitarian ecology. In other words, the Bible emphasizes human autonomy over the natural world, and that autonomy is to be used for the development of mankind. Furthermore, after the birth of Western science in the Christian Middle Ages, it was especially the Protestant Reformation and the Enlightenment that emphasized this utilitarian view of nature which opened up the door for the industrial revolution and free market capitalism, the two greatest forces of the modern world which have, according to environmentalists, left the Earth in ecological shambles.

Thus, in opposition to this theocentric-anthropocentric (God-man centered) dominion view of nature, environmentalists have increasingly pushed for a nature-based agenda that gives rights to ecosystems and animals on a par with basic human rights. This, at once, denies the fundamental distinction between man and nature. Modern environmentalists use ecological holism to subvert or trump man's responsibility to subdue and fill the Earth. Environmental holism is the exact opposite of the Judeo-Christian worldview that posits a dualistic distinction between man and nature. Ecology as a holistic science sees all of nature as one interdependent whole that even man is subject to and cannot rise above. The circle of life thus encapsulates everything under its all-pervading influence, and this law of nature must be obeyed. Once man begins to tinker with the circle of life and elevate himself above it, this will invariably create mayhem in the natural order. Man must therefore learn to respect the holistic laws of nature. Such an environmental attitude today is generally called *deep ecology*, which "invites us to overturn the paradigms that dominate Western Society."[14] Deep ecology thus demands that man, especially Western man, be far more humble with the natural surroundings in which he lives.

It is of great irony that the father of deep ecology, Aldo Leopold (1887-1948), began strongly pushing for such a nature-based agenda upon returning home to America from his visit to Nazi Germany in 1935. In the

---

13   White Jr., p. 1,207.
14   Ferry, Luc. *The New Ecological Order*. University of Chicago Press, 1995, p. 59.

mid-1930s, Nazi Germany was the greenest regime on the planet. Leopold went there to observe the new environmental direction the Third Reich was inaugurating. In America, Leopold was the Henry David Thoreau of the 20th century. His influence preceded Rachel Carson (1907-1964) by two decades. The *deep* ecological legacy he left America in the late 1940s was to "think like a mountain." This is the epitome of environmental existentialism.[15] While existentialist philosophy prides itself on its strong emphasis upon subjective freedom, its contingency upon existence as such places many limitations upon that freedom that it remains blindly unaware of. In particular, environmental existentialism reduces human beings to mere natural existence they cannot rise above thanks largely to its hatred of spiritual values that are deemed inauthentic abstractions and unreal to what really exists this side of the grave. In a natural world permeated with environmental existentialism, there is no place for the Judeo-Christian God of the universe to rule over nature or history from His sovereign throne. Neither does it allow man to rule over nature as commanded and assumed throughout the entire Bible. While nature is viewed as free in environmental circles, the same cannot be said of man himself who must always limit his freedoms – particularly of the capitalistic variety – in light of nature's laws or ways that are presumed to be inviolable. If more understood that environmental holism means totalism they would be much more wary of its existential threat. The leap from holism, to totalism, to totalitarianism and fascism is a relatively minor one.

Leopold's green existential worldview, so typical of many modern environmentalists, is also an attack on the rational faculties of the human soul. Many environmentalists hold that Western man's hubristic over-emphasis upon rationality, coupled with the dominion mandate given in Genesis, is precisely the reason why the modern world has been

---

15   *Baker's Encyclopedia of Christian Apologetics* writes an "eclectic group of philosophers and theologians contributed to what became modern existentialism. They include Lutheran theist Soren Kierkegaard (1813-1855), German atheist Friedrich Nietzsche (1844-1900), French atheists Jean Paul Sartre (1905-1980) and Albert Camus (1913-1960), German-Jewish theist Martin Buber (1878-1965), German non-theist Martin Heidegger (1889-1976), French Roman Catholic Gabriel Marcel (1889-1964), and German Eastern Orthodox layman Karl Jaspers (1883-1969). Existentialism emphasizes living over knowing, willing over thinking, the concrete over the abstract, and the dynamic over the static, love over law, the personal over the propositional, the individual over society, the subjective over the objective, the non-rational over the rational, and freedom over necessity. At the heart of existentialism is the belief that existence has precedence over essence," edited by Norman Geisler. Grand Rapids, Michigan: Baker Book House, 1999, p. 234.

left irreversibly sick from an ecological point of view. Reason, rationality and dominion over nature are certainly at the heart of the scientific and industrial revolutions of the modern era. As such, many greens often use the existential realities of nature to try and slow down environmental pollution that has been generated by the scientific age and its subsequent industrialism. Thanks to all of their efforts, scientific rationality is thus no longer king. Natural existence is now king, especially since it has been holistically defined by modern ecology.

As the Christian faith became more nominal and superficial throughout the 1900s, deep ecology established firm roots in both Europe and America. Surprisingly enough, through the rise of this green existentialism, the pantheistic nature worship of the ancients has come roaring back from the shadows of the pagan forest in a powerful, haunting way. Today, much like their ancient forebearers, people increasingly fear the wrath of Mother Nature against them for daring to upset the natural balance of the delicate ecosystems of planet Earth.

The razor's edge of life, confirmed by the physical sciences, has left modern environmentalists in panic palace. The sciences have demonstrated that life indeed hangs in the balance. Non-life or death is everywhere abundant in the universe, and the greens believe that modern man has traumatized the fragile balance of nature. In particular, Western progress over the last 200 years has shattered gradual evolutionary development so that the natural world is unable to cope with all of the massive changes. "The naturalist atheistic worldview sees earth and all its ecosystems as the result of chance processes and therefore inherently unstable and fragile, vulnerable to enormous harm from tiny causes."[16] Worse, all of their environmental worries, concerns,[17] and general unbelief are now being foisted upon an unsuspecting world with unprecedented scaremongering tactics. Instead of fostering panic, however, the extremely narrow frontier between

---

16   Beisner, Dr. E. Calvin, "Testimony of Dr. E. Calvin Beisner to the Subcommittee on Energy and Environment of the Committee on Energy and Commerce of the United States House of Representatives," Wednesday, March 25, 2009.

17   Bramwell, *Ecology in the 20ᵗʰ Century: A History* … "The distinctive qualities of ecologism arose in the late nineteenth century, and consisted of two distinct strands. One was an anti-mechanistic, holistic approach to biology, deriving from the German zoologist, Ernst Haeckel. The second strand was a new approach to economics called energy economics. This focused on the problem of scarce and non-renewable resources. These two strands fused together in the 1970's. The scientific element in energy economics gave impetus to the biologically based ecological movement, which had lost its credibility because of its links with Germany," p. 4.

life and non-life in the universe should be a tremendous testimony to the existence of an ultimate Designer that only the infinite personal God of the Bible can adequately explain. Unfortunately, such a theistic prospect is considered out of the question.

Modern environmentalism refuses to accept man's dominion and reasoning powers over nature. In particular, it has placed a full court press on the capitalistic development of the Western world. Many environmentalists are more than willing to sacrifice human culture and development, especially of the Western sort built upon Judeo-Christian foundations. They wish to do this for the sake of maintaining a natural balance, which Genesis says has never existed. Such a replacement of norms and standards has already led the contemporary West down a path where human concerns are increasingly taking a back seat to environmental anxieties with a *green gone wild*.[18] Still even more disconcerting is that a green gone wild could perhaps easily mutate into a much darker shade of green, perhaps even comparable to what happened in the ancient world when nature worshipers sacrificed human beings on occasion.[19] Even the Aztecs sacrificed thousands of people for the sake of fair weather and the appeasement of the nature gods.[20] Most disturbing, one can also look to the historical experience of Nazi

---

[18] See *Green Gone Wild: Elevating Nature Above Human Rights* by M. David Stirling. Bellevue, Washington: Merril Press, 2008. Stirling demonstrates how the Endangered Species Act, borrowing heavily from a politicized biology, has trampled upon constitutional property rights, threatened the livelihoods, businesses and health of everyday people at enormous financial costs and, on top of this, has done a poor job in saving endangered species.

[19] Myers, John Myers. *The Saga of Hugh Glass: Pirate, Pawnee and Mountain Man*. Lincoln, Nebraska: University of Nebraska Press, 1976. For a much more modern account of human sacrifice and nature worship, John Myers Myers discusses the capture of Hugh Glass by the Pawnees of the early 1800s in the American West. Glass and his partner were captured by the Wolf Pawnees, who "were given to human sacrifice, both for the purposes of pleasing tribal gods and for pyromancy. The latter practices called for using human ashes as tea leaves, in order to read the future. A favored ceremony of these Pawnees was the burning of a young girl as a tribute to the planet Venus in its capacity as the Morning Star ... to win a smile from the Morning Star.... But men and boys were also used as burnt offerings. In the course of his published *Personal Recollections*, James Ohio Pattie reported the rescue of a captured youngster by his father, Sylvester, in 1824. On this occasion the child was to have been sacrificed as the climax of a Pawnee scalp dance." Though Hugh Glass was barely saved from such an arsonist ritualistic ceremony, his partner was not, and Hugh saw it all, "In place of being burned at the stake, as per common executions by fire, the white man was transformed into a living column of kindling by slivers of pine, each rich in resin, thrust in all regions of his bare body. Touched off, they scorched the victim's every part at once, as opposed to have destruction by fire begin at the feet and creep upwards." pp. 52-54.

[20] Ambrose, Jay, "Human Sacrifices to Climate god," *Orange County Register*, March 29, 2009.

Germany in the 1930s and '40s to see how something like human sacrifice may actually play itself out in the modernized world with Romanticism, Naturalism, holism, *progressive* science, pantheism, existentialism, nature mysticism and eco-fascism leading the way.

The Green Nazi Smoke Pouring out from the Chimneys of Auschwitz

Albert Speer (1905-1981), Hitler's architect and armaments minister (1942-45), gave a famous defense at the Nuremberg trials that bizarrely concluded with a warning about the potential destructive powers of science and technology.[21] He pointed out that such technology could easily be used to dominate people. Speer even spoke of intercontinental super rockets that could now rain down atomic fire upon cities without warning. He went on to say, "Science will be able to spread pestilence among humans and animals," and, "Chemistry will be capable of inflicting unspeakable suffering upon an increasingly helpless humanity." With the shockwaves of the nuclear age being recently imposed upon the entire world, Speer was virtually warning everyone present at the trial.

Sounding like a preface to the entire modern environmental movement which sprang into worldwide action in the 1960s, Speer thus managed to deflect some responsibility away from himself and the German people by shoving blame upon Western man's technological prowess to dominate *helpless* people. Thus, oddly enough, environmental concerns are a part of the historical record at Nuremberg attached to the very architect of the Third Reich. More surprising, Speer's defense worked. Although he was certainly one of the primary players in the Holocaust and all of the wanton destruction that was World War II, he eluded the death penalty. He wound up serving 20 years at Spandau Prison with Deputy *Fuhrer* Rudolf Hess, one of Nazi Germany's original green mystics going all the way back to the party's origins.

Even stranger still, many have naively followed in the footsteps of Albert Speer's defense, always blaming Nazi technology, industry and the economy for the Holocaust. At the time of his defense, this is precisely what Albert Speer wanted others to believe about the horrific consequences of the Nazi regime. This should give great pause to all scholars and commentators

---

21   See especially *Albert Speer: His Battle with Truth* by Gitta Sereny. New York: Alfred A. Knopf, 1995, pp. 594-596.

that grapple with the extraordinary historical complications of National Socialism and the Holocaust. More crucial, Speer's defense did not express repentance, but was a perpetuation of what he already believed. Even though he is famously known as being the technocrat of the Nazi war machine, in the innermost core of his very being, Albert Speer was a German Romantic. His defense was, in fact, a perfect exhibition of his own green thinking where he managed to shift some blame upon Western progress and technology to cloud his own accountability in one of the greatest murdering sprees witnessed in history.

Nazi existentialist philosopher Martin Heidegger (1889-1976) also employed the same argument after the war. In a speech given in 1949, which he was careful not to have published until after his death, Heidegger opined, "Agriculture today is a motorized industry of alimentation (process of nourishment), the same thing in essence as the fabrication of corpses in the gas chambers and the death camps, the same as blockading and the reducing of countries to famine, the same things as fabrication of hydrogen bombs."[22] The capitalistic mechanization of the modern farm was a major green concern among some of the leading Nazi ideologues. They were convinced this would bring about the destruction of the soil and landscape of the fatherland. Thus, in his speech, Heidegger continued this Nazi diatribe after the war. He complained of a global technology that had run amok producing corpses, famine and hydrogen bombs. While Heidegger is famously known for becoming anti-technology after the war, the words of this particular speech are virtually unknown. His green anti-technology crusade thus has a connection to the Holocaust in his own twisted view of the world. As far as Heidegger is concerned, Nazism was not the problem per se, but the globalization of technology that was driving over the top of everyone. He "uses the planetary nature of modern technology to deny the irreducible specificity of the Nazi genocide and to associate it with one of the most banal manifestations of the technological transformation of existence—namely the transformation of agriculture into mechanized food industry."[23] The superficial banality of modern life brought on by the industrial revolution on a global scale is therefore the real culprit for the Holocaust.

---

[22] Faye, Emmanuel. *Heidegger: The Introduction of Nazism into Philosophy in the Light of the Unpublished Seminars of 1933-35.* New Haven & London: Yale University Press, 2009, p. 304.

[23] Ibid.

What many do not appreciate is that such an attitude bears all the typical brand marks of what could easily be described as classic Nazi ideology, particularly of the dreaded SS,[24] Heinrich Himmler's (1900-1945) *green* praetorian guard. The SS was the greenest faction of National Socialism. Such sentiments about the dangers of global technology as expressed by both Speer and Heidegger go to the very core of what National Socialism was largely all about. National Socialism prided itself in being uniquely German against the backdrop of a world gone mad with global capitalism and communism competing for industrial domination.

Both Speer and Heidegger also believed National Socialism had gone astray.[25] Thanks to the war effort, the Nazis found themselves in the same industrial rat race that they often complained about during the 1920s and '30s. International competition and survival trumped Nazi values that originally helped catapult them into power. By the late 1930s, Heidegger "concluded that the historical form taken by National Socialism, including its crude naturalistic, biological, and racist views, was another expression of technological modernity, but he never abandoned his conviction that there was a great potential at the core of the movement."[26] Even years after the war, Speer greatly struggled with this very issue in coming to grips with the horrors of his own complicity in National Socialism. With such compromised men, the very concern they bring out in their discussions about the terrors of Nazism should be the very item that is the most thoroughly investigated. In other words, they are to be caught by their own denials, particularly with regard to the very concerns they are protecting. Their dual attraction to both National Socialism and environmentalism is far more significant than most would care to admit.

As far as Heidegger is concerned, global technology uproots people from their natural foundations. Not only does this lead to a dominating view of nature, but it also alienates people from their local environs found in the Earth and soil. It therefore turns them into mechanized cogs of a lifeless machine that has no meaningful specificity. This, in turn, reduces them to

---

[24] SS is an abbreviated form that stands for *Schutzstaffel*, which means a protectorate staff. The notoriously stylized SS letters and its flag were borrowed from Austrian nature mystic Guido Von List (1848-1919) and rooted in Aryan folklore. The SS was the protectorate of the Aryans, its mystical folklore and its Germanic lands.

[25] Joseph Goebbels, the Nazi Propaganda Minister, argued the problem was the German army was not National Socialist enough.

[26] Zimmerman, Michael, "Rethinking the Heidegger-Deep Ecology Relationship," *Environmental Ethics*, Vol. 15, p. 204, 1994.

a life of triviality as the gimmicks of modern industrial society glitzes over their otherwise hollow lives. Such an international homogenization of the same thus prevents them from living what Heidegger considered to be an *authentic* lifestyle, or what he often called the *essence of being*.

Heidegger believed wholeheartedly that essence has no meaning apart from a specific context. In fact, Heidegger reduced the meaning of essence to a localized specific context. Hence his great emphasis throughout his career was upon the essence of existence in one's own localized *dwelling*. With international global capitalism and technology, Heidegger believed modern Western man had lost contact with the world in which he lives so that he no longer has a real home. Instead of being immersed in the existential world around him, particularly in his own localized environs where he can properly serve the needs of the nation, he has become an alien in his own country. As such, he lives an inauthentic lifestyle. To Heidegger, such a person never really authentically lives, nor is able to authentically die. This doctrine would have a particularly repulsive derivative in some of Heidegger's statements about the Holocaust precisely because he considered the Jews to be nomads in Europe.

Indeed, Heidegger's naturist existentialism comes to the Nazi rescue in denying the true horrors of the Holocaust. In a lecture he wrote in 1949, but apparently never delivered, Heidegger goes so far as to deny the very *being* of the Jews. For Heidegger, this means that the Jews were not authentic and were thus not able to really die in the Holocaust:

> Hundreds of thousands die *en masse*. Do they die? They perish. They are put down. Do they die? They become supply pieces for stock in the fabrication of corpses. Do they die? They are liquidated unnoticed in death camps. And also, without such (camps)—millions in China sunken in poverty perish from hunger. But to die means to carry out death in its essence. To be able to die means to be able to carry out this resolution. We can do this only if our essence likes the essence of death. But in the middle of the innumerable deaths the essence of death remains unrecognizable.[27]

First of all, Heidegger reduces the magnitude of the holocaust by speaking of hundreds of thousands of victims instead of millions. Secondly, he virtually

---

[27] Faye, p. 305.

says the Jews were not even able to die in the death camps.[28] According to Heidegger's philosophy, this is because their own inauthentic existence, i.e., their unnatural way of life, denied the true essence of their *being*.

When Heidegger says, "Hundreds of thousands die *en masse*," this is very derogatory. To die "en masse" is to die inauthentically like a homogenous capitalist item made by factories that can only reproduce exact replicas of the same. Therefore, the Jews who died in death camps had no real identity. They were an amorphous blob of *unnoticed* corpses that was liquidated beyond any kind of authentic recognition. More telling, Heidegger does not even mention the Jews, but identifies millions of Chinese. "This makes his silence with respect to the Jewish victims all the more odious. Now, while the famines in China are a terrible reality, they are not the result of willful genocide. The association Heidegger makes is therefore doubly negationist: it denies the actual scale as well as the genocidal intention of the Nazi extermination."[29] Indeed, Heidegger virtually stated the Jewish massacre in the Holocaust was unrecognizable.

Austrian Nazi Franz Stangl (1908-1971), euthanasia specialist and death camp commandant of both Sobibor and Treblinka, gave testimony to the same attitude toward the Jewish mass graves as Heidegger: "They were cargo. I think it started the first day I saw the death camp extermination area in Treblinka. I remember Wirth standing there, next to the pits full of blue-black corpses. It had nothing to do with humanity—It could not have. It was a mass—a mass of rotting flesh."[30]

As such, the destruction of the Jews in the Nazi era was an unrecognizable non-event in human history comparable to supply-side economics homogenized by modern industrial capitalism. Herein lies the existential epitome of Nazi environmental ethics. "Those who presided over the actions of *Einsatzgruppen* (mass shootings) and the mass gassings, were determined that such experiences would be virtually non-events."[31] Nazi crimes were never perpetrated and thus were never accompanied with guilt.[32] Heidegger's own thoughts after the war are a continuation of this gruesome logic.

---

[28]   Ibid.
[29]   Faye, "Being, History, Technology, and Extermination in Heidegger."
[30]   Sereny, *Into that Darkness: An Examination of Conscience*. New York: Vintage Books, 1974, p. 201.
[31]   Pois, *National Socialism and the Religion of Nature*. London & Sydney: Croom Helm, 1986, p. 145.
[32]   Ibid.

Heidegger's thrice repetition of the question "Do they die?" even echoes the bafflement of Rudolf Hoess (1901-1947), the commandant of Auschwitz, when he commented, "The Jews' way of living and dying was a true riddle which I never managed to solve."[33] Hoess was shocked by the behavior of the Special Detachment Jews whose job it was to supervise the prisoners going into the gas chambers and then drag their dead bodies to be burned in the crematoriums. Before the crematoriums were built, they were ordered to dig up the mass graves and burn them, "They carried out all these tasks with a callous indifference as though it were all part of an ordinary day's work. While they dragged the corpses about, they ate or they smoked. They did not stop eating even when engaged on the grisly job of burning corpses which had been lying for some time in mass graves."[34]

Without even considering the Nazi regime itself was responsible for orchestrating such ghastliness, Hoess's anti-Semitism is vividly showcased here with his absolute contempt for the Special Detachment Jews, "They carried out their grisly task with dumb indifference. Their one object was to finish the work as quickly as possible so that they could have a long interval in which to search the clothing of gassed victims for something to smoke or eat. Although they were well fed and given many additional allowances, they could often be seen shifting corpses with one hand while they gnawed at something they held in the other. Even when they were engaged in the most gruesome work of digging out and burning the corpses buried in the mass graves, they never stopped eating."[35]

Hoess would recover from such horrifying scenes by finding some solace in nature. "If I was deeply affected by some incident, I found it impossible to go back to my home and my family. I would mount my horse and ride, until I had chased the terrible picture away. Often at night, I would walk through the stables and seek relief among my beloved animals."[36] Stangl acted likewise as he had the SS side of the Treblinka death camp constructed into what he described as a *really beautiful* place with flowers, gardens, benches and rustic buildings together with zoo animals, stating "We had any number of marvelous birds there."[37] When he was at Sobibor, the SS

---

[33]   Hoess, Rudolf. *Commandant of Auschwitz*. Great Britain: Weidenfeld & Nicholson, 1959, p. 153.

[34]   Ibid., p. 152.

[35]   Ibid., pp. 198-99.

[36]   Ibid., p. 155.

[37]   Sereny, *Into that Darkness*, p. 166.

officer's quarters was called "The Bird's Nest."[38] This is precisely how the authentic natural men of Nazi Germany walked down the barbaric road to Auschwitz. Indeed, "There have been hundreds of descriptions of the SS camp officials as good family men who loved animals and who went home after work to putter in the garden."[39]

Hoess's nature loving tendencies is far more revealing than most scholars would care to admit. While Jews went up in sacrificial smoke in the chimneys of Auschwitz, Hoess said his family lived "a free and untrammeled life. My wife's garden was a paradise of flowers."[40] Hoess was more concerned about untreated stormwater discharging directly into the nearby Sola River from the camp[41] than he was over the incredible slaughterhouse plans that Himmler was foisting upon him. "As a camp commandant I saw all my plans for making Auschwitz a clean and healthy place begin to dwindle," he said.[42] The cunning of nature was indeed an escape route from moral responsibility and culpability. Nature by itself does not judge a man. It is therefore not surprising that Hoess found relief among his animals. As the Nazis understood things, "The person who lives in harmony with, or better, embodies the laws of nature, is authentic and necessarily, all of his actions must be as well."[43]

An ethic based on nature is a dangerous ethic at best. At worst it is no ethic at all. This was perfectly showcased by the barbarism of the Nazi regime. At Auschwitz is seen the epitome of a green Nazi biological ethic laden with heavy doses of natural existentialism.[44] The facticity of the *Fuhrer's* existence coupled with his alleged iron will was often enthusiastically submitted to without question, even under the gruesomeness of brutally liquidating millions of Jews who were deemed biologically and culturally dangerous to the German people by the Nazi regime. The mad scientist, Dr. Mengele (1911-1979), otherwise known as the Angel of Death who performed horrific experiments on human beings, protested that "he

---

38   Ibid., pp. 94-95.

39   Feig, *Hitler's Death Camps: The Sanity of Madness*. New York & London: Holmes & Meier Publishers, 1981, p. 14.

40   Sereny, p. 156.

41   Ibid., p. 209.

42   Ibid., p. 204.

43   Pois, p. 121.

44   On the connection between German existentialism and the Holocaust, see especially chapter 5 entitled "The Natural, Authentic Man and the Road to Auschwitz" in *National Socialism and the Religion of Nature* by Robert Pois, pp. 117-136.

did not invent Auschwitz and that he was not personally responsible for the incidents there. Auschwitz already existed."[45]

Indeed, Hoess was informed of the *Final Solution* in the summer of 1941 by Himmler himself and was warned to get prepared for it. "Every Jew that we can lay our hands on is to be destroyed now during the war, without exception. If we cannot now obliterate the biological basis of Jewry, the Jews will one day destroy the German people."[46] Himmler also added in the same conversation that he had "earmarked Auschwitz for this purpose." Auschwitz, a fort built by the Austrian army dating back to World War I, had to be greatly expanded. The construction of Auschwitz-Birkenau began in October of 1941 to accommodate Himmler's sinister SS plan to destroy the Jews. The German name *Birkenau* is named after the beautiful birch trees that populated the remote area which many Polish people considered to be an "inhospitable place to live in."[47] One of the small villages torn down in order to build the gigantic camp was named after the birch trees, which the SS used for the namesake of Auschwitz II, the very camp that would become a byword for the biggest atrocity committed in the Western world in the 20th century.

When Rudolf Hoess's testimony was presented at Nuremberg, he concluded, "Let the public continue to regard me as the blood thirsty beast, the cruel sadist and the mass murderer; for the masses could never imagine the commandment of Auschwitz in any other light. They could never understand that he, too, had a heart and that he was not evil."[48] Hoess exonerated himself by saying, "I have sufficiently explained how the horrors of the concentration camps could come about. I for my part never sanctioned them. I myself never maltreated a prisoner, far less killed one. Nor have I ever tolerated maltreatment by my subordinates."[49] He was even incensed by the fact that after he was arrested, he was thrashed with his own whip during the interrogation process. "It hardly ever touched my horse, far less the prisoners. Nevertheless, one of my interrogators was convinced that I had perpetually used it for flogging the prisoners."[50]

---

[45] Posner, Gerald & Ware, John. *Mengele: The Complete Story.* New York: Cooper Square Press, 1986, p. 30.
[46] Hoess, p. 183.
[47] Posner & Ware, p. 19.
[48] Hoess, p. 181.
[49] Ibid., p. 179.
[50] Ibid., p. 174.

Rudolf Hoess, the commandant of Auschwitz, the man directly responsible for more than one million deaths, really did not believe that he committed crimes under the banner of National Socialism. He was even proud of how humane the gassing process was at Auschwitz compared to Treblinka. He stated: "So far as Auschwitz is concerned, I have never known or heard of a single person being found alive when the gas chambers were opened half an hour after the gas had been inducted."[51] Concerning the gas chambers at Treblinka, Hoess said, "The exhaust gases were often insufficiently strong to kill everyone in the chambers. Many of them were only rendered unconscious and had to be finished off by shooting." Auschwitz used Zyklon B rather than diesel fumes to kill the Jews.

In July 1942, Himmler visited Auschwitz. He demanded all those murdered and buried in mass graves to be exhumed and burned. Part of the reason why Himmler wanted to burn up the corpses was not only because of the intolerable stench that permeated the summer air throughout the whole area, but also because SS Nazi administrators "of nearby fish farms complained that the presence of poisonous contaminants in the ground water was causing the fish in their ponds to die off."[52] The SS at Auschwitz was far more concerned about fish die offs than they were over murdering innumerable Jewish victims along with many Polish political prisoners. Himmler, no doubt, would have also wanted to burn up his SS crimes in smoke, but in July 1942 this may not have been as big of a concern as it may have become later when the Nazis began to realize they were going to lose the war. The summer of 1942 was the high-water mark of the German blitzkrieg as the *Wehrmacht* had pushed deep into the Russian steppe as they approached Stalingrad on the Volga River. By 1943, the crematoriums at Auschwitz were often working night and day operating in high gear, yet still overloaded with so many corpses that many of them continued to be burned in outdoor pits.

The Term 'Holocaust' Casts a Dark Religious Shadow Over Nazism

The word *Holocaust* itself is derived from an ancient Hebrew word meaning *whole burnt offering*. According to the Old Testament Levitical code, whole burnt offerings were animal sacrifices offered to God for religious

---

51   Ibid., p. 197.
52   *Auschwitz From A to Z: An Illustrated History of the Camp.* Auschwitz-Birkenau State Museum, 2013, p. 34.

purposes.[53] Thus, the selection of this particular term to describe the Nazi crime strongly suggests both the sacrificial and religious nature of the most heinous act committed in human history. While the Jewish religious motivation for using this word to describe the unspeakable atrocity that was the Holocaust is certainly warranted, the problem with using such a term is that it has often bordered on an ineffable holy word. "As the holocaust is sacralized, comparisons are perceived as blasphemy."[54] The unintended consequence is that it has tended to place a damper on discovering the roots of what the Holocaust was all about. In other words, to describe the Holocaust as a whole burnt offering brings up many interesting questions but fails to answer them all. If the Holocaust was a burnt offering, this brings up the question as to who exactly the priestly perpetrators of such a human sacrifice were? Secondly, for what purpose was the human sacrifice offered?

Nonetheless, the term Holocaust is helpful in answering the question *what?* It was a religious whole burnt offering. Moreover, since it was people who went up in smoke, this means at once the Holocaust must necessarily be a human sacrifice. The question *how?* has been answered as well—first by indiscriminate shooting, but then later via cattle cars to the ghettos and gas chambers. The question *by whom?* has almost been answered—by Hitler and the Nazis, of course. The great problem here is the reasoning behind the Nazi atrocities has not been well understood or appreciated, much less even promoted. "Studies of the holocaust have been marred by a poor understanding and an under-theorizing of anti-Semitism."[55] Answers have rightly dwelled upon the racial aspect of it all, but the *scientific* evolutionary pantheism upon which Nazism was based on has often been overlooked. As such, few have bothered to notice that Nazi *scientific* racism was built on a biological-ecological foundation wrapped around a core of German Romanticism, existentialism and nature worship.

Purely secular histories on the Third Reich have also downplayed or ignored the religious-ideological element of National Socialism.[56] The overzealous leftist holy war against ideas that absurdly reduces all thought to

---

53 Leviticus 1:4 says that they were offered "to make atonement" for their souls. An animal substitute died in place of the worshiper according to God's grace.

54 Sax, Boria. *Animals in the Third Reich: Pets, Scapegoats, and the Holocaust.* New York: Continuum, 2000, p. 19.

55 Goldhagen, Daniel Jonah. *Hitler's Willing Executioners: Ordinary Germans and the Holocaust.* New York: Vintage Press, 1996, p. 7.

56 See especially Robert Pois' discussion on this in *National Socialism and the Religion of Nature*, pp. 13-33.

materialistic causes has clouded the fact that Nazi ideology did indeed have sinister and religious consequences. "It would be dangerously misleading to assume that ideas, however abstruse or absurd they might be, cannot develop extraordinary powers of their own."[57] Historical scholarship permeated with leftist materialism, modern existentialism and nihilism has only compounded this problem further. Too many scholars have presumed the Nazis did not have a coherent set of beliefs[58] that should be seriously investigated. "For many historians and political commentators, it has been and will continue to be extraordinarily difficult to believe that individuals and movements, perceived of as being evil, mean what they say."[59] As such, many historians simply assume "the National Socialist party officials, and the SS, was either a sham or, at most, a poorly contrived rationalization for motives rooted in economic self-interest, personal aggrandizement, or nihilistic drives towards self-destruction, essentially opaque to meaningful historical investigation."[60]

Perhaps more pertinent, to untangle the labyrinth of National Socialist ideology reveals many uncomfortable comparisons between Nazism and modern Western man's obsession with nature. The Nazi emphasis upon nature and the natural man, largely rooted in the German Romanticism and Existentialism of the 1800s, continues to reverberate throughout modern culture. Its strong religious or Romantic sentiments are often hidden beneath layers of natural existentialism and the naturalistic sciences of the modern age:

> National Socialism was a religion of nature, one that was rooted in fundamental existential concerns of alienated 20th century man. Its content was German, but the form it assumed could well prove to be congruent with the spiritual needs of all people, who, rejecting Marxist solutions necessitating class-warfare, have been unable to deal successfully with the necessarily alienating character of modern society. In a word, National Socialism was one response to a general problem which has haunted western *bourgeois* culture during the industrial and, for that matter, post-industrial age.[61]

---

[57] Pois, p. 145.
[58] Redles, David. *Hitler's Millennial Reich: Apocalyptic Belief and the Search for Salvation.* New York: New York University Press, 2005, pp. 8-10.
[59] Pois, p. 13.
[60] Ibid., p. 14.
[61] Ibid., p. 10.

That many people are completely unaware of the Nazi infatuation with all things natural is something that needs correction. While the Nazi movement was certainly unique to Germany, "we must not, however, lose sight of the fact that, in its concern that man, or at least Aryan man, regain his place in the natural order of things, National Socialism was simply, albeit in a more pointed fashion, expressing the wishes of a substantial portion of western humanity."[62] This, perhaps, is another reason why modern scholarship has not taken Nazi ideology seriously. Not only will such an investigation remove the simplistic caricatures that many people have with regard to National Socialism, but it will also expose some troubling similarities between Nazi yesteryear and today's environmental movement.

People do not want to be told that their beliefs, particularly when it comes to nature and modern environmentalism, were actually harbored by Nazis as well. That such ideas even played an important role in National Socialism, not to mention the Holocaust itself, is simply inconceivable to them. They are completely unaware that most modern historical scholarship has largely ignored the natural ideology of the Nazis. Most books dealing with National Socialism speak far more about historical events wrapped around raw power politics without ever describing what it was the Nazis actually thought they were doing:

> For the historian, confronting a phenomenon whose central ideological precepts were never abandoned and which were indeed translated into reality once the movement attained power, it is absolutely necessary to accept the somber fact that, even if committed Nazis did not in an ultimate sense say what they meant, they most assuredly meant what they said.[63]

While history is often tragic, this does not mean it is nihilistic or that ideas have no real consequences. Too many scholars have deemed the ideology of National Socialism as largely irrelevant. This has left a huge gaping hole in the minds of many as to what the National Socialist experiment was all about. The vacuum was then filled with socialist/Marxist and existentialist propaganda that touted the Nazis as capitalists even though they called themselves National Socialists.

---

[62] Ibid., p. 29.
[63] Ibid., p. 23.

The Great Weaknesses of the 'Local Only' Nazi Economy

All of this this has led to great problems in answering the question *why?* the Holocaust. Even though the Nazis by and large hated capitalism and Christianity, both of them have often been routinely blamed for the Holocaust. Leftist-Marxist historical interpreters routinely wax eloquently about the terrors of Nazi industrialism and capitalism, even though one of the few bright spots that can be found anywhere during the Holocaust was undertaken by industrialist Oskar Schindler (1908-1974) in Poland and Czechoslovakia. In spite of his character flaws, Schindler protected more than 1,000 of his Jewish workers throughout the war by massive bribery of the SS and other Nazi officials. His great fortunes amassed during the war were almost all spent on protecting his Jewish workers under his authority. He asked to be buried in Jerusalem. He is considered by the Jews to be a hero.

Leftists and Marxists are also quick to show any kind of Christian language the *Fuhrer* made use of from time to time in his public speeches. Unlike many people in general, leftists are fully aware that capitalism and modern industry are based upon a Judeo-Christian worldview with no small thanks to the Protestant work ethic that emanated from Calvin's Geneva. Leftists are therefore eager to show Nazism was both Christian and capitalist. While historically speaking, Catholics and Protestants were often anti-Semitic,[64] and all too many Christians quietly watched what was happening to the Jews from a distance during the Nazi era, both the Old and New Testaments are strongly opposed to human sacrifice that became the hallmark of Nazi slave labor and *euthanasia* practices, where countless victims were either worked to death, shot or gassed. Outside of the one great exception of Jesus Christ and the cross, Christians do not believe in human sacrifice. In fact, thanks to Christianity, the universal practice of even animal sacrifice eventually came to an end in many parts of the world. Yet SS General Oswald Pohl developed an "Extermination by Labor" program for Nazi Germany's concentration camp system. During the Holocaust, Pohl even complained "that expeditiously gassing Jews deprived the Reich of an important resource. His idea, 'Extermination by Labor,' quite simply meant working Jews to death. Only after outliving their usefulness would they be deported to death camps for gassing."[65]

---

[64] Goldhagen, pp. 106-115.

[65] Black, Edwin. *IBM and the Holocaust: The Strategic Alliance between Nazi Germany and America's Most Powerful Corporation.* Washington D.C.: Diaolog Press, 2011, p. 21.

Normally, without SS generals like Oswald Pohl exerting considerable state influence and regulation over industry as the chief of the main bureau of administration and economy in Nazi Germany, most capitalists would rather employ people than sacrifice them. They are at least smart enough to realize that one cannot take advantage of a dead person. While this does not excuse the German industrialists' culpability with regard to the brutal treatment of all the slave labor available to them during the war, Albert Speer and others did point out that starving workers do not make very good ones. Not surprisingly, "over the course of the war, labor was to emerge as a critical constraint in the German war economy."[66] Yet, it was precisely the *local only* racist economy that ransacked the potential workforce of the Nazis by abusing and/or liquidating it. Irrational Nazi policies were suicidal to the war effort. Nazi racist beliefs often compromised the war effort by brutalizing many workers who could have otherwise helped them become more industrially capable of beating back the enemy.

In his book, *German Big Business and the Rise of Hitler*, Yale university professor Dr. Henry Ashby Turner contends:

> Most publications that explain the rise of Nazism in terms of capitalism have no need to rely heavily on evidence. They take as their point of departure a reductive assumption that obviates the necessity for a tightly argued and closely documented analysis of the causes of events: the primacy of economics. If that assumption is granted, the traditional focuses of inquiry into the origins of the Third Reich—intellectual traditions, government policies, national elections, the political behavior of social groups, and the actions of parties and politicians, including Hitler and the Nazis—become relegated to the status of mere epiphenomena located in the "superstructure" of society. Far from determining the source of events, such epiphenomena at most reflect developments taking places in the decisive economic sphere. Since most of what occurs in the economic sphere is assumed to remain concealed from the public and even from the historian, much must be surmised from a few clues rather than demonstrated by a sustained marshaling of the evidence, as in traditional historical scholarship. . . . Through

---

[66] Tooze, Adam. *The Wages of Destruction: The Making and Breaking of the Nazi Economy.* New York: Penguin Books, 2006, p. 358.

circular reasoning the Nazi's acquisition of power is presented as proof that the forces at work in Germany's capitalist economy had of necessity to eventuate in the creation of the Third Reich. Alternatively, recourse is had to a functionalist argument basically similar to that employed by 19th century anti-Semites who insisted that Jews must have caused the French Revolution since they benefitted so greatly from it: Since the capitalists profited under the Third Reich, they must have surely have been behind its creation. The function of Nazism must, according to such reasoning, therefore have been to rescue German capitalism.[67]

Such historical scholarship on Nazi Germany is very typical and continues unabated even today. The false assumption underlying much leftist historiography on the Third Reich is that if one details the economic record of National Socialism, the most significant factors leading up to Nazi tyranny and the Holocaust will be explained. However, under classical liberal values of the American Revolution, capitalism has generally advocated the *invisible hand* of liberty and deregulated free markets, but leftist historians all too easily convert the heritage of free enterprise into vehicles of tyranny. With regard to National Socialism, they do this by ignoring the obvious reality that the Nazis used the state to control, regulate and direct Germany's economy in ways that would not have developed otherwise:

> Hitler never allowed financial considerations to affect his decisions. The industrial barons did not buy him and bend him to their will. Far from it. On the contrary, he slowly but surely imposed his will upon business. He fitted business into a planned economy and placed it under absolute government control which in the long run could only smother all economic initiative and which culminated in a total war economy.[68]

Moreover, the National Socialist government richly rewarded the industrialists who went along with the regime. It was not capitalism per se or free enterprise that led to the horrors of the Holocaust. According to Nazi press

---

[67]   Turner, Henry Ashby. *German Big Business and the Rise of Hitler.* Oxford University Press, 1985, p. 354.
[68]   Dietrich, Otto. *The Hitler I Knew: Memoirs of the Third Reich's Press Chief.* New York: Skyhorse Publishing, 2010, p. 143.

chief Otto Dietrich, Hitler presumed "that in its course of evolution society had outgrown the traditional form of autonomous, private capitalism, and that reason demanded a new and more functional economic order, in other words, a planned economy."[69]

Thus, the notion that Nazi Germany was an economic, capitalistic juggernaut is purely fictitious.[70] Upon the Nazi accession to power, Germany owed almost 20 billion marks to foreign creditors.[71] The value of currency and debt was the great concern of the Nazi government throughout much of its 12-year duration. The Nazi economy was never a strong one, and from 1938 on, faced severe problems.

The Nazis also put into practice some government-sponsored jobs creation programs. Hitler "promised to reform the German state apparatus and to bring order to the ramshackle division of labor between the Reich, states, and local authorities. By the way of social policy, he offered the promise of an agrarian resettlement program, labor service, and a guarantee to maintain health care and pensions. Promoting work and economy in the public services would in turn provide a guarantee against any danger"[72] to the Reichsmark.

What the Nazis really wanted was a nationalistic self-sufficient economy based on race that would be extended over most of Europe through the propagation of war. This meant that capitalism could not and would not be completely set aside, even though many Nazis loathed it. Capitalism and industry were needed to build up the German Army. As such, the National Socialist's primary interest in business and industry was to make weapons in order to prepare the entire nation for war. Moreover, the state-sponsored military industrial complex of the *Wehrmacht*[73] was the primary reason why German unemployment was drastically reduced in the later 1930s, not so much because of their socialist public works programs. With regard to labor and the social economy, therefore, the choice was largely "between recruiting

---

[69] Ibid.

[70] Adam Tooze's monumental book called *The Wages of Destruction: The Making and Breaking of the Nazi Economy* is perhaps the best book that has ever been written describing the National Socialist economy. Tooze masterfully shows the great weaknesses and struggles of the Nazi economy throughout its 12-year tenure.

[71] Tooze, p. 27.

[72] Ibid., p. 37.

[73] This is the designated name for the armed forces of Germany dating back to the Weimar Republic created in 1919 after the Reich's defeat in World War I.

a man into the armed forces, or leaving him in a factory to produce for the war effort."[74]

What the Nazis especially hated about capitalism was its alleged connections to Jewish international finance. This hatred placed the Nazi regime on a suicidal path of national autarky, economic isolation and destruction. National autarky means economic self-sufficiency, and this emphasis placed Nazi Germany under a siege of its own making. Ominously, by 1938, the German finance ministry began "living from 'hand to mouth' and the *Reichsbank* had been forced into an inflationary creation of money"[75] because of reckless Nazi spending habits on the military. Both Adolf Hitler and Hermann Goering[76] were far more willing to sacrifice the entire Nazi economy[77] on the Nordic altar of the Greco-Roman god of war. They were never interested in expanding capitalistic power for its own sake. Sound financial decisions were seldom made during the Third Reich, something which Hjalmar Schacht, the chief financial architect of the regime, repeatedly warned against. Indeed, Otto Dietrich pointed out, "The armaments plants swallowed many billions which in spite of prosperity and high taxes, did not return to the state treasury."[78] In short, "in economic as well as military terms, Nazi Germany was going for broke."[79]

The Nazis detested the whole concept of international capitalism. Hitler once remarked, "Free trade was simply the smokescreen behind which imperialist Britain, the favored vehicle of Jewish parliamentarianism and liberalism, attempted to monopolize the riches of the entire world."[80] Hitler was captivated by a state-directed economy, stating: "The Venetian Republic affords an excellent example of how successful a state can be. For 500 years the price of bread in Venice never varied, and it was left to the Jews with the predatory motto of free trade to wreck this stability."[81]

---

[74]   Tooze, p. 360.
[75]   Ibid., p. 286.
[76]   Hermann Goering was the leader of the *Luftwaffe* (Air Force) and later became the *Reichsmarschall* (top general) of the entire Germany army. He was an aristocrat of sorts who goes back to the very origins of the Nazi Party.
[77]   Tooze, pp. 333-34, 357.
[78]   Dietrich, p. 24.
[79]   Tooze, p. 347.
[80]   Ibid., p. 174.
[81]   *Hitler's Table Talk: 1941-44*, preface and essay by H.R. Trevor Roper, translated by Norman Cameron and R.H. Stevens. New York: Enigma Books, 2000, midday of July 5, 1942, p. 421.

Hitler would rather conquer nations than freely trade or do business with them. The Nazis sought a *local only* economic autarky in Germany itself to counteract the Jewish disease of international finance which they presumed had fleeced the nation of its wealth in the economic catastrophe of the 1920s. Hitler once said, "Judaism, this form of mental depravation that must at all costs be abolished, has made the fixing of prices depend on the laws of supply and demand—things which have nothing to do with the intrinsic value of an article."[82] After mocking the American economy based on capitalistic rationalization that he said invariably leads to poverty, Hitler then exclaimed, "Obviously the Jew thinks as a capitalist, and not as an economist."[83] While Hitler did believe in private property, he still proclaimed, "I am a socialist."[84] As such, Hitler characterized the capitalistic business world as "made up of everywhere of the same rogues. Gold-hearted money-grubbers. The business world gets idealistic only when the workers ask for higher wages."[85] Hitler's ideas on taxation were along the same socialist lines: "Despite all the taxes, there's a lot of money left."[86]

The Nazis took control of the economy not only by subsidizing Germany's exports in a complicated trading scheme, but also by restricting its imports with a highly-regulated government permission program.[87] This, in effect, created corporate welfare which led to a corrupt relationship between the Nazi Party and big business that became ever entwined in a corporatism of growing terror.[88] While this state-sponsored corporatism greatly enriched the big industrialists and gave the appearance of a strong rebounding economy throughout the 1930s, it also squeezed out the bourgeois middle class and subjected the average German consumer to increased rationing, especially as the war kicked into high gear.[89] The Nazi economy was all guns without butter. The consumers did have money, but fewer items were available for purchase. As such, these economic

---

82   Ibid., evening of March 29, 1942. p. 283.

83   Ibid., evening of Jan. 27, 1942, p. 196.

84   Hitler, Adolf. *Zweites Buch*, p. 26.

85   *Hitler's Table Talk*, evening of Oct. 18, 1941, p. 57.

86   Ibid.

87   Tooze, p 81.

88   Goldberg, Jonah. *Liberal Fascism: The Secret History of the American Left from Mussolini to the Politics of Change*. New York: Doubleday, 2007. Goldberg defines corporatism as a left-wing phenomenon where industry is either nationalized by the government or so heavily regulated that it is effectively nationalized in practice, p. 51.

89   Tooze, pp. 355-56.

practices virtually destroyed foreign competition in German markets[90] so that "the disastrous proliferation of protectionism fractured the bedrock of economic liberalism."[91] With no small irony, by 1939, increasing foreign isolation forced Nazi Germany to make a huge economic deal with its arch nemesis—Soviet Russia—to help keep their economy afloat,[92] another contradiction brought on by unsustainable war-machine spending. After the war, Dietrich said, "Today we know that Hitler purchased economic prosperity with billions in government debt—a debt so staggering that the overloaded credit structure would have made enormous difficulties for him in future years of peace."[93]

Nazi Germany also lacked natural resources. As the imports were increasingly squeezed, the Nazi economy was forced to become an *ersatz* economy. Synthetic substitutes produced locally at home had to be found to fill in the gaping holes. Producing synthetics through the chemical industry became vital to make up for the dearth of imports. This virtually guaranteed that the chemical giant IG Farben would become the heart of the Nazi economy. Worsening foreign relations also meant fewer and fewer imports[94] for German consumers.

Nazi Lebensraum: Looking for Space & Sustainable Development

The territorial acquisitions in western and central Europe by the Nazis only slightly improved their economic predicament. As they swallowed the various economies around them in their drive to obtain continental supremacy, they also inherited all of their economic problems as well. "Despite the extraordinary extent of the *Wehrmacht's* victories, the space under Germany's control in the autumn of 1940 was not the self-sufficient living space of which Hitler had dreamed."[95] Even with all of western and central Europe at its disposal, Nazi Germany still needed to trade with the Soviet Union to make up for their lack of natural resources. Hitler found out the hard way that not even all of western and central Europe can be

---

90   Ibid., p. 107.
91   Ibid., p. 105.
92   Ibid., p. 321.
93   Dietrich, p. 24.
94   Jeffreys, Diarmuid. *Hell's Cartel: IG Farben and the Making of Hitler's War Machine.* New York: Metropolitan Books, 2008, pp. 215-16.
95   Tooze, p. 420.

economically self-sufficient. The drive eastward to take land by force thus became more radical, ominous and sinister, especially as the war effort began to go badly.

The farther east the Germans pushed, the less economic gains there were. The breadbasket that Hitler expected to seize in the Ukraine turned out to be a disastrous mirage. The Nazi brass had not anticipated "how badly forcible collectivization had affected conditions in the Ukraine, or that the grain sent to Germany by Russia in 1939 and 1940 had had to be squeezed out of a near starving peasantry by force."[96] In 1941, the retreating Red Army's scorched Earth policy all but guaranteed the law of steadily diminishing returns as the *Wehrmacht* advanced across the Baltics, Byelorussia, Ukraine and western Russia. "The vast grain reserves the Germans had expected to find in Russia were simply not there."[97] As such, Nazi isolation from international trade only intensified their Malthusian lack of natural resources. The *local only* economy of the Third Reich was a political pipe dream, even with much of Europe under its hegemony.

Though a clergyman of sorts, Thomas Malthus (1766-1834) was a pessimistic political economist. He challenged the gradual perfectibility of man so prevalent among scholars of the Enlightenment. Malthus objected to the liberal hubris of his day primarily by warning against the overpopulation of the laboring classes relative to England's feudalistic property system that he deemed sacrosanct. The upshot of his demographic studies was that exponential population growth of the laboring classes would eventually outstrip the natural resources of the land in any given location. The land, owned by the English aristocracy, will no longer be able to feed its high population densities, invariably inducing tumultuous labor pains upon the progress of the Enlightenment. While Malthus himself was more concerned about labor outstripping local environs more than overpopulation in general, his ideas eventually cross bred with long-term population control measures, including birth control and economic protectionism that could be put into practice to soften nature's harsh ways of naturally reducing the number of people.[98]

---

[96]   Bramwell, *Blood and Soil: Walther Darre and Hitler's Green Party*. Great Britain: The Kensal Press, 1985, p. 127.

[97]   Ibid.

[98]   See "The History of the Population Control Movement 1798-1998" by William Kay on his *Environmentalism is Fascism* website, January 2018.

Malthus thus later became a fundamental figure in Darwinian thought since natural selection thins out the weak from the strong, especially in times of overpopulation. He also could be easily considered one of the founding fathers of eugenics and environmental ethics as well. Many greens have adopted Malthus's overpopulation paradigm relative to scarce natural resources. Adolf Hitler did too. Nazi Interior Minister Wilhelm Frick (1933-43) considered those who were mentally ill, incurably sick or handicapped to be "useless eaters."[99] He was one of the primary authors of the Nazi euthanasia law. "One of Frick's contributions to Nazism was to envisage the monstrous and cloak it in law."[100]

Mein Kampf seethes with Malthusian math in the background.[101] There were too many Germans living in too narrow a living space. Germany itself was running out of environmental breathing room called *lebensraum*, which translated literally means *living space. Lebensraum* could easily be defined as the "natural habitat for Aryans." Running out of habitat, the Nazis believed this was wreaking havoc on the biological health of Germania. In order to reverse this process, the Nazis believed they needed more *living space*. Strong state control and imperialistic military conquest would therefore become necessary in order to stave off the inevitable biological doomsday and rejuvenate the German nation with more environmental living space:

> (Hitler) recognized that unchecked indulgence of the desire for procreation would lead to a shortage of food; he accepted that unquestioningly as an inexorable law of Nature. In his eyes, however, the resultant deprivation had positive value. For hunger drove hardy, vital nations to engage in what he described as "natural imperialism," that is, to stamp out weaker, thus inferior peoples and thereby carry forward the process of human evolution. The quest for more food could only be realized through the acquisition of additional arable land by conquest. . . .[102]

Thus, instead of adopting a pessimistic attitude about life, Hitler would exalt Germany at the expense of other nations just as Nature naturally weeded

---

[99] Tusa, John and Ann, *The Nuremberg Trial*. New York: Skyhorse Publishing, 2010, p. 327.
[100] Ibid.
[101] Hitler, Adolf. *Mein Kampf*, translated by Ralph Manheim. Boston & New York: Mariner Books, 1999, pp. 130-140.
[102] Turner, p. 71.

out the weak and sickly. Pessimism, therefore, belonged to the frail, not to the strong.

In Nature's grand scheme of the survival of the fittest, including the human races, Hitler believed the very existence of Germany was at stake. The horrific consequences of World War I foisted upon the Weimar Republic by the international community had placed Germany in a most precarious situation. Something needed to be done to relieve this growing existential crisis. Hitler's *Mein Kampf* became the answer. The days of what Hitler called inward colonization and pacifism need to be rejected if Germany wanted a place in the new world order. It was now time for Germany either to live or die. In *Mein Kampf*, Hitler wrote:

> For Germany, consequently, the only possibility for carrying out a healthy territorial policy lay in the acquisition of new land in Europe itself ... it must be said that such a territorial policy cannot be fulfilled in the Cameroons, but today almost exclusively in Europe. We must, therefore coolly and objectively adopt the standpoint that it can certainly not be the intention of Heaven to give one people 50 times as much land and soil in the world as another. In this case we must not let political boundaries obscure for us the boundaries of eternal justice. If this earth really has room for all to live in, let us be given the soil we need for our livelihood.[103]

Hitler's reference to the size of land "50 times as much" can only refer to Soviet Russia. Hitler's socialism also demonstrates itself in this particular quote. He considered it unfair that one group of people could have so much land compared to another. This was also considered to be a geopolitical affront to the *eternal justice* of Nature, which, in this particular instance, Hitler calls *Heaven*. In the process of confusing nature with heaven, Hitler was thus looking for a geopolitical social justice based on some form of Nazi pantheism[104] to help him sort out the *lebensraum* problem. Thus, Hitler was a socialist over race and land, not over class or economics.

---

103 Hitler, *Mein Kampf*, pp. 138-39.
104 Pantheism equates God or the gods with Nature.

What Adolf Hitler did in *Mein Kampf* was to convert Karl Haushofer's (1869-1946)[105] *lebensraum* geopolitical doctrine[106] into a justification to invade Poland, Byelorussia and the Ukraine. On the Eastern Front, both Jews and Slavs, who did not know how to relate properly to Nature and her *scientific* racial laws, would be exterminated and enslaved. Superior Aryans would then resettle the conquered areas and be allowed to culturally develop the land into a grand frontier of sustainable development where German men and Nature could live more harmoniously together. Such a hegemony under Nazi state control would also serve as an effective counterweight against the industrial might of North America,[107] not to mention the growing industrialization of the USSR, which Hitler considered to be an outright declaration of war,[108] stating: "The struggle for the hegemony of the world will be decided in favor of Europe by the possession of Russian space. Thus Europe will be an impregnable fortress, safe from all threat of blockade."[109]

Haushofer was a leader in geopolitical thought in Germany in the early 1900s. Much of his *lebensraum* doctrine came from Friedrich Ratzel (1844-1904). In the late 1800s many believed Ratzel had developed a whole new scientific theory of human existence wrapped around geography called geopolitics. Ratzel believed that history was an evolutionary struggle of the various races looking for space, which was later called *lebensraum*.[110] Ratzel also held that expanding borders reflected the biological health of the nation.

---

[105] Karl Haushofer spent quite some time with Adolf Hitler and Rudolf Hess talking about geopolitics when they were both in prison together back in 1923. Hitler wrote most of *Mein Kampf* while in prison.

[106] Bassin, Mark, "Blood or Soil?: The *Volkisch* Movement, the Nazis, and the Legacy of *Geopolitik*," in *How Green Were the Nazis?: Nature, Environment, and Nation in the Third Reich*, edited by Franz-Josef Bruggenmeier, Mark Cioc, and Thomas Zeller. Athens: Ohio University Press, 2005. Bassin writes, "*Geopolitik* was enthusiastically embraced in the Weimar Republic. Its appeal, indeed, extended across the political spectrum, but was greatest among those radical conservative forces who rejected both the Weimar Republic in toto and the rearrangement of European political space promulgated at Versailles. The principal architect of *Geopolitik* was Karl Haushofer, whose indefatigable academic and organizational efforts brought this new 'science' to prominence across Germany and with whose name it consequently became widely associated. . . . Haushofer's highest ambition was that *Geopolitik* would play the role of an applied political science, which, through an analysis of the natural laws determining the spatial behavior and needs of the political state organism, could indicate the sorts of practical policies that had to be pursued," p. 217.

[107] Tooze, pp. 10-11.

[108] Bramwell, *Blood and Soil: Walther Darre and Hitler's Green Party*, p. 123.

[109] *Hitler's Table Talk*, evening of Sept. 17, 1941, p. 27.

[110] Weikart, Richard. *From Darwin to Hitler: Evolutionary Ethics, Eugenics and Racism in Germany*. New York: Palgrave Macmillan, 2004, p. 193.

Thanks largely to Haushofer, the National Socialists adopted Ratzel's mixing of evolutionary theory, biology and geopolitics with a vengeance in their own version of *lebensraum*. Haushofer was an early advisor to Hitler. Haushofer thus became the geopolitical link between Ratzel and National Socialism. Indeed, Haushofer's father was a friend of Ratzel's. Haushofer was also a member of a proto-Nazi anthropology group called the Thule Society. It was the Thule Society that was later converted into the Nazi Party in 1920. Haushofer was also the mentor of Rudolf Hess, who was Hitler's personal secretary up until 1941. It was Haushofer and Hess who helped Hitler write *Mein Kampf*.

During the 1930s, a fascinating rupture took place inside of Himmler's SS over the true meaning of geopolitics between Karl Haushofer and Walther Darre (1895-1953),[111] Hitler's agricultural minister. Darre claimed Haushofer downplayed the role of race with too much emphasis upon environmental determinism.[112] Haushofer's cardinal sin was that he believed race was primarily determined by geographical space, not by blood.[113] While Darre acknowledged the importance of environmental influences that shape a race of people, he also pointed out the special way in which a racial community "shapes its relationship to the soil, and in what form it owns and manages this native soil."[114]

Henceforth, the idea of geographical causation fell out of favor with the Nazi hierarchy in the mid to late 1930s as some noticed such an approach denied the fact that races can and do culturally develop themselves upon their own living space. The green Nazi philosopher, Martin Heidegger, anticipated a similar argument in the early 1930s when he declared the ideal of a people does not derive entirely from its native soil, stating: "Circulation is equally necessary. Thus, the concrete way in which human beings operate in and shape space includes both en-rootedness in the soil and circulation."[115] By circulation, Professor Heidegger meant cultural development. For Heidegger, cultural knowledge is even necessary to "orient the flow of blood."[116]

---

[111]   Bassin, Mark, "Blood or Soil?: The *Volkisch* Movement, the Nazis, and the Legacy of *Geopolitik*," in *How Green Were the Nazis?* pp. 222-231.

[112]   Not surprisingly, after the war, Karl Haushofer placed as much distance as he possibly could between his geopolitical ideas and Hitler's version of the same. Haushofer claimed that only Rudolf Hess, Hitler's secretary, fully understood his lebensraum doctrine. Haushofer committed suicide in 1946.

[113]   Haushofer was also married to a Jew and never became a Nazi Party member.

[114]   Bassin, Mark, "Blood or Soil?: The *Volkisch* Movement, the Nazis, and the Legacy of *Geopolitik*," in *How Green Were the Nazis?* p. 224.

[115]   Faye, p. 143.

[116]   Ibid., p. 98.

Heidegger even added, "without living space that is sufficient, necessary for its positive development,"[117] to his own definition of *lebensraum*.

Thus, Nazi racism placed somewhat of a damper on some of the early German environmentalists in the Reich. Nonetheless, this did not mean that the Nazis gave up on their green ideas. On the contrary, what emerged in the discussions between racism and environmentalism was a Nazi version of sustainable development. "Racial ideology enabled Nazi planners to reconcile the theoretical tensions between industrial growth and environmental protection by positing a uniquely 'Aryan' ability to sustain the land's appearance and overall productivity."[118] In other words, the *dialectical* relationship between racism, Malthusian math, environmentalism, existentialism, naturalistic science and biology would help give modern birth to the ecological cult of sustainable development. Hitler himself "saw National Socialism as having been assigned the role of overcoming the contradictions of 19th century capitalism and achieving a reconciliation between the German people and the economy that sustained them."[119] This is what *lebensraum* was essentially all about—to reconcile the German race with a larger territory for the sake of cultural development and environmental breathing space that would not be adulterated by the Jewish-American-Soviet industrial complex.

Once again, Heidegger's own views presaged this development. In the winter semester of 1933-34 at the University of Freiburg Heidegger specifically taught:

> ... nature becomes manifest as space of a people, as countryside and homeland, as soil and ground. Nature, as the power and law of that hidden transmission of the inheritance of essential instinctive predispositions and tendencies, is set free. Nature becomes a normative rule in the form of health. The more freely nature reigns, the more it is possible to put at her service, in the most excellent and controlled way, the formative power of authentic technology. By being tied to nature, supported and overarched by her, at once fueled and limited by her, the history of the people is realized.[120]

---

[117] Ibid., p. 143.
[118] Lekan, *Imagining the Nation in Nature: Landscape Preservation and German Identity 1885-1945.* Cambridge, Massachusetts and London: Harvard University Press, 2004, p. 246.
[119] Tooze, p. 174.
[120] Faye, p. 72.

Heidegger thus believed in a form of sustainable technology that was authentically rooted in nature. This natural authenticity would place critical parameters on its development. This would prevent it from spinning out of control into a superficial global homogenization alienating to local populations. As such, Nazi Germany would make plans to industrialize and develop technology, but this would all be done with the latest environmental space planning sciences available at their disposal. Technology was not evil if it was not foisted upon them by the alienating and unnatural ways of international globalism, capitalism and communism. In fact, "Nazi theoreticians argued that Aryans' closeness to nature made them uniquely suited to achieving this organic harmony between modern technology and landscape integrity. The landscape architect Heinrich Wiepking-Jurgensmann described Germans' 'love for plants and the landscape' and their affinity for a 'harmonic landscape' as a result of 'biological laws innate in our *being*.'"[121]

Indeed, the July 1938 edition of a magazine entitled "Space Science and Space Ordering"[122] revealed that the Nazis had planned to regulate Hitler's and Goering's Four Year Plan with very environmentally friendly sustainable development schemes. The Four Year Plan was established in 1936 to get the German army operational within four years that could be sustained by a fit German economy. The magazine even revealed a whole cadre of leading Nazis who signed their names with glowing comments on how the environment is to be respected during the process of development. In fact, this particular edition was celebrating an environmental planning office established in 1935 called "The Work of the Reich Office for Spatial Planning." In reality, what the magazine shows is the birth of environmental social engineering schemes over private property that today has become the hallmark of the green movement. These green Nazi social engineering schemes were far ahead of their time. That they were even implemented over the Third Reich's economic war plan is not without great irony. The Nazi war machine was developed under the green hue of sustainable development.

That the Nazis would thus be heading east in a massive blitzkrieg with environmental planning papers in hand during the barbarous heights of World War II to claim areas where Aryans lived, or had lived in the distant past, is a historical fact that needs to be understood and appreciated more fully. The

---

[121] Lekan, p. 246.
[122] This is found in Heinrich Himmler's environmental planning papers archived at Stanford University.

Nazi doctrine of *lebensraum* merged Aryan biology and green geopolitics with an existential and/or aboriginal tribalism that would not be undone until all the smoke cleared from the battlefields of World War II. Rather than overcome their natural resource deficits through competitive commercialism and international trade, the Nazis decided to subjugate the entire European continent instead. In short, Hitler chose war over capitalism and trade. Victory at war would also allow them to depopulate the east so Germans could move in behind the retreating lines to obtain *lebensraum* for themselves.

However, the Nazi hierarchy and military planners also knew they had no chance of success unless Soviet Russia was defeated within the first year of the war. They were fully aware that the lack of natural resources would doom the *Wehrmacht* if there was a long war of attrition. This also helps explain why Hitler seized the Ukraine in September of 1941 when the war effort began to slow down on the Russian front. He then attempted to take the Caucasus in 1942 because of the vast oil fields there. *Lebensraum* was always more important to him than Moscow, much to the chagrin of the German generals who knew that immediate victory was more crucial at the gates of the Kremlin.

A quick, decisive Nazi victory over Russia, on the other hand, promised the Germans a strong position in what would certainly become a new world order. With their own *lebensraum* in the east, this would allow the Nazis to compete with the American-Anglo industrial complex without having to resort to the corrosive effects of what they deemed international Jewish capitalism. More importantly, they could become self-sufficient with plenty of land in the east to be used for growing food and for sustainable industrial development under Nazi state control that could later be extended throughout the entire Reich.

The Nazi economy and eastern war plans were thus not nearly as antagonistic against green goals as most modern environmental historians would like to believe. Moreover, in between both world wars, Western man's hatred of warfare had only just begun. Solving existential problems militarily was not nearly the stigma that it has become today. In the late 1800s up until World War II many often assumed that evolution and progress were largely accomplished through warfare.

Nazi racism based on crackpot biology, economic protectionism with ecological predilections, was suicidal. "Hitler's proclivity for simplification enabled him to relegate huge areas of economic activity to the periphery of reality. Just as he reduced international affairs to a Darwinian struggle to the death among nations, so he reduced that struggle essentially to the level of biology."[123] The Nazis created a government-controlled *local only* biological economy that was doomed to fail. "For Hitler, the decisive factors in world history were not labor and industry, but struggle for limited means of sustenance."[124] This can readily be seen throughout the entire history of the Third Reich's economy.

Hitler's fascist obsession with Malthusian math, race, *lebensraum*, military spending and Aryan sustainable development eventually destroyed Germany's economy. More to the point, greater *lebensraum* controlled by Nazi biology did not resolve Germany's Malthusian economic problems, but only worsened them. The more territory they conquered, the more they lost control over their own fate. Hitler's grand plan did exactly the opposite of what he had hoped for. By 1942, Germany itself was on the verge of famine with severe food rationing contemplated on the home front. This problem, however, was partially relieved by stoking up the gas chambers on the Eastern Front.[125]

Indeed, even as early as the late 1930s, *Reichsbank* president Hjalmar Schacht tried to pull economic levers to cool down Hitler's drive to total war by confronting him with monetary realities.[126] Schacht's warnings were rewarded with his dismissal. By this time, Hitler "as *Fuhrer* of the German people was given the power to determine the money supply at will."[127] Hitler came to hate the economic advice that Schacht gave him and came up with his own theory of inflation:

> Inflation is not caused by increasing the fiduciary circulation. It begins on the day when the purchaser is obliged to pay, for the same goods, a higher sum than that asked the day before. At that point,

---

123 Turner, p. 73.
124 Tooze, p. 8.
125 Ibid., pp. 543-44.
126 Ibid., p. 299.
127 Ibid.

one must intervene. Even to Schacht, I had to begin by explaining this elementary truth: that the essential cause of the stability of our currency was to be sought for in our concentration camps. The currency remains stable when the speculators are put under lock and key. I also had to make Schacht understand that excess profits must be removed from economic circulation.[128]

Hitler's currency policy is summarized even further by his own words: "To give people money is solely a problem of making paper. The whole question is to know whether the workers are producing goods to match the paper that's made."[129]

To curb extreme inflation, the Nazis were forced to take even greater control of the economy by exacting an unparalleled rationalization of industry to make sure the military industrial complex was as efficient as possible. Thus, surprisingly enough, rash military spending habits forced the Nazis into adopting political measures that they constantly railed against throughout the 1920s. The National *Socialists* turned out to be far worse taskmasters than any capitalist-industrialist of the German past could have ever dreamed of.[130] They became infamous technocrats emphasizing tight state control over industry. This also proved to be very profitable for the German industrialists precisely because they were given powers over the economy that could have never been granted otherwise. The increasing lawlessness of the German industrialists was thus largely promoted by the Nazi state itself, i.e., by government technocratic intervention, not by the capitalists or industrialists per se, much less by the market itself, which was far from free. All of this was based on an obsession with race and geopolitical *lebensraum*, not with industry or capitalism, or with sound financial planning.

Holocaustic Motive Ignored by Marxist/Secular Materialism & Existentialist Obfuscation

To fixate on Nazi technology, industry and the economy as the explanation for all that was evil about the Third Reich is to subvert the means

---

[128] *Hitler's Table Talk*, evening of Oct. 15, 1941. p.52.

[129] Ibid., p. 53.

[130] The Communists in Russia treated their labor force even worse in its mad drive to industrialize a backward peasant society into a progressive Marxist one in direct competition with Anglo-American capitalism.

of Holocaustic murder with the motive. In reality, it is no different than the superficial leftist diatribe of blaming the existence of guns for violence rather than holding the murderer himself accountable. Pencils do not create errors but people do. This is actually very typical of leftist thinking in general which has drawn too much from the wells of Karl Marx's materialism.[131] Reductionist secularism and materialism invariably downplays the role of belief, ideology, human responsibility and morality. In its materialistic atheism, it always manages to find ways to blame the material or economic means of production together with its social structures for all that is evil in the world. This has especially been the case with regard to the leftist interpretation of the Nazi experience. Albert Speer used the same ploy to defend himself at Nuremberg, yet with a green twist to it all. Modern environmental historians who have written books on the green Nazi connection have followed in Speer's footsteps.

Closely related, secular historian Raul Hilberg's (1926-2007) seminal work on *The Destruction of the European Jews* was first of all based on

---

131 Though Adam Tooze's book called *The Wages of Destruction: The Making and Breaking of the Nazi Economy* is a great book describing the Nazi economy, it must also be pointed out that he has strong Marxist/Socialist leanings. This has had a profound impact on how he has interpreted the Nazi experience. Any historical facts that demonstrate Nazi beliefs about nature, Romanticism or environmentalism are ignored in favor of the typical Marxist materialistic explanations that dwell upon economics. He also downplays morality and personal responsibility. Tooze demonstrates the great weaknesses of the Nazi economy, but seems completely unaware that such weaknesses are perhaps best explained by the *green* biology of the Nazis. The Nazi ideal of a *local only* sustainable economy was an Aryan pipedream based on crackpot biology rather than true *progressive* science. While the Nazis may have trumpeted themselves as the rightful modern heirs of the German naturalistic sciences, in reality they were reversing the progressive values of the Enlightenment at some critical junctures. What many do not appreciate is that the naturalistic sciences of the Enlightenment originally based on the Judeo-Christian subject/object distinction were slowly replaced by the Darwinian/environmental sciences of the 1800s. This did away with the subject-object distinction and henceforth promoted semi-pagan ideas of vitalism, pantheism and holism in its place—all in the name of the latest evolutionary or *progressive* science of the day. Since Darwinian science no longer accepted man as truly distinct from nature, it came to adopt the Romantic *scientific* ideal of *nature looking into nature*. While this gave the impression of a more intense naturalistic empiricism, it has instead promoted an environmental existentialist worldview that places great doubt on the whole possibility of observational science, since man no longer is outside the natural processes he observes. That the zoologist Ernst Haeckel, the very father of ecology and German social Darwinism, was at the forefront of this transition is critical (on this, see especially Daniel Gasman's *Haeckel's Monism and the Birth of Fascist Ideology*). In short, the Nazis were reversing Enlightenment progress in the name of fascist *progress*. This, however, turned out to be a backward anti-civilization retrogression into a green biological barbarism that shocked the modern world in World War II with an icy, inhuman cruelty as indifferent as nature herself.

Neo-Marxist Franz Neumann's (1900-1954) scholarship but, secondly, popularized by Heideggerian enthusiast Hannah Arendt (1906-1975), and then, thirdly, overrun by Claude Lanzmann's 1985 nine-hour French existentialist film on the Holocaust entitled *Shoah*. "Shoah" means "destruction." This is the preferred name given to the Holocaust by many Jews, particularly by Lanzmann. In his modern existentialism taken chiefly from Jean-Paul Sartre (1905-1980), Lanzmann accordingly and vehemently denies there is any meaning to the Holocaust. He feels it is virtually immoral or obscene to answer the question of why the Holocaust occurred along any kinds of rational inquiry. Lanzmann is a French Jew and has received many accolades for his indomitable work on the Shoah, particularly through his films and interviews with Holocaust survivors and perpetrators.

There is certainly a truth in Lanzmann's concerns that in some sense the Holocaust defies reason. There is no question that the Nazi Holocaust was an irrational existential reality that is very difficult to analyze rationally, but herein lays the great problem with Lanzmann's *Shoah*. The Nazis were themselves steeped in their own existentialism. Their *Triumph of the Will* was rooted in Friedrich Nietzsche's atheistic existentialism of the 1800s that upheld human willpower as intrinsic to what man truly is as opposed to his rational thought, ethics or spirituality. In other words, the Nazi triumph of the will that emphasized biological instincts and emotions at the expense of human thought and morality found its final fulfillment in the Holocaust—which is otherwise known as the Final Solution, a designation that has great meaning. More to the point, Lanzmann's philosophical hero, Sartre, inherited much from Nietzsche as did Nazi existentialist Martin Heidegger, who once quipped, "When the French want to think they have to think in German."[132]

The result of Lanzmann's work is that he invariably covers up the explosive dangers of Nazi existentialism with a hybridized French-German existentialist interpretation of the Holocaust. This is perfectly showcased in *Shoah*. *Shoah* is just as much a work of existential art as it is based on many personal eyewitness accounts. As such, thanks to the great success of Lanzmann's monumental film, when most people think of the Holocaust, they think of trains. Scenes of trains running up and down the tracks in various Holocaust locations in Poland dominate the film. Rather than depict the irrational existential madness that National Socialism imbibed deeply

---

132   Hirsch, David. *The Deconstruction of Literature: Criticism After Auschwitz*. Hannover and London: Brown University Press, 1991, p. 7.

from, the machinery of destruction, i.e., how the Jews were transported to death camps on trains from the ghettos, is emphasized instead. Why the Germans would do such things in the first place is never entertained, except that secularist Raul Hilberg, who is featured prominently in the film, is quick to blame medieval Christendom together with its anti-Semitic laws, measures and pogroms. Lanzmann thus adds a French existential twist that rests on top of the Marxist and/or secular materialist understanding of the Holocaust. Thus, Hilberg's secular approach to the destruction of the European Jews is artfully blurred and woven into the very fabric of Lanzmann's French-German existentialist interpretation of the Shoah.

While Franz Neumann was an assimilated Jew from the Neo-Marxist Frankfurt School in Germany who popularized the leftist fantasy that National Socialism was the final result of monopoly capitalism, Hannah Arendt, another assimilated German Jew, gave to the western world the "banality of evil" thesis while writing on Nazi SS leader Adolf Eichmann's (1906-1962) trial for the *New Yorker*. Using Hilberg's detailed historical account, which focused on the German bureaucracy that administratively carried out the destruction of the Jews step by step, Arendt added her own existentialist kink to Holocaust interpretation by accentuating the bureaucratic everydayness of Eichmann's evil. Here, all murderous intent is essentially lost in the wilderness of bureaucratic existentialism. Eichmann becomes a mere "cog in a massive bureaucratic machine in which wrongdoing had become the norm—hence, his 'banality.'"[133] As such, the banality of the bureaucratic machinery trumped the everyday personal responsibility of many a German throughout the war as they sent the Jews to their deaths. The machinery of destruction essentially took on a life of its own as the bureaucrats, far removed from the death camps themselves, actually became "impervious to the horror unleashed by their actions."[134] Thus crimes without conscience were an existential routine during the time of the Holocaust.

At this existentialist juncture, one begins to wonder out loud whether or not such researchers, thinkers and writers, including Albert Speer and Martin Heidegger, all have some peculiar phobia concerning machines that has completely absorbed their attention with regard to the Holocaust and has managed to distract them from its distinctly German peculiarity. In particular, Arendt's Holocaust interpretation is extraordinarily compromised

---

[133] Wolin, Richard. *Heidegger's Children: Hannah Arendt, Karl Lowith, Hans Jonas, and Herbert Marcuse.* Princeton and Oxford: Princeton University Press, 2001, p. 55.
[134] Ibid., p. 57.

precisely because she had a torrid affair with Heidegger in the 1920s. After Heidegger dumped her, he later joined the Nazi Party in 1933. In shock, Arendt severely castigated her former existentialist professor and lover for being too ensnared with German Romanticism.[135]

However, after the war, like so many lovers' quarrels that are so existentially rooted in the ups and downs of everyday emotions, Arendt made up with Heidegger. Subsequently, "her tone changed abruptly. Thereafter, she systematically downplayed the gravity and extent of Heidegger's Nazi past."[136] She even became Heidegger's apologist to help rehabilitate him back into Western academia in spite of his Nazi sympathies that continued until the day of his death. "Arendt became Heidegger's de facto American literary agent, diligently overseeing contracts and translations of his books."[137] This allowed Heidegger's brand of Nazi existentialism to seep into Western philosophy and leftist political, historical and literary circles that laid the cornerstone for what today is called Postmodernism.[138]

What is meant by Postmodernism is very difficult to express. First, Postmodernism is a form of existentialism. This by itself makes it very difficult to define because under existentialism, the application and power of rationalism and reason is greatly diminished. Ready-made designations, classifications and descriptions are thus very hard to come by. Furthermore, with Heidegger at the helm, Postmodernism is invariably anti-human since it reduces the critical importance of the rational human mind to the brute level of the natural world and biological instincts together with pagan nature mysticism. After the war, Heidegger's writings became more opaque, which managed to disguise his Nazism. In so doing, Heidegger's racism and anti-Semitism were replaced with anti-humanism, which should by no means be understood as any kind of progress, but a deepening of all the problems connected to his existentialism. With no small thanks to Heidegger's works and efforts, much of Postmodern Western philosophy is deeply committed to various forms of anti-humanism, which, at some point, left unguarded, might easily lead to inhuman actions and behavior—perhaps even similar to the levels of barbarism that were witnessed during the heights of the Holocaust?

---

[135] Ibid., p. 47-48, 50.
[136] Ibid., p. 50.
[137] Ibid., p. 49.
[138] See David Hirsch's book, *The Deconstruction of Literature: Criticism after Auschwitz*, pp. 255-56.

In the *Deconstruction of Literature: Criticism after Auschwitz*, Dr. David Hirsch writes, "It is misleading to disengage contemporary anti-humanism from Nazi dehumanization, for they share (the same) philosophical and cultural origins."[139] In short, Heidegger's Postmodern redirection away from anti-Semitic racism to anti-humanism after the war did not express repentance. On the contrary, it only provided a veritable cover-up of his Nazi past that aided his entrance back into Western academia. Hirsch has thus strongly argued that Postmodernism should best be understood as post-Auschwitz.[140] In other words, Postmodernism is existentialism after Auschwitz. Much more disturbing, according to Hirsch, the goal of Post-modernism is to deconstruct the sober truth that the European academy, particularly in Germany, actually fed the intellectual beast which led to the Holocaust. "In brief, the post-Auschwitz age is one in which the nineteenth century prophecies of Marx and Nietzsche have been realized in the Soviet gulag, on the one hand, and in the Nazi death camps, on the other."[141] Hirsch continues, "Whatever post-modernism may be, the post-Auschwitz age is one of total war, mass murder, and genocide; an age of the death of God and of the eclipse of western culture and Judeo-Christian values."[142]

Neither Europe nor the North American leftist academy have come to grips with the fact the 20th century was a socialist slaughterhouse of epic proportions. Postmodernism thus moved in to save secular Europe from facing up to its own intellectual catastrophe in the face of the apocalyptic abyss of World War II—even though Germany's pre-war Romanticism and existentialism played a powerful role in justifying the inhuman brutality of the Holocaust. That Heidegger had to argue after the war that anti-humanism does not in-variably lead to inhumanity is perhaps far more revealing than most scholars would care to admit.[143] Indeed, "Hitler and Heidegger shared a world outlook. Both sought to return German culture to pagan roots by rupturing that fusion between Hellenism (ancient Greco-Roman culture) and Hebraism (ancient Judaism) that constitutes European humanism (through Christianity)."[144]

Hannah Arendt never acknowledged that her own educational back-ground was deep-rooted in the exact same training that led to the destruction

---

139   Hirsch, p. 255.
140   Ibid., pp. 244-68.
141   Ibid., p. 245.
142   Ibid.
143   Ibid., p. 256.
144   Ibid., p. 262.

of her own people. To admit otherwise would have turned her into a treasonous intellectual collaborator. Many assimilated German Jews, including Franz Neumann and Herbert Marcuse of the Frankfurt School, were somewhat blinded to the growing anti-Semitism that was enveloping them throughout the 1920s precisely because they viewed themselves not as Jews, but as Germans. They actually believed the days of German anti-Semitism were virtually on their way out, but this proved to be a grave misjudgment of what was truly happening. They had become so entrenched into German ways of thinking that they were blindsided and shocked by it all when the Nazis took control of Germany in the 1930s. Even Marcuse was a student of Heidegger, and his well-known attempt to give Marxism a *human face* is based on trying to merge Marxism with Heideggerian existentialism. Thus, even Marcuse also played a critical role in merging Marxism with fascism in the last half of the 20th century that has also been described as a branch of Postmodernism.

In truth, both Arendt and Marcuse were unmindful of what Heidegger's existential philosophy would look like if it were actually fleshed out in the real political world. While Marcuse smartened up somewhat, and Arendt did for a time as well in the 1930s, they both failed to see the inherent dangers of Heidegger's political existentialism in the 1920s. Worse, in Arendt's case, she returned to her old professor after the fires of World War II had died down. In so doing, Arendt went on to deny the inherently specific German character of the Holocaust. She did not want to implicate her own native country that raised her academically in the bloom of her youth, and, "thereby, narcissistically herself. Perhaps it would have been psychologically difficult for Arendt to admit that Auschwitz was in fact a German invention, for such an avowal would have implicated her own early intellectual attachments as an assimilated German Jew, not to mention those of friends, professors, and so forth."[145] Dr. Richard Wolin adds further, "It is as though Arendt looked everywhere except the place that was the most obvious: the deformations of German historical development that facilitated Hitler's rise to power."[146] Existentialism obfuscates. It does not enlighten.

While Hilberg disagreed with Arendt's "banality of evil" interpretation of the Shoah, his own Holocaust bureaucracy thesis was not only rooted in Franz Neumann's scholarship, but also based on standard anti-Christian

---

[145]   Wolin, p. 61.
[146]   Ibid., p. 62.

sentiments that are unsurprisingly typical of many secular Jews. Hilberg opens up his *Deconstruction of the European Jews* by establishing that Nazi Germany's bureaucratic machinery, along with its anti-Semitic laws and measures that were used to destroy the Jews, were all inherited from earlier Christian medieval times throughout the centuries of Christendom in Europe.[147] As such, his Holocaust bureaucracy thesis that blames age-old Christian anti-Semitism also manages to absolve the German academic intelligentsia from any real culpability as well.

Yet, in relative contrast to his own bureaucratic machinery thesis, Hilberg still acknowledged, "In the final analysis, the destruction of the Jews was not so much a product of laws and commands as it was a matter of spirit, of shared comprehension, of consonance and synchronization."[148] Hilberg thus admitted it was the "spirit of shared comprehension" that underlay the bureaucratic destruction of the Jews rather than the bureaucracy per se. While Hilberg perhaps presumed the "spirit of shared comprehension" was Christian anti-Semitism, he nowhere says as much, and falls far short of demonstrating that particular hypothesis for a variety of different reasons. The "spirit of shared comprehension" in 1930s Nazi Germany was not church dogma, but racism couched in scientific social Darwinism and political biology/ecology showered with Romanticism and existentialism that was not only extremely anti-Semitic, but anti-Christian as well. By the 1930s, much of Germany was only nominally Christian, and the German intelligentsia was decidedly both anti-Semitic and anti-Christian. However, such ideological considerations that should have informed the "spirit of shared comprehension" were regrettably left unexplained by Hilberg. In 2006, Hilberg was awarded Germany's Order of Merit for his incredible Holocaust research, the highest award that can be given to a non-German. Hilberg was an assimilated Austrian Jew before he escaped to America from the terrors of National Socialism.

In addition to anti-Christian secularity, leftist materialism, anti-capitalism and Postmodern existentialism that have exerted powerful influences over the historiography of the Third Reich, it must also be pointed out that two giant media conglomerates, Holtzbrinck Publishers and Bertelsmann, both of whom have substantial Nazi pedigrees from their past, have done much to share Holocaustic blame and guilt with other players and

---

[147] Hilberg, Raul. *The Destruction of the European Jews*, vol. 1. New York and London: Holmes & Meier, 1985, pp. 5-28.
[148] Ibid., p. 55.

participants in different countries in order to help launder Germany's past.[149] That these two German publishing giants control most of the big name publishing houses and a sizable selection of all the books produced in the United States today bespeaks of powerful media influences that needs to be much more seriously examined than has previously been considered heretofore. Syndicated columnist William Safire complained in 2002, "I bridle at German book publishing hegemony. Few Americans realize that two German *Gesellschaften* are gaining stranglehold on US books."[150]

In 1946, Georg Von Holtzbrinck (1909-1983) was charged with being a Nazi beneficiary, but his judge decided he was just a passive follower whose motives were economic rather than political.[151] Today, the Holtzbrinck Publishing conglomerate owns Henry Holt and Company, St. Martin's Press, Macmillan Palgrave, Picador, Worth Publishing, W.H. Freeman, Roaring Brook Press, Thomas Dunne Books, Bedford, Griffin, Minotaur, Farrar Strauss & Giroux and Nature Publishing Group.

In 2008, Holtzbrinck published *Hell's Cartel: IG Farben and the Making of Hitler's War Machine*, authored by Diarmuid Jeffreys. This book traces the history of IG Farben, which became a colossal corporate chemical industry conglomerate before the rise of the Third Reich. Throughout the mid to late 1930s, IG Farben was heavily involved in Hitler's Four Year economic plan that laid the industrial groundwork for World War II. During the war, not only did IG Farben build a concentration camp near its plant in the Auschwitz environs named Monowitz that savagely abused its slave workforce for war production and profits, but it also sold massive amounts of Zyklon B to the SS through one of its subsidiaries. Zyklon B was the very pesticide used to exterminate the Jews in the gas chambers at Auschwitz.[152] IG Farben also authorized the financing of Dr. Mengele's genetic research and horrific medical experiments at Auschwitz where an almost endless supply of human guinea pigs was available for *scientific* research.[153] "Mengele's work did not come cheap,"[154] but IG Farben paid his bills. Indeed, IG Farben factory manager Wilhelm Mann (1894-1992)

---

[149] Kaplan, Robert E. *The Soros Connection*. Jerusalem, Israel, 2011, pp. 87-104.
[150] Safire, William, "The German Problem," *The New York Times*, September 19, 2002.
[151] Schuler, Thomas, "Evidence of Opportunistic Behavior: How a German Publisher Maneuvered Himself through the Nazi Era," *The Atlantic Times*, February 2009.
[152] Jeffreys, pp. 325-27.
[153] Ibid., p. 327.
[154] Ibid., p. 328.

wrote to an SS contact, "I have enclosed the first check. Dr. Mengele's first experiments, should, as we both agreed, be pursued. Heil Hitler."[155]

With some interest, Holtzbrinck has also published two books by Discovery Institute's Dr. Richard Weikart, who was otherwise heavily criticized by many academics in North America for daring to associate Darwinism with Hitler. Weikart wrote *From Darwin to Hitler: Evolutionary Ethics, Eugenics, and Racism in Germany* in 2006, and then *Hitler's Ethic: The Nazi Pursuit of Evolutionary Progress* in 2009. His contribution to Ben Stein's controversial documentary, *Expelled*, which made the same argument on film, was also roundly condemned by many. Yet, although Weikart's intelligent design views are further considered an anathema by modern academia, Holtzbrinck had no qualms whatsoever in publishing two books that associated the Holocaust with an English Victorian by the name of Charles Darwin.

Bertelsmann is larger than Holtzbrinck. Bertelsmann's publishing hegemony includes Random House, Doubleday, Bantam, Fawcett, Delacorte Press, Broadway Books, Main Street Books, Alfred E. Knopf, Three Rivers Press, The Dial Press, Villard Books, Everyman's Library, Schocken Books, Ballantine, Anchor Books, Pantheon, Chatto and Windus, Jonathan Cape, Dell, Bodley Head and the Crown Publishing Group. Bertelsmann is controlled by the Mohn family, which had a strong pro-Nazi history in the 1930s.[156] Heinrich Mohn (1921-2009), the director of Bertelsmann during the war, was a financial supporter of Heinrich Himmler's SS. Today the Mohns are strong environmentalists and have been heavily involved in the ultra-green Club of Rome. According to American journalist John Rosenthal in Berlin, "Bertelsmann is considered to be the most politically influential corporation in Germany. Hirsch Fischler, the researcher who uncovered Bertelsmann's ties with the Nazi regime, has said the same, explaining its political power as the result of its great wealth and its ability to influence public opinion through its ownership of several newspapers."[157]

Bertelsmann also likes to publish books that tend to whitewash Germany's Nazi past by sharing fascist blame with other Western countries to help relativize its own guilt. Bertelsmann published *The Lucifer Effect* in 2008, which argues that there was nothing inherently German about the terrors of National Socialism and the Holocaust. Even Jonah Goldberg's *Liberal Fascism*

---

155 Ibid.
156 Manus, Elizabeth, "Bertelsmann's Nazi Past Gets Ho-Hummed in U.S.," *The New York Observer*, January 18, 1999.
157 Kaplan, p. 92.

was published by Bertelsmann in 2009. While *Liberal Fascism* is an illuminating political read, Goldberg roots fascism in the French Revolution (1789-1799), drags in Woodrow Wilson (1856-1924) to declare him the first American fascist, focuses much on Benito Mussolini (1883-1945), and then says National Socialism was a form of fascism with a small case "f." Such an argument could not have been stated any better from a German point of view.

Most noteworthy, however, is Edwin Black's *IBM and the Holocaust: The Strategic Alliance between Nazi Germany and America's Most Powerful Corporation*, published by Random House in 2001. This book makes the powerful case that the staggering numbers of Jewish victims who perished in the Holocaust were largely accomplished through the use of IBM automation census technology. The Nazis used IBM's Hollerith cards to automate, identify and catalogue the names of their Jewish victims through coded eugenic profiles gathered and cross-tabulated from welfare bureaus, social security offices, insurance companies, medical, church and genealogical records, doctors, banks and financial institutions, together with various organizations and registries across the nation. Using Hollerith cards, IBM Germany managed to separate the Jews from the Aryans.[158] Such IBM tabulation technology was then exported into Austria, Czechoslovakia and Poland to organize the Holocaust in central and eastern Europe:

> IBM maintained a customer site, known as the Hollerith Department, in virtually every concentration camp to sort or process punch cards and track prisoners. The codes show IBM's numerical designation for various camps. Auschwitz was 001, Buchenwald was 002; Dachau was 003, and so on. Various prisoner types were reduced to IBM numbers, with 3 signifying homosexual, 9 for anti-social, and 12 for Gypsy. The IBM number 8 designated a Jew. Inmate death was also reduced to an IBM digit: 3 represented death by natural causes, 4 by execution, 5 by suicide, and code 6 designated "special treatment" in gas chambers. IBM engineers had to create Hollerith codes to differentiate between a Jew who had been worked to death and one who had been gassed, then print the cards, configure the machines, train the staff, and continuously maintain the fragile systems every two weeks on site in the concentration camps.[159]

---

[158] Black, *IBM and the Holocaust*, p. 47.
[159] Black, Edwin, "IBM at Auschwitz, New Documents," *Reader Supported News*, Feb. 28, 2012.

In short, "with IBM as a partner, the Hitler regime was able to substantially automate and accelerate all six phases of the 12-year Holocaust: identification, exclusion, confiscation, ghettoization, deportation, and even extermination."[160] Black concludes, "Only at the moment of extermination did the Jews of Europe finally break free from Hitler's Holleriths."[161]

However, whether imported from abroad through IBM or exported into the hellish squalor of Auschwitz as IG Farben was, the Nazi economy, industry and its technology were merely the means by which the Holocaust was paid for and implemented. The Russian Front, including the dwindling food supply, provided the opportunity for murder, but neither IBM's Hollerith cards nor IG Farben's Zyklon B can explain the motive behind the Holocaust. While IBM and IG Farben were malevolently interested in making huge profits at the expense of Jewish victims by selling their wares to a reprehensible national government like Nazi Germany, the Nazis did not kill the Jews for the sake of growing corporate profits, capitalism or growing industry, much less for free enterprise or free markets. Black's thesis can certainly answer the critical question on how such incredible numbers of Jews were rounded up, and Jeffreys can explain who was behind the making of the pesticide that killed those rounded up Jews in Auschwitz, but neither author comes anywhere close in answering the question as to why the Nazis were willing to implement the Final Solution in the first place.

If anything, Black's *IBM and the Holocaust* and Jeffrey's *Hell's Cartel* are most serious warnings to big corporations who prostitute themselves with national governments involved in state-sponsored social engineering machinations. However, this was not the message Black, nor Jeffreys, neither Holtzbrinck nor Bertelsmann, wanted to get across when such books were written and finally published. What is just as troubling is not merely that IBM prostituted itself with the Nazis, but that Black managed to devote himself to a cause that Germany's Bertelsmann published. Dragging an American corporation into the purview of the Holocaust is just another excuse that Germany can easily use to avoid facing a dark historical past that many of its historians have never really taken responsibility for. While Black himself acknowledges this particular problem,[162] his anti-capitalist crusade still gets the best of him. In 2012, Black concluded in an article, "International Business Machines, and

---

160   Black, *Nazi Nexus: America's Corporate Connections to Hitler's Holocaust.* Washington D.C.: Diaolog Press, 2009, p. 130.
161   Black, *IBM and the Holocaust*, p. 372.
162   Black, *Nazi Nexus*, p. vii.

its president Thomas J. Watson, committed genocide by any standard. It was never about the anti-Semitism. It was never about the National Socialism. It was always about the money. Business was their middle name."[163] Such a conclusion could not have been stated any better by a vested German eager to share his past guilt with American corporate sins.

In fact, one of the most disturbing aspects of much historical research directed against the Third Reich is how few authors really bother to explain National Socialist ideology—which is precisely where the motive of the Holocaust will be found. Outside of mentioning a few catch phrases about racism and the master race, the vast majority of scholarship on Nazi Germany and the Holocaust focuses greatly on the means and the opportunity for murder, but largely ignores the motive. In any crime, motive cannot be ignored, but many historians of the Third Reich have done just that. In so doing, they have taken German historian Hans Mommsen's lead. He led the charge in denying any kind of true intentional motive behind the murder of the Jews in the Holocaust. Building on Hilberg's bureaucratic explanation for the Holocaust together with Arendt's "banality of evil" thesis, Mommsen is very skeptical of the idea that the Holocaust was pre-planned by Hitler. Mommsen believes that the Holocaust largely came about through a "cumulative radicalization." People became more accustomed to murder to advance their political goals, which developed into ever more drastic measures as Germany plunged into one emergency crisis after the next like a gigantic snowball rolling down the mountainside that could not be stopped.

While Professor Mommsen has since supposedly softened his earlier stance in admitting that Nazi ideology did play a powerful role in the preparation for the Shoah, he still claims the Holocaust could not have happened without certain social structures, both bureaucratic and political, that the Third Reich instigated to destroy the Jews. In an interview with *Yad Vashem* in 1997, Mommsen remarked it was "primarily structural determinants that produce situations in which the rule of the civil law is endangered and the inherited institutions get undermined, which is the precondition for a reign of terror and of mass murder."[164] Emphasizing the "ambiguity" of the holocaustic destruction process, Mommsen went on to say, "Any disagreement with the genocide could not be officially articulated. Even for members of the government or leading officials in the army it was difficult

---

[163] Black, "IBM at Auschwitz, New Documents," *Reader Supported News*, Feb. 28, 2012.
[164] Yad Vashem Interview with Prof. Hans Mommsen, "The 'Functionalist' and the 'Intentionalist' Schools of Thought," *Shoah Resource Center*, Dec. 12, 1997.

to obtain reliable information. Consequently, opposing interests could not find any leverage, being suffocated with the reprimand that the ongoing elimination was just the outcome of emergency situations." Worst of all, and very revealing, Mommsen then drops this veritable apology of moral equivalence: "This phenomenon was not unique and certainly not restricted to the Nazi system. The case of the Vietnam War shows similarities, because the atrocities committed by American troops happened without any clear responsibility and protests were suffocated in the general disorientation and the fact that nobody was responsible. The effects of informal politics, therefore, cannot be overestimated."

Here, Mommsen virtually equivocates the atrocities of the Holocaust with American Army actions committed during the fog of the Vietnam War in order to help clear the German conscience of its Nazi past. German historians are specialists in sharing the *ambiguities* of their dirty laundry with others without taking serious historical responsibility in what has to be understood as perhaps the biggest crimes ever perpetrated in human history. Such a hollow repentance on the part of Mommsen and others still leaves much left-leaning historical scholarship of the Third Reich with a colossal murder case on its hands without a motive. This is precisely how the commandant of both Sobibor and Treblinka, Franz Stangl, found a way to live with himself after the war: "The only way I could live was by compartmentalizing my thinking. By doing this I could apply it to my own situation; if the 'subject' was the government (bureaucracy), the 'object' the Jews, and the 'action' the gassings, then I could tell myself that for me the fourth element, 'intent' (free will) was missing."[165] How convenient, especially for Germany and its proto Nazi history before the rise of the Third Reich—proto Nazi ideas that continue unabated in the Postmodern West with too little self-reflection on those particular influences, and where they could possibly lead.

While many scholars have time and time again emphasized Nazi industrial modernism as if National Socialism was the superlative example of Western modernization gone awry, German literature expert J.P. Stern cautions, "The call for a 'natural' leader, for the abolition of politics in favor of nationalism, of civilization, in favor of culture, the appeal to Nature, the blood, the iron Will, the appeal to 'Northern,' later 'Aryan' values—all these belong to the temper of the Second German Empire. Indeed, there is not a single tenet of the National Socialist Party program of February 1920 or of its

---

165   Sereny, *Into that Darkness*, p. 164.

later amendments which was not propagated in the political literature before 1914."[166] Nazi press chief Otto Dietrich corroborated this assessment: "Hitler was thoroughly old-fashioned, a hangover from the 19th century."[167]

While Jeffreys and many others have spilled much ink over the industrial nature of the Holocaust at Auschwitz, relatively few authors, if any, have written about the many experimental farms, botanical, organic and otherwise, that were set up by the SS in and around the Auschwitz environs. Even Sobibor Death Camp in eastern Poland was described as "an ordinary farm, except for the barbed-wire fences that surrounded it and some barracks. Actually, it was a farm, with all its buildings, in the midst of a beautiful green forest."[168] One of the SS farms in the immediate proximity of Auschwitz II was named *Birkenau Wirtschaftshof*, which quaintly means "Birch Farmyard." The very name Auschwitz-Birkenau, therefore, means something to the SS leaders who named the camp and its subcamps.

The Nazis seized 40 square kilometers for the Auschwitz concentration camp system.[169] Most of the land was used for farming. Almost 10,000 Poles were removed from the area to make way for Aryan farms. Thanks to all the camps and sub-camps throughout the entire area, the Nazis had many thousands of manual laborers to exploit as slaves. They were brutally worked to death and then quickly replaced with other victims who shared the exact same fate. The Nazi state then rewarded them wages consisting of their own ashes as innumerable dead bodies went up in great flames in the crematoriums. Can such ghastly scenes be adequately explained by a German capitalistic industrialism gone awry? Too many in the modern West, particularly of the leftist persuasion, have presumed the affirmative.

Nazi racism, however, was not based on the classical liberalism of American liberty, limited government, nor free enterprise, much less upon Christianity or the Bible. Nazi racism was deeply rooted in Germany's Romantic and existentialist movements of the 1800s that undergirded its later social Darwinism, where a politicized philosophy about the relationship between man and nature developed into an all-encompassing totalitarian *Weltanschauung* or worldview which captivated the nation by the 1930s

[166]   Stern, J.P. *Hitler: The Fuhrer and the People.* Berkeley & Los Angeles: University of California Press, 1992, p. 37.
[167]   Dietrich, p.11.
[168]   Arad, Yitzhak. *Belzec, Sobibor, Treblinka: The Operation Reinhard Death Camps.* Bloomington and Indianapolis: Indiana University Press, 1987, p. 36.
[169]   *Auschwitz from A to Z*, p. 90.

with a pseudo-scientific spell that degenerated into the Holocaust during the heights of World War II.

German Romanticism and/or existentialism, together with its two daughters, social Darwinism and environmentalism, were largely born in the racist forests of Germany during the 19th century. Hardened by the evolutionary sciences and philosophical existentialism throughout the 1800s and early 1900s, German Romanticism eventually led to the destruction of millions of Jews and Slavs during the heights of World War II. While it is true that, from a logical point of view, the German racial ecology of the 19th century did not inevitably demand that there would be a Nazi Holocaust in the 20th century—meaning that although it was a necessary condition for the Holocaust, it still was not a sufficient cause for the Holocaust—history itself usually pays little attention to such abstract philosophical syllogisms. Certainly, the German Romantics of the 1800s did not have the Holocaust in mind when they spewed forth their anti-Semitic diatribes against the Jews for the sake of racial and environmental purity. Perhaps modern greens can take some solace in this fact?

Geographer and geopolitical expert Mark Bassin rightly points out, "The confluence of ecological and political thinking was complex and multi-faceted, and—importantly—that fascism per se was only one of its possible results."[170] This truth cannot be denied. Jewish-German scholar Karl Lowith summarized such historical problems with this acute observation:

> One cannot charge the initiators of a movement with personal responsibility for its historical results. In history, "responsibility" always has two sides: the responsibility of those who teach and intend something and the responsibility of those who act and respond. But one cannot establish a direct responsibility of an intention for provoking this or that response. Between the latter and the former there is no simple equation but also no independence—both together produce historical results, which are, therefore, ambiguous.[171]

Part of the reason for such ambiguity is precisely because primary responsibility belongs to the individual(s) who commit(s) the crime, not to the people

---

[170] Bassin, Mark, "Blood or Soil?: The *Volkisch* Movement, the Nazis, and the Legacy of *Geopolitik*," in *How Green Were the Nazis?*, p. 204.

[171] Lowith, Karl. *Meaning in History*. Chicago: University of Chicago Press, 1949, pp. 212-13.

who lived and died in the past. Adolf Hitler and the leading Nazis are thus certainly to blame for the Holocaust, not German Romantics, existentialists, nor social Darwinists, biologists or scientists of the 19th century. German Romantics and existentialists, together with their social Darwinian cohorts, may have often expressed themselves in anti-Semitic tones, but with the rise of National Socialism, it became pathological.

Yet the interdependence and ambiguity between the early German green movement, social Darwinism and National Socialism still need to be thoroughly appraised and properly weighed. It is in this particular discussion where the motive behind the Holocaust will be found. While much recent scholarship has exposed the fact that many more regular Germans were involved in the atrocities of the Holocaust than first imagined, armed with a plethora of different individual motives for killing the Jews, the leaders of the Nazi movement have to be considered the primary agents of destruction since they were the very ones who ideologically promoted, bureaucratically set up and politically facilitated the horrors of the Holocaust. Without their lead, the Holocaust could not have occurred.

Hannah Arendt remarked, "The member of the Nazi hierarchy most gifted at solving problems of conscience was Himmler."[172] Indeed, immediately following a horrific shooting scene of Jews in the environs of Minsk, Byelorussia, Himmler reassured the soldiers who shot them "their conscience was in no way impaired, for they were soldiers who had to carry out every order unconditionally. He alone had responsibility before God and Hitler for everything that was happening."[173] Himmler then went on to explain that in spite of the unfortunate circumstances which had befallen them on the Eastern Front, nature herself teaches there is "combat everywhere, not only among men but also in the world of animals and plants."[174] In other words, the romantic and uncivilized lawlessness of nature coupled with her silent existentialism and social Darwinism would absolve them of all guilt. Nazi sins would be atoned for by offering a bloody green sacrifice to rid themselves of the Jewish infection.

Thus, the underlying motive of the Nazi Holocaust was a *green* Aryanism rooted in a Romantic philosophy of man and nature that regarded the Jews as alien to the natural order. As such, the primary motive of the Holocaust

---

[172] Arendt, Hannah, *Eichmann and the Holocaust*. London: Penguin Books, 2005, p. 44.
[173] Hilberg, vol. 1, p. 332.
[174] Ibid., pp. 332-33.

was the racial political ecology of the early German green movement. Although German Romanticism and existentialism cannot be charged with outright Holocaustic extermination, it did indeed play a powerful role in the historical developments that led up to the *Shoah*. Its prophesied anti-Semitism in the 1800s came to a shocking fulfillment under the Nazi regime in the 1940s, all in the name of Nature. While the early German green movement can elude the conviction of murder, it cannot escape the accusatory burden of being considered proto-Nazi.

Unlike their predecessors, the Nazis did not just entertain hateful thoughts. The Nazis actually did something about the perceived problem. In their twisted existentialism, they viewed themselves more *authentic* than many of their forerunners. They were far more willing to turn their fantasies into a political reality through a gigantic triumph of the will. As such, no matter how complex or nuanced the relationship may have been between racism, environmentalism and fascism, the animalism of the Holocaust can best be explained by the naturist ideology of the Nazis that included a robust ecological outlook. In *Black Earth: The Holocaust as History and Warning*, Dr. Timothy Snyder illuminates, "An instructive account of the mass murder of the Jews of Europe must be planetary, because Hitler's thought was ecological, treating Jews as a wound of nature."[175] This "wound" against nature would be cured by the annihilation of the Jews.

The early German green movement thus played a critical role in providing the necessary justification for Nazi barbarism. In short, German Romanticism was converted into eco-imperialism by Nazi racism on the Eastern Front. The quest for *lebensraum* in the east, i.e., the quest for empty environmental breathing room so that Germans would not biologically self-destruct in increasingly overpopulated international cities at home, was a sinister eco-imperial plan that far surpassed the evils committed by the Western powers in their drive for colonial expansionism.

---

[175]   Snyder, Timothy. *Black Earth: The Holocaust as History and Warning*. London: The Bodley Head, 2015, p. xii.

"I would regard it as a crime to have sacrificed the lives of German soldiers simply for the conquest of natural riches to be exploited in capitalist style. According to the laws of nature, the soil belongs to him who conquers it."

Adolf Hitler, Night of 28-29, Jan. 1942

CHAPTER ONE:

BAALISM AS SUBVERSIVE NATURE WORSHIP

Much of ancient Israel's plight, well-documented throughout the Old Testament, was its insatiable thirst for pagan nature worship. This was in direct violation of the first two commandments of the Mosaic Law, which commanded Israel not to worship any other false god or *idol* (Ex. 20:3-4). The reason why Israel was forbidden to worship *other gods*, the natural created order, and idols, is given in the opening chapters of Genesis. Genesis 1 presents an ultimate Creator who made the universe out of nothing through His omnipotent spoken word, and then climaxed the creation process by the making of man *in His own image* (v. 27). This foundational truth is basic to the first two commandments of the Mosaic constitution, the rest of which was summarized by the Son of God Himself: "Love the Lord your God with all your heart and with all your soul and with all your mind.' This is the first and greatest commandment. And the second is like it: 'Love your neighbor as yourself.' All the Law and the Prophets hang on these two commandments.'" (Matt. 22:36-40).

What this means is that the worship of God as the Creator and human ethics went hand in hand in the Mosaic law as both were rooted in the very structures of creation itself. The first four commandments demand love for God. Commandment five demands love for parents, and commandments six through ten demand love for others. Man was thus commanded to worship and love God as His Maker, and the best way to fulfill this was to treat one's neighbor with love and respect, precisely because he too was made in God's image. As such, the entire Mosaic code was written with the reality of Genesis 1 in mind, and once this truth was forgotten or compromised by idolatrous nature worship, love and respect for both God and man inevitably diminished. Nature worship and idolatry saddled Israel with a self-destructive way of life. Focusing on all things superficial, Israel's false worship descended into anti-human asceticism during the divided kingdom stage, and finally bottomed out with human sacrifice and cannibalism at the end of the line for both Israel in the north (722 B.C.) and Judah in the south (586 B.C.).

Israel's Adulterous Affair with the Nature god Baal

During the divided kingdom stage (931-586 B.C.), God punished both the houses of Israel and Judah by sending them into exile because they adopted pagan nature worship as their unofficial national religion, imported from the surrounding Canaanite countryside. Shockingly, this thirst for nature worship is often described in graphic sexual language to heighten the shameful offensiveness of their actions. In Jeremiah, the kingdom of Judah is compared to "a wild donkey accustomed to the wilderness that sniffs the wind in her passion. In *the time* of her heat who can turn her away? All who seek her will not become weary; in her month they will find her" (Jer. 2:24). In the same context just a few verses back, the text reads, "For long ago I broke your yoke *and* tore off your bonds; but you said 'I will not serve!' For on every high hill and under every green tree you have lain down as a harlot" (Jer. 2:20). Worse, the idols which Israel bowed down to were compared to sexual toys: "Because of the lightness of her harlotry, she polluted the land and committed adultery with stones and trees" (Jer. 3:9). Nature worship was thus seen as a form of spiritual adultery. The Old Testament prophets compared it to prostitution. Hence, Israel had broken her *marriage vows* with the Mosaic Covenant, which she had entered into at Mt. Sinai after the Hebrews were freed from Egypt.

This form of paganism was purposefully described with such graphic sexual language precisely because cult prostitution and sexual mysticism was a big part of the nature worship process. Sexual fertility cults and the desire for a corresponding agricultural fertility were weaved together into a pornographic nature worship scheme corrupting the entire nation and its people. Throughout Israel's and Judah's history, this deviant and instinctual behavior, in great contrast to the dictates of the Mosaic law, was most often associated with the worship of the nature god Baal. Baal was the god of grain and the god of thunder. He was, in fact, the god of weather. The name Baal itself simply means *lord*. As the tribal lord of the people and the land,

Baal was not only often confused with the *Lord* of the Old Testament, but he was also in charge of agricultural fertility and the weather.

Baal was not all-powerful like the Hebrew God. On the contrary, he was forced each and every year to have a life and death struggle with the god of death, Mot, reflecting the fate of the seasons. Baal dies every summer under the excessive heat and drought. Baal, however, with the help of sexual and bloody rituals practiced by his worshipers, comes back to life to defeat Mot for the cooler autumn weather and the fall rains. The severe weather was blamed on the struggle between Baal and Mot, which could only be pacified through cultic prostitution on the one hand and strict asceticism on the other. Thus, in addition to sexual abandon, the worshipers of Baal also incorporated harsh ascetic practices into their nature worship as well. Ecstatic pleasure and bloody pain were used to propitiate the nature gods for the sake of fair weather (cf. 1 Kings 18:25-29). Baal nature worship was completely indulgent with regard to sexual mysticism on one hand, but overly strict, harsh and severe on the other hand with regard to ascetic practices, with occasional bouts of human sacrifice (cf. 2 Kings 17:28-41). Worst of all, much energy and riches were spent in the promotion and practice of the cult. Israel wasted its wealth and activities on the worship of Baal, which eventually led to the nation's downfall.

Isaiah 57 records the loss of spiritual leadership that contributed to the suicidal demise of the nation where "the righteous man perishes, and no man takes it to heart; and the devout men are taken away, while no one understands. For the righteous man is taken away from evil" (Isa. 57:1). Here Isaiah notes that while good men die off and are taken away to paradise, on Earth no one replaces them. Left behind are the nature worshiping counterculture rebels of society, "Against whom do you jest? Against whom do you open wide your mouth and stick out your tongue? Are you not children of rebellion, offspring of deceit, *who* inflame yourselves among the oaks, under every luxuriant tree, who slaughter the children in the ravines, under the clefts of the crags?" (Isa. 57:4-5). Here is seen nature worship, sexual abandon and child sacrifice all rolled up into one outdoor whore house of death.

Not surprisingly, this contradictory lifestyle of sexual license and strict asceticism and/or human sacrifice was foisted upon the people by the cultivated crowd, the elites of society. They were far more influenced by the surrounding Canaanite religious culture than by the Mosaic constitution.

Nonetheless, the commoners often enjoyed nature worship as much as their leaders, leaving prophets of the Old Testament sometimes comparing themselves to *jackals* (Mic. 1:8), or roaming the streets of Jerusalem looking for at least one righteous man (Jer. 5:1-14). As such, the population at large was completely oblivious to the approaching doom which the Old Testament prophets foresaw. The fact that this downhill process was more than 200 years in the making only contributed further to their false sense of security.

Israel's Nature Worship Destroyed Their Economy & Agriculture

So addicting were such cultic practices that the Canaanite nature religion slowly and inexorably enveloped the entire country and completely corrupted its religious, political and business institutions, eventually bleeding God's people dry (Hos. 2:1-13). It was a long, painstaking process, but it finally choked off what was left of the Mosaic constitution and the associated blessings of the promised land.[176] This left the country in agricultural and economic misery. The prosperity which God richly gave Israel was wasted on Baal nature worship (Ho. 2:8). Wallowing in such self-induced misery and poverty, the depopulation of the promised land ensued. Finally, nature religion finished Israel off with child sacrifice (cf. 2 Kings 17:1-18). Thus, in the Northern Kingdom of Israel, what started out with freedom under the rule of law (Exodus), devolved into nature mysticism and political tyranny (1 Kings 21), which collapsed under conspiracy and military coups, and finally ended with the Assyrian invasion and exile (cf. 2 Kings 14:28-17:18) in 722 B.C. Even Judah ignominiously ended its days with child sacrifice[177] and ultimately cannibalism (Jer. 19:1-13) during the Babylonian invasion 120 years later.

In the book of Hosea, precisely because of Israel's idolatry and nature worship, the God of the Old Testament promises to turn the agricultural prosperity of the promised-land into a wilderness unable to feed its people. "I will destroy her vines and fig trees, of which she said, 'these are my wages

---

[176] See Appendix – Nature's Economy in the Old Testament.
[177] Much ballyhoo is made of the command to Abraham to sacrifice his only begotten son, Isaac, completely forgetting that when the time actually came for the sacrifice of the child, the Angel of the Lord intervened and stopped the ceremony (Genesis 22). There is thus not one instance of child sacrifice condoned by any of the authors of the Old Testament. It is, in fact, routinely condemned, and portrayed as one of the final stages of national destruction.

which my lovers have given me.' And I will make them a forest, and the beasts of the field will devour them. I will punish her for the days of the Baals when she used to offer sacrifices to them and adorn herself with her earrings and jewelry, and follow her lovers, so that she forgot Me" (Hos. 2:12-13).

The same judgment also befell the southern kingdom of Judah because of her own idolatry and nature worship. Isaiah predicted a Jewish Dust Bowl of Biblical proportions (Isa. 5:6, 10-15, 24). In the book of Micah, God determined that He would turn the Jerusalem temple area into a forest unfit for true religious worship (Mic. 3:12). By Ezekiel's day, at the end of the long road to destruction, nature worship left Judah in a slaughterhouse specifically designed by God to teach the nation a most serious lesson. "Then you will know that I am the LORD, when their slain are among their idols around their altars, on every high hill, on all the tops of the mountains, under every green tree and under every leafy oak—the places where they offered soothing aroma to all their idols" (Ezek. 6:13). In the end, in the name of international pagan culture, nature worship sacrificed the Jewish people with a counterculture religion loaded with backward motivations, goals and practices where creation was worshiped rather than the Creator. Nature worship was both subversive and regressive. The Assyrian and Babylonian exiles of Israel and Judah cannot be properly understood apart from the Baalistic practices that preceded these catastrophes.

Wild Gentile Kingdoms Will Prey Upon the People of God

At this juncture, following on the heels of the Babylonian invasion of Judah and its subsequent exile, one cannot help but think of Nebuchadnezzar's vision of the giant tree found in Daniel 4. This particular tree represented Nebuchadnezzar's own kingdom as lord of the Earth (Dan. 4:20-22), the lone superpower in the Middle East at that time. Immediately prior to the vision of this tree, King Nebuchadnezzar received a troubling Divine revelation in the form of a dream about an impressive human statue. This statue not only predicted and prefigured his own tyrannical empire, but also predicted the rise of the Persians, Greeks and Romans as well (Dan. 2:1-38). In a foolish response to this dream's interpretation given to him by Daniel the prophet, Nebuchadnezzar builds a statue of himself that undoubtedly resembled the one he saw in his dream. He then forced all the citizens of Babylon *to fall down and worship* it (Dan. 3:5; cf. vv. 1-30). For this arrogant usurpation of

Divine sovereignty, Nebuchadnezzar was troubled by another dream, this time not of a manly statue, but of a luxuriant tree. In Nebuchadnezzar's vision, this tree is then cut down by *an angelic watcher* (Dan. 4:23), forecasting what will happen to him in the future.

The leftover stump was designed by God to teach Nebuchadnezzar a great lesson on humility which Daniel the prophet disconcertingly revealed to him:

> This is the interpretation, O king, and this is the decree of the Most High, which has come upon my lord the king: that you be driven away from mankind and your dwelling place be with the beasts of the field, and you be given grass to eat like cattle and be drenched with the dew of heaven; and seven periods of time will pass over you, until you recognize that the Most High is ruler over the realm of mankind and bestows it on whomever He wishes. And in that it was commanded to leave the stump with the roots of the tree, your kingdom will be assured to you after you recognize that *it is* Heaven *that* rules. (Dan. 4:24-26)

What started out as idolatrous statue worship of a mortal man devolved into a fallen tree representing the loss of Nebuchadnezzar's humanity and reason. Instead of the gardens of Babylon, Nebuchadnezzar was thrown out into a wild kingdom where "his body was drenched with the dew of heaven until his hair had grown like eagles' *feathers* and his nails like birds' *claws*" (Dan. 4:33b). His human sanity and dominion were taken away for seven years, at which time he finally acknowledged that God was the Creator and *King* of the universe (Dan. 4:33-37). Thus, not only does the book of Daniel present that human reason is one of the chief characteristics distinguishing man from the natural created order, but it also strongly suggests that those who fail to worship God as the ultimate Creator are setting themselves up for irrational, animalistic, instinctual behavior.

With all this in mind, it is no coincidence that the next vision given to Daniel compares the present and future world empires of Babylon, Persia, Greece and Rome to ferocious wild animals (Dan. 7:1-8). The prediction of the rise of these empires described as savage animals is identical to the previous vision describing the same kingdoms as an awesome human statue. The connections here between human deification, nature worship, tyrannical human governments and beastly instincts are thus unmistakable—all poised to terrorize the inhabitants of the earth, especially God's own people, "Arise, devour much meat!" (Dan. 7:5). While suffering in the aftermath of the Babylonian exile, Daniel predicts that the Jewish nation will suffer even further at the hands of such animalistic Gentile kingdoms for centuries to come, even to the point where its own "Messiah will be cut off and have nothing" (Dan. 9:26). The promised Messianic Kingdom that the Jewish heroes of the faith looked forward to is thus put off into abeyance into the apocalyptic future.

This astonishing pronouncement occurs within the context of a description of a false messianic prince who arises and makes a deceitful covenant with the people of Israel (Dan. 9:24-27). Hence, instead of peace, he brings even further destruction of the Jewish people starting at the mid-point of the final seven-year period of human history known in Christian circles as the great tribulation. In the book of Revelation, this false messianic prince, or the Antichrist, is called the wild *beast*. He will control the free market and demand the entire world to *worship him* (Rev. 13:8). At Armageddon is seen the climax of the barbarous and beastly rebellion against God and His people. The wild Gentile powers have a final solution in mind for God's people Israel, but they will be ultimately thwarted by the return of Messiah to the Earth to save them from catastrophe and set up the Messianic kingdom of peace promised throughout the Old Testament (cf. Isa. 2:1-4; 9:1-7; 11:1-9; Hos. 2:14-23; Mic. 4:1-5; Rev. 19-20).

While Adolf Hitler, the Final Solution and the Holocaust are not specifically predicted by Daniel the prophet, there can be no doubt that Nazi Germany epitomizes Daniel's beastly portrayal of tyrannical Gentile governments rising up across the prophetic horizon until the end of time to prey upon the people of God. The few Jewish victims who survived the Holocaust often compared the Nazi SS perpetrators to cruel wild beasts.[178] Hitler "imagined himself a wolf as he screamed to the adoring crowds."[179] He was captivated with wolves and their predator-prey way of life:

> As a boy he was well pleased with his first name, noting that it came
> from the old German '*Athalwolf*'—a compound of *Athal* (noble) and
> *Wolfa* (wolf). And "noble wolf" he sought to remain. At the start of his

---

[178]   Arad, pp. 184-198.
[179]   Sax, p. 16.

political career he chose "Herr Wolf" as his pseudonym. His favorite dogs were Alsatians—in German *Wolfshunde*. One of the Blondi's pups, born toward the end of the war, he called "Wolf" and would allow no one to touch or feed it. He named his headquarters in France *Wolfsschlucht* (Wolf's Gulch). In the Ukraine his headquarters were *Werwolf* (Man Wolf), and in East Prussia *Wolfsschanze* (Wolf's Lair) as he explained to a servant, "I am the Wolf and this is my den." He called his SS "my pack of wolves." Later he would recall with exaltation how in the early days of the movement his Storm troopers pounced upon the opposition "like wolves" and were soon "covered with blood." He had his sister Paula change her name to Frau Wolf. The special agent he chose to supervise purchases for his Linz Library and Museum was Dr. Wolfhardt (Hard Wolf). He approved of naming the Volkswagen factory "*Wolfsburg*." When he telephoned Winifred Wagner, he would say, "Conductor Wolf calling!" The secretary he kept longer than any other was Johanna Wolf. She recalled that while Hitler addressed all other secretaries formally as "Frau" or "Fraulein," he invariably called her "*Wolfin*" (She-Wolf). One of his favorite tunes came from a Walt Disney movie. Often and absent-mindedly he whistled "Who's Afraid of the Big Bad Wolf?"—an animal, it will be recalled, who wanted to eat people and blow their houses down.[180]

If Hitler could have arranged it, no doubt, he would rather have had wolves outside of the concentration camps than guard dogs. Nazi leader Herman Goering, on the other hand, loved lions. Goering kept pet lions at his side, and they were not always just small, young ones.[181]

Hitler had his own barbaric vision in mind for the Jewish people, which can even be sensed in his early writings:

> In *Mein Kampf*, Hitler was not concerned with outlining any part of a National Socialist religion (at least not consciously so) to a major degree. Indeed he often wallowed in a glutinous mixture of self-pity and cultural despair. However, a foreshadowing of what would

---

[180] Waite, Robert. *The Psychopathic God.* New York: Da Capo Press, (1977) 1993, pp. 26-27.

[181] Irving, David. *Goering: A Biography.* New York: Avon Books, 1989, pp. 123, 128, 172-73, 180, 185, 189.

become the National Socialist "religion of nature" was certainly present. Of importance here was Hitler's deprecation of the role of humanity in a universe run according to pitiless natural laws.[182]

A worldview of pitiless natural laws fits in perfectly with Daniel's beastly prophetic visions. These terrifying visions left Daniel greatly alarmed, *exhausted, sick* and *astonished* (Dan. 7:28; 8:27). Daniel knew that these untamed tyrants and kingdoms would persecute the people of God like wild animals for centuries to come.

Baal nature worship in the divided kingdoms of Israel and Judah greased the skids to help usher in what the Bible calls "the times of the Gentiles" (Luke 21:24). The times of the Gentiles will, in turn, find their culmination in the tyrannical worship of the man of sin, the Antichrist himself, the wild beast of Revelation, who will be empowered by Satan to make "the world like a wilderness and overthrow its cities (Isa. 14:17)."

God will Save Israel from the Apocalyptic Wilderness Wasteland

However, as Hosea and other Old Testament prophets have promised, it will be from this wilderness wasteland of the apocalypse, where the wild Gentile powers viciously preyed upon the people of God, that a future Israel will find grace and mercy. Their future salvation will far exceed even their miraculous exodus out of Egypt (Hos. 2:14). In Hosea 2, God promises to romance Israel once again. He promises to renew their marriage vows as He recalls their original honeymoon period in the wilderness of Sinai. In the future, He promises not only to restore her agricultural and economic fortunes in the promised land, but also to "make a covenant for them with the beasts of the field, the birds of the sky, and the creeping things of the ground. And I will abolish the bow, the sword and war from the land, and will make them lie down in safety. I will betroth you to Me forever; yes, I will betroth you to Me in righteousness and in justice, in lovingkindness and in compassion, and I will betroth you to Me in faithfulness. Then you will know the LORD" (Hos. 2:18-20). Israel's future salvation will recover a holy relationship with nature not seen since the garden of Eden. This will be further complemented by true world peace, love, justice and righteousness.

---

[182] Pois, p. 38.

That this promised eschatological salvation will begin in the wilderness[183] is no coincidence. The wilderness is the place of grace and salvation since the difficult conditions of the environment force the people of God to rely upon Him alone. "Israel, separated from Baal, the nations and the material allurements of the city, can find herself again in the wilderness."[184] Thus, the wilderness can and will have a cleansing effect upon the people of God.

However, in the Bible, returning permanently back to the wilderness is not the ultimate goal of Jewish salvation. It is only a temporary means to help the people of God return to their senses by abandoning the emptiness of Baal worship. Baal was the nature god who left Israel for dead, abandoned and naked in the wilderness before the ferocity of the wild Gentile animals. The goal of Jewish eschatological salvation is a return to the reconstituted promised land. It is a land which will be cultured and developed as a kingdom, yet this time not accompanied with all of the unbelief and unrighteousness that so characterized much of Israel's history throughout the Old Testament. The problem was never with human cultural development per se, but with sin that jaded and hijacked it for its own sinister purposes.

---

[183] For an outstanding summary on true biblical romanticism, please refer to Dr. Duane Garrett's Excursus entitled, "The Ideal of the Wilderness" from his commentary on Hosea and Joel. "Hosea, Joel." *The New American Commentary*, Vol. 19A, Broadman and Holman Publishers, 1997, pp. 88-91.

[184] Ibid., p. 91.

"At that time," declares the LORD, "I will be the God of all the families of Is-rael, and they shall be My people." ² Thus says the LORD, "The people who survived the sword found grace in the wilderness-- Israel, when it went to find its rest." ³ The LORD appeared to him from afar, saying, "I have loved you with an everlasting love; Therefore I have drawn you with lovingkindness. ⁴ "Again I will build you, and you shall be rebuilt, O virgin of Israel! Again you shall take up your tambourines, And go forth to the dances of the merrymak-ers. ⁵ "Again you shall plant vineyards On the hills of Samaria; The planters shall plant And shall enjoy them. ⁶ "For there shall be a day when watchmen On the hills of Ephraim shall call out, 'Arise, and let us go up to Zion, To the LORD our God.'" ⁷ For thus says the LORD, "Sing aloud with gladness for Ja-cob, And shout among the chiefs of the nations; Proclaim, give praise, and say, 'O LORD, save Thy people, The remnant of Israel.' ⁸ "Behold, I am bringing them from the north country, And I will gather them from the remote parts of the earth, Among them the blind and the lame, The woman with child and she who is in labor with child, together; A great company, they shall return here. ⁹ "With weeping they shall come, And by supplication I will lead them; I will make them walk by streams of waters, On a straight path in which they shall not stumble; For I am a father to Israel, And Ephraim is My first-born."

Jeremiah 31:1-9

CHAPTER TWO:

THE ROMANTIC REBELLION AGAINST THE JUDEO-CHRISTIAN WORLDVIEW

While the suicidal tendencies of nature worship are plain for all to read throughout the pages of the Old Testament, the judgments upon Israel and Judah were clearly self-inflicted. As Ezekiel indicates, it will take the Babylonian exile to prove to the Jewish people that nature religion was false. Since that time, the Jews have steered clear of idolatrous nature worship. However, in their rejection of paganism, they began to withdraw into a sheltered world of religious isolation from others, which sometimes shaded into a form of religious racism just as foreign to the Old Testament as was the worship of foreign idols.[185]

Over the centuries, the pagans were increasingly offended by such aloofness, and sometimes viewed the Jews with great suspicion. This antagonism finally developed into what later became known as the Jewish-Gentile controversy that the New Testament dwells on at great length. This was a severe controversy which even the primitive church greatly struggled with (Acts 15:1-30; Galatians), and which climaxed with the destruction of the Jerusalem Temple in 70 A.D. at the hands of the Romans. While the New Testament itself, written by Jews, was not anti-Semitic, the same cannot be said of more than a few Gentile converts to Christianity. The Apostle Paul's own attitude toward the Jews (Rom. 9:1-5) was rarely emulated by pagan converts even though he strongly warned his readers against the dangers of anti-Semitism in his letter to the Romans (Rom. 11:11-33). Paul was often persecuted by his Jewish brethren throughout much of his Christian career (Acts 13-24). However, as *a Hebrew of Hebrews* (Phil. 3:5), he never allowed such maltreatment to interfere with his love for the Jews.

---

[185]   The book of Jonah is classic on this.

The Jewish-Gentile controversy has yet to be resolved in the modern world, even after all these centuries. Worst of all, the church itself often did not permit the Biblical text to correct its irrational anti-Semitic views and practices that stemmed from their previous pagan background.[186] In fact, the church distorted the Biblical text and actually Christianized anti-Semitism[187] so that its very identity could not be separated from it. European anti-Semitism thus became "a corollary of Christianity."[188] Judaism was routinely discredited as the polar opposite of Christianity so that "the Jews came to represent much that was antithetical to the moral order of the Christian world."[189] Many Catholics[190] and prominent Protestants, like Martin Luther, despised the Jews. While much of Christendom has been anti-Semitic since the days of its takeover of the Roman Empire, this is contrary to the teaching of the Bible. Just as many Jews had a hard time submitting to the Old Testament revelation in various areas of Scripture, so too, much the same can be said of many Gentile converts to Christianity with regard to both the Old and New Testaments. Hence, while many Christians have been anti-Semitic throughout church history, such attitudes are not Scriptural and are callously insensitive to the Biblical record.

Yet, Gentile Christians recognized the dangers nature worship posed to Christianity, like many Old Testament prophets. Under the Mosaic law, the Hebrews were commanded to cut down cultic altars to protect the people of Israel from its degenerating influences (Deut. 12:1-6). Much later during the church age, "early Christians cut down the sacred groves and chased the ancient gods from the temples, many of which became sites for Christian churches. In early modern times, the non-sacred character of Creation was emphasized by Reformation Christians, such as John Calvin, who encouraged western 'man' to 'develop' Creation."[191] Catholic churches thus replaced the sacred groves. Later the alleged anti-nature dominion mandate

---

186 On this, see especially the book of Esther in the Old Testament where is seen for the first time the word "Jew" in a pejorative anti-Semitic sense.

187 On the Christianization of Anti-Semitism, see especially *Hitler's Willing Executioners: Ordinary Germans and the Holocaust* by Daniel Jonah Goldhagen, pp. 49-53.

188 Goldhagen, p. 49.

189 Ibid., p. 50.

190 See *The Origins of the Inquisition in 15th Century Spain* by Benzion Netanyahu. New York: New York Review of Books, (1995). Netanyahu's 1,200 page magnum opus shows how the Spanish Catholic Inquisition was primarily designed to declare Christian Jews secret Judaizers so as to remove them from their high royal positions that they enjoyed as converts to Christendom.

191 Zimmerman, Michael, "Possible Political Problems of Earth Based Religiosity."

of Genesis was transformed into a justification for human and economic development by the Protestants. This stress on economic development reached new heights with the spread of Puritan values in North America along with the rise of the Enlightenment and industrial capitalism. Neither should it be missed that this historical revolution was primarily a Western Christian phenomenon. Western Christianity valued action over thought, "The Greek saint contemplates; the western saint acts. The implications of Christianity for the conquest of nature would emerge more easily in the western atmosphere."[192] Under Western Christianity, the natural theology of the Middle Ages gave birth to modern science precisely because it became very interested in discovering how creation actually works.

Thus Hebrews, Catholics and Protestants have been cutting down the sacred groves for centuries on both sides of the Atlantic. Romantics of the early green movement and modern environmentalists believe such behavior showcases an arrogant attitude toward the natural world that led directly to western man's unbridled dominion over nature and its subsequent ecological degradation. "Pagan beliefs were more intimately bound to specific places than those of Jews or Christians. The need to placate the guardians of streams or forests inhibited the growth of urban or industrial civilization."[193] The advent of Christianity in the West largely replaced the pagan hesitations and superstitions of the past. Paganism was often very hostile to the idea of human progress and economic development. "Before one cut a tree, mined a mountain, or dammed a brook, it was important to placate the spirit in charge of that particular situation, and keep it placated. By destroying pagan animism, Christianity made it possible to exploit nature in a mood of indifference to the feelings of natural objects."[194]

As the church increasingly lost more and more of its influence over the Western world throughout the late 1800s and early 1900s, nature mysticism, otherwise known as Romanticism, came roaring back to fill in the spiritual vacuum. Romanticism, which was especially strong in Germany, stressed nature, not reason. Romanticism, nostalgically looking for greener pastures in less troublesome rustic settings, revolted against the cult of reason which the Enlightenment overemphasized. In short, "the sympathies of the

---

[192] White, Jr. Lynn, p. 1,206.
[193] Sax, p. 37.
[194] White, Jr. Lynn, p. 1204.

romantics were with nature, while the philosophies of the Enlightenment glorified the civilization of humankind."[195]

While the Enlightenment had its roots in Greek philosophy and the natural theology of medieval Catholic scholasticism, it increasingly separated itself from its theological underpinnings. During the 1700s, the zenith of the Enlightenment's influence was reached under a secular religion called Deism, which was a belief in God as the Creator, but which rejected the possibility of His miraculous supernatural intervention in either nature or human history. In conjunction with this, the Bible was viewed less and less as a sacred object. In its place was substituted a secular religion based on nature, human reason, and science without reference to any supernatural revelation from God.

Thus, during the Enlightenment the pillars of the Protestant Reformation, i.e., the Scriptures alone, faith alone and grace alone,[196] were replaced by reason alone. In turn, Deism, a strict natural theology based purely on nature and reason, replaced many Protestant values. The Enlightenment profaned and secularized Christianity. The deists did not believe God interfered "with His creation. Rather He designed it to run independent of him by immutable natural laws."[197] Furthermore, these natural laws were described in rationalistic terms so that the created world was compared to a working machine without any reference to God. This particular view of the universe became known as Naturalism. From this time forward, the naturalistic sciences increasingly opposed the Judeo-Christian worldview, relegating it to the ash heap of irrationality like ancient superstitions of the pagan past. With a belief in such a mechanistic view of the natural world, the industrial revolution and scientific human progress jettisoned the religious past in favor of an almost utopian society this side of the grave. However, along with industrial progress came the increasing problem of pollution, the growth of dirty cities, the despoiling of the landscape and the rationalistic exploitation of nature itself that had been reduced to a working machine.

It was against this backdrop of growing alienation from the natural world that the subversive rebellion of modern Romanticism and its ecological emphasis was born. Furthermore, the Romantics did not just rebel

---

[195] Sax, p. 39.
[196] *Sola Scriptura, sola fide* and *sola gratia.*
[197] *The Baker Encyclopedia of Christian Apologetics*, p. 191.

against the Enlightenment, but against Christianity also. However different Christianity and the Enlightenment may have been with regard to doctrinal beliefs, they seemed to have tolerated one another to a certain extent, and even worked closely together with each other during the American Revolution. During this period it is often difficult to tell where Protestant Christianity gives way and Deism takes over. Deists attended Protestant churches in America. Hence the Romantics subversively took aim at both groups, looking to undermine their influence through a nostalgic call to a simpler lifestyle more in harmony with the natural surroundings:

> If ecology is a subversive subject … what is it trying to subvert? Some of the possibilities which come to mind are: the accepted notion of what science does; the values and institutions of expansionary capitalism; the bias against nature in western religion. All of these were targets of the 19th century Romantics; they were the first great subversives of modern times. Understanding their point of view, therefore will contribute to our understanding of the ecology movement today. But the connection between contemporary ecology and Romanticism is even more direct than the sharing of antagonists. The Romantic approach to nature was fundamentally ecological—that is—it was concerned with relation, interdependence, and holism.[198]

Romanticism was all about natural harmony and holism. This is precisely why the Romantics targeted both Christianity and the Enlightenment.

The Romantics were convinced that Christianity and the Enlightenment were responsible for the increasing degradation of the natural world since they both accepted man's dominion over nature as basic to the created order. They believed such a worldview ruptured nature's interdependent whole. While the Christians may have emphasized that man was created in God's image on the one hand, and the deists emphasized human reason on the other hand, to the Romantics either emphasis followed a direct straight line to the exploitation of nature for utilitarian purposes. This utilitarian view reduced nature to an economic commodity that could be bought and sold. This, in turn, left the modern world of that time increasingly alienated from

---

[198] Worster, Donald, *Nature's Economy: A History of Ecological Ideas.* Cambridge University Press, 1985 (1977), p. 58.

its natural surroundings. The Romantics then used this alienation to prick the conscience of both the Enlightenment[199] and Christianity—which paid handsome dividends. As Romanticism wrestled with the Enlightenment, it was later tempered with existentialism and the evolutionary sciences of Darwinism that helped give birth to modern environmentalism as it is known today.

The mechanistic sciences of the Enlightenment were thus slowly replaced with the environmental sciences of the modern age. This greening of the Enlightenment would have just as profound consequences on the modern world as Darwin's theory of evolution. In fact, Romanticism and Naturalism later worked together in breaking through Christianity's defenses with a tremendous cultural pincer movement. The Enlightenment dropped Christian natural theology and its mechanistic view of the universe run by God given laws, and adopted an increasingly romantic view of science that attributed vitalist creative powers to nature itself. The Christian West was thus hit from both sides. Romanticism attacked Christianity for its dominion mandate. Naturalism attacked Christianity for being unscientific, especially after the rise of Darwinism. This pincer movement largely explains why the West has become post-Christian. Judeo-Christian foundations have largely been replaced by evolutionary theory and environmental ethics.

Henry David Thoreau's 'Nature Looking into Nature'

The Romantic who best epitomized such views and concerns in North America was Henry David Thoreau. He was one of the first counterculture environmental eccentrics in America. "Henry Thoreau was not a respectable gentleman in the eyes of his neighbors, in part because New England had no tolerance for the idleness implied by unemployment, and in part because Thoreau had no regard for affluence or the trappings of respectability."[200] Thoreau even spent a night in the Concord jail for refusing to pay taxes to support the war against Mexico.[201] He is most famous, however, for writing his ecological memoirs about Walden Pond where he

---

[199] For an excellent discussion on Romanticism, Environmentalism and the Enlightenment see Jonathan Olsen's *Nature and Nationalism: Right Wing Ecology and the Politics of Identity in Contemporary Germany*. New York: St. Martin's Press, 1999, pp. 19-28, 57-61.

[200] Worster, *Nature's Economy: A History of Ecological Ideas*, p. 62.

[201] Ibid., p. 61.

lived in a simple house he built for himself between 1845 and 1847. Walden Pond became his inspiration to commune with nature in a romantic, yet also scientifically observant way. While many modern environmentalists paint him as an anti-government libertarian free spirit, it must be pointed out the American government of his day was very limited in its powers. It openly espoused individual liberty and Manifest Destiny. In other words, to be a rebel against the limited constitutional powers of the American government suggests that Thoreau was not the libertarian or free individualist that many often make him out to be. Thoreau was not happy with what the Puritans did with their liberty upon the American landscape.

Thoreau saw himself as so united with his natural surroundings that he touted a disciplined ecological empiricism which he characterized as "nature looking into nature."[202] In contrast to the mechanistic science of Newton and the Enlightenment emphasizing a detached and objective observation, Thoreau helped advocate a holistic empiricism when it came to the study of nature. "Throughout the 50's, the main thrust of Thoreau's scientific studies was ecological. Once he had learned the names of his 'neighbors,' the appeal of taxonomy gave way to a desire to understand the interrelations among plants, animals, and their habitats."[203] Communion and holism was what was important to Thoreau. He believed that to be "disconnected from the ecological community was to be incomplete, sick, fragmented, dying." Thoreau's writings also represented some of the very first beginnings of a natural existentialist philosophy of man and nature that wedded itself to scientific empiricism. From Thoreau's time forward, a philosophy of natural existence began to impose itself upon the sciences. The natural laws of the mechanistic sciences governed by God were replaced with the existential reality of nature alone without any reference to a transcendental Creator who stood outside the Earthly processes.

"Thoreau and the Romantics generally believed a renewed, harmonious relation to nature was the only remedy for the spiritual as well as the physical ills that marked their times."[204] Hence, not surprisingly, it was Thoreau who claimed, "In wildness is the preservation of the world," and, "The most

---

[202]   Henry Thoreau from his daily journals quoted by Worster in *Nature's Economy: A History of Ecological Ideas*, p. 78.

[203]   Worster, *Nature's Economy: A History of Ecological Ideas*, p. 65.

[204]   Ibid., p. 83.

alive is the wildest."[205] As such, Thoreau also helped to establish the idea that nature without humans would naturally produce "the greatest regularity and harmony."[206] Thoreau thus aided and abetted the Romantic anti-human diatribe that has since become the trademark of modern environmentalism. It seems that from this time forward, cleansing the landscape from human interference became a common obsession among many who belonged to the Romantic Movement. Instead of cleansing the human being from sin, they want to cleanse nature from man.

Thoreau's most valuable ecological insight from a practical point of view came from his observation about forest succession where timber harvesters could learn from nature itself on how to grow healthy perpetual crops of trees.[207] In such studies and observations, Thoreau was most interested in bringing the New England forests back to their pristine condition. One of Thoreau's most original contributions to early environmental studies was the concept of natural ecological history. "The most important and most poignant purpose of Thoreau's ecological study was historical: to reconstruct 'the actual condition of the place where we dwell, (as it appeared) three centuries ago' before the coming of the white man."[208]

What is so often overlooked is that keeping nature pure and untainted from human development is an archconservative viewpoint at complete odds with the ideals of the American Revolution. Contrary to popular opinion, the American Revolution should be considered classical liberalism, where human liberty and human progress and development were expressly used to limit the authority of kings and despotic governments. In truth, the real *hard right* archconservatives of the 1800s were the Romantics. They were subversively consumed with the notion of keeping things the way they once were. Any kind of change that upset the so-called natural harmony was open season for criticism. Nature was literally seen as king and is still seen that way by modern environmentalists. The connection between Romanticism, holism, nature worship and dictatorial totalitarianism runs deep.

To Romantics like Thoreau, the immigrant non-native Puritans had come in and devastated the New England landscape. He thus endeavored to recreate the original environment from a Romantic ecological point of

---

205   Thoreau, Henry David. *The Writings of Henry David Thoreau*, 1906, p. 275 quoted by Stirling in *Green Gone Wild: Elevating Nature Above Human Rights*, p. 18.
206   Worster, *Nature's Economy: A History of Ecological Ideas*, p. 243.
207   Ibid., p. 71.
208   Ibid., p. 66.

view in order to demonstrate how much natural purity had been lost forever. This is the real reason why Thoreau was so interested in environmental history. By using the natural history of the New England landscape since the arrival of the Puritans, he could use it as a critique of the Protestant New England society around him. Instead of learning lessons from a society's historical past, a society could also be critiqued by discussing how it related to the natural surroundings. Environmental purity thus became the standard by which to judge a society of its shortcomings, especially one embedded deeply in Puritanism:

> In 1857 he urged that "men tread gently through nature. Let us religiously burn stumps and worship in groves, while Christian vandals lay waste the forest temples to build miles of meeting houses and horse sheds and feed their box stoves." And in his "Huckleberries" lecture, he asked his listeners why New England's Puritan fathers could not have preserved at least some remnants of the primeval forests. At the same time that they built meeting houses why did they not preserve from desecration and destruction far grander temples not made with hands? More of the Druid and less of the Protestant creed, and America's great forests might have been saved.[209]

Thoreau's opposition to Christianity went so far as to replace the communion sacraments with eating "wild berries in celebration of nature. His religion was to be a 'heath-en' one, drawing its spiritual nourishment from the heaths and woodlands. It could not be contained in the narrow fold of the Good Shepherd, but would leap the fence."[210] Romantics like Thoreau reserved a special hostility for Christianity. In their minds it was a rival worldview which had sharply disjointed man from the natural world.

The purpose of the Christian was not to merge with nature as the Romantics so desperately wished for, but to develop an obedient loving fellowship with God. Even more troubling for the Romantics, a transcendent personal God created a natural world outside of Himself in the Genesis account. As such, because nature was distinct from God, the Mosaic law also prohibited nature worship. According to the Mosaic law, nature cannot be worshiped for the simple reason that it is created by God. As such, God

---

[209] Ibid., p. 88.
[210] Ibid., p. 87.

and God alone is to be worshiped since He is the Creator. God and nature are thus absolutely distinct in the Bible. They cannot be confused with each other into a holistic one:

> The earliest culture in which the world was disenchanted was the biblical world of the Israelites. When the author of Genesis wrote, "in the beginning God created the heavens and the earth," he was expressing that disenchantment. Creation was seen as devoid of independent divine or magical forces which men had to appease. The world was seen as created by a supra-mundane Creator. As long as men came to terms with the Creator, the world was theirs to do with it as they pleased. No interference need be feared from powers immanent in the natural order.[211]

However, the Mosaic presentation of the creation account was even controversial in the ancient world. For the ancients, nature was not created, but was as eternal as the gods since they ultimately could not be separated from each other. They were inextricably tied into a pantheistic one. Pantheism literally means God is everything. This means nature can and should be worshiped, the exact opposite of the Biblical view. It also strongly implies that nature should not be tampered or tinkered with, since this would amount to tampering or tinkering with the gods.

The Hostility Between Romantic & Christianity Spirituality

"Romanticism has always implied, more or less clearly, an alternative to Christian moral tradition,"[212] and the great controversy between them stems from the creation account. There, the God of Genesis crowns His creative work with the creation of man. With the creation of the world and the universe on each successive day, God calls it all *good*, but after the creation of man, God declares it *very good*. In Genesis, man is God's unique creation. Man is the apex of creation. Adam was made in God's image and thus reflected God's transcendent Person in important ways, like rulership, freedom, work, responsibility and fellowship. Even though man is created by God and hence not God, and is also a part of the created order since he is certainly a creature,

---

[211]   Rubenstein, Richard. *The Cunning of History: The Holocaust and the American Future.* New York: Harper & Row Publishers, 1975, p. 28.

[212]   Stern, p. 39.

man is nonetheless given god-like capacities that are to be exercised in the natural world God made for him. As difficult as this may sound to modern evolutionary environmentalists, while the natural world is ultimately made for God's own glory, it is also made for man. More insulting still, marriage is then instituted by God with a specific mandate to accomplish—subdue and fill the Earth. This is precisely why Adam needed a helpmate in Eve. In short, man is created in God's image, and then commanded to rule the natural world, and the direct means by which to accomplish this is to fill the world with population under the Divine institution of marriage. Moreover, this Divine mandate has not been rescinded. It is still in effect. This is the ecological worldview of Genesis 1, which carries over into the post-flood world after Noah (cf. Gen. 9:1-7; Ps. 8).

Such a worldview was simply too much for the Romantics to bear as they "saw nature as a system of necessary relationships that cannot be disturbed in even the most inconspicuous way without changing, perhaps destroying, the equilibrium of the whole. Nor can any creature exist outside the communal organism."[213] Such a collectivist attitude precludes the possibility of the Genesis account from the very outset. The Romantic rebellion against this dominion mandate was at the same time a rebellion against their God-given responsibility to govern the natural world. In other words, just *letting it be* is an avoidance of responsibility and contradicts precisely what humanity was created for in the first place. Most people simply do not want the great responsibility required of them to be stewards of God's green earth.

Environmentalists are also quick to forget the story of Noah and the animals (Gen. 6-9). There can be no doubt that Noah has a much better track record of saving animals than the Endangered Species Act. God made a covenant with both Noah and a select number of animals (Gen. 9:9-10) that guaranteed their survival through the cataclysm (Gen. 6:17-20) into a new post-flood world in which they were to once again fill the earth through abundant breeding (Gen. 8:17; 9:1-7). This was the first piece of real environmental legislation ever handed down to man. However, very unlike modern environmentalists, who want to reduce human population counts, God wanted both the animals and man to breed and multiply abundantly on the Earth.

Contrary to modern evolutionary and environmental views, God also highlighted yet again that man is made in God's image (Gen. 9:6), and hence

---

[213] Worster, *Nature's Economy: A History of Ecological Ideas*, p. 82.

above the natural world and the animals over which he exercises authority. God also promised in the Noahic covenant that He would never flood the earth again (Gen. 9:15), and that there would be a consistency of seasonal weather cycles that could be counted on. "While the earth remains, seed-time and harvest, and cold and heat, and summer and winter, and day and night shall not cease" (Gen. 8:22). While most scientists, of course, doubt the facticity of Noah's flood, there is a vast array of historical and mytho-logical texts, both ancient and legendary, that universally support the case that there was indeed a great deluge that overwhelmed the Earth.

Perhaps a good case in point to help illustrate the hostility of Roman-ticism toward basic Biblical values is to discuss the difference between classic conservationist Gifford Pinchot (1865-1946) and his environmental counterpart John Muir (1838-1914) around the turn of the century circa 1900. It was Gifford Pinchot who coined the term conservation[214] with regard to natural resource management, and defined it as "the fundamental material policy in human civilization" and as "the development and use of the earth and all its resources for the enduring good of men."[215] Pinchot also said all of the federal western lands "must be made to perform their part in the economy in the Nation. Unless the reserved lands of public domain are made to contribute to the welfare and prosperity of the country, they should be thrown open to settlement and the whole system of reserved lands abandoned."[216] Thus, what Pinchot recommended was the scientific management and conservation of the western lands for future human needs. He also believed if that was not done, then the western lands should be turned over to private hands for the very same purpose.

After the great 1906 earthquake, the citizens of San Francisco wanted to build "a dam and reservoir in the Hetch Hetchy Valley as a source of water for its residents. Lying 15 miles north of Yosemite Valley, and dubbed

---

[214] Stirling, p. 20.

[215] Pinchot, Gifford, *Breaking News* quoted by Worster, *Nature's Economy: A History of Ecological Ideas*, p. 266.

[216] Gifford Pinchot in a report of the National Forest Commission, quoted by Worster, *Nature's Economy: A History of Ecological Ideas*, p. 266. Today those very lands are still in the hands of the federal government, which for all practical purposes, is now controlled by various environmental groups and lobbies, not to mention the EPA as well. Much of today's environmental clout all goes back to the fact that they are in control of millions of acres in the west, especially in Alaska. All of this actually begs the question as to whether or not western states are truly on the same equal footing as the eastern states are. The eastern states have very little federal ownership. The drift away from the Constitutional states' rights began in the western territories.

'Yosemite's twin' by Muir, the San Francisco proposal for the damming of Hetch Hetchy Valley required congressional approval."[217] This led to a nasty fight between Gifford Pinchot, who was Theodore Roosevelt's friend and natural resource advisor,[218] and John Muir, who was also a friend of the president. John Muir was much more romantically attached to the Hetch Hetchy Valley than Pinchot and the citizens of San Francisco. Prior to the great earthquake, President Roosevelt had actually joined with John Muir in the Yosemite Valley where both of them extolled the grand beauty of the area. However, when the San Francisco residents made the dam proposal, a split between Roosevelt and Muir resulted. Muir strongly denounced the building of the dam. "Those temple destroyers, devotees of ravaging commercialism, seem to have a perfect contempt for Nature, and instead of lifting their eyes to the God of the mountains, life to them is the Almighty Dollar. Dam Hetch Hetchy! As well dam for water tanks the people's cathedrals and churches, for no holier temple has ever been consecrated by the heart of man."[219]

Though President Roosevelt dearly loved the Hetch Hetchy area as much as Muir and recognized its great value in being preserved, "his practical side recognized that Pinchot's approach of allowing people to utilize natural resources under government management and supervision was a more realistic compromise position for the demands of the fast-growing west, which included San Francisco's need for water. Roosevelt eventually sided with Pinchot, favoring the dam."[220]

Roosevelt made the only real choice that could have been made that took seriously the needs of the people in San Francisco. Conservationists like Gifford Pinchot and Teddy Roosevelt still held that man had dominion over the earth, something which they certainly learned from their Judeo-Christian heritage, no matter how subconscious some of this may have been. They thus acted upon those beliefs and went ahead with the building of the dam. Their idea of conservationism was that the need for nature preservation should never exclude human beings.

Even today, many Americans still hold to the Roosevelt-Pinchot view of multiple-use conservationism with regard to the environment. What most of them do not understand is that this kind of classic conservationism is

[217] Stirling, p. 20.
[218] Ibid.
[219] John Muir quoted by Fox, *John Muir and His Legacy*, p. 144.
[220] Stirling, pp. 20-21.

heavily criticized by modern greens as being selfish, greedy and utilitarian. In fact, when environmentalists talk, many people are assuming classic conservationist values like either Pinchot or Roosevelt, not archconservative Romantic views about nature that considers any change in the presumed natural order of things a catastrophic sin.

The great issue here is the Judeo-Christian worldview, which classic conservationists like Pinchot and Roosevelt assumed, still allows nature to be used and even sacrificed for the needs of man. This concept is something which Romantics, modern environmentalists and greens bristle at. Sacrifice, of course, is always a messy business and always short on looks, appearances and pleasantries. Much like the Old Testament scapegoat or the Passover lamb where an innocent animal dies in place of the Old Testament worshiper, Roosevelt and Pinchot held true to these Judeo-Christian commitments. The pristine Hetch Hetchy Valley was thus sacrificed for the residents of San Francisco.

In light of modern environmental political correctness, one of the most difficult truths to accept is that in a fallen world, nature often must be sacrificed for the well-being of man. This was the first shocking lesson given to Adam and Eve after they sinned. Ashamed of their nakedness, and wishing to cover themselves with green leaves (Gen. 3:7), God provided animal skins instead (Gen. 3:21). This was the first animal sacrifice in human history. It was also a shocking and heart-wrenching consequence with regard to Adam and Eve's sinful rebellion in the garden. Innocent animals were killed in order to properly clothe Adam and Eve.

Sin is so serious that not only did nature tragically fall, but it must also be sacrificed for the well-being of man as well. Since man is a part of nature, if he falls, then nature must fall with him. In fact, once clothed with animal skins, Adam and Eve were removed from the environmental paradise that was Eden (Gen. 3:24). Where they were going, green leaves would not suffice. A survival mode was now introduced into the natural world requiring sacrifices to be made in order to help man live. While all of Genesis 1 portrays creation as serving man, including the sun, moon and stars to help him tell time (Gen. 1:14), sin and the fall of mankind add into the ecological equation the concept of sacrifice as well—a far-reaching consequence.

Nonetheless, in the Biblical account, it is still far better the innocent animal dies rather than man. This, of course, was a most difficult lesson to learn, one which even Cain struggled with when he tried to offer God green gifts instead of a sacrificial lamb like that of Abel (Gen. 4:1-9). What Cain and so many others fail to understand is that animal sacrifices prefigured and predicted the ultimate sacrifice of all time, the crucifixion of the Son of God. Through this sacrifice, man's conscience can be cleansed of his sin by faith in "the Lamb of God who takes away the sin of the world!" (John 1:29). Thus, after sin and the fall of both mankind and nature, another hated element of the Judeo-Christian worldview enters the ecological equation: nature is sacrificed for man, not man sacrificed for nature. Nature and sacrificial animals do indeed play a critical role in the salvation history of the Bible.

Closely connected, imbibing off of the same Romantic worldview of Thoreau and Muir, modern greens also criticize the shepherd motif emphasized throughout the Bible. Abel, Abraham, Isaac, Jacob, Joseph, Moses and David were not only heroes of the Old Testament faith, but they were also all shepherds. Though the Lord Jesus Christ was initially a carpenter before entering His ministry, He strongly portrayed Himself as "the good shepherd (who) lays down His life for the sheep" (John 10:11; cf. vv. 1-18). Furthermore, these Biblical heroes often stand in direct opposition to those who are more naturally minded. The shepherd Abel is jealously killed by Cain who refused to offer a sacrificial lamb. Cain offered a green offering to God instead (Gen. 4:1-5). Abraham was a nomadic shepherd, uprooted from his homeland, an immigrant in the promised land far ahead of its Hebrew residency (Gen. 15:13-21). Isaac was chosen over the wilderness wanderer Ishmael (Gen. 21). Jacob was chosen by God over Esau the hunter (Gen. 25-27). David killed a lion and a bear to protect his father's sheep before taking on Goliath (1 Sam. 17). On the battle lines, David represented Israel's freedom under the rule of the Mosaic law versus the tyrannical nature worship of the Philistines, perfectly exemplified by the gorilla that was Goliath. The result of the battle would determine which direction the nation would go. Finally, Jesus spoke of protecting His own sheep from the wolves in the parable of the good shepherd (John 10:1-30):

> In the Christian version of the pastoral dream, the shepherd does not merge with nature through his flock nor is his occupation a protest against urban alienation from the natural world, both of which are key themes in the Arcadian (Romantic) version. On the

contrary, he is the defender of the flock against the hostile forces of nature—wolves, lions, bears—and his profession is to lead his lambs out of this sorry world to greener pastures.[221]

Those greener pastures are, of course, ultimately heaven.

Many passages in the Bible, even in the Old Testament, do indeed promise that God will restore nature in the apocalypse during the Messianic kingdom:

> And the wolf will dwell with the lamb, and the leopard will lie down with the young goat, and the calf and the young lion and the fatling together; and a little boy will lead them. Also the cow and the bear will graze, their young will lie down together, and the lion will eat straw like the ox. The nursing child will play by the hole of the cobra, and the weaned child will put his hand on the viper's den. They will not hurt or destroy in all My holy mountain, for the earth will be full of the knowledge of the Lord as the waters cover the sea. (Isa. 11:6-9)

Modern environmentalists treat all such passages as myth, even though they absurdly believe they can bring about harmony with nature through political and environmental regulations and restrictions upon human development. However, Isaiah's prophecy is far more likely of taking place than a political utopian environmental state. Reducing human population, limiting human development and tribalizing people into various sustainable bioregions so that mankind can have a better relationship with the Earth will not lead to utopia. Rather, it will lead to much misery for untold billions of people beyond anything experienced today.

More importantly, in treating Isaiah and books like Genesis as a myth, environmentalists have come up with a mythos all their own based squarely on Biblical data, yet ripped entirely out of context:

> There's an initial Eden, a paradise, a state of grace and unity with nature, there's a fall from grace into a state of pollution as a result of eating from the tree of knowledge, and as a result of our actions there is a judgment day coming for us all. We are all energy sinners,

---

[221] Worster, *Nature's Economy: A History of Ecological Ideas*, p. 26.

doomed to die, unless we seek salvation, which is now called sustainability. Sustainability is salvation in the church of the environment. Just as organic food is its communion, that pesticide-free wafer that the right people with the right beliefs, imbibe.[222]

Modern environmentalists have thus romanticized, ecologized and secularized the garden of Eden for their own green political agenda. The desire to recover some lost harmonious state with the natural world runs deep in Romanticism. However, in great contrast to this utopian view, the God of the Bible promises to provide an ecological wonderland in the Messianic future, where all of the alienation of sin and death in the natural world will be conquered (Hos. 2:16-23).

Even the Apostle Paul in the New Testament harmonizes completely with the Old Testament Messianic promises. Paul categorically teaches that the corruption and decay so prevalent in nature today is not permanent. In Romans 8, Paul anticipates not only the resurrection of the human body, but also a resurrection of nature itself:

> For I consider that the sufferings of this present time are not worthy to be compared with the glory that is to be revealed to us. For the anxious longing of the creation waits eagerly for the revealing of the sons of God. For the creation was subjected to futility, not willingly, but because of Him who subjected it, in hope that the creation itself also will be set free from its slavery to corruption into the freedom of the glory of the children of God. For we know that the whole creation groans and suffers the pains of childbirth together until now. And not only this, but also we ourselves, having the first fruits of the Spirit, even we ourselves groan within ourselves, waiting eagerly for *our* adoption as sons, the redemption of our body. For in hope we have been saved, but hope that is seen is not hope; for who hopes for what he *already* sees? But if we hope for what we do not see, with perseverance we wait eagerly for it. (Rom. 8:18-25)

---

[222] Crichton, Michael, "Environmentalism as a Religion," a speech given to the Commonwealth Club on Sept. 15, 2003, in San Francisco, Calif.

However, this Biblical emphasis of being forced to wait for the new eschaton in the Messianic future is precisely why environmentalists will have nothing to do with such ideas. Another complaint often lodged against the Judeo-Christian worldview by the greens is that it is far too focused on going to heaven. To them, this invariably means that nature will be neglected, if not abandoned. To them, this is precisely the kind of thinking that has brought about such widespread environmental degradation in the first place. This has allegedly given Western man the green light to go ahead and pillage the planet of its natural resources until the Lord returns. Indeed, Solomon himself pointed out, "Where no oxen are, the manger is clean, but much revenue *comes* by the strength of the ox" (Prov. 14:4).

To the modern environmentalist, the Judeo-Christian worldview is an anti-natural religion. Its emphasis upon transcendentalism over holism, freedom of private property over collective ownership, shepherding and farm life over wilderness Romanticism, domesticated animals over wild animals, and sacrificial lambs over animal rights, is all directly counter to modern environmentalism's romantic ideals:

> This … variety of pastoralism illustrates nicely what observers have longed noticed about Christianity (and its Judaic background): of all the major religions of the world, it has been the most insistently anti-natural. In the mind of the average Christian, argues Lynn White, Jr., nature's chief function is to serve man's needs. In extreme cases nature is seen as the source of demonic threats, fleshly appetites, and animal instincts that must be vigorously repressed. No religion, this authority on the medieval period believes, has been more anthropocentric. None has been more rigid in excluding all but man from the realm of divine grace and in denying any moral obligation to the lower species. One thinks, for example, of Pope Pius IX's refusal to allow a society to be organized in Rome to protest the slaughter of bulls for sport and amusement; an animal, he declared, has no soul and thus has no claim on man's moral sympathies. This general animus against nature in Christianity seems to have been most pronounced in Roman Catholicism, and, ironically, its arch-opponent on so many other matters, the Puritan wing of Protestantism. Christian apologists in recent years have sometimes pointed to one outstanding exception: the man who

humbly addressed a canticle to the sun and accepted the birds and beasts as his brethren, St. Francis of Assisi. But such rare exceptions have not disproved the essential truth in the observation that Christianity has maintained a calculated indifference, if not antagonism, toward nature. The good shepherd, the heroic benefactor of man, has almost never been concerned with leading his flock to a broad reverence for life. His pastoral duties have been limited to ensuring the welfare of his human charges, often in the face of a nature that has been corrupt and predatory.[223]

Modern environmentalists strongly criticize this humanistic emphasis of the Bible as an anti-nature agenda. They thus share the same critique of the Puritans their forefather, Henry David Thoreau, espoused.

It was the Puritans in particular who demonstrated the vast difference between Christian ecology and the more *humble* nature-based ethos of the Native Americans. The Puritans looked at America as a vast wilderness which needed to be tamed for the development of mankind in great contrast to the Indians who lived with nature, and who had no inclinations whatsoever to turn their *wilderness* home into a European garden. While the Puritans eventually turned New England into a patchwork of cities, farms and fields for livestock that was better prepared to handle the brutal winters because of some measure of control over the landscape, the Indians had seasons of great want and plenty, reflecting much closer the cycles of nature.[224] In fact, from an ecological point of view, the very name *New England* itself speaks volumes of what the Puritans had done to the northeast coast of America. "As early as 1653, the historian Edward Johnson could count it as one of God's providence that a 'remote, rocky, barren, bushy, wild-woody wilderness' had been transformed into a second England for fertileness. In this vision, the transformation of wilderness betokened the planting of a garden, not the fall from one; any change in the New England environment was divinely ordained and wholly positive. By the end of the 18th century, the metaphors for environmental change had become more humanistic than providential, but were not less enthusiastic about the progress such change represented."[225]

---

223 Worster, *Nature's Economy: A History of Ecological Ideas*, p. 27.
224 Cronon, William. *Changes in the Land: Indians, Colonists, and the Ecology of New England.* New York: Hill and Wang, (1983), pp. 34-53.
225 Ibid., p. 5.

Indeed, the belief in human progress became especially strong in America through the taming of the wilderness. Through progress, the wilderness was transformed into private property and profit for common everyday people never before seen. However, for the Romantics, this progressive transformation amounted to the rape of the land. The Puritans were guilty of a great ecological sin against the natural order. "Town and colony records address the entire range of ecological changes in colonial New England: deforestation, the keeping of livestock, conflicts between Indians and colonists over property boundaries, the extermination of predators such as wolves, and similar matters."[226] Such Puritan attitudes about farming, nature and the economy helped lay the groundwork for the widespread destruction of the North American landscape as the Romantics understood it, beginning with New England, but ever pushing westward. The pioneers eventually conquered both the Indians and the wilderness on their way west.

The Ecological Catastrophe of the Dust Bowl

Many modern greens draw a straight line from Puritan farming practices in New England to the Dust Bowl of the dirty thirties. Thanks to science and the industrial revolution, Puritan farming methods later gave way to the modern mechanistic farm. Worse, nature was increasingly viewed as a capitalistic commodity, if not even loot. Indeed, the wilderness that was the Great Plains of the 1800s was turned into ranches and farms dotted across *the fruited plain*. As far as the modern greens are concerned, this climaxed into the Dust Bowl of the 1930s, one of the worst ecological catastrophes of the 20th century. The Americans broke the Great Plains with the plow, but reaped the Dust Bowl as a consequence. Further, blame for this environmental catastrophe is to be laid at the feet of a humanistic arrogance that ultimately stems from the Judeo-Christian *autonomous* worldview over the natural order:

> The American Plainsmen, it must be made clear, were as intelligent as farmers of any part of the world. They were by no means the first to overrun the limits of their environment. But the reason they did so must be explained not by the vague entity "human nature," but rather by the peculiar culture that shaped their values and actions.

---

[226] Ibid., p. 7.

It is the hand of culture that selects out innate human qualities and thereby gives variety to history. It was culture in the main that created the Dust Bowl. The culture of modern, western man rests on the belief that he is autonomous in nature. He is confident that he is a sovereign creature, independent of the restraints that plague other species—not controlled as they are, but in control. That has not been the view of most people in world history, the American Indians being a proximate case. There has been no more important change in the human condition that the transition from a traditional sense of intimate dependence on the ecological community to the modern feeling of absolute free will and human autonomy. It is not too much to say our entire industrial world was made possible by that change in outlook. We have no way of being absolutely precise about when and where the change took place, but we can be sure that as late as 200 or 300 years ago the dominant fact in man's life everywhere was his need to adapt to more powerful natural forces. Then, out of western culture, came a revolutionary impulse: a desire to throw off the restraining hand of nature and to assert in every way possible the contrived hand of humanity. If similar impulses occurred prior to that point, none of them was so sweeping or so successful. The human species, it was now believed, stood liberated from a bondage to the earth that men of no previous era had been able to escape.[227]

In sum, the Enlightenment and free enterprise capitalism united with Puritanism to create the ecological destruction that was the Dust Bowl. "Explaining the plow that broke the plains requires one to explain the powerful expansionary and autonomous thrust of American society. The historian traces the origins of this extraordinarily determined push into the grassland to Jefferson's outward-moving democracy and to the shaping of American agriculture by an evolving capitalism. There was no sharp break between the two; both were expressions of the same self-minded, individualistic dynamism that ignore complex ecological realities."[228]

The autonomy over nature, everywhere practiced by the Puritans, became the dominating feature of American culture. As far as the Romantics

---

[227] Worster, Donald. *The Dust Bowl: The Southern Plains in the 1930's.* Oxford University Press, 1979, pp. 94-95.
[228] Ibid., pp. 96-97.

were concerned, this way of life had little regard for the ecological complexities of living ecosystems. Worse, this dominating view of nature was greatly exasperated by the industrial revolution. "The attitude of capitalism—industrial and pre-industrial—toward the earth was imperial and commercial; none of its ruling values taught environmental humility, reverence, or restraint."[229] This particular statement perfectly showcases the Romantic rebellion against the Judeo-Christian worldview and its two spoiled unruly twins, the Enlightenment and industrial capitalism. The Puritan sodbuster had finally received the bitter fruit of his unnatural humanistic endeavor to tame the Great Plains. Mother Nature had finally fought back to humble him. Tons and tons of black dust blew vital topsoil away from their farms into other states.

At this juncture, however, conservationist-ecologist Paul Sears, an eyewitness of the Dust Bowl, is very instructive. Understanding full well that much of the environmental destruction of the Great Plains was culturally and economically related, he was nonetheless very cautious about trying to resolve the problem with strict ecological social science as his guide. Paul Sears did not believe the social science of ecology had all the answers:

> "Science," he was ready to grant in 1935, "has the power to illuminate, but not to solve, the deeper problems of mankind." But when he moved beyond science to consider cultural issues, Sears clearly felt himself on shakier ground and stepped along with considerable caution. For him the remedy for the desolated plains lay in a reformed, cleansed private enterprise, not radical initiatives. To be sure, he was compelled to put the entire nation as well as the plains in a most unfavorable light. Peasant farmers in Germany or Flanders, he pointed out, showed a much greater sense of husbandry than did the modern American business farmer or his frontier predecessors... But to Sears, hope for American improvement lay in a more responsible, self-disciplined freedom—in giving the old economic ideas another chance. "Is it not possible that the trouble has not been with private ownership as such, but with the fact that it has not seriously and consistently been the rule in the country?"[230]

---

[229] Ibid., p. 97.

[230] See William Hayward, *How the West Was Lost: The Theft and Usurpation of State's Property Rights.* Springville, Utah: Bonneville Books, 2000. Hayward argues that the U.S. Constitution was contravened in the west as the federal government failed to hand over all

A public domain open to exploiters had led to the worst land abuses on the continent, he believed, momentarily ignoring the dust storms, which had taken place on private property. Although he admitted that in "the more stable socialistic countries of Europe communal ownership had not been all that disastrous, it would mean in the United States the government's taking over the 'white elephants' that private citizens had ruined or not wanted—more 'unwise and indulgent paternalism,' he feared. A better solution, in his view, was simply to teach ecological principles to the new generation and to encourage 'the efficient stewardship of private property' by state tax policies that penalized bad farm practices. That stance was as far as he would go toward a critique and reform of the economy in its relations with nature.[231]

Paul Sear's cautious conservationist values, similar to that of Roosevelt and Pinchot, were in hindsight much wiser than those clamoring for radical solutions. Sears, though an ecologist, still knew the cultural problems of society went far deeper than what the ecological and naturalistic social sciences were prepared to deal with. His skepticism in fusing the social sciences with ecology into a holistic one was fully warranted.

Sears even came to recognize ecology itself was a subversive science[232] in that it was coming to have a "more respected place in the university curriculum."[233] In the mid-1960s, Sears wrote a piece entitled, "Ecology—A Subversive Subject." In the article, he spoke of the fact that ecology had become the *favored* child of the sciences. In part, this is reflective of its *racist* origins in the swirling *scientific* Romanticism of the austere German forests. What could be worse than the Dust Bowl of the 1930s? How about the Holocaust of the 1940s?

Thus, with the black dust storms filling the skies in the southern Great Plains, it is now time to turn to Germany of the 1930s, along with its own

---

land to the western states as it did with regard to the original 13 colonies in violation of the equal footing doctrine. Much of the west is still tied up in federal ownership, very unlike the eastern states. This also led to an unequal and unfair hodgepodge approach to doling out land in the west, and ultimately came to a stop in the name of environmental conservation and preservation.

[231] Worster, *Dust Bowl: The Southern Plains of the 1930's*, pp. 207-08. Worster here quotes Paul Sears in his *Deserts on the March*, pp. 25, 140-56.
[232] See Paul Sears "Ecology – A Subversive Subject," *Biocentric*, 14, July 1964.
[233] Worster, *Dust Bowl: The Southern Plains of the 1930's*, p. 209.

Romantic history. Instead of Thoreau blaming Puritans and capitalists for ecological destruction, German Romantics Arndt and Riehl were blaming the Jews and capitalism for the same destructive tendencies. Instead of non-native Puritans invading the North American landscape, it was the *rootless* Jews who had scarred the German countryside with international cosmopolitan cities. Humboldt, Schopenhauer and Haeckel deepened this anti-Semitic nationalistic path by advocating environmental determinism, natural existentialism and racist biology. These deep thinkers ultimately laid the groundwork for Nazi Germany where a Romantic ecology, natural existentialism and secular science were blended together to create a volatile holistic fascism culminating in the Holocaust of the 1940s. The fusion of nationalistic Romanticism with naturalistic science created an explosive concoction that made the Dust Bowl of the dirty thirties look like children playing in the sandbox.

Then God said, "Let Us make man in Our image, according to Our likeness; and let them rule over the fish of the sea and over the birds of the sky and over the cattle and over all the earth, and over every creeping thing that creeps on the earth." ²⁷ And God created man in His own image, in the image of God He created him; male and female He created them. ²⁸ And God blessed them; and God said to them, "Be fruitful and multiply, and fill the earth, and subdue it; and rule over the fish of the sea and over the birds of the sky, and over every living thing that moves on the earth." ²⁹ Then God said, "Behold, I have given you every plant yielding seed that is on the surface of all the earth, and every tree which has fruit yielding seed; it shall be food for you; ³⁰ and to every beast of the earth and to every bird of the sky and to every thing that moves on the earth which has life, I have given every green plant for food"; and it was so. ³¹ And God saw all that He had made, and behold, it was very good. And there was evening and there was morning, the sixth day.

Genesis 1:26-31

CHAPTER THREE:

GERMAN ECO-FASCISM AS HISTORY—NOT METAPHOR

While the growth of Romanticism was slow to develop in North America and England, and was even kept in check by its strong Protestant values, it was much more robust in Germany. In Germany, Romanticism "became a conservative protest against modernity which was linked to a romantic celebration of wildness."[234] Johann Wolfgang von Goethe (1749-1832), often considered one of the very pioneers of Romanticism, is perhaps the greatest titan of German literature. He was especially interested in nature, biology and art. He also considered himself to be a natural scientist. In his youth, he was very involved in a Romantic group called *Sturm und Drang* or "Storm and Stress." This group radically opposed the Enlightenment's emphasis upon logic, reason and objectivity. In place of these values, *Sturm und Drang* advocated subjective experience, emotions, spirituality and the natural world.

As he grew older, Goethe moved away from his youthful leanings, but his interest in Romanticism did not fade away, nor did his opposition to Christianity diminish. Goethe characterized the spirit of Christianity as evil and damningly unnatural.[235] In fact, Goethe's later fascination with the classics and the classical world can easily be understood as a deepening of his Romanticism. At one point in his career, after complaining about "Jewish nonsense" derived from the Old Testament, Goethe opined, "Had Homer remained our Bible, how different a form would mankind have achieved!"[236] Goethe's great emphasis throughout much of his writings was upon holism and the oneness of the natural world and the reconciliation of opposites. In the poem entitled *"Epirrhenia"* Goethe wrote, "Separateness is illusion, one

---

[234] Sax, p. 40.

[235] Stern, p. 39.

[236] Lowith, Karl. *From Hegel to Nietzsche: The Revolution in 19th Century Thought.* New York: Columbia University Press, 1964, p. 22.

and many are the same." Goethe's natural holism, in great contrast to the dualistic nature of the Judeo-Christian worldview, would anchor German Romanticism for decades to come.

Alexander Humboldt & the Birth of Volkisch Environmentalism

Alexander von Humboldt (1769-1859) was an explorer naturalist. He was one of the first German Romantics to emphasize a thoroughgoing scientific-environmental point of view. Like Goethe before him, who had "erased the boundary between man and nature altogether,"[237] Humboldt also "stressed the overriding unity and harmony of Nature."[238] For Humboldt, culture, humanity, science and nature were knitted tightly together. "No doubt much of the impetus for this resolution came from Humboldt's early acquaintance with Johann von Goethe. For a while they had attended classes together at the university of Jena, and Alexander and his brother Wilhelm had spent many hours talking with Goethe about nature and science. They all had shared a dedication to analytical research, providing such research kept in sight larger, more organic research."[239] The analytical sciences of the Enlightenment, therefore, were to be ruled by a romanticized holism presumably taken from nature herself.

For Humboldt, the scientific study of nature was a quest for religious piety.[240] Humboldt therefore shared in the Romantic rebellion against Christianity, but he was less antagonistic against the Enlightenment. Although he himself recognized some of the contradictions between analytical science and Romantic spirituality, "he never surrendered his faith in the value of the scientific approach to nature, (but) he did admit that there were 'mooted and perhaps unsolvable problems that defy such analysis, and that beyond the realm of positive knowledge lies the 'harmonious unity' of nature, accessible only to the vivid and deep emotions.'"[241]

Humboldt's marriage between Romanticism and the Enlightenment was quietly used against Christianity. Humboldt's basic approach to the environment was based on enlightened naturalistic science without reference to

---

237   Dominick, Raymond. *The Environmental Movement in Germany: Prophets and Pioneers, 1871-1971.* Indiana University Press, 1992, p. 36.
238   Ibid.
239   Worster, *Nature's Economy: A History of Ecological Ideas*, p. 133.
240   Ibid., p. 137.
241   Ibid., p. 136.

114

God on the one hand, and yet a belief in a harmonious, mystic philosophy of nature on the other hand. Humboldt's style has since become the hallmark of environmental thought for more than 200 years. Romantics are fond of using the enlightened naturalistic sciences against Christianity, only to delve into a form of nature mysticism all their own. This process became especially conspicuous in Germany as environmental ideas evolved into a full-scale assault upon the Judeo-Christian worldview.

Humboldt's claim to fame with regard to early environmental thought were his insights into geography and climate, and how they interacted with each other to create distinguished climatic ecosystems. "The central concept of his *Geography of Plants* was that the plants of the world must not only be considered in their taxonomic relations, but also grouped in relation to the geographic conditions in which they live."[242] Humboldt was one of the first explorer scientists who developed an explanation as to why certain plants live in certain habitats and not others. "One of Humboldt's major contributions was the idea of tracing isothermal lines across the earth, which made graphic the distribution of world climate; these in turn suggested laws about what kinds of plants one might expect to find in any region."[243] Humboldt laid the foundation for understanding the differing ecological relationships between localized climate conditions and any given indigenous environment:

> Humboldt taught ... to look at nature comparatively: to see each region as a unique ecological assemblage dependent on local or regional conditions, and to study these by placing them side by side—hence an ecology of deserts, of steppes, of tropical jungles, of arctic wastes. In this way he managed to expand the study of ecology from the abstract, worldwide focus of his predecessors to the concrete diversity of the many natural economic orders. A further and highly significant result was to de-emphasize the role of a Creator who controlled from his heavenly perch the earth and its single chain or economy of being. Attention was directed instead to the importance of natural forces such as climate in the creation of peculiar, limited, organic systems.[244]

---

[242] Ibid., p. 134
[243] Ibid.
[244] Ibid., p. 135.

Thus, with a strong, wild, and musky smell of unbelief that an infinite personal God was somehow unable to create or superintend a diverse living natural world that could also be categorized into unique local environments, Humboldt stressed that the environment itself was a basis for shaping not only the character of the landscape, but also man himself. This process was also considered to be a slow, natural, and evolutionary one, preceding Darwin by almost 50 years.[245] Reference to God was no longer necessary, and with this, man's uniqueness and transcendence over nature was also de-emphasized. Thanks to Humboldt's Romanticism, the environment was now king, not God or man. "I shall collect plants and fossils, and with the best of instruments make astronomic observations. Yet this is not the main purpose of my journey. I shall endeavor to find out how nature's forces act upon one another, and in what manner the geographic environment exerts its influence on animals and plants. In short, I must find out about the harmony of nature."[246]

With such ideas about the environment, local ecosystems, geography and climate, Humboldt also laid the groundwork for fusing holism with nationalism, along with a desire for keeping unique local environments and its indigenous occupants free from non-natives and invasive species. This preoccupation with keeping everything local and indigenous would later become a Nazi infatuation. From this time forward, pride in nature and pride in nation began to go hand in hand in Germany. In 1807, in his *Views of Nature*, Humboldt argued that national character is largely derived from environmental geographical influences:

> For example, a cool and foggy climate might produce a melancholy nation while a sunny and warm climate could produce a cheerful folk. In the same vein, he asserted that seminal cultural works of a nation, such as the epic poems of the Greeks or the folk songs of the Bavarians, reflected the "forms of the plants and animals and of the mountain valleys" wherein the poets and musicians dwelled. In this early 19th century interpretation, Nature shaped humankind in two ways: by determining acquired characteristics of physique and personality that, according to the scientific wisdom of that day, could then be transmitted biologically from one generation to the

---

[245]   Darwin read Humboldt's work with great enthusiasm.
[246]   Humboldt quoted by Worster, *Nature's Economy: A History of Ecological Ideas*, p. 133.

next and by molding the early art, music, literature, and folkways of a people, which in turn shaped the outlook and behavior of future generations. The Germans called the community that resulted from these natural influences *das Volk*, a term for the nation laden with images of mystical and organic unity.[247]

Here is seen the intellectual roots of the German *volk* (people's blood community) Romantically and holistically embedded into their own landscape, exemplified best by the folk peasants, the true indigenous natives of Germany.

While Humboldt was not a racist in the modern sense, broadly speaking, his Romantic philosophy of man and nature became the foundation stone for the infamous *blut und boden* (blood and soil) and *lebensraum* (living space) doctrines, which the Nazis used for their own sinister purposes by intensifying such notions to their maximum limit. Thus, long before Karl Marx emphasized that man is a by-product of economic materialistic realities, German Romantics stressed that the environment shapes the national character of the *volk*. Attitudes about nature and race were one of the important distinctions between National Socialism and Soviet Communism in World War II. While both emphasized socialism, they were socialistic on different grounds.

Not surprisingly, Humboldt was a cultural critic of how the natural world was being treated in his own day. Humboldt long ago noted, "Shortsighted plundering had robbed present and future generations of the manifold material and spiritual benefits that derive from the woodlands."[248] In Humboldt's mind, since his spirituality was attached to the forest, the loss of that forest also meant a loss of spirituality. Humboldt therefore used his Romantic spirituality as a way of judging and critiquing society's economic practices according to a nature-based ethos that was contrary to the Judeo-Christian worldview:

> During his far flung travels, von Humboldt gathered illustrations of complex webs that transmitted the human impact throughout the environment. One example was his depiction of the causes for the dried bed of an enormous lake in Latin America. In that

---

[247] Dominick, p. 22.
[248] Ibid., p. 18.

case, he noted how deforestation along the tributaries to the lake had increased erosion, thereby silting up the beds of local streams and eventually of the lake itself. In addition, he wrote, deforestation had lowered the regional water table and depleted the local springs, thus depriving the suffering lake of essential replenishment.[249]

Along similar lines, Humboldt also discussed how the forests of the Mediterranean had been devastated throughout the centuries by constant human interference. This was the beginning of the human invasion diatribe where man is pictured as an alien in the natural world interfering with its harmonious natural processes. Thus Humboldt used environmental history as a Romantic critique of society a whole generation before Thoreau.

Arndt Deepens Volkisch Environmentalism with Nationalism

Ernst Moritz Arndt (1769-1860), a poet and author, took German Romanticism further down the nationalistic nature road by advocating environmental preservation for the sake of the nation. He not only vigorously complained about the growing menace of modern industrialization that was harming the German *volk*, but far worse, added anti-Semitism into the mix as well. In spite of this early sordid mixture, Arndt is still considered to be one of the earliest examples of ecological thinking in the modern sense.[250]

Arndt was a contemporary of Humboldt, but was also a staunch German nationalist in the face of the French Napoleonic wars in the early 1800s. "As early as 1814, Arndt had proposed a return to the celebration of the summer solstice as a way to return politically fragmented Germans to their cultural and religious roots."[251] Arndt personally contrasted German nationalism with the French Enlightenment as "the collective identification with the natural world was revived and strengthened when Napoleon occupied Germany in the name of civilization."[252] German Romantics like Arndt associated the Enlightenment with the French Revolution along with its

---

[249]   Ibid., p. 36.

[250]   Staudenmaier, Peter and Biehl, Janet, *Ecofascism Revisited*. Porsgrunn, Norway: New Compass Press, 2011, pp. 15-16.

[251]   Noll, Richard. *The Aryan Christ: The Secret Life of Carl Jung*. New York: Random House, 1997, p. 115-16.

[252]   Sax, p. 38.

overemphasis upon rationality and the humanistic manipulation of nature. Arndt even wrote a famous poem entitled "The German Fatherland." Arndt starkly contrasted the progressive civilization of the French Enlightenment with the Romantic fatherland of Germany. Arndt's nationalistic views were so strong that they were even used against the French in both world wars in the 20th century. Arndt's nationalism was completely embedded into the German landscape. Industrial capitalism based on Enlightenment principles of liberty and rationality was assumed to be an invasive destructive force upon Germany's fatherland.

Although Arndt trained for the Lutheran ministry, he rejected this path for himself at the age of 28 for Romanticism. He later wrote a book in 1803 highly critical of the practice of serfdom, which kept the village farmers in constant poverty on the German countryside. "While best known for his fanatical nationalism, Arndt was also dedicated to the cause of the peasantry, which led him to a concern for the welfare of the land itself."[253] In 1815, Arndt wrote an essay entitled "A Word about the Care and Preservation of the Forests and the Peasants in the Consciousness of a Higher, i.e., More Humane Law." Arndt believed the relationship between man and nature was mutually interdependent, and for that reason, nature must be protected in order to protect both the German forests and its peasants. Arndt argued: "The axe that is laid on the tree frequently becomes an axe that is laid on the entire nation."[254]

Arndt complained bitterly about the loss of German forestlands. He contended that nature protection was vital to keep the German nation a healthy and beautiful one. He railed "against shortsighted exploitation of woodlands and soil, condemning deforestation and its economic causes."[255] More than 100 years later, the Nazis would pick up on such nationalistic ecological seeds planted by Arndt precisely because his brand of early environmentalism "was inextricably bound up with virulently xenophobic nationalism. His eloquent and prescient appeals for ecological sensitivity were couched always in terms of well being of the German soil and the German people, and his repeated lunatic polemics against miscegenation, demands for Teutonic racial purity, and epithets against the French, Slavs,

[253] Staudenmaier & Biehl, p. 15.
[254] Arndt, Ernst Moritz, "A Word about the Care and Preservation of the Forests and the Peasants in the Consciousness of a Higher, i.e., More Humane Law," quoted by Dominick, p. 22.
[255] Staudenmaier & Biehl, p. 16.

and Jews marked every aspect of his thought. At the very outset of the 19th century the deadly connection between love of land and militant racist nationalism was firmly set in place."[256]

For Arndt, protecting nature was a nationalistic task.[257] In Arndt's mind, nationalism and nature were seen tightly woven together. His stress on the *fatherland* also meant that German nature protection was originally cast in a masculine light rather than in a more modern feminized *Mother Nature* approach. This masculine emphasis upon nature protection in Germany would continue up until the fallout of World War II. Under the banner of National Socialism, chauvinism, the protection of the fatherland and environmental policies would work hand in hand. The masculinity and militancy of the Nazi regime thus does not call into question its overall concern for the environment. The wedding between masculinity and nature protection is the heritage of Arndt.

Riehl Deepens Volkisch Environmentalism with Socialism

Wilhelm Heinrich Riehl (1823-1897), a student of Arndt, added a more socialist element to this green nationalistic mix: "German public opinion regards the forest as the one great possession that has not yet been completely parceled out. In contrast to farmlands, pasturelands, and garden plots, everyone is deemed to have a certain claim on the forest."[258] Riehl thus postulated a public or socialistic ownership of the forest: "That is why forests are primarily a matter of public finance, and only secondarily of private enterprise. It should be distributed across the countryside as evenly as possible, since its riches resist the mobility of commerce."[259] As far as Riehl was concerned, "Forests have not only an economic but also a socio-political value."[260]

Riehl was Germany's sociologist of *Field and Forest*. Riehl invented a sociology of habitat for Germany, all described in poetic language by writing three books between 1851 and 1855 with the collective title *The*

---

[256]   Ibid.

[257]   Olsen, p. 61.

[258]   Riehl, Wilhelm Heinrich. *Natural History of the German People*, translated by David Diephouse. Lewiston/Queenstown/Lampeter: The Edwin Mellen Press, 1990, p. 48.

[259]   Ibid., p. 51.

[260]   Ibid., p. 48.

Natural History of Germany.[261] Riehl extolled the centrality of the countryside landscape and forests in the development of the German character. "We must retain the forest not only to keep our stoves from going cold in the wintertime but also keep the pulse of our national life beating warmly and happily. We need it to keep Germany German."[262] Riehl warned, "Lay the axe to the forest and you demolish civil society as historically constituted. By wiping out the contrast between field and forest you eliminate a vital component of the German national character."[263]

In other words, according to Riehl, a German was not a German without the forest. Without the forest and mountains, a German actually loses his true identity. "If you wish to see a society reduced to a bland parlor culture, where everything is identical in color and finish, then uproot the forests, level away the mountains, cordon off the sea."[264] This was how seriously Germans like Riehl took their forestlands. "The forests constitute the heartland of folk culture. A village without its forest is like a town without historic buildings or monuments, without art, theater or music—in short, without any form of pleasurable aesthetic stimulus."[265]

Riehl's "green streak went significantly deeper than Arndt's: presaging certain tendencies in recent environmental activism, his 1853 essay 'Field and Forest' ended with a call to fight for 'the rights of the wilderness'"[266] Riehl's ecological holism lessened the distinction between humanity and nature, and in so doing, gave rights to the wilderness itself. He demanded parity between domesticated farmlands and wild forestlands. Riehl commented, "A social theorist schooled in the study of folklore must persevere in fighting for rights of the wilderness as well."[267] Riehl stressed environmental activism as a political cause worthy enough to fight for. He thus stood up for the rights of the wilderness by strongly denouncing industrialization, urbanization and international cosmopolitanism. Indeed, for Romantic spiritual reasons, Riehl strongly believed, "Man does not live by bread alone. Even if we no longer needed the timber we would still need the forest. Once we no longer need dry wood to warm up the outer man, we

---

261 Schama, *Landscape and Memory*. New York: Vintage Books, 1995, pp. 112-114.
262 Riehl, p. 49.
263 Ibid.
264 Ibid.
265 Ibid.
266 Staudenmaeier & Biehl, p. 16.
267 Riehl, p. 54.

will have that much greater need for the green and living wood—to warm the inner man."[268]

Riehl complained the destruction of the German landscape could no longer be ignored, "Our fast paced century seems to allow only about 15 years between years between one revolution and the next, the typical tree requires a much longer period of time to reach maturity."[269] Riehl exhibited an early concern for environmental sustainability against the political backdrop of many social revolutions that plagued Germany in the first half of the 19th century. Nature could not keep up with all the societal chaos Germany was going through. "So short an interval, at any rate, will not be enough for nature to repair the immeasurable losses caused by distress sales, plunder, and wanton destruction of the year 1848." For Riehl, development and so-called *progress* had reached its limit. "If you want to convert society into a ... washed out drawing room society, root out the forest, level the mountains, and bottle up the lakes!"[270] Riehl is perhaps the true father of the ecological cult of sustainable development. He was complaining about industrial development outstripping natural resources long before it became popular in modern environmental circles.

In addition, Riehl's desire to reel in the *progress* of civilization was not only to preserve the German countryside, but also its local indigenous peasants as well. Riehl hated tourists, but loved wetlands.[271] Ponds and small lakes were apparently more valued than people. Although Riehl held great respect for the peasant farmer, the true authentic national character of Germany was represented best by the peasant woodsmen. They were the true *volk* of the nation. "The inhabitants of German forest villages almost invariably manifest a distinctive robustness and mental alertness, much more so than villages in the open countryside."[272] In fact, Riehl believed the German forest villages represented a pristine cultural purity worthy to preserve for the sake of national character. "It is in the forest villages—of which our fatherland still has a good many, as anyone knows who has wandered the German hills—that our society finds the remnants of a

---

[268] Ibid., p. 49.

[269] Ibid., p. 48.

[270] Riehl, *Die Naturgeschichte des deustchen Volkes*, quoted by Dominick, p. 23.

[271] Blackbourn, David, *The Conquest of Nature: Water, Landscape and the Making of Modern Germany*. New York/London: W.W. Norton and Company, 2006, p. 185.

[272] Riehl, p. 49.

primeval civilization, preserved not just in its darker aspects but also in its natural splendor."[273]

Such primeval robust villages stood in great contrast to those cultural influences which were polluting both the landscape and its people, i.e., Jewish capitalism and its twin sister, international cosmopolitanism. Riehl viewed Jews as anti-natural and Germans as natural. He was thus "an implacable opponent of the rise of industrialization and urbanism: his overtly anti-Semitic glorification of the rural peasant values and undifferentiated condemnation of modernity established him as the 'founder of agrarian Romanticism and anti-urbanism.'"[274] Indeed, it was the cosmopolitan nature of the cities, fostered by the Jewish people in particular, that raised the ire of Riehl. "If, in this scheme, the rootless Jew was a purveyor of this corrupted, citified society, the forester was his antithesis—the embodiment of ethnic authenticity, rooted like his trees in the ancient earth of the Fatherland."[275] The landless and rootless Jews were the very ones who created a polluted citified landscape wrapped around the marketplace, where material gain supplanted the collective Romantic spirit. "Where large numbers of Jews reside, the population as a whole is almost always politically and economically fragmented. The Jewish huckster finds that his paltry capital circulates much more freely among the urbanized and small town *burghers* of central Germany than among the authentic peasants of the mountains or the plains."[276]

Riehl also reveled in Germany's backwardness in the hinterlands, still largely and rigidly controlled by ancient feudal laws. "Nowhere can the fragments of a feudal order be seen more clearly than in our forest regulations. It is the forest alone that enables rural folk to supplement their resources without encumbrance—in the true medieval sense—from the mad rush of commerce and competition."[277] Riehl had apparently forgotten that it was Martin Luther who railed against the nobility for not allowing its citizenry to cut wood so as to keep warm in the winter. In medieval times, it was the king and nobility who owned the forests, not the people.   Riehl's environmentalism was therefore *conservative* to the extreme in that he valued the feudal despotic order over modern life precisely because he believed

---

[273]   Ibid.
[274]   Staudenmaier & Biehl, pp. 16-17.
[275]   Schama, p. 114.
[276]   Riehl, p. 84.
[277]   Ibid., p. 48.

it did a better job preserving the natural world. It was those *conservative* feudal laws that had preserved so much wilderness in Germany, even as late as the mid-1800s. Riehl rejoiced in the size of wilderness still left and believed that "since Germany's interior is so extensive, it requires much more forest than does England."[278] His spiritual "craving was for some idealized, immutable, rural community that had not been prostituted by industrial modernity."[279]

Not surprisingly, Riehl also followed in the footsteps of his teacher Arndt with regard to rejecting church ministry as his life calling at a young age. Like Arndt, Riehl rejected the Christian ministry for Romanticism, this time wedded with the collectivist ideas of the green socialistic sciences:

> What he shared with the sociologists of the left was a bitter hostility to industrial capitalism and metropolitan life, seeing both as corrosive of the moral solidarity he thought inherent in traditional work and community. Riehl was, then, the first to elaborate what a later and much better known sociologist, Karl Tonnies, would define as the opposition between *Gemeinschaft* (on organically bonded community) and *Gesselschaft* (an aggregate of individuals connected only by material interests).[280]

Thus, socialism, nationalism, nature protection and anti-Semitism all were bonded together in the Romantic life of Heinrich Riehl. Riehl's influence upon early German environmentalism was truly profound. He placed Romantic *volkisch* ideas and practices onto a solid political platform that would last up until the Nazi period. "Riehl's complaint that Jews were disproportionately represented in the commercial, urban, and cosmopolitan *Geselleschaft* that he believed was eating away at the true Germany was adopted as prophetic by the founding fathers of Nazi ideology."[281]

---

[278] Ibid.
[279] Schama, p. 117.
[280] Ibid., p. 113.
[281] Ibid., p. 118.

Such pro-nature anti-Semitic views were not all that unusual in Germany during the 1800s, especially among the academics. Even the great German thinker Arthur Schopenhauer (1788-1860), whom Hitler called a genius,[282] held very similar green anti-Semitic views. Not only did Schopenhauer have a great love for nature, but he was also Adolf Hitler's favorite philosopher,[283] "From him I learned a great deal."[284] Indeed, Hitler's spiritual father, Dietrich Eckart (1868-1923), also dearly loved Schopenhauer.[285] Rudolf Hess too was an avid reader of the German philosopher.[286] In Alfred Rosenberg's (1893-1946) *The Myth of the Twentieth Century*, the Nazi ideologue refers to Schopenhauer many times.

The famous opera composer Richard Wagner (1813-1883) was a contemporary disciple of Schopenhauer. What is not well known is Wagner's opera music would later provide the musical background for National Socialism. Wagner was the most highly esteemed musician of the Nazi era. In fact, Hitler and the Wagner family were on very friendly terms. "Beginning in 1923, Hitler visited the Wagner family at Bayreuth and, as *Fuhrer* spent a fortnight at the Wagner festival."[287] Hitler went so far to say that National Socialism could not be understood without Richard Wagner.[288] As such, the Schopenhauer-Hitler connection was a very strong one even though the philosopher himself would have undoubtedly been traumatized by what later happened under National Socialism.

Schopenhauer vehemently spoke of animal rights well before it became fashionable. "It might truly be said that men are the devils of this earth and

---

[282] *Hitler's Table Talk*, midday of March 7, 1942, p. 270.

[283] Kubizek, August. *The Young Hitler I Knew*, p. 136.

[284] *Hitler's Table Talk*, evening of May 16, 1944, p. 547.

[285] Tyson, Joseph Howard. *Hitler's Mentor: Dietrich Eckart, His Life, Times & Milieu*. New York: iUniverse, Inc., 2008, p. 4.

[286] Manvell, Roger and Fraenkel, Heinrich, *Hess: A Biography*. New York: Drake Publishers Inc., 1973, p. 38.

[287] Mitchell, *Hitler's Mountain: The Fuhrer, Obersalzberg and the American Occupation of Berchtesgaden*. Jefferson, North Carolina and London: McFarland and Company Inc. Publishers, 2007, p. 36.

[288] MacLean, French, *2000 Quotes from Hitler's 1,000 Year Reich*. Atglen, Pennsylvania: Schiffer Military History, 2007, p. 154.

animals the tortured souls."[289] Most disconcerting about his animal rights discussion, he loaded it with anti-Semitism. Schopenhauer charged that the source of the barbaric treatment of animals in Europe and in the West was to be found in Judaism:[290]

> The same emotional intensity shows through Schopenhauer's preaching of animal rights to humane treatment. The unity of all creation, the essential bond between man and animal, is one of the cornerstones of Schopenhauer's ethical philosophy. The separation of the human and animal worlds is, for him, the greatest defect of modern European Christianity, something which makes it inferior to Brahminism and Buddhism, which recognize the kinship that makes it possible for the transmigration of souls to take place between animals and humans. And again, as with human intolerance and cruelty, the abuse of animals is ultimately and quintessentially a Jewish phenomenon, which has been passed on to what Schopenhauer calls Jewish Christianity.[291]

Schopenhauer asserted that the natives of the Asiatic uplands would have been horrified about how cruelly the Europeans treated animals.[292] Although Schopenhauer valued Christianity above Judaism, he complained that it too had the same defect. "The morality of Christianity has no consideration for animals."[293] Schopenhauer also complained that Christianity "has most unnaturally separated man from the animal world, to which in essence he nevertheless belongs. It now tries to accept man entirely by himself and regards animals positively as things."[294]

Schopenhauer was one of the first philosophical existentialists in the modern sense. As such, Schopenhauer downplayed the intellect as something truly distinctive in separating man from the animal world. He also rejected the Enlightenment's conception of nature that emphasized it as a Divinely

---

289 Schopenhauer, Arthur. *Parerga and Paralipomena: On Religion*, vol. 2, translated from German. Oxford: Clarendon Press, 1974, p. 371.

290 Schopenhauer, Arthur. *On the Basis of Morality*. Indianapolis/Cambridge: Hackett Publishing Company, translated by E.F.J. Payne, 1995, p. 175.

291 Rose, *Wagner: Race and Revolution*. New Haven & London: Yale University Press, 1992, pp. 93-94.

292 Schopenhauer, *On the Basis of Morality*, p. 177.

293 Ibid., p. 178.

294 Schopenhauer, *Parerga and Paralipomena: On Religion*, p. 370.

created well-ordered machine. "The world is not a piece of machinery and animals are not articles manufactured for our use."[295] Schopenhauer was appalled that John the Baptist wore animal skins.[296] The lack of compassion toward animals was thus used by Schopenhauer to judge both Judaism and Christianity. "Look at the revolting and outrageous wickedness with which our Christian mob treat animals, laughing as they kill them without aim or object, maiming and torturing them, and even working the very marrow out of the bones of their old horses who are their direct bread winners, until they sink and succumb under the lashes."[297]

Schopenhauer's anti-Semitic environmental ethics[298] specifically targeted the domineering attitude towards nature and animals found in the Bible. "The fault lies with the Jewish view that regards the animal as something manufactured for man's use."[299] Schopenhauer even knew precisely which primary text was to blame. "These are the effects of the first chapter of Genesis and generally of the whole Jewish way of looking at nature."[300] Schopenhauer went so far to say that Jewish animal cruelty demanded some form of European retribution. "We owe to the animal not mercy but justice, and the debt often remains unpaid in Europe, the continent that is permeated with *Foeter Judaicus*."[301] In Latin, *Foeter Judaicus* means "Jewish odor." For Schopenhauer the "odor of the Jews" was their cruelty to animals:[302]

> Now the fundamental defect just mentioned is a consequence of creation out of nothing, according to which the Creator (Genesis 1 and 9) hands over to man all the animals, just as if they were mere things and without any recommendations to their being properly treated, such as even the seller of a dog often adds when parting with animal he has reared. The Creator hands them over so that

---

[295] Ibid., p. 375.

[296] Schopenhauer, *On the Basis of Morality*, p. 178.

[297] Schopenhauer, *Parerga and Paralipomena: On Religion*, p. 371.

[298] Varner, G.E., "The Schopenhauerian Challenge in Environmental Ethics," *Environmental Ethics* 7 (3), 1985, pp. 209-229. George Varner introduced this article by pointing out that Schopenhauer anticipated Lynn White Jr.'s famous thesis by some 100 years that the West's Christian heritage is responsible for the regarding of animals as mere things.

[299] Schopenhauer, *Parerga and Paralipomena: On Religion*, pp. 370-71.

[300] Ibid, p. 373.

[301] Ibid., p. 372.

[302] Paul Lawrence Rose goes on to say, "Four times in a few pages Schopenhauer obsessively refers to the Tacitean *Foeter Judaicus*, which he redefines in terms of his own ethics: the archetypal meaning of the 'Jewish odor' is for him cruelty to animals," p. 94.

man may rule over them and thus may do what he likes with them; whereupon in the second chapter he appoints man as the first professor of zoology by commissioning him to give the animals the names they are to bear in the future. Again this is merely a symbol of their entire dependence on him, that is, of their being without any rights. Holy Ganga! Mother of our race! Such stories have on me the same effect as do Jew's pitch and *foeter Judaicus!*[303]

More ominous still was Schopenhauer's solution to the alleged problem. In order to save nature and the animals, the Jewish view of nature must be banished from the European continent. The stench of animal cruelty was too nauseas to allow to continue. "It is obviously high time in Europe that Jewish views on nature were brought to an end."[304] Shockingly, Schopenhauer pronounced a prophecy which was virtually fulfilled by the Nazis almost a century later. "The unconscionable treatment of the animal world must, on account of its immorality, be expelled from Europe!"[305] Such was the conclusion of one of Germany's most important geniuses of the 1800s, the epitome of green ethics. That Richard Wagner also adopted Schopenhauer's animal rights crusade against Judaism all but guaranteed the Nazis would later follow suit. In 1933, Adolf Hitler signed an anti-Semitic animal rights law. This was most certainly done in honor of Arthur Schopenhauer and Richard Wagner.

The Missing Link of Ernst Haeckel's Social Darwinian Biological Ecology

In the latter half of the 19th century, German zoologist Ernst Haeckel provided the missing biological link between nationalism, socialism, nature protection, race and ecology, which later paved the way for the rise of National Socialism. Haeckel did this by mixing up Charles Darwin's evolutionary theory with German racism together with a secularized form of nature worship. Haeckel even coined the term *ecology* in 1866.[306] He also believed that Germans were on top of the evolutionary chain in terms of cultural progress. As such, he was also the father of German Social Darwinism.

---

[303] Schopenhauer, *Parerga and Paralipomena: On Religion*, p. 371.
[304] Ibid., p. 375.
[305] Ibid., p. 377.
[306] Ernst Haeckel coined the term *ecology* in 1866 in his *Generelle Morphologie*.

Incredibly, Haeckel believed his racialist brand of Social Darwinism was strictly based on sound biological science. In this way, German racism became bound up with science, evolutionary theory and nature worship—all three of which were absorbed by the Nazis in one form or another. According to British scholar Simon Schama, it was the Roman historian Tacitus who noted that Germany's isolation made the Germans the least mixed of all Europeans. This "would, of course, become the lethal obsession of the Nazi tyranny. *Germanentum*—the idea of a biologically pure and inviolate race as 'natural' to its terrain as indigenous species of trees and flowers—featured in much of the archaeological and pre-historical literature both before and after the First World War. The catastrophe of defeat in 1918 seemed only to make the hunger for tribal reassertion more desperate."[307]

Alfred Rosenberg, Professor Ernst Lehman, Anthropologist Hans Gunther and many other leading Nazi academics glorified Haeckel as being one of the primary forerunners of National Socialism.[308] Many of the racial ecological ideals of Haeckel and his Social Darwinist followers became part and parcel of what National Socialism later espoused:

> German Social Darwinists rejected the optimistic laissez-faire free-market liberalism so popular in England and America, and stressed instead the need for state intervention to stop what they saw as the beginnings of the supposed "degeneration" of the human species. The degeneration of the race feared by German Social Darwinists was said to have come about for two reasons: first, because medical care for the "weak" had begun to destroy the *natural* struggle for existence; and second, because the poor and misfits of the world were beginning to multiply faster than the talented and fit. The German eugenics, or racial hygiene, movement emerged in the late nineteenth century in response to those fears.[309]

However, while this certainly gives the strong impression that Haeckel was a proto Nazi, many of his followers are quick to point out his books were

---

[307] Schama, p. 118.
[308] Gasman, Daniel. *The Scientific Origins of National Socialism*. New York: Transaction Publishers, 2004 (1971), pp. 170-73.
[309] Proctor, Robert, *Racial Hygiene: Medicine Under the Nazis*, Harvard University Press, 1988, pp. 14-15.

officially banned by the Nazi Party. Haeckel considered himself a pacifist[310] and a social progressive republican, things which the Nazis soundly rejected. Hitler called Haeckel's biographer, Wilhelm Boelsche, an "urban absurdity."[311] Being too urban, Boelsche was apparently not a wild enough Social Darwinist for Hitler's taste. He belonged too much to the corrupt socialist/Marxist ways of the cities.

Nonetheless, Haeckel's broader overall views on Darwinian racial struggle, nature and ecology would still be absorbed and trumpeted by proto Nazis and Nazis alike, particularly members of the SS. "Adolf Hitler came of age during the decade and a half following the publication in 1899 of Ernst Haeckel's *Riddle of the Universe*, a runaway best seller that over the next two or three decades sold more internationally than the Bible, and profoundly shaped the consciousness of the modern world. Haeckel's book imparted a rigid Social Darwinist message purportedly derived from science: politics is applied biology, the Jews were an inferior race compared with Aryans, Christianity was a religion of weakness, and that eugenic action was necessary to protect the racial composition of society."[312] While many scholars have tried to suggest that Hitler never read Haeckel, this is highly unlikely. Both of Hitler's heroes, Richard Wagner and Dietrich Eckart, read Haeckel with great enthusiasm.[313] Moreover, Nazi press chief Otto Dietrich said that Hitler's conception of natural selection and survival the fittest came from both Darwin and Haeckel.[314]

In his Social Darwinism, Haeckel accentuated racial eugenics. "Haeckel proposed a ruthless attack on social problems. He advocated capital punishment for repeat offenders, and mass mercy killings as a solution to the health care crisis. His recommendations were not lost on Hitler, who signed his Euthanasia Decree in September, 1939."[315] Haeckel took the Darwinian evolutionary theory about the origin of the species, and mutated it into a Romantic pseudo-scientific religious quest to recover and preserve that origin through the evolution of race. In other words, the Darwinian the-

---

310   Haeckel, however, enthusiastically embraced the German cause in World War I. His pacifism was also far more concerned over the fact that too much good German blood would be wasted on the battlefield while the weak ones would propagate further racial corruption on the home front. See Weikart, *From Darwin to Hitler*, pp. 175-76.

311   Bramwell, *Ecology in the 20ʰ Century: A History*, p. 50.

312   Gasman, Daniel, "From Haeckel to Hitler: The Anatomy of a Controversy."

313   Tyson, pp. 4, 300.

314   Dietrich, p. 126.

315   Tyson, p. 300.

ory of natural selection mutated into eugenics under Haeckel's Romantic enthusiasm. Instead of relying solely on natural selection, Haeckel believed the science of eugenics coupled with state control, could help improve the races as a proper political-social policy for the future health of the nation. Worse, Haeckel willfully confused race with separate species, so much so that his eugenic concern was over preserving and protecting the indigenous German species from the disorderly mixing of the races. Haeckel actually believed the separate races were developing men into new species and new cultures according to the Social Darwinian laws of nature. To mix the races, therefore, would be a step backward in the evolutionary process. To this, Hitler and the Nazis heartily agreed.

In its natural evolutionary struggle, Haeckel and his adherents presumed the German race had progressed greatly. "According to Haeckel the Germanic race had progressed the furthest from the form of ape-men and thus had been able to surpass other branches of humanity in civilization."[316] On the other hand, many Germans believed their nation was at the crossroads of degeneration if they continue to mix with the other races. Eugenic action was, therefore, necessary to preserve the Germanic race for the sake of its proper evolutionary development. "The Germans, Haeckel and his followers contended, must either accept a new philosophy based on evolution and science and unite with the forces of nature, or cease, through weakness and deterioration, to exist as a nation."[317] This meant that what many deemed to be the superstitions of the Judeo-Christian worldview must be replaced with Social Darwinism and applied political eugenics.

While Darwin, of course, was not necessarily responsible for such a German mutation, it must be pointed out that his evolutionary theory still became the basis for the eugenic movement in general. Darwin's cousin, Francis Galton (1822-1911), was the originator of eugenics. As such, "Not only did many leading Darwinists embrace eugenics, but also most eugenicists—certainly all of the leaders—considered eugenics a straightforward application of Darwinian principles to ethics and society."[318] Haeckel presumed he was on the same side as Darwin. In fact, Haeckel congratulated Darwin on his 70th birthday by saying that he had "shown man his place in

---

[316] Sax, p. 51.
[317] Gasman, *The Scientific Origins of National Socialism*, p. 31.
[318] Weikart, *From Darwin to Hitler*, p. 15.

nature and thereby overthrowing the anthropocentric fable."[319] This mocking statement was certainly directed against both Jews and Christians.

However much Darwin himself may have been more cautious than Haeckel, his evolutionary theory was still used by fellow Europeans to dehumanize other races.[320] In today's politically correct world, Darwin "would be considered a blatant racist."[321] Today, this has been completely ignored in virtually all discussions of modern evolutionary theory:

> The publication of Charles Darwin's *Origin of the Species* in 1859 represented a watershed in the history of biological determinism in general and scientific racism in particular. Prior to Darwin, it was difficult to argue against the Judeo-Christian conception of the unity of man, based on the single creation of Adam and Eve. Darwin's theory suggested that humans had evolved over hundreds of thousands, even millions of years, and that the races of men had diverged while adapting to the particularities of local conditions. The impact of Darwin's theory was enormous. Scholars in both Europe and America, excited by the prospect of founding a science of man on biological principles, began to apply the principles of natural selection to the science and ethics of human society. Opinions differed widely, however, over just how Darwin's theory was to be applied (but) ... Social Darwinists in Germany ... sought to justify a certain political order by a natural order....[322]

Thus, Ernst Haeckel stressed German political biology with a vengeance. In fact, Haeckel took biological Darwinism, which stressed random change and variations through natural selection and mutation, and converted it into holistic Social Darwinism where the Germans of Europe were placed on the top of the indigenous Aryan totem pole. "Biology in Germany, which might have been expected to stand in the way of the mystically false ideas of the Nazis, came rather to their support and much of the basis of that support is directly traceable to the influence of Haeckel himself."[323] Thus, while it is true that "people generally found in Darwin what they wanted to

---

[319] Ernst Haeckel to Charles Darwin, Feb. 9, 1879 quoted by Weikart, p. 12.
[320] Sax, p. 50.
[321] Ibid.
[322] Proctor, *Racial Hygiene: Medicine Under the Nazis*, p. 14.
[323] Gasman, *The Scientific Origins of National Socialism*, p. xlvi.

find,"[324] it must not be forgotten that in Haeckel's case, he helped Germanize Darwinian evolutionary theory for National Socialist consumption.

There was, however, a certain amount of ambivalence among the Nazi ideologues over Darwinism since a strict understanding of natural selection could call into question the whole idea of Aryan superiority. "For all the bonding with nature Haeckel found in the theory of evolution, he most certainly did not like that he himself might be related to apes."[325] Thus the Nazis never had an official position on evolutionary human origins:

> While Darwinism was part of the Nazi educational curriculum in biology, official National Socialist ideology was suspicious of the idea of human evolution and, while not outright denying it, tended to play down the theory of the animal origin of man. It must be remembered that the Nazis had assigned a heroic and eternally superior character and racial constitution to the Aryans. It was therefore hardly ideologically admissible at the same time to allow for the evolution of the Aryans from a group of inferior anthropoid progenitors. Any theory of this kind would have destroyed the notion that the Aryans were in possession of racial superiority from the beginning. This dilemma of the Nazis, however, in regard to the complete acceptance of the idea of evolution was in fact a Haeckelian dilemma magnified many times. Haeckel and the Monists (his later followers) had also tried to disseminate their belief in man's immutability in a world which by the fundamental tenets of their own theory was assumed to be constantly in motion.[326]

Unbelievably, the Nazis made a living out of this Haeckelian contradiction. However, the Nazis overcame this contradiction by presuming that the Social Darwinian laws of evolutionary development were leading to an increasing separation of the races—with the Aryans leading the way progressively forward.

The Nazis also believed they were far more holistically related to nature in general than simply to reduce their origins to apes. Nature with a capital N was primary. The evolution of apes was secondary. "The Nazis

---

[324] Proctor, *Racial Hygiene: Medicine Under the Nazis*, p. 16.
[325] Sax, p 51.
[326] Gasman, *The Scientific Origins of National Socialism*, pp. 173-74.

challenged the unity of the human race so the origin of humanity appeared less important. Since the nation itself was an organism, they felt that their true ancestor was less an ape than a primeval biotic community."[327] That many of the leading Nazis were vegetarians is thus very consistent with such a view.

It is also true the official line of the Nazis was less inclined to accept the idea that man was descended from apes because of its controversial nature with the public.[328] Hitler and the Nazis were surprisingly not interested in creating unnecessary controversies among the people at large. Privately before his henchmen, however, Hitler clearly accepted the doctrine of evolution, including human evolution, as a scientific fact.[329] Hitler even accepted Haeckel's evolutionary recapitulation theory that posited when animals and people develop from embryo to adult, they go through phases representing successive stages in the evolution of their remote ancestors.[330]

Haeckel's Romantic quest to recover the original, to get back to its indigenous roots, was always dressed in Darwinian scientific garb, never in religious terms. Haeckel remained completely unaware that his so-called evolutionary Social Darwinism was actually much more a Romantic philosophy of man and nature than it was true science. He himself ridiculed and criticized those who tried to incorporate forms of mysticism into his circles of influence. He would have never wanted his ideas to be perceived as anything but scientific.

Hence, in the final analysis, whereas Humboldt used topography to promote his Romantic views, and Arndt used poetry to promote his Romantic nationalistic views, and Riehl used sociology in addition to poetic language to deepen Romanticism even further into German culture, and Schopenhauer provided a Romantic environmental ethic based on animal rights, Haeckel used the veneer of Darwinian science to drive his Romantic underpinnings all the way home. "Certainly among the disciples of Darwin, none pursued the ultimate secrets of nature and society more avidly than Ernst Haeckel, the self-appointed spokesman of Darwin and Darwinism in

---

[327] Sax, p. 55.

[328] Proctor, Robert. *Racial Hygeine: Medicine Under the Nazis*, pp. 340-41.

[329] *Hitler's Table Talk*, discussed twice on the evening of Oct. 24, 1941, p. 66.

[330] Weikart, Richard. *Hitler's Ethic: The Nazi Pursuit of Evolutionary Progress.* New York: Palgrave Macmillan, 2009, p. 79.

Germany."[331] Moreover, since Haeckel was Darwin's German interpreter, Germany understood Darwin through Haeckel.[332]

At this juncture, Darwinian science gets inextricably tied up with German nationalism and racism where the myth of the German *volk* now becomes defended by science, rather than seen for what it really was—largely a movement of the occult with the lower peasant classes. Haeckel and his admirers "brought science to the defense of *volkism*, and attached themselves to the pseudo-scientific myth of the racial unity of the Aryans. It may be said that Haeckel gave to the idea of race a modern and scientific guise by the addition of a Social Darwinist ingredient."[333] In reality, underneath the veneer of Darwinian science, Haeckel was advocating a crackpot *volkisch* Romanticism. The Romantic intuitive certainty of German racism rooted in nature was not enough for Haeckel. "What was required was rational support, and this had to be given at all costs in the form which moderns alone consider acceptable, the form of science, no matter that science also happens to be totally unsuitable."[334] The Romantic belief in the German *volk* embedded in its natural environment needed to be undergirded with science to give it authority and credibility. "The form which Social Darwinism took in Germany was a pseudo-scientific religion of nature worship and nature mysticism combined with notions of racism."[335]

As such, the Romantic belief in the German *volk*, the folkish hillbillies of the German villages and forests, was so widespread and strong that it even entered into the science halls of Darwinian evolutionary thought. "Haeckel's ideas on Social Darwinism were brought to fruition in the milieu that was particularly German. His ideas served to unite into a full-bodied ideology the trends of racism, imperialism, Romanticism, anti-Semitism, and nationalism which were floating around among various dissatisfied and

---

[331] Gasman, p. xxxvii.
[332] Gasman maintains the "Germans understood Darwin and Darwinism through the distorted lenses of Haeckel. When the Germans refer to Darwin, more often than not they in fact mean, not Darwin, but Haeckel and his Monist philosophy," *The Scientific Origins of National Socialism*, p. 161.
[333] Ibid., p. xlviii.
[334] Gruner, Rolf. *Philosophies of History: A Critical Essay*. Great Britain: Blackmore Press, 1985. Gruner's quote is discussing Marx's attempt in trying to use the so-called scientific laws of social science to explain the inevitability of the utopian communist state in the future. However, the same quote also fits Haeckel's own false use of science perfectly as well, p. 87.
[335] Gasman, *The Scientific Origins of National Socialism*, p. xlvii.

frustrated groups in German society, especially among the lower middle classes."[336]

While the German word *volk* itself simply means *people*, to the *volkisch* Romantics, the *volk* was a people bound by German racial blood and rooted within the vital life forces of nature. Germans believed this gave them their originality, creativity, emotional feeling and authentic spirituality. It also gave them their identity and membership into a higher overall purpose, standing tall against the alienating onslaught of the modern civilized world. "*Volkists* dreamed of binding the individual German to his natural and topographical surroundings, in short, to his regional landscape. Romantic *volkism* was a deep desire to recover the primeval roots of the German people against the backdrop of mass urbanization and alienation from nature in the city. Nature and individual, they felt, must be tied together in an indissoluble bond."[337]

In truth, the German *volkisch* movement was a dangerous modernized form of neo-pagan tribalism. "There was a cry to recover the *volk*—the mystical union of a people with its blood and landscape—from the degenerate industrialized masses. The iron cage of 'civilization'—Judeo-Christian beliefs and other political and value systems—had to be cast off in order to recover true culture, the primordial ground of the soul, the *volk*. There was only one solution: recover the 'archaic man' within, allowing a rejuvenating return to the chthonic powers of the Edenic, Aryan past."[338] While the *volkisch* movement was exceptionally multi-faceted, it had a "broad plan for German society: at the individual level, the taking of cures, abstinence from alcohol, nudism, vegetarianism, the eating of health foods, contact with the ancestors through spiritualist practices, and hiking through Nature were all remedies to erase the sense of profound loss that so many suffered. At the level of culture, a cleansing of the Aryan race through eugenics and deportations was proposed."[339]

As such, the *volkisch* movement was comprised not only of conservative Romantic values rooted in the soil of the fatherland, but also appealed to the anarchy of the left as both groups took aim at the rise of industrial capitalism. Both camps believed "a spiritual connection with nature and the cosmos had been sacrificed with the rise of a more highly mechanized,

---

[336] Ibid.
[337] Ibid., p. xlviii.
[338] Noll, p. 115.
[339] Ibid.

industrialized, and urbanized civilization."[340] Furthermore, the *volkisch* movement directly associated this growing industrial alienation squarely with the Judeo-Christian tradition. "All of the values that formed the foundation of the industrial order—repressive Judeo-Christian antihedonism, utilitarianism, and rational thought—were confronted with new philosophies of life or of pure experiences that exalted myth over history, impulsive action or deed over conscious reflection, and feeling or intuition over rational thought."[341]

Thus, the uprootedness and alienation of industrial capitalism and city life was especially abhorrent to the *volkisch* movement. At its very heart, it "was a pathological response to modernity. In the face of very real dislocations brought on by the triumph of industrial capitalism and national unification, *volkisch* thinkers preached a return to the land, to the simplicity and wholeness of life attuned to nature's purity."[342] Most ominous of all, the Jewish people in particular were singled out as the primary object of hatred since they were allegedly in charge of the marketplace, the banks and the cities. "Reformulating traditional anti-Semitism into nature friendly terms, the *volkisch* movement carried a volatile amalgam of 19th century cultural prejudices, Romantic obsessions with purity, and anti-Enlightenment sentiment into the 20th century political discourse. The emergence of modern ecology forged the final link in the fateful chain which bound together aggressive nationalism, mystically charged racism, and environmentalist predilections."[343]

Haeckel's Ecological Monism

To Haeckel and those involved with his *volkisch* Romanticism, the name of their philosophical scientific system was called Monism. Today, Monism is popularly described as social Darwinism. Monism is taken from the Greek word *mono*, meaning *one*. The point of Monism therefore is to emphasize unity, holism or oneness. German Monism or social Darwinism was a Romantic-pantheistic-holistic view of man and nature that attempted to explain everything from within the context of nature alone without any reference to a transcendental deity or sacred text. It took holism so seriously

---

[340] Ibid.
[341] Ibid., pp. 114-15.
[342] Staudenmaier & Biehl, p. 17.
[343] Ibid., pp. 2-3.

that the transcendent nature of both man and God were denied. Man was seen as completely rooted into the natural world and thus subject to its evolutionary biological laws without exception:

> Following the teachings of Haeckel directly, the Monists insisted that for man "the same laws must be valid today which have regulated the life of other species for millions of years." And these were to be found exclusively in the natural and not in the historical world. In the construction of any science of society it had to be kept clearly in mind that man could never hope to transcend his animal essence and character and escape into a deceptively idyllic world free from the competition, conflict and aggression that characterized nature. "Natural selection in the struggle of life," Haeckel wrote "acts so as to transform human society just as it modifies animals and plants." … Failure to follow the laws of nature directly can lead to the "crippling" of man and the "deterioration" of the individual and his family." For this reason biology had to "demand" that sociology follow the laws of nature.[344]

Nature was thus king, if not deified into a feudalistic conservative natural order.

The god of the Monists was a pantheistic god, not distinct from nature as was the case with the Judeo-Christian God. In other words, Haeckel reconciled religion with science by cutting out the Judeo-Christian worldview and its God. Haeckel wrote, "The Monistic idea of God which alone is compatible with our present knowledge of nature, recognizes the divine spirit in all things. . . . God is everywhere. . . . Every atom is animated."[345] German pantheism thus replaced the belief in traditional theism. Haeckel thus transferred the creative powers of the God of the Bible to the pantheistic powers of nature itself. Haeckel also suggested his pantheism was a polite form of atheism.

Nature itself and nature alone became the sole basis for the evolutionary development of plants, animals and society. In Haeckel's pantheistic holism,

---

344 Gasman, *The Scientific Origins of National Socialism*, p. 34.
345 Haeckel, Ernst, *Monism as Connecting Religion and Science. The Confession of Faith of a Man of Science*, London, 1894, p. 28 quoted by Gasman, *The Scientific Origins of National Socialism*, p. 65.

the primacy of nature would also dictate the spiritual and political life of people as well:

> It may be said that in no other country of Europe, or for that matter even in the United States, did the ideas of Darwinism develop as seriously as the total explanation of the world as in Germany. But Darwinism in Germany was a system of thought that was often transformed beyond recognition. *Darwinisumus* was far from the biological ideas or underlying moral and philosophical views of Darwin himself. Professing a mystical belief in the forces of nature, insisting on the literal transfer of the laws of biology to the social realm, and calling for a religious reformation in German life, Haeckel and his immediate followers held to ideas which were remote from the familiar naturalism of Spencer, Darwin, and Huxley.[346]

Haeckel's Darwinism was thus a totalitarian Darwinism because it was used as a total explanation for just about anything and everything, including politics. Indeed, Haeckel's Monist League was very active politically.

Haeckel's Romantic pantheism essentially became a pan-everything-ism. Perhaps it may be better to say that for Haeckel, if Darwinism is really true, then it needs to be put to the test, and that he did on an unprecedented scale. Darwin himself was far more hesitant, much more cautious. He was not as instinctively Romantic as Haeckel. Haeckel used strict Darwinian naturalistic explanations to attack the Judeo-Christian worldview on the one hand, but also launched into his own mystical Monism or social Darwinism on the other hand. "Sun worship seems to the modern scientist to be the best of all forms of theism, and one which may be the most easily reconciled with modern Monism."[347] Hence, Haeckel's sun worship is clearly evident, a theme which he continues: "Indeed, the whole of our bodily and mental life depends, in the last resort, like other organic life, on the light and heat rays of the sun. Hence in the light of pure reason, sun worship, as a form of naturalistic monotheism, seems to have a much better foundation than the anthropistic worship of Christians and of other monotheists who conceive their god in human form."[348] Haeckel even called his belief in Monism

---

[346] Gasman, *The Scientific Origins of National Socialism*, pp. xxxvii-xxxviii.
[347] Haeckel, *Riddle of the Universe*, Buffalo, New York: Prometheus Books, 1992, p. 280.
[348] Ibid., p. 281.

religion.[349] Indeed, "the youth organization of the *Monistenbund*—inspired and led by Haeckel—sponsored sun worshiping festivals each summer solstice. Haeckel himself was not a practicing neo-pagan but loved the spirit of the movement."[350]

Haeckel had thus propounded a subversive and secular religion of nature in direct contrast to the Judeo-Christian worldview. "For those who read Haeckel and were convinced, Haeckelian Darwinism assumed the character of a political and religious ideology and faith."[351] In other words, strict scientific naturalism was used to debunk the Old and New Testaments as myth, freeing Haeckel and his followers to propose their own religious philosophy of man and nature:

> The association of Haeckel and the Monists with 19th century naturalistic and materialistic atheism reveals, however, only one side of their relationship with Christianity and traditional religion. Undeniably, they belonged to the school of scientific critics of religion. But at the same time, even primarily, even though this has been overlooked, is that they belonged to the general intellectual movement of nationalistic opposition to traditional Western Christianity which developed in Germany in the last century. The significance of their encounter with religion is to be found in the fact that they played a vital and critical role in the transformation of traditional faith into pagan, racist, and often occult forms of belief which came to life in Germany in the later decades of the 19th century and which continued to flourish later on under National Socialism.[352]

Haeckel thus became the great anti-hero of German pantheism or monism. One Monist claimed that Haeckel was "the greatest theologian the world has ever seen."[353] Haeckel was almost worshiped by his followers. One particular Monist praised Haeckel, "This implacable opponent of all dogmatic Christianity revealed himself to me as the best and most advanced 'Christ' whom

---

[349]   Ibid., p. 344.
[350]   Noll, p. 116.
[351]   Gasman, *The Scientific Origins of National Socialism*, p. 15.
[352]   Ibid., p. 56.
[353]   Schmidt, Heinrich, "Ernst Haeckel als Theolog," *Der Monismus*, VI, 1911, p. 119 quoted by Gasman, *The Scientific Origins of National Socialism*, p. 15.

I personally have known."[354] Another fan eulogized Haeckel as the Nordic god Odin wherein he rediscovered his fatherland and his people.[355]

Haeckel not only paved the way to make his monistic social Darwinism a *fact* of science, he also opened the door into ecological cult worship. Perhaps more importantly, once nature is worshiped, the worship of man invariably follows. At the height of German Romanticism under Haeckel's Monism, ecological holism and environmental totalitarianism went hand in hand, helping pave the way for cult worship under Hitler. While it is true Haeckel himself viewed the ideal state as one that was not coercive,[356] his biological determinism undercuts the potential of human freedom from the outset. Furthermore, how can eugenics be practiced without state coercion? More telling, "Haeckel and the Monists did not support democracy, partly because they did not trust untrained scientists to understand man and society."[357]

Haeckel was "the first biologist to argue duty was a biological impulse. All living organisms, amoeba, apes, primitive and cultivated man, were bound by law of care for the family and collective and the desire to survive."[358] Such deterministic biological ideas based on natural instinct are counterproductive. By reducing man to mere biological impulses, this does nothing to promote human freedom:

> The German Monist League in the years before World War I, became a vitally important clearing house for eugenic proposals and programs, and Haeckel, along with many of his followers, were instrumental in early attempts to foster a policy of racial eugenics in Germany and organize a defense of the European population in general against the onslaught of either non-white or inferior racial elements. Racial eugenics became for them, much against their ideological insistence on a deterministic nature, a weapon against certain but really unnamed corroding forces of evolution as well as a defense against the harmful effects of industrial and urban civilization—ideas and

---

354 Ostwald, Wilhelm, "Was ich Ernst Haeckel verdanke," in Schmidt H. "Was wir Ernst Haeckel verdanken," I, 199, quoted by Gasman, *The Scientific Origins of National Socialism*, pp. 15-16.

355 Wolfsdorf, Eugene, "Odhin und Haeckel," quoted by Gasman, *The Scientific Origins of National Socialism*, p. 17.

356 Bramwell, *Ecology in the 20ʰ Century: A History*, p. 50.

357 Ibid., p. 52.

358 Ibid., p. 50.

aspirations that complemented their sense of an impending apoca-lyptic struggle between the decay that defined contemporary society and the new scientific and biological utopia that would predictably follow in the wake of a triumphant Monism.[359]

With such a eugenic-environmental worldview, nature inevitably becomes man's dictator, in complete contradiction to Genesis 1.

Although Haeckel did attend church, he only attended for the sake of his family and friends.[360] The natural world and the study of that natural world, not church, was his true temple. He stated: "The goddess of truth dwells in the temple of nature, in the green woods, on the blue sea, and on the snowy summits of the hills."[361] In *The Riddle of the Universe*, Haeckel often complained about Christianity's anti-natural sentiments. "One source of countless theoretical errors and practical blemishes, of deplorably crudity and privation, is found in the false anthropism of Christianity—that is in the unique position to all the rest of nature. In this way it has contributed not only to an extremely injurious isolation from our glorious mother nature, but also to a regrettable contempt of all other organisms."[362] In this particular quote, Haeckel sounds very similar to Schopenhauer.

Haeckel's main goal was to return Germany back to its cultural origins embedded within its own holistic landscape well before the Judeo-Christian worldview corrupted all of Europe with its alleged anti-natural, commer-cialistic and religious internationalism. "Monism enters into its strongest opposition to Christianity on the question of beauty."[363] "Holy German nature"[364] was particularly emphasized, which he frequently described as his "true milieu."[365] Haeckel actually believed "Germany could save itself by religious devotion to nature and to natural law."[366]

As such, religious devotion to nature through monistic scientism was the heart and soul of Haeckel's Social Darwinism. This stood in great contrast

---

Gasman, *Haeckel's Monism and the Birth of Fascist Ideology*, pp. 31-33.

[360] Haeckel, Ernst. *My Church Departure*, p. 30 quoted by Gasman, *The Scientific Origins of National Socialism*, p. 59.

[361] Haeckel, p. 337.

[362] Ibid., p. 355.

[363] Ibid., p. 339.

[364] *Ernst Haeckel to Hermann Allmers, Freienwalde, July 13, 1860* in Koop, *Haeckel und Allmers*, p. 52; quoted by Gasman, *The Scientific Origins of National Socialism*, p. 63.

[365] Ibid.

[366] Gasman, *The Scientific Origins of National Socialism*, p. 63.

to what Haeckel labeled as the "gloom of the cloister" and the "clouds of incense of the Christian Churches."[367] Haeckel even advocated that the Christian humanities be replaced with a nature-based curriculum:

> Demanding the secularization of education and the introduction of science into the curriculum, Haeckel sounded like many other naturalistically and progressively inclined thinkers in the 19th century. But lurking beneath his progressive sounding phrases and ideas was a theory of education and a program which actively sought to undermine the entire humanistic tradition of general education based upon instruction in the liberal arts. Haeckel saw in the transformation of the school curriculum a way to attack what he believed were the corrupting roots of Western Civilization itself. The West, with its glorification of man, its sense of civilization as representing the development of the human spirit and ever growing realization of human freedom, were, from Haeckel's point of view, ideas which had to be combated.[368]

Haeckel complained that the study of nature had been completely neglected by Christian humanistic studies. He thus prophesied, "In the school of the future nature will be the chief object of study; man shall learn a correct view of the world he lives in; he will not be made to stand outside of and opposed to nature."[369]

Haeckel's followers even "campaigned vigorously for the abandonment of Christian holidays. They pleaded rather for the establishment and acceptance of new *volk* holidays which would be based upon nature, and which would replace the 'anachronistic' ones of the Middle Ages. In the Christian Churches 'they complained', one hears only empty sermons, mere phrases, and words which no one really believed anyway. The Germans had to be taught that a holiday could fittingly be celebrated by excursions into the countryside or by the cultivation of one's garden."[370] In the end, "by turning away from Christianity to worship nature, the new religionist would experience a higher pitch of feeling and spiritual intensity, an emotional release which would enable him to return to his ordinary life satisfied and

---

[367] Haeckel, p. 337.
[368] Gasman, *The Scientific Origins of National Socialism*, p. 38.
[369] Haeckel, p. 363.
[370] Gasman, *The Scientific Origins of National Socialism*, p. 68.

refreshed."[371] Easter was to be celebrated not by going to church, but "by leaving the confining walls of the city, and by going out into the countryside to observe and live in nature."[372]

In sum, evolution was a religion to the Monists, and this meant the total abandonment of Christianity together with a total "immersion of oneself into nature."[373] This also meant German naturism was of a higher evolutionary order than Christianity. "The young Monists were assured that in the spring the countryside and nature would cure them of all unhappiness and would teach them the undeniable truth that only in the northern Germanic climates have the highest cultures been able to evolve."[374]

While Haeckel was certainly anti-Christian in his nature worship, even worse he was anti-Semitic. In fact, Haeckel bears the primary responsibility of bringing up the Jewish question as a biological problem. The Jews in particular were subjected to *scientific* investigation. Not surprisingly, Haeckel *discovered* they "possessed inborn racial characteristics which apparently were resistant to change."[375] In other words, the racial characteristics of the Jews were harmfully reactionary to the evolutionary laws of the natural world. Their transcendent view of man over nature made them resistant to evolutionary biological change, and hence, they had become a lesser race. Adolf Hitler heartily agreed with this belief: "Where is the people which in the last 2000 years has been exposed to so slight changes of inner disposition, character, etc., as the Jewish people?"[376] Hitler's statement also implies the Jews have failed to evolve.

Haeckel believed anti-Semitism was a racial problem, not a religious one.[377] Adolf Hitler believed likewise: "The Jews have always been a people with definite racial characteristics and never a religion. ... The Jewish religious doctrine consists primarily in prescriptions for keeping the blood of Jewry pure and for regulating the relation of Jews among themselves, but even more with the rest of the world."[378]

[371] Ibid.

[372] Ibid., p. 67.

[373] P. Flaskamper, "Monismus and Naturegefuhl," *Das Monistische Jahrhundert*, II, 1913-14, 58, quoted by Gasman in *The Scientific Origins of National Socialism*, p. 66.

[374] Gasman, *The Scientific Origins of National Socialism*, p. 67.

[375] Ibid., p. 157.

[376] Hitler, *Mein Kampf*, translated by Ralph Manheim. Boston & New York: Mariner Books, 1999, p. 300.

[377] Gasman, *The Scientific Origins of National Socialism*, p. 158.

[378] Hitler, *Mein Kampf*, p. 306.

Haeckel was one of the principle founders of the extreme nationalistic and anti-Semitic Pan German League.[379] Haeckel acknowledged anti-Semitism was widespread among his own students.[380] He was convinced that anti-Semitism was on an inevitable rise throughout all of Europe, not just in Germany. Haeckel believed anti-Semitism was justifiable in order to force the Jews to give up their separatist ways and assimilate into German culture. "Only by disappearing as a separate group could the Jews demonstrate their patriotism and at the same time serve the national interests of Germany."[381] Much like the *volkisch* Romantics before him, Haeckel decried Jewish cosmopolitanism. He "contended that the Jews were alienated from German life and society and that the Germans therefore fell ill at ease among the Jews."[382] In short, the Jews were not properly related to nature from a Social Darwinian point of view. Their biological blood was not properly related to the evolutionary laws of nature, nor properly rooted in the ecological soil of Germany.

Haeckel and his Monist followers were perhaps the first politically involved environmentalists. Many of the same concerns that environmentalists are so fretful about today were prefaced by Haeckel and the Monist League some 100 years earlier. Haeckel is, in fact, the founder of what is today called political ecology:

> Haeckel's link with ecology is not confined to the verbal accident of inventing the term. Ecology, as a conceptual tool, was a term that contained the kernel of its normative usage from the beginning. Its founder became heavily involved in politics. Both his politics and his scientific work touched on concerns fundamental to today's ecologists. They did not touch on all; on the other hand, his immediate followers extended Haeckel's interests to cover soil erosion and resource conservation. Haeckel's most important legacy was his worship of Nature, the belief that man and nature were one, and that to damage one was to damage the other. He offered scientific "proof" that harmony and benevolence were intrinsic to the world,

---

[379] Gasman, *The Scientific Origins of National Socialism*, p. 128.
[380] Ibid., p. 158.
[381] Ibid.
[382] Ibid.

and that man must fit into its framework, while cherishing and caring for nature's wonders.[383]

Haeckel enthusiastically used his Darwinian *science* to uphold holistic *volkisch* environmentalism. aHaWhile many of the modern German greens have dropped racism from their environmental views, Haeckel's influence is still fundamental to their outlook. He is their father and they are his children. "The political relevance for Germany was to be far in the future, decades after the collapse of the Third Reich, when the educated middle-class began to support the Greens."[384]

Blood and Soil

This Monistic or Social Darwinian emphasis on returning to nature against the dictates of the Judeo-Christian worldview also helped mutate into a cultic *volkisch* belief called "*blut und boden*" or "blood and soil." Here, the Aryan *volk* assumed they had a special relationship to the German landscape through their blood. "Blood" stood for racial eugenics, and "soil" stood for the German land itself. While Haeckel himself never used the phrase "blood and soil" he did argue: "Germans were forest evolved while Jews were from a desert ecosystem, hence an invasive species to Europe. He argued that German soil was made of decomposed German sewage, German corpses and German-bred crops and livestock; in other words German blood and soil were chemically united in a single ecosystem."[385] Hence, well before the Nazis had even come to power, Haeckel and the Monists essentially argued for an early version of eugenics and the environment, both of which were pointed directly at Jews and Christians. This combination of eugenics and environmentalism became known as "blood and soil" under the banner of National Socialism.

The Monists believed it was in nature alone that man can find his genuine roots.[386] Monist Eugene Wolfsdorf concluded that it was Haeckel who

---

[383]   Bramwell, *Ecology in the 20ʰ Century: A History*, p. 53.

[384]   Ibid., p. 52.

[385]   Kay, William Walter, "Environmentalism's Environment," written in 2008 for ecofascism.com.

[386]   Gasman, *The Scientific Origins of National Socialism*, p. 66.

was responsible for "rooting me once again in the soil of my homeland and thereby establishing for me my moral existence."[387]

Thus, the interest in pure racial blood was also a quest for roots in a pristine environment. The *volkisch* presumption was that "civilization had ruined human beings by forcing them into unnatural, cramped, urban environments. Diseases physical and mental were hatched in some places, and the medical science of the day believed that such damage could be passed down to successive generations."[388] Since the Monists holistically bound blood or race within the natural world, they came up with all kinds of cockamamie schemes on how to bring about this natural purity—which was understood to be a form of racial renewal.

The Monist emphasis on ecological holism demanded some sort of connection between humanity and nature. What was that connection? Not surprisingly, the Monists chose blood as that natural link. To them, blood represented different races and different species. Put another way, among the German Monists who loved Haeckel, plants and man are *blood* brothers. "All organisms, from the simplest amoebae and bacteria, to plants and animals, all the way up to man, are similar and equal to each other because they follow the same general laws, have the same characteristics, and are blood relations of each other."[389] The same Monist author also said that man desires to be in communion with nature so that he is able to "feel its pulse because he is blood of its blood."[390]

Racial ethnicity and nature was a growing subject of discussion throughout the first part of the 20th century in Germany. It became more ominous after the tragic defeat of World War I. "Racist, *volkisch*, and anti-Semitic voices became significantly more pronounced, moving from a fringe phenomenon to a prominent part of the still quite diverse choir of conservationists."[391] In fact, the monistic fusion between man and nature was so complete that some Germans began to see themselves as an endangered species that needed to be saved, especially after the economic disaster of the 1920s.

---

[387] Wolfsdorf, Eugene, *Odhin und Haeckel* in Schmidt (ed), "Was wir Ernst Haeckel verdanken," II, 47 quoted by Gasman, *The Scientific Origins of National Socialism*, p. 65.

[388] Noll, p. 115.

[389] P. Flaskamper, "Monismus and Naturegefuhl," *Das Monistische Jahrhundert*, II, 1913-14, pp. 60-61, quoted by Gasman, *The Scientific Origins of National Socialism*, p. 66.

[390] Ibid., p. 64, quoted by Gasman, *The Scientific Origins of National Socialism*, p. 66.

[391] Uekoetter, Frank. *The Green and the Brown: A History of Conservation in Nazi Germany.* Cambridge University Press, 2006, p. 25.

Hitler's ultimate goal was essentially a mighty crusade to save the Aryan species from death. He stated: "If I can accept a divine Commandment, it's this one: 'Thou shalt preserve the species.'"[392] Hitler's understanding of man was completely fused with nature. Racial species like the Aryans must be protected from extinction just like animals should be protected from extinction. "Like Haeckel, Hitler believed that mankind was sharply divided from each other as species in the animal and plant kingdom. In the struggle for existence, the lower and weaker races were bound to die out."[393] As such, Hitler promoted the notion that "the consequence of this racial purity, universally valid in Nature, is not only the sharp outward delimitation of the various races, but their uniform character in themselves. The fox is always a fox, the goose a goose, the tiger a tiger, etc."[394] While evolutionists use this particular statement from the *Fuhrer* to demonstrate Hitler did not really believe in evolution, "this is really not the case. Hitler recognized that evolution is such an incredibly slow process that in the limited time of known human history—only several thousand years—little biological change could occur."[395] As such, "for all practical purposes, when dealing with centuries or even millennia rather than eons, races had fixed essences. Thus, even though he believed that races had formed through evolutionary processes, racial characteristics could only change over extremely long periods of time."[396]

Hitler placed both man and animals under the same natural laws which must be obeyed: "You will never find a fox who in his inner attitude might, for example, show humanitarian tendencies toward geese, as similarly there is no cat with a friendly inclination towards mice."[397] Thus, Hitler adopted the Haeckelian-Darwinian survival of the fittest scheme with a vengeance, especially with regard to its application to people: "The struggle is always a means for improving a species' health and power of resistance and, therefore, a cause of its higher development."[398] Hitler believed that natural evolutionary development over time led to a separation of the species. Nature's most patent rule was preserving the purity of the races in which all living species

---

[392] *Hitler's Table Talk*, night of Dec. 1-2, 1941, p. 109.
[393] Gasman, *The Scientific Origins of National Socialism*, p. 164.
[394] Hitler, *Mein Kampf*, p. 285.
[395] Weikart, *Hitler's Ethic*, p. 89.
[396] Ibid.
[397] Hitler, *Mein Kampf*, p. 285.
[398] Ibid.

developed their own "inner segregation."[399] This particular statement also demonstrates how Hitler adopted Haeckel's fusion of evolutionary theory with Social Darwinism. This Social Darwinian movement on the part of Nature is a natural law which must be observed and adhered to at all costs for the preservation of any species, including the different races.

Hitler considered the sick modern world of international capitalism and communism, led by Jews and spread by Christianity, to be disobedient to Nature. Its corrupting influences had become an epidemic threatening the very survival of the indigenous Aryan blood, the true original natives of Europe. Countdown to extinction was looming. Something must be done, and done quickly. "Hitler was in dread of the forces of anti-nature."[400] Hitler was thus defending German Aryan culture against the weakness of Western civilization brought on by its autonomous beliefs and practices over the natural world. "Like Haeckel he sought to curb the 'germs of disintegration' within society by returning to the paths marked out by nature."[401]

By the time of the Nazi period, *blood and soil* had become hardened into a *volkisch* green ideology where the Aryan master race would purify itself by returning to the German landscape away from the alienating asphalt culture of the big cities. "The Nazis, like Haeckel, sought to bring man back within the purview of nature. By stressing in their ideology the importance of rootedness, of *blut und boden*, the Nazis wished to deify the primitive forces of nature."[402] Some got so carried away with this that they wanted to "regard Germany, not Palestine, as the promised land."[403] Here, the Aryan *blood and soil* sentiment functioned as the ultimate environmental counterculture, standing opposite the Old Testament Jews living in the promised land of Israel.

Such quasi-religious views grew out of the German youth movements of the day, especially after World War I, and most notably with a group called the *Artamanen*. This name was derived from the Aryan nature god *Artam*. The *Artamanen* youth movement was a utopian proto-Nazi movement that "propagandized for the creation of a racially pure Germanic peasantry to be fashioned upon the nobility of German blood."[404] They

---

[399]   Ibid., p. 284.
[400]   Gasman, *The Scientific Origins of National Socialism*, p. 162.
[401]   Ibid.
[402]   Ibid., p. xlvi.
[403]   Ibid., p. 156.
[404]   Ibid., p. 152.

strongly believed that "perfection of the race could only take place in intimate connection with the soil of Germany."[405] Such groups synthesized the green peasantry views of Arndt and Riehl with Haeckel's Social Darwinism:

> What it implied most strongly to its supporters at this time was the link between those who held and farmed the land and whose generations of blood, sweat, and tears had made the soil part of their being, and their being integral to the soil. It meant to them the unwritten history of Europe, a history unconnected with trade, the banditry of the aristocracy, and the infinite duplicity of the church and monarchy. It was the antithesis of the mercantile spirit, and still appeals to some basic instinct as a critique of up-rootedness.[406]

Blood and soil was most often associated with German Romanticism and its peasantry. German peasants were considered a hardy group. They lived naturally healthy, but difficult rural lifestyles in the German countryside.

The beliefs of the *Artamanens* were very similar to the views of many National Socialists, particularly of the SS. "Many of the individuals who first received their ideological and social training in this movement later on became officers and leaders in the SS. Among the charter members of the *Artamanen* are Heinrich Himmler, the leader of the SS, Rudolf Hoess, the commandant of Auschwitz, and Walther Darre, Hitler's minister of agriculture and architect of Nazi resettlement policy in the East."[407]

Like Himmler, Rudolf Hoess loved the countryside and was a devoted animal lover.[408] Even though Hoess was responsible for the killing of more than one million people at Auschwitz, he said the best days of his life were spent on a farm with his companion horses riding out the end of the war in hiding.[409] Darre was highly educated in the King's College School and at Wimbledon in England. Darre was a mentor to Himmler. Darre taught that Germany must "bind the best blood among our people irrevocably and as quickly as possible to the soil."[410]

---

405 Ibid.
406 Bramwell, *Blood and Soil: Walther Darre and Hitler's Green Party*, p. 54.
407 Gasman, *The Scientific Origins of National Socialism*, p. 153.
408 Tusa, p. 319.
409 Ibid.
410 *Blut und Boden*, undated documentary film of the SS quoted by Heinz Hohne in *The Order of the Death's Head: The Story of Hitler's SS*. London: Penguin Books, 1969, p. 47.

Darre said the agricultural problems facing Germany in the 1920s were not economic. At root of the crisis was the problem of blood and soil in which Germans had been removed from their native landscapes in the countryside. Worse, Darre believed Germany had been corrupted by the internationalism of the cities run by Jewish capital. Germans must therefore return to the land to save them from such materialistic exploitation:

> The practical present day consequences of this theory were that all influences inimical to the Nordic blood myth must be held at bay, all international *humanist* organizations must be suppressed. . . . Fascinated, Himmler saw opening up before him a world whose existence he had dimly suspected but which he had never been able to visualize clearly. Darre, with his doctrine of blood and soil, opened Himmler's eyes, and what he saw was wonderful—the *volkisch* elite of the future, the lords of the new Germanic tribes, the men of his SS order.[411]

Even as early as 1924, Himmler wrote that the country peasant farmer's worst enemy was international Jewish capital in the cities that divided the townsmen from the countrymen into a corrupting relationship. "By speculation and markets, the Jews ensure that production prices are low and consumer prices are high. The farmer is supposed to earn little, the townsman to pay much."[412]

Henceforth, *blood and soil* became the primary ideological doctrine of the SS. As Himmler rose to power above his mentor in the Nazi Party, he "did not forget his debt to Darre and the *Artamanens*. Later he recruited Darre into the SS. Himmler put him in charge of his new Race and Settlement Office, which Darre used as a stepping stone to the Reich Ministry of Agriculture."[413] Darre became the chief exponent of the blood and soil slogan. So attached was he to the native landscape of Germany that Darre asserted, "To remove the German soul from the natural landscape is to kill it."[414] Darre himself believed that if one lived according to the natural laws of blood and soil, "he would be better, healthier, and happier. The attempt

---

[411] Hohne, p. 48.
[412] Ibid., p. 46.
[413] Ibid.
[414] Mosse, *Nazi Culture* quotes a 1934 speech by Darre, quoted by Dominick, p. 95.

to escape from these bonds could only fail, and lead to a cycle of industrial growth, collapse and misery."[415]

In 1931, a young Albert Speer, who later became Hitler's architect, recalled in his memoirs: "The National Socialist creed held that the roots of renewal were to be found in the native soil of Germany."[416] This was certainly one of the reasons that lured Speer into the new movement. Before he became chancellor of Germany, Speer recalled how Hitler "cried out against the erosion of morals in the big cities. He warned against ill effects of civilization which, he said, damaged the biological substance of the people."[417]

In 1934, Nazi biologist Walther Schoenichen said National Socialism and environmental protection stand "in a tight connection because the *Fuhrer* wills a new German *volksgemeinschaft* whose foundation is drawn from blood and soil, i.e., from the primordial forces of life and soul that are proper to our race, and from the nature-willed bond that subsists between us and the sod of the homeland."[418] He went on to say, "Adolf Hitler demands that man must understand the basic necessity of the rule of nature and must also grasp how much his existence is subjugated from above to these laws of eternal struggle and contest."[419] As such, Schoenichen reminded his environmental readers, "No technology, no rationalism can protect us, together with our civilization, from going under, if we detach ourselves from the natural foundation of life."[420] Schoenichen's writings clearly placed the Nazi *blood and soil* doctrine "within the intellectual history of German Romanticism."[421]

Blood and soil became inextricably tied up with the environmental movement in Germany. Nazi ideologues used the blood and soil slogan for many practical purposes, everything from getting Germans back to the land, to calls for nature preservation and environmental sustainability, to emphasizing a "buy local" self-sufficient economy, and including the upholding of traditional German values. "The celebration of the German woods and animals was a usual feature of the blood and soil literature that

---

[415]   Ibid., p. 73.
[416]   Speer, *Inside the Third Reich*. New York: Bonanza Books, 1982 (1970), p. 14.
[417]   Ibid., p. 15.
[418]   Schoenichen, Walther. *Nature Protection in the Third Reich* (Berlin, 1934) quoted by Zimmerman in "Ecofasicsm: An Enduring Temptation."
[419]   Ibid.
[420]   Ibid., pp.7-8.
[421]   Ferry, p. 91.

anticipated many themes of the Nazi movement."[422] The slogan was also used to complain about capitalism, industrialization, internationalism, Judaism and Christianity.

Fanatical green Nazi Wilhelm Lienenkamper declared a counterculture environmental war against Judaism. He bombastically declared the "First Commandment" of nature protection was the "merciless extermination of the utilitarian perspective."[423] Nazi environmental professionals even trumpeted that the "Third Reich would elevate the ideal values of *heimat* (homeland) and landscape to new heights as part of its commitment to restoring Germany on the basis of *blut und boden*."[424] As early as the 1920s, before the blood and soil doctrine had become a household slogan in Germany, natural historian Konrad Guenther bellowed, "If we did not find German *heimat*, then all efforts to mold the Germans into one nation would be futile."[425] By 1931, he forewarned that if Germany is not successful in their nature protection endeavors, it will mean a "betrayal of Germandon."[426]

Nazi environmentalist Hans Schwenkel glibly pointed out the Mosaic law contained no provisions for nature protection. "Since the first book of Moses, the Jews do not know nature protection, since God has given to the children of Israel all plants and animals for their enjoyment."[427] In other words, the Jews do not protect nature but exploit it as a Divine right of personal selfish enjoyment.

In 1937, Nazi conservationist Hans Stadler complained, "The Jewish merchants specializing in the timber trade—had bought and processed the 'last of the strong oaks and the last of the beautiful walnut trees' in the region and were now seeking to exterminate the pear trees."[428] Walther Schoenichen even wondered whether or not outdoor advertising had its source in Jewish roots. "It would be a worthwhile cause for inquiry in how

---

[422]   Sax, p. 15.

[423]   HStAD NW 60 no. I603, p. 300 quoted by Uekoetter, p. 21.

[424]   Lekan, Thomas, "It Shall be the Whole Landscape!: The Reich Nature Protection Law and Regional Planning in the Third Reich," in *How Green Were the Nazis?*, p. 73.

[425]   Guenther, Konrad, *"Heimatlehre als Quelle neuer deutscher Zukunft,"* (Friebourg, 1922), p. 5 quoted by Uekoetter, p. 25.

[426]   Guenther, Konrad, *"Naturschutz als Wissenschaft and Lehrfach,"* *Blatter fur Naturschutz und Naturpflege* 14 (1931): 16, quoted by Uekoetter, p. 25.

[427]   Closmann, Charles, "Legalizing a Voksgemeinschaft" in *How Green Were the Nazis?*, p. 32.

[428]   StAW Landratsamt Ebern no. 1336, "Der Regierungsbeauftragte fur Naturschutz in Unterfranken to the Bezirksbeauftragten fur Naturschutz in Mainfranken," March 12, 1937, quoted by Uekoetter p. 38.

far this social-psychic disease is the result of an infection with Jewish poison."[429] Hitler himself believed "the oppressive role of Jews in the economy was based on the idea that Jews were biologically predisposed to mercantile activity."[430]

Borrowing from ancient Teutonic mysticism which "posited that German racial identity was essentially tied literally and metaphorically to the land,"[431] and cleansed by Monist scientism, the blood and soil slogan became a rallying cry for a nationalistic environmentalism. It was a dangerous politicized ecology that would spell disaster for the Jewish people in particular. In a speech given on Sept. 6, 1938, Hitler declared that Germany "must be cleansed of all parasites and that, in the process of the struggle against the 'international Jewish world enemy,' 'eternal values of blood and soil' had to be elevated to the 'ruling laws of life.'"[432] The Nazi blood and soil doctrine was thus directly juxtaposed to the rootlessness of the Jewish people living as invasive parasites in Europe.

The Jews were especially prone to being targeted by the Nazis precisely because they were without land or soil. That the Jewish people were rooted at one time within the promised land of Israel during Old Testament times, and removed from their own homeland by other invading powers, was of no consequence. Hitler complained the Jew is the "only human being capable of adapting himself to any climate and of earning a living just as well in Lapland as in the tropics."[433] Hence the Jews were necessarily inferior, a rootless group of people with no environmental or ecological ties. "The concept of the bloodlines of Germany being integrally tied to the soil or land necessitated a German people on a German land, with all others"[434] viewed as intruders, especially if one were a Jew:

> More than mere nationalism or a "back to farming" campaign, it laid the foundation for an anti-Semitism that would not be undone: since the Jews were a nation without a land, they reasoned, the Jews then must be infinitely inferior to the Germans whose national identity and soul were tied to the land. Since Jews were identified

---

429 Schoenichen, Walther, *"Biologie,"* 76, quoted by Uekoetter p. 38.

430 Weikart, *Hitler's Ethic,* p. 98.

431 Kirkley-Best, Elizabeth, "Blood and Soil: *Blut und Boden.*"

432 Hitler quoted in Domarus Zweiter Halbband 1934-38, p. 890 by Pois, p. 49.

433 *Hitler's Table Talk: 1941-44,* midday May 15, 1942, p. 365.

434 Kirkley-Best, "Blood and Soil: *Blut und boden.*"

by race and not religion in the Reich, this land-less people were not to be considered real Germans, and hence one of the first acts of the Reich was to arrest their citizenship and delineate them as a nation which was not German, by race or land.[435]

It is thus no coincidence that environmental laws in Nazi Germany preceded the racially charged Nuremberg laws. "Laws were designed, whether consciously or not, to confirm the identification of the Jews with the decadence of urban civilization."[436] In short, the Nazi racial laws were built upon their environmental laws. They also complemented each other.

Far from eschewing the blood and soil doctrine of the Nazis, Schoenichen even took it upon himself to convert some of his fellow environmentalists to the Nazi camp. Taking the position that other nature conservationists had not been comprehensive or holistic enough to include people into their own way of thinking, Schoenichen played a very important role in winning over more and more greens to the Nazi Party. Schoenichen pointed out, "*Naturschutz* (Nature Protection) concerns more than endangered species of birds and rare plants, more than dunes, moors and forests. . . . It concerns men, and—here with us—German men."[437] After mentioning this, Schoenichen expounded how the racial element had not been nearly as pronounced as it should have been during the Weimar Republic, but, thanks to Hitler, that has all changed. "The words '*volkisch*' or 'national' could only be spoken softly, and whoever spoke them found no listeners in official Germany—until *Der Fuhrer* arrived and won over all hearts with the power of his preaching: away with the liberal-marxist[438] rationalism that had led our whole culture on a course alienated from Nature. . . . And return to the ancient strengths of blood and soil that offers the source of life for our entire people."[439] Thus, even communism was also considered an international nature-hating Jewish heresy.[440] Indeed, Karl Marx was Jewish,

---

[435]   Ibid., p. 2.

[436]   Sax, p. 119.

[437]   *Naturschutz* 15 (1933/34): 8, quoted by Dominick p. 99.

[438]   The Nazis called classical liberalism—the libertarian liberalism of the founding fathers of the United States who strongly believed in the free-market enterprise—liberalism which, oddly enough, today is called the political *right* or *conservative*.

[439]   *Naturschutz* 15 (1933/34): 8, quoted by Dominick p. 99.

[440]   Pois rightly remarks, "It is of some importance to note ... that the Marxian tradition, with its strongly humanistic overtones and its emphasis upon the singularity of the creative human spirit—to say nothing of its own permutation or chiliasm—was very much rooted in that Judeo-Christian tradition which it has felt constrained to combat

and many of the original Bolsheviks who began the Russian Communist revolution were assumed to be Jews. As such, Hitler concluded, "The world of Judeo-Bolshevism must collapse."[441] In his infamous "Total War Speech" given in 1943, Nazi Party propaganda chief Josef Goebbels even went so far as to compare communism and capitalism alike as vast Jewish conspiracies. "The goal of Bolshevism is Jewish world revolution. They want to bring chaos to the Reich and Europe, using the resulting hopelessness and desperation to establish their international, Bolshevist-concealed capitalist tyranny."[442]

Schoenhichen believed, "Capitalism and communism alike pollute air and water, annihilate farmland and forests, destroy the habitats necessary for the preservation of species diversity, and exterminate native peoples."[443] In October 1933, and very typical of Nazi environmentalists in general, Schoenichen wrote in the periodical *Naturshutz* that the German landscape must be cleansed of the "un-German spirit of commerce."[444] Earlier, Schoenichen bemoaned "the unscrupulous thirst for profit that holds nothing as holy or worthy of reverence except the welfare of the cash register."[445]

Like the *volkisch* Romantics and Monists before them, the Nazis blamed the humanistic emphasis found in the Judeo-Christian worldview for this widespread environmental destruction. They believed the Judeo-Christian worldview artificially separated man from nature. "The Nazis retained continuity with the traditions of nature preservationists and Romantic protest in one essential respect—they were not anthropocentric."[446] Hitler

---

in the name of ideological purity. This sharply separates, always hypothetically and usually in practice, the Soviet Communism approach towards religion from that of the National Socialists. In sum, the Marxist approach, hypothetically and in practice, must be seen as emerging dialectically from an ideational background itself Judeo-Christian in character. Thus, the Marxist antipathy to religion cannot be viewed as representing a rebellion against it, even if one bears in mind such quasi-pagan absurdities as worship of Stalin and the placing on permanent display of an at least partially authentic Lenin. Nazism was most definitely a rebellion against the Judeo-Christian tradition," p. 28.

[441] *Hitler's Table Talk*, midday of Feb. 27, 1942, p. 260.

[442] Bytwerk, Randall. *Landmark Speeches of the National Socialism.* College Station: Texas A & M University Press, 2008, p. 117.

[443] Zimmerman, *Ecofascism: An Enduring Temptation*, p. 3.

[444] Schoenichen, Walther, "Das deutsche Volk muß gereinigt werden – Und die deutsche Landschaft?" *Naturshutz* 14, no. 11 (1933): 207, quoted by Charles Closmann, *How Green Were the Nazis?* p. 28.

[445] Shoenichen, Walther. Quoted in Dominick, "Nazis and Nature Conservationists," 514.

[446] Sax, p. 42.

himself flatly stated in 1941: "It's senseless to encourage man in the idea that he's a king of creation."[447]

The Nazis considered the Judeo-Christian belief that man was the king of the created order to be both alien and unnatural. They believed such a position led to an improper arrogation of man over nature that helped foster and promote the disorderly and chaotic city life. This, in turn, invariably led to the biological degradation of society. Hitler especially considered the Jew to be the primary parasite of the city that was leeching off of society like an open sore: "As soon as the Jews were allowed to stick their noses out of the ghetto, the sense of honor and loyalty in trade began to melt away."[448]

The Nazis were trying to eliminate both global capitalism and international communism in order to recover a reverence for nature lost in the modern cosmopolitan world. In the big cities, both international capitalism and communism opposed each other bitterly so that it also divided the German *volk* against itself. In the Nazi mind, both political systems were artificially built on the universal values found in the Judeo-Christian worldview. Both capitalism and communism destroyed man's proper racial relationship to nature. "The Nazi religion ... was singular in its effort to consciously supplant Judeo-Christian forms, and to offer in their place a religion of nature congruent with the perceived needs of a people uprooted from nature."[449]

The Blood and Soil of National Socialism
vs. the Judeo-Christian Worldview

In truth, the Nazi blood and soil ideology was a religious war against the Judeo-Christian worldview, with Jews being the primary target. In his book *The Myth of the 20ᵗʰ Century*, Alfred Rosenberg described history "as a battle between the Aryan and Semitic forces in the world. The Semitic forces included Christianity, which through Paul had been integrated into Judaism."[450] Rosenberg was probably expanding Hitler's statements in *Mein Kampf* when he wrote, "The mightiest counterpart to the Aryan is represented by the Jew."[451] Dr. Mengele of Auschwitz believed the greatest threat

---

[447] *Hitler's Table Talk*, evening of Oct. 24, 1941, p. 68.

[448] Ibid., dinner on March 29, 1942, p. 283.

[449] Pois., p. 28.

[450] Von Campe, Hilmar. *Defeating the Totalitarian Lie*, Crane: HighWay, 2008, p. 46.

[451] Hitler, *Mein Kampf*, p. 300.

to the German race was the Jewish race. Mengele believed there were only two gifted peoples in the world, i.e., Germans and Jews.[452] Could it be that behind the *scientific* veneer of racial eugenics, what was really at stake was a religious war against the Judeo-Christian tradition? Indeed, Holocaust expert Raul Hilberg points out that the Jews were identified and segregated in Nazi Germany not by their race, but by the religion of their grandparents. Hilberg then quips, "After all, the Nazis were not interested in the Jewish nose. They were concerned with the Jewish influence."[453] In short, it was virtually impossible to identify the Jews racially. Thus, contrary to their racist worldview, the Nazis were forced to identify the Jews by their religion.

National Socialism and its religion of nature was a two-pronged rebellion against the Judeo-Christian worldview. It included an overt public attack against the Judeo side of the hyphen for economic and political reasons, and a covert operation against the Christian side of the hyphen for religious reasons. The Nazis charged that Christianity had turned Judaism into a subtle form of international corruption. This, in turn, helped justify the more mundane Jewish exploitation of Germany at the political-economic level:

> At times, the Nazis seemed uncertain as to precisely which aspects of the Judeo-Christian tradition they found most disturbing. Often it was that "otherworldliness" so strongly attacked by Brachman. At other times, though, the Nazis focused attacks upon what they perceived to be the mundane and materialistic aspects of Judaism in particular.[454]

Dr. J. Spelter charged that Christianity masked the hatred of the Jewish God in a "cloak of love."[455] He further charged that Christianity was especially "pernicious since it amounted to a triumph of Judaism, albeit in veiled form."[456]

The infamous conspiratorial tract entitled "The Protocols of the Elders of Zion" propagated a Jewish Zionist conspiracy to take over the world.

---

[452] Posner & Ware, p. 27.

[453] Hilberg, vol. 1, p. 68.

[454] Pois, p. 46.

[455] Spelter, Dr. J. *Der Deutsche Erzjejer als Lehrer der Rassenkunde*, p. 32 quoted by Pois, p. 47.

[456] Pois, p. 47.

Hitler quoted the hoax in *Mein Kampf*[457] as a fact of history. "The Protocols became a key element in Hitler's conspiratorial thinking, for it was used to explain the apocalyptic chaos. The international Jewish bankers, he argued, had created hyperinflation that had forced Germans into epidemic hunger, making them pliant in the face of a Jewish-Bolshevik type revolution and thereby taking another step toward the creation of the Jewish millennial paradise of world domination."[458] The Jewish eschaton of world domination and peace under the leadership of the Messiah is specifically taught throughout the Old Testament, and even everywhere assumed in the New Testament, as well. It was this Judeo-Christian eschaton which the Nazis willfully confused with Judeo-Christian Bolshevism (Soviet Communism) that they so violently opposed. The Nazis were thus plotting an apocalyptic counteroffensive based on their own blood and soil to stop it.

In his "Bolshevism from Moses to Lenin" pamphlet that was supposedly based on a conversation with Hitler, Dietrich Eckart often used Old Testament historical passages depicting Hebrew victory over their enemies as a tool to show how violent, prejudiced and bloodthirsty the Jews really were. Though Eckart died in December of 1923, he was the spiritual fountainhead of National Socialism. He mentored and inspired Hitler to take on a greater political leadership role. Hitler dedicated *Mein Kampf* to Eckart in memory of all that he had done for him and the National Socialist revolution. Not surprisingly, in his dialogue with Hitler, Eckart always sided against the Jews.

Joshua's conquest of the promised land was depicted by Eckart as a Jewish desire to crush the Gentiles. According to Eckart, the fall of Jericho was a vicious attack of cold-blooded mass murder. Elijah murdered 450 pagan priests and had the Israelites commit genocide against the followers of Baalism. Queen Esther and Mordecai conspired to murder 75,000 Persians. Israel's exodus from Egypt was used by Eckart as a justification to expel the Jews from Germany. In fact, as far as Eckart was concerned, the entire Old Testament was a book of hate. In his review of the New Testament, Eckart even claimed that Jesus was anti-Semitic, but this fact was later obscured by the mass murderer, the Apostle Paul. Eckart then continued his interpretive escapade throughout the centuries to lead his readers to the doorstep of Jewish Bolshevism orchestrated by Karl Marx

---

[457] Hitler, *Mein Kampf*, p. 307.
[458] Redles, p. 58.

and Vladimir Lenin. Eckart then concluded, "The Jews first utilized the Mosaic Law, then Christianity, and now Bolshevism to inspire commoners to overthrow the nations."[459]

The communist takeover of the world was thus viewed by the Nazis as a Jewish-Christian conspiracy that must be stopped at all costs to protect the German *volk* from international extinction. Hitler believed that primitive Christianity was the "first Jewish-Communistic cell."[460] The Nazis therefore propounded their own Millennium, the 1,000-year Reich. Revelation 20 promises to its readers a 1,000-year Judeo-Christian millennium at the end of history under the Messiah's rule. The Nazi 1,000-year Reich was propagated as a counterculture millenarianism directly opposed to the very originators of the millennial/apocalyptic worldview—Jews and Christians.

Instead of the Jewish-Christian apocalypse based on Biblical history and prophecy, the Nazi millennium was based on the evolutionary progress of the German race as it submits to the tenets of Nature. "What was of ultimate, indeed chiliastic, significance was the emergence, one totally in keeping with the laws of nature."[461] Even the Nazi blood and soil doctrine countered the history of the Jewish race living in the promised land of Israel. Instead of the Mosaic law which commanded love for both God and man, the blood and soil doctrine of the Nazis promoted survival of the fittest and a racial hatred in the name of Nature—a veritable environmental ethic of barbaric proportions. Instead of the promised land of Abraham, Isaac and Jacob, many Nazis considered the German fatherland to be the promised land of Europe. Instead of being elected solely by God's grace as the chosen people of God, the Nazi salvation program was based on a fascist understanding of progressive evolutionary pantheism. Perhaps worst of all, the Nazis purposefully blurred the distinction between secular history and the apocalypse. They believed they had to help usher in the final eschaton. This is at complete odds with the Biblical view that predicts almost all people will be caught completely surprised by its inauguration (1 Thess. 5:1-3).

Leading Nazis were hell-bent on bringing about the "Final Solution" of the Jewish question, which sharply distinguishes other genocides from the Holocaust. In great contrast to the many genocides of the 20th century,

---

[459] Tyson, p. 363.
[460] Dietrich, p. 127.
[461] Pois, p. 117.

only the Holocaust was carried out with a *final solution* in mind. In short, as far as leading Nazis were concerned, the Final Solution was eschatological. It was an invention of misplaced Nazi eschatology that believed the total annihilation of European Jewry would bring about a sunny era of Aryan salvation that would relinquish both capitalism and communism from Jewish control that had infected the continent for centuries with artificial values and practices alien to Germany, in particular. The Nazis actually believed they were providentially ushering in a new world order of racial salvation that likewise included the protection of its native homeland and environment. "The Nazis hoped to stop the decomposing effects of chaos, renew the spiritual health of the *volk*, and usher in the millennial Reich."[462] This, however, required a final apocalyptic battle against what the Nazis called Judeo-Christian Bolshevism. As such, instead of the great tribulation predicting God's ultimate judgment upon the Earth to cleanse it from sin, the Nazis looked forward to a final battle to the death with Jewish Bolshevism[463] that would open up Aryan *lebensraum* to sustain them for centuries to come. Indeed, during the heights of World War II, SS Jewish *expert* Adolf Eichmann was "absolutely convinced that if he could succeed in destroying the biological basis of Jewry in the east by complete extermination, then Jewry as a whole would never recover from the blow. The assimilated Jews in the West, including America, would, in his opinion, be in no position to make up this enormous loss of blood and there would be no future generation worth mentioning."[464]

While it is true that Hitler saw the whole so-called Jewish problem as a strict racial one, even to the point of denying the Jews their religion,[465] his own views on race were anything but scientific. They were, in fact, very religious and *volkisch*, even though he sometimes tried to distance himself from the naivety of some *volkisch* circles. Though Hitler himself was not a mystical blood and soil ideologue like so many of his SS followers, he certainly did not disparage the slogan.[466] Hitler had a final solution in mind for the unnatural, uprooted conditions of modern Germany—get rid of the

---

[462] Redles, p. 73.
[463] Ibid., p. 65.
[464] Hoess, p. 215.
[465] Hitler, *Mein Kampf*, pp. 306-308.
[466] Dominick, p. 93. Gasman points out "in *Mein Kampf*, Hitler, despite his criticism of the political ineptitude and naivete of the *Volkists*, made use of the broad concept of the *Volk* and of the *Volkisch* state to describe his vision of a racially powerful and united Germany," *The Scientific Origins of National Socialism*, p. xlvii.

Jew—and the secular religion of nature that was National Socialism would be the very vehicle to do just that. "For Hitler the bringer of the knowledge of good and evil on the earth, the destroyer of Eden, was the Jew. It was the Jew who told humans that they were above other animals, and had the capacity to decide their future for themselves. It was the Jew who introduced the false distinction between politics and nature, between humanity and struggle. Hitler's destiny, as he saw it, was to redeem the original sin of Jewish spirituality and restore the paradise of blood."[467]

As such, Hitler viewed the Jew as the unnatural man incarnate[468] who bred humanistic chaos and confusion into nature by attempting to overturn her Social Darwinian racial laws of bloody struggle and survival:

> Races followed nature and fought for land and food, whereas Jews followed the alien logic of "un-nature." They resisted nature's basic imperative by refusing to be satisfied by the conquest of a certain habitat, and they persuaded others to behave similarly. They insisted on dominating the entire planet and its peoples, and for this purpose invented general ideas that draw the races away from the natural struggle. The planet had nothing to offer except blood and soil, and yet Jews uncannily generated concepts that allowed the world to be seen less as an ecological trap and more as a human order. Ideas of political reciprocity, practices in which humans recognize other humans as such, came from Jews. Hitler's basic critique was not the usual one that human beings were good but had been corrupted by an overly Jewish civilization. It was rather that humans were animals and that any exercise of ethical deliberation was in itself a sign of Jewish corruption. The very attempt to set a universal ideal and strain towards it was precisely what was hateful.[469]

Hitler complained that the Jews tried to conquer nature through what he considered an international *pacifism*, which was contrary to natural law.[470] By this, Hitler meant that the Jews tried to pacify the laws of nature through their false economic materialism, whether of capitalistic or communistic variety. While capitalism led to superficial commercialism,

---

[467] Snyder, p. 4.
[468] Stern, p. 40.
[469] Snyder, p. 5.
[470] Hitler, *Mein Kampf*, p. 287.

communism too was based on the industrial economic theories of Karl Marx. Hitler considered both capitalism and communism to be helplessly materialistic. Worse, they both try to tame or pacify nature in the name of economic materialism in one way or another. "Here of course we encounter the objection of the modern pacifist, as truly Jewish in its effrontery as it is stupid! Man's role is to overcome Nature! Millions thoughtlessly parrot this Jewish nonsense and end up by really imagining that they themselves represent a kind of conqueror of Nature."[471]

Heinrich Himmler often complained how Christianity was also in-debted to the same Jewish heresy of domination over nature.[472] The Nazi philosopher Martin Heidegger disqualified Christianity as a Jewish phe-nomenon now dominating the world through democratization in the West or communism in the East.[473] According to Hitler, Jewish materialism was a gigantic vain attempt to pacify or tame nature. "Assuredly, however, by far the harder fate is that which strikes the man who thinks he can overcome Nature, but in the last analysis only mocks her. Distress, misfortune, and disease are her answer."[474] Hitler, of course, was more than willing to give nature a helping hand in this evolutionary process through a violent form of anti-Semitic eugenics.

Hitler also viewed Christianity as a similar "rebellion against natural law, a protest against nature."[475] Hitler thus strongly believed that when man conforms to nature, he will eventually do away with the Judeo-Christian worldview that had led to the ruin of Europe by proliferating weakness and pacifism. Hitler and the Nazis were hell-bent on reinvigorating Europe by shedding the Judeo-Christian worldview which contradicted nature:

> Hitler argued that Western civilization had obscured the true re-lationship between man and nature. Somewhere along the line man's knowledge and understanding of himself had gone awry. Not surprisingly, for Hitler, the culprit was Christianity. For 2,000 years Europe had been trying to convince itself that man was not really part of nature, and that had led to the continual decline of civilization after the fall of the ancient world. Consequently, in

---

[471] Ibid, p. 287.
[472] Pois, p. 48.
[473] Faye, p. 283.
[474] Hitler, *Mein Kampf*, p. 289.
[475] *Hitler's Table Talk*, midday Oct. 10, 1941, p. 41.

Tischgesprache, Hitler dwelt inordinately on the evils of Christianity and offered the Germans a new faith which was to be rooted in nature.[476]

Joseph Goebbels concluded, "Both (Judaism and Christianity) have no point of contact to the animal element, and thus, they will be destroyed."[477]

For Hitler, pacifism was not the way of Nature. Nature cannot be tamed by man, but on the contrary, man must obey Nature. In Hitler's holistic social Darwinism, this meant the survival of the fittest applied to human beings as well, and Jewish pacifism was a false attempt to overthrow this pantheistic natural law. In other words, the Jews tried to avoid or escape natural instinct through pacifism. They were thus not authentic. "In Hitler's ecology, the planet was despoiled by the presence of the Jews who defied the laws of nature by introducing corrupting ideas. The solution was to expose Jews to a purified nature, a place where bloody struggle rather than abstract thought mattered, where Jews could not manipulate others with their ideas because there would be no others."[478]

In Hitler's mind, Jewish pacifism also allowed weaklings to live, which led to the degeneration of races and nations. Hitler believed it is the strong who should starve the weak, but bitterly complained it was the Jews who "could arrange matters so that weak starve the strong." This weakening of the race from within would thus be corrected by getting Nazi Germany back to the bloody laws of the jungle. In other words, Hitler would use the power of the state to force the hand of nature upon its citizenry through the social scientific application of eugenics. Hitler wrote, "In general, Nature herself usually makes certain corrective decisions with regard to racial purity of earthly creatures. She has little love for bastards."[479] As such, the state is required to follow nature's lead and "demand the subordination of the inferior and weaker in accordance with the eternal will that dominates this universe. Thus, in principle, it serves the basic aristocratic idea of Nature and believes in the validity of this law down to the last individual."[480] The

---

[476] Gasman, *The Scientific Origins of National Socialism*, p. 165.
[477] Arnold Arluke and Boria Sax, "Understanding Nazi Animal Protection and the Holocaust," *Anthrozoos* 5 (1992); 18, quoted by Proctor. *The Nazi War on Cancer*, Princeton University Press, 1999, p. 136.
[478] Snyder, p. 28.
[479] Hitler, *Mein Kampf*, p. 400.
[480] Ibid., p. 383.

rebellion of man against nature must, therefore, be quelled by the state. Nature is a king or dictator which must be obeyed with the coercive help of the state. Hitler strongly believed "nature was a singular, brutal, and overwhelming truth, and the whole history of attempting to think otherwise was an illusion."[481]

Hitler and the Nazis strangely reversed the English Victorian beliefs which held that civilization was orderly but nature was both lawless and chaotic. "Nature became a realm of absolute order, opposed to the anarchy brought on by civilization. In imposing inflexible authoritarian rule, the Nazis believed they were restoring the natural order to society."[482] Social Darwinism demanded the political application of eugenics to society at large. In *Mein Kampf*, Hitler said, "In the struggle for daily bread all those who are weak and sickly or less determined, succumb, while the struggle of the males for the female grants the right or opportunity to propagate only to the healthiest. And struggle is always a means for improving a species' health and power of resistance, and therefore, a cause of its higher development."[483] Because of his evolutionary racial naturalism, Hitler was amoral. In great contrast to Judeo-Christian ethics, Hitler "embraced an evolutionary ethic that made Darwinian fitness and health the only criteria for moral standards. The Darwinian struggle for existence, especially the struggle between different races, became the sole arbiter for morality."[484]

Nazi press chief Otto Dietrich credited Hitler's lack of morality to be specifically attributed to his philosophy of nature. Dietrich asserted, "Both in public speeches and private conversation he would repeatedly refer to this philosophy, his purpose being to convince his listeners that this philosophy represented the final truth about life. He took such principles as the struggle for existence, the survival of the fittest and strongest, for the law of nature, and considered them a 'higher imperative' which should also rule in the community life of men. It followed for him that might was right, that his own violent methods were therefore absolutely in keeping with the laws of nature."[485] Based on what is often observed in nature, Hitler concluded that racial Social Darwinism was an ethic to be adhered to at all costs.

---

[481]   Snyder, p. 2.
[482]   Sax, p. 41.
[483]   Hitler, *Mein Kampf,* p. 285.
[484]   Weikart, *From Darwin to Hitler,* p. 210.
[485]   Dietrich, p. 11.

In reality, Hitler's evolutionary scientism was a naturalistic religion, even though he prided himself in the secularity of modern German thought. "For Hitler ... Social Darwinism was not simply the idea of struggle. It was the holy conception of nature."[486] It was thus an evolving secular religion of nature opposed to the transcendentalism of the Judeo-Christian worldview. "What Hitler had done was to wed a putatively scientific view of the universe to a form of pantheistic mysticism presumably congruent with adherence to 'natural laws.' In this, he bore a marked resemblance to such Darwinians as Ernst Haeckel who, as is well known, informed their scientific endeavors with large doses of Romanticism."[487] Hitler was a pantheist of sorts.[488] His holistic vision between man and nature was total and comprehensive. "The broad masses are only a piece of Nature."[489] Man is completely subject to the natural world. He must obey its stern laws which he cannot rise above, and Hitler himself would see to it that this was indeed the case. "By extending control almost without limit the Nazis thought they would become nature itself, harsh and implacable yet always orderly."[490]

In short, while following along *scientific* Monistic lines, Hitler believed salvation was to be found in the "study of nature and in the worship of its diverse forms and beauties."[491] Hitler stated, "I think the man who contemplates the universe with his eyes wide open is the man with the greatest amount of natural piety; not in the religious sense, but in the sense of an intimate harmony with things."[492] He also believed, "It is possible to satisfy the needs of the inner life by an intimate communion with nature."[493]

At the same time, Hitler specifically stated, "The man who lives in communion with nature necessarily finds himself in opposition to the Churches. And that's why they're heading for ruin—for science is bound to win."[494] Hitler thus believed the scientific study of nature would destroy what he considered to be the superstitions of the Judeo-Christian worldview.[495]

---

[486] Gasman, *The Scientific Origins of National Socialism*, p. 162.

[487] Pois, pp. 39-40.

[488] For the most authoritative book on this discussion, please see Dr. Richard Weikart's *Hitler's Religion: The Twisted Beliefs that Drove the Third Reich*. Washington D.C.: Regnery History, 2016.

[489] Hitler, *Mein Kampf*, p. 338.

[490] Sax, p. 42.

[491] Gasman, *The Scientific Origins of National Socialism*, p. 169.

[492] *Hitler's Table Talk*, night of July 11-12, 1941, p. 7.

[493] Ibid., midday of Oct. 14, 1941, p. 48.

[494] Ibid., p. 49.

[495] Gasman, *The Scientific Origins of National Socialism*, p. 169.

Along similar lines, Nazi Party leader Martin Bormann said, "When we National Socialists speak of a belief in God, we do not mean what naïve Christians and their clerical expositors have in mind … the power of Nature's law is what we call the omnipotent force or God."[496] The Nazis believed in an evolutionary pantheism where biology, ecology and a religion of nature were all hotwired together in a violent survival of the fittest scheme that would not be undone until the Allies declared victory in the spring of 1945. In great contrast to the Judeo-Christian God of love, what the Nazis emphasized was "the cruel struggle for existence, one in which the most natural of peoples would survive."[497]

Martin Heidegger's Blood and Soil Existentialism

Friedrich Nietzsche's (1844-1900) anti-Christian existentialist philosophy was also used by the Nazis. Next to Schopenhauer, Hitler's second favorite philosopher was Friedrich Nietzsche.[498] The Nazis essentially made the Nietzsche Archives of Weimar the "official shrine of their regime after 1933"[499] where the green Nazi philosopher[500] Martin Heidegger (1889-1976)[501] spent much time (1935-42).[502] Many scholars have tried to show that Heidegger resigned from his philosophical chair from the University of Freiburg in 1934 as some kind of token opposition against the Nazis, but this is simply untrue. On the contrary, Heidegger did not resign because he opposed the Nazis, but because his attempt to Nazify the university met with stiff opposition. Heidegger decided to devote himself more fully to Nietzsche. Why? To Nazify Nietzsche for National Socialist consumption. Even as late

---

[496]   Sax, p. 106.

[497]   Pois., p. 43.

[498]   Kubizek, August. *The Young Hitler I Knew*, p. 136. Strangely, more than a few scholars have stated that there is no evidence that Hitler ever read Nietzsche. Yet Hitler's friend in his youth, August Kubizek, clearly said Hitler "always had his Schopenhauer by him, later Nietzsche too." In an earlier edition of his book entitled *The Young Hitler I Knew*, which included a chapter 6 called "School," Kubizek said that Hitler devoured the library in his youth and that, "I remember Adolf as always surrounded by books." In case he be misunderstood, Kubizek said again, "Books were his whole world." p. 134. With such testimony, it is actually hard to believe that Hitler did not read Nietzsche, a popular critical thinker in Germany's history.

[499]   Faye, p. 252.

[500]   See "The Green Nazi Deep Ecology of Martin Heidegger" by Mark Musser, *The American Thinker*, July 10, 2011 (Internet Website).

[501]   Uekoetter calls Martin Heidegger one of the who's who of German conservationism in 1934, p. 93.

[502]   Faye, p. 252.

as 1944, Heidegger claimed that Nietzsche was the spiritual inspiration of Hitler.[503] "As one Nazi functionary said, whoever says 'Heil Hitler!' at the same time is saluting Nietzsche's philosophy."[504]

While it is true that Nietzsche was not a racist anti-Semite, he still "castigated the Jews for their ideas and their ethics, particularly as they manifest themselves in Christianity."[505] Nietzsche considered Christianity a Jewish invention. His scorn for Christianity, therefore, is proof of his dim view of Judaism as well. Following Schopenhauer, Nietzsche sometimes even spoke of the "odor of the Jews" in his writings. Nietzsche considered both Judaism and Christianity to be religious systems of slavery run by slaves that elevate the weak and downtrodden at the expense of the strong and the elite. "From this successful revolution of the unfit issued eventually the French Revolution, democracy, the emancipation of women, socialism, and other manifestations of what Nietzsche saw as the total decadence of society."[506] According to Nietzsche, Judeo-Christian morality invariably promotes mediocrity where mass culture and the herd instinct dominate society so that it invariably becomes superficial, feeble, and worthless. While Marx derided what he deemed to be empty theological abstractions that artificially controlled the masses, "Nietzsche believed the opposite, that Christianity was a means by which the powerless—by manipulating guilt, requiring benevolence, and surpassing natural vitality—could enchain the powerful."[507]

Nature and philosophical existentialism were used by Nietzsche[508] to disguise his hatred for Christianity since its heavenly emphasis mocked the Earth and its real flesh and blood existence. "At the heart of Nietzsche's philosophy is his contempt for abstractions. In his desire to affirm this life, he rejected the transcendental categories of reason and morality."[509] Writing *Thus Spake Zarathustra* from the spectacular Engadine Alps in Switzerland, Nietzsche blurted out, "I beseech you my brothers, remain faithful to the

---

[503] Ibid., p. 105.

[504] Veith, Gene. *Modern Fascism: The Threat to the Judeo-Christian Worldview.* St. Louis: Concordia Press, 1993, p. 82.

[505] Ibid.

[506] Ibid., p. 83.

[507] Ibid., pp. 82-83.

[508] See "Friedrich Nietzsche and his Proto-Nazi Eco-Fascism" by Mark Musser, *The American Thinker,* November 27, 2011.

[509] Veith, p. 82.

earth, and do not believe those who speak to you of other worldly hopes!"[510] This is not far removed from Hitler's own comments, "When man attempts to rebel against the iron logic of Nature, he comes into struggle with the principles to which he himself owes his existence as a man. And this attack must lead to his doom."[511] Nietzsche also added that since God was now dead, "To sin against the earth is now the most dreadful thing."[512] Hitler harmonizes with his philosophical forerunner when he remarked that what is required of man is to "conform to the laws of nature."[513]

Nietzsche's use of the word *Earth* is ever present throughout his most personal work, *Thus Spake Zarathustra*. The existence of the Earth is specifically used by Nietzsche to contrast it with heaven and its alleged corrupting otherworldly emphasis. Nietzsche expert J.P. Stern noted, "The normative idea of Nature—Nature as a model of human existence—exercises a profound attraction on Nietzsche; it is certainly one scheme of values that is not subject to his scathing criticism."[514] Nietzsche's infamous "God is dead" theology is inextricably bound up with this earthly existentialism. His so-called *superman* ethos is also cut from the same cloth. Nietzsche's desire was to replace what he calls the Judeo-Christian slave morality of weakness and meekness with strong masculine values like heroism, strength and courage. This is the heart of Nietzsche's "beyond good and evil" doctrine, if not also his "will to power" creed.

Since God is dead, men must become supermen in order to legislate a new set of values for the future based on biology and instinct rather than upon Western rationality and ethics. Western rationality has shown that God is dead. It therefore must be transcended by a new set of values in order to avoid the dangerous meaningless of nihilism. Since Nietzsche believed the weakest part of man was his rational consciousness, and that biology, body, willpower and instinct were his strengths, these new set of values governing the future would have to transcend the Enlightenment. Nietzsche thus recommended humanity must utilize state-prescribed breeding programs in order to weed out the weak from the strong. Nietzsche also assumed that war and conflict were at the vortex of human evolution and growth.

---

510 Nietzsche, *Thus Spake Zarathustra: A Book for None and All*, translated by Walter Kaufmann. New York: Penguin Books, 1966 (1954), p. 13.
511 Hitler, Adolf. *Mein Kampf*, p. 287.
512 Nietzsche, *Thus Spake Zarathustra*, p. 13.
513 *Hitler's Table Talk*, midday Sept. 23, 1941, p. 32.
514 Stern, p. 39.

Thus, Nietzsche's "will to power" was not an attempt to dominate nature, but was to be in accordance with nature, and rooted in an Earth-based evolutionary existentialism.

Nietzsche ridiculed the Christian emphasis on love as being womanly and weak, very much like Nazi chauvinistic values. In the place of Judeo-Christian love, Nietzsche emphasized harsh male virtues and even strongly stated Christianity "is the greatest of all conceivable corruptions. . . . I call it the one immortal blemish of mankind."[515] Heinrich Himmler agreed. He said Christianity was "a perverse *Weltanschauung* (worldview) estranged from life (nature & its natural laws)"[516]and was "the greatest pestilence in history which has befallen us."[517]

In his lesser-known second book called *Zweites Buch* or *Second Book*, Hitler said religious ascetics cannot avoid the realities of natural instinct because, "though the fleshless aesthete may lodge a thousand protests against such an assertion, the fact of his own existence is already a refutation of his protest. Nothing that is made of flesh and blood can escape the laws which determined its coming into being. As soon as the human mind believes itself to be superior to them, it destroys that real substance which is the bearer of the mind."[518] The *Fuhrer's* statement strongly suggests that Hitler's Social Darwinism was not just informed by Ernst Haeckel's biological scientism, but also by Nietzsche's natural existentialism.[519] Where Haeckel trails off and Nietzsche begins is actually very difficult to decipher.

Martin Heidegger's strong interest in Nietzsche during his tenure under National Socialism is thus no trifling matter. Martin Heidegger built the fascist bridge between Nietzsche's natural existentialism and what is

---

[515] Nietzsche, Friedrich. *Antichrist: A Criticism of Christianity*, translated by Anthony Ludovici. New York: Barnes & Noble, 2006, (1895), pp. 74-75.

[516] Ackerman, Josef. *Heinrich Himmler*, p. 92 quoted by Pois, p. 55.

[517] Ibid.

[518] Hitler, *Zweites Buch*, p. 4.

[519] The subtle nuances that exist between Haeckel's Social Darwinism and National Socialism is best explained by this nature-based existentialism. Hitler's love for Arthur Schopenhauer only strengthens the existential connection even further. Schopenhauer could easily be considered one of the first existentialists in the modern sense, and Nietzsche borrowed heavily from his teacher. In fact, Nietzsche's "Will to Power" was certainly mined from Schopenhauer's pessimistic masterpiece, *The World as Will and Representation*. For both men, the concept of natural will was more important than thought. Hitler kept Schopenhauer's book with him during World War I on the despairing front lines of trench warfare. Herein lies the academic background to the cultic Nazi will to power emphasis. This was perfectly showcased in Leni Riefenstahl's infamous documentary film, *Triumph of the Will*.

today called deep ecology. Heidegger was a green existentialist philosopher who was far more compromised with Nazism than many scholars have presumed. Many Western students of Heidegger have been so enamored with his existentialist philosophy that it has been very difficult for them to accept the fact that he could be a real Nazi.

Environmental historians in particular have been quick to cover[520] for Heidegger because he is such a critical figure in modern existential green philosophy. Others have tried to place distance between Heidegger's existentialism and deep ecology.[521] They are anxious to spare deep ecology the charge of environmental fascism. Heidegger is known among environmental philosophers for later advocating an anti-technology *let it be* attitude toward nature after his so-called turning from National Socialism. However, Heidegger's turning from National Socialism is a modern myth built on outright lies and the later redaction of his earlier materials hidden under dense language and opaque existentialism.[522] Even today, some of Heidegger's works are strictly controlled by his family.[523] Martin Heidegger was an unrepentant Nazi. Even after the war he spoke of the inner truth and greatness of National Socialism.

The idea that Heidegger temporarily strayed into Nazism only to later recover himself with a much more mature existentialist philosophy is simply untenable. In fact, it is far more likely Heidegger managed to infiltrate much of the postmodern world with a more developed Nazi political philosophy,[524] and his brand of environmental existentialism is at the heart of the cover-up. Even after the war, Heidegger still believed in order to save the planet, Western philosophy built on the Judeo-Christian worldview must be extinguished. With its transcendental emphasis upon mind, thinking and thought, both classic Western philosophy and the Judeo-Christian worldview elevate rootless contemplation over the reality of existence. As far as Heidegger was concerned, this has led Western man into an inauthentic lifestyle contrary to the natural world grounded in what Heidegger called *being*.

---

[520] See especially "Martin Heidegger, National Socialism, and Environmentalism" by Thomas Rohkramer in *How Green Were the Nazis?*, pp. 171-203.

[521] See "Rethinking the Heidegger Deep Ecology Relationship," by Michael Zimmerman originally written for *Environmental Ethics* in the early 1990s.

[522] See Emmanuel Faye's *Heidegger: The Introduction of Nazism into Philosophy in Light of the Unpublished Seminars 1933-35.*

[523] Faye, p. xvii.

[524] Ibid., pp. 203-322.

Existentialism is very fertile ground upon which to develop an environmental philosophy. Existentialism uses natural existence or *being* to trump rational or religious thought that heightens itself above the natural world. Nature and its holistic interrelatedness thus become trump cards to neutralize both philosophy and religious faith as inconsistent with what actually exists in the real world. Religious and philosophical thought needs to bow to nature and its existence, rather than to try to arrogate itself above them through imaginary ideas and concerns, especially of the Christian theological variety. For Heidegger, religious and Western speculative thought invariably leads to a false, dominating view over nature, which has become especially superficial in the modern mechanized world. For Heidegger, therefore, what needs to be done is to destroy Western philosophy and its Judeo-Christian handmaid. The main thrust of Heidegger's political philosophy is to reduce all metaphysics to the question of *being* or existence.[525] In so doing, Western man's alienating and destructive dominance over nature can be arrested.

In a speech given in November 1933, Heidegger proclaimed, "We are witnessing the end of philosophy that had idolized a thought deprived of soil and power."[526] That modern environmentalism has swept in behind the collapse of classic Western philosophy and the fading Judeo-Christian worldview is thus no accident. It is part and parcel of the whole modern denial of any transcendental truth or God that exists independent and outside of the natural world. Without such transcendental truths, all that is left is amoral nature and its factual existence, and Martin Heidegger has been leading this particular charge since his early days in the camp of National Socialism. As such, Heidegger vehemently attacked both Western morality and philosophy. Because of his radical existential views, "the very principles of philosophy are abolished. No place is left for morality, which is openly and radically annihilated."[527]

Although Heidegger did not join the Nazi Party until 1933, he was certainly very aware and supportive of the movement from its inception. Heidegger's wife, Elfride, was a Nazi enthusiast going back as far as the early 1920s.[528] She was very involved in the naturist Nazi youth groups of the time—a veritable evangelist of National Socialism. With inheritance money, she also purchased what later became known as Heidegger's hut or

---

[525]   Ibid., p. 249.
[526]   Ibid., p. 71.
[527]   Ibid., p. 316.
[528]   Ibid., p. 29.

chalet in the upper reaches of the Black Forest called *Todtnauberg*. The chalet had beautiful nearby valley views topped off by the Alps in the distance. From this very chalet would come the inspiration for much of Heidegger's environmental existentialism throughout his entire career. He also wrote in a newspaper article that he decided to turn down the most prestigious philosophical chair in Berlin to practice his philosophy at *Todtnauberg*, which ironically enough, means "mountain of death."[529] In the same year, Martin Heidegger signed an environmental petition called the "German Landscape in Peril."[530] Other Nazi greens who signed the petition included Paul Schultze-Naumburg, Walther Schoenichen, Hans Schwenkel, Konrad Guenther, Werner Haverbeck and Fritz Todt.[531]

Former students of Heidegger also confirmed he was a Nazi blood and soil environmental enthusiast throughout much of the 1920s.[532] One of them said Heidegger loved to hike and cross-country ski with his students where he often had much to say about the relationship between the German *volk* and nature. "He felt an intimate closeness to the word *volkisch* and said he was tied to the blood and the soil."[533] Heidegger bragged about the Nazi naturist youth movement as one of the keys to a successful future. Around 1930, Heidegger taught in one of his lectures that the essence of truth is *volkischly* rooted in the soil of the *heimat*.[534] Heidegger also believed that universal reason as practiced by modern philosophy since the Renaissance is contrary to the existential realities of blood and soil.[535] This is certainly the essence of Nazi existentialism.

In May of 1933, the Nazi journal called *Der Almanne* said of Heidegger, "We also know that he never made any mystery about his German convictions and that for many years he has supported in the most effective way the party of Adolf Hitler in his struggle for being and power."[536] This journal also affirmed Adolf Hitler's support of existentialism. In August of 1933, Hitler avoided jumping into a blood and soil debate between the Pan

---

[529] Emmanuel Faye says that this was a mask for his real intentions. Heidegger wanted to remain at the University of Freiburg so he could devote himself more fully to the Nazification process of the university there, pp. 46-48.

[530] Uekoetter, p. 92.

[531] Ibid., p. 93.

[532] Faye, p. 30.

[533] Ibid.

[534] Ibid., p. 35.

[535] Ibid., p. 38.

[536] Ibid., p. 31.

Germans who emphasized the importance of Nordic blood in general, and the view of other Nazi eugenicists who held that German blood itself was primary. Hitler rather surprisingly spoke of a racial existentialism that went beyond the typical biological categories.[537]

Many of Hitler's own writings in *Mein Kampf, Zweites Buch* and *Hitler's Table Talk* are peppered with existentialism, albeit a racist one. This is most certainly an inherited legacy from Nietzsche himself, who was later Nazified under Heidegger's own existential categories. There is also the very real possibility that Heidegger wrote some of Hitler's speeches. Heidegger expert Emmanuel Faye points out, "Anyone who, in his or her research, has had to carry out a close reading of Heidegger's speeches, lectures, and courses of the years 1933-34, as well as certain of Hitler's speeches of the same period, cannot but be quite struck by the similarity of style and doctrine between many passages in the two men's speeches."[538] Hitler was thus not a strict Haeckelian biological fundamentalist. He also accepted something similar to Heidegger's racism based on the essence of German *being* rooted in the German soil. How much of this was borrowed from Heidegger is difficult to say. Regardless, like Heidegger, Hitler seemed to have believed in a Social Darwinian existentialism of blood and soil.

Heidegger's Nazi radicalism was also observed in 1931 by another student who claimed the philosopher was convinced only a National Socialist dictatorship could oppose Marxism properly. He also said that violence, if not liquidation and assassination, against opponents was an acceptable solution to political problems.[539] Heidegger openly proclaimed the *Fuhrer* principle, German racism and eugenics, Nazi collectivism, and was even promoted as rector to the University of Freiburg when Jewish professors were being forcibly removed from their posts.

Heidegger proclaimed that the people of Germany were to be governed by an *erotic* love for the Nazi state.[540] Heidegger was also anti-Semitic. He often complained about the growing "Jewification" of society. Heidegger accepted in no uncertain terms the Nazi doctrine of *lebensraum*, and called the Jews in the eastern territories Semitic nomads.[541] This characterization essentially deprived the Jews of their living space in the Slavic East. Many of

---

[537] Ibid., p. 27.
[538] Ibid., p. 147.
[539] Ibid., p. 31.
[540] Ibid., p. 134.
[541] Ibid., pp. 142-144.

Heidegger's students during the 1930s would later fully immerse themselves in the fiery cauldron of World War II on the Eastern Front. Shockingly, many dead German soldiers on the battlefields of the Second World War possessed Heidegger's books in their rucksacks.[542]

In June of 1933, Martin Heidegger spoke at the Freiburg university stadium during a book burning ceremony. While un-German books were being publicly burned, Heidegger stated, "Flame announce to us, light for us, show the path from which there is no turning back."[543] Much of Heidegger's environmental, existential philosophy was specifically designed to do away with all thought he considered to be inauthentic. Heidegger's presence and words at the book burning of 1933 showcases a political ecological fascism in the name of existentialism.

More than a few environmental historians point out that since Heidegger did not believe in biological racism, he cannot be considered a genuine Nazi. However, Heidegger's opposition to biological racism had more to do with the fact he considered Darwinism an Anglo-Saxon construct[544] since Darwin was a Victorian Englishman. More importantly, in place of a literal, fundamentalist view of biological materialism, Heidegger taught a racial rootedness in the German soil that was ontologically or existentially grounded rather than biologically based.[545] Martin Heidegger's *Being and Time*, written in 1927, related authentic existence to the idea of "essence of being" rather than to something as literal as the blood. However, though Heidegger considered himself a philosopher, he never disavowed the Nazi doctrine of blood and soil. He merely repackaged it and undergirded it with philosophical categories rather than biological ones.

More importantly, in some ways, this existential or ontological enrootedness actually deepens his ties to Nazism further. In such a scenario, Nazi biologism could also easily fall under Heidegger's German existentialism without a contradiction per se. It also provides a philosophical justification for German racism without it being necessarily tied to the fundamentalism of Nazi scientism. This, in turn, provides a broader foundation for Nazi

---

[542] Heidegger critic Paul Hühnerfeld (1926-1960) stated, "These books, whose meaning was barely decipherable when they appeared, were devoured. And the young German soldiers in the Second World War who died somewhere in Russia or Africa with the writings of Hölderlin and Heidegger in their knapsacks can never be counted. Heidegger loved the German Romantic writer Friedrich Hölderlin (1770-1843).

[543] Faye, p. 53.

[544] Ibid., p. 36.

[545] Ibid., pp. 258-262.

doctrines to rest upon, pollinate and grow. Heidegger's fascism is thus built on environmental existentialism rather than biological scientism. Indeed, in his Heidelberg courses he enlightened his audience by saying, "The Fatherland is being itself."[546]

Nazi Biology as Eco-Fascism

More than a few Nazi ideologues characterized National Socialism as "politically applied biology." As such, the Nazis adopted an extreme literal reading of nature.[547] They were naturist fundamentalists. Since biology is a part of ecology, what the Nazis meant with regard to politically applied biology was that nature was to have primacy over politics. This would have devastating consequences with regard to the Jews in particular. To many Nazis, the great sin of Western Civilization was its incessant concern in trying to overcome nature according to Judeo-Christian values, something which the *Fuhrer* branded as "Jewish nonsense."[548] In the eyes of the Nazis, this self-defeating effort would finally come to an end through National Socialism. Indeed, natural instinct and will was more authentic than forced morality and behavior, especially as prescribed by the Judeo-Christian religion. "Man," Himmler stated before the SS in Berlin in a 1942 speech, "is nothing special."[549] To Nazis like Himmler, man was just a piece of Earth.[550]

In 1931, the National Socialists Physician League declared "the primacy of national biology over national economy." Moreover, the environmental concern of keeping the German landscape clean also fit in perfectly with the racial hygiene emphasis of the medical community. The Jews were considered a source of both medical and environmental pollution. Just as Nazi biology would therefore lead to dreadful consequences with regard to racial theory and medical hygiene, it would also have sordid ramifications with regard to environmentalism as well.

Nazi professor Ernst Lehman stated, "We recognize that separating humanity from nature, from the whole of life, leads to humankind's own destruction and to the death of nations. Only through a reintegration of

---

[546] Ibid., p. 104.

[547] Gasman, *The Scientific Origins of National Socialism*, pp. 162, 169.

[548] Hitler, *Mein Kampf*, p. 287.

[549] Himmler, Heinrich, *Himmler: Geheimreden: 1933 bis 1945*, herausgegeben von Bradley F. Smith und Agnes F. Peterson (Frankfurt/ M, Berlin, Propylaen Verlag, 1974), p. 160, quoted by Pois, p. 48.

[550] Ibid.

humanity into the whole of nature can our people be made stronger. That is the fundamental point of the biological tasks of our age. . . . This striving toward connectedness with the totality of life, with nature itself, a nature into which we are born, this is the deepest meaning and the true essence of National Socialist thought."[551] Biology and ecology were not seen as separate categories to be pursued independently of each other. "Biology was important to the Nazis: the Nazis appealed to biology to provide support for their idea that nature rather than nurture, was the key to the development of human talents and institutions."[552] "German scientists of the Nazi period maintained that their science was that of northern peoples. They insisted that their science was holistic and not based on a duality of matter and spirit, in contrast to the mechanism of Judaic thinking."[553]

As such, social lessons were invariably drawn from the fields and forests of Germany.[554] Biology and ecology were everywhere applied socially and politically. Worse, the applications were literal. Natural metaphors, very useful in illustrating and teaching many important concepts in everyday life, were not metaphors for the Nazis. When Nazi biologists described the natural landscape as *sick* or *wounded* or *tamed*, they meant it literally. The natural landscape was as much an organism as anything else.

Nazi biologists militarized the natural world as well. "The spruce trees, hardened by battle with the elements are the first line of defense for the forest in the high mountains." Furthermore, "The confusion of branches reaching in all directions marks the forest of spruce as a battle zone." Likewise, teachers in schools throughout the Nazi period would invoke all kinds of naturist socialistic lessons for children to learn from. For example, rose thorns were "weapons to protect their own lives and those of their descendants." Woodpeckers are like the police. They are extremely important for the health of the forest because they eat up parasites. In their opposition to the Judeo-Christian worldview, the Nazis humanized nature in order to blend in with their natural surroundings.

National Socialism was therefore a political ecology where politics was inappropriately and dangerously hotwired with *scientific* biological racism into a totalitarian wholeness. "Over and over, the Nazi celebrated

---

[551] Lehmann, Ernst, *Biologischer Wille. Wege und Ziele biologischer Arbeit im neuen Reich,* Munich, 1934, pp. 10-11, quoted by Staudenmaier & Biehl, p. 13.

[552] Proctor, Robert. *Racial Hygiene: Medicine Under the Nazis,* p. 38.

[553] Sax, p. 104.

[554] Ibid., pp. 108-09.

the creativity of Aryan science with its putative power to move beyond dispassionate analysis and grasp the whole … they sought to overcome the fragmentation of knowledge and experience by integrating everything into a single structure."[555] The Nazis associated the fragmentation of knowledge in the West to the dualistic matter-spirit division so characteristic of the Judeo-Christian worldview. Thus, it was time to move away from this Jewish-Christian fragmentation of knowledge onto higher ground with a progressive synthesis. The problem was that such a synthesis led to a forced mixture that blew up the circuitry of all of Europe.

In order to encapsulate all its various tenets, National Socialism is best understood as a secular religion of nature that can go so far so as to explain the madness of the concentration camp system:

> However weak and inconsistent the natural religion grounded *Welt-anschauung* appears when it is subject to reason informed scrutiny, the Nazis were convinced that they had succeeded in fusing the realms of nature and spirit, that the product of this fusion was or would be natural, Aryan man, and that the process of re-informing a decadent, bourgeois world with a new nature *Mythus* necessitated extermination of those whose very existence was an insult to the (natural – *sic*) laws of life. It was no accident that the most successful purveyors of political mysticism to date provided that the last sight which greeted those who were to be exterminated, before they confronted the expression which crowned the gate of Auschwitz, "*Arbeit macht frei*", was that of a large tree, striking in its luxuriance.[556]

The phrase *Arbeit macht frei* literally means *work makes free*. In reality, of course, the Jews were much more often gassed to death than worked to death, but the same sign greeted those at the entrance of Buchenwald as well—which was not a death camp, though many still died there. The *work makes free* slogan was actually the title of a novel written by a German nationalist in the 1920s and then used in the Weimar Republic as a means to advertise its public works programs to end unemployment. Weimar's public works department used it to mock the medieval phrase *stadtluft macht frei*, which literally means *city*

---

[555] Ibid., p. 104.
[556] Pois, p. 134.

air makes free. That the Nazis would incorporate this same mocking environmental slogan against the Jews is hardly surprising.

Work makes free therefore fit in perfectly with their own *Weltanschauung*, or holistic biological-ecological-socialistic worldview. This was especially true with regard to their racist biological view of life, which was epitomized best by Ernst Haeckel's Social Darwinian *science*. Ernst Haeckel's so-called science, allegedly built on Darwin's theory of evolution, is more appropriately understood as a holistic philosophy of man and nature. It was, in fact, just as much religion as it was science. Much of Nazi science was short-circuited by politics and religion based on socialism, racism, ecological holism and existentialism. Their crackpot science was not a science at all, but the most pernicious form of scientism yet to date.[557] It was something that Winston Churchill himself characterized toward the end of his famous "Their Finest Hour" speech presented to the House of Commons on June 18, 1940 as reading by the "lights of perverted science." Behind the veneer of progressive modern science was a subversive political and religious mysticism about nature that was as socially regressive as it was totalitarian.

Throughout the tenure of the Third Reich, much of Europe became gradually converted into a gigantic outdoor camping complex. Countless camps—whether work, concentration or death camps—were set up for a variety of different reasons all over Germany, Austria, France, Czechoslovakia and Poland. In the early to mid-1930s, work and indoctrination camps were established in rural parts of Germany to help unemployed city dwellers get back to work, but also get back to the land—which included university students. They were called on to farm the land and grow crops for the Reich, and also to help with land reclamation projects—all of which was designed to root the presumed *green* social economy of Germany into the soil of the fatherland. Bourgeoning concentration camps, of course,

---

[557] Barrett, William, *Death of the Soul: From Descartes to the Computer*. Garden City, New York: Anchor Press/Doubleday, 1987. Barrett writes, "What is this peculiar phenomenon we call scientism? It is not science, any more than the shadow is anything identical with the substance of a thing. Nor is science ever evidence of scientism. At most, science merely serves to heat up the imagination of certain minds—and they are not few—who are too prone to sweeping and unqualified generalizations in the first place. Scientism is pseudoscience or misinterpreted science. Its conclusions are sweeping and large, and therefore sometimes pretend to be philosophical. But it is not a part of philosophy, if by philosophy we mean the effort to think soberly within the restrictions that human reflection must impose for itself. No, scientism is a malady—an ideology. And as such, along with other ideologies that beset us, it has become a permanent part of our modern culture," p. xv.

were also set up for criminals, but increasingly for political prisoners—most of whom were also required to work. During the war, prison labor was extensively used to keep the Nazi war machine afloat in the face of severe labor shortages. Many prisoners were worked to death and only then became free of National Socialist tyranny. Those that lived through it barely survived. As such, and as time wore on, the concentration camp system and its slave labor became more dark, cruel, brutal and even macabre as it was inextricably linked up with eugenics, human medical experimentation and even euthanasia practices that finally reached its climax in the notorious death camps in Poland.

Yet many of the most notorious camps were located in strikingly beautiful surroundings. The most outstanding example of this was Buchenwald concentration camp. Buchenwald means *beech forest*. It was located in the lush greeneries, valleys and hills of the Weimar countryside of Thuringia. In the heart of the beech forest near the top of a mountainous hill called *Ettersberg* was a giant oak tree that Goethe himself often visited back in the late 1700s. Even in Goethe's day, this giant oak tree was already several hundred years old. It had become a legendary oak for a growing number of Romantics. It was a popular forest destination for many writers who extolled the oak as a nationalistic symbol that reflected the life, history and fate of the German Reich. "The legend was that the fate of Germany was connected with the life of the oak of the *Ettersberg*: when the oak died, the German Reich would also fall."[558] Purchased from an aristocrat's estate,[559] it was this romantic location the Nazis chose to set up Buchenwald concentration camp. The beech forest was cleared to make room for Buchenwald, but the Nazis saved Goethe's Oak and built the camp around it.

While the SS themselves enjoyed stunning vistas from villas they occupied below the camp, many prisoners grievously suffered and/or died in Buchenwald. More than a few political and religious prisoners were hanged on the branches of Goethe's Oak. So many prisoners were hanged over the years that SS guard dogs had managed to scratch off all the bark around the butt of Goethe's Oak trying to reach and take a bite out of those hanging from its limbs. Using sacrificial language, Buchenwald prisoners cursed Goethe's Oak as "the martyrs mound." By 1942, the oak tree stopped putting forth its leaves. It was later burnt in 1944 by

---

[558] This testimony was taken from anonymous Buchenwald Prisoner number 4935.
[559] Feig, p. 92.

an Allied bombing raid. The Nazis then took meticulous care to protect the stump that still can be seen today at the Buchenwald museum. The romantic prophecy about Goethe's oak symbolizing the fate of the nation was thus historically fulfilled when the Allies declared victory in 1945 as Germany lay in ruins.

Many Buchenwald prisoners were pitilessly worked to death. Such agonizing slow death was not only a form of SS entertainment, but also a very gratifying form of applied biological social Darwinism that included environmental social justice as well. In addition to being worked to death, many prisoners were experimented upon, quickly discarded and replaced with a seemingly endless supply of human guinea pigs instead of experimental animals. Shrunken skulls inspired from the African jungle together with lampshades made of human skin placed upon lampstands supported by human bones were specialty items of the SS at Buchenwald. More curious, the SS built a zoological garden and game preserve in the camp, including an expensive aristocratic falconry area.[560] The falcon house was carved out of solid oak. Zoo animals received far better treatment than the prisoners. Not only were the animals given better rations than the prisoners, but sometimes the prisoners were given as food to the animals. "As a favorite pastime Commandant Koch threw prisoners into the bears' cages. Survivors remember the excellent diet the animals enjoyed. Although the camp suffered from a serious food shortage, the zoo animals received a daily meat ration from the prisoner mess. Bears ate honey and jam, and the monkeys consumed mashed potatoes with milk, oat flakes, and other delicacies."[561] While most of the prisoners of Buchenwald were allegedly incalcitrant Germans during the pre-war years, the Jews that were there had a special obligation with regard to the zoo animals that had died—they were forced to sacrificially pay for their replacement.[562]

It was into this ferocious jungle of Social Darwinism, biology, eugenics and environmentalism that the Jewish people in particular found themselves increasingly devoured throughout the tenure of the Third Reich. The Nazi enterprise was a socialist slaughterhouse based on a secularized form of nature worship that holistically bled into a variety of different directions. That this evolutionary Nazi nature religion was clothed in secular biology

---

[560] Ibid., pp. 103-04.
[561] Ibid.
[562] Ibid., p. 104.

and colored by environmental policies and practices is a historical truth that has been ignored and underreported for too long a time in all of the discussions about the Holocaust. The Jewish people became unwilling sacrificial victims during the heights of World War II in a National Socialist bioregional[563] plan, later known as the Final Solution. The *lebensraum* bioregion in which the slaughter would take place would be directed from Germany, but carried out in the occupied territories of the East behind the Russian Front in Poland, Ukraine, Byelorussia and the Baltic states. The biological and ecological aspects of it were steeped in German Social Darwinism, *volkisch* Romanticism and natural existentialism, all of which targeted especially the Jews. However, the Nazis also took aim at the Slavs, Bolsheviks and Christians as well. "The Nazis murdered in the name of nature, invoking animals and landscapes."[564]

Sacrificial Nazi Oak Trees

There is a luxuriant oak tree standing just inside the gated entrance into Auschwitz Camp I where the sign reads, "Work makes you free." In fact, there are many stately oaks inside the camp and just outside the entrance. There were also oak trees in the immediate proximity of a few of the gas chambers and crematoriums as well. More ominous, the gas chamber doors at both Auschwitz and Treblinka were made of solid oak. At Auschwitz, the Nazis made double oak doors[565] that sealed the sacrificial fate of all the victims when they were shut. The intimate proximity of such oak symbolism to concentration and death camps like Auschwitz, Treblinka and Belzec, is not likely to be merely coincidental. There was a certain method to the Nazi madness. That Adolf Eichmann was placed in charge of the logistics of the Holocaust in the eastern territories is incredibly ironic. His last name virtually means "man of the oaks."

No matter how industrial the gas chambers may have been so often characterized, the ancient symbolism of human sacrifice being practiced under the

---

[563] Bioregional.org defines bioregionalism as an area that shares similar topography, plant and animal life, and human culture. Bioregions are often organized around watersheds, and they can be nested within each other. Bioregional boundaries are usually not rigid, and often differ from political borders around counties, states, provinces and nations. Ideally, bioregions are places that could be largely self-sufficient in terms of food, products and services, and would have a sustainable impact on the environment.

[564] Sax, p. 43.

[565] Nyiszli, p. 36.

oak trees bleeds through the veneer of Nazi modernism. Konnilyn Feig, the author of *Hitler's Death Camps: The Sanity of Madness*, depicted Nazi concentration camps as "high altars of expiation" where prisoners were often "consecrated to death."[566] Many Nazi concentration and death camps were metaphorical *high places* of nature worship and human sacrifice that dominated the European landscape in all directions during the heights of World War II.

At Auschwitz, eyewitness accounts depict conspicuous lightning rods that were attached to each of the four sides of the crematorium chimneys.[567] The massive flames that burst out from the chimney tops accentuated the lightning rods, especially at night. The Nazi SS letters themselves were iconically stylized after lightning bolts borrowed from nature mystic Guido von List (1848-1919). Guido von List believed in a pan-German nature mysticism called Ariosophy. Ariosophy simply means "wisdom of the Aryans." It was both anti-modern and anti-Semitic. Ariosophy mixed apocalypticism, occultic mythology, paganism, racism, evolution, eugenics and ecology into its worldview. Not surprisingly, Guido von List was also an expert on Norse mythology. Through Guido von List's writings and influences, Himmler was likewise devoted to ancient Norse mythology. Himmler was well aware the Norse god Thor was not only the god of thunder and lightning, but also the god of the oaks. That Himmler's SS was in charge of the Nazi concentration camp system makes the oak and lightning symbolism at Auschwitz anything but trivial or coincidental, but very ominous indeed. The SS leadership mindset itself was rife with ancient paganism.

Oak trees were considered especially sacred to ancient Germans. "Of all European trees none has such claims as the oak to be considered as pre-eminently the sacred tree of the Aryans. Its worship is attested for all the great branches of the Aryan stock in Europe."[568] In German paganism, the oak tree symbolized fertility, power and sacrifice—and sacrifice was the means by which fertility and power were obtained. Sexual fertility and male virility were symbolized by oaks as well. The oaks were also considered mighty because of their sheer size, with no small thanks to their powerful roots anchored deep into the soil. Pagan sacrifices were offered in the sacred oak groves in order to help guarantee the fertility of nature and her harvest cycles.

---

[566] Feig, pp. 93-94.

[567] Nyiszli, p. 10.

[568] Frazer, Sir James George, *The Golden Bough: A Study in Magic and Religion.* Oxford University Press, 2009 (1994), pp. 753-54.

Fertility, sacrifice and power were all virtually worshiped by the National Socialists in one form or another, no matter how scientific or secular many of its adherents would try to couch their ideology. While Himmler was not embarrassed by his semi-occultic underpinnings, others like Hitler, were very adept in covering up their nature mysticism with racial scientism and/or existentialist philosophies. Yet both men loved oak trees and the fertility, power and sacrifice they symbolized. Indeed, the great desire of National Socialism was to become fertile and powerful through sacrificial eugenic measures.

The weaknesses of the modern Western world were presumed to have its crumbling foundations within the longstanding influences of the Judeo-Christian tradition, with the Jews in particular being at the very core of the problem. The *green* sacrifice of the Jews would therefore be required to help the European world return back to Nature and her eugenic racial laws of evolutionary development that the Judeo-Christian worldview interrupted. What the Nazis labeled "Judeo-Bolshevism" would likewise have to be exterminated in the process. Judeo-Christian universalism denied racism by tracing all humanity back to Adam. The Nazis believed that such universalist values had also infected Soviet Communism with false international values.

In his youth, while trying to enroll in a Vienna architectural school in 1908, Adolf Hitler wrote up a play about religious sacrifice centering on the differences between Christianity and German paganism. In fact, he feverishly spent all night working on it. When his roommate, August Kubizek, was awakened, he asked Adolf what he was doing. Kubizek wondered what Adolf could possibly be working on, and what would be the end result of all of his work. Was Adolf's architectural school that difficult? Hitler did not respond to him, but instead gave him a piece of paper with these words written on it: "Holy Mountain in the background, before it the mighty sacrificial block surrounded by huge oaks; two powerful warriors hold the black bull, which is to be sacrificed, firmly by the horns, and press the beast's mighty head against the hollow in the sacrificial block. Behind them, erect in light-colored robes, stands the priest. He holds the sword with which he will slaughter the bull. All around, solemn, bearded men, leaning on their shields, their lances ready, are watching the ceremony intently."[569] Hitler

---

[569] Kubizek, p. 110.

was clearly very aware of the practice of religious sacrifice under the oak trees in ancient paganism.

Astounded by Hitler's passion, Kubizek asked him what it was. Hitler finally responded, "A play." Kubizek, of course, was mystified by the connection between the play and his architectural studies:

> Then, in stirring words, he described the action to me. Unfortunately, I have long since forgotten it. I only remember that it was set in the Bavarian mountains at the time of the bringing of Christianity to those parts. The men who lived on the mountain did not want to accept the new faith. On the contrary! They had bound themselves by oath to kill the Christian missionaries. On this was based the conflict of the drama.[570]

Hitler's play was borrowed from the ariosophist Guido von List's *Die Armanenschaft der Ario-Germanen*, published earlier in the same year.[571] Guido von List's ariosophical works had become cult classics in Vienna in the early 1900s when Hitler lived there at the time. Kubizek said that in addition to philosophers Schopenhauer and Nietzsche, Hitler loved German mythology.[572]

That Adolf Hitler would later rule Germany from the majesty of the Bavarian Alps at his mountain chalet in the *Obersalzberg* fits in with the play that he wrote up many years earlier. Many of Hitler's plans were envisaged in the Bavarian Alps where he spent much time brooding over the mountain landscape. Could it be that Hitler believed his beloved SS was protecting Germany as a pagan mountain priest or shaman? When Kubizek wrote his autobiography after the war, he sensed that there was something very significant that particular night when Hitler composed his play. Kubizek probably did not think too much about it until years later. Looking back, he sensed that it had a strong connection to what later became known as the Holocaust. Could it be that paganism, mountains, oak trees and human sacrifice are hiding behind the shadows of the firelight blazing around the camp of National Socialism?

---

[570] Ibid., pp. 110-11.
[571] Goodrick-Clarke, Nicholas. *The Occult Roots of Nazism: Secret Aryan Cults and their Influence on Nazi Ideology, 1890-1935*. New York: New York University Press, 1985, 1992, p. 199.
[572] Kubizek, pp. 135-37.

Indeed, many of the actual leading perpetrators of the Holocaust were Austrian Nazi mountain men from the Carinthian Alps.[573] It was they who administered Operation *Reinhard* from the Lublin district of Poland, where perhaps more than two million Polish Jews perished in notorious death camps like Treblinka, Sobibor, Belzec and Majdanek. Plans for Sobibor were discussed and finalized between Globocnik and Stangl in a charming park area that surrounded the SS Headquarters in Lublin. Years later, Stangl fondly recalled, "It was a beautiful spring day. The grass was very green, the trees in bud and there were new flowers everywhere. I came upon Globocnik sitting by himself on a bench about ten meters away from—and with his back to—the building. There was a lovely view across lawns and trees to buildings far away."[574] Before being later transferred to Treblinka, Stangl lived in a forester's cabin near Sobibor. In the Sobibor death camp itself, Jews were forced to sing, "Our life is happy here. We receive good food. How happy we are in the green forest where I stay." Sobibor was located in a beautiful area.

Auschwitz itself did not kill as many Jews as Operation *Reinhard*, but has received most of the attention because of its proximity to the IG Farben chemical factory that was exported into the area. Perhaps too many anti-capitalist leftist historians have been involved in characterizing the Holocaust as a modern industrial killing machine. The fact of the matter is, the conditions in which the Jews were murdered were extremely primitive, even in places like Auschwitz, let alone in the more remote areas of Treblinka and Sobibor.

Dr. Franz Grassler, the SS Deputy Commissioner of the Warsaw Ghetto in Poland, was an avid German mountaineer and alpinist in addition to being a lawyer. During the early part of the war, Grassler worked closely with the leaders of the *Judenrat* of the Warsaw Ghetto. The *Judenrat* were Jewish community leaders who were given the gruesome job of administering the horrors of the ghettos set up by the Nazis to corral the Jews before they were eventually *evacuated* to various death and/or concentration camps. In Claude Lanzmann's famous documentary film *Shoah*, Grassler conveniently had some bouts of amnesia when specifically confronted about his past responsibilities in the Warsaw Ghetto. When Lanzmann pressed Grassler about how much he remembered, he responded, "Not much. I recall more

---

[573]   Rieger, Berndt, *Creator of the Nazi Death Camps: The Life of Odilo Globocnik*. London and Portland, Oregon: Vallentine Mitchell, 2007, pp. 65, 89.

[574]   Sereny, *Into that Darkness*, p. 102.

clearly my pre-war mountaineering trips than the entire war period and those days in Warsaw. All, in all, those were bad times. It's a fact we tend to forget, thank god, the bad times more easily than the good. The bad times are repressed." By willfully repressing his memory, Grassler downplayed his authoritative role in the Warsaw Ghetto, and concluded Lanzmann's interview by saying the clean alpine air of the mountains he loved so much was far better than the "ghetto air."

After the war, Grassler worked at a mountain guide publishing company that extolled the great beauties of the Alps. In 1951, Grassler wrote an elitist pro-environmental anti-modern skiing article. In the article, Grassler pointed out that "alpine skiing had originally been an elite practice, undertaken by those who had the time, money, courage, and physical toughness to confront the Alps in winter. The spread of lift infrastructure," argued Grassler, "submitted this formerly elite sport to the 'herd instinct.' Skiing on heavily groomed *pistes* carried all the nobility of mass transit."[575] With such highbrowed sarcasm, Grassler elevated himself above the rest, and applied Nietzsche's superman earth-based ethos to skiing by ridiculing the herd character of the modern ski slopes. There were too many people on the slopes nowadays ruining the snow and the true alpine character of the Alps. In the Nazi mind, mass culture was a Jewish disease foisted upon Germany stemming from the inner cities where a corrupt globalism artificially dominated politics, the economy and the fatherland. That Jews were stuffed in ghettos *en masse* before being finished off in the gas chambers and crematoriums of the Nazi death camp system was not merely a matter of biological racism, but also a form of environmental social justice.

Hitler's Oaks, Nazi Racism & the Green Aryan Crusade

The nationalistic ecological road to Auschwitz symbolically began in the 1936 Berlin Olympic Games when Adolf Hitler gave "oak seedlings,[576] potted and presented as a gift of the German people to each of the 130 gold medal winners. . . . These Olympic oaks—sometimes dubbed Hitler Trees because of the Nazi leader's association with the Berlin games—were proudly accepted by such Americans as Jesse Owens, taken to their home

---

[575] Denning, Andrew. *Skiing into Modernity: A Cultural and Environmental History.* Oakland: University of California Press, 2015, p. 175.

[576] The gold medal winners received potted oak saplings. The stage was decorated with oak leaves.

countries and planted as living symbols of the Olympic spirit."[577] While Hitler himself did not personally present the oak trees to the gold medal winners, the Nazis certainly worked with the Olympic Games committee to make sure that such gifts were granted. Today, several decades later, a few of these oaks are still alive and growing, including one at Jesse Owens' high school practice field in Cleveland, Ohio.[578] Jesse Owens was the great star of the 1936 Olympics, winning four gold medals.

Much racist ballyhoo was made of the fact that Hitler allegedly ignored Jesse Owens at the Olympics. However, Jesse Owens himself provided a much different perspective: "Hitler didn't snub me—it was [FDR] who snubbed me. The president didn't even send me a telegram."[579] In fact, Jesse Owens was warmly received by the German public at the games, signed autographs for them, and was even able to stay with whites in the hotels during the games. He himself stated, "When I passed the Chancellor he arose, waved his hand at me, and I waved back at him. I think the writers showed bad taste in criticizing the man of the hour in Germany."[580] Thus according to Jesse Owens, in practice, Franklin Delano Roosevelt was more racist than the *Fuhrer* himself. Ironically enough, Jesse Owens was buried in Chicago's south side at Oak Woods Cemetery when he died in 1980.

According to Albert Speer, Hitler was clearly annoyed by Owens' victories but then shrugged his shoulders. "People whose antecedents came from the jungle were primitive ... their physiques were stronger than those of civilized whites."[581] Hitler considered Jesse Owens stronger because he was closer to nature. Hitler, faced with the fact of Owens' obvious physical superiority, was still able to interpret the event within his own nature-based *Weltanschauung*. Indeed, the racism of the *Fuhrer* was more nuanced than a simplistic preoccupation with skin color. Somehow, many have forgotten that Hitler's most intense hatred was directed not against people of different skin color per se, but against Jews in particular, and then more generally against Slavs in the East, neither of whom were black. This is not to say that Hitler was not a white racist, as he most certainly was, but it is to say that his racism was far more nuanced than many have glibly attributed to him.

[577] Boswell, Randy, "Hitler's Tree: An Ottawa Professor Searches for Canada's vanished Olympic Oak," *Canada.com*, Aug. 18, 2008.

[578] Ibid.

[579] Schaap, Jeremy. *Triumph: The Untold Story of Jesse Owens and Hitler's Olympics.* New York: Houghton Mifflin Company, 2007, p. 211.

[580] Ibid., p. 193.

[581] Speer, Albert. *Inside the Third Reich*, p.73.

Adolf Hitler's green gifts to the 1936 gold medal champions were a symbol of a German nationalism and pride, rooted deep in nature like the roots of an oak tree. Aryan Germany was thought to be superior to the other nations of the international Olympic Games. The Nazis thought of themselves as being properly related to nature and its social Darwinian laws. They starkly contrasted themselves with much of the West, which still held to the Judeo-Christian tradition that distinguished man from nature. In a most ironic but sordid twist, far from elevating themselves above nature, the Nazi master race was considered the best precisely because it was most in harmony with the laws of an all-inclusive holistic natural world. Hitler seamlessly talks about German racial superiority in one breath, and then quickly denounces the Jews for their vain attempt to conquer nature in another breath, without any pause or consideration that he might be contradicting himself.[582] That Nazi Germany walked away with most of the gold medals in the 1936 Olympics, notwithstanding Jesse Owens' heroic performance, confirmed this prejudice. "The goal of the National Socialist movement was the creation of a new human type, the natural man."[583] This natural man "was a being who was totally in harmony with a natural world of which he, through understanding its totality, was the highest expression."[584]

Colonel Hans-Ulrich Rudel (1916-1982) was the "first and only recipient of Germany's highest military decoration—specially created for him by Hitler in December 1944—the Iron Cross with Golden Oak Leaves, Swords and Diamonds."[585] This man was decorated as Germany's best ace of all time. He sank a battleship, "dispatched two cruisers, one destroyer, 70 landing craft, and more than 500 Russian tanks."[586] Grounded in German pride, oak leaves and acorns were the primary symbols of the SS,[587] whose leader, Heinrich Himmler, was a green pagan mystic. Historically, the oak tree itself had often been described as Germany's national tree or even characterized as its holy tree rooted in the pagan past.

With the oak tree serving as such a powerful spiritual symbol of German nationalism and its natural landscape, Hitler had oaks planted all over the

[582]   Hitler, *Mein Kampf*, pp. 286-287.
[583]   Pois, p. 118.
[584]   Ibid.
[585]   Goodricke-Clark, Nicholas. *Hitler's Priestess: Savitri Devi, the Hindu-Aryan Myth and Neo-Nazism.* New York: New York University Press, 1998, p. 171.
[586]   Ibid.
[587]   Bramwell, *Ecology in the 20ʰ Century: A History*, p. 200.

Reich in hundreds of towns and villages. This practice was later dubbed by many Nazi environmentalists as "concordant with the spirit of the *Fuhrer*."[588] Furthermore, this symbol of natural strength borrowed upon a hallowed German tradition going back hundreds of years to ancient pagan times before the rise of the Judeo-Christian civilization in Europe. It was this ancient Germanic culture, embedded in the primeval natural world that more and more Germans were trying to romantically recover throughout much of the 19th century. Indeed, Herman Goering's wife Carin, who died in 1931, was initially buried in Sweden. She was later exhumed and reburied between two giant oak trees on Goering's beautiful nature reserve in June of 1934, on the first day of summer. The reburial was attended by many of the leading Nazis, including Hitler himself. June 20, 1934, was chosen as the day of reburial precisely because the summer solstice was a day in which the "the pagan ideology of the National Socialists" was "freighted with symbolic importance."[589]

This basic *volkisch* spirit, in great contrast to the Judeo-Christian worldview, was absorbed by the Nazis into its own movement as a backlash against modernity that has only become even more popular in Western societies:

> ... even the core of the National Socialist religion of nature was not something utterly alien to Western/Central European cultural history in general, and that of Germany in particular. In part it was rooted in a general malaise that was a byproduct of material progress, a malaise which found articulation in the "return to nature." It received much of its specifically German center from a "group fantasy" that constituted a substantial portion of at least the bourgeois response to rapid economic growth, social displacement, military humiliation, and cultural and political upheaval. Implicit in any fantasy is the guiding notion of freezing time, of a certain flight from historical reality. . . . In their efforts to assure the emergence and advancement of the "new Aryan man", the bearers of National Socialist religiosity had to set the stage for a frozen, anti-transcendent world in which archetypal suppositions became truths grounded in "nature's eternal laws." Here, the National Socialists

588 Uekoetter, p. 52.
589 Larson, Erik. *In the Garden of Beasts: Love, Terror, and an American Family in Hitler's Berlin*. New York: Broadway Paperbacks, 2011, p. 281.

went beyond bourgeois fantasizing in their determination to push matters through to a logical, if not rational, conclusion: in a word, to the point at which the literally "fantastic" became real.[590]

The Nazis were more than willing to turn this fantasy into political reality. Indeed, the first step to return Germany back to nature and its holistic natural laws was to get rid of its Jewish element. Second, it must move east to capture environmental living space to relieve their own overpopulated country. Third, it must then subvert, or remove if necessary, the Christian faith which was just as anti-natural as Judaism.

Hence throughout the 1930s, the Nazis began an Aryan crusade to purify their own country. They deemed Germany to be polluted by a foreign international globalism fostered by a soft Judeo-Christian political-religious worldview. The Nazis not only blamed international capitalism but also international communism/socialism as well—both of which had borrowed heavily from the Bible. To Hitler and the Nazis, such religious and political movements tied to the Judeo-Christian tradition had greatly weakened all of Europe. In Germany itself, the class warfare between the capitalists and the communists/socialists had divided the *volk* so much that the nation had been greatly destabilized. Both capitalist and socialist societies had become feeble because of their refusal to bow to nature's social Darwinian laws. As far as the Nazis were concerned, both free market and socialistic liberalism had falsely presumed the basic humanistic position of man's dominion over nature. They were thus to be strongly opposed precisely because they were both a byproduct of the alleged weaknesses of Judeo-Christianity. "The Nazis condemned Judaism and Christianity for being nature hating, life despising, and otherworldly."[591]

Adolf Hitler himself juxtaposed his own religion of nature with Christianity. "There are some who say the world is evil, and that they wish to depart from this life. For my part, I like the world! ... To make death easier for people, the Church holds out to them the bait of a better world. We, for our part, confine ourselves to asking man to fashion life worthily. For this, it is sufficient for him to conform to the laws of nature. Let's seek inspiration in these principles, and in the long run we'll triumph over religion."[592]

---

590   Pois, p. 170.
591   Zimmerman, Michael, "Possible Political Problems of Earth Based Religiosity."
592   *Hitler's Table Talk: 1941-44*, evening of Sept. 23, 1941, pp. 31-32.

Hitler also charged the Jews with the same otherworldliness in contrast to nature: "It was necessary for the Jew to appear on the scene and introduce that mad conception of a life that continues into an alleged Beyond! It enables one to regard life as a thing that is negligible here below. . . . The Jew plays in nature the role of a catalyzing element. A people that is rid of its Jews returns spontaneously to the natural order."[593]

This chilling statement from the lips of the *Fuhrer* himself gives a nature-based justification for cleansing the Jews from the landscape. "The Nazis identified civilization with the Judeo-Christian tradition and identified with the pagan past. By claiming a special bond with nature, the Nazis stigmatized their adversaries as unnatural."[594]

Shockingly, on the way down the green camouflaged fence corridors into the gas chambers of the death camps at Treblinka and Sobibor, the Jewish sacrificial victims walked under a sign in Hebrew that read, "This is the way to heaven." This sign was an absolute mockery of the heavenly and transcendental background of the Hebrew Bible and its people. At Treblinka, after the Jews passed under the sign, they were greeted with the prettiest flower garden of the entire camp. These flowers were the last spectacle the Jewish people saw before entering the gas chambers to be euthanized to death. Even more sadistic, Treblinka Commandant Franz Stangl referred to the gas chambers themselves as Jewish cities.[595] The Nazis often characterized city areas populated by Jews as dirty ghettos, devoid of flowers, parks and green areas, indicative of their alleged financial greed that strove to live above the blood and soil of Germania.

After Treblinka and Belzec were torn down by the SS, lupine wildflowers, which are wolf flowers, were planted on the remains of the Jewish victims[596] where almost 750,000 people were sacrificed. Hitler's wolf-like nature religion was thus much more at the heart of the Holocaust than most would care to admit. Ironically enough, SS General Odilo Globocnik (1904-1945), the very man who was in charge of Operation *Reinhard* that claimed more than two million Jewish lives, was originally from Wolf Mountain (*Wolfsberg*) in the Austrian Alps of Carinthia. After the SS virtually liquidated Polish Jewry, the death camps of Belzec, Sobibor and Treblinka were completely

---

[593] Ibid., midday Feb. 17, 1942, p. 238.
[594] Sax, p. 41.
[595] Arad, p. 184.
[596] Ibid., pp. 371-73.

dismantled, cleaned up, re-afforested and converted into farms by the fall of 1943 to provide green cover for its colossal crimes.[597]

On Nov. 3, 1943, some 43,000 Jews were gathered, shot and killed from various death and concentration camps in Poland. This concluded Operation *Reinhard* (1941-43) that had made Belzec, Sobibor and Treblinka the primary extermination centers of Polish Jewry. The SS called the final action "Operation *Erntefest*," which means "Harvest Festival."[598] While countless historians, commentators and books have time and time again emphasized the industrial nature of the Holocaust, SS Nazis understood the concluding action of Operation *Reinhard* to be a special day on the farm comparable to an annual harvest celebration. In the twisted Nazi mind, Jewish weeds had to be eradicated from the blood and soil of Germany's *lebensraum*. Operation *Erntefest* was the single largest Nazi Jewish massacre conducted throughout the entire war.

On Jan. 14, 1944, a few unruly members of Police Battalion 101, who would have most certainly been involved in Operation *Erntefest*, received a special reprimand for illegally poaching wild boars during the harvest season itself. "Members of the Order Police who were assigned to the protection of the harvest unlawfully hunted wild boars." The commander of the memo then reminded them: "I must point out that every kind of illegal hunting will be treated as poaching. Repeaters will be called to account."[599] While the *harvest* referred to could have very well been a cryptic reference to Operation *Erntefest*, regardless, German police battalions were still thoroughly engaged in the wanton slaughter and torture of countless Jews and other undesirables throughout Poland. Yet the commander of Police Battalion 101 saw no contradiction between reprimanding poachers and carrying out the murder of unarmed human beings. While poaching boars was forbidden, hunting Jews was ordered and carried out with great enthusiasm. When environmental legalism trumps the wholesale slaughter of people, it is time to pause and reassess what the intent of the Holocaust was truly all about, especially in the eyes of the Nazi leadership. "What appears to be ironies, so obvious that they could be missed by none, so cruel that they should have shaken any involved, were undoubtedly lost on the perpetrators. They were

---

[597] Ibid., pp. 171, 370-72.
[598] Ibid., pp. 365-69.
[599] Goldhagen, p. 266.

too far gone. Their cognitive framework was such that the juxtaposition could not register."[600]

At the close of the war in 1945, Odilo Globocnik, together with some SS team members who helped him administer Operation *Reinhard*, returned to the Carinthian Alps to hide out. Globocnik hiked up the Mosslacher Alm to a mountain hut which offered a breathtaking view of the turquoise-colored Wiessensee Lake in the valley below. The night before Globocnik was captured by British soldiers, who discovered his whereabouts through an informant, the SS General discussed with his friend "that the task of the Nazis after the war was to preserve the German way of life; that is, they should have no contact with Jews, and lead a simple and natural family life."[601] After being captured, Globocnik committed suicide by swallowing cyanide poison.

National Socialism's Evolutionary Naturalism/Existentialism

National Socialism's secularized religion of nature was not a codified set of doctrines which can be described in a clear ideological system. Not only would this be contrary to their existentialism, but many believed National Socialism was developing or evolving as one studies and learns from nature. Indeed, the whole point of many Nazis was to shy away from Judaistic or *legalistic* ideas of truth which had already been discredited by a long list of philosophers, skeptics, agnostics, pantheists, atheists, evolutionists, *volkisch* romantics, biologists and ecologists coming out of the academic halls of Germany from the late 1700s to the early 1900s. Goethe's Romanticism and Kant's (1724-1804) skepticism concerning the possibility of delineating objective rational knowledge laid the foundation stones for a nature based German worldview. Following suit was Friedrich Schleiermacher (1768-1834). His theological Romanticism emphasized a religion of feeling over a rational belief system of set doctrines. Humboldt then emphasized environmental holism and the birth of the German nature *volker*. Arndt and Riehl then added a nationalistic anti-Semitic environmentalism into the mix that fired up the German stoves even more.

Georg Wilhelm Friedrich Hegel (1770-1831) taught that history was an evolutionary struggle in which the semi-pantheistic World Spirit progressively develops man through historical contradictions between ideas and states.

---

[600]   Ibid., p. 270.
[601]   Rieger, p. 164

His belief in the evolutionary development of religious history would have profound effects upon men like Ferdinand Christian Baur (1792-1860) and Julius Wellhausen (1844-1918), who used Hegel's philosophy to criticize the historical foundations of both the New and Old Testaments, respectively. Ludwig Feuerbach (1804-1872) posited that the God of the Bible was merely a projection of human consciousness. Presuming Feuerbach's basic thesis to be true, Karl Marx's (1818-1883) atheistic materialism and exaltation of all things human then reduced all life to the miserable realm of economics, capitalistic exploitation and class warfare.

At about the same time, Arthur Schopenhauer's existentialist philosophy laid the groundwork for environmental ethics. This was followed by Friedrich Nietzsche's atheistic existentialism that vehemently denounced the belief in God as a declaration of war against nature. Ernst Haeckel then superimposed a scientific holistic pantheism called Monism upon Darwin's evolutionary theory. Martin Heidegger then rounded off this long drawn-out German escapade by emphasizing environmental existentialism.

With such a list of academic superstars placed in the most important halls of influence for a sustained 125 years, is it any wonder that National Socialism became the capstone of such a legacy? Granted, the Nazis crudely mixed these ingredients together into an explosive *scientific* concoction that blew up all of Europe, but the ideas that lay behind the National Socialist experiment were previously propounded by its academic forefathers.

Hitler himself was a very eclectic figure who adopted all kinds of different views and positions into his own way of thinking. He awkwardly absorbed well over 100 years of German naturalistic, *volkisch* and existential thought into his own person as the culminating representative of the *volksgemeinschaft*. As such, Hitler was vehemently antagonistic against all forms of Christian dogma. He was a firm believer that truth was something growing and evolutionary which will eventually leave Christianity behind. "Our epoch will certainly see the end of the disease of Christianity. It will last another 100 years, 200 years perhaps. My regret will have been that I couldn't, like whoever the prophet was, behold the promised land from afar. We are entering into a conception of the world that will be a sunny era, an era of tolerance."[602]

Under the guise of a National Socialist version of political correctness, Hitler preached tolerance in great contrast to the Christian emphasis upon

---

[602] *Hitler's Table Talk*, midday of Feb. 27, 1942, p. 260.

truth. "It's probable that, as regards religion, we are about to enter an era of tolerance. Everybody will be able to seek his own salvation in the way that suits him best."[603] Thus, surprisingly enough, many liberal scholars and leftist academics do not realize that their own views on religious toleration were also shared by the *Fuhrer* himself:

> The *Fuhrer* has consciously avoided allowing his National Socialism to develop into a stationary doctrine. It should and it must remain a revolutionary idea. Each doctrine leads all too easily to dogmatism and through that to alienation from the world.[604]

This particular quote reeks of Nietzsche's existentialist philosophy. The Nazis continued and emphasized Germany's evolutionary legacy of unbelief, naturalism, Romanticism, existentialism and Biblical skepticism in eschewing any ideas of an absolute truth. Hitler even complained about the Bible's alleged inconsistent dogmas, repression and intolerance.[605] While it is true that Hitler often sounded pro-Christian or pro-church in his public speeches, "there can be no question that he said these things cynically, for political gain. In private, he possessed an unblemished record of statements against Christianity and Christians."[606]

For Hitler and the Nazis, true knowledge was a knowledge based strictly on nature. Furthermore, since nature was in a state of perpetual development, dogmatic assertions about transcendent realities like God were simply out of the question. "In its fusion of a well-nigh positivistic view of science with general mystical and pantheistic concerns usually and correctly associated with Germany's romantic past, National Socialism proffered a religion of nature necessarily secular in many ways."[607] Indeed, Hitler asserted, "The dogma of Christianity gets worn away before the advances of science. Religion will have to make more and more concessions. Gradually the myths crumble."[608] Hitler then concluded, "Consequently, the more Christianity clings to its dogmas, the quicker it will decline."

---

603   Ibid., p. 259.
604   Institute For Zeitgeschichte, reel no. MA 138/1, frame 301789, quoted by Pois, p. 48.
605   Gasman, *The Scientific Origins of National Socialism*, p. 167.
606   Metaxas, *Bonhoeffer: Pastor, Martyr, Prophet, Spy*. Nashville, Tennessee: Thomas Nelson Publishers, 2010, p. 165.
607   Pois, p. 70.
608   *Hitler's Table Talk*, midday of Oct. 14, 1941, p. 48.

Thus, in the 1930s and '40s the Nazi political leadership decided it was time to return Germany to its primeval cultural and natural purity. However, this was not perceived as a backward movement, but a forward one—a great progressive evolutionary advance into a new world order. In their racism, Hitler and the Nazis believed they were the vanguard of societal evolution in great contrast to the religious superstitions of the past. Their backward barbarity was thus obscured by many modern progressive ideas:

> Nazi barbarism was motivated by an ethic that prided itself on being scientific. The evolutionary process became the arbiter of all morality. Whatever promoted the evolutionary progress of humanity was deemed good. Multitudes must perish in this Malthusian struggle anyway, they reasoned, so why not improve humanity by speeding up the destruction of the disabled and the inferior races? According to this logic, the extermination of individuals and races deemed inferior and unfit was not only morally justified, but indeed morally praiseworthy.[609]

While the Nazis justified their cause on the basis of the evolutionary progress of the German man, they remained completely unaware of its atavistic character. Their primitivism was dressed up with enough progressive language that it deceived many people, including the Nazis themselves.

National Socialism was a German hybrid of Romanticism, existentialism, evolution, political biology and eugenic science—all dressed up in progressive naturalistic ethics, nihilistic power with strong ecological inclinations. Such a rich concoction is perhaps better understood as a religion of nature. It was directly opposed to the transcendental Judeo-Christian worldview. "National Socialism ... can be understood in part as a perverted religion of nature, which rejected Jewish and Christian otherworldliness as well as progressive political ideologies that are indebted to Christian ideas about divine purpose actualizing itself in history."[610] This would include Marxism. In Hitler's mind, Christianity and Marxism were one in the same. The humanistic emphasis found in Marxism is derived from the theocentric-anthropocentric view of man found in the Bible. As far as Hitler was concerned they are very close to each other because they both try to live

---

[609] Weikart, *From Darwin to Hitler*, p. 227.
[610] Zimmerman, Michael, "Possible Political Problems of Earth Based Religiosity," p. 2.

above Nature. Hitler once remarked, "Burgdorff has just given me a paper which deals with the relationship between communism and Christianity. It is comforting to see how, even in these days, the fatal relationship between the two is daily becoming clearer to the human intelligence."[611] Ultimately for Hitler this meant the persecution, if not the extermination, of the Judeo-Christian tradition, together with many of its adherents.

That Christians were also personally targeted under Hitler's Nazi Germany is another one of those historical truths which has been either forgotten, or simply denied.[612] While not subjected, of course, to the same degree of persecution the Jews received, practicing Christians were often isolated from Nazi society. Hilmar Von Campe, a former member of the Hitler Youth and war veteran, recalled how anti-Christian the Nazi Party originally was: "I cannot help but remember the German Gestapo (Secret State Police) agents on Sunday mornings. They would gather in front of our church attempting to intimidate those of us who came to worship God by writing down our names in full view of everyone."[613]

Church harassment was commonplace even early on in the Nazi regime, something which the *National Encyclopedia* of 1934 quickly acknowledged.[614] However, "the persecution of the Christians, unlike the Jews, was not publicized to the outside world."[615] The attack on the church was therefore much more covert, but still very real. "The Nazis knew that God's moral absolutes were an obstacle to their total control because you can only manipulate morally weak people who care only for themselves. Therefore, the Christian religion and its moral absolutes had to be destroyed. During the first years of power and during the war, Hitler could only weaken their impact. The final destruction he had planned was meant to occur after the war was won."[616] Contrary to popular opinion, Hitler was very sensitive to the fact that every time he criticized and attacked Christianity, his popularity declined.[617] The elimination of Christianity would thus have to wait until after the war.

---

[611] *Hitler's Table Talk*, night of Nov. 29-30, 1944.

[612] See *The Swastika Against the Cross: The Nazi War on Christianity*. Denver: Outskirts Press, 2007, by Bruce Walker.

[613] Von Campe, Hilmar, *Defeating the Totalitarian Lie*, p. 2.

[614] Black, William Harman, *If I Were a Jew*, p. 115; quoted by Walker in *The Swastika Against the Cross*, p. 34.

[615] Walker, Bruce, *The Swastika Against the Cross*, p. 33.

[616] Von Campe, p. 45.

[617] Metaxas, p. 167.

"Let no German ever forget this, nor rest until these parasites (tribe of Juda) have been wiped out from German soil and been exterminated. This poisonous mushroom on the German oak-tree!"

Kaiser Wilhelm II, German Emperor

CHAPTER FOUR:

THE GREEN NAZI POLITICAL ECOLOGY OF THE THIRD REICH

Underneath the Nazi umbrella of a secular religion of nature, the German environmentalists of the day, many of whom were already *volkisch*, decided to set up shop in the 1930s. German ecology became politicized under Nazi biology. The German greens had finally found a political platform in the biologically based Social Darwinism and natural existentialism of the Nazi Party. Theirs was a voice which had been so often neglected during the social-democratic days of the 1920s. It was time for a change. In fact, they purposefully looked to the Nazis for something that Hitler might have said that would have helped their cause. German Conservationists[618] combed Hitler's "pronouncements for some nod of favor toward their ideas, and two different defenders of nature cited the following remark as evidence of support from *Der Fuhrer*: 'Man should never fall into the misconception that he has really risen to be lord and Master of Nature … rather he must understand the fundamental necessity of the rule of Nature and comprehend how even his own existence is subordinated to these laws of eternal struggle."[619] This was one of Hitler's pet peeves about modern Western society in general—that it had arrogated itself above nature and her natural laws, thanks largely to the Judeo-Christian tradition. The early German greens, of course, shared this environmental point of view, though not always or necessarily in social Darwinian terms. Nonetheless, they still looked to Hitler to see if he would take any interest in their cause. And he most certainly did.

The previous Weimar Republic left natural resource management to the responsibility of the local states. This invariably weighed down the nature

---

[618] German conservationism is not to be directly equated with the Gifford Pinchot-Teddy Roosevelt views and practices of American conservationism.

[619] Dominick, p. 90.

protection movement with a hodgepodge approach at the local level as it was subject to a myriad of competing interests, especially that of private property. The greens thus tried many times to make a breakthrough with environmental legislation at the federal level throughout the 1920s, but always came up short. Private property was the trump card that lay in the path of many environmental dreams. However, in 1935, Bernard Rust, the Prussian minister of education, claimed Adolf Hitler had agreed with him that private property rights had always interfered with a comprehensive federal nature protection law.[620] This became a boon for the environmental cause in Germany. During the Nazi era, the greens were very busy in establishing one nature reserve upon another. "Never in German history have so many nature reserves been designated within such a brief period of time."[621] Rather surprisingly, "the Nazi government accomplished much in the way of conservation."[622]

Because of Hitler's *aristocratic* view that nature was king over man, and not the other way around, he offered the early German greens a place at his political table. The political flower of Nazi environmentalism is certainly the result of the natural foundations sowed in Germany throughout the 1800s. Philosophical Romanticism, Darwinism and existentialism helped to promote a nature-based ethic that fully displayed itself with new environmental rules in the Third Reich. From 1933-35, Hitler signed very significant environmental legislation. As such, Nazi Germany actually began in a green cloak. In the early to mid-1930s, the Third Reich emphasized a brand new era of political ecology. In fact, compared to any other country on Earth at the time, the greens made the deepest inroads into Nazi Germany.

Furthermore, this political activity on the part of the greens also represented a fundamental shift in their previous undertakings during the Weimar Republic.[623] During the 1920s the greens were largely apolitical, and hence, unsuccessful. However, during the 1930s, many of the greens were Nazis. The German conservationists were even given a considerable amount of freedom and independence,[624] something which the Nazis did not always do with many other groups:

---

620   Reich Ministry of Science, Education, and Culture, "Betrifft: Entwurf eines Natur-schutzgesetzes," March 6, 1935, BAP, R II 43/27, quoted by Closmann, "Legalizing a Volksgemeinschaft," in *How Green Were the Nazis?*, p. 29.
621   Uekoetter, p. 142.
622   Sax, p. 44.
623   Uekoetter, p. 193.
624   Ibid., p. 42.

The distance between the conservation community and the Nazis was much smaller in practice than one would expect from the background of the divergent philosophies: cooperation was far too intensive, and far too cordial, to be explained by a partial coincidence of goals. Thus an analysis of the ideological relationship needs to be supplemented by a discussion of institutional ties. For the conservation movement, the Nazi regime offered a number of unprecedented opportunities, which conservationists tried to seize to the greatest extent possible. It was the institutional links that created the atmosphere of sustained sympathy, if not unbridled enthusiasm that permeated the conservation literature of the Nazi era.[625]

As such, the *gap* between the greens and the Nazis was not only bridged by the mid-1930s, but was also well used and traveled. Thanks to National Socialism, the green movement became a political player in its own right. Indeed, in 1948, environmentalist Hans Klose gave a speech in which he expressed his hankering for the good old days of National Socialist environmentalism.[626] By the late '40s, the heyday of working for the *Fuhrer* circa 1936-39 was clearly missed. That Hans Klose was not even a Nazi Party member is perhaps even more revealing.

Though the greens would wind up very disappointed in the end of the Nazi regime, Hitler still had a certain respect for environmentalism in spite of his apparent ambivalence on the issue. Hitler once remarked, "As far as possible, one must avoid ruining landscapes with networks of high tension wires, telpher railways and machines of that sort."[627] Even in July of 1941 when the blitzkrieg was devastating Soviet forces on the Russian front, Hitler remarked, "At the end of the last century the progress of science and technique led liberalism astray into proclaiming man's mastery over nature and announcing that he would soon have dominion over space. But a simple storm—and everything collapses like a pack of cards."[628] That this would be prophetic with regard to the *Wehrmacht* within a matter of a few months was something that Hitler had not considered at the time.

---

[625] Ibid., p. 44.
[626] Klose, "Weg," 43, quoted by Uekoetter, p. 161.
[627] *Hitler's Table Talk*, midday of Feb. 9, 1942.
[628] Ibid., night of July 11-12, 1941, p.7.

The brutal natural forces of the Russian winter would prove to be just as implacable as the Soviet army.

Thus, in the end, it was not just the German environmentalists who were deeply disappointed, but the entire Third Reich. Like most everything the Nazis did, they started out with stunning success at the beginning, only to get mired in the mud of a bitter disillusionment later. They were great on blitzes, but not so good over the long haul. The Nazis seemed to have a great difficulty in putting many of their ideas into practice over a sustained period of time, including their environmental plans for Germany and the occupied territories in the East during the heights of World War II. In a word, the collective *volksgemeinschaft* was not up to the job, but was often characterized by polycentric infighting that compromised almost everything the Nazis attempted. The idea of the collective Nazi *volk* was a myth. As Albert Speer acutely noted, "What eventually developed was a society of totally isolated individuals."[629]

The Green Nazis

The Nazis were widely represented by a whole host of differing facets of the early German green movement. The *Fuhrer* himself was a self-proclaimed animal lover who became a vegetarian at some point during his political career. An intimate associate of Hitler going all the way back to 1923 was veterinarian Friedrich Weber. Weber was "Hitler's primary advisor on policy involving animals."[630] When Hitler signed a series of new environmental laws for the Reich he stated, "The German countryside must be preserved under all circumstances, for it is and has forever been the source of the strength and greatness of our people."[631]

Next in line was Hermann Goering, the Nazi Reich forest minister. He was a mountaineer, huntsman, hiker, animal lover and forester who loved the great outdoors. As a young man, after pioneering a new route up the twin Wild Sander peaks with his two friends, Goering wrote in his mountaineering diary the next day, "Alone with nature and nice people. I thought of the hot, dusty cities, particularly of Berlin; I thought of the bare walls and

---

629 Speer, *Inside the Third Reich* p. 33.

630 Sax, p. 146.

631 Hitler, Adolf quoted from the *Reichszeitung der deutschen Erzieher/Nationalsozialistischen Lehrerzeitung* in Groning and Wolschke, "*Naturshutz and Okologie im Nationalsozialismus,*" quoted by Domonick, p. 81.

drab parade ground of the corps and thanked God I could enjoy the heights of nature."[632] Goering was followed by the much more mystic homeopath and vegetarian Rudolf Hess, Hitler's secretary and Deputy *Fuhrer*. "Hess's office contained several ecologists …who wrote on the need for carefully planned, organic, ecologically sound land use and planning."[633] The fact that both Goering and Hess were very close to Hitler, and were also two of the most powerful figures in the Nazi Party throughout most of its history, would all but guarantee that the Reich would be painted green along with the brown. Hess himself characterized his personal "interests as those of a mountaineer" who loved alpine chalets and "countrified pursuits."[634]

Heinrich Himmler, the infamous SS leader, was a strong green pagan mystic and animal lover. "SS training included a respect for animal life of near Buddhist proportions."[635] Himmler was obsessed with blood and soil ideology[636] and its emphasis upon the green peasantry. Himmler began his political career in the 1920s as a backwoods Nazi leader from the forests and countryside of Bavaria.[637] Himmler and the SS dreaded over what they called *land flight*. Thanks to Himmler and the SS, the Nazis incorporated a modernized agrarian Romanticism into their movement. Himmler and his agricultural mentor, Richard Walther Darre, actually believed German racial biology was being destroyed by the cosmopolitan life of the cities. Germans were being uprooted from their homeland and enslaved to the artificial values of the Jewish international market on one hand, and Jewish Bolshevism on the other. Himmler opined "The yeoman on his own acre is the backbone of the German people's strength and character."[638] To counteract this existential crisis, Darre and Himmler came up with a cockamamie racial green doctrine called blood and soil. The idea was to get German blood back out of the city into the soil of the countryside where they could become self-sufficient farmers in a *buy local* scheme of racist proportions.

Himmler was considered by the German greens of the day to be on their side. He was the ultimate go-to man to finally put a stop to a controversial

---

632   Irving, p. 32.
633   Bramwell, *Ecology in the 20ᵗʰ Century: A History*, p. 197.
634   Manvell and Fraenkel, p. 138.
635   Bramwell, *Blood and Soil: Walther Darre and Hitler's Green Party*, p. 134.
636   Hohne, p. 44.
637   Ibid., pp. 43-44.
638   Heinrich Himmler: *Volkische Bauernpolitik*, undated, Central Archives, Microfilm 98; quoted by Hohne, p. 44.

mining operation on the Hohenstoffeln Mountain in southern Germany near Lake Constance.[639] In spite of the fact that Nazi Germany was in dire need of natural resources to build their military machine, Himmler was used by green Nazi Dr. Ludwig Finckh to get the mining operation finally shut down after a two-decade dispute. Himmler wrote to Goering calling for the quarry's closure and "in spite of protests from the company and the chamber of commerce, mining operations finally ceased on the Hohenstoffeln by the end of 1939."[640] The quarry was essentially confiscated at great cost to the mining company. After the mine was shut down, Dr. Finckh wrote in a magazine article that his victory was a "symbol: the *Fuhrer's* principles are not simply written on paper, they become a fact, a truth, they lead towards realization."[641]

In 1940, Himmler established experimental organic farms called biodynamic plantations at concentration camps like Dachau and Ravensbruck. Such plantations were also established in Poland as well. These organic plantations grew biodynamic herbs, medicines and other goods for the SS. The year before, Himmler organized a new SS corporation named the German Research Facility for Food and Nutrition otherwise known as the DVA. "A substantial portion of its operations consisted of biodynamic plantations growing products for the SS and the German military, with production monitored by representatives of the Reich League for Biodynamic Agriculture."[642] The Reich League for Biodynamic Agriculture was set up in 1933 under the authority of organic farming enthusiast Erhard Bartsch. Organic farm devotees like Bartsch considered their holistic farming practices to be the application of spiritual peasant wisdom that stood in great contrast to the corrupting influences of "civilization, technology, and modern urban culture."[643]

In an instructional letter sent to Dachau and *Ester-wegen*, Himmler stated, "I wish the SS and the police also will be exemplary in the love of nature. Within the course of a few years the property of the SS and the police must become paradises for animals and Nature."[644] Although Himmler did have a

---

[639] See especially Uekoetter, pp. 85-99.

[640] Uekoetter, pp. 96.

[641] Ibid., p. 97.

[642] Staudenmaier & Biehl, p. 122.

[643] Willmann, Kurt, "Vom Wesen des deutschen Bauerntums," *Demeter*, August 1939, p. 147; quoted by Staudenmaier & Biehl, p. 116.

[644] Degregori, Thomas, "Environmentalism, Animal Rights Activism, and Eco-Nazism," April 1, 2001.

secret plan to turn Poland and Russia into an independent industrial empire outside of Germany to sustain the SS,[645] he was nonetheless heavily involved in a horrific green master plan for the occupied East as well. In fact, one of the reasons Himmler wanted to seize heavy industry in the East was to use it as a fundraiser to help pay for this plan. As the SS leader, Himmler was in charge of the resettlement policies in the East. He wanted to Germanize the eastern steppes by growing large tracts of forestlands to make the new German settlers feel more at home.[646]

These high-ranking Nazi leaders, including the *Fuhrer*, clearly demonstrate that the green streak of the Reich was no trifling matter. Even without Hitler's own environmental predilections, with the likes of Goering, Hess and Himmler, no other country could boast of such a green triumvirate at the highest echelons of society. In fact, it is highly doubtful that such a concentration of green power at the pinnacle of any Western society has existed since. Indeed, in November of 1937, Lord Halifax confessed that Goering was "like a schoolboy, full of life and pride in all he was doing, showing off his forest and animals, and then talking high politics out of the setting of green jerkin' and red dagger."[647]

In addition to Goering, Hess, and Himmler, biologist Walther Schoenichen was perhaps the most thoroughgoing ecologically minded Nazi environmentalist, followed closely by Dr. Alwin Seifert. Dr. Seifert was known as "Mr. Mother Nature" among his Nazi colleagues and worked out of Hess's ecology department. Seifert successfully prevented the most ecologically devastating plans of a power plant dam in the Austrian Alps in spite of the Nazi thirst for energy to supply their war machine. The dam was not fully operational until 1944. Like many shrill environmentalists today, Seifert feared "irreparable damage" to the area. Dr. Seifert worked for the highly praised Nazi civil engineer, Dr. Fritz Todt, as the state attorney for landscape.[648]

---

[645] See Albert Speer's book called *Infiltration* (New York: MacMillan Books, 1981) which deals with this very topic. Speer was unimpressed with Himmler's attempt to build an industrial empire in the East. According to Speer, Himmler was a backward Romantic with too many mediocre Nazi deadbeats under his authority to have accomplished such a feat. In other words, an industrial empire based on concentration camp slave labor run by backwater Nazis is an oxymoron. Worse, Speer also suggested that Himmler was forced by Hitler to keep gassing the very workers who were supposed to build his industrial empire.

[646] Bramwell, *Blood and Soil: Walther Darre and Hitler's Green Party*, p. 134.

[647] Irving, p. 193.

[648] Olsen, p. 76.

Dr. Todt was appointed inspector general for the German roadways by Hitler and built the *Autobahnen*. He was not only a friend of Seifert's but also was sympathetic to ecological ideas and early environmental engineering experiments. Dr. Todt loved mountain climbing and was an avid skier. He became the leader of the Nazi construction industry. He was placed in charge of building the West Wall, and later became Hitler's armaments minister. Dr. Seifert used his position under Dr. Todt "to argue for environmentally sensitive building projects that would protect forests, rivers, and wetlands."[649] Seifert is thus one of the primary fathers of what is trumpeted today as green building. "He believed that while human intervention into nature was absolutely necessary for continued technological, scientific, and economic advance, such intrusions should be limited and should preserve as much as possible the natural characteristics of a particular eco-system."[650] As such, according to Seifert, "Intervention into nature ... should be guided by a holistic view of the relationship between nature and human beings."[651] Seifert thus presaged the modern environmental technocratic emphasis upon green building and sustainable development.

Albert Speer, who replaced Todt after his death in a mysterious plane crash in 1942, said he had much in common with him. "We loved nature, life in alpine shelters, ski tours."[652] Speer went on to say that he and his wife were frequent guests of the Todts and that they "lived in a small unpretentious place off the beaten track on *Hintersee* near *Berchtesgaden*. No one would have guessed that the famous road builder and creator of the autobahns lived there."[653] While many blame Speer for his technocratic ways and labeled him an industrialist, he himself saw no contradiction between being a technocrat and being a Romantic.[654] In fact, Speer was proud of his *green* accomplishments as chief of the beauty of work office.[655] Researcher Gitta Sereny characterized Speer as a very private man who once told her, "I have never liked to live in places where I look out on houses or where people can, heaven forbid, drop in. I like waking up to smell the grass and the sight of the mountains, and I like to choose who I see, in my own house or elsewhere."[656]

---

[649]   Ibid., p. 77.
[650]   Ibid.
[651]   Ibid.
[652]   Speer, *Inside the Third Reich*, p. 193.
[653]   Ibid.
[654]   Sereny, Gitta. *Albert Speer's Battle with Truth*, p. 41.
[655]   Speer, *Spandau: The Secret Diaries*, p. 399.
[656]   Sereny, *Albert Speer's Battle with Truth*, p. 119.

Wilhelm Lienenkamper represented the preservationist camp in helping to set aside nature preserves. Hans Schwenkel was a conservationist professor. Wiepking-Jurgensmann was a Nazi environmental planner who had the best-laid plans designed for the occupied eastern territories. For the newly reclaimed land in Poland, western Russia and the Ukraine, he and Konrad Meyer "proposed a synthesis of nature and technology"[657] where a shaping of nature was respectfully pursued without disrupting it so that man, wildlife and plants could live harmoniously together. Like Seifert, they were big believers in sustainable development. "German planners in the East always maintained that they wanted to balance modern economic needs with the claims of nature."[658]

Dr. Paul Schultze-Naumburg was one of the first prominent early environmentalists to join the Nazi Party in the 1920s. Both he and Alwin Seifert were in the Thule Society together before they became Nazis.[659] The Thule Society was an Aryan secret lodge that emphasized Pan Germanism and semi-occultic beliefs together with working class values.[660] The Thule Society emphasized an anthropology rooted in ancient Germanic studies. It became the ideological basis upon which Nazism was later built. In fact, it seems as though the Thule Society disbanded in 1919 and re-organized itself as the Nazi Party (NSDAP). Not only did Schultze-Naumburg work with Alfred Rosenberg, who attended Thule Society meetings and was the doctrinaire on all things Nazi, but he was also later elected to the Reichstag as a Nazi Party delegate in 1932. Like Rosenberg, Schultze-Naumburg became one of the most important authors of Nazi political culture. Goebbels considered Schultze-Naumburg one of the national treasures of National Socialism by placing him within the top ranks of what was called the *Gottbegnadeten* List.

Like Hitler, Schultze-Naumburg loved art and railed against modern architecture. He was also heavily involved in the *Heimat* movement in the early 20th century. He was the chairman of the German Federation for the Protection of the Homeland (DBH) between 1904 and 1914.[661] *Heimat* means homeland, and so the early German greens were considerably involved with this movement long before the Nazis rose to power. The DBH's "un-

---

657 Blackbourn, p. 289.
658 Ibid., p. 287.
659 Olsen, p. 68.
660 Tyson, p. 110.
661 Olsen, p. 65.

derstanding of nature was inherited from Romanticism, and like Romantic thinkers leading representatives of the *heimat* movement articulated themes of the organic society, a stress on the naturalness of the nation, and a rejection of fundamental Enlightenment beliefs."[662] Here, the fateful connection between racism and environmental protection of the homeland later became the foundational basis upon which many *right wing* greens in contemporary Germany have built their ecological views upon.[663] That a rough and ready line can be drawn between the Thule Society and modern *right wing* ecologists, with a few evolutionary bumps along the way, is certainly disconcerting to say the least. This is especially true since today many facets of the so-called German *right wing* ecology movement are in step with the *left wing* environmentalism of the German Green Party. This is the legacy of Dr. Paul Schultze-Naumburg.

The Hitler Youth cannot be ignored either. The veritable bible of the Hitler Youth was Nietzsche's earthy existentialist book called, "Thus Spake Zarathustra."[664] The Hitler Youth was built upon the *volkisch* youth movement of the early 1900s called the *wandervogel*. The *wandervogel* movement began in 1894. It was one of the first environmentally conscious movements in Germany. The term *wandervogel* itself literally means "free wandering bird." Much of the early German green movement before World War I emphasized birds and bird-watching. The *wandervogel* movement provided opportunities for German youth to explore the great outdoors with a spirit of adventure and rugged self-discipline. German folklore, nationalism and an intense appreciation for nature were emphasized. *Volkisch* nationalism and environmentalism together with a regressive rejection of modernity characterized the *wandervogel* movement:

> The chief vehicle for carrying this ideological constellation to prominence was the youth movement, an amorphous phenomenon which played a decisive but highly ambivalent role in shaping German popular culture during the first three tumultuous decades of this (20th) century. Also known as the *wandervogel*, the youth movement was a hodge-podge of countercultural elements, blending neo-Romanticism, Eastern Philosophies, nature mysticism, hostility to

---

662 Ibid.
663 Ibid., pp. 53-109.
664 Peters, H.F. *Zarathustra's Sister: The Case of Elisabeth and Friedrich Nietzsche.* New York: Crown Publishers, 1977, p. 221.

reason, and a strong communal impulse in a confused but no less ardent search for authentic, non-alienated social relations. Their back-to-the-land emphasis spurred a passionate sensitivity to the natural world and the damage it suffered. They have been aptly characterized as "right wing hippies," for although some sectors of the movement gravitated toward various forms of emancipatory politics, most of the *wandervogel* were eventually absorbed by the Nazis.[665]

The *wandervogels* took part in festivals that reminded "them of the inner connection between the landscape and customs of the various German tribes."[666] In the late 1930s and early 40s, school children regularly sang nature songs National Socialist style. While the Hitler Youth later replaced the *wandervogels* during the Nazi regime, one could also easily argue the SS itself was a grown-up version of the *wandervogel* movement. Heinrich Himmler and Walther Darre were both involved in one of the *wandervogel* groups called the *Artamanens*. *Artaman* basically means "agricultural man" or "country man" with certain racial connotations.

The 'Back to the Land' Movement of the SS

In 1930, Richard Walther Darre, Himmler's mentor and close associate of Dr. Paul Schultze-Naumburg, declared, "The unity of blood and soil must be restored."[667] Through such Nazi slogans, Darre became the champion of the *green* peasant farmer. He forcefully pitted himself against the cultural bankruptcy of the international cosmopolitan city. Darre strongly believed the modern city was corrupting Germany with international capitalism and communism. "Harking back to Arndt and Riehl, he envisioned a thoroughgoing ruralization of Germany and Europe, predicated on a revitalized yeoman peasantry, in order to ensure racial health and ecological sustainability."[668] Darre "saw the re-ruralization of Germany as the only viable alternative to inevitable national destruction."[669] To overcome severe cultural decay,

---

[665] Staudenmaier & Biehl, pp. 20-21.

[666] Zimmerman, *Ecofascism: An Enduring Temptation*, p. 8.

[667] Darre announced this in a speech called "Blood and Soil as the foundations of the life of the Nordic race," quoted in Staudenmaier & Biehl, p. 31.

[668] Staudenmaier & Biehl, p. 31.

[669] Bramwell, Anna, *Blood and Soil: Walther Darre and Hitler's Green Party*, p. 74.

Germany must become a socialist rural state built on the *green* peasantry. Thus, move over proletariat for the pristine Nazi *volkisch* peasant farmers! Now was the time to get back to the land.

Darre had "radical proposals to de-industrialize Germany, to leave the cities to decay, and to concentrate resources on the land."[670] He was adamantly convinced that industrialization, urbanization, and cosmopolitanism were destroying German culture. Darre believed that such a lifestyle had removed people from the countryside and made them dependent upon the international exploitation of industrial capitalism in the city that invariably fostered an unnecessary communist backlash to alleviate the social grievances.

Thanks to the Treaty of Versailles that concluded World War I, the capitalistic powers of the West condemned Germany to extreme economic deprivation that lasted almost a decade. Those who lived in poverty in the cities faced grave difficulties. They had no land to fall back on to grow their own food. Thus, Darre's "back to the land" impetus found many adherents. "The argument was if man lived according to the laws of nature, becoming aware intuitively of his links with the world around him, he would be better and happier. The attempt to escape these bonds could only fail, and lead to a cycle of industrial growth, collapse and misery."[671]

Without Darre and his "back to the land" movement, the Nazis would not have garnered the necessary votes that catapulted them into power. It was Darre who presented to Hitler's Nazi Party a united *green* front of peasant farmers.[672] "By the fall of 1932 the demands of Germany's agrarian organizations had become more radical and threatening from the standpoint of industry and banking. The Nazis themselves had a hand in that process of radicalization, as they had infiltrated the largest and most vocal of the agrarian organizations, the *Reichslandbund* (RNS), within which their spokesman consistently assumed extreme positions."[673] Darre even wrote a letter to Hitler in the early 1930s speaking of the possibility of making a

---

[670] Ibid., p. 105.

[671] Ibid., p. 73.

[672] Gerhard, "Breeding Pigs and People for the Third Reich" in *How Green Were the Nazis?*, p. 133. Gerhard then goes on to argue that Darre was really not green after all, but was rather a typical Nazi racist instead, almost as if the two categories must be a priori mutually exclusive, pp. 136-40.

[673] Turner, p. 282.

peasant coup "to be carried out by force, if necessary, against Germany's big cities."[674]

Informed by the *volkisch* nationalism of the 1800s, German farmers rebelled against the urbanism and industrialization of the modern capitalistic world. "When in the fall of 1932, the *Reichslandbund* and other organizations comprising the 'Green Front' that championed agrarian interests demanded a thoroughgoing system of stringent import quotas for agricultural products and a downward adjustment of the interest rates on outstanding farm mortgages, the Nazis emphatically endorsed their demands."[675] These anti-predatory lending concerns coupled with a buy-local farm push was designed to mobilize discontent in the countryside against the German government for allegedly ignoring their interests.[676] Later, the German farmers' opposition to capitalistic farming practices was confirmed by the ecological catastrophe of the Dust Bowl.[677] Hitler rewarded Darre for his efforts by appointing him as the Third Reich's agricultural minister in 1933. Darre held this position until 1942, at which time he was finally deposed. The food crisis in 1941-42 forced him to start drawing up plans to begin severe rationing for Germans on the home front.[678] Because of Darre's failure to feed Germany appropriately, Hitler retired him.

Yet one year before Darre's dismissal, Hitler lauded his efforts: "Darre has done two good things: the law of agrarian inheritance, and the regulation of markets."[679] The post-war opinion, however, described his agrarian inheritance efforts as "Teutonic breeding centers."[680] Darre was SS. He was as racist as they come. His law of agrarian inheritance was designed to protect the peasant blood of Germany who lived closely to the soil. The "law proposed to create a new category of farm, the *Erbhof* (hereditary farm), protected against debt, insulated from market forces and passed down from generation to generation within racially pure peasant families."[681] These hereditary farms could not be sold, nor "used as a security against mortgages."[682] Closely connected, Darre also "proposed that the *Erbhof*

---

674   Bramwell, *Blood and Soil: Walther Darre and Hitler's Green Party*, p. 76.
675   Turner, p. 282.
676   Ibid.
677   Bramwell, Anna, *Ecology in the 20ᵗʰ Century: A History*, p. 207.
678   Tooze, p. 543.
679   *Hitler's Table Talk*, night of July 27-28, 1941, p. 15.
680   Bramwell, *Blood and Soil: Walther Darre and Hitler's Green Party*, p. 183.
681   Tooze, p. 182.
682   Ibid., p. 183.

farmers should assume collective responsibility for each other's debts," which were then "to be transferred to the *Rentenbank Kreditanstalt*, a state sponsored mortgage bank."[683] To help keep the *Erbhof* farmers out of debt, Darre also set up a strict "system of price and production controls" which "marked the end of the free market for agricultural produce in Germany."[684] Indeed, prices were no longer to be determined by supply and demand, and this required Darre's RNS to extend "its control and supervision into every field, barnyard and milking shed in the country."[685] There was even a ban on corrugated iron roofing for farm buildings[686] to help prevent roof stormwater from polluting the countryside.

While Darre was at first interested in establishing self-sufficient Aryan farms, he later became increasingly attracted to low-tech organic farming. Darre's change of attitude about organic farming came from the strong influences of Hess, Seifert[687] and others from the Reich League of Biodynamic Agriculture[688] so that his blood and soil mystique got mixed up with organic farming. "Biodynamic publications combined anthroposophical,[689] organic, and National Socialist vocabularies, including *Lebensraum* and blood and soil terminology, and touted the abundant contributions made by biodynamic practices to the environmental policy of the Third Reich. Such ideological combinations carried a potent message; biodynamic representatives blamed profit-oriented chemical agriculture on the Jews, and their anti-materialist stance won them praise from Nazi anti-Semites."[690] Much publishing help on biodynamic themes came from Hanns Mueller. Mueller was heavily involved in the Nazi *Lebensreform* movement, which was a popular crusade within the party promoting lifestyle reform. Thanks to Muller and other *Lebensreform* officials, "biodynamic growers were presented as pioneers of the natural German method of cultivation that had finally come into its own under the leadership of the Third Reich."[691]

However, Darre's plans to make Germany self-sufficient in terms of growing food required more land to be subjected to the plow. Such widespread

---

683 Ibid.
684 Ibid., p. 186.
685 Ibid., p. 187.
686 Speer, *Spandau: The Secret Diaries*, p. 399.
687 Bramwell, *Ecology in the 20ʰ Century: A History*, pp. 197-204.
688 See Staudenmaier & Biehl, pp. 108-123.
689 See footnote 1058 for the meaning of anthroposophy.
690 Staudenmaier & Biehl, p. 117.
691 Ibid., p. 118.

practices across the entire German countryside began to raise the ire of Seifert and other green Nazis. They complained that draining all the swamps and regulating the rivers for the sake of making the land more arable for farming would dry up Germany's water table and threaten the land with a potential dust bowl. As a strong proponent of organic farming, Seifert wanted to "rid the countryside of artificial fertilizers and insecticides. He advocated composting organic waste to enrich the soil, and establishing hedgerows as habitats for pest-eating birds and animals."[692] As the 1930s wore on, therefore, Darre began to think more seriously about implementing organic farming in the Reich to help offset some of these ecological concerns.

This desire to organicize German agriculture, however, met with much opposition in the Nazi hierarchy and thus was never carried out. While there is no little controversy over this particular issue among environmental historians, what is known for sure is that Goering, Hess, Darre, Seifert, Bormann and others were having heated discussions over whether or not German farms should go organic, even during the early part of the war. "A similar result in other countries seems improbable, especially during war time, and demonstrates the extent to which interest in organic farming had permeated the Nazi as well as the German establishment."[693] While Bormann was antagonistic to organic farming because of its ties to mysticism, Goering opposed it because "he feared a drop in German food production."[694] Himmler, however, took organic farming under his wing in the occupied East during the war. Herbert Backe, who replaced Darre as the Reich's agricultural minister, said "The SS have already installed their own agricultural and market gardening enterprises, and it really looks as though leadership has been transferred to Himmler."[695] Thus, surprisingly enough, organic farming headed east during the war.

At one time, Darre had the fourth largest budget in the Third Reich at his disposal, but he was never able to truly implement his *volkisch* agrarian dreams, nor seriously get the Reich to pursue a path of organic farming, especially as the war effort set aside all other concerns. The great problem with Darre's plans was that he essentially wrote off a sizable population slice of Germany since most people lived in the city. Darre was also a Nordicist

---

[692] Lekan, p. 231.
[693] Bramwell, *Ecology in the 20ʰ Century: A History*, p. 204.
[694] Ibid., p. 201.
[695] Backe papers; BA NL75/10 quoted in Bramwell, *Ecology in the 20ʰ Century: A History*, p. 199.

who spoke glowingly of the white race of the far north. Not all Nazis agreed with the Nordic racist position. Hitler himself was from Austria.

Darre "argued that peasant cultural continuity, the living tradition, was lost in urbanization. But he also argued that peasantness was genetically inherent in the Nordic people. If this was so, then there was no reason why sound Nordic stock could not be rescued from the towns and returned back to the land. By arguing that peasantness could not re-emerge from submergence in town life, he subordinated his racialist argument to his concept of spiritual peasantness, and, by inference, wrote off the 70% urban population of Germany."[696] Such proposals proved to be far too radical even for many of the Nazis. Shockingly, Darre was more fascist than the Nazis themselves.[697] While Hitler used Darre to help himself gain power over Germany, he was not willing to allow him to carry out his entire *blood and soil* program, largely because of certain political and economic realities which had to be faced in order to get Germany on an all-out war footing.

Yet, many of Darre's *back to the land* government programs were still implemented by the Reich on a grand scale.[698] In the early to mid-1930s the Nazi government began setting up labor camps all over the Reich to help Germany become more arable and self-sufficient. The SS set up an office for the express purpose of "selecting desirable people for settlement in rural districts as farmers, farm laborers and peasants, which, working on the lines of the new biological revaluation, granted permits, land and sometimes credits, only to the best people from the standpoint of descent, health and capacity."[699] These labor camps became filled with workers. Not only were many still suffering from displacement problems brought on by the Treaty of Versailles, which redrew Germany's borders, but unemployment continued to be a huge problem in the early to mid-1930s, especially as the Great Depression set in. Many young Germans entered the labor service between the ages of 17 and 25. They then served for six months in such capacity before going on to serve the military.

Nietzsche expert and Nazi sympathizer Anthony Ludovici from England gave this glowing eyewitness report in 1936: "Life in the camps is divided between manual labor with spade and hoe, in which all must take part, strenuous drilling exercises, and period of leisure given to reading

---

[696]   Bramwell, p. 74.
[697]   Ibid., p. 89.
[698]   Ludovici, Anthony, "Hitler and the Third Reich," *English Review*, 63, 1936, p. 148.
[699]   Ibid., pp. 148-49.

and the study of contemporary events and problems. The day starts at 5 a.m. in the summer and 6 a.m. in the winter, and ends at 10:00 p.m.—the time after supper and short intervals during the day being devoted to rest and leisurely pursuits."[700] The books that would have been read by the laborers were undoubtedly racially charged propaganda books. "Darre wanted farmers and their families to be educated into racial consciousness—White is Beautiful—as part of the process of instilling a sense of identity. It was seen as a rescue operation of a vanishing breed."[701]

By 1935, there were 1,300 camps in Germany which consisted of about 150 men each.[702] This gave the Reich 200,000 workers whose labor was basically unpaid.[703] Ludovici was very impressed with the results of this unpaid labor: "The net annual proceeds derived from the work done by the Labor Service organization have already exceeded 10% of the cost of the organization. But the full value of what they are now creating in the form of new agricultural areas, new farmsteads and new peasant population will, of course, not be realized for perhaps a generation or two."[704] Ludovici also pointed out the Labor Service slowed down the great migrations to the cities, and the results of such practices led to more wholesome lifestyles: "Thanks to the right spirit and the right values, and in spite of a world that has too long worshipped only money and the successful stockbroker and financier, it somehow comes true. It can already be seen in the faces and manners of the people, and it is evidenced in every relationship of high and humble in the life of modern Germany."[705]

Ludovici then made this conclusion: "Withdrawing the human being from a close touch with the realities of nature's work and laws, from the everyday and obvious lessons to be learnt by watching cultivated plants and animals grow, and observing the conditions essential to their prosperity, town life must in time foster a fantastic or unrealistic attitude to life and its problems, which of itself constitutes mental or intellectual unsoundness. Over and above this, however, in towns and cities, the very roots of human life tend to wither."[706] Ludovici thus praised the new Nazi laws and

---

[700] Ibid., p. 150.
[701] Bramwell, *Blood and Soil: Walther Darre and Hitler's Green Party*, p. 72.
[702] Ludovici, "Hitler and the Third Reich," *English Review*, 63, 1936, p. 150.
[703] Ibid.
[704] Ibid., p. 151.
[705] Ibid., p. 152.
[706] Ibid., pp. 231-32.

practices to get people back to the land: "Three influences—urbanization, industrialism, and the negative Socratic values which began to prevail with the spread of Protestantism, and happened to be favorable to the former two—have now, for almost two centuries, been inclining the people of Europe, and all countries like Europe, to set their faces ever more steadfastly against a biological attitude towards man."[707] By negative Socratic values, Ludovici meant that Western Civilization's emphasis upon mind over body can be attributed back to Socrates. According to Ludovici, Socrates, the ancient philosopher of Greece, was a man of poor physique and bad health. To make up for his physical weaknesses, he magnified his philosophical mind over his wretched body—a tradition which was later spiritualized by the Protestants. As far as Ludovici was concerned, this trend needs to be stopped in order to stave off the decline of Europe, and the Nazis were on the right path to do just that very thing.

The Nazi blood and soil *back to the land* movement was celebrated annually at the Buckeberg Harvest Festival in central Germany for five years running. Following on the heels of the all-German Party rallies that took place at Nuremberg in early September on the National Socialist calendar,[708] the Reich harvest festival, the so-called Nazi day of thanksgiving, became known as the "Nuremberg of the north" because it was so widely attended. By 1937, 1.2 million people had gathered to celebrate the harvest festival. Only the demands of the war effort from 1938 onward put a stop to the festival as the *Wehrmacht* increasingly took control of the transportation system of Germany. The Buckeberg blood and soil festival was so large that it created great transportation challenges because of its rural setting.

Originally organized by Goebbels and Darre in 1933, and administered by the SS with some planning advice coming from Speer, on these festive occasions, "50,000 farmers and peasants in ancient folk costumes (the beautiful, strong, healthy-hard men of our *Landvolk*) trooped to the Buckeberg and there erected a giant German crown-like wheat sheaf."[709] The peasant folklore was strongly accentuated with singing, folk dancing, and great color, but also mixed in with demonstrations by the armed forces. This festival thus perfectly symbolized the *volkisch* unity between the farmers and soldiers of Germany. As the German farmers feed the nation, the army

---

[707] Ibid., p. 231.
[708] For a good summary detailing the Nazi Party calendar year, see Stern's chapter entitled "The Religious Expectation and its Ritual," pp. 70-75.
[709] Stern, p. 72.

protects the *volk* and the land, i.e., its blood and soil. During the festivities both Hitler and Darre were crowned with harvest wreaths. Goebbels and Darre gave short talks before giving way to Hitler's speech that usually lasted 30 minutes. The content of Hitler's speeches at the festivals consisted on how the foundation for the economy is rooted in its farmers who will help make Germany strong and self-sufficient. Closely connected, Hitler would then sharply pillory the forces of international Jewish finances and Bolshevism that artificially worked against the critical need of developing a self-sufficient Aryan economy. The audience often cried out with thunderous outbursts of "*Sieg Heil!*" in response to the *Fuhrer's* tirades.

Adolf in the Alps

Before Hitler came to power, he fell in love with an area called the Obersalzberg. It was located in the Bavarian Alps above a beautiful mountain hamlet named Berchtesgaden. Hitler remained strongly attached to the alpine serenity of the Obersalzlberg until his death. In fact, many people assumed, both inside and outside of Germany, that the last stand of the Nazis would take place at the alpine redoubt in the Obersalzberg.[710] The first time Hitler saw it he exclaimed, "What a lovely view over the valley! A countryside of indescribable beauty."[711] Even the naturalist explorer Alexander von Humboldt, one of the original *volkisch* environmental thinkers in Germany of the 1800s, stated the Obersalzberg was the most beautiful spot on earth.[712]

Hitler's fatherly sage, Dietrich Eckart, was the very man who introduced Hitler to the spectacular region in April of 1923. "Hitler stayed at Pension Moritz with Eckart, registering him under the name 'Wolf.'" Eckart also loved "Berchtesgaden, an alpine village with no industries beside dairy farming, toy manufacture clock-making, salt mining, and tourism. He shuttled back and forth between Munich and Berchtesgaden several times between 1922 and 1923."[713] At the time, Berchtesgaden served as a retreat, if not hideout[714] for Eckart. It was even stated: "There

---

[710]   Mitchell, p. 1.
[711]   Ibid., p. 18.
[712]   Ibid, p 8.
[713]   Tyson, p. 403.
[714]   *Hitler's Table Talk*, night of Jan. 16-17, 1942.

are no traitors in Obersalzberg!"[715] The town was situated in the extreme southeast of Germany virtually on the border of Austria surrounded by craggy mountain peaks that appear much taller than they actually are. The failing Eckart died of heart failure the day after Christmas 1923. "Nearly 100 gathered to bury Eckart in Berchtesgaden's old cemetery on December 30th. 10 speakers paid tribute. In accordance with his wishes, the headstone faced Obersalzberg's massive peak."[716] Many Nazi leaders did not attend the funeral because of strong police surveillance. One of them "viewed the burial through binoculars from a distant point."[717]

In the 1920s when Hitler was younger, he did go on hikes in the area. He also climbed Mt. Jenner and enjoyed skiing. Hitler's rambling habits would continue up until the mid-1930s when he "had always enjoyed long mountain walks around the Obersalzberg and mixed freely with the local population, but enormous numbers of admirers eventually posed problems of organization and security."[718] Although Speer was unimpressed with Hitler's mountain climbing abilities, he recalled that "between 1934 and 1936 Hitler still took tramps on the public forest paths accompanied by his guests and three or four plainclothes detectives belonging to the SS."[719] This activity slowed considerably as Hitler tightened his control over Germany. Along with this came strict national security measures. By the late 1930s Hitler's health declined so that his walks were far less common and held to a minimum. While some environmental historians cynically hold that Hitler had little interest in such beautiful settings beyond the postcard image,[720] this is simply untrue. Hitler fell in love with the beautiful scenic area as early as 1923.[721] Even Goebbels "was entranced by the lake and mountain scenery which had such a life-long attraction for the *Fuhrer*."[722]

On one of his earlier hikes, Hitler "stumbled upon *Haus Wachenfeld*, a rustic cabin where he would build his *Berghof* (mountain home) chalet in

---

[715] Tyson, p. 404.
[716] Ibid., p. 413.
[717] Ibid.
[718] Goodrick-Clarke, *Hitler's Priestess*, pp. 155-56.
[719] Speer, *Inside the Third Reich*, p. 47.
[720] Uekoetter, p. 32.
[721] Ibid., p. 179.
[722] Manvell and Fraenkel, p. 39.

1936."[723] Hitler later bought the mountain hut in 1933. Early pictures[724] of the Obersalzberg area show *Haus Wachenfeld* off to the side of about a dozen quaint houses and sheds overlooking the valley below where Berchtesgaden sits. From this perch there were breathtaking views toward the southeast into Austria itself. The houses and sheds sat slightly above *Haus Wachenfeld* on a beautiful pastoral shelf. This serene area would later become a security fortress after Hitler became chancellor of Germany. By 1945, the Nazis had filled this mountain meadow with 16 oversized buildings including many barracks, administration buildings, living quarters, a kindergarten, a post office, a hotel, a model architectural house, a nursery and a Gestapo office.[725] A model farm was also built in the area for Hitler. Dr. Alwin Seifert even designed a greenhouse so that the *Fuhrer* could eat organic vegetables all year long despite the mountain weather.[726]

It was Martin Bormann who developed the idyllic Obersalzberg into a maximum security complex in the mid-to-late-1930s. Speer remarked that Bormann became "the real master of the *Obersalzberg*. He forcibly bought up centuries old farms and had the buildings torn down. The same was done to the numerous votive chapels, despite the objections of the parishes. He also confiscated state forests, until the private area reached from the top of the mountain ... to the valley ... and embraced an area of 2.7 square miles."[727] However, Hitler himself had a different view of the situation, "I am buying up all these hills and making it forbidden property so that Himmler can quit worrying."[728] Hitler hated walking with Himmler's SS security men. He also once complained that giving up his Bavarian leather walking shorts was one of the biggest political sacrifices he had to make.[729]

Bormann was in fact always building and developing the Obersalzberg. He never finished it. Speer complained, "With total insensitivity to the natural surroundings, Bormann laid out a network of roads through this magnificent landscape. He turned forest paths, hitherto carpeted by pine needles and penetrated by roots, into paved promenades A barracks, a vast

---

[723]   Tyson, p. 405.

[724]   See *Hitler's Alpine Retreat*. South Yorkshire, United Kingdom: Pen & Sword Military, 2010, by James Wilson, pp. 39-42.

[725]   Ibid., pp. 6-7.

[726]   Zeller, Thomas, "Molding the Landscape of Nazi Environmentalism," in *How Green Were the Nazis?*, p. 168.

[727]   Speer, *Inside the Third Reich*, p. 84.

[728]   Mitchell, p. 26.

[729]   Ibid., p. 22.

garage building, a hotel for Hitler's guests, a new manor house, a complex for the constantly growing number of employees, sprang up as rapidly as in a suddenly fashionable resort."[730] There were even plans to build public scenic roads below Mt. Jenner high above Konigssee.[731] In fact, after Bormann overspent tens of millions of marks developing the Obersalzberg, Hitler was somewhat embarrassed by it all: "When it's all finished I'll look for a quiet valley and build another small wooden house there like the first."[732] Bormann's extravagance was best exemplified when he built the Eagle's Nest for Hitler on top of a mountain directly above the Obersalzberg at an elevation of almost 7,000 feet above sea level.

As such, many complained about Bormann's nonstop clumsy building activities and lavish expenditures. After the war, Otto Dietrich called Hitler's mountain retreat an "industrial oasis" and an "artificial park with driveways and gravel paths."[733] Even Dr. Todt was incensed by what Bormann had done. He "repeatedly had serious run-ins with Bormann, protesting his despoiling of the landscape around Obersalzberg."[734] Speer remarked, "Hitler regretted the hubbub but commented: it's Bormann's doing. I do not want to interfere."[735]

However, in spite of all of Bormann's construction activities, Hitler's *Berghof* was still a majestic place. Speer begrudgingly acknowledged the *Berghof* did have a strong personality to it: "The place was still geared to the simple activities of a former weekend cottage, merely expanded to vast proportions."[736] A picture taken before the buildings were bombed by the United States Air Force in 1945 shows how beautiful the area still was. Hitler certainly used it as a showcase to entertain the likes of "the Duke and Duchess of Windsor, Neville Chamberlain, David Lloyd George, Mussolini, Eduard Daladier, Kurt von Schuschnigg, and Admiral Miklos Horthy."[737]

Environmental historians, of course, have a field day describing how the *Fuhrer* overdeveloped the Obersalzberg. They are quick to emphasize how much building took place there throughout much of the Third Reich's duration. They are also giddy over the fact that Hitler kept on expanding the

730   Speer, *Inside the Third Reich*, p. 84.
731   Dietrich, p. 167.
732   Speer, *Inside the Third Reich*, p. 85.
733   Dietrich, p. 164.
734   Speer, *Inside the Third Reich*, p. 193.
735   Ibid., p. 85.
736   Ibid., p. 86.
737   Goodrick-Clarke, *Hitler's Priestess*, p. 156.

size of his chalet. It is such a topic of discussion the reader is left with the idea that Bormann and Hitler tore up the entire mountainside in total disregard of any environmental concerns.

However, the environmental scrutiny on this is far overblown, and much of the eyewitness testimony that complained of the overdevelopment of the Obersalzberg comes from the Nazis themselves. More to the point, those 16 buildings sit on a shelf of perhaps 50 to 75 acres or so, which is very small when one considers that the Obersalzberg essentially became the second capitol of Germany. The fact of the matter is, "The area which later formed the Nazi central zone on the Obersalzberg and accommodated most of the buildings they erected following the takeover was in fact, quite a small area."[738]

One could easily argue that Hollywood actor/environmental activist Robert Redford has developed his Sundance Mountain Resort in Utah that he bought in 1969 on the back side of Park City far more than the *Fuhrer* overdeveloped the Obersalzberg. There are more than 100 houses and studios at the resort. Redford also has an incredible plush alpine home that sits above the Sundance resort in the valley below with a network of good roads mantling his environs. The Redford home is a veritable mountain castle that has an outstanding view of the +11,752 foot Mt. Timpanogos and its satellites—the very massif that provides much of the background to his favorite film that he starred in in 1972 called *Jeremiah Johnson*. The movie is largely based on an historical novel of sorts by Raymond Tharp and Robert Bunker, entitled *Crow Killer: The Saga of Liver-Eating Johnson*. According to mountain-man folklore of the 1800s, "Liver-Eating Johnson" ate the livers of countless Crow warriors after he killed them as revenge for murdering his wife while he was out trapping one season. While *Jeremiah Johnson* leaves such cannibalistic details out of the film, it does manage to blame a prudish Christian minister for the death of his Indian wife in the Hollywood revisionist version of the saga.

While Redford prides himself in making the Sundance Mountain Resort a model for sustainable development, it must be granted the Obersalzberg was also to be constructed along similar lines. "On Hitler's instructions, the landscape and all the wildlife contained within the area of the Obersalzberg were to be preserved. Furthermore, he stated that all construction on the mountain should be unobtrusive in an attempt to maintain a degree

---

[738]   Wilson, p. 49.

of harmony with the natural surroundings."[739] Hitler himself stated the dimensions of the *Berghof* "made me somewhat afraid that it would clash with the landscape. I was very glad to notice that, on the contrary, it fitted in very well. I had already restricted myself for that reason—for, to my taste, it should have been still bigger."[740] Even Hess, who spent much time at the Obersalzberg, later began to make plans for his own "elaborate mountain residence he hoped to establish in Germany after the war."[741] Hermann Goering had already built a house in the immediate area in 1933 upon a ridge which he called "Adolf Hitler Peak."[742]

Hitler had the place developed precisely because he wanted to spend considerable time up in the mountains. Its proximity to Salzburg on the Austrian border was just as important to the *Fuhrer*. In fact, Odilo Globocnik, who was an avid hiker and helped Hitler take Austria for the Nazis before he was charged with being the commander of the Final Solution in Poland, walked all the way from the Obersalzberg to Salzberg in one night.[743] As Hitler had plans to become the *Fuhrer* of both Germany and Austria, the Obersalzberg was the perfect location from which to govern a greater Reich. Hitler was also an Austrian, and he "used his Obersalzberg as a base for repeated sorties around Bavaria, and ... throughout the 1930s he spent a week at Bayreuth for the Wagner festival in August."[744] In fact, Hitler spent almost half of his time enjoying the mountains, living a virtual Bohemian lifestyle far above the hubbub of Germany where "he was out of reach of the bureaucrats."[745] According to the administrator of the *Berghof*, Hitler spent only two to three hours a day on government affairs.[746] Ernst Roehm (1887-1934), the leader of the Nazi paramilitary SA complained, "All he wants to do is sit up in the mountains and play God."[747] Roehm was later arrested and executed by other Nazi rivals, yet with Hitler's hesitant consent.

For political purposes, Hitler presented himself as the veritable mountain man of Germany. At the time, the *Berghof* itself was simply known as "Hitler's

739   Ibid., p. 43.
740   *Hitler's Table Talk: 1941-44*, night of Jan. 16-17, 1942, p. 161.
741   Manvell and Fraenkel, p. 139.
742   Dietrich, p. 169.
743   Rieger, p. 163.
744   Mitchell, p. 29.
745   Ibid.
746   Ibid., p. 28.
747   Ibid., p. 22.

Berg" or "Hitler's Mountain."[748] He was the *Fuhrer* who ruled the country from the alpine heights. "The image of the *Fuhrer* up on the Obersalzberg had a powerful impact on the imagination of the German people."[749] The German cult of the mountains and forest was certainly something that Hitler cultivated for his own political purposes, but he was no less a cult enthusiast. "Up in the great Bavarian mountains he could retreat for refreshment, for thought and planning. The alpine location was most appealing to many German people. Up on his *berg* he could define himself as a healthy, natural sort of man who relished the simple pleasures of life."[750]

In 1935, one visitor said Hitler was a man of the alpine people: "There sitting on the hard chairs hewn by peasant hands, Hitler drank hot milk and chatted about mountains and weather and cows with the bearded mountain men who might be having their daily restoratives of schnapps at that moment."[751] After visiting the *Berghof* in 1938, British diplomat Ivone Kirkpatrick stated, "For days and even weeks this idyllic existence goes on. Hitler may claim that it is no holiday, but every German soldier and every German workman would gladly give up his leave for a few days' rest in the enchanting atmosphere of Berchtesgaden."[752]

Hitler extolled his alpine retreat, stating: "There's nothing lovelier in the world than a mountain landscape. There was a time when I could have wept for grief on having to leave Berchtesgaden."[753] Such a sentiment stated before Albert Speer shows that Hitler had some emotional attachment to the beauties of nature. He was not all red, tooth and claw with regard to his social Darwinism. One Nazi publication wrote:

> One who has been there understands that there is probably no place in Germany where, despite the nearness of the surrounding mountains, one has so wide and unhindered view of the beauties of nature. The *Fuhrer* lives here in the midst of the beauties of nature, a metaphor for human events. Here he writes his major speeches which affect not only Germany, but give new direction to events in the entire world. Far from the confusion and noise of

---

[748]   Sereny, *Albert Speer's Battle with Truth*, p. 118.
[749]   Mitchell, p. 7.
[750]   Ibid., p. 6.
[751]   Ibid., p. 27.
[752]   Ibid., p. 29.
[753]   *Hitler's Table Talk*, midday Feb. 9, 1942, p. 232.

everyday life, the seeking spirit, surrounded by the vastness of the landscape, finds the right paths for the people and fatherland. As the mountains remain eternal despite the passing of millennia, so too the work the *Fuhrer* has begun here will live for millennia in the history of the people."[754]

Speer himself at first assumed that Hitler's choice to often stay at the Obersalzberg was because of his love for nature. In fact, many Germans simply took it at face value that the *Fuhrer* sought "rest and recreation in secluded, untouched nature."[755] After all, at this time, Nazi leaders were talking green and Hitler was signing major green laws. However, after more careful reflection, perhaps after many years sitting in Spandau prison, Speer stated he was mistaken about Hitler: "He did frequently admire a beautiful view, but as a rule he was more affected by the awesomeness of the abysses than by the harmony of the landscape."[756] In other words, Speer intuitively knew that Hitler had much darker views of nature. He stated: "When I look back today, the image of a romantic and also cruel and ruthless world rises before me—romanticism in its unruliness and wildness, not in its pleasant *Bierdermeier Gemutlichkeit*."[757] Thus Speer did not doubt Hitler's basic romantic spirit. Speer just later realized that Hitler was far more attracted to the struggle of nature rather than to its harmony, something which even Darwin himself wrestled with.[758] Love for nature's harmony is thus too strong of a term to characterize Hitler. However, Speer also cautiously remarked, "It may be that he felt more than he allowed himself to express."[759] Neither did Speer know Hitler in the 1920s when the *Fuhrer* was largely unbothered by political and state responsibilities. In other words, with regard to environmentalism and nature, Hitler was very hard to read, even by one of his most trusted associates. Nature itself is hard to read. It can easily be both cruel and non-cruel at the same time, usually depending on the mood of the weather.

Whatever the exact case may be, Hitler himself did strongly believe the Obersalzberg was a beautiful place which gave him better imagination,

---

[754] Mitchell, pp. 26-27.
[755] Uekoetter, p. 117.
[756] Speer, *Inside the Third Reich*, p. 47.
[757] Speer, *Infiltration*, p. 13.
[758] Worster, *Nature's Economy: A History of Ecological Ideas*, pp. 125-27, 180-81.
[759] Speer, *Inside the Third Reich*, p. 47.

inspiration and clearer thinking. "By night, at the *Berghof*, I often remain for hours with eyes wide open, contemplating from my bed the mountains lit up by the moon. It's at such moments that brightness enters my mind."[760] Speer said, "Hitler's stays on the mountain provided him, as he often stressed, with the inner calm and assurance for his surprising decisions. He also composed his most important speeches there."[761] This certainly does not sound like one who is completely disinterested in natural beauty. Hitler declared, "Our duty is to teach men to see whatever is lovely and truly wonderful in life, and not to become prematurely ill-tempered and spiteful. We wish fully to enjoy what is beautiful, and cling to it."[762] For Hitler, lovely beautiful settings in nature and creative imagination went hand in hand.

Furthermore, it is no coincidence that "whenever possible, Hitler, the *Reichforstmeister* (Reich Forestry Minister) Goering, and Himmler were photographed in sylvan settings."[763] In 1935, a book was published by Heinrich Hoffmann called *Hitler in the Mountains*.[764] There were 88 photographs of the *Fuhrer* against the background of beautiful natural settings. This was far more than just propaganda that so many modern environmental historians wish to believe. In fact, in Hitler's racial ecology, the beauties of nature were something to sacrifice oneself for. He said, "What inexhaustible riches the world contains for the man who knows how to enjoy his senses! Moreover, Nature has given man the desire to make others share in the joy he feels. The beautiful always claims its right to primacy. Otherwise how is one to explain the fact that in periods of misfortune so many beings are ready to sacrifice their lives simply to ensure the continuity of their races?"[765] In light of all that is known about Hitler's racism, this is a stunning statement coming from the lips of the *Fuhrer*. In 1938, Hitler asked Leni Riefenstahl to produce a film on the beauties of the Obersalzberg.[766] Riefenstahl starred in popular mountain films in the 1920s and early 1930s. In the mid-1930s she produced two infamous pro-Nazi documentary films, along with one of the best movies on the Olympic Games ever made, called *Olympia*.

---

[760]   *Hitler's Table Talk*, night of Jan. 2-3, 1942, p. 128.

[761]   Speer, *Inside the Third Reich*. p. 88.

[762]   *Hitler's Table Talk*, evening of Sept. 23, 1941, p. 32.

[763]   Schama, p. 118.

[764]   Kershaw, Ian. *Hitler 1889-1936: Hubris*. New York: W. W. Norton & Company, 1999, photograph insert between pp. 418-19.

[765]   *Hitler's Table Talk*, night of Dec. 1-2, 1941, pp. 109-110.

[766]   Mitchell, p. 37.

In 1840, philosopher Arthur Schopenhauer, the anti-Semitic German guru of animal rights, wrote, "In Europe a sense of the right of animals is gradually awakening, in proportion to the slow dying and disappearing of the strange notions that the animal world came into existence simply for the benefit and pleasure of man."[767] Schopenhauer recognized a slow changing of the guard in Europe with regard to animal rights: "Societies for the protection of animals are today being formed all over Europe and America. On the other hand, such would be the most superfluous thing in the world in the whole uncircumcised Asia, where religion affords sufficient protection for animals and even makes them the subject of positive beneficence."[768] That this uncircumcised development would find an anti-Semitic culmination during the Nazi era would have undoubtedly shocked Schopenhauer. Nonetheless, in November of 1933, Adolf Hitler signed a law for the protection of animals called the *Tierschutzrecht*. Before the law was passed, Hitler had declared in a speech Schopenhauer's great romantic wish: "In the new Reich cruelty to animals should no longer exist."[769] Just two months after Hitler signed the law, he was awarded the Eichelberger Humane Award by a Seattle-based United States animal rights foundation.[770] That same year, postcards were sold in Germany showing Hitler feeding two deer fawns.[771] The words on the postcard read that the *Fuhrer* was the friend of the animals.

Section I opened up with two major principles with regard to animal cruelty: (1) It is forbidden to unnecessarily torment or roughly mishandle an animal; and (2) One torments an animal in so far as it does not serve any rational, justifiable purpose. One mishandles an animal when one causes appreciable pain; mishandling is rough when it corresponds to an unfeeling state of mind. Section II dealt with animal protection measures. It prohibited the general neglect of animals, and practices like using them in demonstrations, spectacles or in films in which they might be abused. The law forbade an owner from getting rid of his or her pet. The Nazi

---

767   Schopenhauer, *On the Basis of Morality*, p. 180.
768   Schopenhauer, *Parerga and Paralipomena*, p. 371.
769   Ferry, p. 91.
770   Radkau, Joachim & Frank Uekötter, "*Naturschutz und Nationalsozialismus*," Frankfurt/M. et al. 2003 (*Geschichte des Natur und Umweltschutzes*, vol. 1).
771   Kershaw, photograph insert between pp. 418-19.

regime also prohibited dog fighting and other cruelties to animals. They even set age limits when domesticated animals like horses, cows and pigs could be castrated.

Section III went so far as to provide strict, complex guidelines for animal experimentation:

> Especially in the early years of the Nazi regime, the government sometimes tried to uphold fastidious standards for animal protection. The famous zoologist Karl Von Frisch was reprimanded by the Ministry of the Interior when he cut up anesthetized earthworms in an experiment. One of the worms moved slightly in spite of being numbed, and this was reported to the Ministry by a student.[772]

As such, animal lab researchers often conducted their experiments discreetly. "Researchers at the University of Freiburg once conducted a frantic search for a cat with electrode implants in its brain that had escaped during a nighttime experiment."[773] Section IV threatened punishments of up to two years in prison together with substantial fines. In 1938, the animal rights law was updated and expanded.

Much of the contents of this law are certainly the result of the legacy of Arthur Schopenhauer, who hotly railed against animal cruelty and experimentation. He strongly believed that vivisection should be held to a bare minimum, and that much of it could be avoided by simply reading books on the subject:

> When I was a student at Gottingen, Blumenbach in his lectures on physiology spoke very seriously to us about the horrors of vivisection and pointed out to us what a cruel and shocking thing it was. He therefore said that it should be very rarely resorted to and only in the case of very important investigations that are of direct use. But it must then be done with the greatest publicity in the large lecture hall after an invitation has been sent to all the medical students, so that the cruel sacrifice on the altar of science may be of the greatest possible use. Every quack, however, now considers himself entitled to carry out the cruelest tortures on animals in

---

[772] Sax, p. 117.
[773] Uekoetter, pp. 56-57.

order to decide problems whose solution has long since appeared in books, but which he is too lazy and ignorant to look up.[774]

Lest Schopenhauer be misunderstood, he then fervently compares vivisection to extortion and medieval torture when he writes, "To extort the final answers on the path of cruelty is to put nature on the rack in order to enrich his knowledge, to extort her secrets which have probably long been known. For such knowledge there are still many other innocent sources without his having to torture to death poor helpless animals."[775] Schopenhauer further asserted, "No one is justified in practicing vivisection who does not already know and understand all that is to be found in books on the question under investigation."[776]

Thus, with regard to animal experimentation, the empirical sciences were to take a back seat to the older books that have allegedly already resolved most scientific concerns. After having compared vivisection to wanton sacrifice, extortion and torture, Schopenhauer then drops this jaw-dropping conclusion upon his readers: "A man must be bereft of all his senses or completely chloroformed by the *foetor Judaicus* (the odor of the Jews), not to see that, in all essential respects, the animal is absolutely identical with us and that the difference lies merely in the accident, the intellect, not in the substance which is the will."[777] Hitler no doubt would have heartily agreed with Schopenhauer in all of this. Otto Dietrich said of the *Fuhrer*, "In peacetime he spoke often and intensely about the protection of animals and antivivisection. He vigorously opposed vivisection—which won him much applause from the ladies—unless experiments with animals served some military purpose."[778]

In keeping with Schopenhauer's anti-Semitism, the Nazi animal rights protection law even devoted an entire chapter over to the alleged Jewish barbarity of ritual slaughter. As such, it was henceforth prohibited.[779] By definition, this would, in effect, also outlaw the Jewish practice of Passover. In fact, thanks to the animal protection law, the slaughter of animals

---

[774]   Schopenhauer, *Parerga and Paralipomena*, p. 373.
[775]   Ibid., pp. 374-75.
[776]   Ibid., p. 375.
[777]   Ibid.
[778]   Dietrich, p. 172.
[779]   The Antichrist, i.e., the wild *beast* of Daniel, the gospels, 2 Thessalonians and Revelation, will bring an end to the Jewish sacrifices in the temple at the midpoint of the great tribulation (cf. Dan. 9:27).

had to be supervised by professional veterinarians. As such, "employment at slaughter yards had become a particularly lucrative and prestigious veterinary specialty."[780]

Not surprisingly, many German veterinarians considered Jewish kosher slaughter to be a form of barbarism, if not torture.[781] Nazi propaganda graphically heightened the gore and animal suffering being carried out by uncaring, merciless Jews.[782] Here again is seen the trail of Schopenhauer's anti-Semitic environmental ethics: "Such notions result in animals being treated exactly like things, for they are the source of their rough and quite ruthless treatment in Europe. In the second volume of the *Pererga* 177, I have shown they are of Old Testament origin."[783] Animal rights and Jewish bigotry were very typical in northern Europe,[784] but Nazi Germany raised them to an entirely new level.

The realization that love for animals does not mean a love for fellow man becomes strikingly apparent, especially if you were a Jew who believed in a false, unnatural religion:

> There can be little doubt that, while most Nazis usually allowed the Jew to participate in nature at the lowest possible level, the image of the Jew as utterly alien to nature also entered into the picture from time to time. This could help explain why someone like Himmler, who loved defenseless animals, could engage in politics of mass extermination. As Josef Ackerman has said, the qualities of love for animals and contempt for human life often go together. The Jew as an unnatural, anti-natural being who willfully inflicts pain upon creatures of nature, can be seen in a review of "The Eternal Jew," which appeared in the *Volkischer Beobachter* on December 9, 1938. The review ended with a condemnation of the Jewish ritual slaughter of animals. Emphasized here was the brutality of the Jews, who did not allow the animals to be stunned before they were slaughtered. Such practices were unthinkable in National Socialist Germany. In this context, the Jew is made to appear utterly life-alien, unnatural humanoid, the at first seemingly curious combination

---

[780] Sax, p. 144.
[781] Ibid.
[782] Ibid.
[783] Schopenhauer, *On the Basis of Morality*, p. 180.
[784] Sax, pp. 143-44.

of love of animals and contempt for certain humans becomes, on reflection, not so curious.[785]

Otto Dietrich expounded further that for many years even Hitler "strongly promoted humane treatment of animals; in conversation he repeatedly stressed his love for animals. And this same man, given the comprehensive powers that were his, must have known of, tolerated, and ordered the horrible cruelties which have been inflicted on men."[786]

The elevation of animals often comes at the expense of human beings, and with the Nazis came the most sinister form of dehumanization ever seen on such a grand scale. In fact, for the Nazis, their antagonism toward the Jews is perhaps better described as a form of denaturalization rather than dehumanization. *The Eternal Jew* documentary film quoted above was an attack on the transcendent nature of man, with which the Jews had allegedly sickened Europe. This the Nazis ruthlessly and emotionally rebelled against. They were bound and determined to restrict man's constitution to a purely natural order without any connections to transcendent beliefs that may lie outside of it.

In fact, the shocking climax of the infamous *The Eternal Jew* stunningly reveals a strong green rationalization based on animal rights for the looming destruction of the Jews. The hour-long documentary keeps a steady pace throughout, going from one anti-Semitic line of reasoning to the next. The Jews do not possess hardworking countryside values. Nor do they produce anything of real value. All they do is buy and sell goods in markets produced by the locals, which artificially places them on top of the financial food chain. Jews are much more at home bartering and selling on dirty city streets than they are in performing hardy and healthy outdoor tasks. Their capitalistic international trade is comparable to a massive infestation of rats characterized like an invasive species overwhelming Germany and spreading disease everywhere they go.

International communistic values are also negatively explored in the film. Here the Nazis eschew the universalism and equality that the Marxists falsely emphasize because of its Jewish *eternal* roots. Such unnatural ideas invariably lead to class warfare, which wears down the health of the nation. The propaganda film also strongly expresses the Nazi diatribe against

---

785 Pois, p. 126.
786 Dietrich, p. 5.

Jewish arts and entertainment, which have allegedly poisoned the public with international cosmopolitan values.

However, the real shocker is carefully and purposefully placed at the climax of the film, where the Nazis spend an inordinate amount of time showing the practice of Jewish kosher slaughter of cows and sheep. The Nazis even warn viewers beforehand about the traumatic forthcoming scenes. They then graphically show the kosher ritual slaughter. The documentary shows three different cows in three different settings being slaughtered in this way. Neither do they fail to mention that the Jewish Mosaic Law "has no love or respect for animals in the Germanic sense."

After showing all this blood and gore *cruelty* against animals, the Nazi narrator finally brings up the *Fuhrer* for the first time in the 1940 version of the film. The narrator then lauds Hitler's efforts to bring to an end such *cruel* practices in Germany because of his animal protection laws. This praise for Hitler's outstanding animal protection law then shades into his famous speech given in 1939 before the Reichstag in Berlin. This scandalous speech was a virtual warning that Hitler was about to send the Jews into hell on Earth. In it, he promised to hold the Jews personally responsible if they initiate another global war with their international finances. At this, Hitler received a rousing ovation.

That the Jews were soon to be corralled in cattle cars and sent to death and concentration camps set up like stockyards where they were often herded with whips,[787] and then ultimately sacrificed to death en masse for their *unnatural* ways, is a gruesome truth that has been too long ignored. The Nazi *punishment* of treating the Jews like stock animals headed for the slaughterhouse supposedly matched their *crime* of animal cruelty—the very charge *The Eternal Jew* singles out as the most heinous of all.

In the later 1930s, the Nazis updated their animal protection laws by regulating animal transportation. "These included an elaborate law on animal protection in trains, passed on September 8, 1938."[788] They made up all kinds of detailed regulations on how much space was to be afforded to animals, and how much water and feed they should have. Thus, with regard to the Jews, the Nazis willfully confused stockyards with concentration camps. "German officials occasionally held their men accountable for cruelty to animals. Meanwhile, they were taking Jews and other political prisoners off

---

[787] Arad, pp. 186-202.
[788] Sax, p. 114.

to concentration camps in trains and trucks under conditions of extreme crowding and privation that would certainly not have passed inspection under the laws governing transportation of animals."[789]

Thus, the Nazis broke their own highly regulated animal transport protection protocols when they stuffed Jews like sardines in train cars to be sent to their appointed doom. Even more sadistic, on June 11, 1943, the commander of Police Regiment 25 scolded his squadron for not "posting the information sheets regarding animal protection"[790] as they were loaded into train cars for transport. The commander then went on to say, "Special attention is to be devoted to the beef cattle, since through over-crowding in the railway cars great losses of animals have occurred." No such considerations were given to the Jews when they were jam-packed into cattle cars. How many Jews can a railway car hold during the height of the Holocaust? One more. So suffocating were the conditions that sliding doors could only be closed with great strain, and many Jews were literally kicked into place as they were finally shut.[791] "Orders not to cram Jews too tightly into cattle cars never came the way of the Germans in Poland who deported Jews to their deaths, typically by using kicks and blows to force as many Jews into the railway cars as was possible. The freight cars carried both cattle and Jews. Which of the two was to be handled more decently, more humanely, was clear to all involved."[792]

Neither was such concern for cattle strictly for food. "The Germans, throughout this period, took great pains to ensure that animals were treated decently. In their minds, it was a moral imperative."[793] For example, Nazi guard dog care was extremely meticulous. Dog managers closely watched their canines for the slightest indications of sickness or behavioral change, whereupon a visit to the veterinarian was required.[794] On the other hand, "Jews who were sick, especially the gravely ill, or those who gave the slightest indication of having a contagious illness, like typhus, made no visits to the doctor. As a rule, the Germans fought Jewish illnesses with a bullet or a social-biological 'sanitizing' trip to the gas chamber."[795]

---

789   Ibid., p. 115.
790   Goldhagen, p. 269.
791   Ibid., p. 270.
792   Ibid.
793   Ibid.
794   Ibid., p. 269.
795   Ibid.

Thus, Schopenhauer's naïve conviction that the humane treatment of animals and people went hand in hand[796] was thus completely shattered by the Nazi regime. Somehow Schopenhauer overlooked the fact that if a premium is not placed on people, they will inevitably be neglected, devalued and diminished, and the Nazis showed just how low the dehumanization process can go. In fact, thanks to his romantic love for nature, Schopenhauer was blinded by his own anti-Semitism.

Even more nightmarish, many Jews would also soon be treated like experimental animals at Auschwitz where human experimentation replaced vivisection on an incredible scale. This was not an oversight. The infamous Dr. Mengele, who performed an untold number of cruel experiments on human guinea pigs at Auschwitz, but later managed to escape Europe, would often opine to his Nazi friends after the war in South America about "the future of mankind, the evolution of man, archaeology, and the ecological problems, i.e., the destruction of nature and about the evil of materialism."[797] Dr. Mengele, what about the evil of treating Jews like experimental animals? Mengele even had a lab inside the Auschwitz gas chambers to make human experimentation and autopsies more convenient. Mengele's favorite guinea pigs, twins, were contained in Birkenau's Barrack 14 of Camp F which was sadistically nicknamed "The Zoo."[798]

At best, the Jews were compared to the lowest forms of life—like germs. They were thus worthy of extermination since the "National Socialists chose to view at least one group of people, the Jews, as at best existing at a level of nature so low as to be comparable with disease-bearing germs, or even as essentially outside of nature."[799] Himmler compared the Jews to parasitic blood suckers.[800] At the height of the war on the Eastern Front, with lice plaguing many German soldiers, Himmler also compared the Jews to lice: "As far as Anti-Semitism is concerned, it is exactly the same as with delousing. No question of *Weltanschauung* is involved in removing lice. It is a matter of cleanliness.... Soon we will be deloused."[801] In the presence of Himmler, Hitler himself compared the Jews to a virus, saying: "The discovery of the

---

796   Schopenhauer, *On the Basis of Morality*, p. 179.
797   Posner & Ware, p. 226
798   Ibid., p. 35.
799   Pois, p. 123.
800   Ackerman, Josef, *Himmler as Idealogue*, p. 159; quoted by Pois, p. 123.
801   Himmler, Heinrich. *Geheimreden*, pp. 200-01; quoted by Pois p, p. 136.

Jewish virus is one of the greatest revolutions that have taken place in the world ... we shall regain our health only by eliminating the Jew."[802]

To the Nazis, the so-called *Eternal Jew* was an alien to the natural order:

> The elevation of nature to the position of divinity, and the setting apart of a portion of humanity as being, at least partially more natural than others, allowed genuine nature mystics to pursue the most ruthless policies in dealing with beings of a low order. Hence, sensitive souls like Himmler, for whom every aspect of the natural world throbbed with sacred mystery, could pursue a policy very much in keeping with the coldest and yet "fairest" of natural laws: that the weak or degenerate must perish. .... As opposed to urban civilization developed from Jewish liberalism, the Nazis posited a re-mystified world whose eternal tensions and rhythms pulsed in the veins of the chosen. Nature herself, acting through the agencies of those living in harmony with her, would defend this world by purging it of the unclean.[803]

Hence, the Nazis believed they were defending Nature from a Jewish disease which had been rotting Germany from the inside out, and their nature conservation laws, including the *Tierschutzrecht*, was a part of this whole process. Indeed, on Oct. 4, 1943, Himmler declared in a speech before the SS that Germany was "the only nation of the world with a decent attitude toward animals."[804]

Some environmental historians have tried to point out that the Nazis were not serious about the animal protection law, or that it was used as a disguise to go after the Jews.[805] The enforcement of its provisions "was erratic, which is hardly surprising in view of the turmoil in Germany."[806] However, even in normal times the enforcement of any law has always been a problem since time immemorial. Furthermore, environmental laws are perhaps the least enforceable of all from a practical human standpoint.

---

[802]   *Hitler's Table Talk*, evening of Feb. 22, 1942, p. 251.

[803]   Pois, p. 125.

[804]   *Internationaler Militar-Gerichtshof Nurnberg*, "Der Prozess gegen die Hauptkriegsverbrecher vor dem Internationalen Militargerichtshof," vol. 29, p. 123; quoted by Uekoetter, p. 57.

[805]   Uekoetter, pp. 55-57.

[806]   Sax, p. 117.

"The very complexity of the Law for Animal Protection of 1933 was an obstacle to consistent enforcement."[807] When the scientific community vigorously complained against the law, the Nazis quickly realized that university research was of course very dependent upon the practice.[808] In fact, Hitler had originally intended to completely ban animal experimentation altogether, but his personal doctor talked him out of such a draconian measure for the sake of German scientific research.[809] The real moral of the story, therefore, is not that the Nazis were unserious about animal protection rights, but that environmental regulations hastily passed quickly become a moronic laughingstock. In fact, a cartoon was posted in the *Kladderadatsch*, showing a picture of a whole host of experimental rabbits and squirrels saluting Hermann Goering. This political cartoon was "published at a time when the Nazis were producing one animal protection law after another."[810]

Goering himself was forced to water down his own anti-vivisection decree of August of 1933 within a matter of three weeks, "being revised by a decree of September 5 with more lenient provisions. In the end, the ministry of the interior handed out blank permits to university institutes to conduct experiments with animals and refrained from any closer supervision of experimental practice."[811] Thus reality always has a way of making a mockery out of absolutist regulations at such a mundane level, and this is especially true with regard to environmental rules. However, even as late as 1940, Adolf Hitler himself put a stop to a law that was designed to protect the food supply by prohibiting useless pets.[812] This should not be surprising since Hitler "showed little or no emotion at the death of friends, but wept when his canary died."[813] Nor was this something unusual with Hitler. He "showed much more affection of a lost dog he adopted on the western front in the Great War than he did for the members of his beloved list regiment, who died in large numbers and who were wounded in horrific ways."[814]

---

[807] Ibid., p. 118.
[808] Uekoetter, pp. 55-56.
[809] Sax, p. 112.
[810] Uekoetter, p. 56.
[811] Ibid.
[812] Ibid., p. 57.
[813] Sax, p. 121.
[814] Walker, *Sinisterism: Secular Religion of the Lie*. Denver: Outskirts Press, 2006, p. 150.

When Hitler lived in Vienna, he often fed bread to the squirrels and ravens.[815] "Throughout his life he had expressed affection for animals."[816]

Nazi Vegetarianism

That Hess, Himmler and Hitler were all vegetarians is also part of the historical record that fits in perfectly with their animal loving tendencies. It was the great Swiss theologian Karl Barth (1886-1968) who smartly quipped about the *Fuhrer*, "A powerful ascetic can be a vessel of much greater wickedness than even the most indulgent. We cannot forget so easily that one may be a non-smoker, abstainer, and vegetarian, and yet be called Adolf Hitler."[817] Indeed, on a romantic date in the 1920s, Hitler "scolded his female companion for having ordered *Wienerschnitzel*."[818] Taken aback, the woman did not know how to respond, but Hitler did not demand her to change the order, saying: "No, go ahead and have it, but I don't understand why you want it. I didn't think you wanted to devour a corpse ... the flesh of dead animals. Cadavers!"[819] So much for the idea of romancing with the *Fuhrer*. Hitler went so far to call any kind of meat broth as "corpse tea."[820]

Nazi press chief Otto Dietrich confirmed that Hitler was "a complete vegetarian; he never ate meat or fish. He lived almost entirely on vegetables and certain cereals."[821] In his vegetarianism,[822] Hitler said he was following Richard Wagner's advice: "I don't touch meat largely because of what Wagner says on the subject."[823] Wagner, in turn, as stated earlier, was greatly influenced by Arthur Schopenhauer. Wagner even preached a racist socialism based on vegetarianism that would cleanse Germany from the corrupting influence of the Jews.[824]

---

[815] Sax, p. 121.

[816] Waite, p. 413.

[817] Barth, Karl. *Church Dogmatics*, III.4. Edinburgh: T & T Clark, 1977, p. 348.

[818] Proctor, *The Nazi War on Cancer*, p. 135.

[819] Waite, p. 19.

[820] Ibid.

[821] Dietrich, p. 170.

[822] There can be no doubt that for the most part, Hitler was a vegetarian. *Hitler's Table Talk* shows that Hitler routinely claimed to be a vegetarian, p. 156, 168, 176-77, 333-34, 430-31, 465, 483. While Proctor shows that there is some testimony that suggests Hitler also ate sausage, dumplings, ham and some seafood on occasion, it still cannot be denied that he became a vegetarian at some point in his political career. See Proctor, *The Nazi War on Cancer*, pp. 134-141.

[823] Waite, p. 26.

[824] Proctor, *The Nazi War on Cancer*, p. 135.

Rudolf Hess was such a fanatic vegetarian that he would not even eat food prepared for him by Hitler's cook. He brought his own biodynamic concoction to the chancellery meetings.[825] Hess eventually wore out his welcome. "Hitler suggested to Hess in return that maybe he might rather stay home for lunch from now on."[826] Even years after the war while in prison, Hess continued to worry about the effects of canned food on human health.[827]

Heinrich Himmler tried to convert the *Waffen* SS into vegetarian non-smokers.[828] He also looked forward to the day when all of Germany would become vegetarian.[829] Apparently, he and Hitler had plans to require a vegetarian diet to be enforced on the German populace in the future, but this would have to wait until victory had been achieved. "Hitler himself told Goebbels (in April 1942) that he would wait until after the war to tackle the issue of vegetarianism."[830] Hitler also had draconian plans in mind for the meat industry after the war, as well.

Hitler complained that pasturelands for cattle took up too much farmland. "Pasturages cover 37% of the surface of the soil in Germany. So it's not the man who eats grass, it's his cattle."[831] Hitler clearly felt that Germany would be far better served with the growing of more vegetable gardens than setting aside so much land to feed stock animals. Hitler even pointed out how animals with vegetarian diets have great endurance: "As regards animals, the dog, which is carnivorous, cannot compare in performance with the horse, which is vegetarian. In the same way, the lion shows signs of fatigue after covering two or three kilometers, while the camel marches for six or seven days before even his tongue begins to hang out."

Hitler even looked forward to the day when his own sheep dog would eventually become completely vegetarian via evolution.[832] He was also a strong advocate of eating raw foods: "Those who adopt a vegetarian diet must remember that it is in their raw state that vegetables have their greatest nutritive value. The fly feeds on fresh leaves, the frog swallows the fly as it is, and the stork eats the living frog. Nature thus teaches us that a

---

825 Ibid., p. 139.
826 Goldberg, p. 386.
827 Speer, *Spandau: The Secret Diaries*, p. 407.
828 Proctor, *The Nazi War on Cancer*, p. 139.
829 Ibid., p. 138.
830 Ibid., p. 139.
831 *Hitler's Table Talk*, evening of Jan. 22, 1942, p. 176.
832 Ibid., dinner on July 8, 1942, p. 431.

rational diet should be based on eating things in their raw state."[833] Hitler complained, "Cooking destroys the vitamins, which are the most valuable part of our food."[834]

Never Cry Wolf—Hermann Goering, Aldo Leopold & the Green Nazi Hunting Law

Hermann Goering was an avid hunter, which environmental historians try to use to demonstrate that he was not really serious about animal rights or other environmental causes. They are quick to glibly show pictures of Goering standing over trophies that he had shot. What they fail to appreciate is that, number one, Hitler also chided Goering for the same alleged inconsistency: "First you protect the animals, then you shoot them dead."[835] In fact, Hitler loved to ridicule Goering's penchant for hunting before his minions at the *Obersalzberg*: "If only there were some danger connected with hunting, as in the days when men used spears for killing game. But today, when anybody with a fat belly can safely shoot the animal down from a distance."[836]

Hitler detested hunting.[837] He stated: "How can a person be excited about such a thing? Killing animals, if it must be done, is the butcher's business."[838] Even in 1942, with the most barbaric war in human history blazing across the Russian steppe, Hitler claimed, "I have never fired at a hare in my life. I am neither poacher nor sportsman."[839] Himmler himself had a hysterical reaction to the practice of hunting. Himmler even asked his personal doctor, "How can you find pleasure in shooting from behind cover at poor creatures browsing on the edge of a wood, innocent, defenseless, and unsuspecting? It's really pure murder."[840] For Himmler, hunting animals was murder, but slaughtering Jews was not.

Modern environmentalists oppose Native Americans for their own love of the hunt as well. Yet no one questions the strong commitment that

---

[833] Ibid., midday on April 25, 1942, p. 333.
[834] Ibid.
[835] Klose, Hans "Wie das Reichnaturschutzgesetz wurde," 9-14, quoted by Dominick, p. 107.
[836] Speer, *Inside the Third Reich* p. 97.
[837] Irving, p. 180.
[838] Speer, *Inside the Third Reich*, p. 97.
[839] *Hitler's Table Talk*, midday Sept. 2, 1942, p. 516.
[840] Sax, p. 121.

Native Americans have toward green ideals and practices. In 2007, off the northwest coast of Washington State, the Makah Indians riddled a gray whale with harpoons and huge bullets only to be turned away at gunpoint by the coast guard.[841] The Makah Indians got tired of waiting for an environmental permit to legally hunt the whale and took matters into their hands. They were not allowed to finish the whale off. It later died and sunk down into the water to a depth of 700 feet.

Native Americans love to hunt. Hunting was and is still a deeply religious practice to them. It was for Hermann Goering too.[842] There is therefore nothing necessarily inconsistent between hunting, respect for animals, and nature protection as even many hunters will indeed testify. The worldwide hunter and nature conservationist Teddy Roosevelt himself is a great testament to this fact. Aldo Leopold, the father of deep ecology, was also an avid huntsman. In his famous work entitled *A Sand County Almanac*, Leopold pointed out that the distinctively American tradition of self-reliance, hardihood, woodcraft and marksmanship was well expressed by the 26th president of the United States: "Theodore Roosevelt was a great sportsman, not because he hung up many trophies, but because he expressed this intangible American tradition in words any schoolboy could understand."[843]

Aldo Leopold's environmental views moved sharply away from the Roosevelt-Pinchot style of conservationism toward a deeper ecology in the 1930s. In fact, his complete conversion to deep ecology coincided with his 1935 three-month stay in Nazi Germany. He certainly would have had the opportunity to meet with Nazi environmentalists, including Hermann Goering. How much Leopold influenced Nazi environmentalists or how much he was influenced by them would be difficult to decipher. Whatever the exact case may be, Leopold certainly echoed Nazi environmentalism when he wrote in the foreword of his *Sand County Almanac*, "Conservation is getting nowhere because it is incompatible with our *Abrahamic* concept of the land. We abuse the land because we regard it as a commodity belonging to us. When we see the land as a community to which we belong, we may begin to use it with love and respect."[844] By "Abrahamic concept

---

[841] "Animal Welfare Institute Condemns Illegal Whale Hunt By Makah Tribal Members," *Animal Welfare Institute*, Sept. 10, 2007.

[842] Irving, pp. 182, 188-190.

[843] Leopold, Aldo. *A Sand County Almanac*. New York and Oxford: Oxford University Press, 1949, p. 179.

[844] Ibid., p. viii.

of the land," Leopold certainly meant Jewish-American capitalism. While Thoreau primarily complained about the Puritans, Leopold reverberates the Nazi diatribe against Judaism, all garbed in typical green anti-capitalism rhetoric.

The Wilderness Society, which Leopold co-founded in 1935 with socialists like Norman Thomas and Benton MacKaye, reveals a natural disposition toward green socialistic standards. Even Bob Marshall, the other co-founder of the Wilderness Society, had the same green socialistic leanings. Leopold chimed in with the National Socialists when he said, "The Germans realized the increment bought at the expense of soil health, landscape beauty, and wildlife is poor economics as well as poor public policy."[845]

While sitting in his hotel room in Berlin, Leopold wrote about the need for interdisciplinary thinking when it came to ecology. It was time to do away with the fragmentation of knowledge fostered by Western thought that had artificially separated history, economic studies and the social sciences from ecology. Leopold looked forward to the day when these disciplines could be fascistly fused together. There can be no doubt this was certainly a great topic of discussion among his Nazi colleagues.

Leopold's *Sand County Almanac* even shows some *volkisch* cultural undertones mixed in with environmental existentialism that can be seen here and there throughout the book. Although his writings were much more succinct and clear than Martin Heidegger, Leopold demonstrates a serious concern for preserving a folkish-culture rooted in the land against the backdrop of the growing homogenization of international capitalism:

> Wilderness is the raw material out of which man has hammered the artifact called civilization. Wilderness was never a homogenous raw material. It was very diverse. These differences in the end-product are known as cultures. The rich diversity of the world's cultures reflects a corresponding diversity in the wilds that gave them birth. For the first time in history of the human species, two changes are now impending. One is the exhaustion of wilderness in the more habitable portions of the globe. The other is the worldwide hybridization of cultures through modern transport and industrialization. Neither can be prevented, and perhaps should not be, but the question whether, by some slight amelioration of

---

[845] Imort, Michael, "Eternal Forest – Eternal Volk" in *How Green Were the Nazis*, p. 47.

the impending changes, certain values can be preserved that would otherwise be lost.[846]

His environmental anxiety over the capitalistic homogenization of world-wide culture also led Leopold down the road of a soft nationalism as well: "There are cultural values in the sports, customs, and experiences that renew contacts with wild things. . . . First there is value in any experience that reminds us of our distinctive national origins and evolution, i.e., that stimulates awareness of history. Such awareness is nationalism in its best sense. For lack of any other short name, I shall call this, in our case, the split rail value."[847]

This is not to say that Leopold was some kind of closet Nazi, but his later views on deep ecology still coincided with many National Socialist environmental values. There is a reason why he visited Nazi Germany in 1935. Leopold and Nazi conservationists shared many of the same environmental concerns. While critical of many of Germany's past game management efforts, Leopold was, in fact, generally impressed with what the Nazis were doing. Leopold claimed that Nazi environmentalists were actually doing something about ecological problems, not just talking about them like American conservationists. "Leopold expressed strong admiration for the nature protection movement in Germany, which was already introducing raptors and some predators."[848] His insistence upon wilderness preservation in America after his visit was largely due to the fact he was shocked by how little wilderness was left in Germany proper. A strong push, therefore, was necessary in America to avoid the same fate.

For many greens, there can be no true wilderness without predators. After Leopold returned home, he began to consider how to bring wolves back into America. Once again, Leopold was following in the footsteps of National Socialism. In 1934, Germany became the first nation to place the wolf under protection.[849] This Nazi action was largely symbolic, however, as the wolves had been killed to extinction as early as the 1850s. Nonetheless, "the Nazis were already looking toward Poland and other countries where wolves could still be found."[850] That the push to reintroduce wolves

---

846   Ibid., p. 188.
847   Ibid., p. 177.
848   Sax, p. 79.
849   Ibid., p. 75.
850   Ibid.

in America was in part inspired by Leopold's visit to Nazi Germany receives little press. Nonetheless, "since the Nazi period the cult of the predator, especially the wolf, has not faded."[851] It later continued on in North America with Farley Mowatt's best-selling novel, *Never Cry Wolf*, which stated: "The caribou feeds the wolf, but it is the wolf who keeps the caribou strong. We know that if it were not for the wolf there would be no caribou at all for they would die as weakness spread among them."[852] The wolf, of course, was Hitler's favorite predator.[853]

In some important ways, therefore, Aldo Leopold looks more like America's version of Hermann Goering,[854] just far less brutal and much more congenial. "Leopold showed no trace of the brutality or the chauvinism that characterized the Nazi movement."[855] In spite of his great push toward deep ecology in the latter years of his life, Leopold was still very much influenced by the pervasiveness of Judeo-Christian values in the United States of America that he slowly began to oppose more and more as the years passed by.

Nonetheless, from a strict environmental perspective, Leopold and Goering shared many similarities and interests. Both of them loved hunting. Both of them were very ecologically and environmentally minded. Both of them bought abandoned parcels in the 1930s upon which to set up ecological experiments in order to restore them into more environmentally sound ecosystems. Both of them struggled in their efforts to naturally restore the parcels. Goering was partially successful in reintroducing bison, wild horses, beaver, otter, night owls, wood grouse, heathcocks, ravens and gray goose, but completely failed to get a moose herd going.[856] Leopold planted 40,000 trees on his place near Baraboo in Sand County, Wis.

In addition to personal demeanor, another major difference between them was that Goering's efforts were far more extravagant than Leopold's. Goering built a huge mansion at Carinhall near the beautiful Schorfheide Heath area north of Berlin. This became a veritable aristocratic hunting lodge for all of his visitors, but it was an outstanding green area of forests,

851   Ibid., p. 80.
852   Mowatt, Farley, *Never Cry Wolf*, pp. 199-200; quoted by Sax, p. 80.
853   Sax, p. 76.
854   Kay, William Walter, "The Sacred Nature Bund: Review of Encyclopedia of Religion and Nature," 2008, on ecofascism.com.
855   Sax, p. 79.
856   Uekoetter, pp. 100-109 and Irving p. 182.

glades, ponds and lakes of which Goering was particularly proud. Conversely, Leopold remodeled an old chicken coop into a humble lodging where he and his family could spend much time outdoors. It was here that he wrote his famous *Sand County Almanac*. With its strong emphasis upon deep ecology, this book has increasingly become the environmental conscience of America.

The other notable difference between the two men was that Leopold was spared the destructive ecological indignity of having the Red Army roll its tank tracks across his back porch. With great enthusiasm, when the Red Army arrived at Carinhall in 1945, they decimated "the game population. According to Erwin Bucholz and Ferdinand Coninx, the Red Army employed tanks to drive the game out of the forest and then used machine guns for the kill, extinguishing the last of the wild horses in the process."[857]

With all this in mind, to make a big fuss over Goering's love for the hunt misses the point with regard to his environmental interests and concerns. It is too convenient and self-serving for modern greens to quickly pass off Goering as not being a true environmentalist or friend of the animals because of his love for bagging trophies. Hitler, who knew Goering much better, never doubted Goering's commitment to green policies even though he was a hunter. He called Goering's hunting fraternity "that green Freemasonry."[858] In spite of his love for the hunt, Goering was devoted to transforming his Schorfheide Heath into a "forest reserve that would reproduce the conditions of primeval Germany, complete with primeval animals."[859] He was also a bird lover as well.[860]

Goering had a much deeper respect and love for animals than he did for people. "There was an unsuspected empathy between this man, Hermann Goering, and the animal kingdom, and there was no phoniness about it."[861] Goering even used human guinea pigs in weaponry tryouts instead of experimental animals. "While in Britain defense scientists contented themselves with testing blast bombs on goats and chimpanzees, in 1942 Goering's high altitude aviation experts would show no qualms in conducting lethal low temperature and low pressure experiments on human beings (criminals under the sentence of death supplied by Himmler's concentration

---

857 Uekoetter, p. 108.
858 Irving, p. 180.
859 Larson, p. 279.
860 Ibid., p. 280.
861 Irving., p. 180.

camps)."[862] In fact, so serious was Goering about animal protection that he warned the nation that he would throw people into concentration camps who were abusive to them:[863]

> In order to prevent the spreading of torture to animals before such law, I issued this decree, making use of a right that is accorded to me, to put violators who still think that they can treat animals as a lifeless commodity into protective custody or a concentration camp. The German people have always shown great compassion for animals and issues concerning animal-rights. They always saw in animals, especially those which became their compatriots in house, homes or battles for thousands of years, yes, we can say; in many ways their co-workers and—one need only to think about the horses— even comrades in arms, creatures of God. For the German people, animals are not just living things in an organic sense, but creatures who have their own unique feelings, who feel pain, joy, and show loyalty and affection. Never would the German people's love for animals permit them to treat animals as objects without feelings or souls, to be used only as tools, or to be exploited, to be discarded, whether for reasons of usefulness or not, or to be tortured or destroyed for the same reasons.[864]

Even before the animal rights law was passed, Goering warned in a broadcast that he would toss violators into a concentration camp.[865] For Goering, anticipated animal rights laws were just as valid as signed animal rights laws. Vesting rights were thrown out as soon as he made his public announcement. Once Goering took charge, the passing of the law was a mere formality.

Such sentiments, of course, are miles apart from the idea that Goering was some kind of modern American sport hunter who enjoyed killing animals. In May of 1937, a Professor Burckhardt of Berlin overheard a heated conversation over the phone between Goering and a forester.[866] The forester

---

[862]   Ibid., p. 182.

[863]   Reported in *Journal of the American Medical Association*, Sept. 30, 1933, p. 1087; quoted by Proctor, *Racial Hygiene: Medicine Under the Nazis*, p. 227.

[864]   Walker, Bruce, "Nazis, the First Ecologists and the First PETA nuts," *Web Commentary*, April 27, 2006.

[865]   Irving, p. 182.

[866]   Ibid., p. 181-82.

was under pressure by some local farmers who wanted to kill some wild boars for creating havoc on their farms. Goering angrily lashed out at him, "One more word and I'll blast a shotgun up your snout!" Goering was even well known to be an animal lover years after his death.[867]

Most telling of all, on the very same night that Hitler finally reported the execution of 43 traitors on the *Night of the Long Knives*, "Goering celebrated the passage of the Reich Game Law."[868] Following on the heels of the *Tierschutzrecht*, the Reich Game Law was the second important piece of environmental legislation passed by the Nazis in July of 1934. Goering helped draft the Nazi law for limiting hunting called the *Das Reichsjagdgesetz*. Neither was it an oversight that the animal rights protection legislation preceded the new Reich hunting law. This was part of a plan to obtain bigger and better environmental prizes. For Goering the next green prize was to pass a hunting law for Germany at the federal level:

> In 1933 he found the hunting scene to be a microcosm of Germany itself—plagued by petty rivalries and self-interest. Each humble parish or great estate seemed to have its own hunting laws and taxes. Wildlife could be hunted down at will. Conservation and breeding of the dwindling species were impossible. In Germany, the eagle, bear, bison, and wild horse were almost extinct.[869]

Thanks to the green Nazi hunting law, hunters were now not only required to have licenses, but also to feed game animals during the winter.[870] As part of the provisions of the new law, hunting with painful traps was outlawed.[871] "With one stroke of the pen he made it a criminal offense to kill an eagle, or hunt with poisons, artificial light, or the steel trap—that medieval instrument of torture."[872]

Das Reichsjagdgesetz was envied well beyond Germany's borders. In 1937, the International Game Committee congratulated Goering for his efforts on regulating hunting.[873] It had many restrictions and provisions.

---

[867]   Goodrick-Clarke, *Hitler's Priestess*, p. 128.
[868]   Irving, p. 183.
[869]   Ibid., p. 181.
[870]   Sax, p. 116.
[871]   Ferry, p. 107.
[872]   Irving, p. 183.
[873]   Ibid.

"The sixth section of the law is devoted to establishing limitations on the right to hunt, limitations based not only on the need for security, public order, and even protection of the landscape, but also on the need to 'avoid cruelty to animals.'"[874] Endangered species were also off limits to hunters. The only drawback of the law was that as long as one abided by the hunting rules, a sportsman could kill as many animals he wished.[875] Goering, of course, loved to hunt.

The Nazi hunting law was green. Not only was it expressly passed to protect wild animals but it was also designed to educate people to develop a love and understanding for nature and its creatures as important *cultural* assets. "The *Reichsjagdgesetz* turns out to be the key pin of the National Socialist ecological platform: in it, man is no longer positioned as master and possessor of nature which he humanizes and cultivates, but as responsible for an original wild state endowed with intrinsic rights, the richness of diversity of which it is his responsibility to preserve forever."[876] With regard to the Nazi hunting law, once again is seen the National Socialist fusion between German culture, nature and animals in a very holistic understanding:

> We should specify right away that the goal of the law is not only to introduce legal unity to culture and nature, but also to separate it within the framework of an authentic ecological system of thought. Thus it is necessary to limit the right of hunting in order that it concurs with the stated need for preserving the natural environment. In this sense, the law of 1934 is undoubtedly the first to redefine the role of the hunter in modern terms. According to a theme destined to long posterity, the hunter goes from being a simple predator to one of the main architects of environmental protection, even of a restoration of original diversity forever threatened by modern uniformization.[877]

In short, for Goering, hunting and concern for animals went hand in hand. "He insisted that the new game officials must be animal lovers, dedicated National Socialists."[878] Goering was thus a *volkisch* hunter.

---

[874] Ferry, p. 107.
[875] Sax, p. 116.
[876] Ferry, p. 107.
[877] Ibid., pp. 106-07.
[878] Irving, p. 181.

Furthermore, this law on limiting hunting did not go unnoticed by Hitler. He was fully aware of its prohibitive regulations against poaching: "As it is, a poacher kills a hare and goes to prison for three months!"[879] Worried over losing so many soldiers in battle, Hitler then goes on to say that those poachers who have gone to prison should be released to serve the Nazi state behind the front lines by fighting partisans in the forest. Lest he be misunderstood that he was perhaps being lax on poaching with regard to such a proposal, he then clarifies: "Do not imagine that I condone the wholesale depredations of poachers among the wildlife of the forests. On the contrary, my sympathies are entirely with the gamekeepers."[880] In fact, Hitler wanted to send the poachers into the forest for the express purpose that they would pay for their National Socialist poaching crimes: "Of course we must suppress the activities of the poachers. But as I have said, let the punishment fit the crime—send them to fight the guerillas, make them into a marksman's coup d'elite."[881] This was apparently arranged. As was so typical of many leading Nazis, murdering Jews was far less troubling to Hitler's conscience than poaching animals. More to the point, to the Nazi mind, the word *partisans* was a euphemism for *Jews* who were caught in behind German front lines on the Eastern Front. Poachers were thus converted into Jew hunters.

Nazi Forest Protection

On Saint Hubert's Day in 1936, before his hunting fraternity, Goering bellowed, "For us, the forest is God's cathedral."[882] Goering was a lover of the forest as well. He was also known to have gone on hiking and climbing excursions in the Watzmann Mountain Range near Hitler's alpine retreat.[883] Goering became Germany's self-appointed Reich Forestry Minister and his environmental legacy was not a small one with regard to nature conservation. "The nature conservancy branch in the *Reichforstamt* pursued three national park projects, until all had to be shelved as nonessential to the war effort. By the beginning of the war, nonetheless, almost 800 smaller-scale nature protection areas had been created, many of them in forested

---

[879] *Hitler's Table Talk*, midday of Aug. 20, 1942, p. 483.
[880] Ibid., p. 484.
[881] Ibid., midday September 2, 1942, p. 516.
[882] Irving, p. 182.
[883] Uekoetter, p. 32.

areas."[884] Thanks to Goering's efforts, children were everywhere taught all about the woodland ecosystem in forest ecology programs implemented in schools.

Under Goering's leadership, the Nazis also made a sharp break from forestry practices of the Weimar Republic by emphasizing a new environmentally sensitive model called *Dauerwald*.[885] *Dauerwald* means *eternal forest*. German environmentalists of the 1920s had fought hard for this forestry concept and practice, but without success. Once again, it was National Socialism who granted the greens their wishes when they came to power in the 1930s. By January of 1934, the Nazis passed the Law against the Devastation of Forests.[886]

Along totalitarian lines, *Dauerwald* was mandated for all German forests, including private forest owners as well. In fact, thanks to the totalitarian nature of the Nazi rule, Germany never looked at private forests the same. "This is largely the result of a fundamental re-conceptualization of the German forest from a private commodity to a public ecological resource, a process that, cynically enough, was facilitated by the dictatorship's ability to disregard the objections of private forest owners."[887] Indeed, during the Nazi rule, a private German forester might find himself in jail for cutting down a conifer tree under 50 years of age.[888]

The main thrust of *Dauerwald* was not the scientific maximization of wood production for human consumption but the desire to make the forest ecosystem healthier in the long run. The idea was to promote more sustainable yields in the future without destroying the forest. The modern lingo for this is called sustainable forestry. "The *Dauerwald* decrees thus had a positive ecological legacy in that they introduced foresters at all levels to a holistic view of the forest that emphasized the forest rather than the stand or individual trees as the basic management unit."[889] This holistic thrust was intended to do away with previous scientific monoculture tree growing models. *Dauerwald* introduced forestry practices to develop organic and diverse timberland ecosystems consistent with its local environs.

---

[884] Imort, Michael in "Eternal Forest – Eternal Volk: The Rhetoric and Reality of National Socialist Forest Policy," in *How Green Were the Nazis?*, p. 62.

[885] Ibid., p. 45.

[886] Lekan, p. 157.

[887] Imort, Michael in "Eternal Forest—Eternal Volk: The Rhetoric and Reality of National Socialist Forest Policy," in *How Green Were the Nazis?*, p. 63.

[888] Ibid., p. 49.

[889] Ibid., p. 59

They also planned to curtail the ecological shock of clear-cutting and to protect the overall forest canopy as much as possible. This was to be done by emphasizing single tree selection rather than clear-cutting and to refrain from cutting the youngest and oldest trees. Nazi foresters were also very concerned about eradicating diseased trees, not to mention invasive species, both of which they deemed detrimental to the German landscape. Thus, the forest ecosystem must be kept consistent with its local Aryan environment: "Ask the trees, they will teach you how to become National Socialists!"[890]

Natural historian Konrad Guenther said, "The source of Germanic national character was inexhaustible since … it lay in the darkness of the forests, where it is beyond the reach of enemy hands."[891] Their forestry and Aryan views were thus fused together with no small thanks to their holistic Social-Darwinian views on both man and nature:

> In 1936, a propaganda film with the title *Ewiger Wald* (Eternal Forest) premiered in German cinemas. It presented a sequence of vignettes on the 2,000 year history of the German *volk* with images of historical figures and events emerging from the forest. Using the technique of fading, the film suggested the interchangeability of Germans and trees by dissolving one into the other. The film was not coy about telling the audience how it should further connect the specifics of forestry, and particularly the practice of improvement cutting as employed in *Dauerwald* forestry and as shown in the film, to the life-or-death question of race, blood and soil. Thus, one scene shows an axe in close-up while a chorus exhorts the audience from the off: "Excise what is of foreign race and sick." In the next shot, the axe cleaves the dead wood of a dry tree. Before the tree crashes to the ground, the axe appears once more in a close-up and the chorus spells out the mission of the New Germany: "From the multitude of species, create the new community of the eternal forest, create the eternal forest of the new community." This carefully selected new community was the racially pure *Volksgemeinschaft*, its eternal

---

[890] Modersohn, A.W., "Weltauschauung und beruflicher Einsatz," Deutsche Forst-Zeitung 8, no. 15 (1939) 602-03; quoted by Imort in "Eternal Forest—Eternal Volk: The Rhetoric and Reality of National Socialist Forest Policy," in *How Green Were the Nazis?*, p. 54.

[891] Guenther, Konrad, "*Naturschutz als Wissenschaft and Lehrfach," Blatter fur Naturschutz und Naturpflege* 14 (1931): 16; quoted by Uekoetter, p. 25.

forest the *Dauerwald*. Both were to protect and help reproduce one another: the *Volksgemeinschaft* maintained the eternal forest, which in turn provided the physically challenging and spiritually nourishing environment that was necessary for the continual honing of the German race.[892]

Getting back to the primeval forest was viewed to have a cleansing indigenous effect upon Germany. The healthy forest was the organic forest which stood in great contrast to the monotony of the scientific commercial forest.

Dauerwald was such a sharp break from previous efforts that even Aldo Leopold took notice: "The Germans, who taught the world to plant trees like cabbages, have scrapped their own teachings and gone back to mixed woods of native species, selectively cut and naturally produced."[893] This was, in fact, the very reason Leopold traveled to Nazi Germany in 1935 with an all-expenses paid three-month trip. Though he returned with some criticism over some of their longstanding contradictory forestry and game practices, Leopold still praised the Nazis. "The foresters of Germany were already making attempts to restore their original landscapes which resembled those Leopold would propose in the United States."[894] Germany's lack of wilderness areas due to constant human interference over the centuries became the impetus for Leopold's drive to set aside wilderness areas in America before it was too late. That 1935 was also the very same year the Nazis passed the Reich Nature Protection Act, which began a brand-new era in German environmentalism, shows just how ecologically eventful that particular year was.

However, the forest policy of *dauerwald* proved too draconian to work in the real world, especially as the economy began to rebound with an ever-growing demand for wood, along with the preparation for war. This, of course, created problems and inconsistencies that went contrary to *dauerwald* theory. In fact, the *dauerwald* regulations were so strict that even German foresters disliked it. At a 1937 forestry conference, "a high ranking official

---

[892] Imort, "Eternal Forest—Eternal Volk: The Rhetoric and Reality of National Socialist Forest Policy," in *How Green Were the Nazis?*, pp. 56-57.

[893] Leopold, Aldo, "A Biotic View of Life" (paper given at the Meeting of the Ecological Society of America on June 21, 1939); quoted by Michael Imort in "Eternal Forest—Eternal Volk: The Rhetoric and Reality of National Socialist Forest Policy in *How Green Were the Nazis?*, p. 48.

[894] Sax, p. 79.

forester delivered a thinly veiled attack on the *dauerwald* rules in the presence of Von Keudell (the Nazi architect of *dauerwald*) and received thunderous applause."[895] This ecological pipe dream that a forester is required to refrain from cutting conifer stands under 50 years of age, refrain from clear-cutting more than two-and-a-half percent of the forest, use single-tree selection cutting principles rather than clear-cuts, cut the worst rather than the best trees, and refrain from cutting the oldest and the biggest trees,[896] all at the same time, could have only worked in the depressed times that character-ized Germany during the early-to-mid-1930s. Hence by 1937, von Keudell was forced to resign because he was unwilling to relax the *dauerwald* forest regulations. Thus, in spite of its promising beginning, "Goering now had to sacrifice his love of *dauerwald* principles and take measures to ramp up the wood output of the German forests at all costs. To avoid violating its own regulations, the *Reichforstamt* was forced to issue new regulations that allowed cuts to exceed the limit set by the 1934 *dauerwald* regulations."

This, however, does not mean the *dauerwald* concept was completely rejected, but that a much more practical compromise was reached. "The new regulations repeated the stipulation that forestry had to be 'close to nature,' which in essence meant that the composition, structure, and man-agement of the German forest had to be appropriate for the ecological site conditions—even though the primary function of the forest was to supply wood."[897] The strict *dauerwald* concept was therefore replaced by *naturgem-aBer Wirtschaftwald*—which literally means a "close to nature commercial forest."[898]

With no small interest, as the war began in earnest on the Russian Front, the stress on Germany to become self-sufficient with regard to wood production was greatly eased. The forests of Austria and Poland could now be used as well. This meant further compromises of *dauerwald* would not have to be made, though they were contemplated. Perhaps more to the point, this is also one of the reasons why the Germans were heading east in the first place—to help relieve the environmental stresses on their own countryside. The Aryan obsession with economic self-sufficiency had the unintended consequence of placing more environmental stress on the

---

[895] Uekoetter, p. 71.

[896] Imort, "Eternal Forest—Eternal Volk: The Rhetoric and Reality of National Socialist Forest Policy," in *How Green Were the Nazis?*, p. 49.

[897] Ibid., p. 58.

[898] Ibid.

homeland. "Conquest in the east made it possible to think about relaxing the 'Battle for Production.'"[899] The quest for *lebensraum* or *living space* in the East was far more than just a plan of conquest. It was also a pre-meditated ecological plan as well: "The east was a safety valve."[900]

The Reich Nature Protection Law & Environmental Totalitarianism

The high-water mark for environmentalism in Nazi Germany came in June and July of 1935 with the passage of the RNG—the Reich Nature Protection Law called the *Reichnaturschutzgesetz*. The RNG was laden with ecological social engineering schemes. The RNG "created a Nature Protection Office at the national level, empowered to implement unified *Naturschutz* regulations for the entire Reich."[901] The RNG required comprehensive land use plans called *environmental effects reports* before new construction projects could be built. Section 20 of the RNG stipulated that all "national, state and local officials consult" with the proper nature protection authorities "prior to conducting any project which might lead to essential alterations in the free landscape."[902] These were essentially early forms of what is today called environmental impact statements. They created a huge bureaucratic paper chase:

> Going through the surviving files, the most striking feature is the enormous diversity of conservation work. The agenda of the national conservation law had ranged from small-scale natural monuments to the landscape in general, and that left a great deal of leeway for local peculiarities and personal preferences. Some used the new option to protect the countryside in general and created large landscape protection reserves. Others focused on small issues like the protection of hedgerows that were important for birdlife and erosion control.[903]

The RNG placed a premium on the holistic or organic integrity of the environment. The green Nazi environmental slogan on this was

---

[899] Blackbourn, p. 287.
[900] Ibid., p. 286.
[901] Closmann, "Legalizing a Volksgemeinschaft" in *How Green Were the Nazis?*, p. 27.
[902] Ibid., p. 21.
[903] Uekoetter pp. 138-39.

all-encompassing: "It shall be the whole landscape!" With such sentiments, the emphasis upon environmental totalitarianism cannot be missed.

Nazi environmentalism was holistic, fascist and intrusive to the core. "Dictatorial regimes can achieve many goals including those of conservation more effectively in the short run than can democracies, which require elaborate processes of negotiation."[904] Nazi conservationist Wilhelm Lienenkamper clearly understood the RNG imposed "a new postulate for totality."[905] As a necessary part of this environmental scheming, sections 18 and 24, respectively, allowed the expropriation of land. It even "denied indemnification claims by aggrieved parties who lost land to the state under the law."[906] While environmental historians are quick to point out the Nazi greens rarely used the right to expropriate property without compensation, they still used the clause to pressure property owners into compliance. They could always legally threaten to take away property if necessary, so "life was much easier with paragraph 24."[907]

Nazi environmentalists working under the auspices of the RNG saw themselves to be an environmental police force. "When the Association for the Swabian Alb decided to set up a conservation watch in April 1940, the result was an impressive documentation of the enduring vibrancy of nature protection during the first year of the war: more than 700 members volunteered for patrol service in scenic areas to prevent unruly or destructive behavior."[908]

A small list of specific examples of what the RNG wrought upon the German landscape is illuminating. For example, a slovenly tavern was attacked by officials in the *Weissenburg* district for damaging the beauty of the landscape.[909] Karl Oberkirch went after private animal collections and compared them to concentration camps.[910] Jewish cemeteries were screened to see if they could be confiscated for natural monuments.[911] Hunters were told by Nazi greens to make their shooting blinds blend into the landscape.[912] The Reich Conservation Agency and the German Institute for Agricultural

---

[904] Sax, p. 44.
[905] Uekoetter, p. 1.
[906] Closmann, "Legalizing a Volksgemeinschaft," in *How Green Were the Nazis?*, p. 21.
[907] Uekoetter, p. 145.
[908] Ibid., p. 153.
[909] Ibid., p. 138.
[910] Ibid.
[911] Ibid., p. 139.
[912] Ibid., p. 139.

Studies decided they would perform a joint study on how mouse poison was impacting birdlife.[913] Nazi biologist Walther Schoenichen demanded a study on leeches because medical practitioners had pushed them to the point of extinction in the previous century.[914]

In September of 1941, the military had to request a special permit to build a secret national security installation in the *Kahler Austen* nature reserve.[915] The ministry of education was consulted "in a conflict over a concrete wall on a lot bordering Lake Constance."[916] In 1943, a *Westphalian* farmer was threatened with a trip to the Russian front by a county commissioner because he cut down a scenic hedgerow. He needed to be taught a serious lesson on the "true value of the German *heimat*."[917] Environmentalists were even seen as important enough to be among the last considered for military service.[918]

Such a list of concrete examples is undoubtedly just the tip of the iceberg. The RNG is thus no footnote in environmental history. The RNG was the first of its kind precisely because of its landscape planning provisions over already developed areas that went way beyond the typical conservationist and preservationist models of environmental thinking. That such a comprehensive environmental law was passed at the federal or national level makes it stand out even further. In fact, the RNG was so far ahead of its time that even many Nazi greens did not really know what to do with it. "The usual response from the conservationist rank and file remained somewhat lukewarm: nature reserves and natural monuments, not landscape planning on a grand scale, remained the mainstay of conservation work. After all, landscape planning was very different from the traditional core activity of the conservation community."[919] Schoenichen pointed this problem out by arguing, "The task of landscape preservation was to influence the human use of landscapes in a certain way."[920] In other words, the RNG legalized environmental social engineering schemes along totalitarian lines.

Because this environmental social engineering was rather new in its approach at such a high level, the RNG was never utilized to the extent that

---

913 Ibid., p. 151.
914 Ibid.
915 Ibid., p. 153.
916 Ibid.
917 Ibid.
918 Ibid., p. 154.
919 Ibid., p. 141.
920 Ibid.

it could have been. It remained in embryonic stage during the Nazi era in Germany and was handed over to the likes of Alwin Seifert and Heinrich Wiepking Jurgensmann.[921] In contrast to the many greens of his day, Seifert strongly held that since there was no wilderness left in Germany, the desire to preserve second-rate landscapes that were long ago destroyed by modernism and liberalism was not only ill-conceived, but also outmoded.

Seifert believed it was far better to mitigate, restore, remedy and rejuvenate environmental damage through ecological planning than try to preserve mediocre or second-rate landscapes. In fact, environmental planners like Seifert "viewed themselves as technicians of sick landscapes, who, like the Third Reich's racial scientists, public health experts, and medical doctors, promised to heal the nation's biological foundations. They believed that the German *Lebensraum*, like the German *Volk*, needed to be brought more closely in line with natural laws to sustain itself over time."[922] Seifert thus dedicated "himself to seeking state assistance for restoring landscape diversity, native vegetation, and indigenous habitat along streets, railways, canals, and rivers."[923] In fact, thanks to his dedication, Seifert's environmental planning efforts began to overrun nature preservation practices in Nazi Germany.

Even today in America, environmental landscape planning has eclipsed nature protection activities with a plethora of land use regulations that have greatly constrained private property rights. The more socialistic the modern Western world has become, the more totalitarian the environmental movement has become as well. It is one thing to set aside federal lands for preservation where no one lives, but quite another to regulate private property where people actually do live. In effect, this turns private property into state parks for the public, and green Nazi Alwin Seifert is at the heart of this transformation in the modern Western world teeming with environmental social engineering schemes.

This is why the Weimar Republic was not so keen about passing environmental laws to satisfy the German greens of the 1920s. How will they compensate private property owners for the loss of using their property because of environmental restrictions? For Hitler and the Nazis, this was less of a problem. As such, with regard to the RNG, one is talking about a

---

[921] Ibid.
[922] Lekan, p. 244.
[923] Ibid., pp. 236-37.

lot more than just preserving national parks or wilderness areas. Nazi environmental laws were holistic, organic and totalitarian enough to trump private property rights. The RNG thus struck at the heart of freedom and private property. Once entire landscapes and ecosystems are subject to environmental rules, private property invariably falls by the wayside under the stress of green totalitarian policies and schemes. Because of this, "even though the RNG looked like laws drafted under the Weimar Republic, only the Nazis could have adopted this measure. The comments of those Nazi officials who justified the RNG based upon emergency legislation of 1933, or appealed to notions of 'common good' taking precedence over the 'individual good,' underscore this point."[924] That Adolf Hitler was not against private property rights per se on the one hand, but then would turn around and subvert it for environmental reasons on the other hand, reveals an interesting green socialism that tugged at his heart strings.

Most telling of all, with private property rights in doubt, and with the ministries of the interior, education and justice fighting over the right to control the RNG, Hermann Goering seized it for himself. In a very illuminating phone conversation between Goering and Bernhard Rust, the minister of education in the Reich, the *Reichforsteister*, asked, "Listen Herr Rust,[925] what's happening with *Naturschutz*? I am the only one who pursues proper *Naturschutz*. Are you agreed that it goes over to my jurisdiction? (pause) Oh but I have the forests and the animals, so *Naturschutz* fits much better in my jurisdiction than yours.... OK, you are agreed.... Thanks."[926] Here, Hermann Goering represents the epitome of environmental totalitarianism.

Goering was thus heavily involved in all three federal Nazi environmental laws, even with regard to the RNG. While all of this may be seen by many as a simple power grab, for Goering, it was much deeper than that. "The animal world remained his own private kingdom."[927] Goering's high position in the Nazi Party also meant that such environmental laws like the RNG were anything but trivial. For all of his faults and inconsistencies, which are too many to count, and which would also show up in his administration over the RNG, Goering was deeply committed to green ideas as he understood them. Though not always successful in his endeavors, he

---

[924] Clossman, "Legalizing a Volksgemeinschaft," in *How Green Were the Nazis?*, p. 30.

[925] Rust was the Nazi minister of science and education.

[926] Dominick, p. 107.

[927] Irving., p. 180.

was "keen to pioneer new techniques."[928] He did establish nature reserves in various places, and his most successful habitat restoration project was just outside of Berlin. "The whole *Schorf Heath* experiment worked. From its *Werbellin* Lake Game Research Laboratory he reintroduced the rarer fauna into the heath."[929] Had not many of his animals been machine-gunned down by the Red Army when it surrounded Berlin in 1945, his environmental experiment could have been hailed as a huge success. In Spandau prison, Rudolf Hess later bragged about Goering's environmental accomplishments with regard to hunting and nature preserves.[930]

While environmental historians today do not take Goering's conservation efforts seriously, the greens of his day did. In fact, with the passage of the RNG at the hands of Goering, the gap between the conservationists and the Nazis was completely bridged—"giving way to a strong affection, if not enthusiasm, for the Nazis."[931] The law was universally praised.[932]

Schoenichen enthusiastically asserted that the RNG was a culmination of Romanticism.[933] He believed it was necessary to protect Germany because of "the leveling influence of the general culture and of urbanization, which constantly and increasingly presses back the particular and the original essence of the nation, while economic rationalization gradually eats away at the original specificity of the landscape."[934] German environmentalist Hans Klose, even though he was not a Nazi party member because he was married to a Jew, still called the RNG the "Magna Carta"[935] of German nature protection. Klose even declared that previous regimes were unable to pass such a measure because "those essential political and worldview assumptions were lacking."[936] What they lacked, of course, was a holistic totalitarian view of the natural world at the political level, which was succinctly summarized by Hitler himself: "From now on, one may consider that there is no gap between the organic and the inorganic

---

[928] Ibid.
[929] Ibid.
[930] Speer, *Spandau: The Secret Diaries*. New York: Macmillan Books, 1976, p. 399.
[931] Uekoetter p. 61.
[932] Ibid., p. 62.
[933] Ferry, p. 94.
[934] Schoenichen is quoted by Ferry, p. 103.
[935] Closmann, "Legalizing a Volksgemeinschaft," in *How Green Were the Nazis?*, p. 32.
[936] Klose, Hans, "Der Schutz der Landschaft nach 5 des Reichnaturgesetzes," 5, 7, quoted by Closmann, "Legalizing a Volksgemeinschaft," in *How Green Were the Nazis?*, p. 32.

world."[937] Severing the gap between man and nature was the hallmark of the Nazi regime, and this is precisely why environmentalism did, in fact, find an important niche in the Third Reich. Hitler and the Nazis wanted to cut man down to size and plunge him back into the natural world where he rightfully belonged, and the RNG was part of this naturist campaign against the Judeo-Christian worldview.

---

[937] *Hitler's Table Talk*, evening of Oct. 24, 1941, p.66.

"The German people have always had a great love for animals and have always been conscious of our strong ethical obligations toward them. And yet, only thanks to the National Socialist leadership has the widely shared wish for an improvement in the legal provisions affecting the protection of animals, the wish for the establishment of a specific law that would recognize the right of animals inherently possess to be protected in and of themselves, been achieved in reality."

November 1933 – Nazi Law for
the Protection of Animals

CHAPTER FIVE:

THE 'STEELY' ROMANTICISM OF NATIONAL SOCIALISM

All this green testimony, however, does not mean that National Socialism was completely consistent with all things environmental. The Nazi economy, technology and the war machine have all been used by environmental historians to discredit the authenticity of the green streak of National Socialism. In reality, however, the alleged inconsistencies between Nazism and environmentalism have far more to do with the fact that National Socialism was too green for its own era. Compared to all of the other Western nations at the time, the Nazis were far ahead of the curve when it came to environmental policy and protection. National Socialism was a vanguard of political ecology that the world of its day, steeped in industrialism and technological progress, often conflicted with. It should, therefore, be hardly surprising that National Socialism was inconsistent with regard to the application of its environmental programs. Furthermore, pioneering movements are usually extolled for all they have done with minimal resources available to them, but in the case of National Socialism and its ties to environmentalism—perish the thought.

Few environmentalists, if any, would ever want to admit there was indeed a strong collusion between their forefathers and one of the most brutal regimes of the 20th century. For obvious reasons, environmental historians have accentuated as much as possible the inconsistencies between Nazism and the modern green movement. However, none of their relativizing attempts are fatal to the historical reality that the Third Reich had a very strong undercurrent of green motives, attitudes, perceptions and practices that continue to reverberate into the contemporary Western world. It is far too easy for modern environmental historians to judge the Nazi experiment in hindsight than it was for those greens who actually lived through it. No matter how inconsistent National Socialism may have been from a contemporary environmental point of view, this does not change the historical fact that many German conservationists still supported the Third Reich with great enthusiasm, and many of the leading Nazis played significant roles in the development of the modern green movement from a variety of different angles.

Nazi Population Growth, the Battle for Production and Public Works

Environmental historians are quick to point out the Nazi push for population growth is contrary to the modern green movement since it strongly advocates a reduction in the number of inhabitants on the planet. Hitler's drive for robust birth rates is abhorrent to modern greens. Yet, the *Fuhrer* believed population growth was a matter of racial survival, not a question of fulfilling the Genesis mandate to subdue and fill the Earth. Hitler's stress on Aryan breeding was to carry out nature's evolutionary law, i.e., the survival of the fittest. The push for population growth was therefore not done for humanistic reasons since Nazi racism was rooted in nature. Rather, the National Socialist impulse for greater birth rates strongly resembles the ancient pagan fertility cults—ancient cults of nature worship which modern greens have drawn deeply from.

The Nazis even set up breeding centers outside the institution of marriage so that strong Aryan men and women could come together, copulate and help improve the racial stock of Germany. In the long shadows of the Eastern Front where many women were sent to serve the Reich, "office romances were common, and marriage was not the only result. Many children were born out of wedlock. Such promiscuous behavior was not frowned upon; on the contrary, propagation of the Aryan race was a patriotic duty."[938] The wartime atmosphere and Holocaustic violence "intertwined with a sexual revolution that tested boundaries and definitions of matrimony, procreation, childbearing, femininity, and pleasure."[939]

Yet Hitler's push for population growth cannot be properly understood without appreciating the backdrop of his eugenics program that was saddled with euthanasia practices and policies. In truth, the whole eugenics program matches up with population control far better than it does with population growth. Hitler knew that Germany needed many babies precisely

---

[938] Lower, Wendy, *Hitler's Furies: German Women in the Nazi Killing Fields*. Boston and New York: Houghton Mifflin Harcourt, 2013, p. 136.
[939] Ibid.

because his eugenics program demanded the elimination of the weak and sickly—and in the Nazi worldview, the weak, sick and infectious were very broadly understood. "With Hitler's backing, medical health professionals and their technical experts developed a new genocidal expertise, which they applied to ever-larger operations of mass murder, especially in the more remote eastern territories."[940] Early on in the war, there was even a top-secret mission ordered by the *Fuhrer* and sworn to utmost secrecy that mobilized euthanasia experts to the Eastern Front where German soldiers were relieved of their suffering through mercy killings.[941]

As far as Hitler was concerned, nature herself demands the state implement eugenic programs to weed out the weak from the strong. Hitler, of course, would be the very wolf who would keep the German herd healthy. He often went by the nickname of "Uncle Wolf":

> The measures of annihilation were not to be confined to the war. German physicians, nutritional scientists and university teachers vied with each other in their eagerness to supply Hitler and Himmler with long-term schemes regulating education, sanitation, food supplies, medical services and birth control in the conquered Eastern territories, designed to reduce their populations, keep the survivors at subsistence levels, and turn them into ignorant and abject slaves. There was nothing very remote about these plans. Experiments of mass sterilization (by drugs, X-rays, and surgical means), conducted on several hundreds of Jewish concentration-camp prisoners and on Eastern civilians and prisoners of war, were so successful that one professor of medicine, Clauberg, claimed in a letter to Himmler (June 7, 1943) that the use of this method made it possible to sterilize one thousand women a day.[942]

Hitler's eugenic plans for Germany and his genocidal plans to destroy the Jews and Slavs in the eastern territories make his push for population growth less inconsistent with environmental goals of reducing overall population counts. Indeed, like all too many modern environmental leaders today, Hitler "spoke of human beings as planetary bacilli."[943]

---

[940] Ibid., p. 122.
[941] Ibid.
[942] Stern, pp. 197-98.
[943] Dietrich, p. 126.

Between 1939 and 1945, some 50 million Europeans were weeded out. If Germany had won the war, many millions more would have died as the "Nazi genocidal program was not directed just against Jews, but also against other categories of people despised by the Darwinian eugenicists, including invalids, Slavs, and Gypsies. Had the Nazis prevailed, it would have unquestionably have been expanded to include other non-Nordic Europeans, Africans, and Asians—that is, the entire target list of the eugenics movement."[944] Moreover, in truth, the modern environmental resolve to lessen birth rates and reduce the number of people on the planet is not all that far removed from a form of eugenics anyway. After the Nazi doomsday when eugenics could no longer be defended, many eugenicists in the West converted their concerns to overpopulation. It was the eugenicists who laid down the foundation stones for the dreaded concern about overpopulation that now undergirds most of the ideas, policies and practices of modern environmentalism.[945] In a word, all of the propaganda surrounding overpopulation is the new eugenics dressed up in more modern environmentalist garb.

Hitler once said his ultimate political objective was "to make the German people rich and Germany beautiful."[946] While environmentalists would appreciate the last part of Hitler's statement, they would have a hard time with the first part. Even though many modern promoters of environmentalism are actually quite rich, they publicly lambaste the power of money as greedy and corrupt. They believe there is a one-to-one relationship between being rich and the degradation of the environment. Furthermore, when Hitler asserted he wanted to make Germany rich, one must keep in mind that the economic depression of the 1920s had a profound impact on the psyche of all Germans. No one wanted poverty. Even many of the greens of the time "accepted the dominant view that drastic measures were necessary to renew the country's economic vitality."[947] For all too many, the first half of the 1920s Weimar Republic was hell on Earth.

Moreover, Hitler clearly understood that, without financing, it would be impossible to make Germany beautiful. It is also truly amazing to listen

944   Zubrin, Robert. *Merchants of Despair: Radical Environmentalists, Criminal Pseudo-Scientists, and the Fatal Cult of Antihumanism.* New York, London: New Atlantis Books, 2012, p. 72.
945   Ibid., pp. 81-92.
946   Tooze, p. 135.
947   Lekan, p. 206.

to extremely rich environmentalists like Prince Charles, Al Gore, James Cameron, Robert Redford and many other Hollywood actors castigate money and capitalism. Hitler routinely did the same even though he later became financially well off. While environmentalists find it all too easy to criticize Hitler on such points, they themselves need to take a look in the mirror.[948] Moreover, Hitler actually lived in poverty for more than half of his life. His personal fortune only rose with the fortunes of the Nazi Party from the mid-1920s until his death in 1945.

Nazi propaganda minister Josef Goebbels (1897-1945) suffered an environmental gauntlet all his own when he tried to build a mansion in a protected area near Berlin. Without the repeated intervention of Goering, he would not have been able to finish it.[949] Nonetheless, Goebbels was also an animal lover and a vegetarian. He strongly advocated a "steely romanticism" that would tame unbridled capitalistic technology and "fill it inwardly with soul, to discipline it and to place it in the service of our people and their cultural level."[950]

Nazi Party leaders did sacrifice their own environmental rules in the later 1930s to place Germany on an all-out war footing. In the great Battle for Production, Germany rapidly emphasized a self-sufficient Aryan economy. This actually forced Germany to reclaim more of their own land for the sake of greater industrial development and farming. Worse, some of the places they needed for such purposes were the exact same places that had previously been set aside as environmental protection areas.[951] The *local only* economy forced Nazi Germany to intensify their own industrialism to make up for the lack of imports coming into the country.

As a part of the same endeavor, the SS emphasis upon self-sufficient farming required more German soil to be reclaimed to grow food for the Reich. Furthermore, as the drive for war became ever more ominous, the need

---

[948] Kay, William. "Petropoulos' Royals and the Reich" written in 2011 on ecofascism. com. Kay argues, "An important feature environmentalism shares with fascism is the centrality, within each movement, of the European aristocracy." Book Review 25 at *Environmentalism is Fascism* Internet Website.

[949] Uekoetter, p. 147.

[950] Goebbels, Joseph, "Deutsche Technik," March 1939, pp. 105-06, based on a speech given by Goebbels at the Berlin Auto Show in February of 1939: quoted in *Reactionary Modernism* by Jeffrey Herf, p. 196.

[951] For a good example of this, see Sandra Chaney's *Nature of the Miracle Years: Conservation in West Germany 1945-1975* (New York & Oxford: Berghahn Books, 2008) where she discusses how the Nazis began building a hospital and planted mines in the Luneburg Heath Nature Reserve in 1942. Other development plans they considered never materialized, pp. 60-61.

to grow food for the sake of growing food became more important than Darre's blood and soil agrarian pipedream. As such, under the influence of Herbert Backe's (1896-1947) pragmatism, the blood and soil farm plans envisioned by Darre had been severely eroded by the return of capitalistic farming practices.[952] After Darre was dismissed in 1942, he complained in his diary, "First of all I was considered an idealist, then a romantic, then a rebel, then a defeatist, and last of all a fool."[953]

However, the Battle for Production, otherwise known as the *Four Year Plan*, was not designed to be a permanent economic strategy for the Third Reich. Hitler had plans to scale the Four Year Plan down "to a more modest scope of activity."[954] Furthermore, the Four Year Plan was to be regulated by environmental planning guidelines which the Nazi brass called "Space Science and Space Planning." These environmental plans were specifically designed to improve the biological strength of the German *volk*, to show the best way to use the powers of the soil, to arrange a harmony between man and nature, and to improve the willingness of Germans to fight hard for their own fatherland. The plans required the various ministries of the Nazi government to work together to bring about profitable *volkisch* cooperation.

Nazi spatial planning policies were a very early attempt at what is today trumpeted as sustainable development and/or green building. Interior minister Wilhelm Frick declared that such environmental plans were necessary because modern industry had ignored the importance of national life too long, and that Germans receive power from untouched nature. Another minister said Germany had been subjected to poor planning in the past, but now this could be reversed thanks to the new requirement of inter-departmental cooperation. Even Albert Speer chimed in when he wrote the new environmental plans were the basis for retrofitting and remodeling old towns and farms for the sake of a new Germany. Spatial planning was also designed to regulate new construction as well. As such, even the dreaded Four Year Plan, which environmental historians always use to discredit the green streak of the National Socialism, was all to be carried out under a cooperative green supervision between the various ministries of the Reich.

---

[952] Bramwell, *Blood and Soil: Walther Darre and Hitler's Green Party*, p. 178.
[953] Ibid., p. 182.
[954] *Hitler's Table Talk*, Night of Feb. 26-27, 1942, p. 257.

Adolf Hitler loved architecture. He loved to have monumental building projects constructed National Socialism-style that, at first blush, seems contrary to the anti-development obsession of the modern green movement. Hitler was also very proud of the hard-working industrious German spirit. The Nazis saluted the German workers far more than the Marxists because they associated their labor with the development of the racial community. Hitler also dropped Gottfried Feder's (1883-1941) green garden village plans for architectural megalomania on the streets of Berlin.[955] "Once in power, Hitler jettisoned much of Feder's program for de-concentration of urban areas and sent his old mentor off to a respectable semi-retirement. Rather than return to the village past, the Nazis now sought to mold their cities into their own alternative form of modernity."[956]

However, Dr. Fritz Todt was the very man who replaced Feder, and Todt was very concerned about environmental issues. More importantly, Hitler's penchant for grand building projects goes back to his own Romantic lust to bring back the Greco-Roman world of antiquity. Hitler was trying to recover the historic Roman Empire before it had been infected with the Judeo-Christian worldview, and his grand Olympic construction style actually re-digs the Romantic hole even deeper than Feder. Thus while it is true that Nazi public works were certainly employed to modernize Germany under Todt's supervision, it must not be forgotten this was also done with a strong Romantic longing for a greener yesteryear when Greco-Roman man was fully embedded into the natural world. Thus, Nazi public works toiled to modernize the Reich, but this was still all to be done with a Romantic hue to it.[957] In fact, Hitler's great interest in constructing the *Autobahnen* was based on his Romantic fascination with the old Roman roads.[958]

Even though the Nazis did love their own construction projects, Hitler himself frequently complained about over-industrialization. "When speaking of Germany's industrialization he usually employed such adjectives as 'harmful,' 'excessive,' or 'unbridled.'"[959] Hitler also "harbored a profound distaste for the huge urban concentrations of population to which that process had

---

[955]   Speer, *Inside the Third Reich*, pp. 50-70.

[956]   Kotkin, Joel. *The City: A Global History*. New York: The Modern Library, 2005, p. 103.

[957]   See Leni Riefenstahl's propaganda Nazi film *Triumph of the Will* (1934), where an army of Nazi workers with spades on their shoulders are exhibited as a gigantic *green* public works program. This was largely connected to the implementation of the SS *back to the land* movement.

[958]   *Hitler's Table Talk*, evening and night of Nov. 2-3, 1941, p. 86.

[959]   Turner, p. 75.

given rise. He looked on the great industrial cities of Germany with loathing as 'abscesses on the body of the *Volk*, in which evil vices, bad habits and sicknesses seem to converge.'"[960] Moreover, Hitler's ascetic modesty was not based on Judeo-Christian ethics, but squarely on biological determinism where heredity determined morality rather than education.[961]

Environmental historians are also critical of the Nazis for many of their public works projects. They complain Nazi public works construction efforts far outpaced what the environmental landscape planners could keep up with.[962] Thus, ironically enough, it was the National Socialist public works department that was running roughshod over the German landscape, not the *liberal* socialists of the Weimar years who sorely neglected environmental concerns. Ironically, the *back to the land* movement of the SS in particular was the primary culprit. The pipe dream of a self-sufficient agricultural economy required the Reich to make more land arable for farming. This created hydrological upheaval on the land as dams and dikes were built, wetland areas were drained, and streams and rivers straightened in order to grow more food for Germany. "Nature preservationists bemoaned the destruction of swamps and marshes, which the Labor Service deemed 'wastelands,' because these parcels of land provided vital habitat for birds and small mammals."[963]

The nature protection officer for the Ruhr Settlement Association, Karl Oberkirch, grumbled: "The land reclamation projects were upsetting the entire household of nature by changing local climate conditions, lowering the groundwater table, and desiccating the soil."[964] Other regional nature protectionists were concerned that "the new dams created stagnant waters that were intolerable for local fish species, which were accustomed to migrating through swiftly moving stream and river currents."[965] During the very first Reich Nature Protection Conference held in 1937, Hans Klose lamented, "There is no one in this room who will not shudder with horror at the thought of incessant water drainage processes being conducted by agricultural cultivators and the Labor Service, which in many places have already gone too far. In just a few years, such actions will almost completely

---

960   Ibid.
961   Weikart, *Hitler's Ethic*, pp. 87-88.
962   Lekan, Thomas, "It Shall Be the Whole Landscape!" in *How Green Were the Nazis?*, p. 91.
963   Lekan, p. 210.
964   Lekan, Thomas, "It Shall Be the Whole Landscape!" in *How Green Were the Nazis?*, p. 92.
965   Ibid.

disfigure the landscape and thereby take away these natural resources from the Fatherland."[966] All this, however, had far more to do with the law of unintended consequences than a purposeful intention on the part of the SS to harm the countryside. As time wore on, both Himmler and Darre became more sensitive to this growing environmental concern, but the war effort placed it on the shelf.

Closely related, environmental historians also carp the Nazis did not allow conservationists to criticize public works programs or drum up public opposition for some environmental cause. "The Nazi regime clearly encouraged administrative activity and negotiations behind closed doors, whereas anything that smacked of public protest was monitored suspiciously. It was fine for the conservationists to be obstinate in an internal meeting, even if that stalled a war economy project for months; it was not acceptable to voice protest in public."[967] However, National Socialists did not want such divisions to become public primarily because this would be seen as a rupture in the *volk*. That the Nazis allowed internal environmental arguments to be debated actually speaks far more volumes as to how green they actually were. While environmentalists were not allowed to protest the building of such projects informally on the streets, thanks to Nazi conservation regulations, it was not necessary to do so anyway. By law, they were given a consulting role with regard to all construction and development plans on the landscape.

One can also easily argue even today in green states like Washington and California, public works projects are not scrutinized nearly as much as private building projects.[968] Public works seem to have an uncanny habit of getting out of the restrictions that have been foisted upon private individuals. Just for example, outside of Mt. St. Helens,[969] the biggest polluter

---

966   Lekan, p. 211.
967   Uekoetter, p. 136.
968   Cornwall, Warren and Lindblom, Mike. "Some Light Rail Tunnel Debris Polluted," *The Seattle Times*, Sept. 9, 2007, Washington's Department of Ecology has never truly fined Sound Transit for dumping tons of jet grout material in dumpsites not properly geared for such material. The title of this article is understated as evidence from the article itself shows. Moreover, Sound Transit was also finally fined for stormwater violations in excess of $150,000, but these fines were late in coming, thanks largely to a whistleblower who blew his whistle long enough and loud enough that the Department of Ecology could no longer ignore the problem.
969   Doughton, Sandi, "Mount St. Helens is the State's no. 1 Air Polluter," *The Seattle Times*, Dec. 1, 2004.

in Washington State is Sound Transit,[970] a massive public works project which is attempting to build a light rail system in the Puget Sound area for green purposes to get people out of their cars. Hence, the end justifies the means. Should it therefore be surprising that Nazis public works projects seemed to have gone on largely unhindered by environmental concerns? Absolutely not, especially when one considers that since the National Socialist Worker's Party, the quintessential *volkisch* representative of the German countryside, was doing the work.

In 1938, the Nazi brass had what Speer characterized as "vehement discussions" over Hitler's plan to build a gigantic industrial plant near Linz, Austria. "Goering hailed it in the name of the Four Year Plan, but Todt and especially the city planners were against it. Hitler personally had picked out the building site near the city. He brushed aside all objections about the potential problem of industrial fumes, which would be intensified by the prevailing east winds in the Danube."[971] This, of course, is not what most people deliberate about when they think of the Nazi hierarchy arguing over what needs to be done in the greater Reich. Heated environmental discussions with the *Fuhrer* over the building of an industrial plant? Dr. Todt even pleaded with Hitler by complaining, "Beautiful old Linz would be transformed into a sooty industrial and proletarian city."[972] In the heat of the controversy, however, Hitler responded with sober mathematical reasons why the plant should be built and how this project was to be funded.

Yet Speer also recalled how Hitler wanted to reconstruct Linz rather than Vienna as a payback to the capital city for failing him as a youngster.[973] At the time, Vienna was the sixth largest city in the world—a veritable overpopulated mongrel metropolis that needed to be trimmed down with Nazi eugenic measures, including economic ones. Hitler thus told Speer his reconstruction plans for Linz were not out of the ordinary at all, but historically comparable and consistent with what had transpired before. While standing in the famous Renaissance courtyard of the *Landhaus*, Hitler told Speer, "If you compare little Linz of that period with its 3,000 inhabitants with the present day city and consider its future development,

---

[970] Bundy, Emory, "The Carbon Cost of Building and Operating Light Rail," *Crosscut.com*, July 25, 2007. See also the Performance Audit Report of Brian Sonntag, the Washington State Auditor, whose report shows that much of the $5 million of unnecessary expenses were because of environmental negligence.

[971] Speer, *Spandau: The Secret Diaries*, p. 174.

[972] Ibid.

[973] Ibid., p. 96.

you will admit that my plans for this city are no more lavish than theirs."[974] Hitler was thus not oblivious to the development concerns of those under him. Here, he tries to soften an old environmental argument that was not forgotten by him even though he brushed aside their complaints at the time. Indeed, Hitler would later grant the city of Linz "a picture gallery of German Romantic painters, including the finest Spitzwegs in the world. Hitler said he wanted this gallery to be unique of its kind, the equal to any metropolitan gallery and a place of pilgrimage for all lovers of Romantic painting."[975]

Other Minor Environmental Inconsistencies

Another reason why environmental historians are skeptical of the green Nazi connection is that conservationism did not hit its stride with the party elites until the 1930s. Prior to their takeover of Germany, the Nazis only talked sparingly about conservationism.[976] However, this perception that the Nazis paid little attention to environmental motifs during the 1920s completely overlooks Hitler's long associations with Hess. Hess was green through and through. Furthermore, Hess goes all the way back to the very origins of the Nazi Party with Hitler himself. So do Feder and Haushofer. That Hitler and Hess did not talk about green issues together during the 1920s is simply untenable:

> It would be difficult to overestimate Hess's power and centrality in the complex governmental machinery of the National Socialist regime. He joined the party in 1920 as member #16, and for two decades was Hitler's devoted personal deputy. He has been described as "Hitler's closest confidant," and the *Fuhrer* himself referred to Hess as his "closest advisor." Hess was not only the highest party leader and second in line after Goering to succeed Hitler; in addition, all legislation and every decree had to pass through his office before becoming law.[977]

---

974   Ibid., p. 173.
975   Dietrich, p. 149.
976   Dominick, pp. 90-92.
977   Staudenmaier & Biehl, p. 37.

In fact, thanks to Hess, who in 1934 essentially took over much of the conservation movement by placing it under the auspices of the German Labor Front, there is seen a growing alliance between National Socialism and environmentalism that could even be described as a greening of the Nazi Party. While the two groups may have earlier diverged from each other, there was nonetheless enough of a convergence between them that "intellectual vortices began to churn, and they generated powerful currents that eventually swept an apparent majority of the conservationists toward the Nazi camp. In that swirling, central area of shared demands and ideals, both the Nazis and the nature conservationists longed for national regeneration."[978] Both the Nazi hierarchy and environmentalists were on a campaign to get back to nature, however different they may have sometimes been on what this really meant or how this was to be accomplished.

Just for example, at the very beginning of the 1930s, every time an environmental problem was discussed in the Nazi Party's central newspaper, *Der Volkischer Beobachter*,[979] "the editors stood on the side of the preservationists."[980] On the other hand, when the editors explained why it was that they were siding with the conservationist position on a particular environmental concern they "ignored considerations of scientific ecology, public health, or rational calculations. Instead, predictably enough, they preached aesthetic values, or more often still, the *volkisch* argument that nature preservation maintained the strength of the nation."[981] This interesting observation by an environmental historian does show how different motivations can work for the same environmental totalitarian goal.

One must also keep in mind it is more than possible the Nazi editors left out the more ecologically scientific-friendly arguments, not because they were completely disinterested in them, but simply because they assumed the *volkisch* argument would be more effective in getting people to side with their cause. The Nazis actually believed their crackpot *volkisch* arguments were based on science anyway. Racism and eugenics were considered to be big biological science in those days before the Holocaust brought about a sudden worldwide repentance on the subject. In addition, newspapers are in the habit of saying what needs to be said with the fewest words possible, and if they had a choice between a *volkisch* environmental argument and a

---

[978] Dominick, p. 86.
[979] *Der Volkischer Beobachter* means the People's Racial Observer.
[980] Ibid., p. 91.
[981] Ibid.

purely ecological argument, certainly the *volkisch* argument will win. After all, their readers were of the *volkisch*. They strongly believed that without nationalism, the environment could not be properly preserved anyway.

Later, other Nazi Party leaders like Martin Bormann were strongly opposed to those attracted to organic farming, *volkisch* mysticism and occultism, especially after World War II began in earnest. They, of course, were undoubtedly very concerned that such preoccupations would compromise the war effort. Bormann himself called such views "slogans of political soothsayers."[982] Yet, even Bormann himself still acknowledged that true Nazi ideology was "founded on a scientific knowledge of the laws of race, life, and nature."[983] Furthermore, much of the opposition to the Romantic occultists of the Third Reich goes back to an old feud between Ariosophy and Theosophy that was originally launched by Hitler's fatherly mentor, Dietrich Eckart. The only real difference between those two movements was Ariosophy emphasized an Aryan form of Romanticism, whereas Theosophy was more universal. Ariosophy highlighted Pan German nature mysticism, whereas Theosophy highlighted a more generalized form of natural theology.

Just as Bormann quietly began to overshadow Hess as the party secretary, so Herbert Backe increasingly eclipsed Darre's green farming ideas in the later 1930s. Backe even "thought that Himmler's growing Romanticism and mystic interests was a result of Darre's bad influence, and while Darre was not interested in the occult, which he jeered at in the Nordic Ring, he was capable of inspiring others with his own enthusiasms, and many of his ideas re-emerged through Himmler in a perverted form in later years."[984] Such various attitudes among the Nazi Party elites do "reflect a split within National Socialism, between practical men, and the alternative, individualist rebels against the Weimar structures, whose ability to conform to the strictures and precepts of the Third Reich was tempered by their own strongly held beliefs."[985]

Hermann Goering himself was practically a living conflict of interest since he was also in charge of the economy and the war plans in the great Battle for Production. His lavish lifestyle and political maneuverings with

---

[982] Bramwell, *Ecology in the 20ʰ Century: A History*, p. 197.

[983] Lang, J. von, *The Secretary*, pp. 160-61, quoted by Bramwell, *Ecology in the 20ʰ Century: A History*, p. 197.

[984] Bramwell, *Blood and Soil: Walther Darre and Hitler's Green Party*, p. 90.

[985] Bramwell, *Ecology in the 20ʰ Century: A History*, p. 197.

the elites of German industry and banking[986] compromised his otherwise enthusiastic green record.

However, many people have already said as much concerning Al Gore. Al Gore has the arrogant audacity to command Americans to live simpler lifestyles for the sake of the environment while he himself lives in a huge mansion that guzzles more energy[987] by far than the average American home. He also rides around in large SUV's and private jets. Furthermore, Al Gore's fortune was made in big oil. He also ran roughshod over environmentalists in California when he allowed the sale of drilling rights to Occidental Oil on federal lands in the Elk Hills of California.[988] For the past decade, Gore has been scheming to find a way to profit hugely from global warming legislation. Since leaving the vice-presidential office in 2001, his worth has skyrocketed to almost 100 million dollars.[989] He has made a killing on green populism, donations from rich corporations, and government subsides, a veritable 95-percent increase. Just exactly how green is Al Gore? Green hypocrisy is by no means limited to Hermann Goering. Similar arguments have been marshaled against Prince Charles, Ted Turner, Robert Redford and James Cameron—all of whom are super-rich environmental celebrities.

It would therefore be a grave mistake to suggest Hitler and the Nazis were against the environmental movement, or that they had no interest in it.[990] "Although the anti-modern, anti-Enlightenment, anti-industrial, and nature-revering rhetoric of the Nazis in the early 1930s was largely betrayed by their subsequent commitment to rearmament and industrial productivity, the Nazi government passed environmental laws that were the most far-reaching in the developed world at that time. Nazi reverence for and identification with nature were not merely opportunistic"[991] as

---

[986]   Turner, pp. 143-45, 148-49, 152, 156.

[987]   See "Al Gore's Own 'Inconvenient Truth – a $30,000 Utility Bill,'" *ABC News*, February 26, 2007, written by Jake Tapper as Gore's home uses more than 20 times the national average. See also "Al Gore's House Uses More Energy After 'Going Green'" written by the *Tennessee Center for Policy Research*, June 17, 2008.

[988]   Mesler, Bill, "Al Gore: The Other Oil Candidate," *Corp Watch*, Aug. 29, 2000.

[989]   Hanson, Victor Davis, "The New War Against Reason," *National Review*, Nov. 25, 2009.

[990]   Dominick's view is nature protection for Hitler was "little more than a quaint stage prop in his unfolding drama of world domination and racial extermination," p. 91. Bramwell states, "Hitler was not sympathetic to the 'green' wing of his party" in *Ecology in the 20ʰ Century: A History*, p. 51. The problem with this statement is that Bramwell makes Darre the star of Hitler's greeners because of her bias in favor of agrarian green ideals over and against more radical ecological ideals. The fact that there were others in the Reich far more green than Darre, as she herself points out, betrays this assessment.

[991]   Zimmerman, Michael. *Possible Political Problems of Earth-Based Religiosity*, p. 2.

many environmental historians now piously assume. In fact, the Nazis were undoubtedly the first modern regime to take the concept of sustainable development seriously. The Nazis would therefore develop, but they would do so with certain ecological parameters in place to protect them from the destructive effects of the international free market. As such, National Socialism laid the political foundations to bridge the gap between old-style conservationism and social engineering environmentalism that has become the staple of the modern green movement, especially with regard to sustainable development.

Between 1933 and 1935, Hitler did sign four landmark environmental laws. They were the first of their kind because they were comprehensive federal laws. Environmental laws prior to the rise of National Socialism were largely passed at the local level. Hitler essentially nationalized environmentalism with the signing of these particular laws. Furthermore, these environmental laws, "ordered by Hitler, who made them his pet projects—though they also corresponded to the wishes of numerous and powerful ecologist associations of the period—bear the signatures of the principal ministers concerned: Goering, Gurtner, Darre, Frick, and Rust, in addition to that of the chancellor."[992] On occasion, Hitler could even easily pass for a modern environmentalist himself: "Without doubt, man is the most dangerous microbe imaginable. He exploits the grounds beneath his feet without ever asking whether he is disposing thus of products that would perhaps be indispensable to the life of other regions. If one examined the problem closely, one would probably find here the origins of the catastrophes that occur periodically in the earth's surface."[993]

While it is true that in *Mein Kampf* Hitler was far more interested in viewing nature in a Social-Darwinian sense, almost like a pantheistic agent of history, the natural laws of which man must discover and adhere to, this was not exactly what the average environmentalist was trying to preserve.[994] Yet, on the other hand, most environmentalists espouse the Darwinian doctrine of evolution with regard to creation origins. So the distance between these two camps is not that far off in spite of some of the *volkisch* nuances of Social Darwinism. With no little interest, even a cursory comparison of *Mein Kampf* (1920s) with *Hitler's Table Talk* (1940s) shows a greening of Adolf Hitler.

---

[992] Ferry, pp. 91-92.
[993] *Hitler's Table Talk*, night of July 5-6, 1941, p. 6.
[994] Uekoetter, p. 31.

Hitler even told Albert Speer that *Mein Kampf* was already outdated.[995] As such, Speer never bothered to read it. He only flipped through it. Hitler's political ambitions had grown, and environmentalism was one of those areas in which this growth can be seen.

Hitler was even keenly aware of the varying shades of green to be found among the *volksgemeinschaft*: "The real peasant keeps his eye firmly on the land, and he lives by the plough. The beauties of the woods were discovered, not by the peasant, but by the professor."[996] Thus Hitler noticed the differences between peasant Romanticism represented best by Darre, and ecology professors like Seifert, Schoenichen and others. However, in Hitler's statement, he does not disparage either one. Far from it. They both have a valuable role to play in the development of the German *volksgemeinschaft*.

In 1941, Hitler proclaimed, "We will not only create a Germany of power, but also a Germany of beauty."[997] In his Nietzschean "will to power" emphasis, Hitler clearly understood that without power, beauty cannot be achieved. It is also often forgotten that Hitler first and foremost viewed himself primarily as an artist. As far as Hitler was concerned, politics was an unfortunate necessity, especially when one wants to fix the ugliness of a society gone completely awry with Jewish international materialism coming from the both the East and the West. In a speech given at an opera house, Hitler declared, "All this chatter of internationalism in art is as idiotic as it is dangerous."[998] An eyewitness of the speech went on to say Hitler "argued that since art is the expression of a people's life and the bloom on the trees of their values, no man can bear any intimate relation to any cultural achievement which does not have its roots in his own origins and soil."[999]

Hitler also considered himself to be a Romantic. Even as late as 1943, right before the decisive battle of Kursk on the Eastern Front, Hitler commented, "It is perfectly true that we are a people of Romantics, quite different from the Americans, for example, who see nothing beyond their skyscrapers. Our Romanticism has its origins in the intense appreciation of nature that is inherent in us Germans. Properly to appreciate such artists as Weber,

[995] Speer, *Inside the Third Reich* p. 509.
[996] *Hitler's Table Talk*, evening of Aug. 6, 1942, p. 467.
[997] See Hans Schwenkel, *Taschenbuch des Naturschutzes* (Salach/Wurttemberg, 1941), 37 and "Aufgaben der Lanschaftsgestaltung und der Landschaftspflege," *Der Biologie*, 10, (1941), 133 quoted by Uekoetter p. 41.
[998] Ludovici, "Hitler and Nietzsche," *The English Review*, 64, 1937.
[999] Ibid.

Ludwig Eichter and the other Romanticists, one must know the *Franconian Mountains*, for that is the background which gives birth to Romanticism in both music and painting; and, of course, the stories and legends of our folklore also make a potent contribution."[1000]

Another way green historians discredit Hitler's lack of environmental thinking is to point out one of his close associates in the 1920s commented the *Fuhrer* was "a city person who felt only at home on cobblestones."[1001] However, that such a criticism is flimsy is shown by a more recent correspondent who acutely observed, "Unlike every other president stretching all the way back to Theodore Roosevelt, Obama has spent his entire life living in urban areas."[1002] In other words, in spite of President Obama being the quintessential big city Chicago man, he still campaigned on a green agenda. Obama has also given all the appearances that he cares about the subject, yet has on occasion been forced to move away from some of his earlier green rhetoric that he exhibited on the campaign trail.[1003] Political wishes and political reality are very often two different things, even in Nazi Germany. Furthermore, the correspondent above was not trying to say that Obama could not be a very good environmental thinker because he was a big-city person. Yet when it comes to Hitler, he, of course, was a city person, and therefore could not have been much of an environmental thinker.

Hitler himself also had some choice words of his own for the city dweller: "What, think you, would happen if the work of a city worker or an official depended on chance? Work on the land is a schooling which teaches energy, self-confidence, and a readiness to make swift decisions; the town-dweller, on the contrary, must have everything exactly mapped out for him, and he does all he can to eliminate the slightest chance of any risk. As a last resort, he takes out an insurance policy—and the insurance company which issues it to him reinsures itself into the bargain!"[1004]

[1000] *Hitler's Table Talk*, midday of June 15, 1943, p. 536.

[1001] Hansfstaengl, Ernst, *Zwischen, WeiBem und Braunem Haus. Memoiren eines politischen AuBenseiters*, p. 80, quoted by Uekoetter p. 32.

[1002] Sullivan, Amy "Obama's Other Breakthrough: A Big-City President," *Time*, Jan. 13, 2009.

[1003] See Stephen Power and Siobahn Hughes, "Coal Industry Digs Itself out of a Hole in the Capitol: Support from EPA, Energy Nominees Signals Obama Team Headed Toward Center of Matter on Fossil Fuels and Carbon Emissions," *Wall Street Journal*, Jan. 15, 2009.

[1004] Ibid., evening of Aug. 6, 1942, p. 468.

Nazi ideologue Alfred Rosenberg said in his *Myth of the Twentieth Century*, "Those who today rage against technology and heap maledictions upon it forget that its appearance derives from an eternal German impulse which would have to be destroyed along with it. Truly, this would mean a descent into the same barbarism which was the ultimate fate of the Mediterranean cultures."[1005] Rosenberg was thus not against technology per se. However, like so many other leading Nazis, what Rosenberg viewed as a cultural threat was the homogenization of modern technology based on international capitalistic values. Rosenberg complained such technology was alien to the *volk*: "It is not technology which today destroys vitality. It is man himself who has degenerated. He has become inwardly deformed because, at weak moments in his historical experience, alien seductions were dangled before him—world conversion, humanity, universal culture."[1006] As such, as long as Germans were advancing an Aryan technology that did not denigrate the personality of the Teutonic man, technology was a good thing. Green Nazi existentialist philosopher Martin Heidegger held very similar views up until the defeat of Germany.

As such, Rosenberg reacted strongly against an internationalized technology he believed was destroying the modern soul. Worse, Rosenberg believed the Jews were at the heart of a parasitic modernism that was making the world soulless through the technological progress of capitalism.[1007] He and many other leading Nazis contradictorily believed German technology was uniquely Aryan and "must not be confused with the financial swindles of the Jews."[1008] Rosenberg even charged that Americans sought technology for the same characterless reason—for the sake of the Almighty dollar: "The American man still ruthlessly forces his will on society. The ceaseless hunt for the dollar almost exclusively governs his existence. His culture is represented by sport and technology."[1009] Thus for Rosenberg, it was the Jews and Americans who misused technology. Germans, on the other hand, were a resourceful and productive people.

[1005]   Rosenberg, Alfred. *Myth of the Twentieth Century*, p. 129.
[1006]   Ibid.
[1007]   Ibid., p. 324.
[1008]   Herf, Jeffrey. *Reactionary Modernism: Technology, Culture, and Politics in the Weimar and the Third Reich.* Cambridge University Press, 1984, p. 225.
[1009]   Rosenberg, p. 346.

Later on in his book, Rosenberg pointed out how the American drive for unbridled capitalism was leading to increasing cultural mayhem on the streets of New York, especially now that an untold number of cars were driving in and out of the city:

> One needs only to look at the troubles of New York, which touch upon the very vital nerves, to know at once that all is at stake. Things have now gone so far that the erection of multilevel streets has been proposed. Roads for cars have to be laid under the houses and pedestrian stairways arranged above these in passages. Bridges must span one side of the street to another. An entire complex of stairs, passageways and permanently artificially lighted thoroughfares, is planned. The new American three zone law allows a higher development of houses. New designs surpass anything known before, as we see in the work of architects like H. Ferris, R. Hood, M. Rusell and Crosell. The aim of all these technical efforts, which reveal perfect freedom of movement as the foundation of their world view, is a heap of mammoth stone pyramids in which all human life must become desolate, rigid, and must finally perish. Such a foundation for a world view must be cleared away. Only then will the path be clear for the surpassing of technology through technology itself. The great city created ease of transport. It must die from this ease of movement if we do not wish to perish racially and spiritually. The Polis created Greek culture. The small town, the middle sized city made every *volkisch* civilization in Europe. The expanding vision of the former individual peasant grasped the idea of a state, without losing itself into infinity. In this alone could an organic cultural structure arise.

Rosenberg thus demonstrates his reactionary spirit to the modern American lifestyle, a view that is also shared by many today in the green movement. Even though Rosenberg maintained technology itself was a good thing if it was used for the sake of the *volk*, his strong opposition toward international capitalistic progress is clear.

Nazi scholar Dr. Jeffrey Herf has characterized this Nazi stance, so typical of many National Socialists, as a form of reactionary modernism:

Before and after the Nazi seizure of power, an important current within conservative and subsequently Nazi ideology was a reconciliation between the antimodernist, romantic, and irrationalist ideas present in German nationalism and the most obvious manifestation of means–ends rationality, that is, modern technology.[1010]

Nazism thus "incorporated modern technology into the cultural system of German nationalism, without diminishing the latter's romantic antirational aspects."[1011] *Volkisch* science wrapped around the community with the *Fuhrer* as its leader would replace the presumed corruption of the international sciences. "The Nazis had little difficulty using the reactionary modernist tradition to present a biological-racial version of German technology struggling for its freedom."[1012] Hitler himself had no trouble in accepting that "scientists and specialists had purposes within the racial community: to manufacture weapons, to improve communications, to advance hygiene. Stronger races should have better guns, better radios, and better health, the better to dominate the weaker. He saw this as a fulfillment of nature's command to struggle, not as a violation of its laws. Technical achievement was proof of racial superiority, not evidence of the advance of general scientific understanding."[1013]

The Nazis wanted to convert the alien Western civilizing effects of modernity "into an organic part of German culture."[1014] This conversion would be one of the primary responsibilities of the state that would include a fascist environmentalism, but would also certainly involve the rise of the National Socialist industrial military complex:

> The reactionary modernists were nationalists who turned the romantic anti-capitalism of the German Right away from backward-looking pastoralism, pointing instead to the outlines of a beautiful new order replacing the formless chaos due to capitalism in a united, technologically advanced nation. In so doing, they contributed to the persistence of Nazi ideology throughout the Hitler

---

[1010] Herf, p. 1.
[1011] Ibid., p. 2.
[1012] Ibid., p. 221.
[1013] Synder, p. 9.
[1014] Herf, p. 1.

regime. They called for a revolution from the Right[1015] that would restore the primacy of politics and the state over economics and the market, restore the ties between romanticism and rearmament in Germany.[1016]

Indeed, Martin Heidegger went so far as to say that the motorization of the *Wehrmacht* in Nazi Germany's victory over France in 1940 was a "metaphysical act."[1017] Not only does such a sentiment reduce philosophy to the realm of politics and power—the epitome of Nazi existentialism—but more importantly, Germany's conquest over France represented the victory of National Socialist existentialist ideology over the international values of the French Enlightenment that exaggerated human reason over Nature.

Yet with no small irony and just a few years later, Albert Speer became extremely frustrated with Nazi Romanticism that often compromised his ability to keep the war machine going.[1018] At the most critical times, Speer often had to fight against antiquated Nazi ideas which had lost all rational meaning because of the practical demands of war. Even after the catastrophe of Stalingrad, Nazi environmentalists fought against hydroelectric plans to use up more water in Wutach Gorge Scenic Area for the sake of much needed power. Speer threatened to personally intervene if the Forest Service continued to obstruct them. Some of the greens even assumed that Hitler would side with their cause as they tried to reach the *Fuhrer's* attention directly through secret channels.[1019] Himmler was also similarly contacted for help.[1020] Such environmental infighting during the heights of war, even in the wake of a disaster on the scale such as Stalingrad, shows just how environmentally entrenched National Socialism actually was.

In fact, Speer actually concluded Hitler's ideological Romanticism was ultimately detrimental to the war effort. Hitler was simply not a big believer in technology to help Germany win the war:

[1015] Describing the "Right" as anti-capitalistic and desirous of taking state control over the economy cannot be reconciled with modern American conservatism that fully embraces free-market capitalism.

[1016] Herf, p. 2.

[1017] Faye, p. 299.

[1018] Speer, *Infiltration*, pp. 76-84.

[1019] Uekoetter, p. 134.

[1020] Ibid.

Was not Hitler downright anti-modern? After all, the symbol he chose for National Socialist ideology was not the modern sowing machine but the sower, not the tractor but the plow. The thatched roof was preferred over the asbestos cement roof; and modern music as the expression of our technological age was replaced by the folk song. Hitler could polemicize against the "soulless machine." If one is pessimistic about civilization, one may understand some aspects of these strivings. But this anti-modernity prevented Hitler from approaching victory: thatched roofs, old-fashioned ideas about artisan manufacture, division of the land into individual farms—all these things were contrary to the rational exploitation of German production not only in practice but far more in their ideological background. When I began my work as armaments minister in 1942, I kept coming up against such hindrances more and more, or else I fought against a rubber wall, when, for instance, I demanded the promotion of nuclear fission by all possible means, and the party organ, *Der Volkisch Beobachter*, ran an article entitled "Jewish Physics Stirs Again." Typical of this intertwining with a romantic ideology was Hitler's, Goering's, and Sauckel's refusal to let German women work in the armaments industry during the war, something that came about as a matter of course in the Anglo-Saxon countries. The reason given was that the factory work would damage their morals and child bearing capacity. Such unsophisticated feelings were not consistent with Hitler's plans to make Germany the most powerful nation on earth.[1021]

Could it be that National Socialism's reactionary modernism and Aryan sustainability concerns had a significant impact in derailing the National Socialist drive to victory on the European continent? Albert Speer almost says as much here. Right or wrong, Speer certainly pushes the envelope. Whatever the exact case may be, Hitler's Social Darwinism, Malthusian math, racism, and ecological views meant that he limited the promises of science precisely because he saw much of it as an international Jewish disease. Universal science, like universal politics was seen as a Jewish threat,[1022] rather than a means to victory.

[1021] Speer, *Infiltration*, p. 83.
[1022] Snyder, p. 10.

Even Hjalmar Schacht, who was the Reich's minister of economics before the war "warned that National Socialism's preference for political-ideological training at the expense of technical education threatened Germany's technical superiority over other nations, a decline that had grave consequences both because of the importance of exports for the German economy and for military purposes. Schacht's understanding of the relation between science and technology was not widely shared in the regime."[1023] Schacht clearly understood that the Aryan local-only economy endangered the entire Battle for Production that the Nazis emphasized so strongly between 1936 and 1940.

Too many leading Nazis, especially Hitler, believed German willpower was more important in preparing the nation for war than economic realities. They foolishly believed the economic realities on the ground were a Jewish invention designed to enslave the German people. That their emphasis upon an Aryan technology would wind up pushing the best and brightest minds out of the country with regard to nuclear fission is very telling indeed. Nazi Germany lost one of the greatest scientists of all time to America. His name was Albert Einstein. He was a Jew.

Even physicist Pascual Jordan (1902-1980), a key pioneer in the development of quantum mechanics who wanted to help the Nazis develop advanced weaponry for the war effort, was denounced by party leaders for being too involved with Jewish science.[1024] Jordan was even an enthusiastic Nazi who had no qualms whatsoever about politicizing his brand of physics with National Socialist jargon.[1025] Jordan went so far as to advocate that certain microscopic molecules were endowed with dictatorial authority over entire organisms.[1026] In other words, he inserted the *Fuhrer* principle into his brand of politicized physics. Jordan also believed the Nazi "will to power" doctrine was based on physics[1027] and that this would have political repercussions in the upcoming new world order as the Third Reich was in the process of liquidating the liberal values of the Enlightenment[1028] together with the subject-object distinction of the classical sciences.[1029]

[1023] Herf, p. 202.
[1024] *Science, Technology, and National Socialism*, edited by Monika Renneberg and Mark Walker. Cambridge University Press, 1994, p. 247-250.
[1025] Ibid., pp. 224-254.
[1026] Ibid., p. 238.
[1027] Ibid., p. 234.
[1028] Ibid., pp. 224-227.
[1029] Ibid., p. 237.

Yet, this National Socialist stress on "will to power" undercut the famous scientific dictum of the Christian Middle Ages that emphasized "knowledge is power." Because of the Nazi focus on vitalism, life and nature, they replaced "knowledge" with "will." This invariably clouded their approach to technology and science. In Nazi scientific theory, along existential lines, the concept of will was more important than knowledge. Incredibly, more than a few Nazi scientists actually believed that "democratic liberalism was dead, along with its deceptive insistence that the true value of science lay in the world of ideas, not material technology."[1030] Thus, there can be no doubt such reasoning had a negative impact on the development of German technology. While it is true those Nazi academics clamoring for a strict Aryan science were quelled by regular researchers and scientists in the German universities,[1031] no other country in the world at the time was complaining and arguing over the "problem" of Jewish science. Even though the Nazis never took complete charge over German universities and various research departments, such foolishness was still detrimental to the war effort.

The highest achievement of so-called Aryan technology, which took years of trial and error at an enormous cost, was the V2 rocket system, something which Hitler was never completely sold on. Worse, however, because the Nazis had no nuclear capability, the V2 rocket system was essentially worthless from a military point of view. It was merely a weapon of terrorism that had little military threat:

> In the end, despite episodes of disinterest on the part of the *Fuhrer*, almost no one fundamentally questioned the wisdom of an extremely expensive weapons system that was supposed to destroy enemy morale by scattering relatively small amounts of conventional explosives over large urban areas. As a result, the rocket program built an institution and a weapon which made little sense given the Reich's limited research resources and industrial capacity—a perfect symbol of the Nazi regime's pursuit of irrational goals with rational, technocratic means. Because of the infighting in the Third Reich, the guided missile system came not "too late" but ... too

---

[1030] Ibid., p. 250.
[1031] Ibid., p. 10.

early—before electronics, computers and nuclear weapons could make it effective.[1032]

The Nazis would have been far better off building tanks for the Russian front than spending an entire decade trying to figure out how to send conventional weapons by rocket into British cities for the sake of terrorizing the populace into submission. While the rocket system itself was a tremendous technological achievement, it was far surpassed by the Manhattan Project and the development of the nuclear bomb. At the close of the war, many top-notch scientists and rocketeers escaped to the Alps to hide out from the Allies.[1033] Werner von Braun himself surrendered from the scenic Adolf Hitler Pass near the German-Austrian border where he ate, drank, sunbathed and admired "the snow-capped Allgau Alps"[1034] before his capture. While many may presume an apparent incongruence between a rocket program and environmentalism, it should be recalled that the popular songwriter and green activist John Denver loved NASA. Denver wanted to be an astronaut. President Reagan recruited Denver to be a spokesman for NASA. After the spaceship Challenger exploded in 1986, Denver wrote and sang a tribute to the crew who died in the skies entitled, "They were flying for me." Denver's real last name is Dutchendorf.

The fact of the matter is the Nazis were behind in many critical technological areas throughout the war. British radar advances helped sway the Battle of Britain into England's favor. The Brits also managed to decode the presumed unbreakable encryption of the German Enigma machine that gave them superior intelligence throughout the war to help warn the Allies in advance of Germany's military plans. In particular, Nazi naval messages were decoded and were used to set aside the Third Reich's submarine supremacy on the high seas. The Soviets had the best tank on the battlefield in the T-34 until the Nazis finally caught up with it and slightly surpassed it with the Tiger tanks. The problem was the Nazis could not make enough Tiger Tanks to compete against the Russians. Furthermore, the Tiger tank was essentially copied from captured T-34's. According to Franz Stangl, the Fins had the best sub-machine gun.[1035]

1032 Ibid., p. 71.

1033 Jacobsen, Annie. *Operation Paperclip: The Secret Intelligence Program that brought Nazi Scientists to America.* New York: Little, Brown and Company, 2014, p. 33.

1034 Ibid., p. 66.

1035 Sereny, *Into that Darkness*, p. 123.

Nazi press chief Otto Dietrich complained that Hitler's nationalistic nature-based continental philosophy was particularly disastrous with regard to the air campaign: "He lacked all supranational breadth of vision and therefore could not appreciate the international, progressive elements of modern aviation and electronics."[1036] Dietrich remembered how Hitler "would make remarks to the effect that modern developments in aviation—the domination of the soulless, inanimate forces—were depersonalizing human life and cheapening life's essential content. In such a world, he would declare, life no longer seemed to him worth living."[1037] As such, Dietrich concluded that Hitler's backward worldview had a disastrous effect particularly with regard to the air campaign: "He was a figure of the past, not of the future. That, it seems to me, was the deepest cause of his failure in air warfare."[1038] Yet, it must also be pointed out that it was Green Nazi Hermann Goering who was in charge of the *Luftwaffe*. One of the main headquarters for Goering's *Luftwaffe* was at the Romantic Castle Kransberg in the Taunus Mountains. Hitler's own secret castle, designed by Speer, was just a few miles away. It was called *Adlerhorst*, or "Eagle's Nest." From here, Hitler directed the failed campaign of the Battle of the Bulge.[1039]

While it is true the Nazis did come up with a superior jet at the end of the war, it was too little too late. All the Allied pilots had to do was wait until the Nazi jets ran out of gas. They then would go in for the kill when they had to report back to base. The Nazi jets virtually drank up more fuel faster than they could fly—all at a time when they had little gas to spare. More telling, the *Fuhrer* ordered small suicide planes made of plywood that Hitler Youth members could use kamikaze style against allied bomber squads.[1040] When the fuel shortages were worsened, the Nazis came up with the ultimate suicide plane—unpowered gliders! In short, the story about Nazi technology has been overblown. Nazi willpower, racism, biology, and instinct, issues that were far more important to the Nazis than technology per se, were not enough to overcome their technical and industrial deficiencies during the war. On the contrary, their ideology only aggravated their limitations. Even the Third Reich's automated eugenic profiling system to find the Jews relied on foreign IBM cross tabulation technology.

[1036] Dietrich, p. 88.
[1037] Ibid.
[1038] Ibid.
[1039] Jacobsen, p. 18.
[1040] *Science, Technology, and National Socialism*, p. 101.

As such, there can be no doubt Albert Speer's frustration over Nazi Romanticism was very real. Speer believed Nazi ideology often interfered with his ability to weaponize the army to its fullest potential. This continued to be a problem even when pragmatism should have easily trumped ideological considerations:

> If leading members of the Nazi regime actually came to believe that German technology was in fact the expression of an Aryan racial soul or that the will to power was pulsing through and over the *Autobahnen*, then there would be no limit to the strategic miscalculations they could make. Their anti-intellectualism caught up with them. The price to be paid for the reactionary modernist synthesis was severe: declining enrollments, reduced study time, and a glaring deficit of understanding at the highest levels of the Nazi regime concerning the relationship between developments in modern science and technical innovation. The number and quality of German arms were simply insufficient to match those of Nazism's enemies. In this sense, the reconciliation of reactionary modernism came up against the limits imposed by its rejection of the Enlightenment. Reactionary modernism had taught them to neglect strategy for ideology.[1041]

While it is true an isolated Nazi Germany simply did not have enough resources, nor the economic might to keep the army afloat in such a worldwide conflagration, their reactionary modernism only compounded their military problems further. It was the industrial might of both the Soviet Union and the United States that bombed Nazi Germany into oblivion. Goebbels even said as much in his notorious "Total War Speech" delivered after the fall of Stalingrad: "The war of mechanized robots against Germany and Europe has reached its high point."[1042]

Speer himself readily recognized that even his own push for modernization to help Germany keep afloat during the war was completely contrary to the original National Socialist ideology.[1043] He pointed out, "Until 1942 our Reich was only seemingly ruled by standards of technology and

---

[1041] Herf., pp. 222-23.
[1042] Bytwerk, p. 121.
[1043] Speer, *Infiltration*, pp. 76-84.

efficiency."[1044] Lest he be misunderstood, he reiterated further, "Until then mass production had been contrary to the ideological premises of National Socialism."[1045] In fact, he admitted that his re-armament mass production methods were American, not German. This created problems for him with Nazi purists:

> When I review the matter carefully Hitler was anti-modern in his decisions on armaments as well. He opposed the tommy-gun because he said it made soldiers cowardly and made close combat impossible. Or he rejected the jet fighter because he said its extreme speed was an obstacle to fighting. He had little sympathy for jet propulsion as for rockets until 1943. He even distrusted our hesitant attempts at developing an atom bomb by means of nuclear fission, and in private conversations he called such efforts a spawn of pseudoscience. Thus, both Hitler and Ohlendorf, and with them the majority of leading Party bigwigs, paid tribute to seemingly humanitarian ideals. The war was supposed to be won with technology, but actually technology was evil.[1046]

With this statement, Speer puts his finger right on the sorest point of Nazi Germany's drive to total victory. Furthermore, without Speer's modernizing efforts, which was a radical break from what the Nazis were doing before under Dr. Todt,[1047] it is doubtful Germany would have lasted as long as it did.

Hitler even held off on the V2 rocket attacks until late in the war because he feared that such missiles would create an ozone hole which would allow poisonous gasses from outer space to leak into the atmosphere.[1048] He thus waited until the end of the war "when he no longer cared whether or not the world ended, and felt lured by the prospect of universal annihilation, which included his enemies, victims, people and himself."[1049] More surprising still, while German scientists had developed a highly weaponized nerve agent called *tabun*, Hitler never gave permission to use it, even with

---

[1044] Ibid., p. 83.
[1045] Ibid., p. 84.
[1046] Ibid., pp. 83-84.
[1047] Uekoetter, p. 132. Adam Tooze, however, debates this.
[1048] Tyson, p. 329.
[1049] Stern, J.P. *Hitler: Fuhrer of the People*, p. 221 quoted by Tyson, p. 329.

red horde bearing down on Germany's borders from the east.[1050] It will be recalled that Hitler himself barely survived a chemical attack toward the end of World War I.

Many military historians have also strongly pointed out the *Wehrmacht* was not nearly as mechanized as has been generally assumed. In reality, it was the American army that was outfitted with jeeps, tanks and trucks galore—not the Germans. When Operation Barbarossa began against the Soviet Union, the Germans had more horses than vehicles on the Russian front (750,000 to 600,000). German panzer divisions quickly outstripped their supply lines precisely because the *Wehrmacht* lacked vehicles. The farther east the Nazis pushed, the more overstretched they became. As the war progressed, there was one horse for every four German soldiers on the Eastern Front. "More than a million horses were taken by the Germans from the Soviet Union, while vast numbers were also taken from Poland and other captured territories."[1051] Many Nazi soldiers walked across the vast Russian steppe on their way to the front lines which became ever wider as German panzer divisions further outstripped their supply lines. By the end of the summer 1941, the German Army was exhausted and had suffered heavy casualties.

Regardless of all such particular nuances on reactionary modernism, and in spite of the environmental inconsistencies and conflicts that existed within the Nazi Party, as illustrated best by Albert Speer himself, it still cannot be denied that National Socialism was the greenest regime in the world in the 1930s. When they went to war in 1939, their environmental record was quite extensive in spite of the Battle for Production:

> In important respects, of course, Nazi green ideology was a nostalgic appeal to widespread yearning for allegedly simpler times before Bismark's push for German industrialization. Praise for rural life and celebration of the countryside helped bring Hitler to power, while concealing his aim of total industrialization, mobilization, and militarization. Nevertheless, National Socialism's positive attitude toward nature was not merely an instance of cynical political propaganda, because many Nazis did in fact make a connection between healthy races and healthy land.[1052]

[1050] Jacobsen, pp. 24-29, 54-56.

[1051] Sax, p. 93.

[1052] Zimmerman, *Ecofascism: An Enduring Temptation*, pp. 12-13.

It could also be easily argued that underneath the veneer of National Socialist modernism and technological prowess was a regressive naturalistic socialism based on crackpot biology that dug an ecological grave as deep as Auschwitz. The "combination of Romanticism and technocratic brutality was simply heightened to the point of caricature in Nazi Germany."[1053] This racist environmental ambivalence between nostalgia and modernism can be seen throughout the Nazi era. The Nazis struggled to preserve the Aryan race organically embedded in the German soil in great contradistinction to the international commercial industrial complex propagated by what they deemed to be Jewish materialism.

It was leftist thinker Kurt Tucholsky (1890-1935) who strikingly asserted the National Socialist creed "started green but became bloody-red."[1054] Indeed, the green Nazi environmental record of the 1930s preceded their bloody red war record of the 1940s. While many environmental historians use this alleged contradiction to discount the historical possibility that National Socialism was green far ahead of its time, the Nazis themselves believed they could bring about a Romantic modernism for the *volk* through a gigantic triumph of the will that would make Germany both strong and beautiful at the same time. Rather than criticize the Nazi environmental record as something disingenuous or contrived, it is far better to say that National Socialism was simply unable to bring about a synthesis between *volkisch* Romanticism and modern life. Sustainable development turned out to be a pipedream that compromised everything the Nazis did. The Nazis simply overestimated their "will to power." Their existentialism simply could not compete with the technological superiority and industrial might of the Allies.

The 'Steely' Romanticism of Nazism on the Autobahn

One green historian noted Hitler's "political decisions reveal little in the way of environmental thinking."[1055] This statement is very baffling since Hitler ordered and signed three milestone nature conservation laws during the 1930s. The example then given to demonstrate Hitler's shallow environmentalism was he decided "that while beech forests obviously should be

---

[1053] Sax, p. 165.

[1054] Bramwell, *Blood and Soil: Walther Darre and Hitler's Green Party*, pp. 63, 129.

[1055] Uekoetter, p. 32.

preserved as far as possible during the construction of the Autobahn, they would have to yield to the demands of such a great technological project in case of conflict."[1056] That Hitler even responded about the beech forests at all says far more than he is given credit for, especially in light of all the enthusiasm the Nazis had with regard to the Autobahn. The Autobahn was good for propaganda, good for the economy by putting some 100,000 Germans to work and good for transportation. The autobahns were also good for national security since they could be used to quickly mobilize troops and military vehicles and/or equipment to the borders of Germany from the interior.

However, surprisingly enough, the Nazis also promoted the autobahns as good for the environment as well. Many greens were "cautiously optimistic that the *Autobahnen* would help to disperse urban populations away from city centers and slow down, or even reverse Germany's inexorable transformation into an industrial state. Having not yet experienced the problems associated with automobile usage and suburban sprawl, preservationists argued that the new highways would help to relieve congestion along regional roads and city streets and make longer distance travel from suburban garden towns feasible and inexpensive. Furthermore, historic preservationists hoped that the *Autobahnen* would divert traffic away from centuries old-medieval town and city centers, obviating the need for widening streets and destroying cultural monuments."[1057]

While this may all sound counterintuitive today from a contemporary point of view, the Nazis even bragged they would build the autobahns to help bring the German driver closer to nature rather than the other way around.[1058] In reality, cars are certainly more intimate than trains. Hitler even believed roadways were more beautiful and less intrusive than railways. He once commented, "There are other parts of Germany, apart from the Rhineland, which give me intense pleasure to visit—the *Kyffhauser*, the forests of Thuringia, and Harz and Black Forest. It is most exhilarating to drive for miles through the woods and forests, far away from the throngs."[1059] Hitler loved the country roads of Germany. "Longish stops for picnic lunches amid the beauties of the landscape were a part of the enchantment of travel for Hitler."[1060]

[1056] BArch R 43 II/227 p. 41n quoted by Uekoetter, p. 32.
[1057] Lekan, p, 218.
[1058] Ibid., pp. 225-26.
[1059] *Hitler's Table Talk*, midday of March 23, 1944, p. 544.
[1060] Dietrich, p. 121.

The Nazis proclaimed the autobahns to be a reflection of the German love of nature. They proudly touted they were purposefully engineered to be embedded into the natural landscape of Germany's countryside.[1061] Nazi conservationists Walther Schoenichen and Hans Schwenkel both lauded the Autobahn as "a magnificent example of landscape design."[1062] The construction of the Autobahn began in 1933 and its chief civil engineer was Dr. Fritz Todt of the Todt Organization. Dr. Alwin Seifert was the primary environmental consultant on the project.

Even years after the war, Rudolf Hess bragged about Todt's accomplishments on the Autobahn in his conversations with Albert Speer in Spandau prison. Hess claimed Todt's engineering was based on a "philosophy of the beauty of the highway."[1063] He also recalled the Autobahn was to "be kept clear of all disturbing structures, that the bridges were to be built of the natural stone of each region, and that the directional signs should be kept as small as possible. Landscape architects had supervised the plans … to insure that the course of the road should conform to the landscape."[1064] Speer himself recollected that even the Autobahn maintenance buildings were made in half-timber style[1065] to blend in with the countryside.

Such views reflected in their own time, of course, are not enough for environmental historians. They want to judge Nazi environmentalism according to their own more modern views on the subject. Green historians argue that very little environmental money was spent on the Autobahn and that Seifert's advice was routinely ignored, especially at the beginning of the project. "Only by the late 1930's were the landscape architects able to make some headway. The tensions between the engineers and the architects, two distinct professional groups with different agendas, were not resolved during the Nazi years, only covered up by the fast pace of the overall project."[1066] Furthermore, many regional planners who were concerned about autobahn construction activities ripping up the environment in their own local areas and watersheds, felt as if Seifert later ignored them,[1067] even though he sympathized with them at the beginning. However, most of "the

---

[1061] *Dr. Todt: Mission and Achievement*, Nazi documentary film, 1943.
[1062] Schwenkel, Hans *Taschenbuch*, 37, quoted by Uekoetter p. 80.
[1063] Speer, *Spandau: The Secret Diaries*, p. 399.
[1064] Ibid.
[1065] Ibid.
[1066] Zeller, "Molding the Landscape of Nazi Environmentalism," in *How Green Were the Nazis?*, p. 153.
[1067] Lekan, pp. 234-242.

new highways traversed areas that had been thoroughly domesticated for centuries; there was no question of destroying wilderness."[1068]

More to the point, how could there have been an escalating tension between landscape architects and engineers if the engineers always got their own way? The rising acrimony that did exist between the greens and the old school engineers on the Autobahn is actually testimony of the growing power of the environmental movement. Even today, the greens always argue they are ignored even though they control and regulate many facets of the modern economy. They have cried wolf so many times over the years that it is very difficult to take their assertions seriously. Even with the multitude of environmental rules they have foisted upon the modern economy, construction still continues on in spite of the great hidden costs associated with it. Life goes on. Does this mean the greens have no say or influence in modern society?

Whatever the exact case may be, Dr. Alwin Seifert eventually convinced Dr. Todt to build the Autobahn as environmentally sensitive as possible. In the process, Seifert ruffled a lot of engineers' feathers. The mechanical engineers were incensed by Seifert's demands. He prescribed that trees were to be spared as much as possible. Engineers and construction workers must refrain from making straight lines. They must follow the curvature of the landscape. Seifert also insisted the topsoil be saved during excavation so that it could be later used again to replant along the right-of-ways. That such environmental demands would go unchallenged by public works engineers locked into their own way of doing things is simply not conceivable, especially when one considers how weak the German economy was in the early to mid-1930s. Money was in extreme short supply. Because of the tension, Todt had to take a more moderate position on the issue. Todt called Seifert a "fanatical ecologist."[1069]

Todt represented both sides and came up with compromises that forced them to work together. This was not an easy task. There were many struggles between vested parties and interests during the entire construction of the Autobahn. However, rather than complain his fellow Nazis were not green enough as environmental historians do, Todt simply chalked up such tensions on the construction jobsite as inevitable: "Every activity meets with opposition, everyone who acts has his rivals and unfortunately

---

[1068] Staudenmaier & Biehl, p. 106.

[1069] Bramwell, *Blood and Soil: Walther Darre & Hitler's Green Party*, p. 173.

his opponents also. But not because people want to be opponents, rather because the tasks and relationships force different people to take different points of view."[1070] Here, Todt sums up the green Autobahn controversy about as well as could be stated.

Dr. Todt was an early environmental engineer. Even though he was not as radical as Seifert, he was still very concerned about ecological integrity. "Todt demanded of the completed work of technology a harmony with nature and with the landscape, thereby fulfilling modern ecological principles of engineering as well as the organological principles of his own era along with their roots in *volkisch* ideology."[1071] Thus, while Todt was forced to balance Seifert's environmentalism with his own mechanical engineers, he still strongly believed "the fulfillment of mere transportation purposes is not the final aim of German highway construction. The German highway must be an expression of its surrounding landscape and an expression of German essence."[1072]

Much is made of the bureaucratic confusion that existed on the Autobahn between the engineers and landscape architects. According to one environmental historian, neither group really understood their role.[1073] The ambivalence between mechanical engineers and landscape architects is thus used to suggest the Autobahn was not nearly as green of a project as the Nazis touted. However, this is actually what happens all the time on any construction project these days thanks to an ever-increasing plethora of environmental regulations. The greener the construction project, the more bureaucratic, confusing and expensive it all becomes. The environmental paper chase has become mind-numbing. As such, it is hardly surprising the Nazi public works department did everything in their power to sideline distracting landscape architect plans as much as possible. Such bureaucratic overlap and chaos is not a strike against the reality of green polices in Nazi Germany, but actually one of its classic symptoms. Moreover, the fact such environmental bureaucratic chaos may have actually been born

---

[1070] Speer, *Inside the Third Reich*, pp. 194-95.

[1071] Ludwig, Karl Heinz. *Technik und Ingenieure im Dritten Reich*, Dusseldorf, 1974, p. 337; quoted by Staudenmaier & Biehl, p. 35.

[1072] Sierferle, Rolf Peter. *Fortschrittsfeinde? Opposition gegen Technik und Industrie von der Romantik bis zur Gegenwart*, Munich, 1984, p. 220; quoted by Staudenmaier & Biehl, p. 35.

[1073] Zeller, "Molding the Landscape of Nazi Environmentalism," in *How Green Were the Nazis?*, pp. 152-53.

in Nazi Germany on the Autobahn is far more significant than most are willing to admit.

With regard to the Autobahn, Alwin Seifert hollered loud and long enough to ensure that it was built with some of the latest bio-engineering designs. Seifert thus had his work cut out for him. He took on the public works bureaucratic mindset which often resented his environmental advice. He was thus not always successful, nor always listened to, but the fact the Nazis even allowed Dr. Seifert to be in a position to often criticize how things were built shows how open the Third Reich was to green suggestions. In 1934, Dr. Todt even "arranged for Seifert to address his construction supervisors. Shortly thereafter, he arranged for Seifert the honor of a personal audience with Hitler. Seifert then joined the party in 1937, and a year later Hitler personally granted him the honorary title of professor."[1074]

Seifert wholeheartedly believed in holistic environmental planning and design for any building project. However, much to the dismay of his Nazi colleagues, Seifert especially criticized the SS "back to the land" public works projects he believed were drying up the German water table. In fact, Seifert strongly warned Germany of the same desertification problems that occurred in America with the Dust Bowl if civil engineers do not change their ways on how to build environmentally sensitive structures. Seifert went so far to say that "short-sighted government programs threatened to create the same problems in authoritarian Germany as in America, where capitalist indifference and 'big Jewish finance' had created an environmental catastrophe that displaced thousands of rural farmers."[1075]

Just like many modern environmentalists today,[1076] the ecological catastrophe that was the Dust Bowl was one of Seifert's rallying cries to environmental humility. "He lashed out against the hydrological engineers 'mechanistic' approach and called for a holistic view that gave sufficient attention to the interconnectedness of nature."[1077] Seifert claimed that "through dredging, straightening, narrowing, and denuding riverbeds, hydraulic engineers had created a 'machine landscape' with unforeseen ecological consequences."[1078] In an effort to get rid of water as fast as possible, hydraulic engineers rooted in the Enlightenment sciences and the Industrial

---

[1074] Dominick, p. 109.
[1075] Lekan, p. 231.
[1076] See Worster, Donald. *Dust Bowl: The Southern Plains in the 1930's.*
[1077] Uekoetter p. 77.
[1078] Lekan, p. 231.

Revolution were lowering the groundwater table that was leading to what he called the 'steppification' of all of Central Europe. He sharply censured engineers for exacerbating flooding problems downstream that invariably spawned more erosion and deeper riverbeds:

> His particular line of attack was against the current theory and practice of hydraulic engineering. For decades, Seifert claimed that the goal of water experts had been to lead rainwater out of the countryside as fast as possible—and the result had been a diminishment of local water supplies. River straightening and dam construction led to more and faster higher water, leading in turn to destruction downstream. But the devastating effects of hydraulic engineering could also be seen upstream, where coppices growing on the banks had been cut down, upsetting the natural balance of water circulation in the valleys. The effect of all these measures was the draining of Germany, with destructive ecological and economic results ... the solution Seifert offered was a technology close to nature: instead of building large dams, Germany needed to build mill and fish ponds that would retain water and re-naturalize its streams.[1079]

Such talk, of course, enraged the business as usual public works engineers, but Seifert did not back down. He continued his pointed attacks against them, even though he was not necessarily always successful in being heard.

While such new ways of environmental thinking may have been opposed by the civil engineers at the time, Seifert's scathing criticisms eventually made an impact on men like Himmler and Darre. Even the *Fuhrer* himself took notice. Moreover, Seifert's holistic views that development ruptures the hydrological water cycle in ecosystems have today become the staple of environmental policy with regard to all construction activities. The modern public works department is increasingly adopting greener views of development all the time. Seifert was also one of the leading pioneers in what is today called stormwater management. All of the stormwater ponds seen today on virtually every new construction project and housing development are a tribute to Alwin Seifert's influences. That this tremendous

---

[1079] Zeller, "Molding the Landscape of Nazi Environmentalism," in *How Green Were the Nazis?*, p. 155.

long fought environmental battle largely began in Nazi Germany is not an insignificant fact.

How Green Were the Nazis?

Environmental historians strongly point out Nazi conservationism was not very effective in that it was ultimately trumped by the economy, agricultural autarky, the war effort and by racism which left many greens disappointed in the end. One environmental historian in particular pointed out the Reich Nature Protection Act (RNG) of 1935 was not very effective since the "Reich Office for Nature Conservation was understaffed and much of the work fell to unpaid local commissioners, usually retired officials or teachers, who tried to resist incursions into their protected areas by commercial interests and planning bureaucracies without powers of enforcement and often without typewriters or clerical assistance."[1080] Nazi environmentalist Wilhelm Lienenkamper complained, "Adolf Hitler's highways and the construction of monumental buildings are representative works of National Socialism, for whose construction money is readily available. The preservation of the actual remaining traces of primordial Germany through the Reich Nature Protection Law is an equally important task that cannot be carried out with enough money."[1081]

However, in truth, how many environmental laws are even very effective today? The EPA's Endangered Species Act has an extremely poor record. It has run roughshod over constitutional property rights, and has cost businesses, property owners and American taxpayers enormous sums of money over the years. Of the 1,355 plants and wildlife species that have been placed on the Endangered Species list since 1973, only 46 have been delisted, and of the 46, 16 of those were improperly placed on the list in the first place.[1082] Thus one could easily ask how effective is the Endangered Species Act? Not very. In fact, what it seems to do best is restrict private property and liberty. Its holistic view on nature has no real place for individual human needs and concerns.[1083] How green is the Endangered Species Act? It looks good on paper, but has worked very poorly in practice. Furthermore, the Endangered Species Act has had much more cash available on hand to pay

---

[1080] Blackbourn, p. 280.
[1081] Lekan, pp. 207-08.
[1082] Stirling, p. 163.
[1083] Ibid., pp. 93-115.

for its policies since it has had a vast capitalistic network to leech off of. The Nazis never had such a luxury as they used National Socialism to come out of a depression far worse than the Great Depression in America.

How green are modern smart growth plans? For example, against the wishes of the electorate, the Washington State Legislature passed a very green growth management act in the early '90s called the GMA. It is in many ways very similar to the Nazi RNG. Almost 20 years later, the Puget Sound area is now increasingly being called Pugetopolis. The GMA has been a miserable failure. It has not stopped growth, nor really protected the environment. In fact, environmentalists in Washington state today are now all alarmed that Puget Sound is being threatened by widespread stormwater pollution runoff from private properties into state waterways, with asphalt roadways and parking areas being the conduit of that pollution. Thus, in the end, all the environmental planning has gone for naught, and did exactly the opposite of what its original planners had envisaged.[1084] As such, the discussion about how effective the Nazis were with regard to their environmental policies to try and demonstrate they were not all that green remains unconvincing.

In fact, all the very same arguments environmental historians use to debunk the idea the Nazis were green can also be leveled against modern greens as well. How green is renewable windmill energy? Not only do ugly windmills fill the wide-open horizon for miles and miles (at least cities have their places), but they also annually kill hundreds of thousands of birds[1085] and bats. They even make the coal/natural gas plants far less efficient by making them slow down and speed up precisely because the blowing of the wind is so erratic. These huge wind mills are also full of oil to keep them lubricated, and require massive foundations of concrete to be built upon. Worst of all, precious metals needed for windmill technology are mined in places like Mongolia and China that have led to devastating ecological problems in both of those countries where the mining takes place.

[1084] Kresovich, Greg, "Dumb Growth: The Smart Development Movement has made Sprawl Worse, not Better." Kresovich pointedly remarks, "Nearly 20 years after its inception, Washington's Growth Management Act (GMA) is a dismal failure. Instead of reducing sprawl by limiting development to designated urban areas, as the Legislature intended, we have subdivisions from Arlington to Tumwater housing people who work in King County," *Washington CEO*, November 2008.

[1085] "Green Power Collides with Endangered Species Act," *Oregon Natural Resources Report*, Aug. 9, 2009.

How green is the new ethanol push as a substitute for traditional oil and gas? Much like the Nazi "back to the land" drive for agricultural autarky, more land has been converted to crops in order to provide corn for both cars and stomachs. Furthermore, what about all the wasted energy used in the production of renewable energy? The search for renewable energy as some kind of holy grail for the future often does more damage to the environment than simply drilling for gas and oil. Renewable energy is very land intensive. Drilling for gas and oil these days does minimal environmental damage compared to yesteryear. Moreover, the development of gas and oil saved the forestlands. People use oil and natural gas to heat their homes today rather than wood. The litany on such green dilemmas is unending. Just how green is green power anyway?

How green are the modern stormwater rules? Unbeknownst to many, stormwater was the environmental pet project of the 1990s and the first half of the first decade of the new millennium right before the global warming/climate change diatribe took center stage. While $CO2$ is currently being touted as a form of air pollution in the global warming debate, not many people understand that back on the ground, dirt and mud churned up from construction activities have also been deemed pollutants as well. Hence straw is now being used far more on construction sites these days than in horse barns. Unworked bare soils must be protected from soil erosion by covering them with straw, mulch and/or seed. Hence both straw and seed prices have skyrocketed. Thus, much of what has been mandated on construction sites to help prevent soil erosion has only intensified further agricultural activity since the EPA wants contractors to act more like farmers when they rip up the ground for the building of houses.

Worse, most of the huge stockpiles of dirt that are seen on the average construction site today, which are especially prone to erosion when it rains, are there precisely because massive stormwater ponds are required by environmental laws on many sites. It is also true that all of the soil erosion devices implemented on the jobsite during the construction phase of the project wind up in the landfill when all is said and done, including tons of plastic sheeting. Exactly what all is being accomplished from an overall sound environmental point of view is difficult to understand. It looks more like an environmental exchange program of one problem for another with lots of cash hemorrhaging out of contractors' and homeowners' back pockets to pay for such ecological demands.

At this juncture, President Vaclav Klaus of the Czech Republic strongly points out, "It should be clear by now to everyone that environmental activism is becoming a general ideology about humans, about their freedom, about the relationship between the individuals and the state, and about manipulation of people under the guise of a 'noble' idea. It is not an honest pursuit of 'sustainable development,' a matter of elementary environmental protection, or a search for rational mechanisms designed to achieve a healthy environment."[1086] Klaus then adds further, "I consider environmentalism to be the most significant illiberal populist ideology of the present era."[1087]

Perhaps worst of all, many environmentalists actually believe they are performing their ecological duties democratically, all the while using taxes, laws, prohibitive regulations, public policy meetings and lawyers to bully people and drag them into their green totalitarian agenda. Dr. Anna Bramwell starkly points out that modern greens are "levelers rather than true conservationists."[1088] She then complains their environmental "prescriptions are often as unrelated to the environmental issues as they are draconian."[1089] In conclusion, she asserts that modern environmentalists "bear more resemblance to those pre and proto-Nazi groups that sprang up during the 1920's in an outbreak of quasi religious prophecy and radicalism."[1090]

Such questions about how green were the Nazis could go on and on ad infinitum. How red was Vladimir Lenin? Within a very short time he had to pass the New Economic Policy, which relaxed communistic controls over the economy. He was forced to do so to help prevent his Soviet comrades from starving to death. How totalitarian was National Socialism? Believe it or not, some historians even debate this because the Nazis often had a hard time implementing their totalitarian system over German society. It is simply not true that Germans always followed Nazi orders. Many Germans bucked the National Socialist authorities in a variety of different ways, often without consequences.[1091] Between 1936 and 1937 alone, there were some 200 or so successful worker strikes against the Nazi regime.[1092] As such,

---

[1086] Klaus, p. 99.
[1087] Ibid., p. 18.
[1088] Bramwell, *Blood and Soil: Walther Darre and Hitler's Green Party*, p. 200.
[1089] Ibid.
[1090] Ibid.
[1091] Goldhagen, pp. 118-21.
[1092] Ibid., p. 118.

does this really mean that National Socialism cannot be characterized as a totalitarian regime?

National Socialists also had to rescind a law to ban crucifixes in public schools.[1093] They also failed to remove the popular Lutheran leader Hans Meiser of Nuremberg.[1094] Does this mean that Nazis were not anti-Christian? In 1935, Hitler also ordered that violent individual actions against Jews must be stopped.[1095] This was quickly followed up by Interior Minister Dr. Wilhelm Frick's harsh threats against those who ignored Hitler's decree.[1096] Does this mean that Hitler was concerned about the Jews? Hitler also had to finally call off his pet construction projects because of the war effort, "including those at the *Obersalzberg*."[1097] Does this mean he did not care about them? In fact, Speer and Hitler were incredibly ineffective in bringing to fruition many of their building plans for Nazi Germany. Does this mean that they were not very architecturally minded? Certainly not. Speer categorically stated that architecture was certainly Hitler's great love.

How effective was the German war machine in the East? Like the Nazi environmental laws, they started out with spectacular gains at the beginning, only to be gravely disappointed in the end. Does this mean the Nazis did not care about the war? Speer acutely noted, "It remains one of the oddities of this war that Hitler demanded far less from his people than Churchill and Roosevelt did from their respective nations. The discrepancy between the total mobilization of labor in authoritarian Germany is proof of the regime's anxiety not to risk any shift in the popular mood."[1098]

Before the war with Russia ever began, Hitler himself had acknowledged the Siberians must be stronger because of the harsh, primitive climate in which they live. Nonetheless, "when the campaign in the East began, he thrust down his own thesis, for it ran counter to his plans."[1099] Does this mean Hitler really did not believe in his social Darwinian survival of the fittest motif? Even Dr. Todt was sorely depressed by the social Darwinian facts on the ground in Russia: "It is a struggle in which primitive people will prove superior. They can endure everything, including the harsh-

---

[1093] Pois, p. 165.
[1094] Ibid.
[1095] Kershaw, p. 563.
[1096] Ibid.
[1097] Speer, *Inside the Third Reich*, p. 215.
[1098] Ibid., p. 214.
[1099] Ibid., p. 185.

ness of the climate. We are too sensitive and are bound to be defeated."[1100] Moreover, when one reads through the plethora of military books about the *Wehrmacht*, one cannot help but notice the infighting between Hitler and his generals perhaps prevented them from potentially winning the war. Goering's colossal failures during the war far surpassed his failures as an environmentalist. Both the Reich Hunting Law and the RNG outlived the Nazi regime to survive in some form in postwar Germany.

The fact of the matter is that most of human history is a tale of people acting inconsistently with what they say they believe, including a sizeable portion of church history as well. "Every man, therefore, is caught. As he tries intellectually to extend his position in a logical way and then lives within it, he is caught by the two things which, as it were, slap him across the face—the external world with its structure, and those things which well up from inside himself. Non-Christian presuppositions simply do not fit into what God has made, including what man is. This being so, every man is in a place of tension. Man cannot make his own universe and live in it."[1101] Jesus summarizes this conundrum the best when He commanded, "Make no oath at all ... for you cannot make one hair white or black" (Matt. 5:34, 36).

In short, it is all too easy to demonstrate one is not living up to his own standards. Thus with regard to Nazi ecology, it is much easier to argue the Nazis failed to fulfill their environmental commitments because they simply were not able to do so, rather than suggest the Nazis did not care about them. The former is far more likely than the latter. The latter argument has to set aside too much of the historical record to be considered a viable theory.

With regard to lax environmental enforcement and the economy, these are not in any way unique to Nazi Germany. Speer pointed out that if the economy had been left in the hands of the original Nazi Party members of the 1920s, Germany would have never come out of their depression precisely because they were so *volkischly* backward in their economic thinking. The German industrial intelligentsia showed up to help the *Fuhrer* in the 1930s. What is more, Hitler and the Nazis needed them for the simple reason that was where the cash was. Goering and Bormann were master manipulators of the business community. Thus, it should surprise no one that Nazi environmental rules and regulations were contravened by other interests. Even

---

[1100] Ibid.
[1101] Schaeffer, Francis. *The God Who is There.* Chicago: InterVarsity Press, 1968, p. 132.

304

in very green states like California and Washington, environmental rules are regularly contravened by a whole variety of business and government groups, not to mention competing political and economic interests, as well. Unfunded mandates are a way of life for environmentalism even in modern America, and without taxes and rich corporations and foundations feeding the green movement copious amounts of red meat, their situation would be far more dire.

Many environmental rules are essentially unenforceable almost by definition. They are often used to try and correct the minutest details of private life. The more recent preoccupation with stormwater nonpoint source pollution is so complex that it is impossible to keep track of. Everything one does on his private piece of property is potentially under suspicion because stormwater at some point washes down into watersheds every time it rains. Thus, it is no coincidence the EPA allows other private citizens to file third-party lawsuits against those who are not even their neighbors. Even the EPA, state and local jurisdictions combined cannot possibly keep track of everything that happens on private property.

The charge the Nazis were not very green because they were racist simply does not hold any water. Racism and environmentalism are not mutually exclusive categories; something which German Romantics resoundingly proved for more than 100 years before the Nazis even came to power. The Nazi environmental laws thus "lead us to reflect that an interest in nature, while it may not imply a hatred of men ipso facto, does not exclude one either."[1102] Logically, of course, the existence of environmentalism does not mean Nazism is inevitable. However, Murphy's Law does have a logic all its own. In the real world of life, high logical standards are the exception, not the rule, as all too many existentialists are quick to remind everyone. Worse, anti-humanism has become the hallmark of modern environmentalism, and racism is just one form of anti-humanism.

While in Spandau prison, Albert Speer concluded the Nazi regime's interest in environmental concerns and beauty was "very marked."[1103] He went on to say, "The ruthlessness and inhumanity of the regime went hand in hand with a remarkable feeling for beauty, for the virginal and unspoiled, although that feeling quite often degenerated into the sentimentality of a

---

[1102] Ferry, p. 93.
[1103] Speer, *Spandau: The Secret Diaries*, p. 399.

postcard idyll."[1104] Speer even discounted the possibility the Nazis were disingenuous about their environmentalism: "Today I sometimes read statements to the effect that all this was merely camouflage, a calculated maneuver to distract the attention of the suppressed masses. But that was not so."[1105] Seifert himself, who was very "involved in *volkisch* organizations well before 1933 and published extensively in Nazi periodicals,"[1106] routinely praised the environmental accomplishments of the Third Reich.

Speer singled out Hitler's anti-modern diabolical fear as a factor which colored and compromised the Nazi love for beauty: "Of course the regime's craving for beauty also had to do with Hitler's personal taste, with his hatred for the modern world, his fear of the future. But there was an unselfish social impulse at work, an effort to reconcile the unavoidable ugliness of the technological world with familiar aesthetic forms, with beauty."[1107] While Speer sharply contrasts the inhumanity of the Nazis with their strong interest in natural beauty, he does not consider the possibility that they could potentially explain each other. The Nazis took nature far too seriously by basing their ethics upon it. In so doing, they opened up a wild *volkisch* Romanticism and Existentialism that ended up treating people like social Darwinian beasts rather than human beings made in the image of God.

[1104] Ibid.
[1105] Ibid.
[1106] Staudenmaier & Biehl, p. 107.
[1107] Speer, *Spandau: The Secret Diaries*, p. 399.

"It's lucky we don't understand the language of hares. They might talk about you (hunters) something like this: 'He couldn't run at all, the fat hog!' What can an old hare, with a whole lifetime's experience, think about it all? The greatest joy must prevail amongst the hares when they see that a beater has been shot (Social Darwinism at work in Nature— perhaps the hunter is also an old beater worthy of the same fate?) ... For two or three years they've (Goering & the SS) been preserving foxes. What damage they have caused! On the one hand, they're preserved for the sake of the hunter (an inconsistency—why should hunters like to preserve animals?), which means a loss of I don't know how many hundred million eggs; and, on the other hand, they (Goering & the SS) make a Four Year Plan! What madness!"

Adolf Hitler, midday Oct. 30, 1941

CHAPTER SIX:

THE BROWN ROAD TO AUSCHWITZ WAS LINED WITH GREEN TREES

Men like Rudolf Hess, Dr. Fritz Todt and Dr. Alwin Seifert played a valuable role in the greening of the Nazi Party throughout the 1930s. However, World War II placed a damper on many of the original Nazi environmental plans envisaged in the early to mid-1930s. In May of 1941, one month before the fateful launch of Operation Barbarossa, Deputy *Fuhrer* Rudolf Hess mysteriously flew to Great Britain in a haphazard attempt to negotiate peace with England so that Germany could have a free hand to carry out a full-scale invasion of Russia.[1108] Hess' mission failed. His airplane crashed in Scotland where he was arrested. Hess did not return to Germany until after the war when he was put on trial at Nuremberg for war crimes. The upshot of his reckless gamble was that green Nazis like Seifert were subsequently sidelined by other party leaders like Martin Bormann because Hess was no longer there to defend or protect them. Dr. Todt then died in a plane crash on the Russian front in early 1942.

Although Hess was Hitler's Deputy *Fuhrer*, he had been increasingly pushed aside by his ruthless undersecretary Martin Bormann. The replacement of Hess with Bormann coupled with the wartime atmosphere of the early 1940s considerably darkened the green emphasis of the Nazi Party.

[1108] Day, Matthew, "Rudolf Hess Flight to Britain Approved by Hitler," *The UK Telegraph*, May 31, 2011. Hess' flight to Britain in May of 1941 was an unresolved mystery for many years. Recently, however, documents have been uncovered from the Moscow archives which show Hitler was fully aware of his flight and even ordered Hess to "use all means at his disposal to achieve, if not a German military alliance with England against Russia, at least the neutralization of England." See also *Hess, Hitler, and Churchill: The Real Turning Point of the Second World War—A Secret History*, by Peter Padfield (London: Icon Books Limited, 2013). Padfield makes the same case, but on different grounds where an anonymous witness saw the peace plans that Hitler and Hess wanted to offer England through its powerful appeasers.

With Bormann exerting a powerful sway in the upper hierarchy of the party, the influences of men like Seifert and Todt waned, especially as the war kicked into high gear. While Bormann seized power for himself in light of the Deputy *Fuhrer's* absence, Hess sulked under POW house arrest where the bare, rocky and grassy English landscapes made him yearn for the great stretches of the German forests.[1109]

According to Speer and other Nazi leaders, Bormann's unexpected rise to power also had a bad influence on Hitler. Dr. Hans Frank, Hitler's personal attorney, stated that Hess' departure led to a "kind of iron curtain" which "descended between Hitler and the German people."[1110] Hess, who was understood to be the conscience of the Nazi Party,[1111] was Hitler's point man who provided intimate contact between the *Fuhrer* and his people. Without Hess, Hitler increasingly became aloof from the average German—a barrier which Bormann could never remedy. However, many leading Nazis like Goebbels, Goering, Rosenberg, Ley, Himmler, Ribbentrop or even Hess himself, simply did not recognize "a threat in the shape of trusty Bormann. He had succeeded in representing himself as insignificant while imperceptibly building up his bastions."[1112]

Bormann was a master manipulator and pulled many strings, especially financial ones, to get where he wanted to be. "Even among so many ruthless men, he stood out by his brutality and coarseness."[1113] He used his personal proximity to Hitler to amass a considerable amount of power for himself, especially after Hess' departure:

> Rudolf Hess's flight to Britain opened the way for the "Brown Eminence" to step into his shoes on 12 May 1941 as head of the *Parteikanzlei* and to gather the reins of the Party into his own hands and steadily undermine all his rivals for power. Until the end of the war, the short, squat Bormann, working in the anonymity of his seemingly unimportant office, proved himself a master of intrigue, manipulation, and political in-fighting. Always the "narrow Party man" and a fierce guardian of Nazi orthodoxy (he was an arch-fanatic when it came to racial policy, anti-Semitism and the

---

[1109]   Manvell and Fraenkel, p. 144.
[1110]   Ibid., p. 122.
[1111]   Ibid., pp. 46-80.
[1112]   Speer, *Inside the Third Reich*, p. 87.
[1113]   Ibid.

Kirchenkampf—war between the churches), Bormann strengthened the position of the Party against the *Wehrmacht* and the SS, and increased his grip on domestic policy. Increasingly he controlled all questions concerning the security of the regime, acts of legislation, appointments and promotions, especially if they concerned Party personnel. He also established espionage in the army, getting younger officers promoted to spy on the political attitudes of their colleagues. He reopened the fight against the Christian churches, declaring in a confidential memo to Gauleiters in 1942 that their power "must absolutely and finally be broken." Nazism, based as it was on a "scientific" world-view, was completely incompatible with Christianity whose influence was regarded by Bormann as a serious obstacle to totalitarian rule. The sharpest anti-cleric in the Nazi leadership (he collected all the files of cases against the clergy that he could lay his hands on), Bormann was the driving force of the *Kirchenkampf*, which Hitler for tactical reasons had wished to postpone until after the war.[1114]

Bormann was extremely antagonistic to all forms of spiritual mysticism, Christian or otherwise, including nature mysticism.

Bormann especially despised Hess's infatuation with homeopathic nature remedies. As such, after his sudden departure, the Nazi push for natural medicines also slowed down considerably.[1115] Some Nazi Party leaders deemed such practices as medical quackery.[1116] That Hess also had some connections to the mystic homeopath and anthroposophist[1117] Rudolf

---

[1114] See *Martin Bormann* at http://www.jewishvirtuallibrary.org/jsource/Holocaust/bormann.html.

[1115] Proctor, Robert. *The Nazi War on Cancer*, p. 55.

[1116] Ibid., p. 56.

[1117] Peter Staudenmaier points out in *Anthroposophy and Ecofascism*: "The very name Anthroposophy suggests to many outsiders a humanist orientation. But Anthroposophy is, in fact, a deeply anti-humanist worldview." Although many modern Anthroposophists today deny any connections to the Nazi Party, Hess was a practicing Anthroposophist and tried to co-opt the movement and its institutions under the Nazi umbrella, but Himmler finally banned it in 1935, even though he himself grew fond of organic farming practices. Himmler viewed Anthroposophism as a rival to his own pagan nature mysticism. According to Bramwell, Darre protected the Anthroposophists from the Nazis, but Staudenmaier strongly asserts, "Even after the ban there was no general persecution of Anthroposophists. Their publishing activities continued uninterrupted. Anthroposophist professors, teachers, and civil servants kept their jobs; Waldorf schools and biodynamic farms continued to operate. Many of these establishments were shut down in the course of the later 1930's, despite the pro-Anthroposophist intervention

Steiner only further strained the relationship between Alwin Seifert and other Nazi Party leaders. Seifert was a follower of Steiner—whom many leading Nazis considered an ideological enemy.

Rudolf Steiner (1861-1925) founded the German Anthroposophical Society in the early 1900s. His philosophy was an eclectic amalgam of the occult, nature mysticism, racism, anti-Semitism and Haeckelian ecology. Steiner and Haeckel originally had a cordial relationship, but Haeckel eventually parted company with him over his excessive mysticism. Steiner also founded biodynamic farming, which is a very specialized form of organic gardening. More than likely, Hess' strong interest in organic farming was fueled by Seifert, who himself was very intrigued by some of Steiner's ideas. However, during World War I, Hitler's spiritual mentor, Dietrich Eckart, had developed a personal feud with Steiner. Eckart hated Steiner's pacifism, his brand of social liberalism, his Waldorf schools and even some of his semi-occultic leanings.[1118] Neither was Steiner anti-Semitic enough for Eckart's standards.[1119] Nor could Eckart tolerate Steiner's characterization of Guido von List as a false prophet.[1120] Guido von List was an Ariosophist who emphasized Aryan Pan-German nature mysticism[1121] in contrast to Steiner's Anthroposophy. While both men were strong lovers of nature and all things natural, Guido von List's Ariosophy was decidedly pro-Aryan. While it is true Steiner was certainly a German racist, he was also semi-Protestant. As such, Steiner considered Ariosophy to be a pagan cult "which exalted one's lower self at the expense of the spirit."[1122]

Eckart's reprisals against Steiner were loaded with ridicule and slander. As such, thanks largely to this antagonistic debate between Eckart and Steiner, National Socialism and Anthroposophy were often on unfriendly

---

of influential Nazis like SS war criminal Otto Ohlendohrf. But the final blow didn't come about until 1941, when Hess, Anthroposophy's protector, flew to Britain. After that point the last Waldorf school was closed for good, and biodynamic farming lost its official support, and several leading Anthroposophists were imprisoned for a time."

[1118] Tyson, p. 230.

[1119] Ibid., p. 231.

[1120] Ibid., p. 233.

[1121] See especially *The Occultic Roots of Nazism: Secret Aryan Cults and Their Influence on Nazi Ideology, 1890-1935*. New York: New York University Press, 1985, 1992, by Nicholas Goodrick-Clarke. Goodricke-Clark says that Guido von List's Pan German Aryan nature mysticism influenced Heinrich Himmler more than any other Nazi leader. Hitler was influenced somewhat by Ariosophy when he was a young man in Vienna, but according to Clarke, he was far more interested in political street activism than developing a Teutonic spirituality.

[1122] Tyson, p. 233.

terms. As early as 1922, Nazi SA Brownshirts crashed an Anthroposophical meeting with clubs and brass knuckles in which Steiner "barely escaped with his life."[1123] As soon as Hitler came to power in 1933, he banned the Anthroposophical Society.[1124] Anthroposophists were some of the first to be interned into Nazi concentration camps. While much has been made of the Nazi-Steiner feud by environmental historians, the ideologies of Anthroposophy and Ariosophy were actually very similar in many ways. They were rivals of each other.

Since Seifert was a follower of Steiner, he was put under surveillance. "He was aware that he was being watched and once even mockingly volunteered, in a letter to Oswald Pohl, the main SS business manager, to work in the organic herb farm in Dachau in the event he was arrested."[1125] Dr. Todt's sudden death in 1942 in a surprising airplane crash compounded Seifert's isolation further. Dr. Todt, "had planned to give Seifert a country retreat as a reward for his work—a feudal gesture sponsored by the construction industry, Todt's profiteers. But after Todt died, Seifert rallied his academic friends at the Technical University in Munich in order to obtain a chair there in lieu of the Alpine abode."[1126] Seifert initially had Hitler's backing on this particular move, but because of his apparent connection to student dissent in 1943, he was put on probation by the Reich Chancellery and declared unfit for the job.[1127] Yet his authority over natural resource conservation matters in Nazi Germany was never in doubt. In 1944, Seifert became the Reich Landscape Advocate for water and energy.[1128] He was also "promoted to the rank of General within the *Organisation Todt*."[1129] He received a very high salary up until the last months of the war.[1130]

After the war, during the de-Nazification process, Seifert proudly proclaimed himself to be "the trustee, the faithful savior of the German landscape."[1131] Thanks to Bormann's conduct, Seifert was able to distance himself

---

[1123] Ibid.

[1124] Ibid., p. 234.

[1125] Zeller, "Molding the Landscape of Nazi Environmentalism" in *How Green Were the Nazis?*, p. 159.

[1126] Ibid.

[1127] Ibid.

[1128] Lekan, p. 243.

[1129] Staudenmaier & Biehl, pp. 106-07.

[1130] BArch Berlin Document Center Speer Listen Best. 8461 E 0104 pp. 32-68; quoted by Uekoetter, p. 76.

[1131] Seifert to the chair, Spruchkammer VII Munchen, 8 April 1947, 20 AGM, VII 3702; quoted by Zeller in "Molding the Landscape of Nazi Environmentalism" in *How Green*

from the Nazi Party in later years, which should have been far more difficult than it turned out to be. The proud designation he claimed for himself was *getreuer Eckhart*, "which alludes to the sage figure in the *Tannhauser* myth who warned erring humans not to enter the tempting Mountain of Venus. Evidently, Seifert deemed himself to be the guardian of the German landscape, warning humans not to fall for the trappings of modernization—a position as lofty as his former role in Nazi Germany."[1132]

Obviously, with such a statement, and very typical of many Nazi greens, his passion for nature far exceeded his passion for people. "There can be little doubt that Seifert was one of the most prominent environmentalists in Nazi Germany. He owed his position to his patronage and his personality as well as to his skills in maneuvering his way through the fragmented body politic. In his quest to restore what he saw as truly German landscape, he was willing to engage in coalitions that would further his professional, personal, and political goals, even if they involved the most murderous agencies of Nazi Germany."[1133] Indeed, he "insisted on extirpating all foreign plants, comparing this to the battle against human invaders."[1134] The anti-invasive species diatribe that is currently one of the pillars of modern environmentalism can also be attributed to the fascist legacy of green Nazis like Alwin Seifert.

Eco-Imperialism—New Environmental Horizons in the East

The environmental streak of the Nazi Party, however, did not die with the loss of Hess and Todt and the sidelining of Seifert. Not only was Goering still around, but environmentalism headed east under Heinrich Himmler's authority and the banner of the SS. Speer recalled after an evening dinner in 1943 how Himmler "talked glowingly about the future border villages for German peasants in the East, *Wehrbauerndorfer*. There would be village ponds, village greens, window boxes of geraniums at the farmhouses; there must certainly be a village linden tree, and oaks lining the streets. The new settler was to feel at home immediately in a kind of ideal German landscape.

Were the Nazis?, p. 160.

[1132] Zeller, "Molding the Landscape of Nazi Environmentalism" in *How Green Were the Nazis?*, p. 170, footnote 75.

[1133] Ibid.

[1134] Sax, p. 109.

Hitler saw eye to eye with him on all this."[1135] Since Seifert was SS, he too would play an ideological role in the greening Nazification plans that were to be unleashed on the unsuspecting populaces of Poland, Byelorussia and the Ukraine.

Beginning in 1939, World War II opened up brand new horizons for environmental landscape planning in the East. Hitler told Goering, "Our real future lies on the Baltic and in the open spaces of Russia. Better to sacrifice another two million men in war, if this will give us the room to breathe."[1136] Hitler, highly concerned about overpopulation and over-industrialization at home, saw *lebensraum* as environmental breathing space. In fact, once the war began in earnest, the newly acquired territories were so wide open that environmental planning in the East was superseding environmental plans back at home. "The conquered spaces in the East were supposed to provide a reprieve for the relentless pressure on land in Germany. Instead, the East had primacy, as Himmler's planners devoted themselves to designing utopian landscapes whose principles would only later be applied to the Old Reich."[1137]

Because of the war effort, green plans would have to be temporally shelved at home until after victory. Ironically enough, outside of Germany proper, SS planners were far more free to make the best laid plans for the East. These plans included many environmental landscape provisions together with an air pollution policy. They also included newly developed technocratic spatial planning theories derived from the Reich Office of Spatial Planning that showcased the critical importance of sustainable development.

All such plans were designed to Germanize Poland, Byelorussia and Ukraine so that "the Germanic-German man feels at home, settles down, falls in love with his new *heimat* and becomes ready to defend it."[1138] This meant the East would have to be greened up for the incoming Germans. Thus, the green emphasis of the Nazi Party found new vigor under Himmler's leadership in the occupied territories of Poland, Byelorussia and Ukraine. Indeed, Himmler told his SS officials, "The destruction of 30 million Slavs was a pre-requisite for German planning in the East."[1139] Henceforth, Slavs

---

[1135] Speer, *Spandau: The Secret Diaries*, pp. 399-400.
[1136] Irving, p. 187.
[1137] Blackbourn, p. 290.
[1138] BArch B 245/88, p. 4; quoted by Uekoetter, p. 158.
[1139] Koehl, RKFDV, 146n.; quoted by Uekoetter, p. 158.

would be purposefully depopulated so the master race could take root in the eastern territories.

According to Speer, Himmler had always wanted to have the SS become independent in the occupied territories, a veritable state within a state. Hitler did not give his approval for this until 1944, but it was something that Himmler coveted for years. Himmler desired a totally free hand in the East. As such, the SS would take complete charge of the occupied territories, especially over industry. Himmler and Hitler had plans to use industry to fund a gigantic construction project that would take over a century to build. "Programs on this scale, as Himmler established, could not be carried out by the German construction industry. They were too expensive and they greatly exceeded its capacities."[1140] As such, Himmler fantasized construction costs could be kept to a minimum by using concentration camp prisoners as slave labor to do the work.

What exactly was this huge construction plan? Shockingly, Hitler and Himmler wanted to convert the Russian steppe into a beautiful Germanic garden park through environmental planning and sustainable development. Hitler clearly understood this plan would far outlive his existence, stating: "Within 20 years the area will comprise 20 million people. In 300 years, it will be a flourishing park landscape of extraordinary beauty."[1141] Hitler even wanted to reforest large portions of Ukraine.[1142] While Hitler may have ignored Feder's green utopian village plans in large cities back home in Berlin, such ideas were revived for the eastern territories. "Not all of Feder's ideas were discarded. In their plans for their new occupied eastern territories, the Nazis envisioned an archipelago of compact German dominated industrial centers, surrounded by agricultural settlements and traditional villages"[1143] with pristine natural areas outside their perimeters.

As the city of Kiev was under siege in September of 1941 in the biggest encirclement in military history, Hitler himself remarked, "We torment ourselves cultivating marshes—and in the Ukraine an inexhaustibly fertile soil, with a thickness, in places, often meters of humus, lies waiting for us."[1144] Hitler's comments show environmental sensitivities for German wetlands. *Torment* is a strong emotional term. Moreover, Hitler was undoubtedly

---

[1140] Speer, *Infiltration*, p. 298.
[1141] Ibid. See also *Hitler's Table Talk*, evening of Oct. 17, 1941, p. 54.
[1142] Sax, p. 117.
[1143] Kotkin, p. 104.
[1144] *Hitler's Table Talk*, evening of Sept. 23, 1941, p. 31.

thinking of Seifert and many others like him when he stated, "We torment ourselves." Furthermore, when Hitler says "we," he even includes himself in the torment. Hitler thus indicates that Seifert's shrillness was perhaps far more effective than some environmental historians have presumed.[1145] After making his statement about marsh areas, Hitler then goes on to justify the removing of Ukrainians from their land because their race is not worthy of such rich soil: "It's inconceivable that a higher people should painfully exist on a soil too narrow for it (Germans), whilst amorphous masses, which constitute nothing to civilization (Slavs in Ukraine) occupy infinite tracts of a soil that is one of the richest of the world."[1146] The Nazis shipped tons of Ukrainian soil back to Germany via rail to help amend their own overused soils back home. With such a practice, *blood and soil* could not be illustrated any better.

In a ravine called *Babi Yar* just to the north of Kiev, thousands upon thousands of Jews were shot, killed and buried. During the initial stage of this gruesome operation in September 1941, Hitler made some environmentally sensitive statements with regard to how Ukraine should be managed:

> It would be a mistake to decree that in the Ukraine the quality of the soil means that we should sow nothing but wheat. No, we must also leave room for pastures. Nature has made the various regions of the earth in such a way as to ensure a sort of autarky for each, and man must respect this modified kind of order. We shall therefore let the marshlands continue to exist, not only because they will be useful to us as fields for maneuvers, but also in order to respect the local climatological conditions, and to prevent the desert from gradually encroaching on the fertile regions. The marshes play the role of a sponge. Without them, it might happen that a whole crop was wiped out by a wave of heat.[1147]

Hitler's environmental concerns for respecting local environs, wetlands and the encroaching problems of desertification show how much Seifert

---

[1145] Bramwell notes, "Seifert was probably the unnamed but influential ecologist in the Todt Organization who, according to Backe, in 1939 persuaded Hitler to put a stop to any further land improvements in Germany, on the grounds that drainage and similar projects would ruin Germany's water table," *Blood and Soil: Walther Darre and Hitler's Green Party*, p. 173.

[1146] *Hitler's Table Talk*, evening of Sept. 23, 1941, p. 31.

[1147] Ibid., midday of Sept. 28, 1941.

influenced him.[1148] Hitler was well aware of what happened to America in the Dust Bowl.

In the mid-1930s, Seifert sharply criticized Darre for plowing under wetlands. To some extent, Seifert opposed Darre's "back to the land" SS plans to convert much of Germany into one big countryside farm for the *volk*. Seifert "wanted agricultural practice to mimic nature according to the most stringent organic farm prescriptions, avoiding weeding, ploughing or monoculture."[1149] Darre slowly warmed to Seifert's ideas. By 1941, even Hitler seems to have synthesized Seifert and Darre with regard to ecologically sensitive farming methods. By showing his concern for desertification, Hitler clearly did not want Ukraine to turn into an American Dust Bowl. Indeed, even Martin Burgener's great hydrological engineering plan to dike and drain the vast Pripit Marshes in Ukraine was shelved as early as 1941.[1150] Burgener had been planning this huge public works project for years. However, his gigantic land reclamation venture came to an abrupt end—a veritable harbinger of much anticipated environmental plans to come.

At the height of the Nazi blitzkrieg in the summer of 1941, Hitler summarized his desire to conquer the East for green purposes, not for riches: "At the outbreak of the First World War, many people thought we ought to look towards the mineral riches of the West, the raw materials of the colonies, and the gold. For my part, I always thought that having the sun in the East was the essential thing for us, and today I have no reason to modify my point of view."[1151]

There can be no doubt the thirst for *lebensraum* in the East had a green hue to it. "Hitler consistently accorded a subordinate role to the non-agrarian potentialities of his dream of *lebensraum* in the East. His conception of economic autarky remained narrowly and archaically agrarian, assigning at most a secondary status to the vast and immensely valuable industrial resources which the realization of his grandiose scheme for conquest would have placed at Germany's disposal."[1152] As far as Hitler was concerned, "Russia deserved invasion, because her attempt to industrialize was tantamount to an act of war against the West. Her ordained role was to produce

---

[1148] Blackbourn, p. 287.
[1149] Bramwell, *Blood and Soil: Walther Darre and Hitler's Green Party*, p. 173.
[1150] See Blackbourn, pp. 250-279.
[1151] *Hitler's Table Talk*, night of July 27-28, 1941, pp. 15-16.
[1152] Turner, p. 74.

food for Europe."[1153] That Hitler would spend more than three months in his military field headquarters just to the southwest of Kiev was indicative of his great concerns and plans for the East. The bunker itself was called *Wehrwolf*. The location was specifically selected because of the proximity of some oaks in a secluded pine forest that was originally known as Oak Grove. Slave labor was cruelly used to build the complex under the auspices of the Todt Organization, and it included an organic vegetable garden to suit the *Fuhrer's* palate. Wolves, oaks, and organic vegetable gardens thus served the backdrop for the great eastern campaign on the Russian front.

Himmler's SS *purged* the anthroposophical elements of organic farming inherited from Steiner, and renamed it *natural farming*.[1154] While the Reich League for Biodynamic Agriculture was dissolved in 1941, and a few of its representatives were temporarily imprisoned because of their Steiner connections, organic farming was purposefully protected by Himmler to be put into practice in the occupied eastern territories. The relationship between the SS and organic farming was fairly deep by 1941. Himmler and Darre's SS had incorporated many organic farming specialists and their organic farming methods into their back-to-the-land program, especially by the late 1930s. In "1939, the SS requisitioned a large farmstead in the occupied province of Posen to turn it into an agricultural training facility based on biodynamic principles."[1155] Many leading organic farmers in the SS wanted to turn Poland into a green organic farming paradise.

Even Oswald Pohl, Gunther Pancke and Otto Ohlendorf, three of some of the most powerful men in Himmler's entire SS, were dedicated to organic farming:

> Pancke was Darre's successor as head of the SS Office of Race and Settlement and played a leading role in the effort to alter conquered lands in the East according to Himmler's Germanic model once the racially unfit inhabitants were forcibly removed. One of Pancke's goals was the establishment of agricultural estates in the Eastern territories governed by so-called soldier-farmers. He considered biodynamic cultivation the suitable method for this would-be vanguard, pioneers of a racially dependable peasantry in

---

[1153] Bramwell, Anna, *Blood and Soil: Walther Darre and Hitler's Green Party*, p. 123.
[1154] Staudenmaier & Biehl, p. 121.
[1155] Ibid., pp. 120-21.

the ethnically cleansed East, and the SS sent its personnel to attend courses provided by the Reich League for Biodynamic Agriculture. Pancke's colleague Oswald Pohl was in charge of the economic enterprises of the SS and administrator for the concentration camp system. Pohl was a friend of Seifert and had his own estate farmed biodynamically.[1156]

In 1943, SS officer Carl Grund was appointed to evaluate how organic farming could be imported into the Russian provinces. "On Himmler's orders, Grund was given a variety of special tasks and prerogatives as an expert for 'natural farming' in the East. Himmler also directed that former members of the Reich League for Biodynamic Agriculture be engaged in the re-organization of agriculture in the Eastern territories and thus contribute to the 'practical work of reconstruction' being carried out by German forces. SS sponsorship of biodynamics continued until the camps were liberated."[1157]

Himmler was also on the lookout for a few Slavs who had enough residual German blood to make them worthy to save. The operation was called "Hay Harvest Festival" in which SS men fanned out across Poland, Ukraine and Byelorussia in search of able young men and women to kidnap them for future services to the Reich.[1158] Once SS racial examiners determined the children were German enough, they were handed over to adoption services, or given to women who were infertile or who had miscarried. Such women were also "desperate to prove their racial merit by becoming mothers."[1159] Those children not deemed German enough were "sent to children's homes and forced labor camps or, in some cases, used as guinea pigs in Nazi medical experiments."[1160] Himmler's SS had so merged people with nature that such despicable actions were compared to harvesting people where the chaff was separated from the wheat. Worthy people were farmed like animals for the improvement of racial stock. Those deemed unworthy were often treated either like work and/or experimental animals.

Being the SS man he was, Darre declared, "The concept of blood and soil gives us the moral right to take back as much land in the East as is necessary

---

[1156] Ibid., p. 121.
[1157] Ibid., pp. 123-24.
[1158] Lower, p. 36.
[1159] Ibid.
[1160] Ibid.

to establish a harmony between the body of our *volk* and the geopolitical space."[1161] Darre and Himmler had been planning for such an eastward expansion as far back as the 1920s. In their minds, the only way they could get Germans out of the polluted city and back to nature was through a massive displacement of Jewish and Slavic populations from the eastern territories. Himmler, worried about German overpopulation and massive Slavic immigration, coldly stated, "Increase of our peasant population is the only effective defense against the influx of the Slav working-class masses from the East. As 600 years ago, the German peasant's destiny must be to preserve and increase the German people's patrimony in their holy mother earth in battle against the Slav race."[1162]

Both Himmler and Darre would provide green camouflage[1163] to justify Nazi operations on the Eastern Front. Their belief in the master race and environmental predilections was at the heart of why they were so obsessed with *lebensraum*. That Hitler made operation *Barbarossa* the primary linchpin of Nazi actions demonstrates his concerns very similar. In spite of some of the environmental ambivalence and inconsistencies within the Nazi Party, "the existence of competing and shifting priorities over the 12 years of the Third Reich did not ... weaken the centrality of blood and soil ideology or its persistence as a justification for territorial expansion and racial extermination. From the early days of Darre's rural campaign in 1930 to his service as the head of the SS Race and Settlement Office and even beyond Darre's 'retirement' in 1942, blood and soil was one of the ideologies that fueled Nazi action."[1164]

Even as late as 1944, with Austria, Bohemia and Moravia now under the Reich's authority, Hitler himself observed: "It is a great pity that Germans know so little of their own country. Since 1938 the number of beauty spots within the boundaries of the Reich has increased considerably. . . . To visit all the beauties of his country, a German today would require to take a holiday in a different district each year for the rest of his life."[1165] Hitler was also very grateful to Goering for pushing hard to obtain Austria for

1161 Bergmann, *Agrarromantik und Grobstadtfeindschaft*, p. 312; quoted by Staudenmaier & Biehl, p. 32.
1162 Himmler: *Volkisch Bauernpolitik*, Central Archives, Microfilm 98; quoted by Hohne, p. 46.
1163 Staudenmaier and Biehl, p. 32.
1164 Gerhard, "Breeding Pigs and People for the Third Reich: Richard Walther Darre's Agrarian Ideology" in *How Green Were the Nazis?*, p. 129.
1165 *Hitler's Table Talk*, midday of March 23, 1944, pp. 544-45.

the Nazis. Goering loved Austria. He loved her mountains, forests, hunting grounds and castles. Once Austria was firmly in the hands of the Nazis, Hitler, choked up with great emotion, called Goering and said, "You cannot imagine. I had completely forgotten how beautiful my country is."[1166] Hitler thus clearly understood the great campaigns in the East included the taking of the ecological spoils of war. Environmental imperialism was one of the primary reasons why Nazi Germany decided to conquer the eastern territories. "The luxury of environmental deliberation on this scale was, like genocide, a by-product of conquest."[1167] The Nazis could now both sustainably industrialize and get back to nature at the same time. This was the whole intent of obtaining *lebensraum,* or living space in the East.

National Parks, Landscape Cleansing & Genocide

Nazi environmentalism merged with genocide and terrorism on the Eastern Front. While German forester Lutz Heck shelved the idea of setting aside large national parks within Germany itself until after the war,[1168] Nazi biologist Walther Schoenichen had expansive dreams for the austere *Bialowieza* Forest in Poland and Lithuania. Schoenichen wanted to cleanse Jews and Slavs out of the *Bialowieza* Forest in order to turn it into a giant national park, much bigger than what the Poles had already designated for the area. For Schoenichen, the *Bialowieza* Forest would provide an opportunity to make up for the primeval jungles Germany lost in colonial Africa after its defeat in the First World War.[1169] Not surprisingly, the Nazis showed much more love for trees than for people: "It is, of course, painful to acknowledge how ecologically conscientious the most barbaric regime in modern history actually was. Exterminating millions of lives was not at all incompatible with passionate protection for millions of trees."[1170]

The Nazi *blood and soil* doctrine provided new environmental horizons to mold Polish and Lithuanian landscapes after the German image. In the process, racial genocide coincided with landscape cleansing in the great northern forests of Poland, Lithuania and Byelorussia:

[1166] Irving, p. 209.
[1167] Blackbourn, p. 287.
[1168] Uekoetter, pp. 72-73.
[1169] Schama, p. 71.
[1170] Ibid., p. 119.

The first task toward realizing this "total landscape plan," as it was designated, was to empty villages. Between late June and mid August 1941 thousands of farmers and foresters from the old, timbered villages on the edge of the forest were deported out of the area; trudging along the roads with a battered bag, their houses in flames behind them, their animals wasted in the burning barns. Around the villages of Narew, northwest of *Bialowieza*, Battalion 322 behaved with characteristically brisk cruelty, rounding up the population on the pretext of checking papers, then driving the men off into the *puszcza Ladka* nearby and shooting about a hundred after the usual excavation of a forest pit by the prisoners. One or two men managed to escape by feigning death. And when the news passed around, villagers returned to the site at night, dug amidst the mass grave for their family members, and brought them back clandestinely to Narew for burial in the local cemetery.[1171]

This was how the Nazis went about establishing nature reserves and parks. They first had to be freed of Jewish and Slavic occupancy.[1172]

At the forefront of this operation was the infamous *Einsatzgruppen*, which were mobile death squads that fanned out all across the Baltics, Byelorussia, western Russia and Ukraine. Very unlike Europe and Poland where most of the Jews were murdered in death and/or concentration camps, it was the *Einsatzgruppen* who hunted them down in the East. Up to a million Jewish victims were shot, brutalized or burned alive by the *Einsatzgruppen* during the early part of Operation *Barbarossa*. The *Einsatzgruppen* hunted Jews wherever they could be found, even as far as the remote forests and swamps which often provided green shelter for their colossal crimes. Ironically enough, "the great majority of the officers of the *Einsatzgruppen* were professional men. They included a physician, a professional opera singer, and a large number of lawyers. These men were in no sense hoodlums, delinquents, common criminals or sex maniacs. Most were intellectuals."[1173] In other words, they were steeped in the *science* of social Darwinian biology and the

---

[1171] Ibid, p. 71.

[1172] Joachim Wolschke-Buhlman says in "Violence as the Basis of National Socialist Landscape Planning," in *How Green Were the Nazis?*: "Native Americans were forcefully removed to create Yellowstone National Park in Wyoming, just as native blacks were displaced to establish Serengeti National Park in Tanzania," p. 244.

[1173] Hilberg, vol. 1, p. 289.

ecological *intellectualism* of Romanticism and existentialism that dominated the German academy for well over a century.

The Teutonic pagan hunter and Master of the German Forests, Hermann Goering, virtually took the *Bialowieza* as his own personal property.[1174] He wanted to turn the entire area into a vast hunting reserve. However, in the early part of the war, the Nazis hunted people in the forest instead of animals. Jew hunts were common:

> In the summer of 1941 open season was declared on the Jews who made up about 12% of *Bialowieza's* population. The procedure was routine, not just for the SS but for the regular troops of the German army; in this case Battalion 322 of General Fedor von Bock's Army Division of the Center. The 550 Jews were lined up in the forecourt of the hunting palace, the women and children were separated from men and boys over 16. The next day the males were taken into the deep forest and somewhere amidst the old oaks and lindens were shot beside their mass grave. Their families were deported to the ghetto at *Pruzhany* and ended up in the extermination ovens of Treblinka, where massed freestanding stones mark their monument.[1175]

More telling, even though the *Bialowieza* was full of enemy hideouts, the SS was not allowed to flametorch "the forest to purge it of any possible shelter for partisans."[1176]

Such shocking schemes show just how seriously some of the Nazi leaders took nature preservation even in time of war. "As for the primeval forest, it was a *heiliger Hain*, 'a sacred grove'. Not a leaf was to suffer hurt. Fur and feathers were to be strictly protected. For the elk and bison were now his (Goering's) elk and bison—German elk and bison."[1177] The suffering and harm would be foisted upon the human occupants of the forest. "If the creatures' woods live undisturbed under the regime of Scherping's German forest guards, the same protection was not extended to the local population."[1178]

[1174] Wolschke-Buhlman, "Violence as the Basis of National Socialist Landscape Planning," in *How Green Were the Nazis?*, p. 244.

[1175] Schama, p. 70.

[1176] Ibid., p. 69.

[1177] Ibid.

[1178] Ibid., pp. 69-70.

Even after the catastrophic defeat of Stalingrad, in March of 1943, environmentalist Hans Klose proposed an inventory of nature reserves in the Caucasus Mountains.[1179] The Caucasus Mountains were south of Stalingrad. In the winter of 1942-43, the Nazi troops fighting there barely escaped. Hans Klose also wanted to implement "existing *Naturshutz* laws into occupied portions of Poland. Indeed, the Nazis installed their own nature protection officials in occupied Eastern Europe, and these officials immediately attempted to extend German conservation laws into captured lands."[1180] Much later in 1944 when the war was all but lost, the Nazis published for the *Wehrmacht* a special edition of Wilhlem Riehl's *Natural History of the German People*.[1181] The *Wehrmacht* needed to be reminded why they were fighting for *lebensraum* in the first place. Riehl was one of the most important *volkisch* environmental thinkers of Germany in the 1800s—the very father of German green socialism and sustainable development.

While environmental historians strongly point out the Third Reich was an ecological catastrophe because of all its wartime destruction, the Nazis themselves viewed things much differently. The Nazis saw the war as a necessary means to a noble end. Even during the height of the war, Himmler himself longed for peace "when people could be educated again. Kersten, his masseur and perhaps most intimate friend, seriously thought that in his heart of hearts Himmler would have preferred to educate rather than exterminate the subject peoples of the East."[1182] By this time, gone were the good old days of Nazi ascendancy when Himmler and Darre were the great teachers of blood and soil ideology. Thus, the war was not an end in itself. It was a means to get Germans back to more natural and healthy lifestyles with plenty of environmental breathing space to enjoy. The quest for *lebensraum* was far more than just imperialism and colonialism. It was also a geographical-ecological extension of Aryan blood and soil mysticism outside of Germany's borders.[1183]

The Nazis were not just interested in establishing nature reserves or parks in the *Bialowieza* forest. They also had green sustainable development plans for the entire landscape—even over areas that were heavily populated.

1179 Uekoetter, p. 81.
1180 Closmann, "Legalizing a Volksgemeinschaft," in *How Green Were the Nazis?*, p. 34.
1181 Dominick, p. 87.
1182 Hohne, p. 45.
1183 See Kirkley-Best, Elizabeth, "Blood and Soil: *Blut und Boden*," 2003, p. 1.

Environmental totalitarianism and sustainable development were to be used to shape and mold the landscape from a German point of view:

> Once World War II began, Nazi experts followed the German army into occupied Poland and immediately began to implement National Socialist planning concepts on a massive scale. They justified the forced removal of thousands of Poles from their homes on the grounds that such an allegedly degenerate race of people could never have a proper relationship to nature and those portions of the countryside occupied by the Germany army.[1184]

While Seifert himself was not in charge of environmental landscape planning in the East, Himmler and the SS certainly were. Either way, both men had the same basic ecological view that the eastern territories had to be Germanized in order to restore the natural landscape, and this meant that Nazi spatial environmental plans would be implemented on a titanic scale.

As one of the great spoils of war, landscape planners were not beset by any foreign constitution, laws, regulations or private property. They were given absolute freedom to plan to their hearts' content. The Nazis called such ethnic landscape cleansing *planning freedom*:[1185]

> No doubt these architects and planners had mixed and overlapping motives. Many probably just wanted to enhance their status as civilian soldiers of the Third Reich. Others were probably just frustrated by the way in which existing social structures and property relations thwarted their ability to redesign their home cities and regions to the degree they would have liked. A few, however, were already beginning to take this logic to its ultimate extreme and embrace the notion that an empty landscape offered unique opportunities.[1186]

Some Nazis believed the occupied East was an urban and environmental planners' paradise where all of the sins of landscape development of the past could be ameliorated.

[1184] Closmann, "Legalizing a Volksgemeinschaft" in *How Green Were the Nazis?*, p. 34

[1185] Wolschke-Buhlman, "Violence as the Basis of National Socialist Landscape Planning," in *How Green Were the Nazis?*, p. 247.

[1186] Ibid., p. 244.

All of this was simply too tempting not to take advantage of. Landscape planners rushed into the annexed territories with climatic-geographical surveys and "transfer of population" exhibits in their hands, ready for implementation. Even as early as "1939, they were no longer thinking simply in terms of designing individual projects such as gardens and parks but in terms of redesigning entire regions."[1187] Environmental holism and totalitarianism took on a scale never considered before. "Many of the planners were apparently thrilled by the opportunity to re-sculpt the eastern territories in their totality, even if it meant the suppression, exploitation, and extermination of the people who lived there."[1188]

Emil Meynen (1902-1994), one of the primary geographers and environmental spatial planners working for the SS, attended the infamous Wannsee Conference in 1942 where the destruction of the Jews was discussed from a legal and technocratic point of view. Eliminating the Jews was certainly a top priority in order to prepare the groundwork for total landscape planning:

> Landscape architects and urban planners enjoyed an unusually high status within the political and social structures of Nazi Germany, and nowhere was their influence more apparent than in the so-called Annexed Eastern Areas of the former Republic of Poland. After defeating Poland in September 1939, Nazi leaders set out to Germanize their annexed territories through murder, expulsion, expropriation, and other forms of ethnic cleansing. Nazi-era architects and planners, for their part, welcomed the opportunity to re-sculpt Poland's rural and urban landscape as they saw fit. Ultimately, Nazi exterminationists created an empty space that landscape and urban planners filled in accordance with the conceptual ideas they had developed inside Germany.[1189]

Landscape Planner Heinrich Friedrich Wiepking Jurgensmann, who was the chair of the Institute for Landscape Design at the University of Berlin, wrote in 1939 the war in Poland promised "a golden age for the German

---

[1187] Ibid., pp. 244-45.
[1188] Ibid., p. 245.
[1189] Ibid., p. 243.

landscape and garden designer that will surpass everything that even the most enthusiastic among us had previously known."[1190]

A close confidant of the *Fuhrer*, Dr. Hans Frank was made the governor-general of Poland. In April 1930 Frank had publicly attacked the Jews for their kosher slaughter practices before a group of animal lovers in Munich.[1191] After other activists from England and a medical expert spoke at the conference, Frank stood up and gave a lecture about the evil inhumanity of the Jews most cherished religious celebration, i.e., the Passover. After he finished his tirade, the assembly adopted a resolution which stated, "The time will come for the salvation of animals from the perverse persecution of retarded subhumans."[1192] The prophetic insight of that animal lovers' conference in 1930 is truly shocking. With regard to the Jews, the resolution became a self-fulfilling prophecy after World War II began. This was especially true in Poland, the very place where blood and soil *lebensraum* and death camps would come together on a barbarous scale unimaginable at the time the resolution was adopted. Indeed, in February of 1942, the Nazis passed a decree which prohibited Jews from having pets as a preliminary step toward their deportation "to concentration camps, where conditions (particularly on the trains) would not be compatible with the animal protection laws."[1193]

In 1941 Seifert himself sermonized, "If the East is to become home for Germans from all over Germany, and if it is to flourish and become as beautiful as the rest of the Reich, then it is not enough just to cleanse the towns of past Polish mismanagement and construct clean and pleasant villages. The entire landscape must be Germanized."[1194] Seifert's statement perfectly reflects the complete fusion between Nazi ecological views and its nationalism, racism and pride. They were one in the same. Echoing the earlier rants of Riehl about the vital importance of forests to Germans, Seifert advocated re-afforesting the newly acquired eastern territories to bring to a halt the steppification process of Poland, Byelorussia and Ukraine

---

[1190] Wiepking-Jurgensmann, Heinrich Friedrich, "Der Deutsche Osten: Eine vordringliche Aufgabe fur unsere Studierenden," *Die Gartenkunst* 52, 1939, 193; quoted in Wolschke-Buhlman, "Violence as a Basis of National Socialist Landscape Planning," pp. 246-47.

[1191] Dominick, p. 92.

[1192] *Volkischer Beobachter*, April 9, 1930 quoted by Dominick, p. 92.

[1193] Sax, p. 119.

[1194] Wolschke-Buhlman, "Violence as the Basis of National Socialist Landscape Planning," in *How Green Were the Nazis?*, p. 245.

brought on by the negligence of its Slavic residents: "The German must have a forest, where he can be happy, not pine forests or acres of rod-thin trees, but rather real forest, rich, diverse, green forest."[1195] Conversely, but not surprisingly, Seifert considered the Slav as "a man of the bare steppes."

Hitler noted, "With the beauties accumulated in central Germany, the new territories in the East seem to us like a desert. . . . We'll take away its character of an Asiatic steppe, we'll Europeanize it."[1196] The *Fuhrer* was well aware of how much human culture and development had spawned increasing deforestation and desertification over the centuries.[1197] Hitler believed Germanizing the East was a great improvement over what had transpired before, even from an environmental point of view.

Likewise, Professor Heidegger told his students in the 1930s: "History teaches us that nomads did not become what they are because of the bleakness of the desert and the steppes, but that they have even left numerous wastelands behind them that had been fertile and cultivated land when they arrived, and that men rooted in the soil have been able to create for themselves a native land, even in the wilderness."[1198] SS environmental planner Konrad Meyer "used the supposed depravity of the Polish plains"[1199] to justify German conquest together with the need for superior Aryan land management. "Seifert himself described Poles and Russians as racial groups incapable of proper land-use management and referred to the degraded state of Polish towns as justification for the invasion and transformation of those areas."[1200] In fact, Seifert believed Aryanism itself "depended on halting the process of steppification, rejecting the mechanistic past, and restoring the healthy cultural landscape that had once flourished in preindustrial Central Europe."[1201]

Seifert advocated, "Every village must be embedded in a grove of fruit trees and lindens. Every stream, every river, and every man-made ditch"[1202] would be overshadowed by poplar and ash trees to break up the meadows. "Such measures would not only beautify the area but also gradually make the climate moister and offer shelter for protection for predators that

---

[1195] Lekan, p. 233.
[1196] *Hitler's Table Talk*, evening of Oct. 17, 1941, p. 54.
[1197] Ibid., midday of July 7, 1942, p. 427.
[1198] Faye, p. 143.
[1199] Lekan, p. 245.
[1200] Ibid.
[1201] Ibid., p. 233.
[1202] Ibid., p. 244.

would keep in check harmful insects and vermin that might otherwise destroy newly planted crops."[1203] In other words, in the eyes of the Nazis, Germanizing the landscape meant caring for it by creating garden cities, nature reserves, national parks and green landscape development plans for its inhabitants. Indeed, master planned communities were to be built without Jews and Slavs. Cities would be redone with attractive green areas.

Beautiful pastoral farms would replace the huts that were scattered across the eastern landscape. Small Polish farms with many families were to be converted into much larger farms for just one German family.[1204] Ukraine would become the agrarian bread basket of the Reich dotted with romantic frontier farms. Hitler also wanted to be careful not to over-industrialize the Ukraine in the process of setting up an infrastructure to export its future wheat supply: "We should rather build windmills all over the place, to supply regional needs—and export only the wheat demanded by the large centers."[1205] Hitler thus also understood the green dream of renewable wind energy long before it became environmentally popular.

In the spring of 1942, the SS proposed[1206] spending over 13 billion Reichsmarks for the sake of agricultural and rural renewal in the eastern territories which demanded a complete makeover. They were also planning on spending an additional three billion Reichmarks on landscape amelioration, which would include the re-afforesting of 11,000 square kilometers together with the mitigation of 20,000 square kilometers of improperly drained agricultural lands. More than a half a billion Reichsmarks were to be spent on re-afforesting agricultural areas and protect them with hedgerows. All these *green* plans represented almost 40 percent of the proposed budget that the SS wanted to spend in remaking the eastern territories. The rest of the budget would be spent on redesigning urban areas, which they presumed would be much more expensive to fix.

With regard to urban designs, planning schemes based on Walter Christaller's Central Place Theory would also be applied on a scale unachievable in Germany thanks to the fact that the Nazis were first going to cleanse the landscape of its Slavic and Jewish populations. Christaller advocated a

---

1203 Ibid., pp. 244-45.
1204 Wolschke-Buhlman, "Violence as the Basis of National Socialist Landscape Planning," in *How Green Were the Nazis?*, p. 249.
1205 *Hitler's Table Talk*, evening of Oct. 17, 1941, p. 55.
1206 Tooze, pp. 474-75.

hierarchy of towns and villages wrapped around a central city that was to maximize economic and administrative efficiency for state planners.

Landscape cleansing reached its zenith under National Socialism.[1207] Environmental planners were well aware of the existence of concentration and death camps.[1208] Indeed, SS agrarian economist and environmental planner Konrad Meyer worked closely with General Odilo Globocnik,[1209] who was in charge of Operation *Reinhard* administered from Lublin, Poland, where some two million Jews were rounded up and murdered in numerous concentration and death camps located throughout the country. Cleaning out Jews and Slavs for Aryan sustainable development and the preservation of nature shows the great campaign in Poland and Russia was also fought for ecological reasons as well. "Proper landscape planning, in other words, would sustain Blood and Soil across time and space."[1210] By cleansing the landscape of inferior races through a massive euthanasia program, the eastern territories could then be used to rebuild the natural health of the German people. "The evidence of environmentally conscious thinking is all over the plans, not just in proposals to set aside conservation lands in every village and establish a conservation area in every district, but in the larger governing principles."[1211] The war was thus seen by many to be a means to a green end. Indeed, just as the cauldron of Stalingrad was initially exploding in Germany's favor in August of 1942, Hitler looked forward to the environmental spoils of conquest: "Our country today is overpopulated ... once we are in a position to start colonizing in the East, most of our difficulties will disappear."[1212]

As Jews were being crammed into dirty ghettos, a place befitting of their alleged nature hating tendencies, organic farms were being set up in various places in Poland for new German settlers. SS leader Gustav Pancke "visited Polish farms in October and November 1939, two months after the German invasion and conquest of Poland, in search of farms that could be farmed organically, and sent detailed reports to Himmler on each one, its fertility, productivity and potential."[1213] SS Deputy Georg Halbe, an avid devotee

---

1207 Wolschke-Buhlman, "Violence as the Basis of National Socialist Landscape Planning," in *How Green Were the Nazis?*, p. 249.
1208 Ibid., p. 249.
1209 Rieger, p. 105.
1210 Lekan, p. 247.
1211 Blackbourn, p. 290.
1212 *Hitler's Table Talk*, evening of Aug. 6, 1942.
1213 Bramwell, *Ecology in the 20ʰ Century: A History*, p. 204.

of peasant Romanticism and organic farming, moved to the Ministry for the Occupied Territories after Darre was replaced by Backe.[1214] Hermann Reischle, the SS department head of the Race Bureau in the Office of Race and Settlement, was heavily involved in the planning stages of converting the eastern territories into a healthy environment suitable for Aryan colonizers.[1215] Before moving to their new environs, new German settlers were to receive training from biodynamic plantations like the one in Dachau to prepare them to become organic cultivators.[1216]

Shockingly, once re-settled in the eastern territories, farms and villas in Poland and Ukraine often became killing fields where German settlers themselves often joined in on the action by using Jews as target practice in their gardens.[1217] In other rural killing fields farther east, local Ukrainian girls were "routinely used at mass shootings to assist in the collection and mending of victims' clothes. As 'packers' in the pits, girls pressed down on corpses with their bare feet; as 'hemp collectors' they gathered hay and sunflower stalks to be used for hastening the burning of the corpses."[1218]

Nature reserves, green landscape plans, organic farms, garden variety killing fields, even composting the dead[1219] in concentration and death camps—it is all here in the most grisly set of circumstances imaginable. SS leadership, racial hygiene, genocide, and environmentalism were inextricably bound up with each other on the Eastern Front. When Auschwitz crematoriums were burning Jewish victims at a rapid pace in 1943, the camp building department wrote to the Prussian Institute for Water, Soil, and Air Hygiene asking for an expert opinion on air pollution problems and questions with regard to the "construction of a heating plant."[1220] The Prussian air quality hygiene institute, in turn, requested a map from Auschwitz that was to show the surroundings of the projected plant within a five-kilometer radius. At this juncture, the letter exchange apparently came to an abrupt end because the heating plant was most likely a crematorium that would have exposed the Auschwitz death camp itself.[1221] Regardless, the gray smoke of Auschwitz dirtied the skies and environs with sooty human ashes. While

---

[1214] Staudenmaier & Biehl, p. 113.
[1215] Ibid., p. 115.
[1216] Ibid., p. 123.
[1217] Lower, pp. 131-38.
[1218] Ibid., p. 141.
[1219] Rieger, p. 101.
[1220] Uekoetter, "Polycentrism in Full Swing," in *How Green Were the Nazis?*, p. 118.
[1221] Ibid., pp. 118-19.

mass burials generated water pollution problems for Nazi fish farms that SS administrators earlier complained about in 1942, the answer to burn the corpses up in crematorium *heating plants* did not alleviate the environmental concerns of those living in the Auschwitz vicinity.

At Treblinka, on one side of the death camp, there was a picnic area and a zoo with wild foxes for the SS staff to enjoy while countless Jews went up in smoke on the other side of the camp. Auschwitz itself "contained a botanical station for the breeding and testing of newly discovered flora."[1222] In order to Germanize the eastern landscape, much research was committed to finding plants that were similar to the fauna found in Germany that could also thrive in the eastern climate. "Just as Nazi racial policies promised to restore and perpetuate Germany's 'natural' Aryan stock, so did the landscape advocates pledge to re-create and maintain Germany's 'primordial' habitat, the 'source of power for the people.'"[1223]

Not surprisingly, many of the SS death camp commandants and officers were euthanasia specialists.[1224] Auschwitz, Treblinka and Belzec death camps, thanks to their gargantuan euthanasia practices, became colossal recycling centers where all of the victims' belongings that were carried on the trains to their final destination were not only confiscated and stolen, but salvaged as well. In fact, human hair shaved from euthanized victims was later recycled and sown into Nazi army uniforms to help keep the Germans warm on the battle front. Hair was also recycled to help seal German submarines.[1225] More sickening still, there is a pair of gloves made of human skin on display in the World War II museum in Kiev. All of the robbed jewelry, gold rings, bracelets and teeth were, of course, a financial bonanza, but nothing was to be wasted. The Nazi recycling fetish went so far so as to include the attempt to generate gas from inmate's feces in sludge experiments that apparently claimed thousands of lives.[1226] Even the grease of human fat that oozed from the piles of corpses when they were burned was sometimes thrown back into the hellish fires to stoke the flames even more. In Auschwitz, the human ashes were placed in a stormwater mill pond and later recycled as fertilizer.

[1222] Sax, p. 109.

[1223] Lekan, p. 247.

[1224] Arad, pp. 181-198.

[1225] Rieger, p. 126.

[1226] Zeller, "Molding the Landscape of Nazi Environmentalism," in *How Green Were the Nazis?*, pp. 158-59.

On Sept. 4, 1943, regimental order 37 was handed down from the German commander of Police Battalion 101 in Lublin, Poland, demanding his men clean up their litter and recycle whatever can be reused. He had become aware that "large quantities of wrapping material, mineral water, and other bottles lie about."[1227] He then threatened punishment upon those who wasted any reusable materials: "It is irresponsible that in the present raw material and supply conditions, the responsible persons do not endeavor to make immediate renewed use of the empty containers and the wrapping material."

Situated in eastern Poland, Lublin was the command center of Operation *Reinhard* where the notorious death camps of Belzec, Sobibor, Majdanek, and Treblinka all received their directives. At these death camps, just like Auschwitz, recycling and murderous euthanasia practices went hand in hand. T-4 euthanasia experts, who originally set up the gassing system where tens of thousands of *unfit* Germans had been euthanized to death until public outrage put a stop to the operation, were transferred from the homeland and assigned to SS General Odilo Globocnik in Lublin, Poland. It was most probably Globocnik and his T-4 euthanasia experts who came up with the monstrous blueprints on how to liquidate Polish Jewry through the organization and construction of death camps replete with shower room facilities. After a Berlin speech given in 1940, Globocnik was extolled for his "healthy agricultural"[1228] style of speaking that was highly valued as is fitting for the natural authenticity of the German *volk*.

While the Poles were being herded around, and the Jews were being sacrificed en masse, organic farms were being set up to feed the SS so they could continue their landscape cleansing in the East:

> In December 1942, Heinrich Himmler issued a "General Directive on the Shaping of the Landscape in the Annexed Eastern Territories." Ostensibly, this was a "green" order par excellence. Himmler offered guidelines on how to deal properly with flora and fauna, and how to conserve the landscape while building streets, villages, cities and even industrial zones. At the same time, he asserted that the countryside and natural surroundings had been largely destroyed by local, nonnative populations. Settling the "living space"

[1227] Goldhagen, p. 265.
[1228] Rieger, p. 80.

with ethnic Germans, on the one hand, and getting rid of these foreign populations, on the other, was thus an integral part of Nazi "ecology." It was no coincidence that the Nazis sought to "cleanse" and "purify" their *lebensraum* first and foremost of Jews. It was no coincidence that Jews were identified as a genuine environmental threat, and called "polluted," "diseased" and "parasitic."[1229]

Thus, in Poland and Russia, Jews and Slavs were sacrificed by the social Darwinian nature religion of the Nazis, and environmentalism played a ghastly role in the process. The Jews, Poles, Russians, Byelorussians and Ukrainians were all considered unfit from both a racial and an environmental point of view.

Even before the war began, German spies in Poland reported in 1937 "an outbreak of pine bud mite, which destroyed vast tracts of forest along the German-Polish border, as tantamount to an act of war—the Poles had not only taken their trees, they had neglected and destroyed them."[1230] Such an attitude was certainly borrowed from the 19th century Romantic writers Arndt and Riehl, who believed the Slavs had ruined the landscapes of Eastern Europe. Following their ecological forefathers, the Nazis carried this belief to its logical conclusion:

> … Generalplan Ost (East) was about bringing humans, nature and race into a harmony in order to establish a new agrarian way of life for Aryan colonists. Here green and Nazi thinking came together to a degree not seen elsewhere. In order to achieve this vision, the landscape had to be made anew, first by forcibly removing the Slavic population, then by bulldozing away the past, and finally by moving Germans into the newly emptied space. Annexation exposed a side of Nazi conservationism that was as ugly as it was logical. It was ugly because it was exterminatory. It was logical because only the clearance of the new territories created the opportunity to build a new, green Germany. Polish forests were therefore turned into Nazi hunting grounds, eastern agrarian lands were transformed

---

[1229] Neumann, Boaz, "Green, Brown and Bloody all Over," *Haaretz. News,* March 7, 2008.
[1230] Bramwell, *Ecology in the 20th Century: A History*, p. 200.

into German settlement areas, and inferior Jews and Slavs were weeded out to make room for superior Aryans.[1231]

In fact, environmental degradation was also used to justify the ethnic cleansing of people not properly suited to their natural surroundings. Landscape Planner Heinrich Friedrich Wiepking Jurgensmann handily summarized this Jewish-Slavic conundrum, complete with pictures in hand and full of commentary:

> The landscape is always a form, an expression, and a characteristic of the *volk* living within it. It can be a gentle countenance of its spirit and soul, just as it can be the grimace of its soullessness and of human and spiritual depravity. In any case, it is the infallible, distinctive mark of what a people feels, thinks, creates, and does. It shows, divine creative power, or part of a destructive force. The German landscape—like the German people—differs in every way from those of the Poles and the Russians. The murders and atrocities of the Eastern peoples are engraved in a razor sharp manner, in the grimaces of their native landscapes.[1232]

In short, the Jews, Poles and Russians were not properly related to nature and thus deserved to be liquidated.

Even the Nazi governor general of Poland, Hans Frank, spoke of the liquidation of the Poles along environmentalist lines as early as 1940: "If I had to put up a poster for every seven Poles shot, the forests in Poland would not be sufficient to manufacture the paper." Frank did not believe that liquidated Poles in the name of a greater Reich were worth even one poster or piece of paper that could be processed out of one tree. While Frank justified his virulent anti-Semitism on animal rights, the green forests of central and eastern Europe were far more precious than giving murdered Poles at least some recognition with regard to their dastardly fate. Frank did not believe a dead Pole was worth the piece of paper written on it.

1231 Zeller, *How Green Were the Nazis?*, p. 14.

1232 Wiepking-Jurgensmann, Heinrich Friedrich, "Die Landshaftsfibel, 1942, 13; quoted by Wolschke-Buhlman in, "Violence as a Basis of National Socialist Landscape Planning," in *How Green Were the Nazis?*, p. 251.

Worst of all, the Nazis presumed they were the descendants of the original natives of Europe, i.e., the Aryans. Such a presumption was one of the primary justifications the Nazis used to extend German hegemony far into Eastern Europe. Since the Nazis assumed the Aryans came from the east and settled in the west, their eastern conquests were viewed as less problematic. The Nazis believed the Aryans were Indo-Europeans who had originally come from the hinterlands of southwest Russia.[1233] Over the course of the centuries the Aryans had settled farther and farther west into the heart of Europe. Hitler himself certainly connected Aryanism to ancient Hellenistic Greek culture. Furthermore, it was this ancient culture that he was most interested in restoring—a rough-hewn Spartan ethos embedded in the natural world, which had not yet been destabilized and corrupted by the alienating Judeo-Christian transcendental worldview. Even Seifert went so far to argue that "19th century industrialization had broken the connection between 'tribe' and 'living space.'"[1234]

This meant Hitler and the Nazis were trying to save the original or indigenous German people from Western capitalism on the one hand, and Eastern communism on the other hand. Both were deemed dangerously materialistic because of their presumed false ties to Judaism and Christianity. Western capitalism was viewed as materialistic because of its superficial emphasis upon finances—which had been degraded by international Jewry. Eastern communism was also viewed as materialistic because it emphasized political industrial economy and class warfare. Christianity was merely an international form of Judaism. Capitalism, communism, Judaism and Christianity were all judged to be dangerous to Germany because each emphasized universal values alien to the *volk*.

As such, Nazi Germany believed it was protecting the indigenous Aryans from the disorderliness of international cosmopolitanism. National Socialism was extremely concerned about preserving the original or indigenous Aryan man, who represented a natural purity long before the Judeo-Christian worldview corrupted Europe. In fact, Seifert originally

---

[1233] Some Nazis were very attracted to the occult story that Aryans originated in the north of Iceland from a Nordic Atlantis that had since been covered with water because of a cataclysmic meteor strike coupled with severe climate change. Other Nazis, especially the SS, simply believed in Nordic superiority.

[1234] Lekan, p. 189.

viewed the National Socialist revolution as "nothing less than the final confrontation between an exhausted Western and Bolshevist materialism that adores the measurable and countable, on the one side, and on the other side a worldview based on simple truths such as soul, belief, honor, *heimat*, and nature."[1235]

On occasion, Hitler himself did compare the fight against the Poles and partisans in the eastern territories to a war against Indians comparable to the American West.[1236] While this seems to suggest that Hitler identified with the American destruction of the Indians as something to be modeled by the Nazis in World War II, there are some important distinctions that need to be brought out in this discussion. First of all, Hitler hated America. Secondly, he also hated the very capitalism that ran roughshod over the Indians. Thirdly, Hitler did not believe in a limited form of government as America originally did when Manifest Destiny was in full swing. Neither did Hitler like the individualism of Americans. Hitler was thus not pro-American by any stretch of the imagination, but in his racism, he did certainly believe the Americans were superior to the Indians. What is actually more surprising, Hitler compared the Slavs, who are white, to red-skinned Indians. Perhaps more importantly, Hitler never considered the Poles, who were certainly indigenous to their own country, to be Romantically tied to nature like that of the Indians of North America.[1237] The Slavs had been ruined by the heresy of the unnatural Judeo-Christian worldview, and therefore were doomed to a social Darwinian death.

Hitler loved Karl May's (1842-1912) Germanized Romantic Westerns that often portrayed cowboys as evil and Indians as good.[1238] In fact, Germany learned about all the evils of Western cowboy imperialism from Karl May. He was extremely popular with German readers. Karl May Germanized James Fenimore Cooper's *The Last of the Mohicans*. In the place of Cooper's Mohican hero *Chingachgook*, Karl May extolled his Apache warrior Winnetou. Instead of Hawkeye, *Winnetou* is befriended by a strong German frontiersman by the name of Shatterhand. However, the Apaches, unlike

---

[1235] Seifert, "*Natur und Technik*, p. 10, quoted in Lekan, p. 232.

[1236] See especially Blackbourn's discussion on this, pp. 303-06.

[1237] One must also always keep in mind Native American Indians fought amongst themselves. Some Indian tribes like the Blackfeet, the Sioux, the Pawnee, the Apache, the Yakima, the Cayuse, the Arikara, and the Huron, were notorious for their tribalism and cruelty.

[1238] For this fascinating discussion see especially "Karl May's Imaginary America" at the Internet site http://www.ibaradio.org/Europe/winnetou/may/May1.htm.

the Mohicans, were notorious warriors. Karl May glorified the warrior ethos of the Apaches, something which James Fenimore Cooper does not do with regard to the Mohicans. In fact, Cooper demonizes the warlike Hurons that are the enemies of the Mohicans.

When Hitler was young, he did read *The Last of the Mohicans*. After reading James Fenimore Cooper, someone then introduced Hitler to Karl May's works. Hitler said, "The first book of his I read was *Ride Through the Desert*. I was carried away by it. And I went on to devour at once the other books by the same author. The immediate result was a falling off in my school reports."[1239]

Hitler's Romantic fascination with Karl May was life-long. Not only did the young Hitler attend one of May's lectures in Vienna in 1912, but he also kept his books by his bedside. He even passed them out to his military commanders. Albert Speer commented, "Any account of Hitler as commander of troops should not omit reference to Karl May. Hitler was wont to say that he had always been deeply impressed by the tactical finesse and circumspection that Karl May conferred upon his character *Winnetou*. Such a man was the very model of a company commander, Hitler would say."[1240] The *Fuhrer* would even turn to Karl May's books at the most hopeless times to regain courage and use *Winnetou* as a great "model of a noble spirit."[1241] Speer even blamed Hitler's passion for Karl May's books as one of the reasons why the *Wehrmacht* was often unprepared on the battlefield.

The Nazis had propagandized Karl May so much that his person and books were persona non grata in East Germany after the communist takeover in the post-war period. The communists assumed Karl May's books were fascist. The Nazis even managed to turn Shatterhand into an Aryan, and they also compared the evil Yankees to Jews.

Praising Karl May, Hitler once stated: "The only romance which stirs the heart of the North American is that of the Redskin; but it is curious to note that the writer who has produced the most vivid Redskin romances is a German."[1242] Hitler also noted in the same discussion that German nostalgia for wild Romanticism is different "from the Americans ... who see nothing beyond their skyscrapers. Our Romanticism has its origins in the intense appreciation of nature that is inherent in us Germans." Hitler then

---

1239 *Hitler's Table Talk*, evening of Feb. 17. 1942, p. 240.
1240 Speer, *Spandau: The Secret Diaries*, p. 347.
1241 Ibid.
1242 *Hitler's Table Talk*, midday of June 15, 1943, p. 536.

concluded by saying that this Romantic German nostalgia now requires a drive for *lebensraum* in the east to satisfy its cultural longings.

More importantly, unlike the Americans who crossed the frontier to build a better life with Manifest Destiny and individual liberty as their guides, the Nazis were trying to return Germans to a more natural healthy state by converting the eastern territories into an Aryan frontier where social Darwinian laws could rule both people and nature. In the Nazi mind, this would rejuvenate the nation and restore natural harmony through sustainable development and economic prosperity without the excesses of the Jewish-American commercial industrial complex. Such a picture was certainly not what the Americans were looking for when they conquered the western frontier and took it away from the Indians. Hitler and the Nazis wanted to conquer Eastern Europe National Socialism style, and this meant it had to be subjugated without creating an unfettered capitalistic Dust Bowl in the process.

The Nazis were not white supremacists as is typically understood. The Slavs were white and yet still suffered greatly and tragically under the Nazi regime. The Nazis considered some Czechs, Poles, Ukrainians, and Russians to be Aryans, but most were not considered as such.[1243] Hitler's pecking order, of course, was a white man's totem pole—but with the Germans on top with little deference given to white Slavic populations in Eastern Europe. The Germans were then followed closely by the Scandinavians, the Dutch, the Britons and then perhaps the Americans. The blacks were considered to be Semites and the Jews were placed on the bottom rung of the racial ladder. Yet many Jews are white-skinned. In *Mein Kampf*, Hitler did sometimes appear to have broadly categorized many whites as Aryans, but there can be no doubt he still believed in a Germanic superiority over the rest of the whites.

What the Nazis desired was to return to their pristine Aryan roots before the Judeo-Christian worldview ruined Europe. They believed if they could recover their primeval roots, they could get Europe back on track by

---

[1243] Weikart, *Hitler's Ethic*. Weikart says, "Ambiguity and inconsistency dogged this enterprise, since neither Hitler nor the anthropologists and other racial experts assisting the Nazis in making racial determinations had a coherent, consistent way to discern racial fitness. All the racial terms of the Nazis—Aryan, German or related race, and so on—were ill-defined and highly subjective in application. Nonetheless, in theory, Hitler's racism always trumped nationalism. Nazi policies made a valiant effort to follow this ideology, but it was always bedeviled by the practical difficulty in categorizing people racially," p. 68.

leaving behind the disastrous effects of the Judeo-Christian international worldview. In truth, the Nazis wanted to become more indigenous in biological communion with nature according to the evolutionary laws of social Darwinism together with a natural existentialism. Thus, their racism, in spite of promoting cultural development, had a strong ecological ring to it. The Nazis believed the Judeo-Christian tradition brought about an unnatural weakening of the races. In the eyes of the Nazis, this backward process had to be reversed so that Aryan evolution could resume once again.

Lest some presume this entire discussion over the top, consider Charles Lindbergh, the famous American pilot who was the first in the world to cross the Atlantic solo in 1927 in an airplane.[1244] Lindbergh's heroic legacy was forever tarnished by his Nazi sympathies. During the 1930s he spent a considerable amount of time in Germany. He inspected the German Air Force under Goering's leadership and extolled the invincibility of the *Luftwaffe*. In 1938, he also received the Service Cross of the German Eagle from the Nazis for his heroic flight on the *Spirit of St. Louis*. Later it became clear Lindbergh was not only a white racist and a political isolationist, but he also strongly opposed entering the war against Germany that created much controversy in America.

In 1974 Lindbergh died in Maui an extreme environmentalist.[1245] Before he passed away he demanded he be buried naked so he would not pollute the earth. He also had become "an enthusiastic visitor to Africa, interested in indigenous tribes, even as he was becoming less enthusiastic about aviation, once his life's passion. He had become a kind of true believer now in the faith that machines were destroyers—enemies of the natural world."[1246]

The man who became a notorious recluse due to the political firestorm he created by becoming a national spokesman for an isolationist organization with Nazi sympathies called "America First," finally began to open up again to the public late in life over environmental issues. Throughout the 1960s, Lindbergh became increasingly concerned about deforestation, the extinction of species and marine wildlife. He also held a special soft spot for primitive peoples, i.e., the preservation of indigenous races in wild areas. He became heavily involved in protecting polar bears, blue whales

---

1244 Musser, Mark, "Lindbergh, Nazism and Environmental Fascism," *The American Thinker*, Oct. 19, 2013.

1245 Rabinowitz, Dorothy, "The Lindbergh Nobody Knew," *The Wall Street Journal*, July 24, 2009.

1246 Ibid.

and coral reefs. He was a director of the World Wildlife Fund, an advisor to the Nature Conservancy organization, a representative of the International Union for the Conservation of Nature, and also worked with the Oceanic Foundation. *The New York Times* reported in 1969, "Beyond these organizational affiliations, he pursues conservation as a private person making use of a worldwide network of friendships that he has amassed in a lifetime of aviation. This network includes political leaders, business executives, and men of science."[1247]

Thanks to his environmental passion, the "Lone Eagle" became an international star for the fledgling green movement of the 1960s. Lindbergh played a very significant role in developing the green movement into a global phenomenon. Yet Lindbergh's outspoken views on National Socialism and his later worship of all things environmental are by no means inconsistent with each other. It is no coincidence that his willingness to speak out publicly about white racism, eugenics, excessive Jewish influences over society and isolationism to keep America out of World War II would later yield to vigorous environmental campaigning in the late 1960s.

Lindbergh held onto his racist beliefs throughout his life. In the 1950s and '60s, he secretly sired three different families through three different German women in addition to his American wife. "The man so determined that the genes of the white race must be preserved had in the end, perhaps, found a way to contribute to the cause."[1248] Could it be that he was doing his part to recover Aryanism because of all that had happened to Nazi Germany in World War II? Indeed, Lindbergh was very upset with the Nuremberg trial proceedings, and his first German romantic encounter began in 1957 just outside the famous *Feldherrenhalle* in Munich. This is the very location of the infamous Beer Hall Putsch confrontation of 1923 between Nazi revolutionaries and the Bavarian State Police that ended in Adolf Hitler's arrest. Lindbergh's family members were shocked when his secret affairs and children were revealed—especially because two of the lovers were physically disabled. This cut against the grain of Lindbergh's otherwise strongly held belief in eugenics.

Late in life Lindbergh said, "The primitive developed life. Civilization must be based on life. We should never forget that human life was created

---

[1247] White, Alden, "Lindbergh Traveling Widely as a Conservationist," *The New York Times*, June 23, 1969.

[1248] Rabinowitz, Dorothy, "The Lindbergh Nobody Knew," *The Wall Street Journal*, July 24, 2009.

in and for millions of centuries, was nourished by primitive wildness. We cannot separate ourselves from this ancestral background. It is folly to attempt to do so. I believe that many of the social troubles we face today result from our being already too far removed from our ancestral environment. . . . I think there is nothing more important for modern man than to merge his intellectual knowledge of science with the instinctive wisdom of wildness."[1249] In short, in order for man to cleanse himself, he must root himself in Nature, and make Nature the ethos of his *civilized* life. Such a fascist blending of anthropology, social Darwinism, romanticism, existentialism, environmentalism and science was, of course, the very ideological bread and butter of National Socialism.

As such, for Lindbergh, racial and environmental purity went hand in hand. His increased interest in environmentalism did not deter his interest in preserving the purity of the races. It is also very likely that Lindbergh's introduction to *volkisch* environmentalism took place when he wined, dined and *green jerked* with Hermann Goering at Carinhall. It thus stands to reason that Charles Lindbergh was an environmental fascist dating back to the 1930s. Consistent with some modern green Neo-Nazis, his strong interest in preserving black indigenous tribes was probably due to the fact he did not wish them to mix with other races. They should keep to themselves in their own bioregion. Preservation of the races in their indigenous homeland and environmentalism were undoubtedly intertwined in Lindbergh's worldview.

Nazi biologist Walther Schoenichen himself clearly advertised his great concern for the indigenous when he said, "Indeed, the enslavement of primitive peoples in the cultural history of the *white race* constitutes one of its most shameful chapters, which is not only streaked with rivers of blood, but of cruelty and torture of the worst kind. And its final pages were not written in the distant past, but at the beginning of the 20th century ... the natural policy for National Socialism to follow is clear. The policy of repression and extermination, the models for which are furnished by the early days of America or Australia, are just as unthinkable as the French theory of assimilation. Rather it is appropriate for the natives to flourish in conformity with their own racial stock."[1250] In this quote, Schoenichen clearly distinguishes between the white American conquest of nature and

---

[1249] White, Alden, "Lindbergh Traveling Widely as a Conservationist," *The New York Times*, June 23, 1969.

[1250] Schoenichen quoted in Ferry, p. 105.

National Socialism, notwithstanding the fact the Nazis would later prove to be far more cruel to the Jews and indigenous Poles than the Americans were with the Indians. Thus, contrary to popular opinion, the Nazis sometimes even celebrated the differences between cultures in opposition to global international assimilation.[1251] In sum, when one tries to save the indigenous, he will invariably celebrate the multicultural differences.

Schoenichen's concern for the indigenous is not too far removed from many of the stories that have been presented over the years in *National Geographic* on a monthly basis. Just how different is *National* Socialism from *National* Geographic?[1252] Perhaps not nearly as different as many people would like to presume:

> Like the aesthetics of sentiment and deep ecology, which also place new value on primitive peoples, mountain folk, or American Indians, the National Socialist conception of ecology encompasses the notion that the *Naturvolker*, "the natural peoples" achieve a perfect harmony between their surroundings and their customs. This is even the most certain sign of superiority of their ways over the "liberal" world of uprootedness and perpetual mobility. Their culture, similar to animal ways of life, is a prolongation of nature.[1253]

Nazi racism thus was strongly tied to ecology. They wanted to preserve "the ethnic, cultural and natural milieu of peoples, beginning of course with one's own."[1254] In so doing, the Nazis also believed such a process would lead them to greater evolutionary racial progress in the struggle of all life.

[1251] Ferry, p. 105.

[1252] For an interesting discussion on a similar theme see "Blood or Soil?: The *Volkisch* Movement, the Nazis, and the Legacy of *Geopolitik*," by Mark Bassin in *How Green Were the Nazis?*, pp. 204-242. Mark Bassin shows the different angles that many Nazi *greens* emphasized from their *blood and soil* perspective. According to Bassin, SS *blood and soil* men like Darre emphasized *blood* rather than *soil*. Bassin also suggests that other *green* Nazis like Haushofer emphasized *soil* rather than *blood*. Many *green* Nazis were therefore caught in between both camps, sometimes emphasizing the priority of the German *blood* over the environment, while others emphasized environmental determinism over *blood*. While Bassin makes excellent points and shows yet another layer of environmental nuance among Nazi *green* thinkers, he downplays the word *and* that fits in between *blood* and *soil*. Darre never taught *blood or soil* as two mutually exclusive categories. He taught *blood and soil*.

[1253] Ferry, p. 105.

[1254] Ibid.

Nazi racism was couched in *scientific* social-Darwinian terms mixed in with ecology and indigenous ethnicity. National Socialism's strong interest in preserving the naturally indigenous is one of the primary reasons why it mutated Darwinism into social Darwinism. Although evolution was taught in Nazi Germany, the Nazis were not necessarily strict Darwinists who believed in random evolution through natural selection. The unpredictability of natural selection and the attempt to preserve the original or indigenous are somewhat difficult concepts to reconcile. Nonetheless, the existential concept of *will* was far more important to the Nazis than natural selection. National Socialism's brand of evolutionary theory was thus imbued with a heavy dosage of existential willpower. This is precisely why eugenics and strong state control did not conflict with evolutionary theory in the Nazi mind. Yet the Darwinian survival of the fittest was still the primary paradigm of National Socialism, and the Nazis did believe their racism was based on the progressive evolutionary sciences—yet with an indigenous existentialism inserted into the mix. Such a redirection moves Nazism away from the doctrine of evolution and pushes it back toward German Romanticism. Moreover, in reality, German existentialism is merely a hardened form of German Romanticism. German literature expert J.P. Stern defines existentialism as the final and most extreme form of Romanticism.[1255]

The upshot of steering National Socialism into the camp of Romanticism is that it also shades the Holocaust green. The Nazi *lebensraum* experiment was a racially green socialist campaign to save the indigenous German people. The Jews in particular were sacrificed en masse for this grand *volkisch* cause. As such, nature religion and human sacrifice found a stunning way to reassert itself in the modern civilized world. The Final Solution and ecological *living space* in the eastern territories was in fact a fulfillment of racist passions about indigenous peoples and the environment, both of which came at the expense of Jews and Slavs. This, of course, was all couched in social-Darwinian environmental terms, neither of which can be neatly separated from the other. During the war on the Russian front, the Germans were motivated by a dark green racist philosophy of man and nature. The Nazis used a secular Darwinian nature religion to justify cleansing the East from Jews and Slavs.

As such, to suggest, as some environmental historians often do, that the Nazi war effort trumped ecological concerns, completely misses the whole

---

[1255] Stern, p. 33.

point of what Word War II on the Russian front was all about. Even as the aftermath of the Stalingrad defeat began to sink deeply into the German consciousness against the backdrop of an ominous red menace invading from the east, Josef Goebbels strongly reminded his audience in his *Total War Speech*, "The German nation is fighting for everything it has. We know that the German people are defending their holiest possessions: their families, women and children, the beautiful and untouched countryside, their cities and villages, their two thousand year old culture, everything indeed that makes life worth living."[1256] In other words, in the Nazi mind, defending the fatherland included defending its environmental treasures.

[1256] Bytwerk, p. 122.

"After the war, equally, we must not let control of the economy of the country slip from our hands. If we do, then once more all the various private interests will concentrate on their own particular objectives. The coastal population, for example, from the viewpoint of life as they see it, still regard land reclamation by means of dam construction as the last word in wisdom; in point of fact, however, land reclamation by this method is the purest folly, for we have all the land we need in the East. On the other hand, enrichment of the soil is still most important, and it must not be impeded by the interests of industry. When once we are convinced that slime from the seabed is, on account of higher nitrogen content, a better fertilizer than any artificial manure, we must transport whole trainloads of it, in spite of the protests of our chemical industry. As most people are egoists at heart, any efficient functioning of a national economy is not possible without State direction and control."

Adolf Hitler, July 5, 1942 midday

CHAPTER SEVEN:

ENVIRONMENTAL HISTORIANS & THEIR ENVIRONMENTAL CORRECTNESS

In 2000, a swastika made of larch trees, 200 feet in diameter, was cut down in a German forest 60 miles north of Berlin near Brandenburg. Larch trees are very unique among coniferous trees. In the autumn, their needles turn a stunning gold and fall to the ground like deciduous trees. The Brandenburg larch trees distinguished themselves from the evergreen forest around them every autumn turning into a golden swastika visible only from the air. The trees were likely planted in the 1930s as a sign of environmental collectivist solidarity with the Nazi Party. "It was seen as a modest tribute to the *Fuhrer* every time he flew over the woodland of Brandenburg."[1257] These larch trees were not *discovered* until after the fall of the Berlin Wall in 1992. They were finally cut down.

In a very similar way, green historians seem to be trying to figuratively cut down the environmental trees planted by the Nazis to cleanse themselves from such sordid connections. Green historians, very sensitive to the convergence between Nazism and environmentalism, and very sympathetic to their own cause, have been quick to point out the divergences between themselves and the Nazis wherever they can be found. Environmental historians often present many distinctions which are trivial, while ignoring many greater similarities.

Thus, the whiff of environmental correctness can be sensed when one reads much of the recent material on the subject. In the process, green historians make a valiant attempt to cleanse the environmental historical record of any real Nazi connections much like those foresters who cut down the

---

1257 Boyes, Roger, "Polish Village Mayor is Determined Hitler Birthday Oak Will Not Last 1,000 Years," *Times Online*, July 8, 2009.

golden swastika of larch trees. In some cases, environmental authors go so far as to deny any collusion between Nazism and environmentalism.

One group of green historians smartly put together an anthology of the various Nazi environmental policies and practices, and placed a picture of the golden swastika of larch trees on its cover entitled, *How Green Were the Nazis?* The picture of the golden swastika in the midst of green trees is perfectly consistent with the theme of the book—that while the Nazis did adopt many green policies within their political agenda, their environmental inconsistencies and polycentric infighting show that they were not as green as they might have sometimes trumpeted themselves to be. Green historians eloquently argue that since German environmentalism existed both before and after the Nazi period, there is no inherent connection to National Socialism.

Dr. Anna Bramwell: The Origins of the Green Nazi Debate

Dr. Anna Bramwell of Britain is a self-proclaimed environmental sympathizer, but she began to openly talk about the Nazi connections to the ecology movement in the early to mid-1980s. In 1985 she published *Blood and Soil: Walther Darre and Hitler's Green Party*. The basic gist of her controversial work was that Richard Walther Darre was a green nationalist dove in the SS who was later sidelined by the Nazi hierarchy for his *back to the land* utopianism. The great problem with her work is it is very difficult to believe Darre was some kind of green dove inside the SS. Nonetheless, Darre was never convicted as an outright war criminal like other leading Nazis. The Nuremberg trials found Darre guilty of racial callousness with regard to food rationing schemes, plunder and spoliation in Poland.[1258] Darre's defense attorney, Hans Merkel, was not only an organic farming enthusiast, but also a specialist in the SS agrarian law that was passed as a part of the *back to the land* movement. Merkel had been with Darre since 1934. Merkel was one of the key influencers that turned Darre into an organic farming convert. Merkel "published widely on farming policy and wrote regularly for Darre's blood and soil journal *Odal*, combining organic metaphors with calls for expanded German *Lebensraum*."[1259]

[1258] Bramwell, *Blood and Soil: Walther Darre and Hitler's Green Party*, pp. 184-193.
[1259] Staudenmaier & Biehl, p. 112.

More troubling, however, Bramwell "consistently downplays the virulently fascist elements in his thinking, portraying him instead as a misguided agrarian radical. This grave error of judgment indicates the powerfully disorientating pull of an ecological aura."[1260] Indeed, according to Reich historians Roger Manvell and Heinrich Fraenkel, it was Darre who "finally convinced Hitler and Himmler that the Jewish and Slav peoples, in particular, had to be purged from the Germanic lands which the Nazi regime came to dominate between 1938 and 1944. They saw no solution as they moved east but genocide of those whom they regarded as racially inferior or degenerate."[1261] This has been further corroborated by recently released archived materials. In 1936, Darre gave a speech where he stated that Germany will settle as far east as the Urals bordered on the south by the Caucasus Mountains, the Caspian and Black Seas respectively, and all the way to the Baltic Sea in the north.[1262]

There were other characters within the Nazi Party who were just as green, and in many ways, far greener than Darre, who would have made Bramwell's case much stronger. However, Bramwell chose Darre because of his self-proclaimed dovish attitudes during the Nuremberg trials. She thus portrayed him as an anti-Hitler of sorts. If Darre was both green and dovish, it would make the connections between Nazi greens and modern greens far less troublesome. Greens could also take some solace in the fact that Darre was later dismissed by Hitler. However, Bramwell was also forced to distinguish Darre from Himmler as the proverbial good Nazi even though she acknowledged Darre was Himmler's teacher. Manvell and Fraenkel called Darre Himmler's "friend and advisor."[1263] Yet, Bramwell claims that Himmler carried out many of Darre's plans "in a perverted form in later years."[1264] Regardless, both men were SS leaders and they both shared the same Haeckelian Monist background from the nature-orientated youth groups of their past. This complicated scheme in and of itself actually shows the depths of the issues involved when it comes to the green Nazi connection.[1265]

[1260] Ibid., pp. 33-34.

[1261] Manvell and Fraenkel, p. 34.

[1262] Tooze, p. 198.

[1263] Manvell and Fraenkel, p. 34.

[1264] Bramwell, *Blood and Soil: Walther Darre and Hitler's Green Party*, p. 90.

[1265] See especially William Walter Kay's "Review of Bramwell's Hidden History of Environmentalism," on his website found at www.ecofascism.com.

More importantly, Bramwell purposefully chose Darre because she believed his agrarian radicalism represents more authentic green thinking than many modern greens whose environmental "prescriptions are as often unrelated to environmental issues as they are draconian."[1266] So, she wanted to promote Darre's agrarian radicalism as something positive. In order to do this, however, she had to cleanse the rural-based green thinking of Darre from outright connections to Nazism as much as possible. She accomplished this by not only juxtaposing Darre's utopian plans with that of Hitler's, but she also dragged environmentalism into the Nazi debate precisely because she wanted to discredit certain aspects of the modern green movement. Bramwell's biography on Darre is thus a very complex thesis as she points out, "Darre disassociated himself from the 'Nature-before-man' arguments of the extreme ecologists. His emphasis on the essential artificiality of human life, the need to direct nature, parallels his belief in the need to protect man."[1267] In effect, what Bramwell manages to do is relive the same arguments Darre had with his more radical Nazi ecological friends in the 1930s. As such, her work has often been met with what she calls vituperation.[1268]

Blowback Against Bramwell's Perspective on the Green Nazis

The fallout from Bramwell's writings is it opened up a hornet's nest amidst a certain group of environmental historians, however localized it may have been. In fact, it has taken environmental historians almost 20 years to get on top of the debate.[1269] Now, finally, environmental historians have published various books which have largely defended the early German green movement from Nazi contamination. This publishing spree was a result of a 2002 symposium on the subject sponsored by the German minister for the environment, Jurgin Trittin:

1266 Bramwell, *Blood and Soil: Walther Darre and Hitler's Green Party*, p. 200.
1267 Ibid., p. 174.
1268 Bramwell, *Ecology in the 20ʰ Century: A History*, p. 96.
1269 Environmental historian Raymond Dominick gave an early rebuttal to Bramwell in 1992, "The argument developed here has tried to reduce the damage done to the reputation of the conservation campaign by its highly visible ties to Nazism. Nevertheless, it remains true that Germany's conservation movement sustained a heavy blow from those associations," p. 115.

... the German minister for the environment, Jurgen Trittin, pushed aggressively for a conference on the topic, a remarkable move given the fact that public interest in the Nazi past of conservation was almost nonexistent ... the result was a symposium on "Conservation in Nazi Germany," which took place in July 2002. The first conference of its kind, it attracted a surprisingly large number of participants, along with intensive coverage by the media, demonstrating that the issue was clearly more than an academic topic.[1270]

Trittin's symposium was an interesting move since many greens had long before dismissed the environmental policies of the Nazi era as largely trivial and irrelevant.[1271] Environmentalists "would have liked to ignore this past, but that turned out to be difficult: history kept coming back to haunt them. However, instead of trying to face up to its own responsibility, the conservation movement developed a set of ideas and attitudes that, though highly dubious from a historical standpoint, managed to quell the nascent discussion within a matter of years. Briefly the argument was that conservation was not a political issue and that the national conservation law of 1935 had only coincidentally been passed under the Nazi regime—thus there was no further need for soul-searching."[1272] As such, many smart greens, including the German environmental minister Jurgen Trittin himself, knew such a course of denial would ultimately be counterproductive. The results of this symposium would therefore take the German green connections to the Nazis much more seriously than before. They would admit and confess the collusion between them, but also find ways to distance them from National Socialism.

With no small interest, even though Dr. Anna Bramwell's work has been roundly and routinely discredited by environmental historians, she laid down a strategy on how to rescue Darre's radical green agrarianism from the Nazis as early as 1989. While environmental historians dismiss all too quickly Darre's SS *back to the land* movement as being something authentically ecological—though it was perhaps the most radical attempt in Germany's history to transform the countryside into a green *volkisch* mecca— in a most subtle move, they took note of Bramwell's general methodology

---

1270 Uekoetter, p. ix.
1271 Bramwell, *Ecology in the 20ʰ Century: A History*, p. 197.
1272 Uekoetter, p. 14.

laid out in her second book, entitled *Ecology in the 20ʰ Century: A History*, to save other Nazi environmentalists from National Socialism. This damage control plan to disassociate the German green movement from Nazism was clearly spelled out by Bramwell in 1989 when she wrote the following:

> Given that ecological ideas in Germany did not begin with the Nazis, would their proponents have come to power in any case under a non-Nazi government? Would their policies have been made law? Was a radical revolutionary government necessary for the activists to attain office? ... Again, how far was their continuity of ideas and personnel with the past, or should all legislation and activity under the Third Reich be seen as manifestations of Nazism? Another problem is how important the various ecological legislation and activities were in terms of the overall program. So far, they have been dismissed as trivial and irrelevant. Was this true, or was this dismissal because academics did not want to draw comparisons with today's green ideas? Has there been a paradigm shift? How far did the Nazis implement their ecological policies? These are questions which are not always posed in the discussions of ideology and practices, but they are important, and all discussions on this issue need to take account of methodological difficulties, which will be borne in mind as the account continues.[1273]

It is ironic Bramwell's basic approach to slacken the green Nazi connections was later used by the same environmental historians who criticized her work. The environmental historians just applied this same strategy to the German green movement in general, but not with regard to Darre himself. Thus Bramwell's general historical method was used, but was given a different application to a different cast of green Nazi historical figures and actions.

As such, since that time, green historians have taken the lead with a growing number of books coming out on this most troubling episode of environmental history. Much the same way Bramwell talked about Darre in isolation from uniforms and swastikas,[1274] so too environmental historians have followed suit. They found ways to place distance between the Nazis

---

1273   Bramwell, *Ecology in the 20ʰ Century: A History*, pp. 196-97.
1274   Bramwell, *Blood and Soil: Walther Darre and Hitler's Green Party*, p. 12.

and the environmentalists, and minimized the convergences wherever convenient. In so doing, they managed to relativize the green connections to the Nazis by dispelling "the notion that there is a clear-cut, black-and-white approach to Nazi-era conservationism."[1275]

This is the basic methodology of the book entitled *How Green Were the Nazis?* This book is an anthology written by various environmental historians. They systematically deal with many aspects of Nazi environmentalism, everything from the Reich Nature Protection Law of 1935, their forestry practices, their air pollution laws, their agricultural practices, the *blood and soil* doctrine, construction on the Autobahn and even Martin Heidegger's foray into Nazism.

The book concludes by discussing the environmental landscape planners' involvement in the Holocaust. It is the only chapter where all possible defenses of the environmental cause in Nazi Germany are conspicuously missing. This chapter on landscape cleansing is also the shortest chapter of the book even though it is discussing the darkest episode in all of environmental history. Worst of all, although "these racist landscape planners really came into their own during the Nazi years, they did not suddenly disappear with death of Hitler in 1945. Wiepking-Jurgensmann, Meyer, Wickop, and many others continued their careers as professors and consultants. A genuine de-Nazification of landscape architecture never really took place."[1276]

In fact, toward the end of the war, Nazi spatial and environmental planners destroyed massive quantities of records.[1277] They then reorganized themselves into the "Academy for Area Research and Regional Planning" and the "Institute for Spatial Planning."[1278] Although Karl Haushofer committed suicide in 1946, Konrad Meyer survived Nuremberg and later continued his work in spatial planning and sustainable development. Another key SS spatial planner, Walter Christaller, joined the Communist Party in 1951.[1279] His Central Place Theory on regional and urban planning largely developed under the auspices of the Nazi regime is sometimes even considered a model for sustainable development and the

---

[1275] Zeller, *How Green Were the Nazis?*, p. 14.

[1276] Wolschke-Buhlman, "Violence as a Basis of National Socialist Landscape Planning," in *How Green Were the Nazis?*, p. 253.

[1277] *Science, Technology and National Socialism*, p. 136.

[1278] Ibid.

[1279] Frantzman, Zeth, "Hitler's Geographer: Walter Christaller and Nazi Academics," *The Jerusalem Post*, August 27, 2010.

so-called Green Economy. As such, after the war, social engineering based on Aryan biology was replaced with a blander form of socialism, but its ties to environmentalism and sustainable development continued unabated and grew exponentially in the decades to come.[1280] German environmental spatial planners thus played an early critical role in the promotion of the European Union's green sustainable development policies.

One glaring weakness of *How Green Were the Nazis?* is it never bothers to define what *green* is. Yet the overall argument of the book suggests the Nazis were not all that green. In the first chapter, author Charles Closmann focuses on the Reich Nature Protection legislation (RNG) of 1935. He is the only historian in the book who takes seriously the notion that the RNG was "indeed a green law in the sense that it echoed progressive ideas about nature preservation and landscape protection from the standpoint of the 1930's. The RNG also reflected key elements of the National Socialist worldview when one takes into account the broader ideological context in which German officials drafted this law."[1281] While Closmann does say that one cannot glibly equate Nazi environmental goals with the greens today,[1282] he seems to suggest that those historians who take issue with the possibility that the Nazis were green do so because they are interpreting the environmental history of National Socialism from their own much more modern point of view. In the chapter entitled, "Eternal Forest—Eternal *Volk*," Michael Imort concedes, "While German nature conservancy may have been at the mercy of the Nazi state, it should not be overlooked that the Reich Nature Protection Law helped slow the deterioration of overall ecological conditions in Germany. In terms of its ecological legacy, the law provided for measures toward the *in situ* protection of plant and animal species, in effect amounting to an early form of habitat protection."[1283]

The Nazi Party was in control of Germany for only 12 years, half of which involved the biggest war in human history, which certainly compromised National Socialism's environmental legacy. However, it is also true the Nazis would have turned their newly acquired *lebensraum* into a green utopian state of sustainable development for Germans. However, during

---

[1280] See "Green Lebensraum: The Nazi Roots of Sustainable Development" by Mark Musser, *The American Thinker*, Jan. 27, 2012.

[1281] Closmann, "Legalizing a Volksgemeinschaft" in *How Green Were the Nazis?*, pp. 20-21.

[1282] Ibid., p. 21.

[1283] Imort, Michael, "Eternal Forest – Eternal Volk: The Rhetoric and Reality of National Socialist Forest Policy," in *How Green Were the Nazis?*, p. 62.

wartime, many high ideals must be sacrificed until after the shooting stops. Environmental historians ignore this reality as something unimportant. They are very unforgiving in their attitudes toward the Nazis and hold them to the strictest of standards, something which they have failed to do with their own modern compatriots. One of the authors in the book concluded, "Nazi agriculture and environmental policies cannot simply be called green."[1284] Here he admits the Nazis were green, but not *simply green*. Does this mean they were complexly green?

Boria Sax, a self-proclaimed animal lover, wrote *Animals in the Third Reich: Pets, Scapegoats, and the Holocaust* in 2000 (updated and re-published in 2013). This book is often brutally honest about the environmental emphasis of the Nazis. While Sax accepts the green streak of National Socialism as fact, he does strongly point out how much animals did suffer under Nazi authority in spite of their animal protection laws, largely because of the war. However, Sax's acceptance of the fact of Nazi environmentalism does not mean for him that green ideas should therefore be rejected. On the contrary, "The example of the Nazis should not, therefore, turn us against animal welfare."[1285] He goes on to say that not everything the Nazis did was completely evil, and that Nazi crimes do not "discredit regard for the natural world. We should admit that the Nazis, whatever their motives, were right in much of their humane legislation."[1286] In other words, Nazi environmentalism was good, but their crimes were not. This is exactly the same view that Albert Speer maintains.[1287]

In the book called *The Green and the Brown*, German environmental historian Frank Uekoetter admits his "book is the product of an intellectual journey that had far more resemblance to a roller-coaster ride than I, or anyone, could have imagined when I came to the topic in 2001."[1288] Uekoetter thus acknowledges that his damage control effort was a very rocky one at best. Even with all the historical examples he manages to scrape up from what is left of the Nazi archives, Uekoetter acknowledges, "Seeing a cause

---

[1284] Gerhard, Gesine, "Breeding Pigs and People for the Third Reich," in *How Green Were the Nazis?*, p. 138.

[1285] Sax, p. 164.

[1286] Ibid., p. 165.

[1287] Speer, *Spandau: The Secret Diaries*, p. 399.

[1288] Uekoetter, p. ix.

dear to one's heart aligned with such a regime is painful, and many readers will have read this book with a sentiment of 'never again.'"[1289]

The sentiment, "never again," demonstrates beyond a shadow of a doubt that environmental history does have a blemish on its record, and a rather ignominious one at that. Moreover, what Uekoetter wrote for the sake of damage control can also be easily seen as a case of *friendly fire*:

> Culture wars like real wars have direct hits, collateral damage, and friendly fire. Professor Uekoetter's *The Green and the Brown: a History of Conservation in Nazi Germany* is an example of friendly fire. The book was written to contain damage caused by growing awareness that Nazism is the forbearer of German environmentalism but it is yet another trove of facts affirming the Nazi-environmentalist connection. German conservationism, and its attendant tendencies and sentiments, was not a distinct social movement separable from German fascism. Parallel to the Gestapo's nightmarish dragnet ran a green reign of terror of intrusive eco-activism.[1290]

While, of course, one must be "wary of the kind of demagogy that invokes the horrors of Nazism to disqualify any ecological concern *a priori*,"[1291] it is also true the connection between Nazism and environmentalism must not be denied to the point that one is prevented from considering its significance.[1292] Bramwell calls attention to the fact it is not necessary to "strain at gnats to show that there was a strain of ecological ideas among the Nazis: the evidence is ample."[1293] A whole series of books are now available on the subject. One of the contributors of the Nazi conservationist symposium in Germany sarcastically remarked, "A conference on conservationism and Stalinism would certainly be much shorter than this one."[1294] Indeed.

The National Socialists were well represented by the greens of the day. To say that such an environmental entourage, however disparate they may

---

[1289] Ibid., p. 202.

[1290] Kay, William Walter, "The Nazi-Enviro Connection: Uekoetter's Green and Brown" written in 2009 found on ecofascism.com.

[1291] Ferry, p. 92.

[1292] Ibid., p. 93.

[1293] Bramwell, *Ecology in the 20ʰ Century: A History*, p. 195.

[1294] Blackbourn, David, "'Die Natur als historisch zu etablieren.' Natur, Heimat und Land-schaft in der modernen deutschen Geshichte," in Radkau and Uekoetter, *Naturschutz und Nationalsozialismus*; quoted in Uekoetter, *The Green and the Brown*, p. 8.

have been at times, only played a minor role in the Third Reich, would be an understatement. One historian even went so far to say that the Nazis were the first "radical environmentalists in charge of a state."[1295] Bramwell said there was a loose green party among the Nazis.[1296] Others such as Dr. Peter Staudenmaier are more comfortable in saying that the Nazis had a green wing in their party,[1297] "The green 'wing' of the Nazis represents the historical fulfillment of the dreams of reactionary ecology: eco-fascism in power."[1298]

Staudenmaier himself has spent much time in studying the Nazi "back to the land" movement and its historical ancestry. Staudenmaier strongly asserts, "Nothing could be more wrong than to suppose that most of the leading National Socialist ideologues had cynically feigned an agrarian romanticism and hostility to urban culture, without any inner conviction and for merely electoral and propaganda purposes, in order to hoodwink the public."[1299] While Staudenmaier himself is an environmentalist and a fan of organicism, he has been dogged in reminding his fellow greens of the dangers posed by eco-fascism:

> … too many of the recent contributions to this ongoing debate are oriented toward debunking the notion that authentic ecological elements played a significant role in the Nazi regime. I consider this approach a mistake. Much of Nazism based both its destructive and its constructive aspects on a specifically naturalist vision, one that bore compelling and substantive parallels to ecological values, and these similarities were reflected in an expansive spectrum of institutions and practices. Minimizing Nazism's especially disturbing and unanticipated features does not relieve the burden for ecological activists today but conceals the continuities between some of the twentieth century's most cherished ideals and some of its most shameful crimes. Neglecting the "green" features of

---

1295 Hauner, M. "A German Racial Revolution?" *Journal of Contemporary History*, 1984, p. 685, n.46; quoted in Bramwell, *Ecology in the 20th Century: A History*, p. 11.

1296 See Bramwell, *Blood and Soil, R. Walther Darre and Hitler's Green Party.*

1297 Staudenmaier & Biehl, p. 34. See also Jost Hermand, *Grune Utopien in Deutschland: Zur Geschichte, des okologishcen BewuBstseins.*

1298 Staudenmaier, Peter, "Anthroposophy and Ecofascism."

1299 Bergmann, *Agrarromantik and GroBstadtfeindschaft*, p. 334; quoted in Staudenmaier & Biehl, p. 30.

Nazism is a deceptive way of shielding ourselves from what is most unsettling about the history of the topic.[1300]

Staudenmaier then sharply points out, "The close proximity—ideological as well as geographic—between Nazi programs for ecological renewal and Nazi programs for racial extermination suggests that further attention to this unlikely conjunction is called for."[1301]

Staudenmaier himself is a self-proclaimed anarchist. He therefore may be opposed to big government environmental authoritarianism. Yet he concludes his book by saying, "I remain a social ecologist fully committed to a thoroughgoing transformation of society and of human relations with the natural world."[1302] How a thoroughgoing transformation of society can be accomplished without big government authoritarianism is itself another fantasy of some greens who consider themselves independent and libertarian.

Michael Zimmerman, a deep ecologist, talks about Nazi eco-fascism as one aspect of the environmental historical record of which modern greens need to be wary:[1303] "Unhappily, National Socialism was in some respects a green movement."[1304] Raymond Dominick narrows the green association with National Socialism to the *volkisch* variety of nature conservation.[1305] In spite of all this testimony, all coming from those sympathetic to the environmental cause, some environmental apologists outright deny that there is any association between Nazism and being green.[1306]

In *Imagining the Nation in Nature: Landscape Preservation and German Identity 1885-1945*, Thomas Lekan takes issue with Jeffrey Herf's reactionary modernism thesis as being too simplistic or monocausal.[1307] As such, Lekan drives a wedge between preservationists on the one hand and technocratic environmental planners on the other hand. He characterizes the preservationists of the Third Reich as the true heirs of Romanticism. The Nazi environmental planners, represented best by SS Nazis Alwin Seifert

---

[1300] Staudenmaier & Biehl, p. 128.
[1301] Ibid., p. 125.
[1302] Ibid., p. 132.
[1303] Zimmerman, Michael, "Ecofascism: An Enduring Temptation."
[1304] Zimmerman, Michael, "Possible Political Problems of Earth Based Religiosity."
[1305] Dominick, p. 114.
[1306] Guha, Ramachandra. *Environmentalism: A Global History*, p. 19; quoted in *How Green Were the Nazis?*, p. 2.
[1307] Lekan, p. 224.

and Konrad Meyer, are depicted as racialists and progressive innovators. To Lekan, environmental planners like Seifert *construct* nature artificially in order to rejuvenate the landscape rather than try to preserve it as true Romantics desire.[1308] Lekan then points out how such technocratic environmental planners eclipsed the preservationists in terms of power, prestige and authority, leaving them very disappointed and frustrated as they were constantly ignored. With such a long-winded and extremely nuanced discussion, Lekan manages to convert Seifert into a modernizer,[1309] even though those who worked closest with him considered him to be a fanatical ecologist. Seifert clearly thought of himself to be on the Romantic side of the spectrum with his love for holism and his continual denigration of the mechanistic sciences of the Enlightenment.

Lekan also exaggerates the juxtaposition between strict preservationists and other greens attracted to environmental restoration, green engineering, sustainable development and racism, as if the latter categories are really not a part of Romanticism. He thus conveniently tries to suggest that social Darwinism, racism and Romanticism are inconsistent with each other. In order to spare the green movement the charge of proto-fascism,[1310] Lekan strains to separate Romanticism from racist environmentalism by suggesting that green Nazis like Schoenichen, Schultze-Naumburg, Seifert and Meyer were actually artificially constructing and racializing the landscape through technocratic means rather than preserving it.[1311] However, such a convoluted storyline is, in reality, a reflection of just how deeply entrenched the early German green movement really was in the Third Reich. Such distinctions between preservationists and environmental planners only demonstrate the Nazi green movement was far from monolithic. It suffered from its own polycratic infighting and complexities, something which Lekan himself even admits: "What is clear, however, is that German environmentalism has had a variety of cultural meanings and political implications that complicate progressivist accounts of the rise of ecological consciousness in modern industrial societies."[1312] This is an understatement.

The very word *ecology* itself was not only born in the racist social Darwinism of Ernst Haeckel's evolutionary biology, but also rooted in the *volkisch*

[1308] Ibid., pp. 232-247.
[1309] Ibid., p. 224.
[1310] Ibid., p. 262.
[1311] Ibid., pp. 156-168, 232-247.
[1312] Ibid., p. 263.

Romanticism of Goethe, Arndt, Humboldt and Riehl. Indeed, German literature expert J.P. Stern reminds his readers, "The Romantics had preached the unity of science and poetic inspiration: at the turn of the century the doctrines of race and of Social Darwinism derive their authority in equal measure from their 'scientific' pretensions and from their claims to be a true reflection of the processes of Nature herself. This is the era of Hitler's formative years in Vienna."[1313] It was only after the disastrous fallout of World War II that German Romanticism dropped its *volkisch* racism in favor of a more modernized form of international environmentalism. Staudenmaier points out, "The notion of a clear separation between environmental tendencies on the one hand and ruralism and racial ideology on the other hand is a post-1945 imposition, a projection of current values onto the past. From the Wilhelmine era through the Nazi period, these phenomena combined in various amalgamations of rural romanticism, racial utopias, back-to-the-land ideals and proto-ecological sentiments."[1314]

An excellent case in point is German environmentalist Dr. Erich Hornsmann (1909-1999). In 1947, Hornsmann became a founding member of the Protection of German Forests. In 1955, he wrote *The Forest: The Foundation of our Existence*. He warned of spreading desertification problems associated with the cutting down of trees and expanding ski resorts on mountain slopes. Dr. Hornsmann even led the post-war charge on promoting radical water conservation measures. Hornsmann belonged to the Alliance for the Protection of German Waters and wrote extensively on how water was becoming an increasingly scarce commodity.[1315] Hornsmann applied Malthusian math to the waters of Germany. He was convinced water consumption would outstrip water supplies as personal usage of it skyrocketed with ever-increasing showers and baths. Industry itself wasted more water than entire cities combined.

Hornsmann also wrote an apocalyptic environmental book entitled, *Otherwise Collapse: The Answer of the Earth to the Abuse of Her Laws*. To counteract the environmental catastrophe looming just around the corner, Hornsmann was convinced that "comprehensive land use planning was imperative."[1316] He was also one of the first greens to emphasize that environmental calamities were of far bigger concerns than those of even national security.

1313 Stern, pp. 39-40.
1314 Staudenmaier & Biehl, p. 114.
1315 Dominick, p. 142.
1316 Ibid., p. 150.

The destruction of Mother Nature was "Enemy Number One."[1317] Yet such an exemplary German environmentalist sent a postcard to a relative in America on Hitler's 50th birthday stating, "We think of you sincerely on a great Day! We must pity, however, 'God's own country' as long as it is ruled and exploited by Jews and their servants."[1318]

In the excellent read called *The Conquest of Nature: Water, Landscape, and the Making of Modern Germany*, historian David Blackbourn reduces Nazi ecology to questions of race and land reclamation with inconsistent environmental policies and practices fluctuating in the background.[1319] Blackbourn argues the Nazis continued the mastery over nature in spite of some interest in environmentalism. However, this is a very shallow argument. No one, not even the modern greens, can escape the mastery over nature.[1320] In the very act of saving nature, greens demonstrate their own control over it. Romanticism is by definition an illusory dream completely inconsistent with reality. The conquest of nature is in fact a Divine mandate that has been embedded into the constitution of man and into the structures of creation itself. More to the point, that the Nazis continued the mastery of nature has far more to do with the fact that they acted inconsistent with their ideology. They simply were not able to act any other way. Hitler routinely criticized the modern world for trying to conquer Nature, but could not avoid practicing it himself.

Environmental historian Frank Uekoetter simply gives the Nazis mixed reviews.[1321] He claims that since there was so much polycentric infighting among Nazi Party officials, one cannot conclude there was something which can be called a "green wing" of the Nazi Party.[1322] Uekoetter condemns the fascistic opportunism the greens used to gain a much stronger foothold in Germany during the Nazi era, but he does not charge them with outright

---

[1317] Ibid.

[1318] This postcard was sent to a relative in Bloomington, NJ.

[1319] See Blackbourn, pp. 251-303.

[1320] In *Changes in the Land* environmental historian William Cronon asserts, "It is tempting to believe that when the Europeans arrived in the New World they confronted Virgin Land, the Forest Primeval, a wilderness which had existed for eons uninfluenced by human hands. Nothing could be further from the truth. . . . All human groups consciously change their environments to some extent—one might even argue that this, in combination with language, is the crucial trait distinguishing people from other animals. . . ." pp. 12-13.

[1321] Uekoetter analyzes four case studies on Nazi conservationist projects, pp. 83-136.

[1322] Ibid., p. 203.

fascism.[1323] The true fascists are the *brown*, not the *green*. Hence the title of his book:

> The title of the book is "The Green and the Brown." Of course, this title is misleading in a way: the "green" and the "brown" were not two camps at a distance ... but two groups that shared many convictions and came to work together to a stunning extent. The green were brown to some extent—all too many of them. The story that emerges is a complicated one, with many facets that defy a simple narrative or a clear cut explanation. It is a story of ideological convergence, of tactical alliance, of simple careerism, of implication in crimes against humanity, and of deceit and denial after 1945. It is a story that many environmentalists will find disturbing. This is what makes it important.[1324]

Uekoetter asserts his own bias in this particular quote when he says the conservationists of the Nazi era were too *brown* and therefore not *green* enough, almost as if someone who is truly *green* could not have possibly acted in the way the Nazis did. Uekoetter rationalizes that since the environmental historical record of the Nazis is a very complex one, the greens should not be judged too harshly. They were never able to form an independent green party of their own during the Nazi era:

> All in all, it is clear that the German conservation community never merged into a forceful alliance during the Nazi era. Instead, it was a rather chaotic set of actors with three centers of gravity: the Landscape Advocates under Alwin Seifert's charismatic leadership, a second group of landscape planners around Heinrich Wiepking-Jurgensmann, and the Reich Conservation Agency under Schoenichen and Klose, with its vast network of conservation advisors in all parts of Germany.[1325]

No matter how complicated and chaotic the relationships may have been, the Nazis had a sizable group of green adherents within their own

---

[1323] Ibid., p. 16.
[1324] Ibid.
[1325] Ibid., p. 81.

ranks. Even today, environmental thinkers are all over the map. They represent a whole host of different ideas, practices and emphases, which often come into conflict with each other. The environmental movement is far from monolithic today, let alone in Nazi Germany. How this fact shows the Nazis were not very green simply does not add up. Even the church is made up of all kinds of different groups, denominations and cliques, yet they still are all called Christians. What Uekoetter claims is since there was no independent green political party within the ranks of National Socialism, the environmentalists of that day really cannot be judged on their own merits. This is not much of a protective screen.

Summarizing the Green Nazi Controversy

The prevailing shifting winds of analyzing the ideological roots of National Socialism perhaps began with Daniel Gasman's controversial work called *The Scientific Origins of National Socialism* (1971). Gasman's motivation for writing his book was to defend "Charles Darwin and the theory of evolution that he pioneered."[1326] Since National Socialism promoted social Darwinism and emphasized the evolutionary struggle for existence, Gasman wanted to prevent Darwin's theory from being smeared with Nazi blood. Whether or not Gasman was successful in his goal is open to much debate,[1327] but he blamed Germany's interpreter of Darwin, Ernst Haeckel, for promoting an Aryan Social Darwinism that distorted evolutionary theory. In other words, it was Ernst Haeckel who was the true proto-Nazi, not Darwin. While Nazi press chief Otto Dietrich simply stated that Hitler's views on natural selection and survival of the fittest came from both Darwin and Haeckel,[1328] Gasman managed to shift some of the blame away from Darwin onto Haeckel's Romantic philosophy of science and nature called Monism, i.e., social Darwinism: "Central to my argument was the conviction that Haeckel and his theories represented a fundamental distortion of the Darwinian tradition and humanistic science in general, and that this led to dire intellectual, scientific, and political consequences."[1329]

[1326] Gasman, Daniel. *Haeckel's Monism and the Birth of Fascist Ideology.* New York: Peter Lang Publishing, 2008 (1998), p. ix.

[1327] Weikart, *From Darwin to Hitler*, pp. 216-17.

[1328] Dietrich, p. 126.

[1329] Gasman, Daniel. *Haeckel's Monism and the Birth of Fascist Ideology*, pp. ix-x.

However, although it is true Darwin himself has the reputation of being called the dismal scientist, i.e., the man who looks only at scientific explanations, he never divorced himself from the Romanticism that heavily influenced his own thinking.[1330] Nature was at the heart of Darwin's thought just as much as any other Romantic philosopher of the 1800s. Regardless, by shifting blame onto Haeckel's Romanticism, Gasman opens up an ecological can of worms perhaps more controversial than the Nazi-Darwin connection itself. In order to save Darwin's evolutionary theory, Gasman unwittingly implicates the early German green movement instead. Haeckel was not only the father of German social Darwinism, but also of German ecology. Gasman thus exchanges one controversial Nazi connection for another that is potentially even more flammable than the first. In fact, it was Gasman who took note that Himmler, Darre and Hoess, all SS men, were all involved in the *Artamanen* movement. The *Artamanens* were an outgrowth of Haeckel's biologically based ecology.[1331] The *Artamanens* were a part of the German green *wandervogel* movement of the early 1900s.

Others, like Anna Bramwell, began to take notice of such connections, especially after it was revealed by the media in the early 1980s that major players in the founding of the German Green Party were former Nazis. Bramwell spent the entire decade of the 1980s researching the green connections to Nazism. She wrote two books—*Blood and Soil: Walther Darre and Hitler's Green Party* in 1985 and then *Ecology in the 20ᵗʰ Century* in 1989. In *Ecology in the 20ᵗʰ Century*, Bramwell takes a few swipes at Gasman. Bramwell was specifically interested in protecting Darre's green agrarian views from being hopelessly contaminated with the Nazi flag. While readily acknowledging Haeckel's influence on Darre,[1332] Bramwell disassociates Haeckel from Hitler.[1333]

In between Bramwell's two books was a work written by Robert Pois called *National Socialism and the Religion of Nature*. For the most part, Pois left the Darwinian debate alone, but still confirmed and strengthened Gasman's view that the Nazis had incorporated a secular religion of nature as the basis for their *Weltanschauung*. Pois can be credited with relating National Socialism to a form of nature worship that in some respects was independent of Darwinian evolutionary theory. His book emphasizes the religious and

---

[1330] Worster, pp. 180-184.

[1331] Gasman, *The Scientific Origins of National Socialism*, p. 153.

[1332] Bramwell, *Blood and Soil: Walther Darre and Hitler's Green Party*, p. 174.

[1333] Bramwell, *Ecology in the 20ᵗʰ Century: A History*, pp. 50-51.

existential naturalism of the Nazis in great contrast to the transcendentalism of the Judeo-Christian worldview.

Such books as these, of course, invited some kind of response from the environmental movement and their historians. Initially, the only real serious response came from Raymond Dominick. Dominick wrote a history of German environmentalism between the years of 1871 and 1971. While admitting the Nazis had connections to the early German green movement, Dominick completely downplays the idea of a green Nazi. Staudenmaier criticizes Dominick's work as "a naïve refusal to examine the full extent of the ideological overlap between nature conservation and National Socialism."[1334]

Over time, the environmental movement realized a more robust answer was necessary because the Nazi connections to the green movement could no longer be swept under the carpet. Thus began, as already outlined, a whole series of books on Nazi environmentalism. While admitting more overlap between German environmentalism and National Socialism than Dominick did, these particular historians are still skeptical of any such thing as a green Nazi. Their *wandervogel* attitudes have yet to accept any real responsibility in the Holocaust that largely took place in what Bramwell called Germany's Ireland, i.e., Poland.[1335] Ireland, of course, is a very beautiful green country.

Perhaps most critical, German environmentalism has yet to undergo a genuine repentance with regard to its Nazi past. "After the destruction of the Third Reich, the *Naturshutzer* huddled far from the center of the political stage, wondering how they might adopt the protective coloration of a restored democracy. As it turned out, years would have to pass before the embarrassment of Nazi connections would fade and a resurrected ecological vision, one untarnished by blood and soil, could mobilize a new generation of environmental enthusiasts."[1336] What Dominick describes here is not much of a confession. Rather than a true acknowledgement of facing a morbid past, the German environmental movement simply waited until the embarrassment faded from memory. In truth, what Dominick portrays is a death and resurrection of German environmentalism without repentance. "It is no coincidence that the German environmental

---

[1334] Staudenmaier & Biehl, p. 14.
[1335] Bramwell, *Blood and Soil: Walther Darre and Hitler's Green Party*, pp. 151-70.
[1336] Dominick, p. 115.

movement has taken longer than many other groups to recognize its own Nazi past."[1337] In fact, they are the last of all groups. The Nazi environmental symposium in Germany of 2002 was late in coming. The books which have cropped up since do come across as somewhat smug and fairly defensive. They are written more to misdirect than really confess or admit. Something still smells here.

The Green Fascist Wandervogel Alfred Toepfer

While strongly asserting there was indeed a robust relationship between German environmentalism and Nazism, Peter Staudenmaier couches his controversial assertions by carefully pointing out, "Eco-fascism should not be judged as an instance of guilt by association. Rather it ought to be an occasion to reflect on the political susceptibilities of esoteric environmentalism."[1338] He points out many naïve German *wandervogels* somehow found themselves very attracted to Hitler, "This shift from nature worship to *Fuhrer* worship is worth examining."[1339] The so-called wandering free spirits of Germany were strangely captured by Adolf Hitler's wild totalitarianism.

A strong case in point is Alfred Toepfer (1894-1993).[1340] Alfred Toepfer was an extremely successful German tycoon, an avid environmentalist,[1341] and a key influential supporter for the development of the European Union in the post-war years. Toepfer made his fortune in agri-business during the fateful years of the Weimar Republic (1919-1933). In the late 1920s, Alfred's brother, Ernst, was the secretary of a pro-Nazi organization in New York City called *Wehrwolf*. Ernst was also working for his brother's international firm at the same time. During the 1930s, Toepfer was also very loyal to the Nazi regime,[1342] even though he was never a card-carrying member. Toepfer was particularly loyal to Heinrich Himmler's SS.

Alfred Toepfer was born near the Luneburg Heath, a plain full of meadows, forests, peat bogs and sand dunes in northern Germany, just southeast

---

[1337] Uekoetter, p. 14.

[1338] Staudenmaier, "Anthroposophy and Ecofascism."

[1339] Staudenmaier & Biehl, p. 21.

[1340] Much of the rest of this section is taken directly from the internet article entitled, "The Green Nazi Tycoon Alfred Toepfer" by Mark Musser, *The American Thinker*, April 22, 2012.

[1341] Meinecke, Horst, "Hamburg's Prince of Parks," *The Rotarian*, May 1973.

[1342] Pinto-Duschinsky, Michael, "The Prize Lies of a Nazi Tycoon," *Standpoint*, April 2010.

of Hamburg. Historically, the Luneburg Heath was a place of nationalistic pride where rugged old-style farming practices harmonized with the natural surroundings.[1343] It was symbolic of a strong German character nationalistically rooted in the soil of the homeland. Indeed, after Himmler committed suicide, he was buried in the Luneburg Heath in an unmarked grave.[1344] The heath was also where Nazi environmentalists gathered together at the end of the war to find some solace.[1345] From the Luneburg Heath, environmentalist Hans Klose reorganized what was left of the German green movement to facilitate post-war conservation activities in West Germany.

After the war, the Luneburg Heath was an environmental flashpoint between Germany and the Allies.[1346] Not only did Nazi Germany surrender to the Allies on the heath, but the sacred ground was scarred up by British tanks, which used the southwestern portion of it for military maneuvers. Toepfer strongly opposed the presence of the British military in the heath, but the Brits did not leave until 1994. However, thanks largely to the efforts of Toepfer, the Luneburg Heath became the first national park of Germany in 1956.

In the early 1900s, the Luneburg Heath was a natural sanctuary for the *wandervogel* movement because it was especially well known for its wild birds. *Wandervogel* literally means "free wandering bird." Alfred Toepfer became actively involved in the *wandervogel* movement as early as 1913. Later, during the Nazi era, Toepfer was also an SS blood and soil enthusiast.

Alfred Toepfer continued to be a nature-lover until the day of his death. He was the chairman of the Nature Park Society from 1953 to 1985, where he helped develop many new nature parks for Germany from the North Sea to the Alps. His efforts at the Nature Park Society were greatly expanded for all of Europe under the rise of the Europarc Federation, an association which Toepfer's foundation still supports. In 1981, the Alfred Toepfer Academy for Nature Conservation (NNA) was established. It is a state institution that emphasizes sustainable development and environmentalism. Its main office is located at an old farmstead named *Hof Mor* in the Luneburg Health itself.

[1343] Chaney, p. 61.
[1344] "Chilling Picture Emerges of Nazi leader Himmler Taken Just Moments after He Swallowed Cyanide Pill," *Mail Online*, Feb. 17, 2011.
[1345] Dominick, p. 120.
[1346] Chaney, pp. 59-64.

Even Toepfer's most prestigious academic prizes and scholarships he financed are named after men foundational to the German green movement. The Hanseatic Goethe Prize, dedicated to outstanding European scholarship, is named after Johann Wolfgang von Goethe (1749-1832), the father of German Romanticism. The Alexander von Humboldt Foundation in New York is named after Alexander von Humboldt (1769-1859), the father of German *volkisch* environmentalism. It was precisely during the Nazi regime that Toepfer began funding academic awards to European foreign students with much help coming from the infamous Joachim von Ribbentrop (1893-1946), Hitler's foreign minister. Such academic philanthropy has paid Toepfer handsome dividends over the years. Even though Topefer's loyalty to National Socialism continued after the war by employing notorious SS men like Brigadier Edmund Veesenmeyer, Kurt Haller and Major General Hans-Joachim Riecke, all of whom were responsible for hundreds of thousands of atrocities committed during the war, both British and German scholars have been reluctant to admit the full force of Toepfer's Nazi past.

Much has been made of the fact that Toepfer was arrested by the Nazis in 1937 for foreign currency violations that were forbidden under the *local only* National Socialist economy. However, Toepfer was finally released thanks to his SS patronage together with the personal intervention of Goering. Even Goebbels was very complimentary of Toepfer in 1936.

So was German Nazi historian Hans Mommsen in 2007. After an historical examination paid for by the Alfred Toepfer foundation that investigated his Nazi past, Mommsen concluded Toepfer was "a model European." Mommsen is known for advocating the leftist notion that most Germans were pressed into extreme actions during the Nazi period largely because of economic and social factors rather than because of an intentional anti-Semitism. Mommsen emphasizes the institutional infighting between various rival power blocs in the Reich helped foster political and societal chaos that led to extremism. With no small interest, environmental historian Frank Uekoetter resorts to Mommsen's thesis to slacken the compromised relationship the German green movement had with National Socialism.[1347]

[1347] Uekoetter, p. 9. See also "Polycentrism in Full Swing," in *How Green Were the Nazis?*, by Uekoetter, pp. 101-128.

Such nature-based allurements to National Socialism like Alfred Toepfer's was also perfectly illustrated by Albert Speer himself. Though Speer proved himself to be an efficient technocrat, he was still nonetheless sympathetic to green interests, practices and ideas. His environmental views were in fact very similar to Dr. Todt's.[1348] Speer replaced Todt as Hitler's armaments minister after he died in a freak plane crash in 1942. Speer noted in his memoirs that his particular generation, including himself, had a strong and distinctive attraction to get to close to nature.[1349] That this would be the same generation which also foolishly accepted Adolf Hitler as its political leader is highly instructive. These wandering free spirits were essentially trying to escape the responsibilities of the modern world, and found themselves captivated by the *Fuhrer*.

Modernity built on the bustle of the city was a world which Speer's naturist generation really did not understand, nor desired either politically or economically. Speer noted his particular generation's love affair with nature "was not merely a romantic protest against the narrowness of middle-class life. We were also escaping from the demands of a world growing increasingly complicated."[1350] It was, in fact, a world which they disdained, full of varied responsibilities and demands which they would rather not do.

It was also a world which they believed could be overcome by escaping to the great outdoors, if not even through mountain climbing. "Often, from the mountain tops, we looked down upon a gray layer of cloud over the distant plain. Down there lived what to our minds were wretched people; we thought we stood high above them in every sense."[1351] After spending many years in prison, Speer later acknowledged he and his climbing comrades were "young and arrogant." Speer added, "We were convinced that only the finest people went into the mountains. When we returned to the normal life of the lowlands, I was quite confused for a while by the bustle of the cities."[1352]

Speer and his generation of *wandervogels* measured and compared themselves with others based on how close they were to nature. Generally

---

[1348] Speer, *Inside the Third Reich*, p. 193.
[1349] Ibid., p. 10.
[1350] Ibid.
[1351] Ibid.
[1352] Ibid.

speaking, Speer's generation had little appreciation for the difficult realities of what it really meant to live in the modern world. They were looking for purity, simplicity and peace without the modern stress of working and making a living. This was especially difficult in the trying times of the Weimar Republic, "We felt that the world around us was out of balance. In nature, in the mountains and river valleys, the harmony of Creation could still be felt. The more virginal the mountains, the lonelier the river valleys, the more they drew us."[1353] The embarrassment, depression and defeat Speer and his comrades experienced in the Weimar Republic could all be forgotten in the lofty alpine hills. Abandoned and forsaken by the Weimar Republic, they found solace in the isolationist ideology of National Socialism. In the end, their strong interest in nature's lonely places would find a solitary niche in the singleness of Adolf Hitler.

This truth is borne out by the Nazi Party membership roles. In great contrast to other social groups, roughly 60 percent of green leaders in various conservationist groups were Nazi Party members.[1354] "By 1939 at least 59% of the *Naturschutzer* ... had enlisted in the Nazi Party, compared to roughly 10% of all adult males, 45% of medical doctors, and approximately 25% of teachers and lawyers. This indication that conservationists were overrepresented in the Nazi movement is heightened by evidence that, among German professionals of all kinds, foresters had the second highest rate of participation in Hitler's Party, lagging only behind veterinarians."[1355] As early as 1933, 75 percent of the faculty and 50 percent of the students at the Hannover Veterinarian School had joined the Nazi Party. "After the Nazis came to power the veterinary profession policed itself, eliminating dissenters and Jews without even having to be asked."[1356]

More damning than such statistics is the Nazi Party seemed "to have made little effort specifically to recruit *Naturschutzers*"[1357] in the 1920s, yet in the 1930s many greens became National Socialists. It thus becomes very difficult to understand how environmental historians manage to drive a wedge between the greens and National Socialism when in fact the Nazi Party itself had a highly proportional slice of environmentalists within its own ranks. "Clearly the affinities between environmentalism and National

---

[1353] Ibid.
[1354] Walker, *Sinisterism: Secular Religion of the Lie*, p. 149.
[1355] Dominick, p. 113.
[1356] Sax, p. 146.
[1357] Dominick, p. 90.

Socialism ran deep."[1358] This, of course, is not to say that every German environmentalist was a National Socialist[1359] or a Nazi sympathizer. Neither does it mean that every environmentalist joined the Nazi party because of ideological convictions. However, generally speaking, there was a convergence between the Nazis and the greens that cannot and should not be ignored no matter how disturbing this may be. "During most of the Third Reich, most active German conservationists were Nazi Party members and most Nazi Party members were active in conservationist organizations. We are not dealing with two camps of men."[1360]

Speer later recalled how superficial and uncritical he was of Hitler's political views. He admitted he could have easily taken a better look at the *Fuhrer's* abysmal record, but he did not want to.[1361] In fact, at the most critical juncture of Speer's life when he found himself spellbound by the mood of Hitler's peasant-like simplicity and modesty, instead of taking a good hard look at the *Fuhrer's* views by availing himself of all the political news that was accessible to him, his inclination was to withdraw into the woods to think it all over. "I felt I had to straighten things out in my own mind, to master my confusion. I needed to be alone. Shaken, I drove off into the night in my small car, stopped in a pine forest near the Havel, and went for a long walk."

Needless to say, the silence of the woods did not help Speer make the right choice. He would have been far better off reading the newspapers, or talking to his dad, whose traditional *liberal* bourgeois views on freedom and responsibility were in direct contrast to both the Communist and Nazi parties.[1362] Even though Speer was an outstanding intellectual and highly educated, he was politically naïve. Speer commented that his particular "fail-

---

[1358] Staudenmaier & Biehl, p. 30.

[1359] Lubbeck, William and Hurt, David, *At Leningrad's Gates: The Combat Memoirs of a Soldier with Army Group North*. Philadelphia, Pennsylvania: Casemate Publishers, 2006. As a young boy and man, William Lubbeck lived in Nazi Germany on a village farm before being recruited into the *Wehrmacht* to fight for Army Group North. He stated the following observation about Nazi Party membership, "Only a small group of top Nazi leaders dominated government policymaking, but the Nazi Party began to recruit many more people into its ranks as the regime increased control over German society. Probably half of the new members joined for pragmatic reasons like maintaining their job or gaining advancement, while the other half joined out of ideological conviction. Of course many people sought membership in the Nazi Party for a combination of reasons," pp. 35-36.

[1360] Kay, "The Nazi-Enviro Connection: Uekoetter's 'Green and the Brown.'"

[1361] Speer, *Inside the Third Reich*, p. 19.

[1362] Ibid., p. 14.

ure was rooted in my inadequate political schooling. As a result, I remained uncritical, unable to deal with the arguments of my student friends, who were predominantly indoctrinated with National Socialist ideology."

As such, Speer fell prey to the counterculture ideology of National Socialism and, in so doing, rebelled against the normal upper-middle-class upbringing his father had given him.[1363] Albert Speer became a mindless rebel without a cause. "My inclination to be relieved of having to think particularly about unpleasant facts, helped to sway the balance. In this, I did not differ from millions of others. Such mental slackness above all facilitated, established, and finally assured the success of the National Socialist system."[1364] Albert Speer joined the Nazi Party in 1931. "I had no idea that 14 years later I would have to answer for a host of crimes to which I subscribed beforehand by entering the party. I did not yet know that I would atone with 21 years of my life for frivolity and thoughtlessness and breaking with tradition. Still, I will never be rid of that sin."[1365]

Albert Speer's honesty is far closer to the truth than most people who were involved in the Nazi party, including the greens of the day, want to admit. Contrary to the position of Staudenmaier, who tries to alleviate the problem of personal guilt by Nazi association, Speer did recognize that birds of a feather do indeed flock together. Being naïve cannot be used as an excuse to avoid responsibility. Who people associate with usually says much about who that person really is.

Sadly, the same kind of superficial reasoning Speer himself was guilty of seems to have clouded the judgment of environmental historians as well. They have been desperate to remove their pet movement from the tragedy that was the Holocaust. "Every one of the people who had been politically involved, perhaps even every German who had been a party member, had a story prepared that would present him or her in the least damaging light."[1366] Sudden amnesia and self-defense have plagued the study of Nazi Germany for decades now. One enthusiastic Nazi in the early years later said, "I want nothing to do with all those people who now claim they weren't Nazis, that indeed they were resisters. I really sometimes wonder who it was who elected Hitler and fought and won all those battles for him. All of

---

[1363] Ibid., p. 20.
[1364] Ibid.
[1365] Ibid.
[1366] Sereny, *Albert Speer's Battle with Truth*, p. 166.

Germany, it now appears, was nothing but anti-Nazis. Disgusting."[1367] It is far more likely that modern green historians are simply continuing to cover for their environmental forefathers. That they even try to defend the Nazi greens demonstrates that environmental historians recognize the *volkisch* fascists are indeed their intellectual forebears.

The so-called wandering free spirits of the 1920s and '30s ambled squarely into the abyss of the most brutal animalistic regime known in human history. "All that it took to join the conservation community during the Nazi era was a willingness to cooperate with Nazi authorities—and of course, a readiness to be silent about points of disagreement. As it turned out, the vast majority of the German conservationists were willing to pay this price."[1368] A little less green rebellion and more serious-minded thinking about politics and people would have spared Germany her *darkest hour*.

Late in life, Speer wrote that he felt uneasy about his own Romanticism because he recognized how closely it resembled the very political ideology of National Socialism. "Today, however, I advocated demands similar to Ohlendorf's. Yet I feel certain doubts when I now discover that parallels to my thinking may be found in Ohlendorf, of all people."[1369] Otto Ohlendorf was a high-ranking SS member who was heavily involved in the Holocaust. Like many SS leaders, he was an anti-industrial Romantic who stood by the original pure doctrines of Nazi ideology throughout the war. He was executed for war crimes. This honest admission from Speer should make the modern greens much more uneasy about all this than they really are.

Yet Speer's admission is disturbing. Has he really learned the lesson of National Socialism if he still holds to similar views years later? Further, how is it even possible Speer *rediscovered* that his own Romantic views in the 1970s were very similar to Ohlendorf's views of the 1940s? What kind of Nazi spell was cast upon the likes of so many like Albert Speer that they have been able to separate themselves from Nazism, all the while holding to similar views throughout their lives? There is a most serious disconnect here, a cognitive dissonance of Holocaustic proportions.

Speer's comments do indeed show how he separated his own Romanticism from National Socialism, even though he later realized such a distinction was artificial and wrong. As part of his defense after the war during the Nuremberg

---

[1367] Ibid., p. 180.
[1368] Uekoetter, p. 208.
[1369] Speer, *Infiltration*, p. 84.

trial, Speer railed against the dangers of technology since the Nazis techno-cratically used it to control the populace. However, Speer later recognized how hollow this defense was since the Nazis were the very ones who said as much. "Did I realize at that time that I myself had implemented the pre-dominance of technology in Germany? Until then mass production had been contrary to the ideological premises of National Socialism."[1370]

The fact of the matter is the Nazis were forced to sacrifice their own cherished principles because of the demands of war, and it was Speer him-self who led the way in automating Nazi Germany, not SS ideologues like Ohlendorf. In fact, Speer complained the veteran Nazis were so "hidebound that they slowed down development in many areas."[1371] Speer gave credit for modernization to the non-Nazi technocrats and industrialists who volunteered to work for the *Fuhrer* after Hitler's rise to power. Without them, Nazi Germany would have failed. "The incompetence of the National Socialist party functionaries would have led to catastrophically poor per-formances in industry."[1372] Such a vast cadre of the intelligentsia changed the Nazi Party and loosed it from its anti-industrial moorings.

In 1981, Speer wrote a book called *Infiltration*. In it he describes how Himmler was secretly planning on building an independent industrial em-pire in the occupied eastern territories that had Hitler's backing. However, Speer winds up exposing how Romantically unfit Himmler was for such a task. Himmler was anything but an industrialist. Furthermore, according to Speer, the SS hated industry.[1373] In fact, the SS strongly opposed the industrialists who worked for Speer and Goering.[1374] Yet both Himmler and Speer were still technocratic Romantics. This tension between *volkisch* Romanticism on the one hand and technocracy on the other hand, can be seen in virtually everything they did.

Himmler thought he could build a technocratic industrial empire using slave labor, yet the whole concept of slavery is a pre-industrial mentality. Himmler's plans, however, were often thwarted because Hitler was order-ing him to shoot or gas the very people who were supposed to build his industrial empire.[1375] How on Earth can anyone build an industrial empire

---

[1370] Ibid.
[1371] Ibid., p. 4.
[1372] Ibid., p. 5.
[1373] Ibid., p. 110.
[1374] Ibid., pp. 103-116.
[1375] Ibid., pp. 5-6.

upon mass graves and the burnt ashes of places like Treblinka, Sobibor and Auschwitz? Slave labor and human sacrifice belong to the pre-industrial world of agriculture and ancient nature worship, not modern Europe or America.

As such, the real moral of the story of National Socialism is not that industry and technology are hazardous per se, but that it is dangerous in the hands of social Darwinian Romantics and existentialists who do not really believe in it. They will invariably use industry for wrongful purposes, like to gas and burn Jews, for example. Holocaust survivor and Nobel Peace Prize recipient Elie Wiesel was shocked by the sheer brutality of Auschwitz when he arrived there from Hungary on a cattle car in 1944. Drenched in cold sweat, he told his father he "could not believe that human beings were being burned in our times; the world would never tolerate such crimes."[1376] However, the Nazi existential reality on the ground graphically portrayed exactly the opposite against all his *modern* expectations. Jews were being burned, and the world did tolerate it.

The Holocaust itself was and is a stake in the heart of the myth of modern progress. In truth, National Socialism was anything but progressive. It was a giant reversal into a backward racist folklore that led to a grisly nihilism of unparalleled proportions that even caused more than a few Jewish victims to question the very justice of God.[1377] The real facts on the ground in 1944 Auschwitz, however, demonstrated not the injustice of God, but how low humanity can sink when nature itself becomes the sole ethos for life.

Not surprisingly, Speer was greatly confused and troubled by the tension between Romanticism and technocratic inclinations that was part and parcel of the whole Nazi enterprise, especially with regard to the SS. Speer's confusion is readily seen in his writings when he concluded Himmler's animalistic actions on the Eastern Front remained an enigma to him.[1378] Thinking out loud, Speer goes on to say Himmler had a weak moral character that was too much influenced by the likes of Hitler and Bormann. To Speer, Himmler's evil was therefore more of a question of moral weakness rather than Nazi ideology.[1379] However, Speer's reticence to acknowledge that Himmler's Nazi ideology was not really the problem is very revealing precisely because he criticizes him on his backward Romanticism through-

---

[1376] Wiesel, Elie. *Night*. New York: Hill and Wang, 1958, p. 33.
[1377] Ibid., pp. 33-34.
[1378] Speer, *Infiltration*, pp. 12-13.
[1379] Ibid., p. 12.

out the book. Indeed, to characterize Himmler's industrial activities on the Eastern Front, one chapter is entitled, "Semi-precious gems, Poison Gas, and Dandelions." So much for the industrial proclivities of Himmler. The final chapter then discusses how Hitler and Himmler had grandiose construction plans to turn *lebensraum* in the occupied eastern territories into a Romantic Germanized countryside of towns, farms and villages so the Reich peasants might "live in outstandingly beautiful settlements."[1380]

National Socialism was indeed a strange admixture of backwardness and modernism, reflecting both German Romanticism and the German Enlightenment. The blending of these two great movements in German history converged on a scale never seen before or since under the National Socialist regime. A brutal technocracy was implemented by the Nazis in order to create a romanticized greater Germany in the new Reich. As one historian acutely observed, "Perhaps the most striking and novel aspect of technocracy under Hitler was the use of rational means and technocratic principles to achieve both rational and irrational goals."[1381] Such confusion between modern rationality and *volkisch* irrationality haunted Speer throughout much of his life. He was never able to sort through it, even after spending many years in Spandau prison:

> As I lay on my cot trying to sort out the throng of memories and determine which ones had been decisive impressions, I discerned a pattern. It consisted always of romantic elements paralleled with technological elements. When I consider the matter, these elements with all their contradictions and frictions but also with all their interactions, are what have governed my life as a whole. Here I am not so much thinking of the dualistic nature of my position in the Third Reich, which indeed did neatly fit into both my romantic and my technologically oriented needs. Rather, I am referring to the perfectly commonplace experience of divided feelings that I have whenever I read a newspaper. All the new technological achievements fascinate me. I admire the mind that has made the earth subject to itself and now is beginning to reach out into the universe. But faced with the inexorable transformation of the world into modern technological ugliness, I am filled with panic and grief. A still further contradiction

---

[1380] Ibid., p. 297.
[1381] *Science, Technology, and National Socialism*, p. 6.

is that I have experienced in myself all the perils of the romantic relationship to the world, all the blindness, the obscurantism, the reckless enthusiasm, and potential inhumanity of it all—and still I love it and cannot part with it.[1382]

In one paragraph, Albert Speer sums up the entire Nazi conundrum that continues to puzzle scholars even today. He admits Romanticism was at the heart of Nazi inhumanity, but he still finds himself strongly in love with it. Even 20 years in Spandau prison could not shake him of this fatal attraction. The same feelings that initially drew him to Adolf Hitler were still with him in March of 1963. That this basic truth eluded Speer is a mystery as mystical as German Romanticism itself and as deep as the green Nazi hell that was the Holocaust.

Indeed, in the spirit of Martin Heidegger's book *Holzwege*, which means "off the beaten timber paths," Speer counted his steps while in prison. He eventually amassed more than 30,000 kilometers before he was finally released in 1966. In his own mind, he marched across much of the world to help break up the monotonous life of Spandau prison. Speer secretly wrote massive amounts of diary material on toilet paper, old newspapers, etc., that were smuggled out of prison. He signed the diary material with the pseudonym *Holzwege.* On the very last night before he left Spandau, Speer smuggled one last telegram out on a piece of paper to his *old friend* which read, "Please pick me up 35 miles south of Guadalajara, Mexico. *Holzwege.*"[1383] All of the smuggled material later became the basis for his best-selling books.

Nazi Right-Wing Confusion

One of the biggest obstacles many people have in connecting the dots between environmentalism and fascism is the myth that National Socialism was a radical right-wing political party. Environmentalists today, by and large, belong to the left side of the political spectrum. As such, since the Nazis were allegedly hard right conservatives, the connections between them and modern environmentalism must therefore be fairly distant, and hence a bridge too far. However, if it can be shown the Nazis were left of

---

[1382] Speer, *Spandau: The Secret Diaries*, p. 391.
[1383] Ibid., pp. 446-47.

center on the so-called political spectrum, then the break between the environmental movement and National Socialism is not nearly as distant as many have presumed. Indeed, Hilmar von Campe, a former Hitler youth member and veteran of the *Wehrmacht* in Yugoslavia, even ridiculed the idea that modern *right wing* neo-Nazis are comparable to the Nazi Party of his youth. Von Campe bluntly stated, "The idea that some punks, who paint a swastika on some walls, represent the Neo-Nazis in Germany is laughable. They are just punks. The socialist/green government coalition, who held the reins of power for many years in Germany, comes much closer to the definition. They are fellow socialists of the Nazis."[1384]

The notion that National Socialism is a phenomenon of the political right is largely a figment of the Marxist and/or leftist imagination. Secular Marxist and leftist scholars always find ways to focus on the Third Reich's economy so they can paint *right wing* modern industry, capitalism and Euro-American colonialism with Nazi blood. This particular argument became much more plausible thanks to the "Night of the Long Knives" in 1934 when Hitler, Himmler and Goering arrested and later assassinated Ernst Roehm, the homosexual leader of the very left leaning nationalist SA (Nazi Stormtroopers). Throughout the 1920s the Nazi Party was a leftist revolutionary socialist party, and Roehm himself was the leader of the powerful paramilitary organization called the SA. By 1931, the SA had almost 1,000,000 members. Popularly known as the Brownshirts, they were the real thugs of the Nazi Party.

Roehm's execution, however, was much more due to practical considerations than ideological differences. Not only was Roehm a personal friend of Hitler, but the Nazis had originally intended to use the SA as a powerful shock troop to take over the Germany Army. However, in January 1933, Hitler was appointed chancellor of Germany through back door deals. Though the political fallout of the Reichstag Fire in February favored the Nazis, they were still not all that popular. Nazi radicalism increasingly dismayed President Von Hindenburg, who in 1934, threatened to sack Hitler and turn the government over to the military. Furthermore, the German Army hated Roehm and the SA. If news got out to the public that Rohem was a flaming homosexual,[1385] the Nazis would find themselves in more political trouble. Roehm thus became not only expendable, but

---

[1384] Von Campe, p. 139.
[1385] Hohne, p. 98.

also a liability. Von Hindenburg's wrath was finally pacified by Hitler's murderous actions taken against Roehm and the leadership of the SA. In August of 1934, President Von Hindenburg died. Hitler then merged the chancellorship together with the presidency in order to become absolute dictator of Germany.

It is also true the Nazis had moderated their flamboyant leftist rhetoric as the decade of the 1920s wore on in order to present themselves to the public as the reasonable middle way between the capitalists and the socialists and/or communists. The failed Nazi revolution of 1923 caused Hitler to change some of his more radical practices. Neither can it be ignored the Nazis needed money to fund their national regeneration program and secure their positions in power. With a very fragile German economy to draw from, they were thus forced to make some important concessions to big business and industry[1386] that Roehm and the leftist SA considered a betrayal of Nazi values. Many in the SA became very resentful of what the Nazi Party stood for once Hitler took power in Germany.[1387]

Roehm's days were therefore numbered. Too many in Germany hated Roehm and the SA. Furthermore, the power hungry green Nazis—Himmler and Goering—also wanted to eliminate Roehm. In reality, the green arm of the swastika ganged up against the pink arm of the swastika. Furthermore, the Nazi assault against homosexuals cannot be understood apart from the Roehm purge. Both Goering and Himmler were troubled by Roehm's influence in the Nazi Party through the SA. However, after Roehm was arrested, Hitler was very reluctant to execute him. Hitler finally conceded and backed Goering and Himmler.[1388] With Roehm out of the way, Himmler's SS assumed the powerful role the SA once possessed. Himmler also shocked the German intelligentsia when he subsequently began recruiting them into their ranks to help build a greater Germany.[1389] During the recruitment stage, Himmler purposefully contrasted the elitism of the SS with the low lifes of the SA. This surprisingly won many of the intelligentsia to his side. Does

---

[1386] See especially Tooze's discussion on pp. 99-100 where Hitler promised the big industrialists that he would crush the German socialists in February of 1933. At this, the big industrialists opened up their coffers and made a down payment to secure their position in the upcoming Third Reich: "It was the donations in February and March of 1933 that really made the difference. They provided a large cash injection at a moment when the party was severely short of funds and faced, as Goering had predicted, the last competitive election in its history."

[1387] Hohne., pp. 92-94.

[1388] Ibid., pp. 102- 130.

[1389] Ibid., p. 132.

killing Roehm and drafting the intelligentsia make the Nazis hard right conservatives? Hardly.

Hess once stated, "If our voters did not have us to vote for, they would go for the extreme left."[1390] Certainly one of the primary reasons the Nazis were so effective in taking over Germany is precisely because they represented the deep concerns of many people, many of whom were rooted in the leftist tradition. "Nazism was a more subtle phenomenon than we commonly imagine, more seductive, more plausible."[1391] Labor, the economy, the environment, science, nationalism, health and racism were all pressing concerns of the German populace throughout the 1920s and '30s. "In almost every area of political pandering to constituencies, the Nazis blazed the trail for later leftists."[1392] The Nazis catapulted themselves into a position of power by incorporating everyday Western concerns into their political program, and environmentalism played a critical role in that process. "Drawing on the heritage of Arndt, Riehl, Haeckel and others, the Nazi movement's incorporation of environmentalist themes was a crucial factor in its rise to popularity and state power."[1393] Indeed, the constant Nazi "rallying cry against the destructive powers of materialism was always sure to get applause in conservation circles."[1394] Put in another way, "the Hitlerian emphasis upon the 'natural man' found wide resonance among the party faithful."[1395]

Nazi researcher Gitta Sereny pointed out, "Between 1933 and 1937, much of the world admired Hitler's pioneering ideas. Although people were distrustful of Nazi racism, many of the other ideas fostered by Hitler were heralded by those on the left side of the divide. During his first four years as chancellor, Hitler expanded the health, social security and old-age benefits pioneered by Bismarck and later adopted by the Weimar Republic. His elaborate public works included a network of *Autobahnen*, innovations such as traffic-free city centers with strict pollution controls, and he further developed the existing parks and green areas."[1396] Hitler himself was heavily involved in an annual Nazi program called "The Winter Relief Drive" that was specifically designed to nationalistically bind the *volk* together by helping

1390 Manvel and Fraenkel, p. 37.
1391 Proctor, *The Nazi War on Cancer*, p. 7.
1392 Walker, *Sinisterism: Secular Religion of the Lie*, p. 157.
1393 Staudenmaier & Biehl, p. 26.
1394 Uekoetter, p. 21.
1395 Pois, p. 117.
1396 Sereny, *Albert Speer's Battle with Truth*, p. 180.

the poor.[1397] Within the first four years of its existence, it raised 1.5 billion marks. Hitler called it "the greatest social achievement of all time."

In other words, it is not an over exaggeration to say "the Nazis were more like the rest of us than we care to acknowledge."[1398] Western society has falsely prided itself in distancing itself from Nazism, not realizing how much it still shares in common with the regime. Sereny concluded, "The barriers which separate us from them are not as high as some would like to imagine ... there are chilling parallels between those times and ours."[1399]

Strangely, Hitler expert Ian Kershaw stated Hitler had never been a socialist. However, that is only true if one *a priori* excludes the Nazis as socialists. One is also left with the heavy burden of explaining why the Nazis called themselves National Socialists if they were not socialists. "Nationalism and Socialism were inextricably linked in Hitler's mind and he often claimed the two were identical."[1400] Hitler purposefully chose the color red for the Nazi flag to reveal the party's basic socialist underpinnings. Dr. Anna Bramwell acutely observed, "The Nazi Party was a peasant party in Protestant areas, but a proletarian party in Catholic areas."[1401] It is far better to say the Nazis simply practiced a different kind of socialism, which even Kershaw admits, "Any 'socialist' ideas in the Nazi program had to follow the same (Social Darwinian) dictates."[1402]

For Hitler, the state and the economy were to be completely politicized by social Darwinism, a common theme that went as far back as *Mein Kampf*:[1403]

> ... as he stated to the industrialists, economics was of secondary importance, entirely subordinated to politics. His crude Social Darwinism dictated his approach to the economy, as it did his entire political worldview. Since struggle among nations would be decisive for future survival, Germany's economy had to be subordinated to the preparation, then carrying out, of this struggle. That meant that liberal ideas of economic competition (free market enterprise) had

---

1397 Weikart, *Hitler's Ethic*, pp. 101-107.

1398 Sax, p. 164.

1399 Proctor, *The Nazi War on Cancer*, p. 7.

1400 Weikart, *Hitler's Ethic*, p. 107.

1401 Bramwell, *Blood and Soil: Walther Darre and Hitler's Green Party*, p. 83.

1402 Kershaw, p. 448.

1403 Hitler, *Mein Kampf*, pp. 149-50.

to be replaced by the subjection of the economy to the dictates of the national interest.[1404]

To Hitler, struggle in nature and struggle against other nations was an evolutionary law which the state needs to nationalistically promote and regulate. This was the whole point of its eugenics program. The Nazis were socialists over issues related to race and nature, not over class like it was for the Marxists and other socialists. "Race was real, whereas individuals and classes were fleeting and erroneous constructions. Struggle was not a metaphor or an analogy, but a tangible and total truth."[1405] For example, in a 1922 speech, Hitler proclaimed, "There is no class struggle but rather racial struggle."[1406] The Nazis thus did not social engineer people based on class like the Marxists, but they most certainly did with regard to biology and race along with a powerful undercurrent of eco-fascism. Indeed, nature was society and politics, and society and politics was nature. They were all one in the same.

The National Socialist stress on evolutionary racism denied the solidarity of the human race. Hitler and Nazi ideologues believed natural evolutionary development was leading to an increasing separation of humanity into different races. Such an attitude about race is very different than Marxism. Marxists emphasized international communism and the new universal humanity, not racism. The Nazis also valued nature over man. The communists on the other hand were humanists. They therefore valued humanism and materialism over nature. In the final analysis, however, the Nazis opposed Soviet international communism because of its assumed Jewish origin and influence. The Nazis replaced class struggle rooted in the humanist tradition with a race struggle rooted in Nature. Such a political biology does not make National Socialism right wing.

While it is true Hitler stamped out the Marxist/socialist left when he came to power, he did this not because he loved capitalism, but because he believed Marxists were dividing the German *volk*. In other words, Hitler attacked the Marxists because he believed their class warfare was artificially dividing the German body politic between the owners and laborers.[1407] Hitler thus believed Marxian class warfare was weakening Germany before its

---

1404 Kershaw, p. 448.
1405 Snyder, p. 2.
1406 Hitler, speech in Landshut, May 5, 1922; quoted by Weikart in *Hitler's Ethic*, p. 76.
1407 Tooze, p. 99.

enemies. As such, surprisingly enough, Hitler was anti-Marxist in the name of German collectivism, not because he loved *right wing* laissez faire capitalism. Nazi propaganda minister Goebbels spoke of the essential spirit of National Socialist justice in his "Total War Speech" when he said, "We pay no heed to class or standing. Rich and poor, high and low must share the burdens equally. Everyone must do his duty in this grave hour, whether by choice or otherwise."[1408] The Nazis thus believed in the cult of the collective just as much as any communist or socialist, even over economic issues. The Nazi state, "not the market, would determine the shape of economic development."[1409]

In further contrast to the Marxists, the Nazis did not want to own the means of production, nor attempt to equalize the classes:

> For Hitler, Socialism did not mean economic inequality or public ownership of the means of production, but rather it meant an economic system characterized by each working for the sake of the whole nation. Each should sacrifice his or her time, energy, and material goods to promote the common welfare of the German nation and people (defined racially, of course).[1410]

The Marxists wanted to own companies producing goods in order to make life more equal or fair. The Nazis, however, rejected this line of reasoning because nature teaches exactly the opposite—life is not fair. Not surprisingly, Hitler firmly believed economic inequality was naturally rooted in biological inequality.[1411] However, even though the Nazis did not want to own companies, they still wanted to control and regulate them. The Nazis did permit big industrialists handsome profits, but they still did not allow them to do whatever they felt like doing for the sake of economic liberalism and *laissez faire* capitalism. On the other hand, the big industrialists may have sided with the Nazis because of Hitler's anti-Marxist rhetoric, but they soon discovered they would still be socially engineered—just coming from a different angle.

According to Nazi administrator Dr. Hupfauer, the Nazi Party was "intending to change the whole concept of labor relations, based on the

---

1408 Bytwerk, p. 125.
1409 Tooze, p. 99.
1410 Weikart, *Hitler's Ethic*, p. 107.
1411 Ibid., p. 109.

principle of co-determination and shared responsibility between management and workers."[1412] Though management would be allowed their profits, they would still be serving the German *volk* and the Nazi Party. "The first years of Hitler's regime saw the imposition of a series of controls on German business that were unprecedented in peacetime history."[1413] Dr. Hupfauer believed the Nazi Party had "actually succeeded in imbuing management and labor with an awareness of a common purpose. And most important for this country, where labor had been bedeviled for centuries by class warfare, it brought about the abolition of the industrial class or caste system, which is much more significant for the functioning of any country than class differences in social life. The real signal change was that class struggle in industry was replaced by solidarity."[1414] This is why the Nazis attacked both communism and capitalism. In the Nazi mind, both communism and capitalism were directly responsible for the industrial class warfare that divided the nation from its overall *volkisch* purpose. Such politics does not make National Socialism right wing.

Characterizing some group as conservative or *right wing* means nothing until one defines what is to be conserved or preserved. The Nazis were trying to preserve the German race, not free market capitalism. The Nazis believed they needed a strong central government to make this preservation a political reality. A strong state was needed to carry out their eugenics program to improve the German race. In this sense, i.e., conserving or preserving the German race, they can be considered a conservative party of the *right*.

However, the great problem here is most people who are considered *right wingers* today are actually similar to the classical liberals of the past. The Founding Fathers of America were classical liberals who strongly believed in limited government and free enterprise that would eventually become the world's melting pot. This is profoundly different than what the Nazis had envisioned for Germany. Anyone who reads the Nazi Party platform of the 1920s clearly realizes at once that it has nothing in common with the political beliefs of Thomas Jefferson or Barry Goldwater or Ronald Reagan in America.

Regardless of such nuances between National Socialism and Marxism, the Nazis still called themselves socialists, and campaigned as such. They

---

[1412] Sereny, *Albert Speer's Battle with Truth*, p. 181.
[1413] Tooze, p. 106.
[1414] Sereny, *Albert Speer's Battle with Truth*, p. 181.

may have been ambivalent on some issues between the so-called left and the right, but generally speaking, they were left of the political divide. Even before the Nazis came to power, Albert Speer's father "had the darkest foreboding, chiefly in view of the NSDAP's socialist tendencies. He was already disturbed enough by the strength of the Social Democrats and the Communists."[1415] *Wehrmacht* veteran William Lubbeck from Army Group North agreed with Albert Speer's father. Lubbeck described the Nazi Party of his youth as "fringe group filled with crude and dangerous extremists who were only marginally better than the Communist radicals."[1416]

The major difference between Nazism and communism was over whether there should be a German National Socialism based on race/nature or an international socialism based on humanism/materialism. Such a concern may have been a big deal to those involved in the debate at the time, but much of the thinking and tactics of both the Nazis and the Marxists were still virtually the same:

> It will surprise many people but it ought to surprise almost no one that the Communists and the Nazis in Germany generally supported the same policies. They were, after all, competing to a large extent for the same voters. . . . In 1927, the Communists in the Reichstag introduced proposals for an eight hour work day; Nazis and Social Democrats were the only other political parties to support that policy; Nazi party deputies in the Reichstag were the only other members of that body to support Communist proposals to exempt the poor from taxation and to pay additional compensation to iron and steel workers in the Ruhr who had been locked out by industrialists. The next year, when 126,000 metalworkers in Berlin went on strike, the Communist Party, the Nazi Party, and the Social Democrat Party all supported the strike and all provided picketers to help the strikers. At the end of that year in December 1930, the Nazis were the only other members of the Reichstag to support a communist measure to rescind cuts in health insurance, unemployment compensation and extended health insurance for the unemployed. Small wonder that, in spite of the Nazis stated opposition to the Bolsheviks, the conservative financial paper

---

[1415] Speer, p. 14.
[1416] Lubbeck, p. 32.

Berliner Borson-Zeitgun fretted about "Marxist tendencies" in the Nazi Party.[1417]

Hitler himself said, "National Socialism is what Marxism might have been if it could have broken its absurd and artificial ties with the democratic order."[1418] Indeed, in the later 1920s, "Nazi labor unions had more members than communist labor unions."[1419] The Nazis and Marxists both hated the international free market and individual liberty. They both promoted strong state control and government intervention over the economy. Thus, in terms of economic freedom, the Nazis and Communists were cousins, and the practical difference between concentration camps and the *gulag archipelago* is minimal.

That the Nazis and Soviets initially agreed to carve up Poland together is therefore not as shocking or contradictory as it has so often been presented. Stalin even granted the Nazi foreign minister Ribbentrop a personal vast hunting reserve as part of the deal. "At this Goering's hackles rose; he insisted that Stalin could have hardly meant this gift to apply to the Foreign Minister personally. A hot dispute broke out between the two hunters which ended with the Foreign Minister sulking."[1420]

Nazis and Communists were, in fact, gang rivals of the left:

> In reality, pre-Nazi Social Darwinism was not a phenomenon of the conservative right, nor was it the outcome of conventional rightwing conservative political thought or an expression of the final stages of the disintegration of capitalism as some Marxist writers have urged. As an ideology, Nazism was much more a special outgrowth of left-liberalism, positivism, Haeckelian Monist science, aspects especially of leftwing Social Democracy, and lastly, of mystical attributes of the *volkisch* and theosophical movements. There was hardly an unbridgeable gap between extreme Social Darwinism and the political Left....[1421]

[1417] Walker, *Sinisterism: Secular Religion of the Lie*, p. 69.
[1418] Declaration to Hermann Rauschning, the Nazi leader of Danzig; quoted by Walker in *Sinisterism: Secular Religion of the Lie*, p. 70.
[1419] Walker, *Sinisterism: Secular Religion of the Lie*, p. 70.
[1420] Speer, *Inside the Third Reich* p. 168.
[1421] Gasman, *The Scientific Origins of National Socialism*, p. xix.

With this quote collapses the presumed unbridgeable gap between National Socialism and the left together with the alleged distinction between Nazi ecology and modern leftist environmentalism. Nazi Germany was in fact the political bridge between German Romanticism and modern environmentalism, between old-style conservationist values and contemporary deep ecology.

Generally speaking, modern environmentalism was born in the *volkisch* soil of Germany in rebellion against both Protestantism and the Enlightenment in the late 1700s and early 1800s. From there, it spread into philosophical existentialist circles together with the evolutionary, geopolitical and racial sciences of the 1800s and early 1900s. In the 1930s and '40s, the Nazis then built the political bridge between localized ecological concerns into national holistic solutions, albeit under racist categories. Today environmentalism is a strong international movement thanks largely to robust European influences in the United Nations.

While there will always be differences, subtleties and nuances, modern leftist environmentalism and Nazism are still much closer to each other than they are further apart on a whole host of issues. This is true not only politically, but philosophically as well. "Though for the most part eschewing notions of race and racial supremacy, modern environmental concerns are in part rooted in this general tradition. As we have seen, National Socialist ideologues were in no small way concerned that man, or at least some men, live in harmony with the environment."[1422] In 1986, Dr. Robert Pois concluded:

> I must confess that I see certain parallels and analogies—although how alarming they are is a matter of opinion—between elements of the National Socialist "religion" and contemporary phenomena. The "naturalism" of the former certainly has parallels with a sort of fuzzy nature-mysticism which can be observed throughout the West, perhaps, most prominently, in the United States. National Socialism has to be seen as symptomatic of a general, perhaps largely unconscious, discomfiture with the Judeo-Christian tradition, something which attained political expression in Germany but can hardly be seen as confined to it.[1423]

[1422] Pois, p. 58.
[1423] Ibid., p. 3.

Ironically enough, the highway to modern *left wing* environmentalism passed through *right wing* Nazi Germany. Both Europe and North America are thus deceiving themselves if they think they can easily distance themselves from National Socialism by travelling further to the left.

Indeed, the present relationship that currently exists between modern environmentalism and left-wing labor unions may in fact have been born in Nazi Germany. In June of 1933, Rudolf Hess and Walther Schoenichen absorbed many of the environmental groups in the Weimar Republic under Werner Haverbeck's Reich League for *Volkstum und Heimat* (Folk National Character & Landscape).[1424] Werner Haverbeck[1425] was a former Hitler Youth leader, and his Reich League was a subdivision of the German Labor Front. "Because the Reich League usually allowed conservation groups that enrolled under its umbrella to continue with pre-1933 leaders unchanged, large and longstanding Nature groups flocked to its banner. By early 1934, the German League for the Protection of the Homeland, the League for Conservation in Bavaria, and the League for Bird Protection all had re-phrased their titles to indicate that they were now subsidiaries of the Reich League."[1426] The German Labor Front thus adopted the greens into their political organization. The green movement and labor have been working arm in arm together ever since.

After the war, while biding his time in Spandau prison, Rudolf Hess often discussed the problems of the free market economy with Albert Speer. For a time, Speer was the department head of the German Labor Front. He also worked under Hess, who was in charge of Nazi public works projects. The relationship between these two men therefore runs long and deep, which continued in Spandau Prison after Nuremberg. Speer noted that Hess loved to use his knowledge on political economy to critique capitalism. Speer said Hess's "interests center in general on sociology and political economy, but in particular on the ills of civilization. He has been long pursuing the connections between such phenomena and liberal democracy. Again and again he comes to me with examples of overconsumption in the United States. He happily notes reports of misguided investments in the market economy, collects examples of land speculation, criminality, bad posture in children and health damage caused by canned foods."[1427]

[1424] Dominick, p. 102.
[1425] Haverbeck was also a follower of Steiner and his organic green farming ideas.
[1426] Dominick, p. 102.
[1427] Speer, *Spandau: The Secret Diaries*, p. 407.

Hess even came up with a cockamamie energy conservation idea that he shared with Speer and his Nazi fellow prisoners in 1951. Since highway lamps were being placed above roadways, Hess believed it would be unnecessary for cars to turn their headlights on at the same time. Energy could be saved by turning off the headlights when highway lamps were burning. Speer even debated with Hess over the issue: "This would save current he maintains, and the erection and maintenance of the floodlights could easily be financed out of the money thus saved. I object that the car's generators would be running anyhow, to supply the current to the spark plugs. He dismisses that; the generator could shut off automatically as soon as the battery was charged. Thus energy would be stored, fuel saved, and this saving could be spent on financing the illumination of highways."[1428] Such an idea from Hess certainly presages the anti-car renewable energy sentiments that have become one of the trademarks of the modern green movement. Moreover, this is the kind of cockamamie technocracy that National Socialism sometimes emphasized, and it has only grown by leaps and bounds since Hess's conversation with his fellow Nazi prisoners in 1951.

The Curious Green Nazi Connection between
Leni Riefenstahl & James Cameron

Film star/director Leni Riefenstahl (1902-2003) is a perfect case in point[1429] to illustrate how the so-called left/right divide with regard to modern environmentalism is illusory. Although she did not become a Nazi Party member, Riefenstahl became enthralled with the new movement. She became captivated with Hitler the first time she heard him speak. She believed he could lead Germany out of its post-WW I political chaos.

In fact, Hitler was a big boon to her career. Hitler had a close camaraderie with many German artists, and Leni was one of his favorites. As such, Leni Riefenstahl became a famous film director during the Nazi regime. While she later vehemently denied that she had an intimate relationship with the *Fuhrer*, "according to Pierre Huss, Leni sometimes claimed that she had slept with Hitler until she was told to shut up."[1430] In any event, Riefenstahl stayed loyal to Hitler well into the heights of the war. She would spend the rest of

---

1428 Ibid., p. 168.

1429 This section is an expanded version of an *American Thinker* Internet article entitled "The Green Nazis" by Mark Musser, April 22, 2011.

1430 Mitchell, p. 37.

her life in a vain attempt to disassociate herself from her Nazi past. Even though she was officially de-Nazified by both the American and French authorities, her unapologetic defense of her actions during the Nazi era remains unconvincing to this day.

In the 1920s, Leni Riefenstahl was a tomboy movie star who played in popular German mountain films. She starred in such silent, snowy movies as *The Holy Mountain* in 1926 and *The White Hell of Pitz Palu* in 1928, not to mention *S.O.S. Iceberg* in 1933. Weimar Germany was captivated by these realistic nature movies. Albert Speer himself was romantically inspired by Riefenstahl's S.O.S. Iceberg.[1431] In 1932, Riefenstahl made her own Romantic nature film called *Blue Light* highlighting the evils of modernism and capitalism. This was the very film "that brought her to Hitler's attention."[1432] Hitler loved *Blue Light*.

Riefenstahl is infamously known as the director of the notorious 1935 propaganda film *Triumph of the Will* that even manages to showcase the Nazi *back to the land* movement. In one particular scene at the colossal Nuremberg rally, militant, uniformed Germans are shown with shovels in their hands as they cry out, "We plant trees!" Later, Riefenstahl made the highly acclaimed documentary film *Olympia* shot at the 1936 Berlin Olympics. The film strongly emphasized the competitive natural strength of the athletes.

After the war, Leni Riefenstahl followed in the footsteps of Charles Lindbergh. She not only became a radical environmentalist, but she also fell in love with indigenous peoples close to nature. Moving away from Nazi tribalism, Riefenstahl became increasingly fascinated with black indigenous races. Riefenstahl relocated to a remote African village to make a documentary film of an almost extinct group of Sudanese called the *Nuba*. Instead of protecting the indigenous Germans from international Jewish materialism, she believed the primitive *Nuba* needed protection from the corrupting, globalist forces of international capitalism. Her documentary, however, was never completed. Some have speculated the reason why the documentary was never made was because she was a perfectionist. The difficult conditions in which the Nuba lived prevented her from making a top-quality documentary. Late in life, Riefenstahl became involved with Greenpeace. She died in 2003 at the ripe old age of 101 years old.

[1431] Jacobsen, p. 45.
[1432] Sereny, *Albert Speer's Battle with Truth*, p. 129.

Robert von Dassanowsky, the director of Film Studies at the University of Colorado, acutely noticed that James Cameron's 1997 epic movie *Titanic* was based on the German mountain films that Riefenstahl starred in. James Cameron loves Leni Riefenstahl's works. Although largely ignoring Riefenstahl's compromised relationship with the Nazis, von Dassanowsky makes a compelling case that Cameron's *Titanic* is a German mountain film set upon the sea ice of the North Atlantic.[1433] Von Dassanowsky even strongly suggests the heroine in the *Titanic*, Rose, is actually Riefenstahl herself. He then intimates that Cameron may have indeed directed the *Titanic* to show how Riefenstahl's untamed feminism eventually overcame her compromised relationship with the chauvinism of the Nazis. This was represented by Rose's refusal to marry her dictatorial fiancé on the ship. In the end, Riefenstahl, like Rose, redeemed herself from the dictatorial Nazi regime.

Even more startling, Cameron also borrowed from Nazi Germany's own version of the *Titanic* made in 1943. In the Nazi version, the hero of the story was a German officer who blamed the profit-crazed capitalistic owners of the ship for sinking the Titanic. Nature's iceberg proved to be more powerful than all of the superficial worries and concerns of those attached to the manipulations of the stock market. A romance also develops between a German musician and an already engaged woman. This romance, however, is left undeveloped in the Nazi film. Cameron's movie seemingly picks up where the Nazis left off by focusing on the romance between Rose and Jack. Jack Dawson, of course, is the drifter played by Leonardo Dicaprio who upsets the pre-arranged marriage plans of Rose's aristocratic fiancé.

One also wonders if Cameron's *Avatar* was made with Riefenstahl's never-completed *Nuba* documentary film in mind? Instead of the *Nuba*, Cameron calls the nature worshiping indigenous tribe in *Avatar* the *Na'vi*. Just exactly who are these *Na'vi* anyway? The answer to that question may be much more compromising than many might assume. Jewish historian Dr. Harold Brackman noted that what unsettled him the most about Cameron's *Avatar* was that it borrowed heavily from the Neo-Nazism of Savitri Devi.[1434] It was Savitri Devi who helped transition the Nazi blood and soil

1433 Von Dassanowsky, "A Mountain of a Ship: Locating the Bergfilm in James' Cameron's Titanic," *Cinema Journal*, issue 40:4, Summer 2001.

1434 Brackman, Harold, "About Avatars, Caveat Emptors," *Jerusalem Post*, Dec. 30, 2009.

mythology into a Neo-Nazi New Age environmentalism that lurks in the background of the modern green movement.

Furthermore, James Cameron's heroes in both films, Jack and Jake, are based on Jack London himself.[1435] This means that social Darwinism and the call of the wild means something to James Cameron. Although the Nazis did burn Jack London's Marxist-socialist books, they never destroyed his wilderness adventure stories of the far north that he is so famous for.[1436] That Jack London was also a white racist[1437] only compromises the issues further. Thus, James Cameron has managed to give the world two block-buster movies starring Leni Riefenstahl and Jack London, all decorated in green socialist themes and wrapped up with *volkisch* streaks of multicultural, indigenous racism. According to researcher Gitta Sereny, who spent time with Riefenstahl in the 1980s, Horst Kettner, her boyfriend of many years, was "less restrained in his frankly anti-Semitic comments."[1438]

Certainly James Cameron loathes the mythical Hitler of the modern leftist imagination that trumpets the Nazis as an extreme right-wing movement. On the other hand, do we really believe Cameron does not know Hitler was called *Avatar* by Savitri Devi in her 1958 Neo-Nazi manifesto called *The Lightning and the Sun?* Put in another way, can the shift to New Age indigenous environmentalism atone for the racist political biology of the Nazi past like getting out of a previous bad relationship comparable to Rose's refusal to get married? While James Cameron certainly thinks so, the verdict is still out with regard to this particular ecological question. Switching from National Socialism to a *National Geographic* indigenous multiculturalism is not as big a repentance as many would like to presume. Indeed, with regard to finding indigenous or authentic mountain peoples for her films, Hitler once observed that Leni "scours the villages in search of the peasant types she requires."[1439]

1435 Parisi, Paula. *Titanic and the Making of James Cameron*. New York: Newmarket Press (1998) 2012, p. 100.

1436 See Jack London's book burning exhibit on the United States Holocaust Memorial Museum at http://www.ushmm.org/museum/exhibit/online/bookburning/author_detail.php?content=bblondon.xml.

1437 Hari, Johann, "Jack London's Dark Side," *Slate*, Aug. 15, 2010.

1438 Sereny, *Albert Speer's Battle with Truth*, p. 132.

1439 *Hitler's Table Talk*, midday March 13, 1944, p. 543.

How the Nazi Global Warming Apocalypse
led to the German Green Party

While modernity often mocks the Scriptures, especially with regard to its predictions of the apocalypse (cf. 2 Pet. 3:1-9), it remains completely unaware of how fundamental the Biblical eschaton is to its own outlook. In fact, modernity would not be modern without it. Most evolutionary and revolutionary ideas about progress within history which leads to some hopeful goal in the future are firmly rooted in the Biblical tradition. Indeed, Biblical history progresses from the Old to the New Testaments, eventually culminating in a catastrophic, yet victorious, Messianic outcome (Jer. 30-31; Matt. 24-25; 2 Thess. 1-2; Rev. 6-20). Having grown up under Western civilization's strong Christian foundations, modern man has imbibed deeply from the Biblical-eschatological view of history in spite of his secularity. "We of today, concerned with the unity of universal history and with its progress toward an ultimate goal or at least toward a better world, are still in the line of prophetic and messianic monotheism—however little we may think of ourselves in those terms."[1440]

Christian theology about the apocalypse has been transposed into secular progressive ideologies like socialism, Marxism and even National Socialism. Although Hitler's 1,000-year Reich was undoubtedly based on Nietzsche's 1,000-year Zarathustran kingdom[1441] of superman values rooted in the Earth, the Nazis promoted it as a counteraction against the Jewish-Christian millennium predicted by the Apostle John in Revelation 20. As Christianity receded behind the wave of Romanticism, existentialism, Naturalism and secularism in Western culture, apocalyptic political hubris filled the vacuum. "The moderns elaborate a philosophy of history by secularizing theological principles and applying them to an ever increasing number of empirical facts."[1442]

A good case in point of this modern contradiction is the global warming apocalypse being preached by environmentalists. Environmentalists have been particularly guilty of drawing up apocalyptic scenarios and warnings in order to mobilize people into drastic political actions. Ironically enough, this has led to insoluble political burdens which continue to haunt the

---

[1440] Lowith, *Meaning in History*, p. 19.
[1441] Nietzsche, *Thus Spake Zarathustra*, p. 240.
[1442] Lowith, *Meaning in History*, p. 19.

modern mindset as ideologues, policy analysts and politicians foist upon unsuspecting populaces the full crushing weight of their apocalyptic concerns. With global warming/climate change threatening the entire planet so imminently, radical political action must be taken in order to avoid the inevitable catastrophe. Such an apocalyptic outlook has placed unprecedented burdens on modern society and has also left the hard sciences in the lurch by requiring an evidential basis for catastrophic global warming.

In point of fact, one of the original popularizers of the global warming apocalypse was Guenther Schwab[1443] (1904-2006), a former Austrian Nazi.[1444] In 1958, Schwab wrote a fictional novel built on Goethe's Faustian play entitled *Dance with the Devil*. While a few scientists since the late 1800s had contemplated the possibility of minor global warming coming from industrial pollution, Schwab used Goethe's dramatic approach to convert the theory into an apocalyptic crisis. The book outlines many looming environmental emergencies, including anthropogenic global warming. Guenther Schwab's very popular novel was an apocalyptic game changer.[1445] By the early 1970s, it had been translated into several languages and had sold more than a million copies. "Schwab's most important service was in reaching out to a large audience with a spell binding story about a host of environmental problems."[1446]

Schwab was no doubt aware of Hermann Flohn's (1912-97) research efforts with regard to global warming attributed to rising CO_2 levels that began during the Nazi era and continued in Germany throughout most of the 20th century.[1447] While Flohn received his doctorate in 1934 and then began work for the German Meteorological Service, he is now considered to be one of the most important climate researchers of the 20th century. For almost half a century, global warming and rising CO_2 levels became

---

[1443] This section is an expanded version of an article posted on the Internet site American Thinker entitled, "The Nazi Origins of Apocalyptic Global Warming," by Mark Musser, Feb. 15, 2011.

[1444] Gert Gröning, Joachim Wolschke-Bulmahn, Stiftung Naturschutzgeschichte, Naturschutz und Demokratie!?: Dokumentation der Beiträge zur Veranstaltung der Stiftung Naturschutzgeschichte und des Zentrums für Gartenkunst und Landschaftsarchitektur (CGL) der Leibniz Universität Hannover in Kooperation mit dem Institut für Geschichte und Theorie der Gestaltung (GTG) der Universität der Künste Berlin, Martin Meidenbauer Verlag, 2006, p. 113.

[1445] Dominck, pp. 152-157.

[1446] Ibid., p. 156.

[1447] Archibald, David, "The Nazi Origins of Renewable Energy and Global Warming," *American Thinker*, July 20, 2017.

a steady theme in his research that merited several prestigious awards. In 1973, he received the Order of Merit from the Federal Republic of Germany. In 1986 he received the International Meteorological Organization Prize followed by the Order of Merit of North Rhine-Westphalia in 1993. This very Germany odyssey began in 1941 when Flohn published the first German language article on global warming entitled, "The Activity of Man as a Climate Factor." The 1930s, otherwise known as the Dust Bowl years on the American plains, was an exceptionally warm period starring 1934 in particular, which is considered by many to be the hottest year on record. While Flohn was not a Nazi Party member, he became the chief meteorologist under Hermann Goering's Luftwaffe High Command. The great irony is that the global warming of the 1930s came to an abrupt hault just in time for the invasion of Russia in 1941 when the German Army essentially froze to death near the gates of Moscow. Flohn believed that rising CO_2 and global warming was a more dangerous tandem than even the complications associated with nuclear energy. Yet 1940 to 1975 proved to be a significant cool down worldwide before warming up again in the 1980s.

Beyond global warming concerns and before Rachel Carson's *Silent Spring* was published in 1962, touching off American environmentalism, Schwab worried about the growing threat of pesticides in his own book as he believed DDT was poisoning everyone on a regular basis. He also said the population bomb was more dangerous than the atomic bomb. In fact, Schwab's book prefaced the entire litany of modern environmental problems that is everywhere trumpeted today. "This popular book presented the legion of environmental maladies all linked together, and it provided an overwhelming empirical documentation for all of the problems it discussed ... Schwab's 14 page bibliography provided an excellent summary of the substantial literature on environmental issues that was already available in 1958."[1448] At one point in his novel, Schwab even opined over the fragile relationship between oxygen and carbon dioxide in the atmosphere. Assuming the planet had only about 100 years remaining, Schwab fretted over the continuing rise of carbon dioxide which "will absorb and hold fast the warmth given out by the earth. This will cause the climate to become milder and the Polar ice will begin to thaw. As a result, there will be a rise in the level of the ocean and whole continents will be flooded."

[1448] Dominick, p. 156.

Thus, long before the green community spent billions of dollars on global warming research, Schwab had already clearly spelled out the doomsday climate apocalypse. Schwab's book sales skyrocketed from 1960 onward—right about the time when, ironically enough, according to the *hockey stick graph* that became iconic in the 2001 Intergovernmental Panel on Climate Change (IPCC) Third Assessment Report, climate researchers began to "hide the decline" by artificially removing some of their proxy data they earlier relied on. This helped them calibrate their scheme with actual observable temperatures that allegedly showed exponential global warming in the latter half of the 20th century. How scientific was the IPCC consensus? They basically came to the same conclusion about global warming that Schwab promoted in his best-selling fictional novel written some 40 years earlier.

Guenther Schwab had been a strong nature lover since boyhood. By the 1920s, he became very active in the emerging environmental movement in Austria. In the 1930s, he joined the Nazi Party. In the post war 1950s, Guenther Schwab's brand of environmentalism also played a fundamental role in the development of the green anti-nuclear movement in West Germany.[1449] The dropping of the atom bomb and the nuclear fallout of the Cold War helped to globalize the greens into an apocalyptic *peace* movement with Guenther Schwab as one of its original spokesmen. The unprecedented destruction in Germany brought on by industrialized warfare never before seen in the history of the world only served to radicalize the German greens into an apocalyptic movement. Their hatred towards global capitalism became even more vitriolic precisely because the capitalists were now also in charge of a dangerous nuclear arsenal threatening the entire planet.

Later, Guenther Schwab joined the advisory panel of the "Society of Biological Anthropology, Eugenics and Behavior Research."[1450] Schwab was especially concerned with the burgeoning overpopulation explosion in the Third World that he was sure would eventually overrun Europe. By advocating modern racial science based on genetics, Schwab believed the population bomb, together with its associated environmental degradation, could be averted. Here, of course, Schwab's mixing of

---

[1449] Nehring, Holger, "Cold War, Apocalypse, and Peaceful Atoms: Interpretations of Nuclear Energy in the British and West German Anti-Nuclear Weapons Movements, 1955-1964." *Historical Social Research*, vol. 29, 2004, No. 3, pp. 150-170.

[1450] Olsen, p. 82.

environmentalism and eugenics can be directly traced back to the Nazi SS doctrine of blood and soil.

The success of *Dance with the Devil* helped Schwab establish an international environmental organization called The World League for the Defense of Life (WSL). Not surprisingly, Werner Haverbeck, former Hitler Youth member and Nazi environmental leader of The Reich's League for Folk National Character and Landscape, later became the chairman of Schwab's organization.[1451] In 1973, Haverbeck blamed the environmental crisis in Germany on American capitalism.[1452] It was an unnatural colonial import which had infected Germany like a deadly foreign body.[1453] Werner Haverbeck's wife, Ursula, was charged with Holocaust denial in October 2010.

Both Schwab's organization and Haverbeck were also instrumental in establishing the German Green Party in 1980[1454] along with other former Nazis and Nazi sympathizers.[1455] In particular, former Nazi SS officer August Haussleiter (1905-1989) organized the growing number of anti-nuclear ecological groups throughout the 1970s to "create the Green Party, with himself as its first chairman, and Ludwig Klages' 1913 proto-Nazi German youth movement tract *Man and Earth* as its founding manifesto."[1456] Klages promoted Nietzsche's Earth-based existentialist philosophy into the German *wandervogel* movement of the early 20th century.

Ludwig Klages (1872-1956) was at the heart of the early *volkisch* green movement in Bavaria up until the 1920s. Hitler's mentor Dietrich Eckart personally met Klages when he was teaching his biocentric philosophy, at the University of Munich, that regarded modern Western reason as an artificial imposition upon man that separated him from the natural world.[1457] Both Eckart and Hitler met with Klages in 1922 during the early days of the rise of National Socialism.[1458] Like many *volkisch* thinkers of his day, Klages characterized the Judeo-Christian worldview as a false moral spirituality that led to the industrial revolution and pollution of the landscape built upon modern science's Abrahamic concept of the land. Klages railed

---

[1451] Dominick, p. 157.

[1452] Olsen, p. 93.

[1453] Ibid., p. 44.

[1454] Dominick, p. 157.

[1455] Knöfel, Ulrike, "Beuys Biography: Book Accuses Artist of Close Ties to Nazis," *Spiegel Online International*, May 17, 2013.

[1456] Zubrin., p. 197.

[1457] Tyson, p. 53.

[1458] Ibid.

against the destruction of nature under progressive European Christian culture, using the virtual extinction of the buffalo on the American plains as one prime example. In *Man and Earth*, Klages sharply complained about modernity: "An unparalleled orgy of destruction has seized mankind, and it is 'civilization' that has unleashed this lust for murder, so that the earth withers before its noxious breath. These are indeed the fruits of progress!" During the early to mid-1930s Klages was a highly honored academic in Nazi Germany, but Alfred Rosenberg later characterized him as a primitive hedonist[1459] because of his seeming lack of interest in militarization.[1460] Yet Klages was a loyal anti-Semitic Nazi up until the end of the war, and his biopolitics and existentialist *lebensphilosophie* (*life philosophy*) was used and esteemed by certain SS Nazi thinkers during the 1930s and '40s—including August Haussleiter.

After the Nazi underpinnings of the German Green Party were fully exposed in the early 1980s, the greens managed such embarrassing facts with some house cleaning and lots of cosmetics. August Haussleiter resigned in 1981.[1461] On March 14, 1983, 75-year-old Werner Vogel, the oldest Green Party member in Germany at the time, was forced to resign from a seat he won in Parliament because of his Nazi past.[1462] Vogel initially balked at calls for his resignation: "I have done nothing to reproach myself for." However, he was forced to acquiesce and give up his office because had had been a storm trooper and an official in the Nazi Interior Ministry. The German Green Party further distanced themselves by conveniently labeling such Nazi greens as extreme *far-right* ecologists. German ecologists who are nationalists or racists are simply labeled *right wing* as a knee-jerk leftist reaction to the horrors of Nazism. Leftist do-gooders believe they could have never possibly behaved in such a manner. This kind of self-righteousness has blinded the left to its own potential cruelty and misanthropy.

Indeed, in his book on so-called right-wing ecology called *Nature and Nationalism*, Jonathan Olsen inadvertently reveals how close the left and right wings of the environmental movement are to each other in contemporary Germany. For example, in his very revealing chapter called "The Cunning

---

[1459] Ibid.

[1460] See *The Philosophy of Life and Death: Ludwig Klages and the Rise of a Nazi Biopolitics* (New York: Palgrave Macmillan, 2013) by Nitzan Lebovic.

[1461] "Another Member of Germany's Green Party Found to Have Been a Member of the Nazi Party," *JTA*, April 28, 1983.

[1462] "Green Party Member, An Ex-Nazi, to Resign," *New York Times*, March 14, 1983.

of Nature," he talks about ultra conservative right-wing ecologist Herbert Gruhl who, "in contrast to the New Left, did not view capitalism as *a priori* dangerous."[1463] He then discusses Schwab's and Haverbeck's WSL organization as further to the right than Gruhl, but which was filled with anti-capitalist rhetoric.[1464] As such, according to Olsen, the WSL is further to the right than Gruhl, but is anti-capitalist—whereas Gruhl—who is ultra-right, is not anti-capitalist per se. How can the WSL become more anti-capitalist the further they move to the right? If taken literally, it would appear that Schwab and Haverbeck have gone so far to the right they actually went full circle so as to meet up with the extreme left on the other side of the spectrum. It certainly seems the cunning of nature has indeed made the left/right distinction pervious to all kinds of logical inconsistencies.

Olsen digs a deeper hole when he begins to talk about *New Left* environmentalism, which he says has moved away from traditional Marxist thought. This is an understatement of vast proportions. Such a conversion from Marxism to environmentalism was actually a huge transformation of the left in the 1960s and '70s. Many leftists originally considered this makeover to be a betrayal of its humanist heritage.[1465] Instead of promoting pro-socialist and/or Marxian propaganda, many leftists began gravitating to environmental apocalyptic books on overpopulation. Furthermore, how can the *New Left* really be considered left if they have abandoned traditional leftist Marxism for environmentalism? "For many in the New Left, traditional orthodox Marxism shared with capitalism a disastrous view of nature as mere stuff awaiting human completion, a thing to be exploited."[1466] Did not Hitler and the Nazi Party dump Marxism as well for very similar reasons? Did not the Nazis lump both capitalism and Marxism together as a materialistic heresy, albeit a Jewish one? Would not Uncle Stalin himself label such treachery by the *New Left* as right-wing extremism comparable to Mussolini's adoption of fascism? Olsen goes on to compromise his positions even further:

> … the New Left of the 1970's began to turn away from the productivist paradigm of traditional left-wing politics. The disillusionment with Marxism manifested itself in the 1970's as the language of

---

1463   Olsen, p. 91.
1464   Ibid., p. 92.
1465   Zubrin, pp. 125-132.
1466   Ibid., p. 89.

Marxism—class struggle, the iron laws of social development, the primacy of objective structures over subjective will—gave away to the language of Nietzsche, irrationalism, and spirituality. Thus from Nietzsche the New Left took its critique of technology, science and progress.[1467]

Is Olsen completely unaware of the strong National Socialist connections to Nietzsche?

Hitler befriended Nietzsche's pro-fascist sister Elizabeth.[1468] Here is another sore spot among Western scholars who love Nietzsche's philosophy. Many are deeply offended by such inconvenient truths when they discover such historical connections. They quickly deny that any such associations are substantially significant, and often complain about how the Nazis abused Nietzsche's philosophy. Dr. Richard Weikart persuasively argues that Nietzsche became more important to Hitler as time wore on.[1469] Regardless of the debate over how Nietzschian were the Nazis,[1470] many people are shocked that there even is a connection in the first place precisely because they have adopted a simplistic caricature of National Socialism that only exists in the imagination of secular leftist opinion. This erroneous caricature is largely due to the false right/left dichotomy that has been seared into their consciences, and which continues to misdirect all studies on the Third Reich.

In reality, there should be no surprise whatsoever that the global warming apocalypse conjured up by the extreme far *right wing* ecologist Guenther Schwab was later embraced by New Left German environmentalists. The nuances between them, though certainly very real, are still much more superficial than most scholars want to admit. Indeed, the United Nations Secretary General between 1972 and 1981 was former Austrian Nazi Kurt

---

[1467] Ibid.

[1468] See especially *Forgotten Fatherland: The True Story of Nietzsche's Sister and Her Lost Aryan Colony* (New York: Broadway Paperbacks, 1992) by Ben Macintyre. Macintyre's interesting book shows the rocky relationship that Nietzsche had with his racist sister who later became a staunch fascist and heralded Nazism as the heirs of Nietzsche's thought. Macintyre does not believe that Nietzsche was a proto-fascist, and that this perception was foisted upon Nietzsche's legacy largely because of his wayward sister. Perish the thought that there is actually a substantial agreement between Nietzsche's supermen and the Master Race.

[1469] Weikart, *Hitler's Religion*, pp. 25-26.

[1470] See *Nietzsche and the Nazis: A Personal View*. Loves Park, Illinois: Ockham's Razor Publishers, 2010, (2006), by Dr. Stephen Hicks.

Waldheim. Not only did Waldheim emphasize a pro-European United Nations during his tenure, he was also heavily involved in strongly developing its green wing.[1471] At the 1972 UN Conference on the Environment in Stockholm, Waldheim gave the keynote address to kick off the international environmental movement. It was in Stockholm that the UN Environment Programme or UNEP was essentially established. Today, the United Nations has a strong pro-European environmental emphasis that often uses the Third World as a tool to subvert capitalism and international free trade. How is it possible that the *conservative* Kurt Waldheim worked so effectively in the leftist international amalgam that is the United Nations? His green streak is the answer.

The global warming apocalypse is largely a German invention of both so-called right and left-wing ecologists. The original political push to combat the global warming apocalypse began as early as January 1986.[1472] The German Physical Society published a doomsday article entitled, "Warning of an Impending Climate Catastrophe." This report later became the basis for a major article on the subject published in August 1986 on *Der Spiegel* that showed Cologne's famous cathedral half drowned underwater on the cover page. German physicists, armed with such an apocalyptic outlook, were thus prophesying rising waters on a scale that the world has not seen since Noah's flood. The Climate Research Unit (CRU) in East Anglia also kicked off its global warming research in England the very same year.

The incredible global warming campaign that began in the mid-1980s and carried over into the 21st century also received much needed propaganda help from Holtzbrinck Publishers, who purchased *Scientific American* in 1986 and then *Nature* magazine in 1995. Many Western scientists were fed a steady eco-friendly diet of pro-global warming environmental propaganda coming from both *Scientific American* and *Nature* magazines. Yet the founder of this German media giant, Georg von Holtzbrinck, was a former Nazi. He joined the National Socialist German Students League in 1931, and later became a Nazi Party member.[1473] Von Holtzbrinck made his publishing fortune during the heyday of the Third Reich by publishing

---

[1471] See "Waldheim's Monster: United Nations Ecofascist Programme," 2009 by William Walter Kay found on ecofascism.com.

[1472] Rosenthal, John, "The Secret History of Climate Alarmism: A Very German Story of Power Politics Disguised as Environmentalism." *The Weekly Standard*, Vol. 15, No. 44, Aug. 9, 2010.

[1473] Schuler, Thomas, "Evidence of Opportunistic Behavior: How a German publisher maneuvered himself through the Nazi era." *The Atlantic Times*, Feb. 2009.

pro-Nazi magazines and books. In particular, he especially did well selling Hitler's favorite novelist Karl May, who turned Apache warriors and German pioneers into Western heroes. Karl May's anti-cowboy romances have become the hallmark of most dark Hollywood Westerns made in the movies today, especially since the death of John Wayne in 1979.

Far in advance of all the scientific research, the greens, especially those stemming from the German camp, already knew the global warming apocalypse was imminent and that an anti-capitalist call to immediate action was necessary to confront the looming disaster. Long before Al Gore's "Inconvenient Truth," green Nazi Guenther Schwab played an early important role in catalyzing the frightening leftist theory of global warming. With no small thanks to Schwab, the great tribulation of the global warming apocalypse was ushered into the modern consciousness behind the collapse of the millennial 1,000-year Third Reich.

Green Neo-Nazis

Even many neo-Nazis are green. In October of 2009, Jeff Hughes of Nanaimo, British Columbia, was shot to death by the Royal Canadian Mounted Police. He had a Nazi flag in his apartment and belonged to a white supremacist group known as Stormfront. He was a Neo-Nazi environmentalist. He was very religious about recycling. His neighbors described him as "a kind and caring Neo-Nazi who wanted to protect the environment."[1474] Likewise, former KKK leader David Duke from Louisiana is a nature photographer and avid birdwatcher.[1475] He loves to spend much time in the Austrian Alps enjoying the mountain air and superb scenery like a free wandering bird.

Back in 2008, a Neo-Nazi group adopted a half-mile section of a highway in Springfield, Mo., to pick up trash.[1476] This, of course, created quite a controversy as people began to complain about the signs along the roadway showing who indeed cleaned it up. The Neo-Nazi group responded by posting on their website that all the complaints were a "lame attempt

---

[1474] Bellaart, Darrell, "Man Shot by B.C. Police Described as 'Kind, Caring' neo-Nazi," *Canwest News Service*, Oct. 27, 2009.

[1475] "Klu Klux Klan Mastermind Now a Bird Watcher in Austria," *Austrian Times*, April 15, 2009.

[1476] Bellaart, Darrell, "Man Shot by B.C. Police Described as 'Kind, Caring' neo-Nazi," *Canwest News Service*, Oct. 27, 2009.

to insult National Socialist pro-environmental/green policies."[1477] Not surprisingly, the Ku Klux Klan has on occasion picked up the green cross for similar purposes as well.[1478]

There is also a Libertarian National Socialist Green Party in America that touts sustainable development, Indo-European living space, and an Aryan cultural revival all at the same time. The libertarian emphasis comes through in that they are more *liberal* than their Neo-Nazi counterparts. "The forum has a swastika with a green flag on its homepage and promotes itself as an alternative to white supremacist sites, a place where people of all races are welcome as long as they oppose racial mixing."[1479] Promoting a Green Nazi flag with a black swastika in the middle of it, its Internet website makes links to other radical environmental groups and showcases the world of Nature:

> Humans originated in the natural world, and are still dependent upon it. While we can perhaps build plastic cities and generate our food artificially, removing us from our environment deprives us of a superior order to anything we've produced so far, as well as something of great beauty and possibilities for learning. Currently the public is in denial of the dire situation of our environment, which can be summarized as follows: humanity is using too much land, over-farming natural animal resources, and creating too much pollution. While the amount of land and food that it produces remains the same, the human population of earth continues to grow exponentially. At some point, we will either expand to fill every space on earth, thus causing starvation and worldwide collapse, or we will learn to limit our population. Further, as we grow, we move more people to first-world lifestyles that are high in energy cost and waste production. The result is like a cancer infesting the globe, in that we will eat it from within and only confront the consequences when they have reached a fatal level. To preserve nature, we must reserve most of the land and sea for the complex interlocking orbits of natural ecosystems that support each other, and through them, the whole. Every creature serves a purpose, from monocellular bacteria to

---

[1477] Ibid.

[1478] "Road Cleaned by Neo-Nazis May be Named for Rabbi," *The Associated Press*, June 21, 2009.

[1479] Davey, Monica, "Behind the Rampage, Loner with a Taste for Nazism," *New York Times*, March 23, 2005.

elephants, and without these different levels of the global eco-system being healthy, the whole collapses structurally and thus, after a delay, falls apart on a visible level. For this reason we must discipline our expansion and habits before we reach a stage of visible failure. Whether or not global warming or any of the other current symptoms of nature collapse are accurately described, the basic mathematics remains the same: if we keep growing in population, and using more resources and producing more waste, eventually we will consume the earth and poison ourselves with our own waste. The primary principle of the LNSG is thus that we must achieve a balance with our environment and grant to it exclusively most of the resources on earth; in order to do this, we must re-organize our thinking toward a naturalistic view of life and impose it on all humanity.

This particular website was a favorite of troubled teenager Jeff Weise. In March of 2005, Weise went on a shooting rampage at the Red Lake Indian Reservation High School in Minnesota.[1480] Incredibly, even though it was "the deadliest school rampage since 15 people died at Columbine High School near Littleton, Colorado, in 1999,"[1481] this teenage slaughter event was only lightly covered in the news media. Ten people were killed including Wiese. "A real Nazi killer commits horrible acts, and much to the media's disappointment, he's linked to green groups. Not convenient, not gonna go down that path."[1482] Jeff Weise was known to have praised Adolf Hitler and considered himself a Native American.[1483] The year before, he even threatened to shoot up the school for Hitler's birthday.[1484] When he actually did do it, he left so many bullet holes they could not be counted by the authorities.

[1480] Morano, Mark "Eco-Extremism Being Ignored in School Shooting Case," *CNS News. com*, March 27, 2005.

[1481] Davey, Monica, "Behind the Rampage, Loner with a Taste for Nazism," *New York Times*, March 23, 2005.

[1482] Morano, Mark "Eco-Extremism Being Ignored in School Shooting Case," *CNS News. com*, March 27, 2005.

[1483] Davey, Monica, "Behind the Rampage, Loner with a Taste for Nazism," *New York Times*, March 23, 2005.

[1484] Ibid.

It is simply not enough to assume that since modern environmentalism is so international and multi-cultural today, and therefore not racist, that it is not eco-fascist in any way. Racism is just one form of anti-humanism, and fascism goes well beyond racism. The environmental movement was largely founded upon the anti-humanism of the German Romantic movement. National Socialism morphed *volkisch* Romanticism into Aryan racism. Today, however, environmentalists hold contempt for mankind in general. Gone are the *good old days* of racist environmentalism. Now the problem is humanity itself. "In practice fundamentalist pantheism seeks to exclude human beings from their own habitat, the property they rightfully own."[1485] In other words, one does not have to be a Nazi environmental racist to cleanse people from their habitat or landscape. One can hold to other forms of landscape cleansing above and beyond the confinements of race.

Former British Prime Minister Gordon Brown's environmental advisor, Jonathan Porritt, warned, "Britain must drastically reduce its population if it is to build a sustainable society."[1486] The Optimum Population Trust, of which Porritt is the patron, calls for Britain to cut its population to 30 million people by 2031.[1487] Today, Britain has 61 million people living within its borders. Reducing Britain's population by 30 million people within two decades is a form of landscape cleansing no matter how clinically the Optimum Population Trust tries to couch it. Furthermore, the environmental push to re-tribalize people into self-sufficient bioregions that are less destructive to ecosystems is eerily similar to the blood and soil doctrine of the Nazis.

When modern environmentalists compare people to a cancer hoping that some plague or virus will come along and reduce the population of mankind,[1488] how is this an improvement upon the Nazis comparing Jews to viruses, bacteria or even invasive weeds?[1489] As bad as the Nazi racist views were, they seemed to at least care about their own German people, but an ever-increasing number of environmentalists have contempt for people in

---

[1485] Stirling, p. 19.

[1486] Leake, Jonathan and Montague, Brendan, "UK Population must fall to 30M, says Poritt," *The Sunday Times*, March 22, 2009.

[1487] Ibid.

[1488] David Graber is a Research Biologist for the National Park Service.

[1489] Pois, p. 124.

general. If left unchecked, this may potentially even mutate into something worse than the National Socialist experiment.

Environmentalist Ingrid Newkirk commented, "Mankind is a cancer; we're the biggest blight on the face of the earth. . . . Phasing out the human race will solve every problem on earth, social and environmental."[1490] This ecological sentiment together with a growing obsession with overpopulation is not a good combination, especially as the green movement usurps more and more political power to itself controlling academia and the media along the way to propagandize environmentalism as the final say on what is existentially true. "Among environmentalists sharing two or three beers, the notion is quite common that if only some calamity could wipe out the entire human race, other species might once again have a chance."[1491] In light of such statements, Dr. Timothy Ball sarcastically pointed out, "The Roman adage 'in wine there is much truth' applies although apparently Ms. Newkirk (quoted above) did not need such liquid courage."[1492] Cleansing people from the landscape for the sake of the environment is a common green dream these days. Furthermore, while it is true the greens today are showing no signs of putting people into concentration camps, at least not at this point, the Son of God Himself does not separate attitudes and intentions from the actual crime itself (cf. Matt. 5:21-30).

Moreover, the green socialists today would not be nearly as crude as their racist National Socialist forefathers. Rather than a "green version of neo-paganism armed with Panzer tanks,"[1493] today's greens are armed with environmental policies, lawyers, regulations, activist groups and taxes:

> Unlike their fascist forbears, environmentalists are cautious about preaching abolition of democracy. However, they are not shy about practicing abolition of democracy. In every western country they have created parallel governance. This diarchy is achieved by appropriating state resources and integrating them with movement-controlled state-like entities in the private sector. Their most visible achievements are the imperious "Environmental" ministries they conjured at all levels of government in the 1970s. These are supplemented by a myriad of agencies and sub-departments involved in

---

1490 Newkirk, Ingrid, *People for the Ethical Treatment of Animals*.
1491 Richard Conniff of the *Audubon Society*.
1492 Ball, Timothy, "The Anti-Human Agenda," *Canada Free Press*, May 19, 2008.
1493 Zimmerman, "Possible Political Problems of Earth-Based Religiosity."

environmental-regulation. Then there is the deliberately inscrutable jumble of quasi-government tribunals and councils conjoined to thousands of environmentalist non-governmental organizations. The upshot is government policies regarding land and water use, fisheries and wildlife, forestry and mining, energy and climate, culture and education, etc. are drafted and implemented by un-elected, unaccountable, and largely unknown people. Wither democracy. . . .[1494]

Rather than horde Jews into the inner-city ghetto via railroad cattle cars, today, the green socialists are doing everything possible to force people out of the suburbs and countryside via light rail through what is called *smart growth* techniques, all in the name of sparing Mother Nature the impacts of human pollution.

The Potential Dangers of Modern Eco-fascism

In July 2009, a controversy erupted in Jaslo, Poland over an oak tree that was scheduled to be taken down due to a construction project.[1495] Come to find out, this particular tree was one of Hitler's oaks planted by the *Wehrmacht* in 1942 to commemorate his birthday. "The southern Polish village of Jaslo was one of several hundred communities to be given a tiny oak from the *Fuhrer's* plantation near his birthplace in *Branau am Inn*."[1496] Planted on April 20, "the ritual was always the same: a brass band and a speech by the German-imposed mayor that would always invoke the metaphor of deep roots, of tiny acorns turning into great oaks, of 1,000 year Reichs. Attendance was compulsory."[1497]

An 81-year-old Polish eyewitness, Kazimierez Polak, watched the ceremony with a few of his friends, saying: "It was part of an effort to make Jaslo German."[1498] Hence, Mr. Polak wanted to save the tree. He stressed the oak tree was "a silent witness to some of the greatest crimes of the 20th

[1494] Kay, William, "Gasman's Haeckel's Monism and the Birth of Fascist Ideology," 2012 found on ecofascism.com.
[1495] Boyes, Roger, "Polish Village Mayor is Determined Hitler Birthday Oak Will Not Last 1,000 Years," *Times Online*, July 8, 2009.
[1496] Ibid.
[1497] Ibid.
[1498] Ibid.

century."[1499] The mayor, however, wanted it taken down to rid the city of its dark Nazi shadow. A Jewish commentator in Israel had a suggestion, "This tree should be cut, put on a train, and incinerated."[1500] Perhaps most intriguing about this particular controversy, is how uninterested so many journalists were in delving into the Nazi environmental record behind the planting of that oak tree. It seems they have become too infatuated with environmental fascism to take notice.

These days, modern environmentalists continue to rush headlong into a dogmatic anti-human nature religion ready to take charge of people's lives. They are more than willing to socially engineer them into their sustainable development ascetic *Weltanschauung*. In *Eco-Imperialism: Green Power Black Death*, Paul Driessen powerfully points out how white rich environmental policies have had devastating consequences upon people living in the Third World. In his chapter entitled, "Cow Dung Forever," Driessen shows how *do-gooder* environmental policies foisted upon the Third World have severely curtailed efforts to develop a basic energy infrastructure for poor countries. This keeps many third-world nations in a position of "misery for millions under the guise of preserving ecological values and traditional lifestyles."[1501] Modern greens thus enforce a miserable indigenous lifestyle upon third-world countries. Rather than allow them to build dams and coal fire electricity plants, the greens offer solar and wind power instead. "Solar panels for huts, and huts forever, seems to be their motto."[1502]

Many people in the Third World actually resent the fact that rich environmental pressure groups in Europe and America have decided that green renewable energy is all that they will get. In the name of environmental activism, the greens have romanticized poverty.[1503] Environmentalists have also prevented genetically modified food and seed shipments from reaching Africa. These genetically modified seeds would greatly alleviate their hunger problems,[1504] but the greens hysterically cry "genetic pollution."[1505] The greens have also required many African countries to ban DDT. This

---

[1499]   Ibid.
[1500]   Ibid.
[1501]   Driessen, Paul. *Eco-Imperialism: Green Power, Black Death*. Bellevue, Washington: Merril Press, 2003-04, p. 35.
[1502]   Ibid.
[1503]   Ibid., p. 42.
[1504]   Ibid., pp. 45-61.
[1505]   Ibid., p. 47.

has sentenced millions of people to their deaths because of malaria.[1506] Unable to control mosquitoes with DDT, malaria is a widespread problem throughout much of Africa. Driessen calls this problem "Sustainable Mosquitoes—Expendable People."

In another chapter, Driessen displays a political cartoon in his book showing one black African talking to another, "Eco-imperialism stinks. At least colonialism did not kill us." According to Driessen, environmental eco-imperialism in Africa indirectly leads to 20 million unnecessary deaths annually.[1507] The modern greens have thus figured out a way to control populations of people of different skin color without panzers or gas chambers. Such environmental policies are bloodless on paper and do not require concentration or death camps.

The more the modern green movement is unwilling to face its National Socialist environmental past, or even remain unaware of it in the first place, the more likely they will open themselves up to eco-Nazi tendencies. Modern greens are becoming increasingly anti-Semitic by joining hands with the Palestinian cause against the nation of Israel.[1508] They have also been gung ho in boycotting Jewish goods internationally. Some modern greens go so far as to characterize the nation of Israel itself as an apartheid state with a false ecological occupation since they have allegedly displaced the indigenous Palestinians from their homeland. To more than a few radical greens, Israel is thus a false colonial import.

Such greens even accuse the Jews of polluting the promised land with development contrary to the native landscape: "The Israeli occupation is one of urban expansion, pollution, settler industrial agriculture, environmental racism, and ecological devastation. It has uprooted the indigenous flora and fauna, including the Palestinian people, and the indigenous food systems that existed prior to European settlement."[1509] Furthermore, many are unaware a green rationale has entered the anti-Jewish settlement discourse that continues to be acrimonious between Jews and Arabs as environmentalists argue Israel should not be allowed to build on *occupied* Palestinian soil. Thus, an environmental anti-Semitic anti-building campaign is alive and well in Israel as they oppose Jewish settlements and industrial development. "Although illegal under international law, Israel has established

---

[1506] Ibid., pp. 65-76.
[1507] Ibid., p. 86.
[1508] Meotti, Giulio, "Ecologists Against Jews," *Frontpage Magazine*, March 1, 2012.
[1509] "Animal Liberation Against Israeli Occupation," *Resistance Ecology*, Aug. 9, 2014.

over 18 industrial zones, implicated in worker exploitation and chemical waste contamination. The expansion of settlements and industrial zones in the occupied territories require an extensive road network that dissects and further seizes the land. The apartheid wall, 90% of which is in the occupied territories, has uprooted native woodlands and contaminated water supplies."[1510] Perhaps worst of all, some environmentalists declare Israel's conservationist practices as an outright sham: "Although there is a growing movement for animals in Israel, it is important to recognize that this cannot be separated from the colonial policies of the occupation."[1511] The Israelis, due to their false non-native ecological occupation of Palestine, are therefore, not true environmentalists: "The reality is that Israel is overwhelmingly destructive to animals, the land, and the people, and has displaced traditional systems and indigenous land to pave way for urban expansion, polluting industries, animal agriculture, road development, water scarcity, and the brutal oppression of the Palestinian people."[1512]

Back in the United States, notice the following *innocent* remarks written on a Seattle-based cable news blogsite by an environmentally minded person about going green:

> I think that making positive lifestyle changes in my (life) has made me LESS stressed. I feel healthier, happier and it has become habitual. It's the easiest thing in the world to just bring burlap bags from home to Safeway, taking the bus I can just sit back and listen to my MP3 player, buying organic and local has made me watch my diet, help out local agriculture, and has definitely encouraged me to start an exercise plan. I think going green has done everything BUT stress me out. It's the Christians and the rich who think that positive environmental compromise is stressful and that just means natural selection will take care of them.[1513]

The whiff of the Nazi environmental cadaver is unmistakable in this quote, everything from his healthy, *buy local* organic farm attitude to the natural selection of the Christians and the rich—lean, mean and green.

[1510] Ibid.

[1511] Ibid.

[1512] Ibid.

[1513] Blog comment on "Feeling Blue Over Going Green?" *Northwest Cable News*, Feb. 21, 2008.

The writer has a green and social Darwinian attitude toward the rich and the Christians with little consideration of where this all originated from. Worse, the blogger is simply thinking out loud. He expresses it so naturally and nonchalantly. Moreover, this opinion is by no means uncommon among many of those who consider themselves to be green.

Environmentalist Michael Zimmerman surprisingly acknowledged, "Because the United States is the world's most liberal democracy and has the highest percentage of church-going Christians of any industrial nation, chances may seem slim that something like a neo-pagan eco-fascism could ever arise here."[1514] Zimmerman thus realizes that Christianity has done much to keep eco-fascism at bay. However, as Christianity increasingly loses its influence over American life, and continues to compromise with many worldly *progressive* issues, like becoming green for example, it will become less of a counterweight to stave off the rise of sinister ideologies. Zimmerman's astute acknowledgment is a false sense of security. Germany used to be very Christian and very Protestant as well, up until about 1900.

In sum, there is a reason why more than a few people are beginning to call environmentalists eco-Nazis.[1515] Even Greenpeace's founder, Patrick Moore, who left the group because of their increasingly extremist views, has warned of a coming eco-fascism "where the planetary police would answer to no one but Mother Nature herself."[1516] However, it is one thing to call someone an eco-Nazi using metaphors, quite another to discover the Nazis had incorporated a green agenda into their political policymaking as well. For obvious reasons, putting these two things together is precisely what modern environmental historians do not want.

[1514] Zimmerman, Michael, "Possible Political Problems of Earth Based Religiosity."

[1515] Delingpole, James, "Why do I call them Eco-Nazis? Because they are Eco Nazis." *UK Telegraph*, Feb. 16, 2011.

[1516] See Patrick Moore's website *Greenspirit for a Sustainable Future*.

"Christianity is our foe. If animal rights is to succeed, we must destroy the Judeo-Christian Religious tradition."

Peter Singer, professor of bioethics
at Princeton University

"Isn't the only hope for the planet that the industrialized civilizations collapse? Isn't it our duty to bring that about?"

Maurice Strong, secretary general of the UNEP

"In our deeply interdependent world today, the iron rule remains—our world is one, unseparated, and interdependent. It is this world that is threatened by the impact of man's unplanned, selfish, and ever growing activities."

Kurt Waldheim, former Austrian Nazi
and UN Secretary General

"We have wished, we eco-freaks, for a disaster or for a social change to come and bomb us into the Stone Age."

Stewart Brand, Whole Earth Catalogue

"If radical environmentalists were to invent a disease to bring human populations back to sanity, it would probably be something like AIDS."

Earth First! Newsletter

Dr. Van den Bosch, University of California, expressed his lack of concern for "all those little brown people in poor countries" who might be saved from disease if DDT were used.

"Human happiness, and certainly human fecundity, is not as important as a wild and healthy planet: Some of us can only hope for the right virus to come along."

David Graber, biologist, National Park Service

"There are too many people and [banning DDT] is as good a way to get rid of them as any."

Charles Wurster, chief scientist,
Environmental Defense Fund

"Given the total, absolute, and final disappearance of Homo Sapiens not only would the Earth's Community of Life continue to exist but the ending of the human epoch on Earth would be greeted with a hearty 'good riddance.'"

Dr. Paul Taylor, professor of philosophy,
City College of New York

"If I could be reincarnated, I would return as a killer virus to lower human population levels."

Prince Philip & Duke of Edinburgh,
patron of World Wildlife Fund

"The earth is a mosque."

Ibrahim Abdul-Matin, Muslim environmentalist

"The earth has a cancer and the cancer is Man."

Club of Rome

"A total population of 250-300 million people, a 95% decline from present levels, would be ideal."

Ted Turner, CNN founder, Global Visionary

"Nature is my god. To me, nature is sacred: trees are my temples and forests my cathedral."

Mikhail Gorbachev, founder of Green Cross International, Club of Rome Member

"The Best of all mosques is nature herself."

Charles, Prince of Wales

"What the climate needs now is a contraction in humanity's use of resources; what our economic model demands is unfettered expansion. Only one of these sets of rules can be changed, and it's not the laws of nature."

Naomi Klein, Canadian social activist and environmentalist

CHAPTER EIGHT:

THE CORROSIVE EFFECTS OF GERMAN THEOLOGICAL ROMANTICISM

Eyewitnesses and historians have been scratching their heads for many decades now over how something as brutal and animalistic as National Socialism could have ever come about in the modern West. "How could one of the chief centers of the civilized world have become a torture chamber for millions of people, a country ruled by criminals so effectively that it conquered most of Europe, moving out toward other continents, planting its swastika from Norway to the Caucasus and Africa before it was brought down at the cost of 30 million lives? What happened to the nation of thinkers and poets, the 'good' Germans that the 19th century knew?"[1517]

Well, for starters, perhaps all those *good* German poets and intellects of the 19th century, most of whom were romantically involved in varying degrees with Romanticism and/or existentialism, and who spent an inordinate amount of time attacking the Biblical faith, were not as *good* as they have been trumpeted to be. If they had bothered to seriously read books like Hosea, Isaiah and Daniel from the archives of the Old Testament, rather than develop all kinds of contrived, complicated evolutionary schemes to doubt their authenticity, perhaps they could have been warned by such works, and thus avoided the Nazi doomsday, especially with regard to their anti-Semitism.

While much has been made of the fact that many Christians voted for Adolph Hitler, and that the church willingly collaborated with the Nazis, and was often co-opted by them, and was virtually silent during the Holocaust, it seems that much less attention is actually given over to the actual proto-Nazis and perpetrators themselves, i.e., the philosophers, Social Darwinists, secularists, socialists, nationalists, scientists, pantheists, doctors,

---

[1517] Davidson, Eugene, p. xiii, introduction to Albert Speer's *Inside the Third Reich*.

lawyers, environmentalists, landscape planners, cultists, policemen, etc., who did a much better job of the laying the groundwork for the Holocaust, and/or were later actually involved in its horrific crimes. While many of the perpetrators would have certainly had some sort of church background, both Protestant and Catholic Christianity had become very nominal by the early 1900s—with no small thanks to all of the *good* German thinkers and intellects of the 1800s who disdained the Bible, including liberal theologians schooled in Schleiermacher's theological Romanticism that valued religious feelings based on natural impulses over the dogmatic content of Scripture rooted in Jewish history.

More to the point, while Christianity had unfortunately institutionalized anti-Semitism in Europe for centuries, it must be pointed out the Holocaust did not occur until after Germany had become completely awash in Biblical skepticism and secularity. In spite of constant Christian anti-Semitism that included severe discrimination, inquisitions and pogroms over the centuries against the Jews, there was no Holocaust in Christian Europe for more than 1,500 years until the Second World War in the 20th century. "Anti-Semitism had existed in Germany—and in many other countries, such as France, Poland, and Russia, sometimes to a much greater extent—for centuries prior to the Holocaust, with no remotely comparable outcome."[1518]

In other words, it was in secular Nazi Germany, in which Judeo-Christian religious restraints were largely cast aside, that the Holocaust occurred. In fact, starting with the French Revolution, modern secularity culminated in the bloodbath that was the 20th century where profane communists, Nazis, and other radical socialists across the globe were responsible for millions upon millions of deaths for the sake of political utopianism that always produced worse results than the alleged injustices that were supposed to be ameliorated. Once the Judeo-Christian ethical worldview was left behind, the madness of secular forms of contrived social justice proved to be anything but. In Nazi Germany, the amoral existence of nature alone without any reference to a transcendental God who stood outside of the historical process as the ultimate Judge, did little to prick the conscience of Germans involved in murdering sprees in the killing fields of Poland, Ukraine, Byelorussia, the Baltics and the Balkans—areas where Germany was already in control, far away from the front lines in western Russia.

[1518] Zubrin, p. 71.

Even Jewish author Daniel Jonah Goldhagen of *Hitler's Willing Execu-tioners*, who does not mince words in his strong denunciation of Christian anti-Semitism, acknowledges that Christianity was not nearly as cruel as secularized Germany later became: "The Jews were left alive because the Church, in recognition of Christianity's and Judaism's common heri-tage, accepted the Jews' right to live and to practice their religion, though they were condemned to live in a degraded state, as punishment for their rejection of Jesus. Ultimately, the Church wanted not to kill the Jews, for they were redeemable, but to convert them. This would reaffirm the supremacy of Christianity. Such was the logic of pre-modern Christian anti-Semitism."[1519]

Because of the historical evidence, Goldhagen is forced to clearly dif-ferentiate pre-modern Christian anti-Semitism from the secular anti-Sem-itism that brewed in Germany after the Bible had lost its credibility in the face of modern philosophy, theology, science and Darwinian evolutionary theory. The fact of the matter is, leading Nazis hated Christianity almost as much as they hated the Jews. Hitler himself often criticized Christianity's *intolerant* dogmas. He was convinced the church was doomed to extinction as modern science races by its antiquated beliefs.

Ironically enough, such *scientific* anti-Christian sentiments actually continue the modern Western assault against Christianity, picking up where Hitler left off, not realizing how the Nazis had already helped blaze the trail for them in more ways than one. This same Nazi hostility toward Christianity is actually becoming more and more mainstream in the Western world, thanks largely to a whole century of German Biblical skepticism and criticism throughout the 1800s that has become the cornerstone of most scholarly discussions about the Christian religion in modern academia.[1520] In great opposition to Biblical theology, it was the natural theology of men like Lessing, Kant, Schleiermacher, Hegel, Baur, Strauss, Ritschl, Wellhausen and Harnack who supplied most of the ammunition against Christianity by eschewing its historical foundations laid in the Old and New Testaments, respectively, which both the Nazis and the moderns have been regularly using against it ever since. German naturalistic interpretations of the Bible catapulted modern secularity above the revelation of God as traditionally

---

[1519] Goldhagen, p. 53.
[1520] Dorrien, Gary. *Kantian Idealism and Hegelian Spirit: The Idealist Logic of Modern Theology*. Great Britain: Wiley Blackwell, 2015, p. 1.

understood, and this *evolutionary* process has gone on unabated throughout the 20th century as well.

Many of the German Protestant theologians of the 1800s were philosophical mystics who based their views on a Romanticized natural theology rather than the Bible. Although they were supposedly very *scientific* and *naturalistic* when it came to subjecting the history of the Bible to the rigors of their modern skepticism, they were extremely loose when it came to their own Romantic mystical beliefs. They were very strict on Christianity, but very soft with regard to their own religious Romanticism. They had little regard for the strong historical basis of the Biblical text. As such, they disparaged the history of the Bible so they could foist upon it their own Romantic and mystical religious ideas and evolutionary interpretations that were also very German.

Schleiermacher's Theological Romanticism was German Theological Liberalism

In the early 1800s, Friedrich Schleiermacher laid the groundwork for what later became known as German theological liberalism—yet was a theological Romantic. So what is the relationship between German theological Romanticism and German theological liberalism? Schleiermacher's emphasis on natural theology universally available to everyone through nature pried German Christianity away from the exclusivism and/or the particularism of the Bible, together with its Jewish foundations, into an ostensibly more open, liberal and progressive theology. While some of Schleiermacher's later followers criticized him on certain points with different theological nuances and directions, the basic structure of Schleiermacher's Romanticized natural theology that debunked the historical revelation of the Bible as myth would become the mainstay of German theological liberalism throughout the 1800s until the First World War.

The upshot of such a relationship between German Romanticism and German theological liberalism particularly revealed itself at the outset of World War I. The entire German liberal theological establishment unreservedly jumped into the barbarism of the Great War. Moreover, it was at this acute juncture that Swiss theologian Karl Barth famously underwent a spiritual nervous breakdown[1521] of sorts as he witnessed all of his liber-

---

[1521] Ibid., pp. 454-89.

al theological professors enthusiastically side with Kaiser Wilhelm II in Germany's declaration of war. In fact, Dr. Adolf Harnack (1851-1930), the quintessential theologian that constituted the climax of German theological liberalism,[1522] actually wrote the Kaiser's declaration of war speech in August of 1914. Many of Harnack's theological friends were very supportive of the war effort. Barth was shocked with incredulity as he came to the realization that German theological liberalism was not liberal, but in truth, not only very Romantic, but also very nationalistic as well. Harnack was the leading academic of Germany up until the advent of the First World War. Under his watch, nationalism was rife during the Kaiser era. In fact, "the Kaiser was seen as ruling by 'divine right' as God's representative for the Christian nation. Soldiers who died in World War I were honored as martyrs for Christ."[1523]

Harnack presumed that all Germans had an "obligation to support and maintain the glorious legacy of German civilization, which rested on superior armed forces and a tradition of scholarly and artistic excellence. He believed that the war had been forced upon Germany and that Western Christian civilization was at stake in Germany's fate. He signed numerous public declarations that said it defiantly."[1524] Harnack went so far to sign a document declaring to all Protestants outside of the Second Reich denying any responsibility for the war as the world had conspired against Germany, "We are deeply convinced that we have to lay the blame on those who for a long time have woven the net of conspiracy against Germany and who have now thrown it on us in order to suffocate us."[1525] On Oct. 3, 1914, Harnack double-downed on what he considered to be the critical importance of showing support for the war effort by garnering further backing from almost 100 of his *liberal* colleagues, theological and otherwise. It was proudly entitled the "Manifesto of Ninety Three German Intellectuals to the Civilized World." In this document, some of the most important prodigies of the Second Reich "denied that Germany caused the war, denied that Belgium was neutral when Germany invaded it, dismissed the militarism verses the culture argument, and fervently concluded: 'Believe us! Believe, that we shall carry on this war to the end as a people of culture to whom the legacy of a Goethe, a Beethoven, and a Kant is as holy as its

---

[1522] Ibid., p. 456.
[1523] Lutzer, p. 134.
[1524] Dorrien, p. 332.
[1525] Ibid.

own hearths and homes.'"[1526] For well over 150 years, German philosophers and theologians were virtually mocking Christians for having faith in the miraculous history of the Bible, but toward the end of this misadventure, Harnack and his geniuses declare a holy war of faith in the name of Goethe, Beethoven and Kant.

Barth called it a very "black day" in which these "German intellectuals came out with a manifesto supporting the war policy of Kaiser Wilhelm II and his counsellors, and among them I found to my horror the names of nearly all my theological teachers whom up to then I religiously honored. Disillusioned by their conduct, I perceived that I should not be able any longer to accept their ethics and dogmatics, their biblical exegesis, their interpretation of history, that at least for me the theology of the 19th century had no future."[1527] While German philosophy and theology had spent well over 150 years in dividing faith from history and natural theology from Biblical theology, Barth witnessed its dissolution into the trenches of World War I. For Barth, German theological liberalism together with its progressive political socialism effectively died in the nationalistic bloodbath of the First World War—the most destructive war to date before that time in all the annals of human history. That Barth was one of the few outspoken theological professors at this time is testament to the fact that his repentance away from German theological liberalism was well-grounded. Barth smelled a rat, and that rat was Schleiermacher, and his ratline was his Romanticized natural theology. Barth became famous for rejecting Schleiermacher's natural theology rooted in theological romanticism.

Barth's spiritual breakdown actually demonstrates the reality that the very label, German theological liberalism, is a misnomer. German theological liberalism should much better be understood as a deepening of Schleiermacher's theological Romanticism. Schleiermacher borrowed much from his Romantic friends. Schleiermacher strongly taught that religious feelings were at the heart of true spirituality, not abstract Christian doctrine or dogmatics alien to the existential reality of everyday life. Schleiermacher's theological writings were largely written to reach his Romantic friends with a Romanticized quasi-Christian religious philosophy of sorts. In other words, for all of Schleiermacher's presumed liberal sentiments of

---

[1526] Ibid.

[1527] Barth, Karl, "God, Grace, and the Gospel: Three Essays by Karl Barth," translated by James McNab. *Scottish Journal of Theology Occasional Papers*, no. 8. Edinburgh: Oliver and Boyd, 1959, p. 58.

theological openness and progressivism, in truth, his theological Romanticism otherwise betrayed his liberalism. In short, with Schleiermacher at the helm, there was/is a very German indigenous tribalism that stands at the very roots of German theological liberalism. Such nationalistic religious feelings manifested themselves time and time again, especially as German theological liberalism invested much time and effort on the destructive critical scholarship of the Bible in a rabid attempt to de-Judaize both the Old and New Testaments. They foolishly believed it was the Jewish historical particularism and exclusivism of the Bible that was keeping their Germanized Christianity from becoming liberal, progressive and universal. Following the First World War, Harnack said old Judaism was a relic of the past that needs to be abandoned for modern Christianity to prosper in the 20th century. Harnack believed those who held onto the Old Testament were having a paralyzing effect on the progress of religion and the church.[1528] Harnack even stated the Hebrew Old Testament was not part of Christian Scripture.[1529] Such statements along with many others were then later enthusiastically used by the German Reich Church during the tenure of National Socialism.[1530]

Thus, the historical attacks against the Bible, otherwise known as German higher criticism, had a strong anti-Semitic ring to them. Back in the day, Schleiermacher himself characterized the institutional Protestant Church as an antiquated form of Judaism too attached to the dead historical letter of the Bible.[1531] The Bible itself upset his overall aesthetic religious views with the vulgarities of its own blunt history that cannot be beautified or glossed over with Romanticism. In a word, the history of the Bible starring the Jews upset the aesthetic idealism of both German philosophy and religiosity, Romantically understood.

The Romantic Anti-Semitism of German Higher Biblical Criticism

At beginning of the 19th century, Schleiermacher helped the renowned Romantic naturist, Alexander von Humboldt, to establish the University of

---

[1528] Dorrien, p. 331.

[1529] Ibid.

[1530] Ibid.

[1531] Gerdmar, Anders. *Roots of Theological Anti-Semitism: German Biblical Interpretation and the Jews, from Herder and Semler to Kittel and Bultmann*. Leiden and Boston: Brill, 2010, p. 63.

Berlin. When the university was opened in 1810-11, Schleiermacher was its main theology professor. As the first rector and dean of the university, Schleiermacher helped organize its theological faculty. Through his fellow Romantic friends, particularly Friedrich Wilhelm Joseph von Schelling (1775-1854), Schleiermacher became acquainted with Georg Wilhelm Friedrich Hegel (1770-1831). After Schelling had taken Hegel under his wing, his writing career began to grow, however slowly it was at the beginning. Schleiermacher saw Hegel's potential. Schleiermacher thus helped bring Hegel on board as Berlin University's philosophy chair to fill in the vacancy left behind by German Idealist philosopher Johann Gottlieb Fichte (1762-1814). The father of German Idealism was Immanuel Kant who propounded a philosophy that is often called today *transcendental idealism*. The major thrust of Kant's philosophy was to keep certain categories of the mind *a priori* relative to the growing scientific empiricism that was threatening the very existence of philosophy itself. In other words, Kant believed that certain categories of the mind were transcendent over all experience and empiricism that were to be properly and cautiously exercised to interpret reality. In this way, the autonomous freedom of the thinking mind, i.e., Idealism, could be rescued from the non-stop pressures of everyday life that regularly forces all knowledge to conform to the unruliness of raw experience.

In 1806, Hegel had written a book called *Phenomenology of the Spirit* that was beginning to garner some attention from German academia. By combining German Romanticism and Idealism with a new field of thought called Historicism—a term coined by Romantic philosopher and friend of both Schleiermacher and Hegel, Karl Wilhelm Friedrich Schlegel (1772-1829)—Hegel became the most dominant philosopher of the 1800s whose thought continues to reverberate throughout the entire West even today. Protagonists and antagonists of his philosophy alike have not been able to free themselves from Hegel's brilliance. The genius of Hegel's thought was its all-encompassing holistic unity that not only brought Idealism, Romanticism and Historicism together, but also aligned it with a secularized form of Judeo-Christian eschatology.

Based on allegedly *scientific* historical research, Historicism emphasizes that people are children of their own times and must be understood as such. This not only means that any given historical context must be rigorously investigated before one can truly understand the past, but it also suggests that man is primarily an historical being rather than an eternal being made in God's image. While Historicism thus tries to present itself as historically objective, the very fact it prejudges past generations as children of their own times still nonetheless presumptuously assumes the idea of progress and the relativity of truth since truth is considered relative to one's own time. Historicism is thus a philosophy of history no matter how much it tries to assert otherwise. Furthermore, latent within the idea of Historicism is also a secular form of eschatology since the progress of history is presumed along both linear and teleological lines. It was this latent eschatology within the concept of Historicism that Hegel not only noticed, but also brought out and pushed to its limits with his own philosophy of history that is often characterized as Absolute Idealism.[1532] Hegel took German Idealism and blended it with Romanticism so that Kant's reason was holistically fused with not only all of life, but all of history as well. Hegel found an eschatological end game for Idealism, Romanticism and Historicism by propounding a forward-looking idealistic future that was no longer viewed as otherworldly or transcendent in the Biblical sense.

Even though Hegel loved philosophy, he was first trained as a theologian at Tubingen University, which would later become world famous after his death under Ferdinand Christian Baur's (1792-1860) leadership. It was Baur who took Hegel's philosophy of history together with the Romanticism of both Schleiermacher and Schelling to lay the foundation stones of German higher criticism. Hegel's religious philosophy of history closely connected his philosophy with religion, "Philosophy became a kind of theology for Hegel because he saw all reality as an expression of the Absolute—who is God. All that exists is the expression of the divine mind."[1533] Yet, Hegel's intention was to progressively replace religion with philosophy. As such,

---

[1532] The online *Encyclopedia Britannica* defines Hegel's Absolute Idealism in this way: "Idealism for Hegel meant that the finite world is a reflection of mind, which alone is truly real. He held that limited being (that which comes to be and passes away) presupposes infinite unlimited being, within which the finite is a dependent element. In this view, truth becomes the relationship of harmony or coherence between thoughts, rather than a correspondence between thoughts and external realities. As one proceeds from the confusing world of sense experience to the more complex and coherent categories of science, the Absolute Idea, of which all other abstract ideas are merely a part, is approached. Hegel also held that this increasing clarity is evident in the fact that later philosophy presupposes and advances from earlier philosophy, ultimately approaching that to which all things are related and which is nevertheless self-contained—i.e., the Absolute Idea."

[1533] *Evangelical Dictionary of Theology*, edited by Walter Elwell. Grand Rapids, Michigan: Baker Book House, 1984, p. 502.

on the one hand, Hegel "spoke of his system as one in which religion and philosophy have at last been reconciled, but on the other hand, he claimed to have eliminated religion in favor of philosophy."[1534] It must also be pointed out that Hegel accomplished this primarily by spiritualizing the secular rather than secularizing the spiritual. Karl Marx, while acknowledging the philosopher's genius, famously said he had to place Hegel's philosophy on its head by removing the spiritual and focusing entirely on the secular. Hegel's philosophy of history thus had an incredible impact even on Western political and social sciences, let alone with regard to philosophy and religion.

What Hegel did was to replace Divine providence in history with the presumption of human spiritual progress being the manifestation of the immanent *Spirit* working through history in the world. Biblically speaking, Divine providence is distinct from the written revelation of the Bible where God silently works behind the scenes in both nature and in history to draw all men to Himself through the sovereign supervision of all circumstances. Such providential supervision on the part of God is understood only very generally, as the Apostle Paul makes so clear in his famous Mars Hill speech given in Athens (Acts 17:24-28). For the most part, Divine providence belongs to God's inscrutable sovereign will that is largely beyond human knowledge (Prov. 15:3; 16:1-11), even though believers are well aware that He is actively involved in all things (Ps. 139; Matt. 6:25-34; Heb. 1:3).

Yet as Hegel left behind the inscrutable transcendence of the Biblical God, he filled providential history with many precise details obtained from his own philosophy of history. For Hegel, "the ultimate design of the world must be perceived. And if theology fails to explain these processes, then philosophy has to vindicate the Christian religion by demonstrating God's execution of His purpose in history."[1535] Hegel did this by speaking about the "cunning of reason" that worked behind the scenes in order to bring to fruition the Spirit's immanent plans for the world to help usher in God's kingdom on the Earth this side of the grave. In spite of the passions of men, the "cunning of reason" is used by the immanent Spirit to bring about Divine goals and accomplishments in history that were not intended. As such, men "act historically by being acted upon by the power and cunning of reason, which is to Hegel a rational expression for divine

---

[1534] Gruner, p. 58.
[1535] Lowith, *Meaning in History*, p. 55.

providence: thus the motives, passions, and interests in history are indeed what they appeared to be at first glance, namely, the human stuff of it, but within the framework of a transcending purpose, promoting an end which was no part of conscious intentions."[1536] One of the great problems of Historicism is how to account for progress, i.e., transcending the past, if men are merely historical beings who are children of their own times. Hegel's semi-pantheism of Absolute Idealism with heavy doses of secular eschatology was propounded to help resolve this dilemma. Reason with a capital letter R became the semi-transcendent Absolute that governed the historical growth and progress of mankind.

The idea of human spiritual progress heading toward a consummate goal is at the heart of Hegel's philosophy of history as the cunning of the *Spirit's* reason teleologically guides man toward an eschatological end that he has been largely unaware of—until the advent of Hegel's philosophy of history. More to the point, since man is spiritually progressing through the cunning of reason, it goes without saying that Christianity as a religion has also been historicized, surpassed and superseded. Just as the New Testament surpassed the Old Testament, so Hegel's philosophy of history has now superseded Christianity. For Hegel, "even though Christianity had grasped the truth, it had grasped it in an imperfect manner, namely in images and symbols and stories, rather than in philosophical concepts."[1537] In other words, "religion for Hegel is simply an imaginative and pictorial way of representing philosophical truth"[1538] so that the evolution from religion to philosophy is part and parcel of the Spirit's use of the "cunning of reason" to transform religious language into true conceptual and/or synthetic knowledge. In this way, Christianity evolves into a superior or higher philosophical synthesis as the Spirit progresses from religion to rational philosophy. Religious mysteries are thus "elevated to the level of reason, and thus cease to be mysteries."[1539] As such, traditional Christianity thus has no future in Hegel's system, but it will live on in philosophical form.[1540] This, of course, means that "Hegel wanted to get rid of religion."[1541]

1536   Ibid., p. 56.
1537   Gruner, p. 58.
1538   *New International Dictionary of the Christian Church*, p. 457.
1539   Gruner, p. 58
1540   Ibid.
1541   Ibid., p. 59.

The providential and teleological outworking of God in man throughout history was the key to Hegel's philosophical system. In the final analysis, the entire history of philosophy becomes an evolutionary development of truth. Hegel called this outworking of God in man the dialectic so that what Hegel calls *God* or *Spirit* or *Reason* progresses dialectically in man throughout history through the holistic synthesizing of opposites—whether those oppositions be religious, social, political, economic, artistic or even warring states against each other. The advancement of the *Spirit* is thus secured by historically synthesizing a thesis and its antithesis that initially lock horns only to produce a higher state of synthesis at the final end of the struggle. For Hegel, "to say that something develops dialectically is saying that it necessarily falls out with itself and releases its own opposite from itself so as to return to itself again, not by becoming the same as it had been originally, but by realizing its unity on a higher level such that it is reconciled with its opposite; it then falls out with itself once more and so on."[1542] As such, the dialectical movements of world history are manifestations of the Spirit's providential direction. "Through divine action contradiction between antithetical movements or cultures are repeatedly resolved into a higher synthesis."[1543] In short, "Hegel thought of history itself as a forum in which the contradictions and inadequacies of finite thought and action are exposed allowing the infinite mind of the Absolute to reach higher levels of cultural and spiritual expression."[1544] Put in another way, true knowledge of ultimate reality is "the product of the Spirit which, in a dynamic development, reconciles the self-contradictions that permeate every aspect of human experience."[1545]

Hegel's Spirit was thus certainly not the God of the Bible. "When Hegel spoke of God, he meant God in man and in the final analysis, he really meant man alone."[1546] In his semi-pantheistic Romantic Idealism of an all-encompassing Monism, Hegel denied the Creator-creature distinction of the God of the Bible, and in so doing, precluded His immutability and transcendence. Hegel rejected static theological ideas about God as being unreal and illusory. Hegel instead viewed God as progressing through the history of man so that He perfects Himself through the historical process.

[1542] Ibid., p. 58.
[1543] *Evangelical Dictionary of Theology*, p. 502.
[1544] Ibid.
[1545] *The New International Dictionary of the Christian Church*, p. 457.
[1546] Gruner, p. 59.

"For in Hegel's teaching it is man in whom God becomes himself."[1547] This, of course, greatly diminishes the God of the Bible, and elevates man at the same time. "If his philosophy, as he said, was a kind of self-worship, it was self-worship, the worship of man by man."[1548] Hegel is thus at the very heart of the progressive mindset so characteristic of the modern age. "Man's self-congratulation, self-admiration, and self-glorification belong to the modern consciousness, and the case of Hegel must count as a prime example."[1549] In a word, Hegel's philosophy of history is the worship of man's self-causing evolution. In effect, what Hegel did was to conflate natural revelation and/or theology to surpass Biblical revelation and/or theology through his own modernized philosophical history. As such, Hegel's philosophy of history was a curious mixture of both the sacred and the profane which degraded sacred history to the level of secular history and exalted secular history to the status of the sacred.[1550]

Closely connected, Hegel's semi-pantheism had enormous significance with regard to the incarnation of Christ. The incarnation is not so much that eternal God became human flesh in the Person of Jesus Christ the Messiah, but that God or Spirit incarnates itself in the world in such a way that it progressively changes with the world and perfects itself through the dialectical process as the very attributes of God are historically worked out in man.[1551] In Hegel's system, the incarnation of Christ is therefore not a one-time historical event that has eternal repercussions as the transcendent immutable God breaks into human history to bridge the chasm between God's holiness and man's sinfulness, but that God constantly incarnates Himself throughout history manifesting a greater and greater philosophy along with it. In other words, as far as Hegel was concerned, the incarnation of Jesus Christ as portrayed in the Bible makes God too limited to a particular setting.[1552] A more general philosophical religion rooted in universal history was the key to Hegel's incarnation of God in man through time that went beyond the historical limits prescribed by the Bible. Relative to the progressive revelation of God in human history, "the figure of Christ thus

---

1547 Ibid.
1548 Ibid.
1549 Ibid.
1550 Lowith, *Meaning in History*, p. 59.
1551 Gruner, p. 59.
1552 *Evangelical Dictionary of Theology*, p. 502.

had no special significance for Hegel; it only marked the point at which the process had become manifest for the first time."[1553]

In spite of the progressive character of Hegel's thought, he was not a relativist. Hegel did believe in a final truth, one that was rapidly coming upon the world scene particularly through his own philosophy of history as the World Spirit was entering into its final phase of progressive development. Hegel thought he had managed to reconcile religion and philosophy that was an inherent sign of the eschaton. Idealistically understood through subjective thought alone, Hegel believed his philosophy as a whole represented a similar, if not superior, holistic reconciliation that rivalled the incarnation of God in Christ with a final comprehended reconciliation of "philosophical theology. It seemed to Hegel that the 'peace of God' was brought about in a rational way through this reconciliation of philosophy with religion."[1554] Hegel thus presumed his great "attempt to translate theology into philosophy" was to "realize the Kingdom of God in terms of the world's real history."[1555]

While many may presume Hegel's philosophy of history to be audacious, it must be granted that one of the reasons why he pushed his dialectical approach was to discourage those who arrogantly presume their fragmented egos and blinded obscurantism[1556] is the whole truth and nothing but the truth (Prov. 8:17). While Hegel did strongly argue that all truth was one, this was not understood dogmatically like an exclusivist religion or differing philosophical positions, but holistically understood from a broad Romantic perspective. "The 'one philosophy' to which Hegel refers is not his own as distinct from others, but rather the whole of philosophic thought, which constitutes a many-faceted though still unitary truth. Indeed perhaps one of Hegel's most significant contributions to philosophy was his demonstration that it could be regarded as a whole instead of a disconnected series of contradictory opinions."[1557]

Yet such a Romantic picture of truth cannot but willfully confuse sacred and secular history that in the end promotes the secular over the sacred. As such, Hegel's philosophy of history played no small role in the development

---

1553 Gruner, p. 59.
1554 Lowith, *From Hegel to Nietzsche*, p. 48.
1555 Lowith, *Meaning in History*, p. 58
1556 Hinchman, Lewis. *Hegel's Critique of the Enlightenment*, Tampa: University of Florida Press, 1984, p. x.
1557 Ibid., p. 11.

of higher Biblical criticism that was launched by Ferdinand Christian Baur at Tubingen University. Sadly and deeply ironic, what Hegel borrows from the Biblical Judeo-Christian worldview, i.e., its sacred history and eschatology, was used against it. In particular, Hegel's secular philosophy of historical progressivism will in fact become confused with the real history of the Bible under Baur's so-called higher criticism of the New Testament. Not only did Baur hold that ancient authors of Scripture were essentially immature religionists who did not have genuine objective standards of Enlightenment historiography, he will also borrow much from Hegel's dialectical progressivism to reconstruct the history of the entire New Testament. In short, the Biblical writers did not have an up-to-date modern historical consciousness, and so lacked the necessary enlightened or scientific acumen to be considered reliable in their historical affirmations. Their theology and superstitious belief in miracles drove their historical testimonies so much that they cannot be taken at face value, but must be vetted under the scientific lens of Enlightenment historiography. Beyond that, the history of the New Testament must also be reconstructed and Hegel's philosophy of history was the very tool used to do just that.

While there is a controversy over how Hegelian was Baur, this particular scholarly dispute is not as critical as it may seem at first glance. Hegel himself was a mishmash of classical philosophy, theology, Kantian Idealism, Romanticism and Historicism. Hegel's holistic philosophy is actually very hard to pin down—which was the primary thrust of his entire outlook. As such, though Hegel's philosophy is called Absolute Idealism, his dialectics and concern with reconciling opposites was found in the Romantic writings of both Schelling and Schleiermacher. While Baur was a fan of both Schleiermacher and Hegel, he did not accept them uncritically. Yet, there is no question that Baur took Hegel's philosophy of history and applied his historical triad of thesis-antithesis-synthesis to reconstruct the history of the early church. While earlier Bible critics were content with simply being skeptical of the Biblical record in general, particularly with regard to miracles, Baur will not only share their skepticism, but will attempt to reconstruct that history along Hegelian lines. This was different, new and radical, and it turned Tubingen University into a major international school of Biblical criticism.

Baur was born in 1792 and died in 1860. He grew up in the rustic town of Blaubeuren[1558]in the beautifully romantic hilly area known as the Swabian Alb not far from the Black Forest. Baur was a bookworm even in his youth. He went to Blaubeuren Seminary at a young age, a Lutheran school that had been a monastery in the Middle Ages. After seminary, Baur became a student of Tubingen University that was in the same general area, and undoubtedly would have been very familiar with the Romantic philosopher Schelling[1559] since his father was the church superintendent of Maulbronn that was also in the Swabian Alb area. In fact, both Schelling and Hegel were students in Tubingen in the late 1700s. When Baur was at Tubingen, the philosophies of Kant, Fichte and Schelling dominated the academic landscape.[1560] At the same time, the grandson of the distinguished Bible scholar Johann Albrecht Bengel, Ernst Gottlieb Bengel, was one of the primary theological professors at Tubingen. While Ernst's grandfather before him had staunchly defended "the authority of the Bible through historical investigation and reasoned argument,"[1561] such an emphasis was far less pronounced in his grandson's teaching. Bengel the younger "portrayed Jesus as a great ethical teacher, 'the highest educator of humanity,' the supernatural element in Jesus's life and work being discreetly pushed into the background. Not that any of the old traditional doctrines were explicitly denied; but Jesus was now regarded as divine in consequence of the divine truths which he taught; his divinity was ascribed to him rather than being inherent in his Person."[1562]

It was Bengel the younger who had the most influence over Baur at Tubingen. Such influences were eventually carried over into his teaching career that began at Blaubeuren Seminary before he later replaced Bengel the younger at Tubingen University after he died in 1826. During the 1820s, Baur was heavily influenced by Schleiermacher's theology as well, although he made his own independent adaptions to his growing theological worldview. Like Schleiermacher before him, Baur conflated natural revelation at the expense of Biblical revelation and used natural theology to interpret Biblical theology. In fact, Baur essentially understood natural revelation as a universal religious consciousness that all people have throughout history:

[1558] Harris, Horton. *The Tubingen School: A Historical and Theological Investigation of the School of F.C. Baur School.* Grand Rapids, Michigan: Baker Book House, 1990 (1975), p. 13.

[1559] Ibid., p. 14.

[1560] Ibid., p. 16.

[1561] Ibid.

[1562] Ibid., pp. 16-17.

"Baur viewed the essence of every religion as lying in the higher religious consciousness, in the consciousness of the higher supra-sensual sphere, in the feeling of absolute dependence upon a power existing outside of natural and sensual perception. This feeling of dependence has its seat in the religious consciousness and finds its expression in the various myths and legends of the many national cultures. Revelation is not to be thought of as supernatural communication from an other-worldly source, but is manifested in history as a general revelation from God, a divine process of education for mankind."[1563] Baur thus held very similar theological views to both Schleiermacher and Hegel in spite of some nuances and differences between them. There was also considerable controversy and deliberation over Baur's semi-pantheistic mysticism which held up his appointment at Tubingen for several months.[1564]

After Hegel's death in 1830, Baur became ever more skeptical the Bible was inspired by God, that Jesus was God manifest in the flesh, or that He was even resurrected. Closely related, Baur had increasing doubts concerning the true origins of Christianity that had been passed down to modern times since its inception. Such doubts, along with his increasing interest in Hegel throughout the 1830s, coalesced into what became known as higher criticism. With no small thanks to one of Baur's prized students from his teaching days at Blaubeuren Seminary, David Strauss (1808-74), Baur became more interested in Hegel's dialectical philosophical theology. Baur identified himself a Hegelian as early as 1833[1565] and mastered his philosophical theology perhaps more than any scholar before or since.

After leaving Blaubeuren Seminary, Strauss went onto Berlin University to learn from Hegel himself. Strauss became a full-blown Hegelian, and then wrote a bombshell book entitled *The Life of Christ Critically Examined* that rocked the theological world of Germany in 1835. In this book, Strauss rejected the miraculous history of the gospels and considered them to be a historical legend or myth that was fashioned, perhaps inadvertently so, by second-century authors far removed from the life of Christ. His book led to such an incredible firestorm that was so controversial even Baur himself had to distance himself from his former student—though he held similar

---

[1563] Ibid., pp. 19-20.
[1564] Ibid., pp. 20-22.
[1565] Ibid., p. 26.

views.[1566] When pressed, Strauss claimed his book was not written to destroy Christianity precisely because true religion, along Kantian Idealistic lines, was based on ideas, not facts.

While Strauss used Hegelian natural theology to historically re-interpret the gospels, Baur will use it to reconstruct the history of Acts and the New Testament epistles. Baur was particularly doubtful of Luke's authorship of the book of Acts, and believed there were bigger rifts in the early church than is generally understood—problems that were theologically glossed over, but now can be investigated properly along strict anti-supernatural historical lines that Hegel's philosophy of history helped establish. What Baur essentially did was to inflate the history of the early Catholic church at the expense of apostolic history. The New Testament as written stands out in sharp relief from the historical background of the times. If it occurred in the way the New Testament reads at face value, it would indeed strongly suggest miraculous beginnings since such a record would be too far advanced compared to the rest of the Greco-Roman world. As such, since modern historiography has shown miracles are mythological, what really happened was that later religionists foisted upon the origins of Christianity legendary fables wrapped around a false miraculous history. In Baur's eyes, such undue conflation needs to be readjusted by a more critical historical investigation.

Using J.S. Semler's (1725-1791) original criticism that first drove a wedge between the theology of Peter and Paul, Baur further developed his hypothesis along Hegelian lines. Baur taught the early church had a thesis, which was a Jewish form of Christianity, which was then followed by its antithesis. This was the Gentile form of Christianity, that was later finally synthesized into the early Catholic church over the course of a few centuries. This Hegelian triad was encapsulated in Baur's book entitled, *Paul the Apostle of Jesus Christ*, a viewpoint that Baur held unchanged throughout the remainder of his life.[1567] Using primarily the Antioch incident recorded in Galatians 2 where Paul charged Peter and Barnabas with hypocrisy for caving into the pressures of the Judaizers, Baur exaggerated this historical incident as indicating a great theological conflict in the early church between what he called the Jewish Petrine party and the Gentile Pauline party. After

---

[1566] Ibid., p. 28.
[1567] *Evangelical Dictionary of Theology*, pp. 128-29.

all, Galatians 2:7-8 speaks of the gospel to the uncircumcised under Paul's ministry, and then the gospel to the circumcised under Peter's ministry.

As such, Baur held there was an early Jewish Christianity that was a pro-Mosaic Law form of Christianity represented by Peter and also by the book of Matthew. Baur considered Matthew as the first gospel written because of its unmistakable Jewish character. However, out of this Jewish Christianity grew its antithesis—the law-free gospel of grace according to the apostle Paul. Baur considers that Paul's Greek anti-Jewish Christianity can readily be seen in Romans, Galatians and in both 1 and 2 Corinthians. These were the only true Pauline epistles that Baur considered genuine. The rest of Paul's epistles were written much later during the times of the early Catholic church, particularly the pastoral epistles that demonstrate church hierarchy. Baur believed that the book of Acts, John's writings and much of the rest of the New Testament was written at this time when a synthesis of Jewish-Greek Catholicism coalesced to bring Peter's and Paul's gospels together sometime in the middle of the second century A.D. Since the Jewish-Gentile split is not seen in much of the rest of the New Testament, Baur presumed it therefore must have been written later. This also meant that much of the New Testament was essentially a forgery in the sense they were not written by who they said they were. Such books were written by early Catholics instead of the apostles as they bridged the schism of Peter and Paul into a higher holistic synthesis. As such, the *World Spirit* was moving forward in classic Hegelian fashion.

Needless to say, only a philosopher could come up with such a fanciful argument that is perhaps even more fantastic than believing in the miraculous history of the New Testament itself. Baur repudiated the miraculous history of the New Testament only to replace it with a secularized and Romantic form of mystical idealism all his own. Even Galatians 2 itself, which Baur considers to be genuinely written by the Apostle Paul, resolves the alleged early split between Jewish and Greek Christianity. Rather than admit that his Hegelianism distorted the historical record of the New Testament, what he did was to throw out all the evidence that suggested otherwise. The remaining letters are thus regarded as late and inauthentic because they do not reflect such Hegelian tendencies. Shockingly, Hegelianism was so strong at the time that Baur's reconstruction of the New Testament was taken all too seriously by all too many. The orthodox Protestants who protested against such a philosophy of history were characterized as rigid anti-progressive legalists of some sort. While there is no question there were certainly problems in the early church, such troubles were not as drastic as Baur made them out to be. What Romantics often do is stress the irrational antinomies and oppositions in life so they can then promote their own spiritual reconciliation programs along holistic lines that are yet presented in plausible secular forms so they do not look as mystical as they really are. In this way, the miraculous, yet rugged, Biblical history was replaced with an aesthetic triad of idealistic beauty that mystically showed the progress of the *World Spirit* working in dialectical fashion.

Even though Baur's Hegelian blitzkrieg had spectacular rapid gains at the beginning, catching many in the theological world off guard, his legacy was not carried forward by the Albrecht Ritschl's (1822-89) liberal school of theology that followed Tubingen's dominance in the mid-1800s. English and Scottish scholars, J.B. Lightfoot (1828-1889) and Sir William Ramsay (1851-1939), rolled back Baur's theory, even though few bothered to take note. Even today Baur's theory is bandied around by many. They are completely unaware that Baur's Hegelian fantasy concerning the origins of Christianity was refuted in rather short order by both of these very serious scholars.[1568] While J.B. Lightfoot was/is one of the great church historians of all time, Sir William Ramsay was an archaeologist who spent many years in Turkey investigating the historical background of the book of Acts. Ramsay was also a historian in his own right who wrote many historical books on the New Testament.

Sir William Ramsay actually studied at Tubingen and was initially convinced Biblical higher criticism was true until hard and empirical historical evidence on the ground in Turkey caused him to repent of his earlier views. When Ramsay finished his incredible research, though he still remained skeptical of miracles, he concluded the New Testament was historically authentic, and that St. Luke was the greatest historian of the Greco-Roman period. One of the primary reasons Sir William Ramsay changed his views was precisely because St. Luke time and time again used first-century names that had changed by the middle of the second century.

[1568] "One of the curious features in German theology is that no ghost is ever laid. A century after his death Baur still walks abroad, and echoes of his ideas are found in all kinds of places. It is still not uncommon to hear references to the 'four undoubted Epistles of Paul' (Galatians, Romans, 1-2 Corinthians), a view which was first put forward by Baur. It is odd that the phrase should have had such a long life," p. 62, from *The Interpretation of the New Testament 1861-1986*. Oxford: Oxford University Press, 1988 (1964) by Stephen Neill and Tom Wright.

Earlier, Lightfoot was able to disprove Baur's theory by finally dating two books written by the early Christian writers Clement and Ignatius. Lighfoot was able to establish that Clement's writings were written in the mid-'90s and that Ignatius' writings were written around 110. Such dates turned out to be very significant because both Clement and Ignatius have strong allusions to almost the entire New Testament in their writings. Meaning that if Clement and Ignatius alluded to most of the New Testament around the turn of the first century, then the New Testament must have been written before that time. Lightfoot's research on Clement and Ignatius thus confirmed the New Testament was a first-century document. Baur's theory thus fell like a house of cards, especially after Harnack acknowledged and corroborated Lightfoot's prodigious research on the topic.[1569] Harnack also wrote a book in 1905 accepting Luke as the author of his gospel and the book of Acts.[1570]

In 1976, John A.T. Robinson then wrote a book entitled *Redating the New Testament* that was/is the final deathblow to radical New Testament historical criticism. Robinson rolled the New Testament even further back than Lightfoot. Robinson strongly pointed out that much of the entire New Testament had to have been written before 70 A.D.—and the reason why is pretty simple, obvious, and hard to miss. Most New Testament authors wrote in such a way that they presumed the Jerusalem temple was still standing. The Jerusalem temple was destroyed in 70 A.D. This means that most of the New Testament must have been largely written before 70 A.D. This, of course, brings the entire discussion back to square one before so-called higher criticism even began. However, rather than acknowledge that the hidebound Bible-believing Protestants were correct all along with regard to the historical authenticity of the New Testament, Robinson's work has for the most part been simply ignored. Archaeologically speaking, gospel fragments have also been found that go all the way back to the first century. A lot of ink was thus foolishly spilled attacking the historicity of the New Testament for some 250 to 300 years, but it was all for nothing with no progressive fruit to show. The historiography of the Enlightenment was wrong, and the German additions of Idealism, Romanticism and Hegelianism only compounded this foolish enterprise by hiding it underneath layers of secular mysticism that were both Romantic and progressivist at

---

[1569] For this fascinating discussion see *The Interpretation of the New Testament 1861-1986*, by Stephen Neill and Tom Wright, pp. 55-62.

[1570] Neill & Wright, p. 62.

the same time. The real fraud was not the New Testament, but the Biblical minimalism that criticized the New Testament without warrant, most of which was of German origin.

However, with the higher criticism of the New Testament being rolled back in the late 1800s, the German theologians and philosophers took up new positions—this time directed against the Old Testament starring Julius Wellhausen (1844-1918). Wellhausen was a Lutheran Bible scholar who propounded the infamous JEPD documentary hypothesis in his book entitled *Prolegomena on the History of Israel* published in 1883.[1571] Presuming that Moses could not have been the author of the Pentateuch, as such a feat would have been too far advanced for its time, Wellhausen postulated that it was not put together until its final form right after the Babylonian captivity around 500 B.C. Even though Genesis-Deuteronomy may look like a composite whole, it is in actuality a piecemeal of different Hebrew traditions and outlooks which were eventually synthetically woven together. Thus, the first five books of Moses were really not written by Moses, but was a process of evolutionary development over a period of almost 1,000 years. According to Keil and Delitzsch, this position was initially promulgated by Orientalist and Hebraist Georg Heinrich August Ewald (1803-75),[1572] whose Biblical criticism originated with his teacher Johann Gottfried Eichhorn (1752-1827), the very founder of Old Testament higher criticism. Wellhausen was a student of Ewald, but he gave most of the credit to Wilhelm Martin Leberecht de Wette (1780-1849) for the establishment of Old Testament higher criticism that his JEPD documentary hypothesis was built upon.[1573]

Wellhausen theorized there were four different Hebrew traditions or strands, i.e., documents, that were finally synthesized together to create the Pentateuch right before the Babylonian exile. The names Wellhausen gave to these four documents were: J, which is the Jahvistic or Yahwistic document, which emphasized God's name Jehovah or Yahweh that represents the earliest source going back to Solomon's reign; E, which was the so-called Elohistic document, written by a group of people or editors who emphasized God's name as Elohim, and came a bit later with the Northern Kingdom of Israel; P, which is what he called the Priestly document

[1571] The original work was entitled *The History of Israel*, published in 1878.
[1572] Keil, C.F. and Delitzsch, Franz, *Commentary on the Old Testament*, Vol. 1. Peabody, Massachusetts: Hendrickson Publishers, 1989, p. 17.
[1573] Gerdmar, p. 77.

that codified the rituals and formalistic religion seen so prevalently in the book of Leviticus that was not completed until as late as 500 B.C., and then finally; D, which was the Deuteronomic document or primarily the book of Deuteronomy, which was compiled during Josiah's reign immediately before the Babylonian exile (1 Kings 22:1-20) in 620 B.C.

Even though the entire Old Testament already shows how the Hebrews developed historically from the times of the patriarchs to their slavery in Egypt followed by the Exodus and the conquest, and then onto the historical periods of the Judges, the united and divided kingdom stages respectively before bottoming out in the Babylonian Exile,[1574] this was not enough evolution for the German higher critics. Wellhausen wanted more evolution within the Old Testament historical record and so provided it as he held that later redactors gradually knitted the different documents (JEPD) together into what is now known as the Pentateuch. As far as Wellhausen was concerned, it is a myth that Moses wrote the Pentateuch, although he and his followers did allow for some kernel of Mosaic history to exist in the ancient past when Moses actually lived.[1575] The reasons given for such an evolutionary makeover is there are too many different Divine names, vocabulary words, styles and differing theologies in the Pentateuch. The other bothersome traits are that two different stories of the same event are seen in passages like Genesis 1-2 along with anachronisms that show Abraham abiding by laws and statutes that did not exist until much later in Old Testament history. For such reasons and others, rather oddly enough, the first five books of Moses, which are naturally assumed to be the foundational books of the Old Testament, are actually the last. In the Wellhausen evolutionary scheme, the foundation becomes the roof in a form of scholarly dyslexia that sees everything backwards or upside down.

Worse, Wellhausen's theory won a broad scholarly consensus that lasted for almost a century,[1576] considerably much longer than the Baur's New Testament higher criticism. Certainly, one of the primary reasons for this is precisely because of the great time gap that exists between modern times and the Old Testament that has proved to be much more difficult to bridge in order to demonstrate the excesses of the Wellhausen theory. Another critical

---

[1574] Compare this to Titus Livy who characterized the entire history of Rome as a vicious circle of conflict between the nobility and the slaves.

[1575] Waltke, Bruce. *Genesis: A Commentary*. Grand Rapids, Michigan: Zondervan, 2001, pp. 24-25.

[1576] Ibid., p. 24.

reason why Wellhausen's theory has proven to be so resilient is because of the doctrine of geological and biological evolution that has allegedly shown Genesis to be a myth in the minds of most people, particularly Genesis 1-11. Meaning that while Hegel's evolutionary philosophy of history was all too easily historicized, Darwinism has proved to be much more difficult to historicize because of its decidedly biological and geological basis, which defies historical analysis. Since geological and biological evolution conveniently predates human history, Darwinism uses naturalistic uniformitarian processes that are observed today to explain past natural history relative to geology and biology. However, the fact that Darwinism requires such incredibly deep time to explain evolution strongly suggests its answers are not all that explanatory as the great problems of biological development and geological upheavals are dissolved in the abyss of deep time. Neither is it a coincidence that Darwinism appeared on the historical scene when virtually anything and everything was explained from an evolutionary point of view—whether that be history, religion, philosophy, society, politics, etc. Geology and biology simply jumped on board along with everyone and everything else. Yet, if Newton's physics was eventually historicized, why not Darwinism? Leftist scientists in particular have fought hard to prevent this from happening because they strongly believe evolution is the truth and nothing but the truth.

With regard to Wellhausen's JEPD theory, Hegel's philosophy of history stood more in the shadows, but still played a role.[1577] As the Hegelian triad of thesis-antithesis-synthesis was increasingly historicized during the 19th century, historians, philosophers and theologians began presuming a much more general evolutionary understanding of religious development that helped establish the History of Religions School under Ritschl's theological influences that replaced Tubingen's radicalism in the later 1800s. What is most peculiar about Wellhausen's JEPD theory, however, is its essential Romantic character. It was strongly rooted in de Wette's Theological Romanticism. As such, Wellhausen's JEPD theory placed Israel's religious development in reverse. Worst of all, the dyslexia and backwardness of Old Testament higher criticism that willfully confuses the superstructure with the foundation, is strongly anti-Semitic precisely because what is historically depicted is not a progressive evolution of Israel's religion, but the very

---

[1577] Albright, W.F., "The War in Europe and the Future of Biblical Studies," in *The Study of the Bible Today and Tomorrow*. Chicago: The University of Chicago Press, 1947, pp. 172-73.

opposite. Along very Romantic lines, the history of Israel degenerates from its simple foundations to restrictive legalism and ritualistic materialism as the Deuteronomists and the priests took over the Jewish religion and fashioned it into a corrupt Judaism far removed from its pure Hebrew beginnings. Similarly, Hegel himself held that most everyone contributed to the progressive growth of the *World Spirit* throughout history except for Judaism. Judaism cut itself off from the progressive evolution of the *World Spirit*, and thus the Jews "will no longer have a history. As the most reprobate people, all that remains of the Jews is ongoing fossilized existence."[1578]

De Wette was a Romantic follower of Schelling. He was a close colleague of Schleiermacher. In fact, Schleiermacher facilitated the finding of a faculty position for de Wette at the University of Berlin.[1579] De Wette's theology of the Old Testament was a Romanticized craving "for the primordial, natural, and simple."[1580] As early as 1804, de Wette argued the Pentateuch was not written by Moses, but developed over time, and was so late on the historical scene that it essentially became the very sourcebook of Rabbinic Judaism. However, this was not seen as process of religious progression, but rather of spiritual deterioration, particularly with regard to what he considered to be the legalism of the book of Deuteronomy. "Whereas the other parts of the Pentateuch represent an early, original, simple, and spontaneous religion, Deuteronomy, with its focus on cultic centralization and ritual action, represent a degeneration of Israelite religion, being a post-exilic development" that was "a gathering of later laws ascribed to Moses through historical fiction."[1581] De Wette Romantically held that ancient Hebrew religion was pure and simple, but was later complicated by a petrified Judaism that promoted the letter of the written word over the freedom of the spirit.[1582] De Wette further criticized "Judaism for having destroyed the aesthetic dimension of religion. The outward, physical and superstitious, and the adherence to a book, were not acceptable to this aestheticism."[1583] De Wette believed that the exile ruined the purity of the Hebrew religion with foreign influences carried back home from Babylon. Judaism was thus

---

[1578] Mack, Michael. *German Idealism and the Jew: The Inner Anti-Semitism of Philosophy and German-Jewish Responses.* Chicago & London: University of Chicago Press, 2003, p. 53.
[1579] Gerdmar, p. 87.
[1580] Ibid., p. 82.
[1581] Ibid., p. 79.
[1582] Ibid., p. 81.
[1583] Ibid., p. 79.

an "unsuccessful restoration of Hebraism" where "metaphysical reflection" had "replaced ethical direction, where concept and letter" had "replaced life and enthusiasm, and where a written source of religion" had "been established."[1584]

Politically, de Wette was a liberal and Romantic German nationalist with strong anti-Semitic sentiments who cherished the ideals of the French Revolution but experienced the invasion of Napoleon instead. While many today may scratch their heads over a nationalist form of liberalism, it represented the heart and soul of Germany throughout much of the 1800s, particularly in the first half of the century before the advent of the Second Reich when the country was finally united:

> The specifically German aspect of the movement was its nationalism: the desire for national independence and the dream of a unified Germany. Whereas in present day politics, nationalism often has a conservative ring to it, in the early 19th century Germany, it was a matter near to the hearts of liberals. The alternative was the old, fragmented, particularistic and partly feudal German-speaking sphere with hundreds of political entities—from territorial states, principalities and free cities, to abbacies and bishoprics. This particularistic structure hindered national unity and obstructed national liberal reforms. The terminology of particularism and universalism so often used in de Wette's (and others') discussions of the Hebrews and Jews directly corresponds to this discussion. German Jews as a particularistic entity, paralleled by post-exilic Judaism, threatened to disturb the universalistic-nationalistic project, the search for national unity and cultural cohesion, with which liberals identified themselves. For a long time, this frustrated passion for a united and great German *volk* meant a growing threat to the freedom of the Jews.[1585]

What originally attracted German liberals to Romantic nationalism was its social collectivism.[1586] In between both world wars, many despised the political fragmentation of the Weimar Republic as well. This brings up

---

[1584] Ibid., p. 82.
[1585] Ibid., p. 87.
[1586] Ibid., p. 89.

the question once again as to how Romantic is theological liberalism? The answer is, very much so.

Thus Schleiermacher's original anti-Judaism cast a long dark shadow over the entire history of German theological liberalism. F.C Baur quipped that none "since Marcion (85-160) had shown so much antipathy towards Judaism as Schleiermacher,"[1587] a spiritual legacy which Harnack himself managed to hand off to a Nazified Christianity. As far as Schleiermacher was concerned, the more Jewish the Biblical text, the less valuable it was, and that Judaism had no connection to Christianity.[1588] Schleiermacher held that the early Christian community's belief in a coming earthly Messianic Kingdom was a childish form of religion, the very last "fruits of Judaism."[1589] Schleiermacher especially hated the historical foundations of the Bible precisely because they were Jewish. He held that "the historical and particular had little value. What Schleiermacher considered important in Christianity is neither the historical nor the teaching of Jesus, but the fact that Christianity was an eternal religion that is the model for eternal humanity."[1590] Closely related, Schleiermacher alleged that Judaism was merely an antiquated bloodthirsty "religion of punishment and recompense, instead of being a religion that challenges and educates people."[1591] He considered Judaism to be a dead historical religion with no future. In the final analysis, Schleiermacher's de-historicization of the Biblical text went hand in hand with his anti-Judaism, a feature that played no small role in the growing higher criticism of the Bible throughout the 19th century. The whole point was to de-Judaize the Bible away from what German Bible scholars considered to be backward, particularistic, legalistic, judgmental and heteronomous in contrast to that which they deemed to be progressive, scientific, open-minded, autonomous and free.

While Schleiermacher himself was not racist, and had some very close Jewish friends,[1592] his real friends were still the fellow Romantics that he ministered[1593] to throughout his life. More to the point, those Jews who were his friends were the enlightened ones who had given up their Judaistic

---

[1587] Ibid., p. 64.

[1588] Ibid., p. 67.

[1589] Ibid., p. 66.

[1590] Ibid.

[1591] Ibid.

[1592] Ibid., pp. 71-72.

[1593] See *On Religion: Speeches to its Cultured Despisers*. New York: Frank Ungar Publishing, 1955 (1799) by Friedrich Schleiermacher.

backgrounds. Schleiermacher suggested that the Jews who were willing to renounce radical observance of the Law and—especially—Messianic expectation, should create a confession of their own, on par with the Christian Church. In other words, Schleiermacher wanted to favor only those Jews who fitted his own ideal picture of religious expression."[1594] Yet at the same time, Schleiermacher was irritable toward enlightened Jews who did not appreciate Christianity. Neither did he care for what he called their "Chaldean view of beauty and wisdom" that was contrary to the "European spirit."[1595]

In spite of the liberalism of Schleiermacher's Christian universalism, he was a strong patriot in the classic spirit of German Romanticism and nationalism, particularly in the face of Napoleon. While Schleiermacher was an original supporter of the French Revolution, the invasion of Napoleon was quite another matter. Indeed, as the "troops fought on the battlefield, so Schleiermacher fought in the pulpit, although interestingly he was also trained in the local militia."[1596] With no small irony, while Schleiermacher denied ancient Jews their particularism, it was quite acceptable for modern Germans to possess their own in the grand scheme of things. Schleiermacher held that the "borders and destiny of the nations were rooted in God's will and creation; each people had been given its calling on earth and its specific spirit, whereby its specific glory would be attained. In political terms, this meant a theological legitimation of the idea of Germany as a nation with a God-given calling, where nationality was linked to the order of creation: only a person who is one with his nation can live as a citizen in God's kingdom."[1597]

Schleiermacher's dialectic between nationalism and liberalism would characterize the entire history of what is otherwise known today as German theological liberalism up until its dissolution during the Great War under Adolf Harnack's watch. This was particularly true during the Second Reich (1871-1918) when Albrecht Ritschl's social gospel of theological liberalism dominated Germany in the late 1800s up until the time of the war. Ritschl's Protestant social gospel not only became very influential, but it was also inextricably tied up with the nationalistic project that established the Second Reich. While Ritschl's school of theological liberalism was opposed

---

[1594] Gerdmar, p. 71.
[1595] Ibid., p. 72.
[1596] Ibid.
[1597] Ibid., p. 73.

to the idea of a state church controlled by conservative confessionalism, it dreamed of a national Protestant culture dominated by Christian ethics[1598] along Kantian idealistic lines that was much more favored because of its secular character. Many believed that liberal Protestantism's social gospel had surpassed the ecclesiastical stage of Christianity's previous history to now enter to its ethical-political spiritual age functioning now as a Divine power in the German nation.[1599]

However, the dominionism of Ritschl's social gospel that pushed for the kingdom of God this side of the grave invariably left the Jews behind as second-class citizens. Protestant liberalism was thus not very liberal toward the Jews, but very nationalistic toward them instead. In fact, the placement of the Jews "was basically the same in the liberal as in the confessional or Catholic vision. For Jews, a Christian state meant relinquishing their religion if they wanted to be assimilated or living as second class citizens, for example, not being admitted to public posts, army training or the field of education."[1600] There was thus no improvement or progress for the Jews. Indeed, "national liberalism required assimilation. From early on liberal Christianity had been a twin to this national liberal project, dreaming of a united Germany where particularistic groups had been assimilated into the body of the people. The refusal of even liberal Jewish groups to assimilate was a thorn in the flesh to liberal Christianity."[1601] Ritschl and other leading liberal Protestants opposed what they considered to be Jewish segregation, backward legalism and restrictive ceremonialism as they hindered their freedoms in a variety of ways. Liberal Protestantism in Germany thus became "an oppressive force against Judaism in the last decades of the 19th century, at the same time as anti-Semitism flourished and Jewish identity was placed within narrow limits."[1602]

In reality, the Second Reich was an anti-Semitic state under the spiritual power of liberal Protestantism where Romanticism, nationalism and socialism all mixed together through the propagation of the social gospel. The great carnage of World War I, however, devastated the optimism of Protestant liberalism that it never recovered from during the post-war years as it began to sink into decline. When nationalism and socialism

---

[1598] Ibid., pp. 133-34.
[1599] Ibid., p. 134.
[1600] Ibid.
[1601] Ibid.
[1602] Ibid., p. 135.

once again came together some 15 years later, Germany was much more secular and pagan the second time around. The pagan underpinnings of Schleiermacher's natural theology dressed up in theological Romanticism became more pronounced as secular Protestantism was replaced with existentialism and political mysticism. The symbol of the cross was replaced with the swastika,[1603] and the mixture of secularity and paganism converted anti-Semitism into a much more murderous enterprise than anyone could have previously envisaged. German theological liberalism did not progress or expand the Protestant Reformation, but managed to put it in reverse as true Romanticism invariably does. As it undermined faith in the miraculous testimony of the Scriptures, it left behind a vast spiritual wasteland after it collapsed in the great tumults of World War I.

The Nature Religion of National Socialism
Overpowered the Weakened Church

Throughout the 1800s and early 1900s, parallel to the rejection of the historical authenticity of the Bible grew up a *volkisch* religion of nature in Germany, sometimes emphasizing ecological holism, nationalism or even a natural existentialism, and other times emphasizing more secular scientific notions about Darwinian biology and racism, all of which in one way or another, was absorbed by the Nazis into their own *Weltanschauung*. Moreover, the primary culprit for the sacrifice of the Jewish people in the Holocaust was this quasi-scientific National Socialist religion of nature, not Christianity per se as liberal Protestantism did much to diminish faith in the Bible. What was left after the fallout of World War I was secular Romanticism and existentialism that had already been growing into a more virulent and ferocious wild animal as the decades passed by.

In other words, the Germanic odyssey that attacked the historicity of the Bible unabated without mercy for well over 100 years did not lead to more liberalism as German liberals originally envisaged, but to its opposite. If such energies had been directed at their own self-criticism, perhaps they would have reaped much better results than the socialist and nationalist slaughterhouse that became the 1930s and '40s:

[1603] See *Hitler's Cross* by Erwin Lutzer.

Perhaps more than in any other modern country, the nation's (Germany) destiny was intertwined with the destiny of Christianity. In contrast with what most modern scholars experience, living their lives on academic islands, German professors of theology and exegesis were no unimportant figures in the life of the nation. In fact, German Protestant theology often saw itself as part of, and key to, the development of Germany. At times it was successful in exerting its influence, not only on theology, but also on politics and cultural life. However, at the same time, the so-called Jewish problem hung as a dark shadow between the Enlightenment and the Holocaust. In the great project of shaping the German nation-state, a project that several leading theologians were involved in, the Jewish minority, whether assimilated or maintaining its integrity, was often regarded as a disturbing phenomenon.[1604]

German theologians and philosophers presumed their secularization project to make the Bible palatable to the modern mindset for the sake of contemporary application to society was all done in the name of religion. However, it never occurred to them that in the process of secularization, they were unleashing the forces of profanization that became much more deadly and lethal, particularly with regard to the Jews. Age old Christian anti-Semitism was secularized into a profane world that was left with few Divine restraints to check the baser instincts, cruelty and passions of men. Anti-Semitism became godless, and as such, became a far more serious problem than heretofore envisaged—particularly after German theological liberalism crashed and burned in the trench warfare of World War I. As bad as the old Christian pogroms were dating back to the Catholicism of Augustine, there was not a Holocaust until the 20th century, and it was German philosophy and theology in response and reaction to the Enlightenment that played no small role in secularizing anti-Semitism into this deep darkness that has no parallels in history.

As such, the historical record of the National Socialist religion of nature desperately needs to be much more a part of the discussion about the Jewish Holocaust. This, however, "has not been done either because National Socialism as a religion of nature has not been taken seriously, or because investigation of such a religion could lead to very disquieting

1604 Gerdmar, p. 23.

conclusions."[1605] Worse, both of these tangents have reinforced each other. Open and honest discussion about the National Socialist religion of nature, therefore, are awfully hard to come by, largely because so many in the modern West have adopted a secular religion of nature all their own. On the one hand, *scientific* Darwinism forms their materialistic views on creation, and on the other hand, environmentalism supplies them with their *spiritual* form of green ethics. While environmental biological racism is no longer being propagated, an international political ecology full of misanthropy has rushed in behind the wake of the battlefields of World War II. More troubling, the best and primary check against environmental misanthropy—Christianity itself—appears to be falling by the wayside in modern life even in America. As Christianity becomes less and less a part of the everyday modern world, Western man is increasingly adopting a secular religion of nature in its place.[1606]

What must not be forgotten is on the eve of the Nazi accession to power, German Christianity had been greatly weakened by more than a century of *volkisch* nature worship on the one hand, and Enlightenment secularization on the other hand, much of which was wrapped up in theological liberalism, and all of which was used by the Nazis against Christianity. The church in Germany was not very strong when Hitler became chancellor in 1933. "Christians of all kinds were deceived by Hitler, at least initially. The liberals, however, who were tossed to and fro by every wind of doctrine, found themselves particularly vulnerable to the vortex of the Nazi whirlwind. Even when Hitler's agenda finally became clear, they were not willing to suffer for the gospel that they had long since abandoned. They were more interested in the miracles of a revived Germany than in the miracles on the pages of the New Testament. Salvation in this world was more important than salvation in an unseen life to come."[1607]

In particular, progressive German theological liberalism was discredited by the defeat and carnage of World War I. Worse, the defeat at war and the great economic suffering that followed in the 1920s did not lead to national repentance, but to a stronger desire for a more secular and political nationalism. Protestant and Catholic nominalism was rampant. "Germans had begun to view themselves as liberated from God. This nation

---

[1605] Pois, p. 11.
[1606] See especially *Resisting The Green Dragon: Dominion not Death*. Burke, VA: Cornwall Alliance for the Stewardship of Creation, 2010 by James Wanliss.
[1607] Lutzer, p. 138.

which had produced a disproportionately large number of great thinkers and inventors came to view these very real achievements as shoving God out of their lives."[1608] As such, German racism based on nature increasingly replaced the Bible and the Judeo-Christian worldview. That many Christians fell for the secular underpinnings of Nazi racism is proof in and of itself how nominal the church had become:

> During the First World War, Germans began in ever greater numbers to turn away from real religious faith, particularly Christianity. . . . After the First World War, in the decades before the Nazis came to power, Christians more and more lost faith in Christianity. Germans began to formally leave the Christian faith in large numbers. In 1920 alone, more than 300,000 people formally resigned from the Christian faith. During the years from 1918 to 1931, 2.4 million Evangelical Christians formally renounced their faith as well as almost half a million Catholics. . . . Between 1908 and 1914, 115,000 Christians in Germany formally renounced their faith; between 1914 and 1918 another 15,000 renounced their Christianity. After the First World War, Protestants were formally abandoning Christianity at an average rate of 186,000 per year, and Catholics at a somewhat lower level. . . . Between 62% and 80% of Germans who were nominally Christian when Hitler came to power had stopped taking communion.[1609]

Hitler himself shared their views, stating: "Since my 14th year I have felt liberated from the superstition the priests used to teach. Apart from a few Holy Joes, I can say that none of my comrades went on believing in the miracle of the Eucharist."[1610] Thus, while Christianity was greatly waning in Germany in the first 30 years of the 20th century, secularists, social Darwinists, pantheists, nationalists, socialists, environmentalists, occultists, counter culturists, etc., were on the rise to replace those declining numbers. More telling, with the loss of Christianity came a naivety about evil that caught them all by surprise during the Nazi era. Thanks to the German

---

[1608] Walker, *The Swastika Against the Cross*, p. 4.
[1609] Ibid., pp. 4-5.
[1610] *Hitler's Table Talk*, night of Feb. 20-21, 1942, p. 246.

emphasis upon Darwinism, race and nature, the concept of evil and sin had been long forgotten.

One of the root causes of such a rejection of Christianity was German nationalism increasingly devoid of Christian values. "To practice a religion which had been imported into Germany from abroad offended the pride of German intellectuals, philosophers, historians, and scientists."[1611] Solomon taught that pride is on top of the list as a special object of the Lord's hatred (Prov. 6:16), and that "pride *goes* before destruction" (Prov. 16:18). The dangers of German nationalism and pride grew as it rejected Christian teaching. The real moral of the story is a sinister ideology eventually filled in the gap behind the retreating lines of Christianity, and the secularized Germans were ill-prepared to handle the situation. They were, in fact, a much bigger part of the problem than they themselves ever realized. They eventually succumbed to the modernized nature religion that was Nazi Germany. In short, without a written, proclaimed and known Divine revelation from God, all one is left with is the silence of the woods and the dangers of religious and/or political mysticism.

In a world without Biblical revelation, German writers and intellects pushed ever deeper into the existential valleys, canyons, and abysses of nature. Germans increasingly eschewed the civilization and the culture that Judeo-Christian values bestowed upon them. The heavenly values of the Judeo-Christian tradition uprooted the Germans from their comfort zones embedded in the soil of their *volkisch* homeland. This high elevation of *heaven's tableland* proved to be too airy for them to handle:

> The dichotomy between a human world, inherently divine due to man's being made in God's image, and a natural world, over which man presumably has some degree of control, has never been a particularly comfortable one with which to live. First of all, as we have seen, the axiological charge to man, as singularly divine creature, situated somewhere between heaven and earth, is an immense one. Secondly, the notion that humans, having certain powers over nature, are themselves responsible for it in some way (rather than simply adjusting to certain "natural laws" beyond their control), places great burden upon them. It has been, and is, a far

---

[1611] Rappoport, Angelo. *The Gauntlet Against the Gospel*, London, 1937, p. 222; quoted by Walker in *The Swastika Against the Cross*, p. 4.

easier choice to see man as not being apart from nature, much less above it, but of nature.[1612]

Shunning such Divine given responsibilities had grave consequences for Germany. The general morass of atheism, agnosticism and unbelief dressed up in Romanticism, existentialism and scientism made Germans far more susceptible to the sordid end that was the National Socialist slaughterhouse. A culture completely embedded in nature without any outside accountability to a transcendent God will end up in self-destruction. By itself nature is amoral. If one builds a culture on such an amoral basis, one will naturally reap the evil consequences of such a foundation. In Nazi Germany, the cunning of nature built a fascist bridge between natural beauty and an amorality that proved to be fatefully popular to many Germans in the 1920s and 1930s.

The Nazis Converted Christian Anti-Semitism into Biological/Environmental Anti-Semitism

Very troubling indeed, Martin Luther's (1483-1546) virulent anti-Semitism would be used as fuel for the fire in the Holocaust. In his later ministry, Luther made extremely harsh comments about the Jews even though he was concerned about their plight in his younger years. Rather than be embarrassed by Luther's tirades against the Jews, Bishop Martin Sasse of Thuringia enthusiastically published a collection of his "Anti-Semitic vitriol shortly after *Kristallnacht's* orgy of anti-Jewish violence. Appallingly, in his foreword, he applauded the burning of the synagogues and the coincidence of the day: 'On November 10, 1938, on Luther's birthday, the synagogues are burning in Germany.'"[1613]

Going all the way back to the early Catholic church, many Christians identified the Jews in general as Christ-killers, even though it was primarily the corrupt political-religious establishment in Jerusalem that handed Jesus over to Pilate and the Gentiles to be crucified. As such, in great contrast to the New Testament (Rom. 9:1-5), Gentile Christians often ridiculed and persecuted the Jews for being stubborn and apostate. Such widespread attitudes played a powerful role "in deciding how far representatives of Christianity

---

[1612] Pois, pp. 57-58.
[1613] Goldhagen, p. 111.

would be willing to go in defending a group of people whose traditional economic and social roles in German life seemed to suggest that an angry God had provided a pariah role for it."[1614] Such an outlook also prevented many a weak and naïve Christian in Nazi Germany from concerning himself too much with the Jewish question. Christian eyewitness Hilmar Von Compe said, "Every German saw this discrimination of a helpless minority and knew what was being done. There was no outcry by the churches, there were no protests on the streets, nor was there any resistance by society. It is an appalling story of a nation of cowards and appeasers, which to my shame, I was a part of, even as a boy. I do not remember ever hearing our church make any reference to the blatantly brutal and godless treatment of the Jewish people."[1615]

Enthusiastic Christian support of the regime, appeasement and relative unconcern for the Jews, paved the way for the National Socialists to take up the banner of anti-Semitism for themselves with relative ease. "Ironically enough, that traditional anti-Semitism which in large measure flowed from Christianity, something which National Socialism supposedly would supplant, helped to assure a general level of support for 'moderate' anti-Semitic measures, e.g., the Nuremberg laws of 1935."[1616] Traditional Christian anti-Semitism, dating back to Catholicism and comments from Martin Luther, would be superseded by Nazi anti-Semitism, which was anti-Semitism on other grounds, i.e., biological and environmental ones which has its deep roots in the paganism of the Greco-Roman era. Nazi anti-Semitism was a secularized version of the former. "Race based anti-Semitism appropriated and reproduced the form of Christian anti-Semitism's cognitive model while injecting it with new content."[1617]

Through German secularity, anti-Semitism adapted, evolved and modernized itself into an ever-growing sinister crusade. Such a secular conversion had increasingly ominous consequences. "Because modern German anti-Semites believed that the Jews were the prime source of disorder and decay, they could assert that until the Jews were vanquished, the world would never be at peace. Medieval Christians could not say this, for even if the Jews were to disappear, the Devil, the ultimate source of evil, would

---

[1614] Pois, p. 166.
[1615] Von Campe, p. 37.
[1616] Pois, p. 169.
[1617] Goldhagen, p. 67.

452

remain."[1618] Nazi secularity thus led directly to a much more extreme version of anti-Semitism. As German anti-Semites replaced Christianity's religious anti-Semitism throughout the 1800s with naturalistic metaphors in organic terms where the Jews were deemed an invasive species threatening the national body politic, the secular concept of race "dictated that a Jew could never become a German."[1619] In Christianity, the Jew could always be converted—at least in theory. Under National Socialism, thanks to a *scientific* racism that believed the races were evolving away from each other into separate progressive species with the Aryans leading the pack, this was impossible.

The Nazis promoted a Darwinian religion of nature and natural existentialism to attack the very foundations of the Jewish faith, i.e., the book of Genesis and its unabashed assertion that man was made in God's image who stood above the created order. That this was also an attack on Christianity is something that many a weak Christian in Nazi Germany had apparently not considered. Neither did the Christian understand that he would have certainly been the next target on the list had the Nazis won the war. In short, for a Christian to be anti-Semitic is to saw off the very limb that is holding him up, something which the Apostle Paul dwells on at great length in Romans 9-11. "The eventual goal of National Socialism had to have been the extirpation of the entire Judeo-Christian tradition, and that only pragmatic demands imposed by social, political, and logistic realities prevented the regime from undertaking an anti-Christian *Kulturkampf* far more pervasive than anything Bismarck could have imagined. Also, and perhaps this is of primary importance, the National Socialist regime survived for but 12 years, hardly enough time to undertake, much less complete, a sustained campaign against Christianity. Thus the average religious German continued to go to church and to pray to the traditional God of battles."[1620]

Christianity's Compromises with National Socialism

Many regular churchgoing parishioners were either blind to the dangers National Socialism posed to Christianity or quietly went along with the

---

[1618] Ibid.
[1619] Ibid., p. 65.
[1620] Pois, p. 28.

regime. All too many actively supported the Nazi state. Some Christians even touted a German Church by lopping off the Jewish Old Testament. They even sometimes turned Jesus into an Aryan anti-Semite. On the academic front, many German theologians and commentators posited Judaism's mixture with the Greek spirit before the time of Christ as the major driving force behind the great spiritual progress of the New Testament. Such views invariably de-Judaize the New Testament in favor of Greek philosophy and/or spiritual mysticism as being superior to the *legalism* of the Old Testament.

On the other hand, however, some Christians also strongly opposed the Nazi regime. In spite of the dark mood of the times, there were occasional shining moments of faith. The fact of the matter is that much of the opposition directed against the Nazis during the 1930s and '40s was most forthcoming from Christian churches rather than from any other segment of German society. Contrary to popular opinion, many of the first occupants thrown into concentration camps were Christians.

In 1934, Karl Barth, who was teaching in Bonn, Germany, was the main contributor to the Barmen's Declaration asserting religious independence from Nazi values. Barth sent the declaration directly to Hitler himself. The contents of the letter affirmed the evangelical churches of Germany were not subject to the *Fuhrer*, but to Jesus Christ. While many evangelical Christians have rightly criticized some of Barth's theological and political leanings, here was a brave moment of truth that gets little attention. The Barmen Declaration was also supported by Dietrich Bonhoeffer, who was later martyred in 1945 for being involved in the 1944 plot to kill Hitler.[1621] However, the Barmen Declaration was not a treatise to rebel against National Socialism per se, but it was a document declaring its heritage of religious freedom dating back to the Protestant Reformation. This document essentially became the charter for an association of like-minded churches in Germany called the Confessional Church. Barth was one of the primary spokesmen of the Confessional Church, but was expelled back to Switzerland by the Nazis in 1935 because he was unwilling to swear an oath to Hitler.

In March 1935, *The New York Times* printed an article[1622] discussing how 700 Prussian pastors were placed under house arrest by the Nazi secret police for reading an anti-pagan manifesto that was certainly aimed

---

[1621] See Eric Metaxas' book entitled *Bonhoeffer: Pastor, Martyr, Prophet, Spy.*

[1622] "700 German Pastors Arrested: Reading of Anti-Pagan Manifesto," *The New York Times*, March 18, 1935.

directly at National Socialism. The manifesto was written to warn Christian churches about the dangers of the new pagan religion spreading across Germany under the National Socialist banner. By reading the anti-pagan manifesto publicly to their congregations, this was one of the ways in which the Confessional Church asserted its religious liberty. Unlike many people today, discerning Christians were well aware of the pagan underpinnings of National Socialism.

However, such cases as Karl Barth, the Barmen Declaration, the opposition of the Confessional Church, and Dietrich Bonhoeffer, as brave as they were, were simply too exceptional during the Nazi era. Much more disturbing, the same bravery the Confessional Church demonstrated against Nazi rule was not exerted with regard to the Jewish *problem*. In fact, it seems that anti-Semitism was the one place where the church and state saw eye to eye. "Indeed, regarding the Jews, there was but little difference between the mainstream Protestant Churches and the breakaway, avowedly racist and anti-Semitic *German Christians* who sought to merge Christian theology with racism and the other principles of Nazism. In many letters that mainstream Protestant pastors wrote explaining their rejection of the German Christian movement, they emphasized the German Christians' impermissible mixing of religion and politics, but not a single one criticized the ongoing persecution of the Jews."[1623]

More telling, while Christians successfully protested against what was called the T-4 Euthanasia program that killed 70,000 German citizens deemed unfit for life because of mental and physical handicaps, there was no outrage directed against Nazi authorities for euthanizing the Jews to death in the Holocaust.[1624] Accordingly, the Nazis stopped the T-4 Euthanasia program within Germany's borders, but the Holocaust itself was never under any danger or pressure to come to a halt. Only the end of the war finally put a stop to it. Yet, many churches and Christians were fully aware what was happening to the Jews by 1941. Even American Pastor Stewart Herman, who ministered in an English-speaking international church in Berlin until December 1941, was fully aware what happened at *Babi Yar* on the outskirts of Kiev just a few months prior to his departure when more than 30,000 Jews were massacred following the destruction of the Soviet Army that failed to protect the city. Herman clearly reported, "It became

---

[1623] Goldhagen, p. 114.
[1624] Ibid., p. 119.

definitely known through the soldiers returning from the front that in occupied Russia, especially at Kiev, Jewish civilians—men, women, and babies—were being lined up and machine gunned by the thousands."[1625]

In fact, Protestant publications and presses during the Nazi era were so routinely imbued with anti-Semitism that it most certainly curtailed Christian feelings for the Jews as human beings. "Small wonder that these Christian readers would look with unpitying eyes upon the Jews as they were being attacked, tormented, degraded, and reduced to social lepers during the Nazi period."[1626] Such Protestant publications even helped catapult Hitler into power. Protestant editors "brought their already virulently anti-Semitic rhetoric into closer concord with that of the Nazis. They did so unbidden, entirely voluntarily, and with unmistakable passion and alacrity."[1627] With such thick propaganda, many Protestants were either entirely sympathetic or eventually won over by Hitler.[1628] Incredibly, they were hoping he would regenerate the nation. They were fooled by Nazi propaganda because in spite of its secular emphasis, their pagan Romanticism presented to the German people a form of spirituality which appeared to offer national restoration. Bonhoeffer looked upon his anti-Semitic theological friends with incredulity, "The most sensible people have lost their heads and their entire Bible."[1629]

Theologian Gerhard Kittel (1888-1948), the editor of the magnum opus *Theological Dictionary of the Greek New Testament* (TDNT), was a Nazi Party member. So was Walter Grundmann (1906-1976) who worked side by side with Kittel on the TDNT and many other New Testament projects and works. Grundmann joined the Nazi Party as early as 1930, and was the academic director of the Eisenach Institute, which was a major driving force behind de-Judaizing German church life.[1630] In 1936, Grundmann essentially became a professor of *volkisch* theology at the University of Jena. As New Testament professor there, Grundmann struck "Hebrew from the curriculum, arguing that the early church had read the Greek Old Testament,

---

[1625] *The Catholic Church and Nazi Germany*, p. 294, quoted by Goldhagen.

[1626] Goldhagen, p. 108.

[1627] Ibid.

[1628] Brown, Courtney, "The Nazi Vote: A National Ecological Study." In her conclusion, Brown points out the Nazis had very strong support coming from rural Protestant peasants.

[1629] Goldhagen, p. 109.

[1630] Gerdmar, pp. 536-38.

not the Hebrew one."[1631] Kittel himself went so far to teach that Jesus was "non-Jewish or anti-Jewish in His preaching,"[1632] and the New Testament itself was an anti-Semitic document.

Shockingly, Kittel characterized Esther from the Old Testament as a book that promoted a false world Jewry bent on international power that artificially demanded the conversion of many Gentile proselytes—which invariably led to racial mixing.[1633] As such, Kittel did not believe the Jews were a race, but a racial mixture, which is why their very existence was such a threat to society. Kittel thus held post-exilic Judaism was a corrupted form of Jewry at complete odds with its earlier foundations that rooted the Hebrew tradition in the blood and soil of the promised land of Israel where racial mixing was forbidden. Such views led Kittel to mine the book of Ezra in particular for modern-day application of Biblical principles since the scribe forbade interracial marriage of the exiles after they returned from Babylon. While much of the Old Testament was taken less seriously, Ezra was a book that Kittel could believe in: "Eliminating mixed blood and intermarriage is sound—the Jews themselves did this."[1634] After Nazi biologist Ernst Lehmann read Kittel's Old Testament historical summary of the Jewish racial problem that had allegedly been threatening world order with its racial mixing since the exile, he concluded, "When the Jewish problem is biologically substantiated in such an unequivocal way as in the following explanation by the theologian Kittel, the biologist can learn something from theologians."[1635] At the time, Lehmann was the academic dean of Tubingen, where Kittel was also professor.

While some scholars have more recently tried to portray Kittel and Grundmann as conservative theologians, the *Theological Dictionary of the New Testament* presumes the liberal fantasy of the Wellhausen JEPD theory that foisted upon the entire Old Testament *historical* evolutionary views completely alien to the text itself. Kittel's New Testament dictionary also presumes the existence of a ghost-like author for Isaiah 40-66 named Deutero-Isaiah, even though such a historical personage has never been found. Kittel purposely disassociated himself from J.B. Lightfoot's (1828-1889)

[1631] Ibid., p. 535.

[1632] Ibid., p. 498.

[1633] Ibid., p. 485.

[1634] Ibid., p. 484.

[1635] Ibid.

Christian apologetic writings coming out of England that sharply opposed Tubingen's higher criticism.[1636]

Even Grundmann presumed German higher critical theories, but he also became deeply inspired by Rudolf Bultmann's (1884-1976) demythological program of the New Testament during the Second World War.[1637] Bultmann's liberalism demythologized the Bible so that it would not have to be accepted at face value. Through Bultmann's demythological approach, the ancient text could be rescued from the great stress brought against it through German higher criticism, and thus find *existential* relevancy once again in the modern world. Yet, it must be pointed out that once Bultmann demythologized the historical Jesus, His Jewishness became irrelevant. No wonder Grundmann found Bultmann's demythologizing program so theologically insightful.

Neither were the Catholics immune to Nazi propaganda and pressures. They often acted worse than the Protestants. Much has been made of Catholic collaboration with the Nazis before, during and after the Third Reich. More astounding, the churches still supported Hitler even after he purposefully stiff-armed them early on. "I adopted a definite attitude on the 21st of March 1933 when I refused to take part in the religious services, organized at Potsdam by the two Churches, for the inauguration of the New Reichstag."[1638] Worst of all, the Nazis had plans to Aryanize or Nazify the German Church, which sometimes proved surprisingly effective.

The real religious madness in the Third Reich was over how many Christians supported National Socialism even though most of the leading Nazis hated Christianity. Hitler was particularly displeased with the Protestant Reformation since it divided Germany for centuries.[1639] Yet in spite of strong Nazi opposition to Christianity, Kittel once remarked, "Adolf Hitler has taught the German people once again to listen to the right instincts and to feel in a sound way."[1640] Such a statement that highlights instincts and feelings as being so politically sound reveals a Romantic and existential heart at work underneath the veneer of Kittel's erudite scholarship.

With German skepticism leading the charge against historic Christianity for more than a century before the rise of National Socialism, spiritual

---

[1636] Ibid., p. 426.
[1637] Ibid., p. 543.
[1638] *Hitler's Table Talk: 1941-44*, midday of Feb. 27, 1942, p. 259.
[1639] Dietrich, p. 127.
[1640] Gerdmar, p. 492.

content slowly disappeared from the pulpit. Empty liturgy inescapably replaced genuine Biblical values. With so many prominent German agnostics, Hegelians, existentialists and skeptics teaching and writing so strongly against Biblical Christianity, the average German pastor's doubts also increased proportionately. German higher criticism had shown the Bible to be a false document historically speaking. When pastors opened their Bible commentaries, they were filled with elaborate theories chock full of German evolutionary skepticism and agnosticism, especially in the Old Testament. Thus, sound Biblical teaching and training was replaced with German evolutionary values, which more often than not were coming forth from the natural theology of the pagan forests. Hence German paganism, nationalism and Christianity became mixed up together in a most shameful way that the Nazis later were able to take complete advantage of.

Hitler especially hated Christians who held fast to their beliefs and refused to adapt their religious views to National Socialism: "The ones we have to fear are the ascetics with rings under their eyes, and the fanatics."[1641] However, the true ascetic was the *Fuhrer* himself being the vegetarian, non-smoker and non-drinker that he was. With regard to the Catholic church, Hitler held it with complete contempt: "Even among those who claim to be good Catholics, very few really believe in this humbug. Only old women, who have given up everything because life has withdrawn from them, go regularly to church."[1642]

Hitler held the Catholic clergy with even greater scorn, "You can bet on anything, if one relies on historical precedents, that the princes of the Church would lick my boots for the value of money."[1643] Hitler sarcastically asserted the Catholic Church "permits the orgies of the Carnival, firstly because she is powerless to prevent them, and secondly, because she recaptures the sinner on Ash Wednesday."[1644] Hitler even bitterly complained about how much money was going to church coffers from the government: "It's a real scandal that we must give the German churches such extraordinarily high subsidies ... unless I am mistaken, our Churches are still at present receiving 900 million marks a year."[1645]

[1641] *Hitler's Table Talk: 1941-44*, dinnertime on April 7, 1942, p. 259.

[1642] Ibid., midday of Feb. 27, 1942, p. 258.

[1643] Ibid.

[1644] Ibid., night of Dec. 1-2, 1941, p. 110.

[1645] Ibid., p. 309.

Hitler even boldly proclaimed before his inner circle, "I promise you that if I wanted to I could destroy the Church in just a few years. It is hollow, it is rotten and false through and through. One push and the whole structure would collapse. We should trap the preachers by their notorious greed and self indulgence. We shall thus be able to settle everything with them in perfect peace and harmony. I shall give them a few years' reprieve. Why should we quarrel? They will swallow anything in order to keep their material advantage. The parsons will be made to dig their own graves; they will betray God for us. They will betray anything for the sake of their miserable jobs and incomes."[1646] Hitler instinctively knew the church was very weak, and one of the primary reasons for its weakness was its historical attachment to the state. Hitler once said, "Therefore, if it's possible to buy the dignitaries of the Church with money, let's do it!"[1647]

After centuries of collaborating with the state, while there were many exceptions to the rule, a considerable portion of German Lutheranism itself had already been run into the ground by its own government connections. In great contrast to Luther's and Melanchthon's overburdened teaching ministry, formalism and liturgy in place of sound Bible doctrine and training had become more and more typical. Lifeless state churches sustained far more by taxes, dead orthodoxy and religious tradition rather than true Biblical spirituality, plagued the Lutheran church off and on in Germany for centuries. Such dead orthodoxy helped fuel the rise of pietism and Christian mysticism. As time went on and unbelief grew, it gave rise to theological Romantics like Friedrich Schleiermacher in the late 1700s. In other words, there was a very good reason why men like Ernst Moritz Arndt and Wilhelm Heinrich Riehl left the state-run religion for Romanticism.

One thing was for sure. There simply were not enough excellent stalwart theologians and Bible scholars like Ernst Wilhelm Hengstenberg (1802-1869), Carl Friedrich Keil (1807-1888), Johann Heinrich Kurtz (1809-1890) and Franz Delitzsch (1813-1890) to go around, especially as the 19th century came to a close. These men provided a Biblical counterweight to the German natural theology, Hegelianism and skepticism so prevalent in the 1800s, but they were vastly outnumbered. Delitzsch viewed the Tubingen school of his day as a university made up of Christian traitors.[1648] Delitzsch was an

---

[1646] Von Campe, p. 46.
[1647] *Hitler's Table Talk*, dinnertime on April 7, 1942, p. 310.
[1648] Gerdmar, p. 226-27.

expert in Hebrew and cooperated with Keil in writing a sound commentary series on the entire Old Testament that has since become a classic. Delitzsch himself strongly opposed the anti-Semitic mood of the times and was very involved in evangelizing Jews.

German Protestantism's Failure to Appreciate Jewish Prophecies

While the Protestant Reformation under Luther rightly used the historical-grammatical contextual method of interpretation to rescue salvation passages in the New Testament from Catholic mysticism, it failed to apply the same sound hermeneutical methods with regard to the prophetic portions of the Scriptures. The numerous prophetic passages throughout the Old and New Testaments, which promise a future national restoration of Israel in the promised land as prescribed by the Abrahamic, Palestinian, Davidic and New Covenants respectively,[1649] were simply ignored. This unfortunately continued the anti-Semitic sentiments of Catholic eschatology since Augustine. Many Old Testament prophecies which bespeak of Israel's future national salvation were confusedly interpreted as references to the church, however problematic and inconsistent with sound hermeneutical principles this was.

The Protestant Reformation stopped short of sound Biblical interpretive exegesis when it came to prophetic passages. In so doing, they in turn revealed an anti-Semitic Gentile bias. The Apostle Paul himself strongly warned the Roman church about this some 2,000 years ago, "But if some of the branches were broken off (Israel), and you (Gentiles), being a wild olive, were grafted in among them and became partaker with them for the rich root of the olive tree, do not be arrogant toward the branches (Rom. 11:17)." Paul then drives his sharp point all the way home:

> … for if you were cut off from what is by nature a wild olive tree, and were grafted contrary to nature into a cultivated olive tree, how much more will these who are the natural branches be grafted into their own olive tree? For I do not want you, brethren, to be uninformed of this mystery – so that you will not be wise in your own estimation – that a partial hardening has happened to Israel until the fullness of the Gentiles has come in; and so all Israel will

---

[1649] See Genesis 12:1-4; Deuteronomy 30:1-9; Psalm 89; and Jeremiah 31:1-40.

be saved; just as it is written, 'the Deliverer will come from Zion, He will remove ungodliness from Jacob. This is My covenant with them, when I take away their sins (Rom. 11:24-27)

Because of arrogance, the early church quickly forgot, "If the first piece *of dough* is holy (Israel), the lump is also; and if the root is holy, the branches are too" (Rom. 11:16). The early church ignored Paul's reminder to the apostolic Roman church that God is not through with His people Israel in spite of their general unbelief in Messiah. In the process of so doing, Paul interpreted Old Testament covenants and prophecies historically and grammatically in context, "From the standpoint of *God's* choice they (Israel) are beloved for sake of the fathers; for the gifts and the calling of God are irrevocable" (Rom. 11:28b-29). Here, echoing the prophets of the Old Testament, the Apostle Paul clearly understood the Jewish people are still God's people in spite of their many sins. Such an understanding as taught by the Apostle Paul would have spared Martin Luther and the Lutheran church from its Gentile pride toward the Old Testament and the Jews.

The Protestant Reformation in Germany did not go far enough in applying sound hermeneutical principles throughout all portions of the Scriptures. While men like Kittel were experts on ancient Judaism and rabbinical literature, they were less interested in the Old Testament texts themselves. With a much better grasp of the great soteriological and eschatological implications of the Old Testament, Romans 9-11, 1-2 Thessalonians, 2 Peter and the book of Revelation, the Lutheran church would have served itself much better during the Nazi era. Romans 9-11 and 2 Thessalonians were the standard the Apostle Paul laid down so many centuries ago where Old Testament prophetic passages were understood historically and grammatically in context—a standard many Protestants in Germany fell short of.

At the same time, as the Protestant Reformation stopped short of applying the historical, grammatical, contextual method of interpretation equally to all portions of Scripture, this opened up a big hole for the Hegelian evolutionary juggernaut. In fact, outside of theologians like Hengstenberg, Kurtz, Keil and Delitzsch, the only influential interpreters who seemed to have applied any kind of serious historical exegesis were the German Hegelians, skeptics and agnostics. As such, their naturalistic and mystical underpinnings attacked the historicity of the Bible rather than expounded it. While Hengstenberg, Kurtz, Keil and Delitzsch tried to correct the deficiencies of their Protestant *cousins* by emphasizing the importance of salvation history, they did not go far enough in that direction to be an effective counterweight to Hegel and his quasi-Christian semi-pantheistic followers. The *historical* evolutionary views of Hegel's semi-pantheism proved to be an almost irresistible tidal wave throughout the 1800s in all the theological halls of Germany.

With no small irony, Jewish apocalyptic prophecies were re-interpreted and eschatologically applied to Germany itself.[1650] By substituting Biblical eschatology for historical progressivism, secular German scholars increasingly positioned themselves as the vanguard of cultural evolution and revolutionary religious and philosophical change. Shockingly, the Jewish-Christian Biblical eschaton was then replaced by a secularized or politicized German one—a veritable Germanic post-millennialism with the propagation of a national social gospel as the very means by which this great eschatological goal would be accomplished. The theology of the Bible was replaced with an evolutionary natural theology that placed Germany on top of the Hegelian totem pole. As such, it is hardly surprising that many German theologians and Bible scholars like Kittel were quick to reject Zionism, even though the Old Testament clearly predicts a Zionistic eschatological future. They did this because of their misinformed German natural theology, not because of what the Biblical texts themselves actually said.

It took the tragedy of World War I to shake up Karl Barth enough to make him realize how shallow and Romantic German theological liberalism based on natural theology really was. However, even Barth himself was not able to shake completely free of the influence of his teachers. Barth rejected many of their theological conclusions, but did not criticize their progressive methods:

> German theologians in the late 19th century, partly because of the onslaught of antireligious Darwinists, but even more in response to the rise of biblical criticism (which they generally embraced), drew a strict line of separation between God and nature. The latter was science's province, while the former belonged to theology. This made their theology impervious to the scientific assault (but also less relevant to the real world).[1651]

1650 See especially Karl Lowith's discussion about Hegel in *Meaning in History*, pp. 52-59.
1651 Weikart, *From Darwin to Hitler*, p. 13.

Barth still accepted the Hegelian *science* of Old and New Testament historical criticism, seemingly unaware of its evolutionary semi-pantheism. This was a fatal flaw in his otherwise deep spiritual understanding. Barth was well known for being extremely antagonistic toward natural theology. However, his wholesale opposition to Schleiermacher's natural theology was fatalistic because he accepted his naturalistic hermeneutic of the Bible as scientific and historical without probing deeper into the evolutionary pantheism such interpretations were based upon.

In fact, his acceptance of so-called *scientific* higher criticism pushed Barth overboard into the realm of pure faith where one could believe in the truth of the Bible but recognize the document itself is fraught with historical mistakes, inaccuracies and inconsistencies. By trying to save the Bible from historical criticism, he undercut its witness still further by teaching one must accept the truth of the Bible by a leap of faith even though the book itself is full of historical mistakes. Along Kantian idealistic lines, Barth did this by placing faith and the truth of the Bible into a non-rational transcendental plane far above the realm of historical criticism.[1652] In so doing, he unwittingly helped to completely separate reality and history from theology into a dichotomous opposition where the average lay person "saw little conflict between National Socialist goals as *they understood them*, and the transcendental claims of Christianity."[1653] This self-defeating theological view is still plaguing the modern church today, and such spiritual and theological confusion only helps to weaken it even further in the face of another pantheistic beast of sorts that is growling and baring its teeth once again.

By the time of the rise of National Socialism, with a flood of unbelief streaming even out of theological schools for well over 100 years, the Lutheran Church of Germany was already greatly weakened. It was wrenched away from its theological moorings of *sola Biblia, sola gratia* and *sola fide*. At the same time, the state Lutheran church had already developed a long habit of rendering unto Caesar much more than rendering unto God. State and church secularization went hand in hand. This mixing of politics, taxes and religion sucked the spiritual life out of the church. It is also true that many clergymen had "never accepted either the fall of the monarchy, or

---

[1652] Schaeffer, pp. 53-54.
[1653] Pois, p. 168.

that liberal abomination, the Weimar Republic."[1654] Protestant presses even claimed the Jews had "caused the collapse of the Christian monarchial order" in Germany.[1655] Many Christians, therefore, were open to the *Fuhrer* and to the new Germany. At the very beginning, National Socialism seemed to have brought back a commitment to national renewal. Lutheran theologian, and friend of Barth, Friedrich Gogarten was a Nazi and called himself a "German Christian."[1656] While Gogarten would later be forced to eat his own words with regard to the praise he originally gave National Socialism, he still nonetheless "became a leader in the secularization movement of Protestantism"[1657] after the war. He thus continued his secular unbelief.

As was the case for many clergymen at that time, working for a state-run church and being paid by state taxes, Gogarten's commitment to true Biblical Protestantism had always been suspect at best. The same strangling secularizing forces which had been corrupting the church for more than a century, were the same secularizing forces which the Nazi Party itself was also promoting. Furthermore, many German Christians at the time were often upholding a secular form of Christianity. They wanted to better reach the secular culture of the day with the gospel, and they believed worldly compromises would help them build a bridge between them and society at large. While the church was thus proffering a secular Christianity, the Nazis were proffering a secular religion of nature. Both of them together were replacing Christian foundations with other foundations hostile to the faith.

Dr. Anna Bramwell notes that modern environmentalism grew the strongest out of the secular mindset established in Northern Europe and North America after the Protestant Reformation: "The scientists concerned with ecology, whether biological or economic, came mostly from Britain, Germany and North America, areas with a Protestant tradition. This suggests that there was some lack felt in the religion of Protestant countries that was not felt elsewhere."[1658] Hitler himself noted, "Protestantism has the warmth of an iceberg."[1659]

[1654] Ibid., p. 167.

[1655] Goldhagen, p. 108.

[1656] Pois, p. 167.

[1657] Ibid.

[1658] Bramwell, *Ecology in the 20ᵗʰ Century: A History*, p. 46.

[1659] *Hitler's Table Talk: 1941-44*, night of Dec. 1-2, 1941, p. 110.

What the Protestant Reformation emphasized was a demystification of nature. As the Protestants returned to the Bible, they de-mystified nature in the process. Though the Christian is to be in awe of God's creation since He created it, it was never to be worshiped. God alone was to be worshiped, not the natural world. Such Biblical truths, however, were largely confused and muddled during the Middle Ages thanks to the recovery of Aristotle and his semi-pantheism that infected Medieval Scholasticism. The Greek Aristotelian view of the cosmos was not overturned until Copernicus, Kepler and Galileo emphasized a mechanistic view of the universe run by natural laws. The Protestants were far less rebellious against this new cosmology than the Catholics. Not only did they believe that a personal, infinite, transcendental God created the world distinct from Himself, but they also believed that He created a rational world that runs according to coherent natural laws.

In short, both the Protestant Reformation together with a scientific mechanistic view of the universe, de-emphasized the miraculous in nature:

> Ironically enough, that Faustian Paganism which has been viewed as apotheosizing man's desire to grasp the totality of the natural world can be traced back to the Judeo-Christian tradition, while imposing ethical obligations upon man with regard to his lordship over the earth, nevertheless placed the earth and all its natural resources and non-human inhabitants at his disposal. In order for man to assert his authority over the earth, the Judeo-Christian tradition had to, in effect, de-spiritualize nature, removing divinity from it through the establishment of a transcendent God. In the sharp dualism between nature and spirit, a sense of magic seemed to have been removed from man's environment. We cannot gainsay the fact that the Judeo-Christian tradition has provided satisfactory solutions to the needs of millions for quite some time. Beginning with modern times, however, that de-spiritualization of the world of nature which had been implicit in this tradition became translated into reality, and, in a world in which mystery seemed increasingly to be replaced by the mundane, those anti-transcendental elements that always had existed as the alter ego to the mainstream of western religious speculation came more and more to the fore.[1660]

[1660] Pois, pp. 26-27.

By desacralizing nature,[1661] the Protestant Reformation placed everyone into a mundane world devoid of spiritual mysticism that was soon to be industrialized, homogenized and commercialized by the Enlightenment. When people began to abandon the tenets of their faith as the decades rolled by throughout the 1800s into the early 1900s, they found themselves left behind in the emptiness of a hollow, ordinary world that could only offer various forms of modern materialism and technological gadgets to dull the conscience. When people abandoned the Protestant Reformation, various forms of nature worship, pantheism and environmentalism necessarily replaced it.

Secularism Opened the Door to German Paganism, Romanticism and Existentialism that Undercut Protestantism

Pantheistic nature worship is the most popular religion in the world and in world history. The Bible is a historical record describing the basic antagonism between the Judeo-Christian worldview and nature worship and/or idolatry. The Jews in the Old Testament struggled with Baalism up until the time of the Babylonian exile. Later in the New Testament, Christians struggled with paganism, which has continued off and on within the halls of the church ever since. Man must and will worship someone or something, and the Bible strongly teaches that he usually worships the wrong object. In fact, the desire to worship is so strong the Bible sometimes compares it to sexual lust which cannot be stopped during the intense heat of the moment.

As such, once Christianity began to wane in Germany, it was just a matter of time before pantheism and the old pagan nature worship returned. Neither was this done unenthusiastically. One of the illegitimate children that came forth from the Protestant Reformation was the birth of Romanticism, a hearkening back for the primeval past of nature worship. This was

---

[1661] In the Bible, nature was never to be confused with God's own Person, much less worshiped. Furthermore, while both Catholics and Protestants have generally taught God is both transcendent above nature and also resides immanently within it, for the Protestants God's immanence was far more related to God's chosen elect people. The Protestants taught that by faith in Christ, God dwells directly within the believer in a special way, something which the Catholics are far more hesitant to say. Thus, the Protestants held that this special immanence of God is restricted to the redeemed or to the elect. This also means that nature does not possess this special indwelling of God, though God of course is still omnipresent and works immanently and providentially within nature and history in a general way.

felt especially strong in Germany, the very fatherland of Martin Luther. Paganism, Romanticism, naturalism, existentialism and Haeckel's social Darwinism quickly filled in the vacuum left behind by the fading of Protestantism. "The extraordinary influence of Haeckel and his successors can be attributed, in part, to the quasi-religious appeal, the incipient pantheism of his picture. But there is a deeper appeal; the return to a god-impregnated nature, which had been banished from the North by Christianity."[1662]

The other illegitimate child of the Protestant Reformation was the Enlightenment, which often prided itself in ancient Greek philosophy. While a part of the Enlightenment secularized Judeo-Christian ethics, particularly with regard to Kant's Transcendental Idealism, another part of it opposed Protestant Christianity's Biblical foundation by hearkening back to the classical Greco-Roman world. Thus, strangely enough, both the *spiritual* Romantic Movement and the *rational* Enlightenment were pining for the good old days of yesteryear before the advent of Christianity interrupted the classical harmony and holism of the Greco-Roman world.

With the long process of removing Biblical foundations coming from both the Enlightenment and Romanticism, Christianity had become very weak in Germany by the early 20th century. Along with a weak faith came an extreme cultural naivety as well. Many Protestants had fallen for the Nazis because they opposed Marxism. Marxists, of course, paraded their atheism. "The Protestant Church welcomed the Hitler Chancellorship since the National Socialists had resolutely fought Marxist 'anti-Church agitation', and now offered new hope for the future and the expectation of a 'favorable impact on the entire people.'"[1663] Many Christians, therefore, believed the Nazis were better than the Marxists. However, many failed to see the *volkisch* and secular dangers of Nazism.

The materialistic secularism of Marxism was simply replaced with the syncretism of *volkisch* secularism of the Nazis. This lack of discernment led to a gullible openness to National Socialism. The Nazis infiltrated the Protestant Church, working hard to replace church traditions with Nazi political ideology. One witness remembered an unwelcome Nazi sermon delivered from the pulpit on a Sunday morning:

[1662] Bramwell, *Ecology in the 20th Century: A History*, p. 45.
[1663] Kershaw, p. 432.

> In 1934, a guest Lutheran pastor visited our church in Puggen. Sitting in our pew, we were shocked when he began to preach Nazi ideology from the pulpit, his loud voice booming throughout the little chapel. Pounding on the lecturn, his sermon proclaimed that God had blessed Germany by bringing Hitler and the Nazis to us. Claiming that everything the Nazis were doing was good for Germany, he told us that we must follow them. My family shook our heads in stunned disbelief at the government's sacrilegious misuse of religion in an attempt to justify its own authority.[1664]

Those sitting in the pews on that day saw with their own eyes and heard with their own ears what Nazi *volkisch* secularization was all about in a most dramatic way.

Some Nazis even tried to promote a political-*volkisch* Christianity together with an Aryan Jesus to replace Biblical Christianity and the Jewish Christ of the gospels. Even well before the Nazi era, many German theologians and philosophers had been working overtime on transforming the historic Christian faith into a secular religious philosophy more in step with modernity. Biblical revelation was increasingly replaced with natural reason and infused with spiritual Romanticism. This was the main thrust of German Protestant Romanticism, existentialism, Hegelian philosophy and the German liberal theology that sprouted from both quarters. Even Schopenhauer promoted an anti-Semitic oriental Christianity. He once opined that European Christians "send missionaries to the Brahmans and Buddhists to inspire them with the 'true faith'; but when these men hear how animals are treated in Europe, they have the deepest loathing for Europeans and their religious doctrines."[1665]

Schopenhauer's favoring of oriental mysticism over Judeo-Christian values had also become somewhat fashionable at that time in Germany. Schopenhauer's disciple, Richard Wagner, whom Hitler championed as the musician of National Socialism, talked about a Greek Jesus. Such bizarre semi-cultic beliefs became all too common even among some Christian circles in Germany as the decades rolled by. Wagner strongly believed that Christianity must be transformed into a modern religion by uprooting it from its Jewish foundations. "For Wagner, the divorce of Christianity from

---

[1664] Lubbeck, p. 35.
[1665] Schopenhauer, *Parerga and Paralipomena*, p. 375.

its Jewish traits of utilizing, dominating and possessing nature is essential if Christianity is to be restored and made the religion of the future."[1666]

The great philosophical master Immanuel Kant was well-known for dispatching with the rationalistic medieval arguments concerning God's existence by emphasizing the limits of natural reason. Kant still held to the moral argument for God's existence otherwise known in philosophical circles as the categorical imperative. Such an approach epitomized the deistic spirit of the age where Judeo-Christian moral values were extolled at the expense of its doctrinal content and miraculous history. When Kant died, his extraordinary work left Germany with a bare naked secularized ethic that was empty of Biblical, doctrinal, historical and religious content that was paper thin and quickly overrun by Romanticism.

Since Kant presumed that objective rational knowledge about God was not possible to obtain, nor historically verifiable as is presumed in Scripture, his theological concentration became more practical. While Kant viewed God as necessary for the sake of human morality to help prevent societal anarchy—theology and religious content were largely ignored since they belonged to another sphere far above human knowledge. In other words, secular morality trumped the importance of religious knowledge and Biblical history. Practical moral considerations coupled with Kant's natural limits to reason thus gutted the whole possibility of theological and religious knowledge from the outset. This invariably contributed to a growing mindlessness regarding theology that was emptied of Biblical meaning and replaced with secularity, subjectivity, feelings and passions rooted in natural experience rather than the text of the Bible. In short, Kant opened the door to German natural theology contrary to the Bible. While reason does have its limits, Kant placed too many restrictions on it. This helped pave the way for the counter Enlightenment in which Romanticism, existentialism and, eventually, postmodernism replaced rationalism and reason in the modern world of philosophy.[1667]

When it came to Jews, Kant blew a gasket, "In Kant's telling, the only moral principle to which Jews subscribed in dealing with their European protectors was 'buyer beware.'"[1668] Not only did Kant call Jews "cowards,

---

[1666] Rose, pp. 57-58.

[1667] See *Explaining Postmodernism: Skepticism and Socialism from Rousseau to Foucault*. Loves Park, Illinois: Ockham's Razor Publishing, 2011, by Dr. Stephen Hicks.

[1668] Dorrien, p. 548.

liars, and cheaters"[1669] in his lectures, but even espoused common anti-Semitic tropes like—Judaism was really not a religion but a political entity,[1670] that the Jews were too attached to this world's goods,[1671] that Hebrew laws were materialistic rather than spiritual, that Christianity did not really have Jewish foundations,[1672] and that Judaist national character stubbornly rooted in the ancient past left them in a backward state as modern progress raced by them. In fact, Kant considered the Jews so tied to their empirical and material history in the Old Testament that he considered them to be non-modern precisely because they were not idealists like himself.[1673] Incredibly, Kant labelled the Jews superstitious because they subjected themselves to the empirical facts and traditions of their backward non-changing Old Testament history.[1674]

Worst of all, Kant's moral system of what he considered to be the liberty of self-sufficient reason was blatantly hostile to Jewish ethics. Kant considered Judaism as heteronomous and slave-like rather than autonomous and free. Jews took commands from outside sources like the Old Testament, the Mosaic Law and Jehovah, and then slavishly obeyed them without any concern about the proper inner autonomy and responsibility to freely carry out those orders. In fact, Kant went so far so as to target "the Jews as the empirical obstacle to the establishment of a rational order in which heteronomy would be overcome."[1675] Here, Kant's Transcendental Idealism casts its shadow over the dark murky waters of an anti-Semitic pro-European secular eschatology that helped later feed German postmillennialism under the auspices of theological Romanticism/liberalism. According to Kant, the money grubbing ways of the Jews provided them security throughout many places in Europe, and such success "threatened to subvert the European hope of an enlightened civil society devoted to the autonomy of life. Jewish aliens, by sneering at the norms of decent society, represented a kind of contagion that contaminated European societies."[1676]

In his *Religion and Rational Theology* written in 1798, Kant spoke on how the practice of his Transcendental Idealism would bring about "the

---

[1669] Mack, p. 5.

[1670] Ibid., p. 23

[1671] Ibid., p. 37.

[1672] Ibid., p. 32

[1673] Ibid., p. 39.

[1674] Ibid., p. 40.

[1675] Ibid.

[1676] Dorrien, p. 548.

euthanasia of Jewishness" with regard to ethics that would lead to moral purity: "The euthanasia of Judaism IS pure moral religion, freed from all the ancient statutory teachings."[1677] Here is a clear example where Kant's secularization did not lead to progress, but rather to destruction instead. Kant profaned the Christian spirit-grace opposition to Jewish law-legalism found in the New Testament and converted that antinomy into the "euthanasia of Jewishness."

Kant was blind to the fact that secularization more often than not leads to godlessness rather than progress. That the Nazis employed euthanasia experts, specialists and practitioners as the primary agents of destruction of European Jewry during the heights of World War II is a bitter irony that Kant himself could have never imagined when he spoke of the "euthanasia of Jewishness." Yet Kant's secularization program did more to promote godlessness in Germany than any other thinker of the modern era. Germany thus took age-old Christian anti-Semitism that had a penchant for pogroms, and secularized it into the Holocaust that was about 150 years in the making.

Hitler himself remarked that Kant's "complete refutation of the teachings which were a heritage from the Middle Ages, and of the dogmatic philosophy of the Church, is the greatest of the services which Kant has rendered to us."[1678] Hitler then pointed out it was "on the foundation of Kant's theory of knowledge that Schopenhauer built the edifice of his philosophy." During the exact same conversation, Hitler extolled Kant, Schopenhauer and Nietzsche as the greatest of Germany's philosophers, "in comparison with whom the British, the French and the Americans have nothing to offer."

As such, it was Schopenhauer who then moved in behind his teacher Kant and substituted his categorical imperative with an environmental ethic that was at first anti-Semitic, and secondly anti-Christian. Schopenhauer supplanted Kant's categorical imperative with what he called pity where one's humane attitude toward animals and nature should be extended to human beings as well. Furthermore, Schopenhauer strongly believed the will of man was far more important than the thought of man. Once again, practical considerations were used to trump the importance of man's reasoning abilities and capacities. A morality based on will in opposition to thought is a highly dangerous foundation upon which to build an ethic.

[1677] Mack, p. 35.
[1678] *Hitler's Table Talk*, evening of May 16, 1944, p.546.

Such an ethical worldview will invariably emphasize natural instinct and biological will over a thoughtful morality.

Friedrich Nietzsche then picked up where Schopenhauer's natural ethics ended, but with a vengeance. Nietzsche vehemently castigated Kant's categorical imperative, the last vestige of God found in modern Western philosophy. While Nietzsche fully agreed with Schopenhauer's thesis that the human will was more important than thought, he rejected his doctrine on pity and humaneness that Schopenhauer advocated to curtail the instinctual excesses of the will. Nietzsche considered such an ethos as womanly and weak. As such, Nietzsche replaced Schopenhauer's pity with his infamous *will to power* doctrine. Nietzsche's *will to power* was a very chauvinistic existential ethic rooted in the Earth where biological instinctual willpower was to dominate all of life. Closely connected, since Nietzsche presumed the Judeo-Christian God was as good as dead, the only place left to develop an ethic was to be found in nature and biology. Nietzsche then attempted to confront such nihilistic despair by promulgating a new natural man with new Earth-based values. This new natural man would be a superman of the Earth who could heroically face the nothingness of life with willpower, strength and vitality.

Thus, strangely enough, even though both Schopenhauer and Nietzsche were great thinkers, they used their great minds to attack thought and the Western philosophical tradition that was once wedded to the Judeo-Christian worldview. This was done in the name of nature under the guise of a natural existentialist philosophy of life. The growing juggernaut of Haeckel's social Darwinism then undergirded such a nature-based ethos with the so-called materialistic sciences of the modern age. All this has only progressively confined the Western world into a totalitarian, holistic fascism from which there is no escape.[1679] From this time forward, the empiricism of the modern science department became increasingly mixed up with evolution, social Darwinism, eugenics, Romanticism, environmentalism and existentialism. Since the catastrophic fallout of World War II, racial eugenics based on Darwinian biology has receded into the background, but the remaining features of the West's modern infatuation with nature still remain strong. While many are confident that the worst features of

---

[1679] For an excellent discussion on Kant, Romanticism, Nature, Schopenhauer, Nietzsche, the ideology of the will and existentialism together with its relationship to fascism and its pseudo-religious form that it took under Hitler's Third Reich, see J.P. Stern's *Hitler: The Fuhrer and the People*, pp. 13-63.

this biological concoction are in the rearview mirror, an environmental ethic based strictly on nature can potentially be just as dangerous as the National Socialist experiment. Environmental misanthropy against human development is by no means morally superior to racism.

"German might has bled to death
Time passed yet the priest remained
To rob the people of its soul
And whether he proselytized Roman or Lutheran
He taught the Jewish faith."

"No, we have not bled anonymous and without fame,
So that the German race will be Judaized
Through Christendom again."

SS festival Songs

CONCLUSION:

ROMANTICISM, ROME, AND ROMANS

On July 5, 1941, as the *Wehrmacht* was making spectacular advances on the Eastern Front into the heart of Byelorussia, the Baltics and the Ukraine, Adolf Hitler announced this stunning definition of fascism: "The fascist movement is a spontaneous return to the traditions of ancient Rome."[1680] With such a nostalgic backward-looking statement, Hitler's Romanticism was not limited to the *volkisch* nature-based ethos of Germany that informed his particular generation. It went all the way back to the Greco-Roman civilization itself before the anti-nature forces of the Judeo-Christian worldview undermined it. Hitler complained, "The Jew can take credit for having corrupted the world."[1681] He then blamed Christianity for the same crime: "It was Christianity that brought about the fall of Rome—not the Germans or the Huns."[1682] In the mind of Hitler, therefore, both Jews and Christians were responsible for the fall of the Greco-Roman world and its Spartan-like warrior culture. Hitler routinely complained Christianity had made the sickening effects of Judaism universal. As such, strong Spartan and Roman warriors were, by and large, missing from the European continent. The Nazis believed their new movement would be the answer to this existential crisis.

The Nazi experiment was therefore a gigantic attempt to bring back the Greco-Roman civilization of the past, all dressed up in modern scientific lingo together with the latest profound German philosophies, and led by the Aryans into a new world order for Europe and beyond. As far as Hitler and the Nazis were concerned, Europe must return to its Greco-Roman traditions before it was diseased with the Judeo-Christian worldview. This

---

1680   *Hitler's Table Talk*, Saturday on July 5, 1941, p. 5.
1681   Ibid., evening of Nov. 5, 1941, p. 91.
1682   Ibid., midday of Jan. 27, 1942.

meant getting rid of the Jews first during the tumult of war and, secondly, the removal of Christians after the war had been won.

Hitler wanted to plunge all of Europe into nature by dispatching with the Judeo-Christian worldview and its cultural traditions. In so doing, Germany would then be governed by the natural laws of life, i.e., social Darwinism, which grew out of Haeckel's Monistic philosophy about man and nature under the guise of evolutionary science. Moreover, since Haeckel was the very man who coined the term *ecology* in 1866, racism and environmentalism were inextricably bound up with one another. Tracking alongside German racism was a *volkisch* environmentalism that culminated in the National Socialist movement under the blood and soil slogan where a mystical connection between biology, racism and ecology were all hotwired together into an explosive amalgam that produced the darkest form of human sacrifice ever witnessed in all of history. It was Hitler's hope that such a green sacrifice would usher in a revived Roman Empire with Aryan Germany restoring Europe back to ancient glory. The sacrifice of the Jews was therefore understood as a prelude to a glorious Aryan future—the 1,000-year millennial Reich.

This herculean endeavor would require a generation of pitiless supermen along the lines of Nietzsche to convert this fantasy into reality through a titanic triumph of the will. In order to bring about the new Aryan man and the 1,000-year German Reich, the false Judeo-Christian emphasis of extolling all things weak had to be callously abandoned to restore natural order back to Europe. The Biblical understanding of a God of love and grace was alien to nature. Such a teaching was understood by the Nazis to have greatly weakened Germany and European culture. The Nazi eugenic laws, rooted in social Darwinism, were thus "designed to strengthen Aryan blood by sterilizing the insane, by killing Jews, Gypsies, homosexuals, and communists, and putting to death the 'sickly,' since in the 'struggle for existence' the 'health' of the organic whole—'blood and soil' could only be won by repudiating the bourgeois and Jewish Christian values of mercy and compassion."[1683] It was the concept of a God of love which allowed weaklings to live that led to the weakening of the races and of society in general. Hitler carped, "Taken to its logical extreme, Christianity would mean the systematic cultivation of human failure."[1684]

[1683] Zimmerman, "Ecofascism: An Enduring Temptation."
[1684] *Hitler's Table Talk*, midday of Oct. 10, 1941, p. 41.

According to Hitler and the Nazis, allowing the weak to live is not what nature teaches or intends. Hitler pointed out that nature itself knows no such moral obligations: "The earth continues to go round, whether it's the man who kills the tiger or the tiger who eats the man. The stronger asserts his will—it's the law of nature."[1685] Instead of ministering to the weak as the church had always done, the state needs to euthanize them instead. "Hitler embraced an evolutionary ethic that made Darwinian fitness and health the only criteria for moral standards. The Darwinian struggle for existence, especially the struggle between different races, became the sole arbiter for morality."[1686] Cutting the weak members out of society will help guarantee the racial strength of the future. Through the euthanization of the Jews, the weak, the sickly, the diseased and the Judeo-Christian Bolsheviks, Germany and Europe can return back to its primeval Greco-Roman roots with the Aryans leading the charge up the Nazi evolutionary mountain. Indeed, Hitler commented, "The Roman Empire, under Germanic influence, would have developed in the direction of world domination, and humanity would not have extinguished fifteen centuries of civilization at a single stroke. Let it not be said that Christianity brought man the life of the soul, for that evolution was in the natural order of things. The result of the collapse of the Roman Empire was a night that lasted for centuries."[1687]

An Aryan Green Sustainable Rome?

In Hitler's mind, racial warfare coupled with a green-based eugenics program would help blaze the trail to revive the Roman Empire. In October of 1941, Hitler declared, "Originally war was nothing but a struggle for pasture grounds. Today war is nothing but a struggle for the riches of nature. By virtue of an inherent law, these riches belong to him who conquers them."[1688] However, this statement from Hitler was not a call for the Nazi master race to exploit nature like Europe had done for so many centuries under a Jewish-Christian ethic.[1689] What would Hitler have done with the riches of nature as the head of the Master Race had the Nazis won the war? The history of the environmental movement under the Nazi's in

---

[1685] Ibid., evening of Sept. 23, 1941, p. 31.
[1686] Weikart, *From Darwin to Hitler*, p. 210.
[1687] *Hitler's Table Talk*, night of July 11-12, 1941, p. 8.
[1688] Ibid., midday of Oct. 10, 1941, p. 41.
[1689] Ibid., night of Jan. 28-29, p. 199.

the 1930s and '40s provides the answer to that question. Hitler had no plans to change Nazi environmental polices after the war, but to continue them, if not reinforce them. The reality of war forced the Nazis to retreat from some of their economic and environmental plans.

In the process of gearing up for the war and fighting the war, the Nazis were forced to experience many shortages of natural resources, which they were able to partially overcome through the development of synthetics. What they had learned about developing synthetics would therefore be put to good use even after victory. Hitler specified, "If in the future we obtain the primary materials that the shortages has compelled us to replace by synthetic products—a thing we could do—thanks to our scientific researches and our superior technique—that will be no reason to stop producing these synthetic products."[1690] Hitler believed the production of synthetic materials would help alleviate the stress on natural resources.

Hitler was, in fact, obsessed with running out of natural resources. He was very serious about conserving them as much as possible by using any scientific and technocratic means necessary. Assuming that coal would soon be exhausted, Hitler anticipated the modern green obsession with natural resources running out well ahead of its time in the 1970s. Hitler believed Western capitalism foolishly wasted natural resources: "Because of the fault of capitalism, which considers only private interests, the exploitation of electricity generated by water-power is in Germany only in its infancy. . . . We shall have to use every method of encouraging whatever might ensure us the gain of a single kilowatt."[1691]

Furthermore, when Hitler spoke of *exploiting* water for the sake of energy, he did not have in mind the construction of huge hydroelectric dams in Germany itself, but a series of small mill ponds built off slight slopes. "Let's not forget the old style mills."[1692] Hitler wanted to turn Norway into the hydroelectric center of Europe, not Germany.[1693] He also planned on limiting hydroelectric usage to the most needed industries like the chemical industry, for example. Why? Because that will be the industry that will help Nazi Germany continue its technocratic conservation methods through the development of synthetic materials. The very idea *ersatz* comes from

---

1690 Ibid., night of July 27-28, 1941, p. 16.
1691 Ibid., evening of Aug. 2, 1941, p. 20.
1692 Ibid.
1693 Ibid.

the Nazi emphasis upon the production of synthetic rubber and fabric.[1694] Hitler, very concerned with overpopulation outstripping natural resources, was certain "the future belongs, surely, to water—to the wind and the tides. As a means of heating, it's probably hydrogen that will be chosen."[1695] Here, Hitler presages the entire green renewable energy fetish that has captivated the entire Western world.

While many modern greens would chide Hitler for some of his ideas, he still had strong environmental technocratic inclinations in the area of energy economics. "There was a department for wind energy production in the Third Reich which was studying windmill technology till the end of the war, while methane gas plants were seen as an energy source of the future."[1696] As a strong exponent of what is today called renewable energy, Hitler wanted to harness science to help the Reich technocratically conserve natural resources. Environmentalists today are great technocrats when it comes to the green economy, smart grid logistics and renewable energy. Much of the growing technocracy in the modern world is largely built on a green foundation.[1697]

With Hitler's romance stretching as far back as the ancient Greco-Roman world, he thus appears to have been interested in establishing a modernized Aryan Green Rome of some sort, with the help of science, technology, renewable energy and sustainable development. However, this *volkisch* dream never materialized thanks to the Allied victory in 1945. With the fall of Nazi Germany came also the demise of *volkisch* environmentalism. "After the war, any talk of holism, or a love of nature that adduced certain values, was suspect."[1698] World War II exploded the racist ecology of the Nazis. After the war, the Allies also burned the nature-loving biological textbooks of the Reich for schoolchildren. "Works on biology, chemistry and landscape planning had to be rewritten."[1699] As such, it took the green movement in Germany almost 30 years to recover, this time and, not surprisingly, emphasize a global environmentalism in its place. "Ecologism in

---

[1694] Bramwell, Anna. *Ecology in the 20ᵗʰ Century: A History*, p. 88.

[1695] *Hitler's Table Talk*, evening of Aug. 2, 1941, p. 20.

[1696] Bramwell, Anna. *Ecology in the 20ᵗʰ Century: A History*, p. 88.

[1697] See especially Patrick Wood's book and website on Technocracy.

[1698] Bramwell, Anna. *The Fading of the Greens*. Yale University Press, 1994, p. 43.

[1699] Ibid.

Germany differs from most European Green movements in its complete break with pre-war ecologism."[1700]

Ironically enough, in 1968, some 23 years after Adolf Hitler's death, the Club of Rome was founded in Rome to promote global environmental sustainability. Today, the Club of Rome is the most powerful environmental think tank in the world. They are zealously trying to resolve what they call the "world *problematique*." The Club of Rome believes the world *problematique* is overpopulation coupled with global capitalism and unsustainable economic growth. There are too many people with too few natural resources. The Club of Rome is one of the primary environmental policy groups that have given teeth to the modern infatuation with sustainable development. This political thrust largely began in 1972 with the publication of its infamous environmental apocalypse entitled *Limits to Growth*. *Limits to Growth* is the best-selling environmental book of all time.

Shockingly, the Club of Rome has its heart set on establishing a future sustainable green society of nature worship. In order to make the planet truly sustainable, they want to stake a twisted and sacrificial verdant cross into the alleged human overpopulation problem. The combination of environmentalism and sustainable development is therefore a form of eugenics. In 1976, using Malthusian math, the Club of Rome asserted in its "Goals for Mankind" that the planet would be best served by reducing human population to anywhere between 500 million to one billion people. This particular population count is apparently ecologically sustainable over time. To help accomplish this, the Club of Rome had a previous plan to divide up the Earth into 10 self-sufficient bioregions of sustainable development.[1701] Bioregions are self-sufficient areas of economic autarky coupled with green sustainable development policies. In order to make the planet more green, each bioregion needs to have its own internal economy based on the natural resources that it possesses. In reality, bioregionalism is built upon the Nazi doctrine of *lebensraum* and *blood and soil*.

The connection, therefore, between Rome and modern environmentalism is thus a very real one, and it was anticipated by the *Fuhrer* himself. In Hitler's own mind, nature worship, eugenics, environmentalism, Caesar worship and *Fuhrer* worship were all wrapped up into a holistic fascism. Hitler himself was very fond of Rome and Italy. In the summer of 1941

[1700] Ibid.
[1701] "Environment: The Club of Rome: Act Two," *Time*, Monday, Oct. 21, 1974.

Hitler said, "Rome really seized hold of me. When the Duce came to Berlin, we gave him a magnificent reception. But our journey in Italy—that was something else!"[1702] Hitler was greatly impressed with Rome and its ancient glorious heritage. In spite of the rivalry that existed between the two dictators earlier in their careers, Hitler regarded Mussolini as a modern Caesar. "As I walked with him in the gardens of the Villa Borghese, I could easily compare his profile with that of the Roman busts, and I realized he was one of the Caesars. There's no doubt at all that Mussolini is the heir of the great men of that period."[1703] Hitler went on to say, "Despite their weaknesses, the Italians have so many qualities that make us like them. Italy is the country where intelligence created the notion of the State. The Roman Empire is a great political creation, the greatest of all."[1704] Hitler's infatuation with Rome was so great he even espoused a twisted form of logic to help maintain his belief in Aryan superiority: "The Romans had no dislike of the Germans. This is shown by the mere fact that blond hair was fashionable with them."[1705]

Hitler even had plans for the future *volkisch* curriculum to include the study of classical antiquities: "Roman history correctly conceived in extremely broad outlines is and remains the best mentor, not only for today, but probably for all time. The Hellenic ideal of culture should also remain preserved for us in its exemplary beauty."[1706] In fact, right before the Soviet counterattack put a stop to the *Wehrmacht's* advances on Moscow, Hitler's Romantic infatuation with the ancient glory of Rome compelled him to say, "What are 2000 years in the life of peoples? Egypt, the Greek world, Rome were dominant in turn. Today we're renewing that tradition. The Germanic race is gaining more and more."[1707] In short, Hitler Romantically fused the Greco-Roman world with his own when he said, "A culture combining millenniums and embracing Hellenism and Germanism is fighting for its existence."[1708]

All of this, of course, begs the question. Who is Hitler really in love with here? Ancient Rome or Nazi Germany or perhaps even a future European

---

[1702] *Hitler's Table Talk*, night of July 21-22, 1941, p. 11.
[1703] Ibid., p. 10.
[1704] Ibid.
[1705] Ibid., night of July 11-12, 1941, p. 8.
[1706] Hitler, *Mein Kampf*, p. 423.
[1707] *Hitler's Table Talk*, evening of Nov. 5, 1941, p. 90.
[1708] Hitler, *Mein Kampf*, p. 423.

supremacy? Hitler keenly asserted, "The reestablishment of German unity was Prussia's task, in the last century. The present task, of building a Greater Germany and leading her to world power, could have been successfully performed only under the guidance of a South German."[1709] Why, one might ask? Because a South German is closer to Rome.

"Following the brilliantly staged 1936 Olympics, Hitler's chief architect, Albert Speer developed elaborate plans to transform Berlin into Germania, a massive metropolis that would serve as a modern day equivalent of ancient Rome or Babylon."[1710] Olympic architecture on a Greco-Roman scale and the handing out of oak saplings to the gold medal winners in 1936 reflects quite a synthesis in the mind of Hitler that has left many historians and commentators, environmental and otherwise, scratching their heads. That Goering once paraded one of his full-grown pet lions during the Olympic Games while onlookers gaped and turned pale[1711] says it all.

Was Hitler a grand rebuilder of ancient Rome? Was he a scientific racist and/or environmentalist who wished to be closer to nature? Or was he a modern secular Caesar who promoted a Greco-Roman warrior ethos mixed together with nature worship? The answer to this question is that Hitler was in fact all three. All three were informed by strong Romantic interests. Hitler's desire to live according to nature's pantheistic laws, his romance over the Greco-Roman world and his lust for cult-like power all went hand in hand. "I'm going to become a religious figure. . . . Already Arabs and Moroccans are mingling my name with their prayers. Amongst the Tartars I shall become Khan. The only thing of which I shall be incapable is to share the sheik's mutton with them. I'm a vegetarian, and they must spare me from their meat!"[1712] Indeed, the Greco-Roman world has often been viewed as a world in harmony with nature. Hitler certainly shared this view, no matter how mythical this belief actually is.[1713] Furthermore, such views of the Greco-Roman world have come down to modern times thanks largely to famous romantic Roman writers like Livy, Virgil and Seneca.[1714]

[1709] Ibid., night of Oct. 21-22, 1941, p. 65.

[1710] Kotkin, p. 103.

[1711] Irving, p. 173.

[1712] *Hitler's Table Talk*, night of Jan. 12-13, 1941, p. 156.

[1713] See *Mythology: Timeless Tales of Gods and Heroes*. New York: A Mentor Book, 1969 (1940) by Edith Hamilton, pp. 13-14.

[1714] See *The Roman Way*. New York and London: W.W. Norton & Co., 1932 by Edith Hamilton, pp. 168-190.

Himmler too was a Romantic religious nut. He was trying to recover ancient Nordic German paganism, sometimes to the consternation of Hitler. Hitler was much more modern or secular in his Romanticism. More to the point, as Hitler wanted to recover the ancient Greco-Roman world in a modernized Nazi way, he would rather use an Aryan or *volkisch* naturism based on social Darwinism to accomplish this great task rather than revive ancient pagan mysticism per se. His secular religion of nature would be his primary political tool to help usher in this great revival of Rome with modern fascism, biological racism, holism, environmentalism and Caesar worship all wrapped into one harmonious synthesis. Himmler was not restricted by such secular caution.

Biblical Prophecy & the Roman Environmental Beast

With the Nazi will to revive the glories of the ancient Roman Empire, a scholar of Biblical prophecy cannot help but think of Psalm 2, the book of Daniel, the Olivet Discourse, Paul's letters to the Thessalonians and even the apocalypse of John. These particular Scriptures presuppose a revived Roman Empire tyrannically ruling the world during the final stage of human history before the Messiah returns to put a stop to man's rebellion and set up the Messianic kingdom of true peace and environmental bliss.[1715] Both Daniel and Revelation even describe this future Gentile power as a beastly wild animal preying upon the people of God. Revelation goes so far to compare the future Roman Empire to a dragon, a fire-breathing dinosaur (Rev. 12-13).

While it certainly seems that National Socialism was a ghastly attempt to bring back the beastly Roman Empire, from a Biblical point of view, its timing and geography were off. First of all, Daniel predicts the Antichrist will be of Roman origin (Dan. 9:26-27), not German. Secondly, the so-called Jewish problem that Hitler and the Nazis were obsessed with, and which the entire world seems to be preoccupied with today, will be resolved on the mountains of Israel at Armageddon (Zech. 12-14; Joel 2:18-3:21; Rev. 16-19), not in Germany, nor in Eastern Europe or Russia. Hitler's Nazi Party membership number also came up short. Rather than 666, Hitler's number was 555.[1716]

[1715] See Psalm 2; Daniel 7-9; Matthew 24-25; 2 Thessalonians 1-2; Revelation 12-20.

[1716] Hitler, *Mein Kampf*, p. xviii.

He later changed his party membership to number seven,[1717] knowing full well its Messianic implications.

The Bible predicts that before the Messiah apocalyptically comes back to rescue His people Israel from all of her enemies (Jer. 30:1-31:40; Mic. 7:14-20), as we learn from both Daniel and St. John, there will be a future divided Roman Empire of 10 kingdoms during a time of great tribulation on the Earth.[1718] The Scriptures thus anticipate kingdoms of tyranny at the end time which will culminate with the reign of the Antichrist, who finally seizes absolute power for himself in the midst of great tumult. As such, according to prophetic determination, at some point in the future, the free democratic institutions of the West must therefore give way to despotic kingdoms of tyranny.

This totalitarian process may have very well begun with the modern rise of fascism in the 20th century, especially with Nazi Germany and its goal of restoring the glory of the Roman Empire. While Aryan biology has been left behind, the present European Union is increasingly taking technocratic and bureaucratic control over all of Europe. Nationalism has been replaced with supra-nationalism. Pan-Germanism has been replaced with Pan-Europeanism. Yet the European Union continues to emphasize the idea of sustainable development as a socialistic compromise between modern industry and the environmental movement—a one-sided compromise which heavily favors environmental concerns over capitalistic profits.

Though Nazi Germany was defeated along with its racist environmentalism, a more universal or generalized fascistic tyranny, together with a more generalized environmental totalitarianism, seems to be on the rise in both Europe and America today. Is it possible a future environmental totalitarianism could indeed help usher in a time of social regression and backwardness that may restore the kings and kingdoms of Europe as predicted by Daniel the prophet and St. John the apostle? Is it possible this totalitarian environmentalism will become the new religion of the future in direct opposition to the Judeo-Christian worldview? Is it possible the prostitute of Revelation 17 who rides these beastly kingdoms of the future "drunk with the blood of the saints, and with the blood of the witnesses of Jesus" (Rev. 17:6), represents a future Roman-Babylonian nature-worship system dressed up in religious and environmental propaganda? Could it

---

[1717] Ibid.
[1718] See Daniel 7; Revelation 12-18

be the woman riding the beast is Mother Nature herself merging with the idolatry of Eastern mysticism that somehow finds a way to pacify or overcome Islam in the Middle East? The European Parliament in Strasbourg, France, even showcases a statue of a woman riding a beastly bull just outside its entrance. Modern Western man's infatuation with environmentalism, technocratic bureaucracy and Eastern religions, which largely began in Germany in the 1800s, may indeed culminate into a future Babylonian nature-worship system placed under the authority of the Western Roman Antichrist. Indeed, Hitler proclaimed in October of 1941, "The great migrations set out from the East. With us begins the ebb, from West to East. That's in accordance with the laws of Nature!"[1719]

When one reads about all of the great environmental catastrophes that comprise most of the book of Revelation (Rev. 6-19), could it be the whole point is that the very natural world that the greens often wish and demand to worship and save will become the same environment that is violently convulsed and traumatically destroyed by the Lord of heaven?[1720] Far from finding harmony in nature, people will suffer from its increasing terrifying imbalances, "Yet once more I will shake not only the earth, but also the heaven" (Heb. 12:26b). During the great tribulation, could it also be that the God of Scripture will put a final stop to the myth of gradual evolutionary change? The massive destructive upheavals on the Earth will push the *survival of the fittest* paradigm to its most extreme limits. In fact, St. John even suggests that present-day environmentalists will save enough wild animals that a sizeable count of human beings will be devoured by them during the apocalypse: "I looked and behold, an ashen horse; and he who sat on it had the name Death; and Hades was following with him. Authority was given to them over a fourth of the earth, to kill with sword and with famine and with pestilence and by the wild beasts of the earth" (Rev. 6:8).

Is it a mere coincidence the "ashen horse" in Revelation 6:8 is better translated from the original Greek as a "green horse"? The first English translator of the Bible, William Tyndale (1494-1536), translated it as a "green horse." The Greek adjective *chloros* is used in Revelation 6:8 to describe the color of the fourth horseman of the apocalypse, from which is derived the modern English word chlorophyll. Though *chloros* also means "pale green" or even "pale" in other Greek usages outside the Bible, it is the

[1719] *Hitler's Table Talk*, Oct. 10, 1941, p. 41.
[1720] See Charlie Clough, "Interpreting Texts on End-Time Geophysical Catastrophes," Dec. 10, 2008.

still the primary Greek word for the color green. In Mark 6:39, it is used to describe the "green grass" that Jesus had his disciples sit down on before He fed the 5,000. Revelation 8:7 likewise speaks of "green grass." In Revelation 9:4 the adjective is used to stand for every "green thing." The Greek Old Testament also often translates *chloros* to mean green. With such Scriptural testimony, especially in the book of Revelation itself, the fourth horseman of the apocalypse should be understood as a "green horse."

Does this mean the fourth horseman of the apocalypse is necessarily connected to environmentalism? No, not necessarily, but the possibility cannot be excluded either, especially when one considers how the modern culture of death has completely permeated the environmental movement.[1721] *Death* and *Hades* follow right behind the "green horse" in Revelation 6:8. Furthermore, the modern West has increasingly placed natural resource management into the hands of environmentalists who have in turn progressively rationed its use so that war, famine and pestilence can easily erupt anywhere on the globe because of so many restrictions attached to the very use of natural resources. Such restrictions, coupled with massive preservation efforts to save animals, will increasingly reap predatory consequences if left unchecked. St. John goes so far to predict that, in the apocalypse, a sizable portion of humanity will not even be able to protect themselves from "the wild beasts of the earth." As the green movement continues to weaken modern infrastructure, especially with regard to energy use, coupled with the bringing back of wild animals, particularly predators, the apocalyptic day may indeed come when men will no longer be able to guard themselves from the destructive dangers of nature—with no small thanks to environmental totalitarian policies that actually forbid them to do so.

Romans Teaches that Nature Judges Mankind Rather than Saves

The book of Revelation presents to the reader an apocalyptic natural world coming apart at the seams as God's ultimate physical judgment on a degenerate human race under a revived Roman Empire of tyranny, mysticism and nature worship. The early chapters of St. Paul's letter to the Romans, on the other hand, speak of God's judgment against nature worshipers that works itself out in everyday life. While Revelation emphasizes

---

[1721] See Stephen Pidgeon's *Behold! A Pale Green Horse!* San Bernardino, California, 2009.

the apocalypse, Romans emphasizes history. Yet both New Testament books have much to say about how God uses nature to judge mankind.

Written upon Nero's accession to the throne, Romans 1-5 describes the relationship between God, nature, nature worship, Jews, Gentiles and salvation. Romans is perhaps the greatest letter ever written describing the salvation history program for both Jews and Gentiles, and God's revelation of Himself in nature plays a critical role in that entire process. In fact, Paul depicts the natural world itself as a revelatory instrument of God's judgment against sin. Contrary to the Nazi contention that one must follow the social Darwinian laws of nature in order to be saved, Paul clearly asserts the opposite. Martin Bormann once bellowed, "We National Socialists demand of ourselves that we live as naturally as possible, that is to say, in accord with the laws of life. The more precisely we understand and observe the laws of Nature and of life and the more we keep them, the more we correspond to the will of this omnipotent force."[1722] In great contrast to this view, Paul presents nature as a revelation from God that works as an instrument of judgment against the Gentiles just as certain as the judgment of the Old Testament law against the Jewish people (Rom. 1:18-2:29). In other words, following the laws of nature is not an avenue of salvation or even renewal. On the contrary, nature condemns those under its revelatory authority just like the Mosaic Law judges those who do not keep it. Far from being something that must be harmonized with, or even must be saved or preserved, nature is used as an instrument of man's condemnation. Man has sinned against his Creator, and creation itself stands as an accusatory witness against him.

Paul strongly asserts in Romans 1-3 that neither nature, nor the Old Covenant law, can save. Rather, both of them condemn mankind instead.[1723] In fact, by Romans 3, the Apostle Paul leaves both groups dead in sin, condemned by both nature and the Old Testament law in the presence of an absolutely holy God. Generally speaking, Gentiles live according to nature, and the Jews trust in their ability to live by the dictates of the Mosaic law. However, because of the insidious and pervasive presence of sin, to trust in either nature or law as the basis for salvation is an illusory pursuit. As such, after dealing with both Gentile and Jewish sins committed under nature's revelation and the Mosaic law, respectively, Paul simply asks the

---

[1722] Sax, p. 106.

[1723] This discussion about nature, law and salvation from Romans 1-3 is not intended to be an exhaustive treatment of this rich, nuanced subject.

rhetorical question, "What then? Are we (Jews) better than they (Gentiles)? Not at all; for we have already charged that both Jews and Greeks are all under sin; as it is written, 'There is none righteous, not even one, there is none who understands, there is none who seeks after God'" (Rom. 3:9-11). Just as the Jews acted sinfully under the auspices of the Mosaic law, so the Gentiles acted inconsistently with what nature had taught them. Paul thus takes both groups to task with regard to their sinful practices. What is more, the problem is not with nature or with the ten commandments, but with people and their sin. Both nature and the Old Testament law reveal the glory of God in great contrast to man's sinfulness.

The Apostle Paul demonstrates that God does not indiscriminately or capriciously judge people. Not only is God very patient and gracious in spite of man's rebellion (Rom. 2:4-5), but He also uses an objective revelatory standard to judge them. This objective standard is typically God's written Word, especially as it reveals His will through the law of Moses. However, Paul also teaches that nature itself is an objective standard by which God judges men. Nature or creation is God's "handiwork" (Ps. 19:1). His glory is revealed through what He has made. God therefore judges men by how they respond to Him based on their experiences with nature. In fact, what Paul points out is that, generally speaking, God uses the law of Moses to judge the Jews, but he uses nature to judge the Gentiles. Furthermore, these two truths were not unique to the Apostle Paul. It was a precedent anticipated in the Old Testament. In addition to the Mosaic law, nature is sometimes appealed to as a witness against the Jewish people as well. For example, when Joshua was commissioned by Moses to be the new leader of Israel, both the Mosaic law and nature were invoked as a double witness against the Hebrews (Deut. 31:24-29). If they failed to live according to the law of Moses, nature would stand as a witness against them and accuse them accordingly. In terms of judgment, nature is therefore also a mirror of God's Person. In fact, nature is a prosecutor of sin just as sure as the law of Moses.

When Paul wrote Romans 1, he was certainly echoing Psalm 19 written by the shepherd boy David who spent many lonely days and nights out-doors taking care of the sheep, "The heavens are telling of the glory of God; and their expanse is declaring the works of His hands. Day to day pours forth speech, and night to night reveals knowledge" (Ps. 19:1-2). Hence Paul's view on nature as a revelation of God is certainly informed by the

Old Testament. In fact, Psalm 19 boldly declares the glory of God is being revealed daily—24 hours a day, seven days a week—without interruption. While Psalm 19 does teach that natural revelation is silent in contrast to God's written Word, it still clearly communicates the glory of God. David also stresses that nature reveals the glory of God universally. No one has been left out, or is exempted from its all-encompassing surveillance: "There is no speech, nor are their words; their voice is not heard. Their line has gone out through all the earth, and their utterance to the end of the world" (Ps. 19:3-4). As such, even though nature is a silent revelation, everyone experiences something of the glory of God through their personal experiences with the natural world.

Unfortunately, this silent revelation has been used by the Gentiles to advocate speculative doctrines. Rather than give glory to God, they glorify the creation instead. Paul says the Gentiles have purposefully *suppressed* the glory of God revealed in nature by idolizing nature. The Gentiles thus ignore the clear truths of nature so they can promote idolatrous doctrines which attribute Divine powers to idols, or to nature itself: "For even though they knew God, they did not honor him as God or give thanks, but they became futile in their speculations, and their foolish heart was darkened. Professing to be wise, they became fools, and exchanged the glory of the incorruptible God for an image in the form of corruptible man and of birds and four-footed animals and crawling creatures" (Rom. 1:21-23). Contrary to popular opinion, nature teaches the glory of its Creator and demands the exclusive worship of that Creator. If man fails to give glory to God, the natural world will rise up as a witness against him to condemn him for his sin. Paul thus posits that nature is a clear revelation of the glory of God. Nature reflects its Creator, and while its spectacular beauties are awe-inspiring, and clearly show the artistic nature of God, nature will still hold man accountable to His glorious Maker.

In short, the Gentiles took something good from God, i.e., nature, and perverted it into nature worship. Paul then points out such idolatry resulted in widespread degenerate behavior among the heathen (Rom. 1:24). He then concludes, "They exchanged the truth of God for a lie, and worshiped and served the creature rather than the Creator, who is blessed forever. Amen" (Rom. 1:25). The Gentiles committed the sin of attributing life-creating powers to nature itself, a contradictory thought which runs contrary to what nature reveals about itself. The Gentiles thus acted completely inconsistent with what nature taught them. They sinned against God by sinning against what nature was teaching them about God.

How does God judge the heathen who have never heard of the Bible? This is not nearly the problem that so many philosophers, atheists and agnostics have made it out to be. St. Paul authoritatively teaches that God uses the reality of nature to judge the heathen Gentiles, "For the wrath of God is revealed from heaven against all ungodliness and unrighteousness of men who suppress the truth in unrighteousness, because that which is known about God is evident within them; for God made it evident to them. For since the creation of the world His invisible attributes, His eternal power and divine nature, have been clearly seen, being understood through that what has been made, so that they are without excuse" (Rom.1:18-20). In other words, Paul says that God does not need a Bible to judge the Gentiles. Nature itself is sufficient to hold the Gentiles accountable to the only true God, their Creator.

As such, outside of the crucified and resurrected body of the Lord Jesus Christ, there is nothing in nature, nor in the Old Testament law itself, that is able to save either the Jews or the Gentiles from their sins. Neither nature, nor natural law, certainly not social Darwinian laws, nor even the much more explicit Mosaic law itself, can save mankind from *the wrath of God*. Why? Because nature or law was never designed by God to be the vehicle of salvation. Both nature and the Mosaic law are objective standards which God uses to condemn sinners, not save them. The Mosaic law demands perfection, which all human beings "fall short of" (Rom. 3:10-23). Nature is no less lenient.

In the book of Romans, since both nature and law work together to condemn rather than save, salvation must therefore come from another source. In Romans 3:19-20, Paul leaves the Jews and Gentiles condemned by the Mosaic law and by nature after a long discussion of the subject beginning in 1:18. Nature judges the Gentiles (Rom. 1:18-2:16) and the Mosaic law judges the Jews (Rom. 2:17-29). Furthermore, both nature and the Old Testament law were designed by God to communicate to all men that they need a Savior,[1724] though neither one of them—as good, important and critical as they may be—provided that salvation. Neither natural revelation or the Mosaic revelation can reverse the indelible effects of the fall of mankind brought upon the world through Adam's sin, "Therefore, just as through one man

---

[1724] See Acts 17:17-31; Romans 3:19-26; Galatians 3:24.

sin entered into the world, and death through sin, and so death spread to all men, because all sinned" (Rom. 5:12).

Because both parties have sinned and have fallen short with respect to the revelation which God gave to them, salvation by works is simply out of the question. A sinner cannot save himself by his own works or by his own religion. This is the heart of the argument in Paul's letter to the Romans. This sets the stage for the necessity of faith in the cross of Christ as the basis for salvation where Paul writes, "But now apart from the Law *the* righteousness of God has been manifested, being witnessed by the Law and the Prophets, even *the* righteousness of God through faith in Jesus Christ for all those who believe; for there is no distinction; for all have sinned and fall short of the glory of God, being justified as a gift by His grace through the redemption which is in Christ Jesus; whom God displayed publicly as a propitiation in His blood through faith" (Rom. 3:21-25a).

In Romans 3:21-31, Paul eliminates the possibility of salvation by works obtained either through natural revelation, natural laws or even the Mosaic law. If salvation is to occur, it must be through the grace of God as exhibited in the cross of Christ. Furthermore, since all forms of religious works, whether heathen or Jewish, have been removed from the salvation equation, faith in the crucified Son of God is the only avenue left open to man. In other words, if men could save themselves by their own works under nature or law, then why did God send His Son to die on the cross? Paul thus strongly intimates that no sinner, heathen or otherwise, will ever be allowed to glory in his own works before an uncompromising holy God, "Where then is boasting? It is excluded. By what kind of law? Of works? No, but by a law of faith" (Rom. 3:27). This also means that faith is a critical spiritual principle, not an irrational method of mysticism that many atheists and agnostic have falsely made it out to be.

In Romans 3:21-26, Paul explains that the only place where God's righteousness or holiness has been propitiated or satisfied is on the cross of Christ—the only human sacrifice acceptable to God with regard to salvation. Man cannot sacrifice himself for salvation because he is a sinner. The cross itself starkly means that man, whether heathen or Jewish, cannot save himself by his own works in any way, shape or form whatsoever. Salvation exclusively belongs to the work of Jesus Christ alone. Jesus Christ was the one who was crucified for their sins.

The word *propitiation* in Romans 3:25 means God's righteousness was satisfied on the cross so that justice has been met with regard to His holiness. Jesus died in the sinner's place as a human substitute sacrifice for the sins of the entire world, something only the Son of God can do since He was without sin. He endured the judgment of God in man's place that man deserved because of his sin. Therefore, if a sinner believes that Jesus died for his sins, God will forgive that man and offer eternal life to him as a free gift. God's justice has been satisfied so that God is free to treat man in grace without compromising His own holy character. Therefore, in order to obtain salvation man must be in relationship with Christ, and the only way that relationship can be initiated is through personal faith in the cross of Jesus Christ.

The Apostle Paul is thus also in complete agreement with the gospel of John where Jesus bluntly told His disciples right before He died, "I am the way, and the truth, and the life; no one comes to the Father but through Me" (John 14:6). As Paul intimates in Romans 3, Jesus Christ has paid the awful penalty for sin, which is death. This was a substitute sacrifice for sin, "For what the Law could not do, weak as it was through the flesh, God *did*: sending His own Son in the likeness of sinful flesh and *as an offering for sin*, He condemned sin in the flesh" (Rom. 8:3). Blood redemption via substitute sacrifice, as prefigured by Old Testament ritual animal sacrifices, is the payment price for sin. This also makes it utterly impossible for any man to pay for his own sins, since this would demand his own death. "For unless you believe that I am *He*, you will die in your sins" (John 8:24). This was the whole point of animal sacrifice. A substitute must be provided in man's place. Thus, if one believes that Jesus Christ died on the cross for his sins, God will forgive him and offer eternal life to him free of charge. This is the good news of the gospel—the greatest news of all time.

Hence in Romans 4, Paul then goes on to explain the great historical significance of Abraham. According to the text of Genesis, the first book of the Mosaic law, Abraham was essentially a saved Gentile before he became a circumcised Jew (Rom. 4:1-17). "For what does the Scripture say? 'Abraham believed God, and it was credited to him as righteousness.' Now to the one who works, his wage is not credited as a favor, but as what is due. But to the one who does not work, but believes in Him who justifies the ungodly, his faith is credited as righteousness" (Rom. 4:3-5). By quoting Genesis 15, Paul teaches that Abraham was justified by grace through faith before he was ritually circumcised as a Jew in Genesis 17. Thus, historically, salvation by faith without works preceded Jewish ritual circumcision. This means that with regard to the means of salvation, Abraham perfectly represents both parties. Paul thus concludes that "Abraham ... is the father of us all" (Rom. 4:16).

Adolf Hitler's suspicion that Christianity has made the Jewish faith universal is much closer to the truth than most Jews and Christians themselves are willing to admit. The great difference is the Old Testament looks forward to the coming of Messiah, whereas the New Testament looks back upon the historic coming of Christ in anticipation of his second coming. Hence, salvation. i.e., justification by faith without works as historically illustrated by Abraham, is something which both the Old and New Testaments teach. Regardless of the particular historical time frame in which one might live, salvation is always by grace through faith.

Moreover, rather than use theological conjecture as the basis for his doctrine of salvation, Paul uses the history of Abraham to make his sharp point. Biblical history and faith go together like glue. Faith in Christ is a faith based on the objective facts of history, and with regard to the crucifixion, one is talking about the most historically attested fact of the ancient world. This is also true with regard to the resurrection. Indeed, Paul even told his Greek audience in Corinth that there were "more than five hundred" historical eyewitnesses to the resurrection of Christ (1 Cor. 15:1-8). Paul then presents a very interesting argument to them: "But someone will say, 'How are the dead raised? And with what kind of body do they come?' You fool! That which you sow does not come to life unless it dies; and that which you sow, you do not sow the body which is to be, but a bare grain, perhaps of wheat or of something else" (1 Cor. 15:35-37). In other words, nature itself teaches the resurrection of the dead. The farmer deals with this year in and year out every time he plants and harvests his garden.

Both natural revelation and the Bible are solid testimonies of God's existence and His righteousness rooted in the objective realties of nature and Biblical history. The great crisis in life, however, is that people willfully, routinely and unwittingly place their faith in the wrong object. The object of their trust is typically their own religious works based on either nature or law or both. Worse, this is an almost universal disease corrupting both Jews and Gentiles in their gigantic quest to obtain their own salvation, utopian dreams or mystical experiences, all in a fallen world that is far too broken to humanly fix. Neither Marxism nor socialism, nor social Darwinism, nor eugenics, nor environmentalism will be able to provide salvation to mankind this side of the grave. To this fallen sinful world full of vanity, the wise preacher of Ecclesiastes concludes, "Behold, I have found only this, that God made men upright, but they have sought out many devices" (Eccl. 7:29).

*Why are the nations in an uproar, and the peoples devising a vain thing?
The kings of the earth take their stand, and the rulers take counsel together
against the LORD and against His Anointed:"Let us tear their fetters apart,
and cast away their cords from us!" He who sits in the heavens laughs, The
Lord scoffs at them. Then He will speak to them in His anger and terrify them
in His fury: "But as for Me, I have installed My King upon Zion, My holy
mountain." "I will surely tell of the decree of the LORD: He said to Me, 'Thou
art My Son, Today I have begotten Thee. 'Ask of Me, and I will surely give the
nations as Thine inheritance, and the very ends of the earth as Thy possession.
'Thou shalt break them with a rod of iron, Thou shalt shatter them like earth-
enware.' "Now therefore, O kings, show discernment; Take warning, O judges
of the earth. Worship the LORD with reverence, and rejoice with trembling.
Do homage to the Son, lest He become angry, and you perish in the way, For
His wrath may soon be kindled. How blessed are all who take refuge in Him!*

Psalm 2

APPENDIX:

NATURE'S ECONOMY IN THE OLD TESTAMENT

- God is Creator/owner of nature (Gen. 1; Ps. 50)
- Polytheism and idolatry and nature worship were forbidden (Ex. 20:1-5; Deut. 4:15-19; Hos. 4:12-13; Jer. 2:20; Ezek. 6:13)
- Nature was made for man to rule, guard and cultivate (Gen. 1:26-28; 2:15; 9:3; Ps. 8)
- The world is designed to be filled with population (Gen. 1:26-28; 9:1)
- Animals are to be cared for (Gen. 6; Ex. 23:19; Prov. 27:23)
- Freedom under the rule of law is assumed (Exodus; Deuteronomy)
- The natural world is to be farmed and mined for human development (Deut. 8:1-20)
- Agricultural and financial blessing based on disciplined obedience to God (Deut. 28; Proverbs)
- Private property is to be protected by redemption rights (Lev. 25:23-34; Deut. 23:24-25; Prov. 23:10-11)
- Mosaic economy extolled the virtues of small business and international trade (Prov. 31:10-31)
- Making wealth provides opportunity for generosity (Prov. 31:20)
- Diversify portfolio for your protection (Eccl. 11:2)
- Credit economy and debt were frowned upon—but not illegal (Lev. 25:1-22; 35-38; Deut. 23:19-23)
- Charging interest was illegal for Hebrews—but not for aliens (Ex. 22:25; Deut. 23:19-20)
- Aliens living in the promised land are to be treated well (Lev. 19:34)

- Hebrews were forbidden to develop idolatrous practices of the multicultural world around them inside the promised land (Deut. 12:1-4; 2 Kings 17:7-18)
- Oppression was forbidden (Deut. 24:14)
- Biblical wisdom is better than riches (Prov. 20:15; 23:4-5)
- Being generous to the poor was not government welfare—but was expected of private individuals—poor people had to work (Lev. 19:10; 23:22; Isa. 58:7-12)
- Government welfare was frowned upon (Num. 11:1-6)
- Election of kings invites the dangers of tyranny and big government leads to oppression (1 Sam. 8:1-22)
- Kings are subject to the Mosaic law just as any other citizen (Deut. 17:14-20)
- Division of powers between king, priest and prophet was assumed (2 Sam. 12:1-15; 2 Chron. 26:16-23)
- Do not be partial to the poor simply because they are poor (Ex. 23:3)
- Poverty is an unfortunate fact of life (Deut. 15:1-11)
- Thorns and thistles result from farming as pollution is also a natural by-product of making wealth (Gen. 3:17-19; Prov. 14:4)

Then the Lord said, "You had compassion on the plant for which you did not work and which you did not cause to grow, which came up overnight and perished overnight. Should I not have compassion on Nineveh, the great city in which there are more than 120,000 persons who do not know the difference between their right and left hand, as well as many animals?"

Jonah 4:10-11

BIBLIOGRAPHY

"700 German Pastors Arrested: Reading of Anti-Pagan Manifesto," *The New York Times*, March 18, 1935.

Albright, W.F., "The War in Europe and the Future of Biblical Studies," in *The Study of the Bible Today and Tomorrow*. Chicago: The University of Chicago Press, 1947.

Ambrose, Jay, "Human Sacrifices to Climate god," *Orange County Register*, March 29, 2009.

"Animal Liberation Against Israeli Occupation," *Resistance Ecology*, Aug. 9, 2014.

"Animal Welfare Institute Condemns Illegal Whale Hunt By Makah Tribal Members," *Animal Welfare Institute*, Sept. 10, 2007.

"Another Member of Germany's Green Party Found to Have Been a Member of the Nazi Party," *JTA*, Bonn, Germany, April 28, 1983.

Arad, Yitzhak. *Belzec, Sobibor, Treblinka: The Operation Reinhard Death Camps*. Bloomington and Indianapolis: Indiana University Press, 1987 (1999).

Archibald, David, "The Nazi Origins of Renewable Energy and Global Warming," *American Thinker*, July 20, 2017.

Arendt, Hannah. *Eichmann and the Holocaust*. London: Penguin Books, 2005 (1963).

Auschwitz A to Z: An Illustrated History of the Camp. Auschwitz-Birkenau State Museum, 2013.

Baker's Encyclopedia of Christian Apologetics, edited by Norman Geisler. Grand Rapids, Michigan: Baker Book House, 1999.

Baker, Peter and Broder, John, "Obama Pledges Public Works on a Vast Scale," *The New York Times*, Dec. 7, 2008.

Ball, Timothy, "The Anti-Human Agenda: Anti-Humanity and Anti-Society Environmentalists," *Canada Free Press*, May 19, 2008.

Barrett, William. *Death of the Soul: From Descartes to the Computer*. Garden City, New York: Anchor Press/Doubleday, 1987.

Barth, Karl. *Church Dogmatics*, 14 volumes. Edinburgh: T & T Clark, 1977.

Barth, Karl. "God, Grace, and the Gospel: Three Essays by Karl Barth," translated by James McNab. *Scottish Journal of Theology Occasional Papers*, no. 8. Edinburgh: Oliver and Boyd, 1959.

Barth, Karl. *The Theology of Schleiermacher*, translated by Geoffrey Bromiley. Grand Rapids, Michigan: William B. Eerdmans Publishing, 1982 (1978).

Beisner, E. Calvin. *Where the Garden Meets the Wilderness: Evangelical Entry into the Environmental Debate*. Grand Rapids, Michigan: William B. Eerdmans Publishing Co., 1997.

Bellaart, Darrell, "Man Shot by B.C. Police Described as 'Kind, Caring' neo-Nazi," *Canwest News Service* (Internet website), Oct. 27, 2009.

Black, Edwin. *IBM and the Holocaust: The Strategic Alliance Between Nazi Germany and America's Most Powerful Corporation*. Washington D.C.: Diaolog Press, 2011, 2001.

Black, Edwin, "IBM at Auschwitz, New Documents," *Reader Supported News*, Feb. 28, 2012.

Black, Edwin. *Nazi Nexus: America's Corporate Connections to Hitler's Holocaust*. Washington D.C.: Diaolog Press, 2009.

Blackbourn, David. *The Conquest of Nature: Water, Landscape, and the Making of Modern Germany*. New York/London: W.W. Norton and Company, 2006.

Boswell, Randy, "Hitler's Tree: An Ottawa Professor Searches for Canada's vanished Olympic Oak," *Canada.com* (Internet website), Aug. 18, 2008.

Boyes, Roger, "Polish Village Mayor is Determined Hitler Birthday Oak Will Not Last 1,000 Years," *Times Online*, July 8, 2009.

Brackman, Harold, "About Avatars, Caveat Emptors," *Jerusalem Post*, Dec. 30, 2009.

Bramwell, Anna. *Blood and Soil. R. Walther Darre and Hitler's Green Party*. Great Britain: The Kensal Press, 1985.

Bramwell, Anna. *Ecology in the 20th Century: A History*. Yale University Press, 1989.

Bramwell, Anna. *The Fading of the Greens*. Yale University Press, 1994.

Brown, Courtney, "The Nazi Vote: A National Ecological Study." *The American Political Science Review*, Vol. 76, No. 2 (June 1982), pp. 285-302.

Bundy, Emory, "The Carbon Cost of Building and Operating Light Rail," *Crosscut. com*, July 25, 2007.

Bytwerk, Randall. *Landmark Speeches of National Socialism*. College Station: Texas A & M University Press, 2008.

Chaney, Sandra. *The Nature of the Miracle Years: Conservation in West Germany 1945-1975*. New York & Oxford: Berghahn Books, 2008.

"Chilling Picture Emerges of Nazi leader Himmler Taken Just Moments After He Swallowed Cyanide Pill," *Mail Online*, Feb. 17, 2011.

Clough, Charles, "Interpreting Texts on End-Time Geophysical Catastrophes," Dec. 10, 2008.

Cornwall, Warren and Lindblom, Mike, "Some Light Rail Tunnel Debris Polluted," *Seattle Times*, Sept. 9, 2007.

Crichton, Michael, "Environmentalism as a Religion," a speech given to the *Commonwealth Club* on Sept.15, 2003, in San Francisco, Calif.

Cronon, William. *Changes in the Land: Indians, Colonists, and the Ecology of New England*. New York: Hill and Wang, (1983).

Davey, Monica, "Behind the Rampage, Loner with a Taste for Nazism," *New York Times*, March 23, 2005.

Day, Matthew, "Rudolf Hess Flight to Britain Approved by Hitler," *The UK Telegraph*, May 31, 2011.

Degregori, Thomas, "Environmentalism, Animal Rights Activism, and Eco-Nazism," April 1, 2001.

Delingpole, James, "Why do I call them Eco-Nazis? Because they are Eco Nazis." *UK Telegraph*, Feb. 16, 2011.

Dietrich, Otto. *The Hitler I Knew: Memoirs of the Third Reich's Press Chief*. New York: Skyhorse Publishing, 2010.

Denning, Andrew. *Skiing into Modernity: A Cultural and Environmental History*. Oakland: University of California Press, 2015.

Dominick, Raymond. *The Environmental Movement in Germany: Prophets and Pioneers, 1871-1971*. Indiana University Press, 1992.

Dorrien, Gary. *Kantian Reason and Hegelian Spirit: The Idealist Logic of Modern Theology*. Great Britain: Wiley Blackwell, 2015.

Driessen, Paul. *Eco-Imperialism: Green Power Black Death*. Bellevue, Washington: Merril Press, 2003-04.

Dr. Todt: Mission and Achievement, Nazi documentary film, 1943.

"Environment: The Club of Rome: Act Two," *Time*, Oct. 21, 1974.

Evangelical Dictionary of Theology, edited by Walter Elwell. Grand Rapids, Michigan: Baker Book House, 1984.

Faye, Emmanuel, "Being, History, Technology, and Extermination in Heidegger."

Faye, Emmanuel. *Heidegger: The Introduction of Nazism into Philosophy in Light of the Unpublished Seminars of 1933-35*. New Haven & London: Yale University Press, 2009.

"Feeling Blue Over Going Green?" *Northwest Cable News*, Feb. 21, 2008.

Feig, Konnilyn G. *Hitler's Death Camps: The Sanity of Madness*. New York & London: Holmes & Meier Publishers, 1981.

Feinberg, Charles. *The Minor Prophets*. Chicago: Moody Press, 1948.

Ferry, Luc. *The New Ecological Order*. University of Chicago Press, 1995 (1992).

Fisher, Maria Sudekum, "Road Cleaned by Neo-Nazis May be Named for Rabbi," *The Associated Press*, June 21, 2009.

Flader, Susan, "Leopold on Wilderness—Aldo Leopold on Germany's Landscape," *American Forests*, May-June, 1991.

Frantzman, Zeth, "Hitler's Geographer: Walter Christaller and Nazi Academics," *The Jerusalem Post*, Aug. 27, 2010.

Frazer, James George. *The Golden Bough: A Study in Magic and Religion*. Oxford University Press, 2009 (1994).

Gasman, Daniel, "From Haeckel to Hitler: The Anatomy of a Controversy," (Internet publication).

Gasman, Daniel. *Haekcel's Monism and the Birth of Fascist Ideology*. New York: Peter Lang Publishing, 2008 (1998).

Gasman, Daniel. *The Scientific Origins of National Socialism*. New York: Transaction Publishers, 2004 (1971).

Garrett, Duane. *Hosea, Joel*. The New American Commentary, Vol. 19A. United States: Broadman and Holman Publishers, 1997.

Geisler, Norman. *Baker Encyclopedia of Christian Apologetics*. Grand Rapids, Michigan: Baker Books, 1999.

"Green Party Member, An Ex-Nazi, to Resign," *The New York Times*, Bonn, Germany, March 14, 1983.

Gerdmar, Anders. *Roots of Theological Anti-Semitism: German Biblical Interpretation and the Jews, from Herder and Semler to Kittel and Bultmann*. Leiden and Boston: Brill, 2010.

Goldberg, Jonah. *Liberal Fascism: The Secret History of the American Left from Mussolini to the Politics of Meaning*. New York: Doubleday, 2007.

Goldhagen, Daniel Jonah. *Hitler's Willing Executioners: Ordinary Germans and the Holocaust*. New York: Vintage Press, 1996.

Goodrick-Clarke, Nicholas. *Hitler's Priestess: Savitri Devi, the Hindu-Aryan Myth, and Neo Nazism*. New York: New York University Press, 1998.

Goodrick-Clarke. *The Occult Roots of Nazism: Secret Aryan Cults and Their Influences on Nazi Ideology, 1890-1935*. New York: New York University Press, 1985, 1992.

"Green Power Collides with Endangered Species Act," *Oregon Natural Resources Report*, Aug. 9, 2009.

Gert Gröning, Joachim Wolschke-Bulmahn, "Stiftung Naturschutzgeschichte, Naturschutz und Demokratie!?: Dokumentation der Beiträge zur Veranstaltung der Stiftung Naturschutzgeschichte und des Zentrums für Gartenkunst und Landschaftsarchitektur (CGL)" der Leibniz Universität Hannover in Kooperation mit dem Institut für Geschichte und Theorie der Gestaltung (GTG) der Universität der Künste Berlin, Martin Meidenbauer Verlag, 2006.

Gruner, Rolf. *Philosophies of History: A Critical Essay*. Great Britain: Blackmore Press, 1985.

Haeckel, Ernst. *The Riddle of the Universe*. Buffalo, New York: Prometheus Books, 1992.

Hamilton, Edith. *Mythology: Timeless Tales of Gods and Heroes*. New York: A Mentor Book, 1969 (1940).

Hamilton, Edith. *The Roman Way*. New York and London: W.W. Norton & Co., 1932.

Hanson, Victor Davis, "The New War Against Reason," *National Review Online*, Nov. 25, 2009.

Hari, Johann, "Jack London's Dark Side," *Slate*, Aug. 15, 2010.

Harris, Horton. *The Tubingen School: A Historical and Theological Investigation of the School of F.C. Baur*. Grand Rapids, Michigan: Baker Book House, 1990 (1975).

Hayward, William. *How the West Was Lost: The Theft and Usurpation of State's Property Rights*. Springville, Utah: Bonneville Books, 2000.

Herf, Jeffrey. *Reactionary Modernism: Technology, Culture, and Politics in the Weimar and the Third Reich*. Cambridge University Press, 1984.

Hicks, Stephen. *Explaining Postmodernism: Skepticism and Socialism from Rousseau to Foucault*. Loves Park, Illinois: Ockham's Razor Publishing, 2011.

Hicks, Stephen. *Nietzsche and the Nazis: A Personal View*. Loves Park, Illinois: Ockham's Razor Publishers, 2010, (2006).

Hilberg, Raul. *The Destruction of the European Jews*, 3 volumes. New York and London: Holmes & Meier, 1985.

Hinchman, Lewis. *Hegel's Critique of the Enlightenment*. Tampa: University of Florida Press, 1984.

Hirsch, David. *The Deconstruction of Literature: Criticism After Auschwitz*. Hannover and London: Brown University Press, 1991.

Hitler, Adolf. *Mein Kampf*, translated by Ralph Manheim. Boston & New York: Mariner Books, 1999.

Hitler, Adolf. *Zweites Buch*. Unpublished, 1928.

Hitler's Table Talk: 1941-44, preface and essay by H.R. Trevor Roper, translated by Norman Cameron and R.H. Stevens. New York: Enigma Books, 2000 (1953).

Hoess, Rudolf. *Commandant of Auschwitz*. Great Britain: Weidenfeld & Nicholson, 1959 (1951).

Hohne, Heinz. *The Order of the Death's Head: The Story of Hitler's SS*. London: Penguin Books, 1969.

How Green Were the Nazis?: Nature, Environment, and Nation in the Third Reich, edited by Franz-Josef Bruggenmeier, Mark Cioc, and Thomas Zeller. Athens: Ohio University Press, 2005.

Hughes, Siobahn and Power, Stephen, "Coal Industry Digs Itself out of a Hole in the Capitol: Support from EPA, Energy Nominees Signals Obama Team Headed Toward Center of Matter on Fossil Fuels and Carbon Emissions," *The Wall Street Journal*, Jan. 15, 2009.

Irving, David. *Goering: A Biography*. New York: Avon Books, 1989.

Jacobsen, Annie. *Operation Paperclip: The Secret Intelligence Program that Brought Nazi Scientists to America*. New York: Little, Brown and Company, 2014.

Jeffreys, Diarmuid. *Hell's Cartel: IG Farben and the Making of Hitler's War Machine*. New York: Metropolitan Books, 2008.

Kaplan, Robert E. *The Soros Connection*. Printed in Israel, 2011.

Kay, William Walter, *Environmentalism is Fascism* Internet website.

Keil, C.F. and Delitzsch, Franz. *Commentary on the Old Testament*, 10 volumes. Peabody, Massachusetts: Hendrickson Publishers, 1989.

Kershaw, Ian. *Hitler 1889–1936: Hubris*. New York: W. W. Norton & Company, 1999.

Kirkley-Best, Elizabeth. *Blood and Soil: Blut & Boden*, 2003.

"Klu Klux Klan Mastermind Now a Bird Watcher in Austria," *Austrian Times*, April 15, 2009.

Knöfel, Ulrike, "Beuys Biography: Book Accuses Artist of Close Ties to Nazis," *Spiegel Online International*, May 17, 2013.

Klaus, Vaclav. *Blue Planet in Green Shackles*. Washington DC: Competitive Enterprise Institute, 2007.

Knöfel, Ulrike, "Beuys Biography: Book Accuses Artist of Close Ties to Nazis," *Spiegel Online International*, May 17, 2013.

Kotkin, Joel, "How Elite Environmentalists Impoverish Blue Collar Americans," *Forbes*, March 16, 2009.

Kotkin, Joel. *The City: A Global History*. New York: The Modern Library, 2005.

Kresovich, George, "Dumb Growth: The Smart Development has Made Sprawl Worse, Not Better," *Washington CEO*, Nov. 2008.

Kubizek, August. *Young Hitler*. Maidstone, United Kingdom: George Mann Limited, (1954) 1973, 204 pages.

Lanzmann, Claude. *Shoah*. Documentary Film: The Criterion Collection, (1985, 2010), 2013.

Larson, Erik. *In the Garden of Beasts: Love, Terror, and an American Family in Hitler's Berlin*. New York: Broadway Paperbacks, 2011.

Leake, Jonathan and Montague, Brendan, "UK Population Must Fall to 30M, Says Porritt," *The Sunday Times*, March 22, 2009.

Lebovic, Nitzan. *The Philosophy of Life and Death: Ludwig Klages and the Rise of a Nazi Biopolitics*. New York: Palgrave Macmillan, 2013.

Lee, Robert and Wilke, Sabine, "Forest as Volk: Eiger Wald and the Religion of Nature in the Third Reich," *Journal of Social and Ecological Boundaries*. University of Washington, 2005.

Lekan, Thomas. *Imagining The Nation in Nature: Landscape Preservation and German Identity 1885-1945*. Cambridge, Massachusetts and London: Harvard University Press, 2004.

Leopold, Aldo. *A Sand County Almanac*. New York and Oxford: Oxford University Press, 1949.

Lower, Wendy. *Hitler's Furies: German Women in the Nazi Killing Fields*. Boston and New York: Houghton Mifflin Harcourt, 2013.

Lowith, Karl. *From Hegel to Nietzsche: The Revolution in 19th Century Thought*. New York: Columbia University Press, 1964.

Lowith, Karl. *Meaning in History*, Chicago: University of Chicago Press, 1949.

Lubbeck, William. *At Leningrad's Gates: The Combat Memoirs of a Soldier with Army Group North*. Philadelphia, Pennsylvania: Casemate Publishers, 2006.

Ludovici, Anthony, "Hitler and Nietzsche," *The English Review*, 64, 1937, pp. 44-52.

Ludovici, Anthony, "Hitler and the Third Reich," *The English Review*, 63, 1936.

Lutzer, Erwin. *Hitler's Cross: How the Cross Was Used to Promote the Nazi Agenda*. Chicago: Moody Publishers, 1995, 2016.

Macintyre, Ben. *Forgotten Fatherland: The True Story of Nietzsche's Sister and Her Lost Aryan Colony*. New York: Broadway Paperbacks, 1992.

Mack, Michael. *German Idealism and the Jew: The Inner Anti-Semitism of Philosophy and German-Jewish Responses*. Chicago & London: University of Chicago Press, 2003.

MacLean, French. *2,000 Quotes from Hitler's 1,000-Year Reich*. Atglen, Pennsylvania: Schiffer Military History, 2007.

Manvell, Roger and Fraenkel, Heinrich, *Hess: A Biography*. New York: Drake Publishers Inc., 1973.

Meinecke, Horst, "Hamburg's Prince of Parks," *The Rotarian*, May 1973.

Meotti, Giulio, "Ecologists Against Jews," *Frontpage Magazine*, March 1, 2012.

Mesler, Bill, "Al Gore: The Other Oil Candidate," *Corp Watch*, Aug. 29, 2000.

Metaxas, Eric. *Bohoeffer: Pastor, Martyr, Prophet, Spy*. Nashville, Tennessee: Thomas Nelson Publishers, 2010.

Macintosh, A.A. *Hosea*, The International Critical Commentary. Edinburgh: T & T Clark, 1997.

Manus, Elizabeth, "Bertelsmann's Nazi Past Gets Ho-Hummed in U.S.," *The New York Observer*, Jan. 18, 1999.

Meotti, Giulio, "Ecologists Against Jews," *Frontpage Mag*, March 1, 2012.

Milloy, Steve. *Green Hell: How Environmentalists Plan to Control Your Life and What You Can Do to Stop Them*. Washington DC: Regnery Publishing, 2009.

Mitchell, Arthur. *Hitler's Mountain: The Fuhrer, Obersalzberg and the American Occupation of Berchtesgaden*. Jefferson, North Carolina and London: McFarland and Company Inc. Publishers, 2007.

Morano, Marc, "Eco-Extremism Being Ignored in School Shooting Case," *Spirithit News CNS News.com*, March 27, 2005.

Musser, Mark, "Friedrich Nietzsche and his Proto-Nazi Eco-fascism," *The American Thinker*, Nov. 27, 2011.

Musser, Mark, "Green Lebensraum: The Nazi Roots of Sustainable Development," *The American Thinker*, January 27, 2012.

Musser, Mark, "Lindbergh, Nazism and Environmental Fascism," *The American Thinker*, Oct. 19, 2013.

Musser, Mark, "The Green Nazi Deep Ecology of Martin Heidegger," *The American Thinker*, July 10, 2011.

Musser, Mark, "The Green Nazi Tycoon Alfred Toepfer," *The American Thinker*, April 22, 2012

Myers, John Myers. *The Saga of Hugh Glass: Pirate, Pawnee and Mountain Man*. Lincoln: University of Nebraska Press, 1976.

Nehring, Holger, "Cold War, Apocalypse, and Peaceful Atoms: Interpretations of Nuclear Energy in the British and West German Anti-Nuclear Weapons Movements, 1955-1964." *Historical Social Research*, vol. 29, 2004, No. 3, pp. 150-170.

Neill, Stephen and Wright, Tom. *The Interpretation of the New Testament 1861-1986*. Oxford: Oxford University Press, 1988 (1964).

Netanyahu, Benzion. *The Origins of the Inquisition in 15th Century Spain*. New York: New York Review of Books, (1995).

Neumann, Boaz, "Green, Brown, and Bloody All Over," *Haaretz News*, March 2008.

New American Standard Bible. Anaheim: Foundation Publications, 1995 (1960).

New International Dictionary of the Christian Church, edited by J.D. Douglas. Grand Rapids, Michigan: Zondervan Publishing House, 1978 (1974).

Nietzsche, Friedrich. *Thus Spake Zarathustra: A Book for None and All*, translated by Walter Kaufmann. New York: Penguin Books, 1966 (1954).

Nietzsche, Friedrich. *Antichrist: A Criticism of Christianity*, translated by Anthony Ludovici. New York: Barnes & Noble, 2006, (1895).

Noll, Richard, *The Aryan Christ: The Secret Life of Carl Jung*. New York: Random House, 1997.

Nyiszli, Miklos. *I Was Doctor Mengele's Assistant*, translated by Witold Zbirohowski-Koscia. Auschwitz, Poland, 2010.

Olsen, Jonathan. *Nature and Nationalism: Right Wing Ecology and the Politics of Identity in Contemporary Germany*. New York: St. Martin's Press, 1999.

Owens, Jesse. *The Jesse Owens Story*. New York: G.P. Putnam Sons, 1970.

Padfield, Peter. *Hess, Hitler, and Churchill: The Real Turning Point of the Second World War – A Secret History*. London: Icon Books Limited, 2013.

Parisi, Paula. *Titanic and the Making of James Cameron*. New York: Newmarket Press (1998) 2012.

Peters, H.F. *Zarathustra's Sister: The Case of Elizabeth and Friedrich Nietzsche*. New York: Crown Publishers, 1977.

Pidgeon, Stephen. *Behold! A Pale Green Horse!* San Bernardino, California, 2009.

Pinto-Duschinsky, Michael, "The Prize Lies of a Nazi Tycoon," *Standpoint*, April 2010.

Pois, Robert. *National Socialism and the Religion of Nature*. London & Sydney: Croom Helm, 1986.

Porritt, Jonathan. *Seeing Green: The Politics of Ecology Explained*. Oxford: Basil Blackwell Ltd, 1985 (1984).

Posner, Gerald and Ware, John. *Mengele: The Complete Story*. New York: Cooper Square Press, 1986 (2000).

Proctor, Robert. *The Nazi War on Cancer*. Princeton University Press, 1999.

Proctor, Robert. *Racial Hygiene: Medicine Under the Nazis*. Harvard University Press, 1988.

Rabinowitz, Dorothy, "The Lindbergh Nobody Knew," *The Wall Street Journal*, July 24, 2009.

Redles, David. *Hitler's Millennial Reich: Apocalyptic Belief and the Search for Salvation*. New York: New York University Press, 2005 (2008).

Richards, Robert. *The Romantic Conception of Life: Science and Philosophy in the Age of Goethe*. Chicago & London: University of Chicago Press, 2002.

Riehl, Wilhelm Heinrich. *Natural History of the German People*, translated by David Diephouse. Lewiston/Queenstown/Lampeter: The Edwin Mellen Press, 1990.

Rieger, Berndt. *Creator of Nazi Death Camps: The Life of Odilo Globocnik*. London and Portland, Oregon: Vallentine Mitchell, 2007.

"Road Cleaned by Neo-Nazis May be Named for Rabbi," *The Associated Press*, June 21, 2009.

Rose, Paul Lawrence. *Wagner: Race and Revolution*. New Haven & London: Yale University Press, 1992.

Rosenberg, Alfred. *The Myth of the Twentieth Century*.

Rosenthal, John, "The Secret History of Climate Alarmism: A Very German Story of Power Politics Disguised as Environmentalism." *The Weekly Standard*, Vol. 15 No. 44, Aug. 9, 2010.

Rubenstein, Richard. *The Cunning of History: The Holocaust and the American Future*. New York: Harper & Row Publishers, 1975.

Safire, William, "The German Problem," *The New York Times*, Sept. 19, 2002.

Sax, Boria. *Animals in the Third Reich: Pets, Scapegoats, and the Holocaust*. New York: Continuum, 2000.

Schaap, Jeremy. *Triumph: The Untold Story of Jesse Owens and Hitler's Olympics*. New York: Houghton Mifflin Company, 2007.

Schabel, Hans, "Deer and Dauerwald in Germany: Any Progress?" *Wildlife Society Bulletin*, 2001 29(3): 888-898.

Schaeffer, Francis. *The God Who is There*. Chicago: InterVarsity Press, 1968.

Schama, Simon. *Landscape and Memory*. New York: Vintage Books, 1995.

Schleiermacher, Friedrich. *On Religion: Speeches to its Cultured Despisers*. New York: Frank Ungar Publishing, 1955 (1799).

Schleiermacher, Friedrich. *The Christian Faith*, 2 vols. New York & Evanston: Harper Torchbooks, 1963 (1822).

Schopenhauer, Arthur. *On the Basis of Morality*. Indianapolis/Cambridge: Hackett Publishing Company, translated by E.F.J. Payne, 1995.

Schopenhauer, Arthur. *Parerga and Paralipomena*, 2 vols., translated from German. Oxford: Clarendon Press, 1974.

Schuler, Thomas, "Evidence of Opportunistic Behavior: How a German publisher maneuvered himself through the Nazi era." *The Atlantic Times*, Feb. 2009.

Schwab, Guenther. *Dance with the Devil*. 1958.

Science, Technology and National Socialism, edited by Monika Renneberg and Mark Walker. Cambridge University Press, 1994, 422 pages.

Sears, Paul, "Ecology—A Subversive Subject," *Biocentric*, 14, July 1964.

Sereny, Gitta. *Albert Speer: His Battle with Truth*. New York: Alfred A. Knopf, 1995.

Sereny, Gitta. *Into that Darkness: An Examination of Conscience.* New York: Vintage Books, 1974.

Snyder, Timothy. *Black Earth: The Holocaust as History and Warning.* London: The Bodley Head, 2015.

Space Science and Space Order. Heidelberg: Kurt Vowinckel Verlag, 1938.

Speer, Albert. *Inside the Third Reich.* New York: Bonanza Books, 1982 (1970).

Speer, Albert. *Infiltration.* New York: MacMillan Books, 1981.

Speer, Albert. *Spandau: The Secret Diaries.* New York: Macmillan Books, 1976.

Staudenmaier, Peter, "Anthroposophy and Ecofascism,"

Staudenmaier, Peter and Biehl, Janet. *Ecofascism Revisited: Lessons from the German Experience.* Porsgrunn, Norway: New Compass Press, 2011.

Stern, J.P. *Hitler: The Fuhrer and the People.* Berkeley & Los Angeles: University of California Press, 1992.

Stirling, M. David. *Green Gone Wild: Elevating Nature Above Human Rights.* Bellevue: Merril Press, 2008.

Stuart, Douglas. *Hosea-Jonah*, Word Biblical Commentary. Colombia: Nelson Reference and Electronic, 1987.

Sullivan, Amy, "Obama's Other Breakthrough: A Big City President," *Time*, Jan. 13, 2009.

Tapper, Jake, "Al Gore's 'Inconvenient Truth'? - A $30,000 Utility Bill," *ABC News*, February 26, 2007.

Tennessee Center for Policy Research, "Al Gore's House Uses More Energy After 'Going Green,'" June 17, 2008.

The Eternal Jew, Nazi documentary film, 1940.

Tooze, Adam. *Wages of Destruction: The Making and Breaking of the Nazi Economy.* New York: Penguin Books, 2006.

Turner, Henry Ashby. *German Big Business and the Rise of Hitler.* Oxford University Press, 1985.

Tusa, Ann and John. *The Nuremberg Trials.* New York: Skyhorse Publishing, 2010.

Tyson, Joseph Howard. *Hitler's Mentor: Dietrich Eckart, His Life, Times and Milieu.* New York: iUniverse, Inc., 2008.

Uekoetter, Frank. *The Green and the Brown: A History of Conservation in Nazi Germany.* Cambridge University Press, 2006.

Varner, G.E., "The Schopenhauerian Challenge in Environmental Ethics," *Environmental Ethics* 7 (3), 1985, pp. 209-229.

Veith, Gene Edward. *Modern Fascism: The Threat to the Judeo-Christian Worldview.* St. Louis: Concordia Press, 1993.

Von Campe, Hilmar. *Defeating the Totalitarian Lie.* Crane: HighWay, 2008.

Von Dassanowsky, "A Mountain of a Ship: Locating the Bergfilm in James' Cameron's Titanic," *Cinema Journal*, issue 40:4, Summer 2001.

Waite, Robert. *The Psychopathic God.* New York: Da Capo Press, (1977) 1993, 482 pages.

Walker, Bruce. *Sinisterism: Secular Religion of the Lie.* Denver: Outskirts Press, 2006.

Walker, Bruce, "Nazis, the First Ecologists and the First PETA Nuts," *Web Commentary*, April 27, 2006.

Walker, Bruce. *The Swastika Against the Cross: The Nazi War on Christianity.* Denver: Outskirts Press, 2007.

Waltke, Bruce. *Genesis: A Commentary.* Grand Rapids, Michigan: Zondervan, 2001.

Wanliss, James. *Resisting the Green Dragon: Dominion not Death.* Burke, VA: Cornwall Alliance for the Stewardship of Creation, 2010.

White Jr. Lynn, "The Historical Roots of Our Ecologic Crisis," *Science*, Vol. 155 (Number 3767), March 10, 1967, pp. 1203–1207.

Weikart, Richard. *From Darwin to Hitler: Evolutionary Ethics, Eugenics and Racism in Germany.* New York: Palgrave Macmillan, 2004.

Weikart, Richard. *Hitler's Ethic: The Nazi Pursuit of Evolutionary Progress.* New York: Palgrave Macmillan, 2009.

Weikart, Richard. *Hitler's Religion: The Twisted Beliefs that Drove the Third Reich.* Washington D.C.: Regnery History, 2016.

White, Alden, "Lindbergh Traveling Widely as a Conservationist," *The New York Times*, June 23, 1969.

Wiesel, Elie. *Night*. New York: Hill and Wang, 1958.

Wilson, James. *Hitler's Alpine Retreat*. South Yorkshire, United Kingdom: Pen & Sword Military, 2010.

Wolff, Hans Walter. *Hosea*, Hermeneia—a Critical and Historical Commentary, translated from German. Philadelphia: Fortress Press, 1974 (1965).

Wolin, Richard. *Heidegger's Children: Hannah Arendt, Karl Lowith, Hans Jonas, and Hebert Marcuse*. Princeton and Oxford: Princeton University Press, 2001.

Work, Telford, "Meager Harvest," *Christianity Today*, Feb. 2009.

Worster, Donald. *Dust Bowl: The Southern Plains of the 1930's*. Oxford University Press, 1979.

Worster, Donald. *Nature's Economy: A History of Ecological Ideas*. Cambridge University Press, 1985 (1977).

Yad Vashem Interview with Prof. Hans Mommsen, "The 'Functionalist' and the 'Intentionalist' Schools of Thought," *Shoah Resource Center*, Dec. 12, 1997.

Zimmerman, Michael, "Ecofascism: An Enduring Temptation—Environmental Philosophy From Animal Rights to Radical Ecology."

Zimmerman, Michael, "Possible Political Problems of Earth-Based Religiosity."

Zimmerman, Michael, "Rethinking the Heidegger-Deep Ecology Relationship."

Zubrin, Robert. *Merchants of Despair: Radical Environmentalists, Criminal Pseudo-Scientists, and the Fatal Cult of Antihumanism*. New York, London: New Atlantis Books, 2012.

Look at the birds of the air, that they do not sow, nor reap nor gather into barns, and yet your heavenly Father feeds them. Are you not worth much more than they? And who of you by being worried can add a single hour to his life? And why are you worried about clothing? Observe how the lilies of the field grow; they do not toil nor do they spin, yet I say to you that not even Solomon in all his glory clothed himself like one of these. But if God so clothes the grass of the field, which is alive today and tomorrow is thrown into the furnace, will He not much more clothe you? You of little faith!

Matthew 6:26-30

INDEX

SCRIPTURE REFERENCES

Made in the USA
Las Vegas, NV
22 October 2022

57984914R00293